Entrepreneur's ULTIMATE START-UP DIRECTORY

Includes
1500
GREAT
BUSINESS
IDEAS!

JAMES
STEPHENSON

EP

Entrepreneur. Press

Managing Editor: Jere Calmes
Cover Design: Beth Hanson-Winter
Composition and production: Eliot House Productions

This publication is designed to provide accurate and authoritative information in regard to the subject matter covered. It is sold with the understanding that the publisher is not engaged in rendering legal, accounting, or other professional services. If legal advice or other expert assistance is required, the services of a competent professional person should be sought.

Library of Congress Cataloging-in-Publication Data

Stephenson, James, 1966–
   Entrepreneur's ultimate start-up directory/James Stephenson.
     p. cm.
   Includes web sites and index.
   ISBN 1-891984-33-0
   1. New business enterprises—United States—Directories. 2. Small business—United States—Directories. 3. Entrepreneurship—United States—Directories. 4. New business enterprises—Canada—Directories. 5. Small business—Canada—Directories. 6. Entrepreneurship—Canada—Directories. I. Title.

HD62.5 .S742 2001
658.1'141—dc21

2001033785

Printed in Canada

09 08 07 06 05 04 03 02 01   10 9 8 7 6 5 4 3 2 1

CONTENTS

38 ADVERTISING
Businesses You Can Start

47 COMPUTER AND HOME OFFICE
Businesses You Can Start

30 CRAFT
Businesses You Can Start

39 DESKTOP PUBISHING
Businesses You Can Start

43 ENTERTAINMENT
Businesses You Can Start

46 FINANCIAL AND PROFESSIONAL
SERVICE Businesses You Can Start

61 FOOD-RELATED
Businesses You Can Start

24 FURNITURE
Businesses You Can Start

37 HEALTH
Businesses You Can Start

29 HOME SERVICE
Businesses You Can Start

30 IMPORT/EXPORT AND
MAIL-ORDER Businesses You Can Start

50 INSTRUCTION
Businesses You Can Start

62 MANUFACTURING
Businesses You Can Start

46 **OUTDOOR SERVICE**
Businesses You Can Start

33 RECREATION
Businesses You Can Start

22 RECYCLING
Businesses You Can Start

26 SECURITY
Businesses You Can Start

76 SPECIAL SERVICE
Businesses You Can Start

39 SPORT AND FITNESS
Businesses You Can Start

60 TRANSPORTATION
Businesses You Can Start

33 TRAVEL
Businesses You Can Start

27 WRITING
Businesses You Can Start

INTRODUCTION

*"What is easy to do is easier not to do.
And most people will take the path of least
resistance!"*
—Brian Tracey

Millions of people want to start their own business, and yes, it is easy to start a business. However, it is easier not to start a business. And the majority of people considering business ownership will take the path of least resistance and simply choose to do nothing about fulfilling a lifelong dream of becoming a successful entrepreneur and operating their own business.

Why? The fear of the unknown, a feeling of being overwhelmed, the loss of security a job or career seemingly provides, and not knowing what business is the right business to start.

That is... until now.

Entrepreneur's *Ultimate Start-Up Directory* has been specifically developed to help you unlock the mysteries about what type of businesses can be started and operated for success. Each business is presented in a straightforward manner with useful information that you can directly apply to starting, managing, and marketing your new business, regardless of your experience or skills.

GETTING STARTED

Every citizen of the United States of America and Canada can start their own business. This is one of the greatest privileges of living in a democratic and free enterprise society. The only way that the vast majority of people living in North America will ever become financially secure and build wealth in less than a lifetime of working a job is to become self-employed operating their own business.

There are exceptions to the rule. You could win the lottery, inherit a million dollars or hit the jackpot in the stock market. However, for the most part wealth and financial stability does not happen by chance or luck, it is the result of careful planning and hard work. Setting personal and business goals and working hard to realize these goals is the only sure way to financial stability. Successful entrepreneurs are no different from you, aside from the fact that they all understood that working for someone else was not going to enable them to reach their goals in life.

The business ventures and information featured in this directory was compiled over a decade-long period and was born from my keen interest in the multitude of business and self-employment opportunities that are available to people from every walk of life to start and operate for success. Sources of information included my own business experiences, personal interviews with many small business owners, government agencies, small business associations, and thousands of hours of research devoted to identifying sound business start-ups.

The objective was to create a business start-up directory listing hundreds of businesses and self-employment opportunities representing a wide cross section of industries. The data and information featured for each business start-up is brief in nature and is meant to give the reader a "snapshot" or short synopsis understanding of the opportunity. Or, in other words, the theme of this directory is not "how to start and operate a business," but rather a collection of business start-up ideas that can be used as a catalyst to get you thinking about the various types of businesses that can be started, and ultimately one that is right for you to start.

ICON SYSTEM

As you read through each business you will notice a line of icons directly beneath the business title. These icons rate each business according to the ease of start-up, the cost to start-up, whether it can be a homebased business, has potential legal issues, part-time possibilities, the franchise or licensing ability and the online opportunity. This system is not to recommend any one business over another, but to give the reader an idea of what might be easier or simpler to start than another.

★ *Stars*

Every business start-up featured in the directory is rated on a scale of one to four stars, with four stars being the highest recommendation a business start-up can receive. The purpose of the rating system is not to predetermine the potential for business success or failure; the ratings system is based purely on logic or common sense to assist you in identifying what might be the right business start-up for you.

The star system is based on the following criteria:

- start-up costs
- market demand and the potential for growth
- competition in the marketplace
- special skill and legal requirements

- operating overhead costs
- potential for profitability
- stability and uniqueness

A business that requires less than a $10,000 investment to start and has the potential to generate income or profits in excess of $50,000 per year receives a high rating. However, if the same business start-up also requires a high degree of specialized skills to operate or is in an extremely competitive industry with declining consumer demand, the rating is reduced.

$ *Start-Up Cost*

The majority of business start-ups featured in the directory include an approximate financial investment that will be needed to start the business. Once again, this is generalized information and should only be used as a yardstick to determine business start-up costs. In most cases the investment indicated will be in the middle of the high-low range, but will vary to factors such as equipment and transportation purchases, licenses and permits, training requirements, operating location, working capital, initial marketing, and advertising budgets. Remember a successful entrepreneur is one who carefully researches and plans every aspect of a new business venture, including the financial investment needed to start a business and the working capital required to achieve positive cash flow.

Start-Up Cost Symbols

$	Less than $1,000
$$	$1,000–$10,000
$$$	$10,000–$25,000
$$$$	Greater than $25,000

PROFIT OR INCOME POTENTIAL. Profit is not a dirty word. Business owners work hard, in fact most entrepreneurs work in excess of 60 hours per week. Where indicated, income or profit potential is considered industry average, thus the amount of income or profit that can be realized by running a particular business may indeed be greater or substantially lower than indicated in the directory. Once again, factors, such as sales volumes, operating overheads, profit margins, management fees, and wages will all have an effect on a business's potential profitability.

🏠 *Homebased*

Do you want to work from the comforts of home, cut your commuting time down to a few seconds, and increase interaction time with your family? If so, you have come to the right place. In the directory you will find hundreds of business start-ups that are ideal candidates to be operated or managed from a homebased location. These homebased business ventures have been specifically identified in the directory with a small house symbol.

Running a business from home has many advantages, including lower operating overheads, less time spent commuting, flexible work hours, a comfortable and familiar work environment, and the ability to create a more balanced schedule in terms of family needs and commitments. However, running a business from home still requires the same amount of planning and research, as any new business venture will. Laws governing the operation of a business from home greatly vary across North America, and some municipalities require no more than the purchase of a simple business license to make the homebased business legitimate. However, other municipalities require fire and safety inspections of the home prior to issuing a business license for a homebased enterprise.

There is no "across the board" set of standard rules and regulations in terms of operating a business from home. It is the responsibility of every entrepreneur considering a homebased business venture to become acquainted with and conform to the rules and regulations governing homebased business enterprises as set forth by local governments.

⊕ *Part-Time Opportunity*

Not too sure that you are ready to jump ship from working for someone else to tackle business ownership on a full-time basis? Or perhaps you would like to "test the waters" and see if you have what it takes to start and succeed in business? Or maybe you are just looking for a way to earn an extra few hundred dollars each month to grow the college education fund?

Regardless of your reason, you will find hundreds of business start-ups in the directory that can be operated on a part-time basis indefinitely or that can be started on a part-time basis and expanded to a full-time going business concern from the profits that the business earns. Almost any business can be operated "part-time," however, business start-ups in the directory featuring the clock symbol are outstanding business venture options for part-time entrepreneurs.

⚖ *Legal Issues*

The scales of justice symbol indicates that there are special permits or certificates of training required to start and operate the business featured. Remember, all new business ventures require that you apply for and receive a business license or permit, as well as registering or incorporating your business at the local or federal level. A major component of starting a business is to research all the legal elements and aspects of the business venture. This includes, but is not limited to, licenses and permits, liability insurance, zoning and building-use codes, fire and health regulations, employee regulations, and certificates of training.

⊕ *Franchise or License Potential*

For entrepreneurs looking for the big business and market opportunities, we have taken the guesswork out of wondering: What is a good business, product, or service to expand nationally on a franchise or license-to-operate basis? Simply look for business start-ups in the directory featuring the globe symbol. These business start-ups have been selected as potentially prime franchise or license opportunities and are purposely included in the directory to appeal to the entrepreneur that is seeking a real business challenge.

☞ *Online Opportunity*

In today's competitive business environment all businesses need some sort of Internet presence: an individual Web site, listed in online industry directories, or part of a community Web site program. The choices are as varied as the individual need or desired exposure. However, with the advent and wide use and acceptance of the Internet, it is very possible to start a business that operates in the "virtual world" only, in terms of marketing and sales of consumer goods and services. Not only is it possible to start a stand-alone Internet business, it is also possible to substantially profit from an Internet business as thousands of individuals, small businesses, and corporations worldwide are now proving.

Business start-ups in the directory featuring a computer mouse symbol have been selected as business ventures that can be started as a stand-alone Internet enterprise or in conjunction with a "bricks and mortar" business venture. Once again, any business enterprise can and should develop an Internet presence via a company Web site or other online marketing options to open the business to a global audience and marketplace. The Internet is a powerful marketing and distribution tool and, in spite of a few recent glitches, no other industry is growing or being embraced by business and consumers alike as quickly as the Internet. Without question, the Internet has changed the way the world does business and will continue to change the way the world does business with every new Internet technology development.

Handy Web Resources

Throughout the directory you will find hundreds of handy Web resources, the purpose of which is not to promote or endorse any one association, program, or business. The resources are there to give you a research tool in terms of "now I am interested in a particular business and how can I find out more?" You will find that the Web resources featured in the directory are a fantastic research tool that enables you to quickly explore and compile further information and data about a particular business opportunity that you would like to learn more about.

Marketing

Every business needs paying customers in order to survive, succeed, and grow. Marketing is the single largest business challenge facing entrepreneurs. Great attention was paid to ensure that each business start-up analyzed in the directory gives you information pertaining to who the target market for the product or service is, and how to reach and secure that market.

In addition to hundreds of sales and marketing ideas and techniques, you will also discover hundreds of useful and practical advertising, management, and business operations strategies and tips that will help you succeed in business.

Research and Planning

Research and planning is vital to the success of every business venture. Research essentials include the business, industry, products, services, and competition on a local and national level as well as the way you will research these topics and compile data. Planning is the function of analyzing the research and developing various plans from the information revealed in the research process. These plans include a business plan, action plans, financial plans, marketing plans, and long- and short-term business goals and objectives.

While the directory does not include information specific to the research and planning aspects of starting a business, you will find suggested reading and information links in the Resource chapter of the directory.

BUSINESS START-UP PREVIEW

The Business Start-Up Preview has been specifically developed to assist you in determining what might be the right new business enterprise for you to start and operate. The purpose of the information and questions featured in the business start-up preview is not to predetermine your ability to start and run a business, but rather a collection of data and information that can be used as a helpful resource in identifying the right new business start-up for you.

What Is the Right Business Start-Up for You?

There is only one person that can answer this question: You. Starting a business is comprised of many elements: What is the right business? When is the best time to start this business? Where is the best place to start? Who will my customers be? How will this business generate income and profits?

Remember, anyone in the United States and Canada can start a business. This is one of the greatest privileges of living in a democratic and free enterprise society. However, the fact remains that many new business ventures fail within the first five years of operation. Businesses fail for a number of reasons, but invariably failure can usually be traced back to lack of planning and research or an unsuitable match between the business owner and the type of enterprise they are operating.

Once again the theme of this directory is not how to start and operate a business, but rather a collection of business start-up ideas that can be used as a catalyst to get you thinking about the various types of businesses that can be started and, ultimately, one that is right for you to start. The Business Start-Up Preview is a tool that you can use to help identify the right new business venture for you. The purpose of the information and questions presented is not to predetermine your ability to start and run a business. The function of the preview is to help you identify the right business start-up that will match your needs, motives, and ambitions.

Personal and Family Situation

One of the most import factors to consider prior to starting or purchasing a business is to carefully analyze your reasons for starting a business, as well as the effect this decision will have on you and your family. No new or existing business can be operated solely by one person. It requires a team effort and family members make up a larger piece of the team than you may think.

Consider the following items to determine what you feel is important to you and your family. If a large percentage of the important aspects of you or your family's lives cannot be satisfied, then the type of business start-up that is being considered may not be appropriate.

• Why do you want to be self-employed and operate your own business?

_____
_____
_____
_____

• I am dissatisfied with my current job or career.

_____
_____
_____
_____

• I want my family to support my business decisions.

_____
_____
_____
_____

• I want to spend more time with my family.

_____
_____
_____
_____

• I am prepared to miss family vacations and special events.

_____
_____
_____
_____

Remember your answers and thoughts are for the purpose of colleting data to help you determine your motives and find the right business venture. If you rank wanting to spend more time with your family as very important to you, then a homebased business would be a better choice then a business that operates outside the home. Remember, when you start a business you are making decisions for more than yourself, so it is important to include family members in the decision-making process. Additionally, never assume that family members will have the same excitement as you about starting or working in the business. This decision must be left up to each individual family member to decide.

Special Skills

What are the special skills that you currently possess, and how can these skills be applied to the new business venture that you would like to start? While you certainly do not have to possess all the skills necessary for running a business, at the same time identifying your strengths and weaknesses prior to starting a business just makes good sense. The skills shown to be the weakest are not reason for concern, they simply just have to be improved. The most successful entrepreneurs are ones that never stop learning or seeking ways to improve their business skills.

	Excellent	Good	Needs Work
• Sales and negotiation skills	——	——	——
• Record and bookkeeping skills	——	——	——
• Organization and management skills	——	——	——
• Computer and software skills	——	——	——
• Ability to listen and seek expert advice	——	——	——
• Problem-solving skills	——	——	——
• Ability to handle stress	——	——	——
• Ability to stay motivated and committed	——	——	——
• Planning and research skills	——	——	——
• Ability to set and achieve goals	——	——	——
• Ability to budget and manage money	——	——	——
• Ability to speak in public	——	——	——
• Decision-making abilities	——	——	——

Income

If your ambition is to earn a six-figure income, then perhaps starting a part-time lawn care service is not the right venture. However, if you aspire to earn an extra $10,000 per year to supplement your family income, a part-time lawn care service would be a wise choice. The key to successfully establishing a required or desired business income is to be completely realistic in your expectations. Yes, a lawn care service can generate a six-figure income for the owner of the business providing the business employs many people, has a substantial customer base, or is expanded geographically. However, it is unrealistic to assume that a part-time lawn care service will generate a six-figure income. Therefore if your ambition is a six-figure income, this would not be a good business opportunity for you to pursue.

If your single largest motivation for starting a business is to get rich, I will guarantee you that you are going to be sadly disappointed. However, if one of the many motivations for starting a business is to build and maintain a long-term comfortable income level, then I will also guarantee that this can be accomplished by using sound business judgment.

Income required per year

$100,000 +	___
$70,000 +	___
$40,000 +	___
$20,000 +	___

Income desired per year
$200,000 +   ___
$100,000 +   ___
$50,000 +   ___

Short- and Long-Term Goals

The only way to know if a business venture has the potential to meet or exceed your short-term and long-term personal and financial goals is to know exactly what your goals are. The best way to identify them is to compile a list of your goals and expectations for you and your family. Keep the list close so that you can reflect back to it in times of business, personal, and financial decisions. If the end result of your decision will mean sacrificing a short-term or long-term goal, then it is safe to assume this would not be a wise decision to make.

Business Location

Where will your new business be located or operated from, and how will this affect your and your family's life? Business location is a very important aspect of finding the right business to start. If you have always dreamed about working from home, then you have already narrowed your choices in terms of a suitable business match. If you feel your current living accommodations are not suitable for a home-based business, then this is also a factor to consider in finding the right business enterprise.

- I want to be able to operate a business from home. Yes___ No___ If yes, why?

  _____
  _____
  _____
  _____

- I am prepared to move to a new community to pursue a business opportunity. Yes___ No___ If yes, how will this decision affect family and myself?

  _____
  _____
  _____
  _____

- My home is suitable for a homebased business. Yes___ No___

- If the business is not suitable to be operated from home, is there a suitable location available in the community? Yes___ No___

- What are the special requirements for the type of business you are considering starting?

  Space _____
  _____
  _____

Budget_____

_____

_____

Fire/Zoning/Safety Codes _____

_____

_____

Existing Resources

What existing resources do you have or have access to that can be utilized in the business? You would be very surprised by what you may have kicking around the house that can be used in establishing a business—and even more surprised by the amount of money you can save in business start-up and operation costs by utilizing existing resources.

	Yes	No
• Do you have computer equipment and software?	___	___
• Do you have a good contact base of people within the community?	___	___
• Do you have suitable transportation for the new business?	___	___
• Do you possess general office equipment and fixtures that can be used in the business?	___	___
• Do you have access to a resource library for research and planning purposes?	___	___
• Are there business clubs, associations, and networking opportunities in your community?	___	___
• Do you know any professionals or current business owners that can assist you with business decisions?	___	___

These are only a few examples of existing resources you may have or have access to. Carefully consider what information, equipment, and research needs to be included to start the business. Compile a list of what is needed and write any existing resources you may have beside the needed item or information.

Start-Up Investment and Working Capital

Do you have or have access to the investment money needed to start the business you are considering? If so, do you also have or have access to further money to be used as working capital for the day-to-day operations of the business. Beyond start-up capital, working capital is needed to achieve positive cash flow. What this means is that I have yet to come across a business opportunity that can be started today and generate a profit tomorrow. Every new business venture requires financing beyond the initial start-up costs in order to achieve positive cash flow, and believe me a lot of time can pass before a business shows a profit or even breaks even.

One of the most common errors entrepreneurs make when starting a business is not calculating the true start-up investment needed to reach positive cash flow. As a rule of thumb use the 75/25 ratio rule, meaning that 75 percent of the total available capital will be used for the hard costs associated with establishing the business such as equipment purchases, initial advertising campaigns, inventory, permits, and transportation the remaining 25 percent of available capital will be held in reserve to be used for working capital in the business. An example of the 75/25 rule would be a business start-up that is calculated to require an initial investment of $60,000 to open for business. A further $15,000 should be held in reserve as working capital for the business, bringing the total start-up costs for the business to $75,000. For anyone considering the purchase of an existing business or franchise this 75/25 rule still applies regardless of financial statements or immediate cash flow projections.

Good Match

A particular interest in a business or industry is not the same as being a well-suited person to start that particular business, or a good match with the business opportunity. While you may have a great understanding and interest in a particular business, that certainly does not ensure that the business is a good match for you. Ask yourself the following questions to ensure a good business match:

- Am I physically and mentally healthy enough to handle the potential physical and mental strains of starting and running this business?

  _____
  _____
  _____
  _____

- Does this business opportunity match my personality type and level of maturity?

  _____
  _____
  _____
  _____

- Can I see myself still excited about this business ten years from now?

  _____
  _____
  _____
  _____

- Does this business opportunity have the potential to help me reach my personal and financial goals?

  _____
  _____
  _____
  _____

• Can I commit to this business and am I prepared to work hard to ensure success?

_____

_____

_____

_____

• Is this the type of business that I initially envisioned as a self-employment venture that would be suitable and a good match for me?

_____

_____

_____

_____

• Do I posses any special skills or abilities that can be utilized in this business?

_____

_____

_____

_____

◆   ◆   ◆

Entrepreneurs and small businesses drives the economies of the United States and Canada, and joining the estimated 30 million business owners may be easier than you think. You have already taken the first step toward becoming an entrepreneur by investing in the most authoritative business start-up directory available. The next step is to harness the power of this book and put it to work for you to find and start the right new business.

KEY

RATINGS	★
START-UP COST	$
HOMEBASED BUSINESS	
PART-TIME	
LEGAL ISSUES	
FRANCHISE OR LICENSE POTENTIAL	
ONLINE	

38

ADVERTISING
Businesses You Can Start

OUTDOOR BICYCLE RACKS

★★ $$ 🏠 🕐 ⚖ 🌐

Are you searching for a unique advertising business opportunity that can be managed from a homebased office, and has the potential to generate a six-figure annual income? If so consider starting a bicycle rack advertising service. The business concept is very straightforward. Simply design and build bicycle lock-up stands that can accommodate four to six bicycles each, and that can be securely fastened to the ground in outdoor locations. The bicycle stands serve two purposes. Firstly, they introduce a terrific advertising medium by creating an advertising space on the top of the stand that can be rented to local merchants and service providers for advertising purposes. The second purpose of the stand is to provide a secure location for cyclists to lock up bicycles while shopping at community retailers.

WEB RESOURCE: www.bikeparking.com Manufacturers of outdoor bicycle lock-up stands.

CAMPUS COUPON BOOKS

★★ $$ 🏠 🕐 🌐

Starting a business that creates and markets campus coupon books directly to university and college students is a fantastic new business venture to put into action. Securing local merchants to be featured in the campus coupon books should not prove difficult as there is no cost to participate, only a requirement to provide honest and generous discounts on products or services that their companies sell. Furthermore, you can enlist students to sell the discount coupon books to other students right on campus, on revenue split basis. The key to success in this unique advertising business is to ensure that the coupon books contain genuine discounts on products and services that students would regularly use and purchase.

WEB RESOURCE: www.couponpros.org Association of Coupon Professionals.

ONLINE CAMPUS COUPONS

★★ $$

The major difference between campus coupon books in print and online campus coupons is how the two business ventures generate revenues and profits. As mentioned above, merchants advertise for free in print coupon books and consumers pay for the coupon books in order to be able to take advantage of the discounts offered within. Online coupons are free for consumers to download and print and merchants pay a fee to have their coupon offer posted on the Web site. The format for this type of Web site is straightforward. The site is indexed into various product and service sections such as apparel and entertainment. Visitors simply click onto the section that is of interest and view the coupon offers. One of the best aspects about providing campus coupons online as opposed to in print format is the fact that you can operate the business from one location and service many regions of the country by employing sales consultants to market the online coupon service to merchants locally.

LITTER CANS

★ $

Purchasing 200 commercial-grade litter cans and securing high-traffic indoor and outdoor locations for the litter cans to be installed can potentially generate advertising revenues of $6,000 per month. In order for this very unique advertising business to succeed, the following two aspects must be considered. First, secure highly visible locations to install the litter cans such as in front of retail stores, inside malls, and inside community and recreation centers. Additionally, the property or business owners must agree to maintain the litter cans in exchange for a portion of the advertising revenues generated. Next, aggressively market the advertising service to local companies who want to participate in a highly effective advertising campaign that costs only $30 per month.

WEB RESOURCE: www.victorstanley.com Manufacturers of commercial grade outdoor litter receptacles.

DOOR HANGER SERVICE

★★★ $

Thousands of renovation and home service companies are missing out on a very effective and extremely low-cost advertising method for their business. And you can capitalize financially by introducing them to this advertising medium by starting your own door hanger design and delivery service. Door hangers are simply a type of marketing brochure that has been designed to fit overtop of an entrance door handle. What makes door hangers such an effective advertising medium is the fact that door hangers are noticed as people enter their homes. Additionally, door hangers can also act as a discount coupon with a company advertising message printed on the front and a coupon or special promotion printed on the back of the door hanger. Current delivery rates are in the range of 25 to 30 cents per door hanger delivered, plus design and printing costs.

WEB RESOURCE: www.laserblanks.com Suppliers of blank door hangers.

INFLATABLE ADVERTISING

★★ $$

Twenty-foot high inflatable gorillas, blimps, and cartoon caricatures get noticed by traffic, especially when these large inflatables are sitting on a retailer's rooftop with a "sale in progress" sign emblazoned across them. Starting a business that rents inflatable advertising objects is a fantastic new business venture to set in motion. The business can be operated on a full- or part-time basis right from home, and clients can include just about any retail business in your community that regularly conducts special sales or promotions. Currently, new inflatables are retailing for approximately $3,000 to $5,000. But as a method to reduce the start-up investment needed to get the business rolling, secondhand inflatables can be purchased for about half the cost of a new one. Rental rates are in the range of $75 to $150 per day including delivery.

WEB RESOURCE: www.windship.com Manufacturers of hot and cold air advertising inflatables.

COMMUNITY DIRECTORY BOARDS
★★ $$ 🏠 🕐 🌐

Do you live in a busy tourist area of the country? If so, perhaps you should consider starting a business that installs, markets, and maintains community directory boards. Community directory boards are simply an outdoor board, covered in protective glass or plastic, featuring information about the local community that they serve. Information featured can include a map of the area, tourist attractions and where they are located, a list of community services, the location of sports complexes and playing fields, and additional information about the community in general. Revenues are earned by selling highly visible advertising spaces on the community directory boards to local merchants wishing to advertise their products and services.

WEB RESOURCE: www.builditworlwide.com Directory service listing manufacturers and designers of specialty products.

FLIER DISTRIBUTION SERVICE
★ $ 🏠 🕐

Not only is a flier delivery service a very easy business to start, it also has the potential to generate a fantastic annual income. Companies have utilized promotional fliers for decades as a low-cost highly effective advertising method. Starting a flier delivery service requires no more than a telephone and a good pair of walking shoes. Currently, flier delivery services are charging delivery rates in the range of 7 to 15 cents per hand-delivered flier. As a method to increase your delivery workforce, consider hiring retirees and students to deliver fliers during busy times.

SPORTS COMPLEX ADVERTISING
★ $$ 🏠 🕐

A very successful advertising business can be built by securing contracts with privately and publicly owned sports complexes to manage and operate their advertising programs. Most sports complexes like arenas, recreation centers, and baseball fields feature some form of interior or exterior advertising space that is rented by local companies to promote their products and services. Generally the owners or operators of the sports complex do not market the advertising spaces for rent. This task is left to an outside contractor who has successfully bid in a tender process for the right to market and manage the advertising program. Be forewarned this is a very competitive segment of the advertising industry that will require careful research and planning prior to establishing a business that specializes in this type of advertising sales. However, with that said, the profit potential is outstanding for the determined entrepreneurs that are awarded these types of advertising contracts.

BENCH ADVERTISING
★ $$ 🏠 🕐

The following three steps can be taken to generate gross sales of $60,000 per year from a part-time business that rents advertising space on park or seating benches.

1. Design and construct 50 outdoor seating benches that feature a large and highly visible advertising space on the back or front of the bench (depending on bench placement).
2. Secure 50 locations to install the benches such as parks, in front of retail stores, etc.
3. Rent the advertising spaces to local merchants wishing to advertise and promote their products and services, and charge $100 per month for each advertising space. Providing the above can be accomplished, the end result will be an advertising business that can be operated from home, and generates yearly revenues of $60,000. In addition to outside benches, indoor advertising benches can also be located in buildings such as recreation centers, public markets, and malls.

WEB RESOURCE: www.victorystanley.com Manufacturers of outdoor park benches.

PROMOTIONAL PRODUCTS
★★★ $$ 🏠

Billions of dollars are spent annually in North America on promotional items such as T-shirts, pens, hats, and calendars by companies that give these promotional items away to existing and potential clients of their business. Securing just a small portion of this very lucrative market can make you rich. The key to success in the promotional products marketing industry is not to manufacture and print the promotional items yourself, but to simply market these items and enlist the services of existing manufacturers and printers to fulfill the orders. This is a business that requires excellent sales and marketing abilities, and this business opportunity is not suitable for an individual who is afraid to go out and ask for business. Aim to achieve yearly sales of $300,000 while maintaining a 50 percent markup on all products sold, and the end result will be a homebased advertising business that generates a pretax and expense earnings of $100,000.

WEB RESOURCE: www.promotionalproducts.com. Directory service listing promotional product manufacturers, printers, and distributors.

TAXI CAB PUBLICATION

Starting a taxi cab publication will take some clever negotiations skills to accomplish, but like any new business venture the effort is generally rewarded financially for the determined entrepreneurs that take the initiative. A taxi cab publication is simply a daily or weekly two-page paper that is distributed free of charge for taxi customers to enjoy during their ride. The paper can feature information about the local community, as well as trivia and games. Revenues are earned by selling display-advertising space in the paper to local business owners and professionals. Ideally, the business could be formed as a joint venture with an established printer who can produce the newspaper, while you concentrate on the marketing and sales aspects of the business. Once established and proven successful, the business could easily be expanded by a franchise or licensed-to-operate basis nationally.

FREE COURTESY TELEPHONES
★★ $$ 🏠 🕐 🌐

Strategically locating courtesy telephones in high-traffic gathering places in your community has the

potential to generate enormous monthly advertising revenues, and best of all the business can be kicked into high gear with an initial investment of less than $10,000. Courtesy telephones resemble commercial pay telephones with one big difference; there is no cost to make local telephone calls. Ideally, the free phones will be installed in high-traffic indoor areas like malls, community centers, and food markets. Income is earned by selling advertising space around the phone booth or enclosure. Alternately, revenues can also be earned by selling advertising space in the form of prerecorded messages that the user of the telephone must listen to before they are able to make their free local call. To ensure the best locations can be secured for the free courtesy telephones, consider splitting the advertising revenue with the owner of the property or business where the courtesy telephones are installed.

TRANSIT ADVERTISING
★ $$$$

Like many advertising service contracts, operating and marketing a transit advertising program is generally awarded by the transit commission or agency that operates the transit service on a tendered basis. Typically, the tenders renew every few years and the decision to award the contract to one particular service provider is made on the basis of reliability, revenue generation, and performance record. This type of advertising service contract can be extremely difficult to acquire. However, for the successful bidding contractor the financial rewards can be outstanding as transit advertising is some of the most sought after advertising media by companies, agencies, and merchants.

HOARDING ADVERTISING SERVICE
★★ $$ 🏠 🕐

For anyone who is not familiar with the term *hoarding*, it is the temporary plywood fencing that is erected around the perimeter of a construction site. Typically, hoarding is used for construction sites in densely populated urban areas to prevent foot traffic from being potentially injured as a result of coming into contact with falling debris or construction equipment. While many people illegally post advertising posters and notices on hoarding fences, a very successful advertising business can be built by legally acquiring permission to post advertising on the fencing. Marketing this type of advertising is very easy as most hoarding is erected in highly visible areas and that is exactly the kind of exposure advertisers are seeking. Additionally, be sure to negotiate a revenue split arrangement with the contractors or property developers of the site, as this will definitely remove any potential objections.

ELEVATOR ADVERTISING
★★ $$ 🏠 ⏰

Elevator advertising is probably the most effective advertising available in terms of consumer awareness, simply because occupants of elevators are a captive audience surrounded by few distractions. The key to successfully operating an advertising service that specializes in marketing elevator advertising spaces is to secure the busiest elevators in the community for the service. Ideally, you should concentrate on securing elevators in commercial buildings such as malls, office towers, and hospitals. The higher the elevator foot traffic the easier it will be to secure advertisers to purchase the advertising spaces. Furthermore, to secure the best elevator locations for the business, consider a revenue split arrangement with the owner of the building or property manager of the building and develop interesting ways to display the advertisements.

SPECIAL OCCASION YARD CUTOUTS
★ $ 🏠 ⏰ 🌐

You can design and build your own special occasion yard cutouts, such as a stork for birth announcements or a happy birthday caricature. Or you can purchase predesigned and constructed special occasion yard cutouts to get this unique advertising business off the ground. Clients typically include people that want to surprise other people by having an announcement placed in their front yard to let everyone in the neighborhood know about the

special occasion. Yard card rental rates are in the range of $30 to $60 per day including delivery, installation, and pickup. A special occasion yard cutout rental business is not likely to make you rich. However, a terrific part-time income can be earned from this homebased specialty advertising business.

WEB RESOURCE: www.lawnexpressions.com Manufacturer of lawn display cards with distributors opportunities.

CHARITY EVENTS
★ $$ 🏠 ⏰

Do you want to start an advertising business that helps local charities raise much needed funding, while building a profitable business for yourself? If so, perhaps you should consider starting a business that organizes community charity events like golf tournaments and craft sales. The charities would receive all event admission fees while you would retain advertising revenues generated by selling advertising spaces in the event's program as well as promotional items such as event hats and T-shirts. The key to success is to build alliances with well-recognized charities in the community, as well as ensuring the events are well promoted and fun for all in attendance.

COMMUNITY BULLETIN BOARDS
★★ $$ 🏠 ⏰ 🌐

High quality 4-foot by 8-foot wall-mounted bulletin boards can be built for about $250 each, and spending $10,000 to construct 40 bulletin boards has the potential to return advertising revenues in excess of $20,000 each month. How? Easy. Simply secure 40 high traffic locations such as food markets, malls, and recreation centers to install the community bulletin boards in. The next step is to secure ten advertisers for each bulletin board and provide the advertisers with an 8-inch by 10-inch high-gloss advertisement on the community bulletin board in exchange for $50 per month. The advertisements can be located around the outside of the bulletin board and be protected by tamper proof glass or plastic, while the inside of the bulletin board is cork and used by people in the community to post notices. To attract advertisers the bulletin boards must be located in high-traffic community gathering places, and to secure the best locations for the boards consider a revenue split arrangement with the owner of the building or business where the community bulletin boards are installed.

WINDOW DISPLAYS

 ★ $ 🏠 🕐

Retailers often must rely on an elaborate window and in-store displays to attract the attention of passing consumers, and starting a business that specializes in creating effective window displays for retail merchants is the focus of this business opportunity. Marketing a window display service can be as easy as approaching local retailers and initially providing your services for free until the owner of the business starts to realize the benefits and increased sales that a well-designed window display can garner. Additionally, the "free" display that you create can also be used as a powerful marketing tool to present to other shop owners. Placing a sign by the display that explains your service and gives contact information will help in getting the word out. Furthermore, be sure to build an inventory of interesting props so that you can provide clients with an "all-inclusive" display service.

SITE SIGN INSTALLATION SERVICE

 ★★ $ 🏠 🕐

Here is a terrific business to start and operate in conjunction with a door hanger service. Company site signs are temporally installed in front of a customer's home telling people in the neighborhood who the company is that is performing work, as well as what business they are in and how to contact the company. Most construction, renovation, and home service companies realize the value of installing site signs. However, time restrictions usually mean the sign never gets installed. Thus, the free advertising benefits never get realized. This is a wise choice for a new business venture especially when combined with a door hanger service, as clients will get a double whammy for their advertising buck.

ONLINE ADVERTISING DIRECTORY

 ★ $ 🏠 ✍

Harness the power of the Internet and start an online advertising directory. Not only will you be providing a valuable service for Web site visitors, but you will also be establishing your own potentially successful business. The business concept is very straightforward. Start by designing a Web site that features information about various advertising mediums including rates, contact information, and any special promotions or discounts in terms of advertising rates. Business owners who visit the site simply locate the type of advertising that suits their marketing program and budgets. Income is earned by charging the advertising companies a fee to be listed on the Web site, as well as by selling banner advertising space featured in the Web site.

WEB RESOURCE: www.entrepreneur.com Create a business Web site with MySite professional Web site builder.

ADVERTISING CLIPPING SERVICE

 ★ $ 🏠 🕐

Did you know that companies that compete within the same industry regularly retain the services of an advertising clipping service to keep them up-to-date on how, why, and where the competition is advertising? Here is your opportunity to capitalize financially by starting an advertising clipping service. The key to success in this business is not to overcharge clients, but to work in volume. Charging clients a mere $30 to $40 per month to belong to the service will guarantee that you retain existing clients and attract new clients to the service very easily. Collect advertisements from newspapers, directories, magazines, and now the Internet and fax them to clients on a weekly basis. Securing and maintaining 100 regular clients can generate an income of as much as $35,000 per year.

AERIAL ADVERTISING

 ★ $$ 🏠 🕐 ⚖

If you are looking for a unique and inexpensive advertising business to start, look no further than starting an aerial advertising service. The best way to initiate this business is to form a joint partnership with a pilot who has, or has access to, an airplane as the pilot can concentrate on the aerial aspect of the business while you can concentrate on marketing the business and selling the advertising service. Demand for the service is not likely to be large enough to operate the business on a full-time basis. However, an aerial advertising service even operated on a part-time basis just a few hours per week can still generate revenues in excess of $50,000 per year, prior to taxes and operating overhead.

RESTAURANT MENUS
★★ $$

How do you provide business owners in your community with highly effective low-cost advertising options, while also providing restaurant owners with high quality menus printed free of charge every month and make a profit for yourself? Easy, start a restaurant menu advertising program in your community. The business concept is very basic. Secure agreements with busy restaurants in your local community that would be prepared to allow advertising to be printed on the front and back covers of their menus in exchange for receiving new and updated menus free of charge each month. Once this has been accomplished, you can set out to market the advertising spaces on the menu covers to local merchants and service providers. The business will take patience to establish, but a terrific annual income could be eventually realized.

COMMUNITY BUSINESS MAPS
★ $$

Community business maps are simply maps featuring information about local attractions and points of interest within a community, as well as highlighting the participating businesses that sponsor or advertise on the maps. Typically, business advertisers will receive a display-size advertisement on the back of the map, and the advertiser's business location will be featured on the front of the map. The maps are given away free of charge to tourists visiting the community, of course with the intention that the tourists will take notice of the advertisers on the maps and purchase their products or services. The maps are generally published once per year, and expanding the business is as easy as introducing the map advertising strategy to new communities.

BILLBOARDS
★ $$$$

Billboards are one of the most competitive segments of the advertising industry, and starting a business that installs billboards and markets billboard advertising will take a lot of research and clever planning. However, with that said, the profit potential for a business that markets billboard advertising is outstanding. The billboard advertising industry works like this. A site to install a billboard is selected based on excellent street visibility and high traffic count. The owner of the building or land where the billboard is installed receives a yearly fee; the amount of money paid to the landowner is based on a percentage of the projected advertising revenues that the billboard will generate. Advertisers wishing to advertise on the billboard pay a one-time art fee to create the ad and a fee for the amount of time the ads are featured on the billboard. One billboard can generate upwards of $10,000 or more each year.

ADVERTISING BROKER
★ $$$

Why pay retail prices to advertise your business? That is the question that you will be asking potential clients if your intentions are to become an independent advertising broker. Purchasing various advertising mediums in advance and in bulk can cut the cost by as much as 50 percent or more. To reinforce this statement, contact your local radio station and ask for the rate for ten 30-second advertising spots versus three hundred 30-second advertising spots. The cost difference will amaze you. Once you have successfully negotiated and secured various advertising mediums in bulk, you can set about reselling the radio advertising spots, display newspaper ads, and more to local businesses in your community at a cost saving to them of 25 percent off the regular advertising rates. Providing clients with a 25 percent discount will still leave you with a 25 percent markup or more on the advertising spots and spaces you have sold.

ONLINE ADVERTISING BROKER
★★ $$$$ 🏠 ✍

Let business owners, professionals, and company marketing representatives decide how much they want to spend on advertising as opposed to being told how much advertising costs. Here is a unique concept—for decades media companies have been setting advertising rates for customers that wish to advertise in their media. Times they are a changing and consumers on all levels are quickly learning that the electronic age of the Internet has created many choices that never existed previously. The concept is basic. Working as an online advertising broker or online advertising club you can develop a Web site focused on letting small business owners and professionals list the type of advertising they are seeking and the price they are prepared to pay for that advertising. Media companies wishing to sell advertising would simply log onto the site and start surfing through the postings or listings to find potential matches. This type of Web site would require careful planning in terms of establishing an operating format that is effective; not to mention some specialized programming and security issues. However, the concept is fresh and without question the demand from small business for this type of online service would certainly be large and welcomed.

PIZZA BOXES
★★ $$ 🏠 🕐

Did you know that pizza boxes are not recyclable due to the grease from the pizza that gets into the cardboard? While this may seem like a useless bit of trivia, it is not, as it can become your greatest and most powerful marketing tool for persuading pizza shop owners and local merchants to partake in a pizza box advertising and recycling program. Here is how it works: Owners of the pizza shop get their pizza boxes for 50 percent of the regular cost for allowing local noncompeting merchants to advertise on the pizza box, and this can potentially save them thousands of dollars each year. Local merchants that advertise on the pizza boxes receive low-cost highly effective advertising and the advertisement can be in the form of a cutout coupon featuring a discount for the merchant's products and services. Consumers still receive a great-tasting pizza, plus valuable discount coupons that can be redeemed at local stores. Last, but not least, the pizza box is partially recycled into coupons and gets a renewed lease on life, which in turn helps us all.

WEB RESOURCE: www.theboxandcontainercorp.com Manufacturers of pizza boxes.

FREE INTERNET TERMINALS
★★ $$$$ 🏠 🕐 ✍

Free Internet terminals are simply kiosks that contain computer equipment capable of connecting to the Internet. The terminals are strategically located in high-traffic community gathering places such as malls and sports complexes, and are free to use for visitors of the location. Due to the fact that the Internet terminals are free to use, the business that owns and operates the terminals sell advertising space on the kiosks to local companies to generate sales and profits for the business. In most cases advertising revenue split will not have to be part of an agreement to secure high-traffic locations throughout the community for the terminals. Participating businesses will benefit from increased foot traffic as a result of the free Internet terminals being installed on the site.

WEB RESOURCE: www.kiosks.org Directory service listing firms that design and construct custom Internet technology kiosks.

RESTAURANT PLACEMATS
★★ $$ 🏠 🕐

Like restaurant menus, many restaurant owners are more than happy to have community businesses featured on their table placemats in exchange for receiving the placemats for free. Here is how the business works. Assume that a busy 50-seat restaurant would use 200 paper placemats each day or approximately 6,000 per month, and the cost to print 6,000 black and white placemats on color paper would be around 10 cents each, or a total of $600. Furthermore, the placemats would feature 16 business card-sized display advertisements around the outside of the placemat, while the inside of the placemat would feature trivia questions. Charging local merchants a mere 1.5 cents per advertisement, per placemat would generate total sales of $1,440 per restaurant each month, or a gross profit of $840. Now times that by ten restaurants, and you would have a great little advertising business generating sales in excess of $100,000 per year.

ONLINE ADVERTISING CONSULTANT
★★★ $$ 🏠 🕐 🖱

The rush to get online is heating up, and some estimates indicate as many as one thousand businesses are going online everyday in the United States. In the real world businesses need to advertise their products and services and the cyberworld is no different, thus creating a fantastic business opportunity working as an Internet advertising consultant. As previously mentioned, 1,000 businesses are going online every day in hopes of cashing in on cyberprofits. In the rush to get a Web site developed and posted, many business owners fail to consider how they will advertise their site once online. In a nutshell, the role of an Internet advertising consultant is to develop an advertising program specifically created to meet a client's particular needs. How do you register a Web site with search engines? What are the benefits of a rotating banner advertising program? What other Web sites should my site be hyperlinked too? What are the best print publications to advertise my Web site in? These are questions that many cyberentrepreneurs are willing to pay top dollar for the answers to.

ADS-THAT-WORK BOOK
★ $$$ 🏠 🕐

Calling all advertising and marketing specialists. The time has never been better than now to write and distribute a book in print and electronic format that teaches business owners and managers how to create effective advertisements that work for their businesses, in terms of creating consumer demand for a product or service and increasing sales. Ideally the book or guide will be broken into sections relating to various advertising mediums such as how to create winning classified ads, how to create effective display advertisements, and information about advertising on the World Wide Web. Once the advertising book or guide has been completed, it can be sold on a wholesale basis to book retailers or distributors or directly to business owners via the Internet. Other avenues for sales are seminars, direct mail campaigns, and business association networking meetings.

HUMAN BILLBOARDS
★★★ $$ 🏠 🕐 🌐

Here is a terrific homebased business start-up for entrepreneurs with good marketing skills, but limited investment capital. Human billboards advertise everything from new home developments to car dealerships and are starting to catch on as a highly effective cost-efficient method of advertising and promoting their products and services. Human billboards are simply people that hold signs or banners emblazoned with promotional and advertising messages in high-traffic areas of the community; usually outside, in front, or in close proximity to the business they are promoting. The objective of a human billboard is twofold. First, get the attention of passing motorists and pedestrians, and once you have their attention, get them to take action. This simply means you want these people to go to the business that is being promoted. There are really two aspects to operating this type of business: marketing and the people who will be the actual human billboards. In terms of the people who will work as the human billboards, seek to hire homemakers, students, actors, musicians, and retirees, basically anyone that is available to work on a part-time, as-needed basis. Additionally, you will want to develop a short training program. Vital to the success of the business will be the ability of the human billboards to get the desired response, which of course is to be noticed. The training program can focus on body language and vocal phrasing, both of which, if used correctly, can be highly effective. Marketing the service can be as easy as setting appointments with local business owners to explain and promote the benefits of your service. Joining community business associations and networking clubs are also good ways to promote the service. Rates for human billboards vary based on factors such as the number of people (billboards), the length of the promotion, and other items like signage and if the people (billboards) require special costumes. Ideally, you will want to develop a few packages. As an example, a basic package could include one person for four hours with two large promotional signs such as "sale today" or "stop here for a great deal" and a dozen helium-filled balloons attached to the signs. The cost of this basic program could be in the range of $75 to $100 and you could have optional upgrade packages. People enlisted to work as the billboards could be paid on a subcontract hourly basis or on a percentage of the value of the contract.

INDOOR AND OUTDOOR SPECIALTY ADVERTISING

★★ $$ 🏠 🕐

Mentioned in this directory are numerous indoor and outdoor advertising businesses that can be started and operated for profit and success. However, in the spirit of being unique, also consider these additional types of indoor and outdoor advertising opportunities that perhaps might be the right new venture for you to specialize in.

Window Billboards

Vacant storefronts and professional offices that do not utilize window space for display purposes are two highly visible and potentially profitable places to display window billboards. Window billboards are two-foot by three-foot color poster advertisements that are laminated in plastic. The minibillboards can be installed in commercial window spaces using small and transparent suction cups. Strike deals with retailers, property owners, and professional offices to join your window billboard advertising program. In exchange for allowing the window billboards to be displayed, participants would receive 40 percent of the monthly revenues the window billboards generate. Solicit local merchants and service providers to rent the advertising spaces at $50 per month plus the cost to create the poster.

Golf Driving Ranges

If your local golf driving range does not have an advertising program in place then you should seriously consider approaching the management of such a facility to initiate one. There are two fantastic locations for highly visible advertising at most golf driving ranges: tee box dividers and distance targets. The golf driving range provides the space for the advertisements and you market the program to local businesses that want this type of advertising exposure. Split the revenues with the golf range and all win.

Telephone Booths

Indoor and outdoor telephone booths and enclosures are fantastic venues to feature advertising place cards. Once again if your local telephone company does not have this type of advertising program in place, then this could be your opportunity to make arrangements to operate the program for them.

Washrooms

Who would want to advertise their business in a washroom? Lots of businesses. Why? A captive audience. Washroom advertising has become extremely popular in the last few years, and many media companies are feverishly working to secure the rights to the busiest washrooms, both public and private, across the country. However, this does not mean that an opportunity does not exist for the small operator to start this type of unique advertising service as there are millions of good locations, and it will take years before the market is saturated. Washroom ads are generally 12-inches wide and 18-inches high, full color, and sealed in an aluminum frame with a plastic covering face. The ads are typically installed beside vanity mirrors, above urinals, and on the back of stall doors. Good washroom locations include airports, restaurants, bars, roadside rest stops, community markets, sports complexes, and arenas.

Planters

Purchase commercial grade, highly attractive rectangular box planters and supply the planters for both indoor and outdoor use complete with plants to retailers, professionals, and restaurants free of charge. Of course in exchange for providing the planters the host location must agree to water and allow a small advertising place card (12" x 12") featuring a noncompeting business ad to be installed on the planter. Solicit local merchants and service providers to rent these highly visible advertising spaces for $25 per month or more.

Delivery Vehicles

In every community across North America there are delivery vehicles of all sizes that make fantastic mobile billboards. Strike a partnership with a courier company, moving company, or basically any company that operates a fleet of service or delivery vehicles to initiate an advertising program. The delivery company allows their vehicles to have advertisements installed on them, and you promote and sell the advertising spaces and split the ad revenues with the delivery company

DRIVE-BY BROADCASTING
★★ $$ 🏠 🕐

You can start an advertising business that rents low-powered FM transmitters for less than a $10,000 initial investment, and the profit potential is outstanding. The Federal Communications Commission allows low-powered FM transmitters to be used without the purchase of a license. There are regulations, such as the maximum broadcasting range is 100 feet and the transmission must not interfere with existing transmissions. However, these regulations are easy to conform to, especially if you purchase the right equipment that has been specifically designed to meet these regulations and to be used for specialty advertising purposes. Typically a sign is used to promote the broadcast, asking people passing by to tune into a frequency on their FM dial and listen to a prerecorded message, which is usually playing on a continuos loop. At one time the quality of these prerecorded messages were at best described as poor, but with the advent of digital technology it is now possible to record the message digitally on a CD-ROM for playback. This type of advertising promotion is excellent for real estate agents to use for promoting a house-for-sale listing, car dealers to promote service specials or car listings, fitness clubs to promote membership sales, and retailers of all sorts to promote sales and clearance events. The cost of each individual broadcasting transmitter is reasonably priced in the $500 range, and rentals for the equipment are typically in the range of $75 to $100 per week. Some operators of these broadcasting businesses will even let clients have use of the equipment at no charge, providing they pay a fee to have their message professionally recorded by their service. There are many options available for the clever entrepreneur to profit in this homebased business on a full- or part-time basis.

WEB RESOURCE: www.fmtransmitters.com Distributor of low-powered FM transmitters and accessories.

PROMOTIONAL BUTTONS
★★ $$ 🏠 🕐

Making promotional buttons is a great home-based business opportunity for the entrepreneur that is looking for a way to generate extra part-time income. The business is easy to start, requires little in the way of experience, equipment, or investment capital, and has the potential to earn you $25 per hour. Promotional buttons have been used by businesses, charities, and organizations for decades as an highly effective, low-cost marketing tool to get a message out about a product, service, or event. Creating promotional buttons could not be easier, especially when you consider that the design or message featured on the button can be supplied in digital format by the customer. It can also be easily created on a computer and then simply transferred via software to a printing stamp or pad to create the finished product. In addition to a computer and software, you will also need a button press, a pad printing press, and a few supplies to get started—all of which add up to an initial investment of less than a few thousand dollars. Market the buttons to businesses, charity organizations, schools, and just about any other business, club, or group that is seeking a way to create a low-cost promotional campaign. Join business and social clubs to network for clients and be sure to hand out a lot of buttons promoting your promotional button business. Much more memorable than handing out a business card, wouldn't you agree?

WEB RESOURCE: www.badgeamint.com Manufacturers and distributors of badge making equipment and supplies.

NOTES

KEY

RATINGS ★
START-UP COST $
HOMEBASED
BUSINESS
PART-TIME
LEGAL ISSUES
FRANCHISE OR
LICENSE POTENTIAL
ONLINE

25
ART
Businesses You Can Start

ART SUPPLIES
★★ $$$$

Millions of people enjoy creating art as a hobby. It is a great way to be creative and reduce stress. All of these people require art supplies to be able to enjoy their hobbies, and this fact creates a terrific opportunity to a start-up art supplies retail store. The store does not have to be large, just well stocked with all the popular art supplies. You can also conduct painting and sculpting classes at night to earn extra income. The investment required to start an art supply store will be in the range of $25,000. However, the profit potential is very good as art supplies are often marked up 100 percent or more. Furthermore, you may also want to occasionally take the business mobile and deliver art supplies to elderly homes and care facilities, as it can often be difficult for these people to get out and pick up supplies for their art projects.

WEB RESOURCE: www.arcat.com/arcatcos/cos37/arc37442.cfm National Art Materials Trade Association.

ONLINE ART SUPPLIES
★ $$$ 🏠 🕐 🖱

Remote or small communities often do not have a store that stocks and sells art supplies, and these are the communities that you will want to target if your intentions are to establish a Web site that features art supplies for sale. In addition to mainstream art supplies like paint, brushes, and canvas, also consider selling more exotic or hard-to-find art supplies. The more varied the selection the better the chances of securing repeat visitors and customers to the site. Furthermore, to keep inventory purchases to a minimum seek to build alliances with manufacturers of art supplies who will ship directly to your customers.

Promote the site in print publications, through art schools and classes, and Internet marketing and advertising options.

WEB RESOURCE: www.entrepreneur.com Create a business Web site with MySite professional Web site builder.

HOTEL ART SUPPLY

Look closely and you will notice that hotels are virtually art galleries. You will find paintings, prints, and sculptures in almost every room, hallway, lounge, and lobby. Assume that one hotel has 150 rooms, one lobby, two banquet rooms, one lounge, and ten hallways. The hotel's art requirements could be as many as 200 paintings or prints alone. Simply supplying one hotel with a complete art decor package can make you thousands of dollars in profits. To activate this business you will want to establish a relationship with at least 15 to 20 different artists who work in various art mediums. Next take digital pictures of the artwork and place it on a CD-ROM and simply start setting meetings and knocking on doors. Placing pictures of the sample artwork on CD-ROM will enable you to do mobile professional presentations right from your laptop computer. Of course, the big profit opportunities are landing art supply contracts with hotels that are being constructed or undergoing total interior renovations.

WEB RESOURCE: www.ahma.com American Hotel and Motel Association.

JUNKYARD SCULPTURES

There are two ways to make money in a junkyard sculpture business. The first, create and sell art sculptures made from junkyard items. The second, supply art schools and artists with interesting junkyard items. In both instances a little bit of innovation can make you a lot of money. When my wife and I were first married, like most newlyweds money was tight. Out of 50 percent inspiration and 50 percent desperation my wife decided to try and remedy the situation by creating a part-time income

to supplement our family income. Her choice was to go to auto recycling yards and purchase old car springs for about 25 cents apiece. Once home she sanded and painted the springs lively colors and placed silk flower arrangements inside. The recycled car springs became known as "Spring's Springs." She sold "Spring's Springs" to gift shops, garden centers, and interior designers on a wholesale basis, and it didn't take long until it became a full-time and very profitable venture. There are a great deal of business opportunities available or that can be created. Sometimes, it just requires us to open our minds to imaginative ideas.

PAINTER

Painting fine works of art definitely requires a great degree of talent, and if you posses this talent what a wonderful way to make a living. As an artist you can paint commissioned and noncommissioned pieces. Commissioned painting for corporations is a very good way to stabilize your income. There are also many art galleries who will accept and display your artwork for a commission on the sale of the artwork. Either way, there is nothing like being self-employed in a business or profession that you enjoy and that you can earn a living at.

ART PRINTS

Whether you are the artist or someone else has created the original art, there is big money in art prints. Art prints are relatively inexpensive to have produced and can retail for as much as $1,000 for a popular piece. Once you have chosen the works that will be reproduced, you can begin to sell the art prints. Set up a sales kiosk in a mall on a busy weekend or rent a booth in a high-traffic flea market. You can also market the art prints to business professionals for office decorations or to interior designers for home decorations. I talked to one gentleman who operated an art print shop in an airport location. He told me that he was selling between 75 and 100 prints per week to business travelers who were taking the prints home as gifts. Assuming he only cleared $15 on each print after all expenses and taxes, he would still be earning more than $60,000 annually.

ONLINE ART PRINTS

Caught up in the excitement of having prints produced from their original artwork, many artists fail to consider how they will market the prints. Herein lies a business opportunity. Develop a Web site that exclusively features art prints for sale. The site can be indexed by print theme and artists from around the world can submit pictures of their prints to be posted. Upon sale of a print the artist would ship it to the purchaser and would receive a percentage of the sales value. Ideally, marketing efforts would be aimed at individuals and organizations that routinely purchase art prints such as decorators, corporations, and property developers. This type of cyberventure is relatively easy to establish and could be operated from home on a part-time basis.

ART AUCTIONS

Every home in North America features some sort of art as decoration. The market for art is enormous and continues to grow as our population expands. Starting an art auction and liquidation sales service is a great way to become your own boss. There are thousands of artists who have works that they cannot, or do not have the ability, to sell. Why not sell it for them? You can advertise the art auctions and liquidation sales in local newspapers, via e-mail, or fax broadcasts, and start making money right away. Start by visiting art schools and associations so you can begin to market your services to artists who want to sell their works. Once you have a few hundred works of art committed, you can hold the first art auction or sale. You will need to rent a temporary location for your "one-day art sale," and good locations include hotel ballrooms or banquet facilities. Room rental may not even cost any money providing you can convince the hotel manager potential

food and drink concession sales will be sufficient for rent payment. The rest is straightforward; hold the first art auction or sale. You do not need to be an auctioneer to start and operate this type of business, just wear formal clothes for a professional appearance. Once you have perfected the business locally, you can duplicate the process and hold art auctions and sales across the country.

REQUIREMENTS: Computer skills and equipment will be advantageous when you start to catalog the art for listing purposes.

START-UP COSTS: The only cost associated with starting an art auction service is time and an initial advertising budget. Once you have established the approximate value of the items to be sold, you will be able to set an advertising budget. I would suggest about 5 to 10 percent of the estimated total sale value of the items to be sold at the art auction or sale. Total start-up costs are $5,000 to $10,000.

PROFIT POTENTIAL: You should be able to use a very basic formula for establishing a billing rate. Charge a 50 percent commission on all sales (no reserve pricing in effect), and allow half of the commissions to cover the total overheads associated with the sale. Providing each sale averages $10,000 in gross revenues, and one show per month is conducted, the business would net $30,000 per year.

ONLINE ART AUCTIONS

Once again, millions of professional and amateur artists are seeking ways to sell their artwork and this fact creates a fantastic opportunity to start an online art auction service. The challenge with operating this type of cyberventure will not be securing works of art to be auctioned, but promoting the site in such a manor that it receives a lot of visitor hits and interest. In terms of marketing and promoting the site, consider building an alliance with a major player on the Web like an ISP or brand name site. Revenues and profits will be created when artwork has been successfully auctioned and I would suggest retaining a commission in the range of 10 to 25 percent of the total selling value for providing the service.

MATTING AND FRAMING SHOP
★★ $$$

There is a lot of competition in the art framing and matting industry, and it can only mean one of two things. No one is making any money. Or, the second and more logical meaning, this is big business and there is plenty of work and profits to go around. Framing stores are relatively inexpensive to start and operate and, like a lot of retail products and services sold, there are gigantic markup percentages placed on the wholesale costs of art and picture framing goods. A large markup allows most retail operations the ability to survive and continue to offer valuable products and services to consumers. Begin with researching your local market to determine if there is a demand for this service or room for an additional framing store. The business requires some special skills, in terms of making custom frames and cutting glass. However, both of these skills can be mastered in a short period of time, and you can generally find instruction classes offered on these subjects in your local community.

WEB RESOURCE: www.framingsupplies.com Distributors of matting and framing supplies and equipment.

WALL MURALS
★ $$ 🏠 🕐 ⚖️

Many building and business owners are turning to having wall murals painted on large areas of their buildings (interior and exterior) for promotional purposes and as a method to deter graffiti. If you have the ability, or can form a group of people with the ability to produce attractive wall murals, then you can make a lot of money operating your own custom wall mural painting service. Paint your first wall mural for free (with permission of course) and use the finished product as your presentation. I will guarantee you that no one else has a presentation portfolio like it. Approach businesses with photographs of your work. Additionally, have a few suggestions and rough drafts of the wall mural you are proposing for their location with you to show during the presentation. It may take a few stops and

presentations, but soon your art services will be in high demand.

CUSTOM AIRBRUSHING
★★★ $$ 🏠 🕐

Paint airbrushing is very popular and has many uses including: customizing cars, creating wall murals, decorating clothing, and creating a one-of-a-kind paint finish on almost any product. The equipment necessary for this business is inexpensive and can be ordered through art supply or paint supply stores. I contacted two businesses that offered custom airbrushing services. One was in the yellow pages, and the second was referred to me by an automotive body shop. In both instances, the charge to create custom airbrushed images was $60 per hour (plus material) with no guarantees on how long it would take to finish the job. Working a mere 25 hours a week providing airbrushing services can earn you as much as $70,000 per year.

WEB RESOURCE: www.airheadairbrush.com Suppliers of airbrushing equipment and supplies.

NATIVE ART
★ $$ 🏠 🕐

Native peoples of the United States and Canada create some of the most beautiful art available, and these artworks are in high demand, especially in overseas markets such as Japan, Germany, and the United Kingdom. The demand for native art creates a great business opportunity for you, if you have a good contact base in foreign countries. This business allows you to work as a highly compensated broker by representing native artists locally and using your international contacts to set up distribution channels in foreign countries. The business can also work in reverse. You can set up distribution channels in North America representing artists from foreign countries. The business does require a lot of research and set up time, but the potential rewards can justify the effort.

WEB RESOURCE: www.iaca.com Indian Arts and Crafts Association.

MOBILE ART GALLERY
★★★ $$

Once again, art is big business, and starting a mobile art gallery can put you on the road to riches. Take a traditional art gallery; place wheels on it and you have this business opportunity in a nutshell. Maybe it is not that simple, but pretty close. In this enterprise you will want to work with perhaps a hundred artists or more. This is a volume-based operation. Once you have selected the artists, begin to establish locations where the artworks will be featured. Good locations include doctor office waiting rooms, office lobbies, restaurants, hospitals, and all other high-traffic gathering places. The art can be displayed in these locations with a small place card on each piece, which reads, "this art is for sale, for further information call (your business name and a toll-free 1-800 number)." When a potential customer calls to inquire about a particular piece of art for sale, you would simply sell the art over the phone and arrange delivery to the purchaser. If a piece sells for $100 then you would give the artist $50, the host location $10 and keep $40 for yourself. As you can see, on a volume basis there is enormous potential for profit. Imagine if you had only 100 locations selling just two pieces of art per month at an average sale price of $150—you would stand to make more than $10,000 every month.

REQUIREMENTS: Operating a mobile art gallery business requires excellent cold calling, presentation, organization, and negotiation skills. You will also need reliable transportation and a computer system to track and maintain customer files and inventory lists.

START-UP COSTS: The investment to set this business enterprise in motion is minimal, in the range of $8,000 to $10,000 will be sufficient to purchase any required equipment and leave enough working capital to operate on for a few months while the business is being established.

PROFIT POTENTIAL: Charging a flat commission of 40 percent for you, and generating gross sales of $250,000 per year will generate business revenues of $100,000. Once again, I stress that you must secure as many art installation locations or "silent salespeople" as you possibly can.

ONLINE ART GALLERY
★ $$$

Like an online art auction, an online art gallery also offers works of art for sale, but not in an auction format. This is the type of art marketing system that many well-established artists prefer to the auction format, as the value of their works cannot be diminished by lack of bids. The site can be indexed into various art mediums, and artists wishing to be featured on the site pay a monthly fee or a commission upon the successful sale of the artwork. Like many online ventures, the key to success often lays within promoting and marketing the site. No visitors, no chance to generate sales. Thus you will have to seek unique and innovative ways to build and maintain site traffic.

HAND-PAINTED CALENDARS
★★ $

Small business and large corporations alike give away millions of calendars every year in hopes that they will be posted in a visible area and remind customers of their products and services. Starting a business that produces hand-painted calendars enables you to fill the growing market demand for calendars while making excellent profits for yourself. Hand-painted calendars make wonderful gifts for business owners to give to special customers and clients. Using watercolor paints to depict landscapes or pictorial themes, you can create the calendars quickly and inexpensively. Marketing the calendars can also be inexpensive. All that is required are a few samples of your work and some time to stop into businesses and present your talents. Or in other words, simply go out and ask for the business.

REQUIREMENTS: Watercolor painting techniques can be learned very easily, and there are many instruction classes available in almost every community to assist you in learning this painting technique. You will also need calendars to practice with, as well as providing you with an initial inventory. Of course if you find that your particular talents are better suited to the marketing side of the business, you can always enlist the services of hungry art students to produce the calendars.

START-UP COSTS: Even if you factor in the cost of art classes and materials to get started, the initial investment into this new venture will still be less than $500. If you choose the route of having others create the calendars for you, the start-up costs could be cut in half, unfortunately so will the profits.

PROFIT POTENTIAL: Hand-painted calendars retail in the price range of $60 to $100 each, and can go even higher if the theme is very elaborate. If you are painting the calendars yourself, you can keep your costs down to around $2 or $3 per calendar, including all materials. In terms of time to paint the 12 pictures required for the calendar, I am told by an artist friend that it would take about three to four hours in total to complete. Based on these figures you would expect to earn about $25 per hour, which is excellent for a business that can be started for less than $500.

HAND-PAINTED GREETING CARDS

★★ $ 🏠 🕐

Like hand-painted calendars, there is large market demand for hand-painted greeting cards and post cards. Once again, if you have the ability to produce the finished product yourself, that's great. If not, there are many artists who will be glad to assist you, for a fee. The greeting and post cards can be wholesaled to retailers or sold directly to companies to give as corporate gifts to clients. If you plan to specialize in hand-painted post cards, you will want to sell them in high-traffic tourist areas like airports, tourist attractions, and beaches. Whichever you decide, this business can be both fun and profitable, and best of all, it can be started for peanuts.

PORTRAIT ARTIST

★ $$ 🏠 🕐

Once again, artistic talent does not need to be on your side for this new business enterprise. Person, pet, or object, many people wish to have something immortalized on canvas for a myriad of reasons. The first step will be to establish a working relationship with a few professional portrait artists or art students seeking income opportunities. Next, you will want to acquire some samples of their artwork and start to market your new business. Simply put, start asking around for businesses, professionals, pet shops, animal breeders, sports celebrities, and anyone else who may be interested in a painted portrait of themselves or of a loved one. The only requirement to get started is a good camera so that once you have secured a paying client you can take a picture of the subject for the artist to work from. This can also be accomplished by using a digital camera and electronic computer file transfer if distance between you, the artist, and the subject is of issue. Revenues for your business will be by way of a 30 to 40 percent commission of the total selling price of the completed artwork.

ARTIST AGENT

★ $$ 🏠 🕐

An artist agent is the same as any other industry agent. You simply represent the talents or skills of an individual or group of individuals. Remuneration is by way of a commission charged on work sold; generally the commission rate is between 10 and 20 percent of the total selling value of the art. Why would an artist seek to be represented by an agent? There are many reasons why artists would need and require professional representation, including greater exposure and recognition, negotiation experience, privacy, marketing abilities, contacts, and various other resources that may not be available to the artists themselves. If you are considering becoming an artists' agent, you will definitely need the aforementioned skills and have to be prepared to research the art industry in great depth. This type of business does have a very steep learning curve. With proper preparation, working as an artist agent can be a very rewarding profession, both financially and personally.

FRAMED MOVIE POSTERS

★★ $$ 🏠 🕐

Movie posters can often be purchased for less than $1 each from video stores and movie theaters. Once framed, these valuable pieces of art can be resold at flea markets, mall kiosks, and to interior designers for terrific profits. Older movie posters are also in high demand as collector items, and this side of the business is best suited for Internet sales. You can develop your own Web site for a small investment and start marketing collectible movie posters. There are guides available that list the value of collectable movie posters depending on condition. These guides will be an invaluable source of information if you intend to offer collectible movie posters for sale.

CHARCOAL PORTRAITS

 ★ $ ◔

Can you produce attractive charcoal portraits of people in a very short time frame? If not, you may want to take some courses so you can, as people portraits created from charcoal drawings is one of the greatest all time "cash" art business that can be started. We have all seen street artists who produce quick charcoal portraits of people. These portraits usually cost $20 and the artist is paid in cash. I live close to a tourist area, and in the summer I have watched street artists draw as many as five portraits in an hour's time. Your math skills do not have to be good to know that adds up to $100 an hour for about $2 or $3 worth of art supplies. Perhaps traveling to foreign destinations is your dream. If so, this is the perfect business opportunity for you. With little more than a passport, suitcase, and a few art supplies, you could easily work your way around the world producing charcoal portraits in every tourist mecca.

CARICATURES

★ $ 🏠 ◔

Big, easily recognizable heads and faces with small bodies is funny stuff, especially if the caricature is of a person we know and do business with. Hire a caricature artist who is prepared to work on a piece-work basis and start to market caricature drawings to local business owners. You will be amazed at the interest you will receive right out of the blocks. Restaurants will purchase caricatures of their staff to adorn the front of menus, professionals will pur-

chase a caricature of themselves to send to clients in the form of a thank-you card, and retail businesses will purchase caricatures of valued regular customers to hang above the cash register. This is a great business enterprise to put into action as it only requires a little bit of creativity to ignite and about $1,000 to start.

ALBUM COVER ART

 ★★ $ 🏠 ◔

Old LP records are not only collectible for the music, but also for the often very elaborate album covers. Once framed, album covers become fantastic pieces of art and are highly sought after home and office decorations. The perfect place to market your music art is to CD music shops. This is a great retail distribution point as the match and fit is ideal. Establishing retail accounts is as simple as booking appointments with music shop managers and presenting finished and framed samples of your music artwork. At first you may even want to locate the artwork in the retail stores on a consignment basis. This can be your way of reassuring retailers that this is a no risk situation. Additional methods to market the product include sales to interior designers, flea markets, mall kiosks, and direct sales to businesses like clothing stores, restaurants, and offices. Whichever marketing method you chose, there will be very little resistance to sales of the art, as there is virtually no competition in this business. The best source for the album covers are garage sales, flea markets, and used record stores (covers must be in good condition).

REQUIREMENTS: I suggest that you not only frame the album covers, but you also manufacture the frames yourself. In doing this you can better suit a frame to the art. Create highly attractive frames from brushed metal, glass, and other interesting materials. You will need a few basic hand tools and framing supplies, but that is about all that is required to get this business rolling.

START-UP COSTS: Including the cost of album covers, basic hand tools, and framing materials, your total initial investment required to get the business rolling will be less than $500.

PROFIT POTENTIAL: Once framed, you will have no problem commanding $30 to $40 for each piece wholesale and more than $60 retail. The profit margins are great when you consider that you can purchase the albums covers for about 50 cents, spend another $5 on framing material and only have a half hour's time into each finished piece. Providing you can tap into the right market to sell your music artwork, you can easily make $1,000 per month or more, and best of all, this can be accomplished with a part-time effort of only 10 to 12 hours per week.

MIRROR ART

 ★ $ 🏠 🕒

Mirror art is simply small pieces of mirror in varying colors and shapes that have been assembled together to resemble a picture, landscape or even abstract design. Mirror art is becoming very trendy for use as home decorations. In most cases a trip to your local glass shop will result in all the mirror you will need for this new venture, and usually at no cost. Why? Most glass shops dispose of mirror cutoff pieces that are too small to sell, but these same pieces of mirror are perfectly sized to create mirror art. The equipment needed to create the art is inexpensive and includes a few hand tools and a glass grinder. Also, patterns are available to make the mirror art or you can create your own. Once completed, the art can be sold via flea market booths and by renting a sales kiosk in malls.

STENCILING

 ★★ $ 🏠 🕒

Specializing in custom stenciling is a fantastic low-investment business you can start and manage right from a homebased office. In the past few years stenciling has once again become a popular interior decorating art medium. The uses vary from decorative wall borders to creating beautiful patterns on cabinet doors. To get started all you have to do is practice. There are many how-to books and videos available that will teach you specific secrets and methods about creative paint stenciling. Basic materials that will be required include paint, paintbrushes, additional paint

applicators, and predesigned stenciling templates. Of course if you have creative flair, you can design your own custom stenciling templates. A paint stenciling service is best marketed by way of referral or word-of-mouth advertising. It may take a little longer to establish a client base this way, however, the extra time will enable you to gain valuable stenciling practice and experience for your new service.

WEB RESOURCE: www.colonialcrafts.com Suppliers of paint stencils and equipment.

NOTES

KEY

RATINGS	★
START-UP COST	$
HOMEBASED BUSINESS	
PART-TIME	
LEGAL ISSUES	
FRANCHISE OR LICENSE POTENTIAL	
ONLINE	

CHILD-RELATED
Businesses You Can Start

CLOTH DIAPER SERVICE
★★★ $$

The not so sweet smells of success. Disposable diapers are not environmentally friendly and can often irritate a baby's skin. The solution? Environmentally-friendly cloth diapers made of natural fibers. A baby can go through as many as 4,000 diapers before being fully toilet-trained, and this fact of life creates an outstanding business opportunity. Depending on your business start-up budget, there are two methods of pursuing this venture. In the first, you offer a complete service, meaning, you supply, deliver, and pick up the cloth diapers, and you also clean the diapers. The second start-up method is to simply supply delivery and pickup of the diapers and have an established commercial laundry clean them. If start-up capital is not a problem, the first option will definitely leave more profits for you. To market a cloth diaper service, try to obtain a list of new baby births from local hospitals. If these lists are not available, start to scan newspapers

for birth announcements. Once you have compiled a list of potential clients, simply drop off or mail a marketing presentation to parents outlining the benefits of your service and how they can contact you.

BICYCLE SAFETY COURSES
★★ $

Thousands of children are seriously injured each year as a result of bicycling accidents. Most of these accidents and injuries could have been avoided had the children and parents attended a cycling safety instruction course. Here is your opportunity to not only start your own business, but also provide a service that can help prevent needless cycling accidents involving children. A bicycle safety instruction service can be initiated on a shoestring budget and operated on a year-round basis using all of the latest bicycling safety methods and equipment. The total investment cost to get you going will be under a $1,000 including marketing and promotional material, as well as bicycle safety equipment. In terms of an operating location, a roped off section of a mall parking lot would be ideal in the summer, and an indoor school gymnasium or a recreation center would be great for wintertime classes. In both cases you will be required to get permission and possibly pay a small amount of rent. Also incorporate bicycle repairs and maintenance tips into your cycling safety course as this can be used as a terrific marketing tool.

WEB RESOURCE: www.cdc.gov/ncipc/bike/ National Bicycle Safety Network.

BRONZE BABY SHOES

Preserving baby shoes, toys, keepsakes, or soothers, a bronzing service is a surefire winner. Low investment, low overhead, unique, and little competition means big profits for you. To get started in a bronzing service you will need to invest a small amount of money into equipment and samples, but that's about it. Start by simply producing samples of your bronzing work and locate the sample items in every baby or child-related store in your community. Provide the retailers with order forms, bags, and nametags for the items to be bronzed. The retailers' customers will simply drop off the items they want bronzed and pick up the items from the same retailer a week later. In exchange for the retailer providing this service for you, give them a 35 percent commission of the total sale. Of course, you will also need to provide the retailer with a sales price list. There should be no problem in getting retailers on board as they are not required to buy or warehouse any inventory for you.

PARTY ENTERTAINER
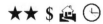

There are a couple of options available in terms of starting a party entertaining service. You can work as an agency representing entertainers for children's parties. Or, you can be an entertainer yourself, if you have the required skills. The different types of entertainers for children's parties include clowns, magicians, trained pet shows, singers, and skit plays. This is a relatively low-investment business to start and operate, and the profit potential is very good. I contacted four different agencies and found the average rate for party entertainers to be $50 per hour with a minimum charge for one and a half hours including travel. One of the more unique agencies even had a dancing troop of monkeys available for children's parties. An agency representing entertainers for parties or being an entertainer yourself is a good home-based business that allows for flexible hours, good income potential, and loads of fun.

DAY-CARE CENTER
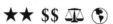

The rising cost of living has made child day care a booming industry simply due to the fact that most families today require two full-time incomes just to survive financially. There are various types of day-care centers, such as homebased, storefront locations, mall and business locations, and mobile day care, and all have their benefits and drawbacks. Once you have determined the operating location and type of day care, the next step will be to get parents to bring their children. This can be accomplished in many ways, and a good starting point is a strong marketing presentation. Parents today want to know their children will be safe, happy, well cared for, and mentally stimulated. I recently visited a day-care center that was very successful, and the key to their success was the fact they installed video cameras in every part of their day-care facility. The digital video cameras gave the daycare the ability to broadcast live over the Internet via their Web site. What a great idea. Parents at work were able to check on and watch their children anytime they wanted to simply by logging onto the day-care Web site.

REQUIREMENTS: In almost all areas of North America, day-care centers and staff require certification. It is very important that you meet all requirements, and in most cases you strive to exceed these legal requirements. You will also be required to carry liability insurance and have on-site safety equipment such as first-aid kits, fire safety equipment, and emergency action plans. Once again, if your approach is professional and very well planned, you will have no difficulty in charging a premium over other competing day-care services in your community.

START-UP COSTS: Homebased day-care facilities can cost as little as $5,000 to establish, while full-scale day-care centers operating from an independent business location can cost as much as $100,000 to start.

PROFIT POTENTIAL: Once you have established the type of day care you will be operating, the next step will be to factor in all overheads and establish a cost per child to provide your service. You will then add a markup or profit margin onto this cost to establish a retail price. Regardless of the size or type of service you provide, you can expect a healthy return on investment. You should have no difficulties earning in excess of $40,000 per year.

WEB RESOURCE: www.nccanet.org National Child Care Association.

CHILDREN'S PARTY SERVICE
★★ $$

Every day thousands of children have birthdays, graduate to the next grade, or just deserve some fun, and all of these events are a very good reason to celebrate and have a party. The main consideration for starting this type of party service is whether the business be operated from a fixed location or on a mobile basis? Once you have established the base of operations, you can begin to market the party service. A great starting point will be a well-designed and colorful marketing brochure describing your service. These brochures can be circulated to daycare centers, kids sports association meetings, and recreation centers. Remember not to overlook elderly groups and associations as this can be a very lucrative market to tap into. After all, grandparents love to spoil their grandchildren. Try to make the party service a one-stop shopping experience, and include items such as a location for the party, theme, party favors, activities, transportation, food, entertainment, and prizes. It's not a bad idea to include some educational value too, if you can make the kids think it's fun.

EDUCATIONAL TOYS
★ $$

Traditional educational toys and games for children will always be popular and in-demand. You can design and develop the toys and games yourself or act as an agent for manufacturers. Both methods can be a very profitable way to earn an income and be self-employed. There are various approaches to marketing educational toys and games including the Internet, mail order, home parties, flea markets, and sales to specialty retailers on a wholesale basis. A unique marketing method may be to hold free seminars for parents with a central theme—perhaps "improve your child's reading skills." The seminar would state all the facts and benefits that improved reading comprehension has for their children. Of course, during the "free seminar" you would promote the products you want the parents to purchase at the end of the seminar. If you choose this route, be sure to establish alliances with experts in the field of child education to speak at the seminars on the subject of the benefits of educational children's toys and games.

PIÑATA SALES
★★ $

This is one of my favorite business start-up enterprises of all the opportunities featured in the children's chapter of the directory. What a great business and concept—homebased, unique, low overhead, minimal start-up costs, virtually no competition, and no limitations on business growth and expansion. Thousands of children's parties take place every day, and tapping into this very lucrative market is easy. Simply develop samples of your products and start knocking on doors. I will guarantee that you will find little resistance to your product, and chances are the biggest business challenge you will face is trying to keep up with the demand for the piñatas. I suggest that you strictly focus on the wholesale market and establish accounts with retail children's stores, party planners, and Internet malls. Try to get your product into as many mail-order catalogs as possible.

REQUIREMENTS: There are very few requirements in terms of qualifications to start and run this business. The largest would be your creative ability in both manufacturing the piñatas and how you will market the product. Of course, there are always the safety concerns, so be sure to place prizes inside that cannot harm, spoil, or create potential liability for you.

START-UP COSTS: It should cost you less than $100 to develop your samples and possibly another $200 to begin marketing your products. This is the ultimate quick return on investment business.

PROFIT POTENTIAL: After an exhaustive search I finally found a piñata for sale in a children's retail store (in excess of 30 telephone calls and an hour's drive). The piñata retailed for $80 and was based on a birthday sports theme. Upon returning home and careful examination, I determined that it would require about an hour to make the piñata, and $5 worth of materials. Inside this particular piñata was hard candy and a toy prize, maybe another $2 to $3 worth. Even at $25 per hour, the total cost to manufacture this product would be in the $30 range. This still allows for a 30 percent markup on your material costs and labor, while the retailer can maintain a 100 percent markup. Now you see why there will be no problem in establishing wholesale accounts with retailers.

PERSONALIZED STORY TIME BOOKS
★★★ $$$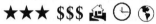

The market for personalized story time books for children is enormous. Every child in the world loves to hear stories, and the best aspect of this new venture is the fact that this business enables you to create books to include children into the story. This is a business that once you have established a relationship with a client you will want to keep that relationship strong as the product has the ability to almost be classified as a consumable. This means that once you form the relationship with the client, it is a given that the relationship will continue to generate revenues for the business, providing the quality of service and product remains excellent. The average child can easily have five or six favorite books, and these books change on a year-by-year basis. This can add up to 20 to 30 different story time books that can be sold to the same client, and that number can multiply by the number of children the client has. There are software applications available including the reprint rights for creating this type of book, or of course you can use the customer's and your imagination to create original stories. A marketing technique

that can help get you started is to pick relatives and friends with children and customize books using their children's names. Once you have the books produced, simply show the story time books to your friends and relatives. It will be nearly impossible for them to say no once they see the finished product and how much work you put into creating the book.

REQUIREMENTS: You will need a good computer system and printer if you plan to produce the books yourself. It can be very costly to have a print shop run a single copy of one item. Additional requirements will include software that legally allows you to reprint the books or good writing skills to create your own stories. The latter is more fun, and you can base the stories on your local community and community events.

START-UP COSTS: The business can be started on a modest budget of less than $10,000, which will include all the necessary computer equipment, software programs, and an initial supplies inventory.

PROFIT POTENTIAL: Once you have established a solid client base, this business venture has the ability to return excellent profits on a part- or full-time effort. As with any business, be sure to use a bottom up approach to product pricing. Factor in all costs, including materials, labor, and overheads, and multiply by the desired markup. The end result of this formula will give you your retail selling price.

WEB RESOURCE: www.hefty.com Distributors of create-a-book software and printing equipment.

COLORING BOOKS
★★ $$$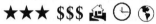

The main focus of this business enterprise is to personalize children's coloring books. The equipment requirements and approach to marketing are very similar to that of the story time book venture. However, an additional marketing technique that can be employed is to design a retail sales kiosk, and locate the kiosk in a busy community mall on weekends. This kind of retail location will enable you to personalize and sell the coloring books right on site. Remember, do not limit your ability to generate revenue. With specialized printing equipment you can also produce children's "u-color-it posters," restaurant placemats, and even specialty greeting cards, all of which can also be sold via the sales kiosk to increase revenues and profits.

ONLINE COLORING BOOKS
★★ $$$$ 📷 ⚲

Online coloring books for kids is a very unique and interesting opportunity that could prove to be both fun and profitable. This online business concept is very straightforward. Simply develop a Web site that features custom designed software that enables kids to chose from a wide selection of images and pictures of animals, people, buildings, and landscapes. These images are downloaded, printed from their desktop printer, and colored using crayons. Alternately you could design a color pallet and tools that would enable kids to color their pictures right on the Web site and print it when they are finished. Kids could print multiple pages and even create their own coloring books to provide them with hours of fun. To generate income to cover the cost for maintaining the site and providing you with a profit, you could license the rights to the Web site to other cyberentrepreneurs to feature a link from their Web sites to yours. In other words this unique interactive tool for kids would be an item that would draw visitors to their site thus increasing hits and the opportunity to create larger revenues.

CHILDREN'S BOOKS AND SOFTWARE STORE
★★ $$$$

The name says it all. In terms of a specialty retail business, this is one of the best. The book side of the business will be of interest to traditional parents. Try to stock hard-to-find titles covering a wide range of topics revolving around or that include children's interaction and involvement. On the software side of the business, try to include software applications for children and for parents with children. Good topics include games, education, how to, instruction, music, sports, and family relationships. You will not need a lot of floor space for the store as all of the items that are stocked are very compact. However, as a traditional retail business there are three words to

live by "location, location, and location." Be sure the store is located in a high-traffic and visible area of the community. Furthermore, you may even want to consider being a "retail store within a retail store." Excellent matches for this type of retailing arrangement include grocery stores, large children's clothing retailers, and family entertainment centers.

CHILDREN'S BOOKS BY CHILDREN
★★ $$$ 📷 🕐

Starting a publishing business that specializes in publishing children's books written by children is a very unique and interesting business enterprise to set in motion. In addition to the books being available in print, they can also be on CD-ROM as well as in an e-book format sold via the Internet. The books can be on numerous topics and subjects such as puzzles and games, short stories, and comics. Marketing the books can be by way of establishing wholesale accounts with retailers, and this should not prove difficult purely due to the unique nature of the product. Furthermore, establishing an alliance with a children's charity group can also be used as an excellent marketing tool, as well as assisting the charity by way of donations on total sales volume.

NURSERY DESIGNER
★★★ $$ 📷 🕐 ⚖

The recent surges in world stock markets have created a lot of new wealth, and with that, a lot of new ways for parents to indulge their children. I recently visited a designer who works from her home and exclusively designs baby nurseries for expecting parents. During this meeting, I gained great insights into this business and how to market this service. First lesson is to throw away everything you know about marketing and promote your service solely on "goo goo ga ga" (as the designer puts it). What she means is that most of the decisions expecting parents make in terms of a baby nursery defy logic and are made on an emotional basis. Her secret to business success is to promote her design talents using elaborate displays at any trade show that is even closely associated with babies and children. This method of marketing enabled her to build a solid client and referral base, with very little (if any) competition at these trade shows. Of course, there are additional marketing options that are open to you in terms of promoting the design service, including working with architects, interior designers, retail children's stores, and custom homebuilders. If you can afford to purchase special designing software, do it. This will give you an advantage when you present your ideas and concepts to potential clients. Most of this software allows you to build a 3-D virtual tour model of the new room right on your computer. Also, make sure that your notebook computer will support these programs so you have the ability to make your presentations mobile.

REQUIREMENTS: Like any design business, you will need a flair for the dramatic and solid design skills. You don't need formal training in most areas of the country as you are not generally changing the structure of the building. However, any certification credentials that you have will definitely be a great marketing tool to use in the business.

START-UP COSTS: Providing you already have access to computer equipment and programs, the investment capital required to get a nursery design service up and rolling will be less than $10,000.

PROFIT POTENTIAL: The profits that can be earned as a nursery designer are excellent. The above-mentioned nursery designer is netting in excess of $80,000 per year after expenses.

CARDBOARD PLAYHOUSES
★★★ $$ 🏠 🕐

Have you ever purchased a new refrigerator, only to find that your children play with the empty box for weeks, instead of playing with their expensive toys? Now is your chance to capitalize on this strange phenomenon. Custom cardboard playhouses are great for kids. They are mobile and can be packed up easily and moved to the beach, Gramma's house, or outside in the summer. To get mobilized in this business, simply design your own playhouse and visit a box manufacturer for an estimate to produce the cardboard playhouses in volume. The playhouses can be sold via retail accounts, mail order, the Internet, craft shows, and flea markets.

DESIGN TIP: Be sure the cardboard playhouses will be interesting to children, and make sure there are a lot of colorful images and themes printed on them.

WEB RESOURCE: www.corrugatedboxes.com Manufacturer and distributor of made-to-order cardboard boxes.

SANDBOX MANUFACTURING
★★★ $$$ 🏠 🕐

Custom sandboxes are the new hot product in the children's play equipment industry. Not the normal 5-foot by 5-foot poorly crafted sandboxes, but new megasandboxes based on a theme, such as outer space, cowboys, or racecars. One manufacturer I recently spoke to expanded his operation of six full-time employees to more than ten, just to keep up with the demand of building and installing his custom "Sand Play Centers" as he refers to them. This may be a great opportunity for you to introduce custom sandboxes into your area, given the number of children and backyards in this country. Even if there is competition, there should still be enough business to go around. The first step will be to design and develop your own products or to find an existing manufacturer and promote their products, preferably under your own company and brand name. Selling the sandboxes should not be difficult. Basically, once you have a sample simply start to establish alliances with other companies in your community that also specialize in children's products. Likewise, displaying and marketing your products at home and garden trade shows can also be an excellent forum to introduce and promote your new products.

REQUIREMENTS: If you plan to design and manufacture your own custom sandboxes, you will probably be required to register the product to safety standards. You may also need specialized manufacturing equipment and skilled staff. Research various kinds of manufacturing material to find out what will best suit your particular application, and make your product safe, durable, and easy to maintain.

START-UP COSTS: Beware. This type of new business venture has a way of costing two or even three times as much as anticipated to start. The reason is that when you are dealing with an item that is custom designed, the process of building a prototype can be very long and include many changes throughout the design process. All of this starts to add up in terms of development costs. However, with careful planning, and keeping a tight control on budgets, a business that manufactures and installs custom sandboxes can be successfully initiated for $25,000.

KITE BUILDING AND SALES
★★★ $$

Starting part-time from your home you can manufacture "one of a kind" kites and sell the kites locally through retail accounts, kiosks, mail order, and the Internet. The investment needed to put this business in action is less than $500, and the operating overheads are virtually nonexistent. On a recent vacation to Cannon Beach, Oregon, I was amazed to find a retail store that specialized only in kite sales. For the hour or so that I was there browsing around at least 15 to 20 people walked through the door and many left with a purchase. To get started you can buy some sample kites to find out what material is used to manufacture the kites and how they are constructed. The store I visited even had "how to build kites" books, videos, and kits. A great promotional idea for the business may be to have a "try before you buy" kite sale. Simply advertise the event in local newspapers, and let potential customers try out the kites before they purchase one. You can hold this event in a local park or at the beach. One thing is for sure it will not take long before a crowd assembles to see what is going on.

WEB RESOURCE: www.aka.kite.org American Kite Fliers Association.

DOLL MAKING
★★ $

It may not seem like it, but doll making and repairs is a giant segment of the craft and toy industry. To reinforce this, simply visit an antique shop that specializes in antique dolls or a retailer of new custom "one of a kind" dolls, and you will soon see that the prices are out of this world. Like kite building, doll making can be started from home on a part-time basis. Once again, the dolls you make can be sold through retail accounts, kiosks, mail order, craft shows, and the Internet. This is an enterprise that requires very little in the way of start-up investment, and the ongoing monthly overhead adds up to what it costs to buy a bag of groceries. Once you have sharpened your skills in doll making, you can proceed to antique doll repairs. Some of the antique dolls that I came across were selling for as much as $500 for the "real thing" and $300 for replicas of the original version. To get started in this aspect of the business, find out if doll making classes are available in your local community. If you find that these types of classes are not available in your community, then once you have mastered the art of doll making and repairs you can begin to hold your own "how to" classes on nights and weekends to earn additional income. Do not forget that in the doll world all of these creations need accessories, houses, cars, clothes, kitchens, and other doll friends, thus a further opportunity exists.

WEB RESOURCE: www.thedollnet.com Directory service with links to suppliers and industry information.

CAMPS FOR CHILDREN
★★ $$$$

Every year millions of parents shuffle their children off to various types of camps for a myriad of reasons. This is an age-old and gigantic industry, but always has room for new and fresh ideas. One of my favorite camps in this industry is a weeklong children's acting camp. Every child wants to be a star and ham it up for friends and family. Of course, the side benefit to this type of training and education is that it builds confidence and socialization skills. Child acting camps generally take place in the summer over the course of a week, and are based on a day camp platform. You can also run this camp during different times of the year. The camps can take place on nights and weekends spread out over longer periods of time. Try to make your camp all-inclusive, which in the case of an acting camp would include a child's acting resume, head shot, and on-air tape. All of these items, with the addition of a completion certificate, can be presented to the students and parents at the end of the camp during the graduation ceremonies. Marketing will require a savvy campaign including brochures, free information seminars, and possibly even a noted professional spokesperson in the profession of the camp you are hosting.

ONLINE CHILDREN'S CAMPS
★★ $$$$ 🏠 🖱

Worldwide, parents have thousands of options in terms of what type and what style of camp they can choose to send their children to. However, due to the fact that there are thousands of choices, most parents will only learn about a very small percentage of these camps, thus potentially missing out on an opportunity to send their children to a camp that would be beneficial in terms of development. Herein lies the business opportunity. Create a Web site that operates as a directory for children's camps located around the globe. The site could be indexed by the style of camp and geographic area. This would enable parents or kids to log on to the site and locate camps that are of interest to them within close proximity to their community. You could literally employ sales consultants in every state, or even country for that matter, to contact camps in their area and solicit the camps to become members featured on the Web site. Given the fact that there are thousands of various camps worldwide it would only require that a small percentage of these camps pay a minimal yearly listing fee to be featured on the site for this online venture to become profitable.

CHILDREN'S PERSONAL SAFETY COURSES
★★ $$ 🏠 🕐

Generally speaking we live in a relatively safe society. However, crime still affects all of our lives at some point. Of course, we always hope that our children are not victims of criminal acts. Criminal acts can be in the form of personal attacks on our children or in the form of having children involved in a criminal act. This scenario can be the basis of your new business. You can hold courses for parents and children on how to prevent, react to, and understand criminal behavior. The courses can be conducted in a group environment or in an in-home "one on one" basis. A great method for marketing these services can be to "tag on" to similar children's courses in your community. For example, if a business, association, or group is holding neighborhood watch meetings, you can attend as a guest speaker with the focus of your presentation aimed at promoting your service. Additional methods to market this service include utilizing press releases about the business to gain interest and establishing alliances with police services and home alarm companies. Also, you will want to design a complete child personal safety guide that can be included in the cost of the course or consulting visit. The guide can become an invaluable marketing tool for promoting your business. Promote the guide as "professional" and "exclusive" to your business. Furthermore, a police, military, or psychology background would be recommended for this business.

USED CHILDRENS CLOTHING SALES
★★ $$ 🕐

Children's clothes are expensive. All parents want the best clothes for their children, but unfortunately, financial budgets do not always allow for the purchase of children's designer clothing. Not to mention the fact that children grow out of their new clothes within a month. The solution to these very real facts are to open a secondhand clothing store featuring apparel for children or rent a booth at a local flea market and sell secondhand children's clothing. In both cases, you can purchase good quality secondhand children's clothing at bargain basement prices and resell the clothing for a profit. Accepting consignment clothing is one way to reduce business start-up costs.

REQUIREMENTS: Selling secondhand clothing will require a retail store location or booth at a busy weekend flea market. Additionally, all the clothing will need to be washed prior to offering the garments for sale. Be sure you have catalogs and other resources available to properly estimate the value of the clothing you will be purchasing for resale purposes.

START-UP COSTS: If you decide to operate from a fixed retail store location you will need in the range of $15,000 to $25,000 to start, stock, and operate the business. If you choose the route of the weekend flea market booth, the business start-up costs will be greatly reduced and you could get started for less than a $3,000 initial investment.

PROFIT POTENTIAL: To be profitable in this type of retail business venture always attempt to maintain a 100 percent markup on clothing items you purchase for resale, and charge a 40 to 50 percent commission for any consignments you accept and sell. If you can maintain yearly gross sales of $100,000 you should have no problem netting $30,000 per year after expenses. If the business is operating from a fixed location, you can add additional revenues from renting children's costumes. There will be a one-time expense to purchase the costumes, however, the costumes will last a long time and generate sizable rental revenues for a great number of years.

WEB RESOURCE: www.smallbizbooks.com Business specific start-up guides and books.

CUSTOM PLAY SETS
★★ $$$+ 🏠 🕐

The demand for custom designed and constructed children's play sets started to boom a few years ago, and these play sets still continue to be a hot seller today. In order to compete for market share in this industry, you will need some very elaborate play set designs and very ingenious marketing strategies. The higher-end multistation play centers seem to be the most popular, thus commanding the largest retail dollar. This may indeed create your niche. You can design and manufacture a smaller, more compact, and affordable version of the large play sets to promote and market. Home and garden trade shows are probably the best bet, in terms of marketing the play sets. Displaying unique and interesting products at trade shows can generate substantial sales leads and interest in the products.

REQUIREMENTS: The main requirements to launching this type of business endeavor are as follows: design abilities, manufacturing equipment, skilled staff, and adequate transportation. Likewise, you will also

have to commit a large amount of time into researching the market and consumer buying habits and trends prior to starting the business.

START-UP COSTS: The start-up investment required for this type of business can greatly vary. However, on a smaller scale the business can be successfully established for less than $25,000. A full-scale operation that includes a fully equipped manufacturing facility could easily cost in excess of $100,000 to establish.

PROFIT POTENTIAL: This type of specialized manufacturing business can generate profits greater than $100,000 per year, providing the business and market have been properly researched and established.

CHILDREN'S TOYS
★★ $$ 🏠 🕐

A few years ago, I spent five days at a home and garden show promoting my home renovation service and generating sales leads. Beside my booth was a gentleman selling windup flying toy helicopters that he had imported from China. Not exactly the type of product you would expect to see at a home improvement trade show. I remember asking him at the beginning of the show how long he had been doing this; he replied that he had been traveling the home show circuit to various cities around the country for two years selling only the windup toy helicopters. At that time I couldn't understand how he could make a living selling $10 toys at trade shows when the booth rent alone was more than $150 per day, not including the additional cost to travel from show to show. By the end of the first day I learned a valuable lesson from this innovative entrepreneur in terms of marketing and promotion, for he sold more than 500 toy helicopters. He told me the cost to purchase the toy helicopters was $2.25 each and the cost to be at the show for the day including travel and accommodations was an additional $300 dollars, bringing his total cost to $2.85 for each helicopter. In one day by himself he had netted more than $3,500 after expenses. By the end of the five-day show, he sold more than 2,000 windup flying toy helicopters. The secret to his success? Simple. He had a unique and uncomplicated product in an environment that had no competition for his product and was surrounded by items that retailed for 100 times more than his did. More important was his ability to demonstrate his product and grab the attention of the show's audience. Imagine being two or three aisles away and seeing flying helicopters overhead. Human nature says you have no choice but to see what all the commotion is about.

WEB RESOURCE: www.nahpco.com Directory service listing toy manufacturers, distributors, and links to toy industry information.

USED BABY EQUIPMENT
★ $$$

Similar to children's clothing, baby equipment such as strollers, car seats, and cribs are very expensive and often out of the financial reach of many parents. So why not start your own business that specializes in clean, good-quality secondhand equipment for babies? The business can be started for less than $15,000 and can be operated from a small retail store location. You can purchase items from parents and mark them up by at least 100 percent for resale purposes. Likewise, you can also take in items on a consignment basis to reduce business start-up costs. This business is ideally suited for a person who has a good number of contacts with parents within the community. Additional income and profits can also be earned by adding a cloth diaper delivery service, which is also covered in this chapter of the directory.

MARKETING TIP: If your business specializes in used products, always refer to your merchandise as refurbished or renewed. This will give your business a more professional appearance and even allow you to charge a premium for your used, I mean refurbished, merchandise.

COMPUTER TRAINING CAMP
★★ $$$ 🕒 🌎

Starting a computer training camp for children is a terrific new business venture to set in motion. In spite of the fact that many children now receive computer training in school, attending computer camps

ensures parents and children a better and more complete understanding of the course material. The computer camps can be operated on a year-round basis or in the summer only. Typically these camps are one or two days in length and available for various training needs from beginner to advanced. Once again, this is the kind of children's business that can be operated as an independent business venture or operated in conjunction with a community program or community center.

WOODEN TOY MANUFACTURING AND SALES
★★★ $$ 🏭 🕒

Wooden toys not only appeal to children for play, but also to adults for home and office decorations. Manufacturing wooden toys is a wonderful home-based business opportunity that can be activated for peanuts and has the potential to return big profits. Marketing the toys can be accomplished by way of wholesale sales to merchants, the Internet, mail-order catalogs, craft shows, mall kiosks, and home shopping parties. Traditionally, wooden toys that have been popular include trains, jigsaw puzzles, cars, numbered building blocks, and wooden soldiers. But that's just the tip of the iceberg. The only limitation to the different kinds of wooden toys that can be designed and manufactured is your own imagination. Additionally, approach local building and home improvement centers to see if they will let you set up a mini-manufacturing facility right in their store. If this can be accomplished, it would be a great marketing tool to be able to build the toys in front of a live audience.

REQUIREMENTS: The requirements for this type of woodworking business enterprise are relatively basic, and include woodworking skills and a well-equipped woodworking shop. Design and building plans are available for various types of wooden toys, or you can design your own toys as your skills improve. In the age of being politically correct, it is not a bad idea if you were to use only recycled wood to make your toys. Not only would you be helping the environment and saving money on material costs, but it can also be a useful and powerful marketing tool.

Recyclable wood material includes beach driftwood, used building materials, cedar rail fencing, pallets, packing crates, and fallen forest brush, and most, if not all, of these waste wood materials can be acquired for free.

START-UP COSTS: If you already have the woodworking equipment that is required for this manufacturing business, you can get going for less than $500 in total investment. If you have to purchase equipment, the start-up costs will be substantially higher, in the range of $1,500 to $2,000.

PROFIT POTENTIAL: There are very little raw material costs involved to produce wooden toys. This type of business is mostly time-based and you will have to assess your own requirements when it comes to establishing an hourly rate. However, you still have to add a markup percentage onto the finished product costs to cover overheads, equipment repairs, and replacements. In terms of establishing an hourly rate, I would suggest at least $25 per hour, thus you could easily generate an income of $20,000+ per year, and best of all, have a whole lot of fun in the wooden toy manufacturing business.

WEB RESOURCE: www.woodentoyplans.com Wooden toy construction plans and links to information about the wooden toy building industry.

ONLINE WOODEN TOYS

★ $$$ 🏠 🕐 🖱️

Unite the wooden toy makers of the world by developing a Web site that features wooden toys and games for sale. Fear not if you do not know how to make wooden toys because there are thousands of people and small manufacturing firms worldwide that specialize in designing and making wooden toys. Like any small enterprise, the largest single challenge these entrepreneurs face is marketing and distributing their products. In a nutshell, the Web site would feature all sorts of wooden toys and games constructed by numerous individuals and small-manufacturing firms. You have two options in terms of earning income. The first is to create an online wooden toy store and charge a commission on all sales generated. The second option would be to establish the Web site

in a directory format and charge wooden toy makers to be listed in the Web site.

MANNERS TRAINING

★ $$ 🏠 🕐

Well-behaved children with excellent manners are the pride, and some times envy of all parents. Starting a child's manners instruction service is a terrific way to get into business for yourself. The market for manners training is large and easily obtained. To get rolling you will need to learn everything about manners that you can. This information is best gathered through reading books on manners and proper etiquette or attending a competitor's class. I would suggest initially that you hold your classes in conjunction with a community or recreation center. You will probably have to work out a split of the revenues with the center. However, this is a fast start method as you will have access to the recreation center's membership base for promotional purposes.

MARKETING TIP: Holding free information sessions on this subject is a great way to gain exposure and potential clients.

PARTY BALLOON SERVICE

★★ $ 🏠 🕐 🌐

Less than $500 will set you up in your own Party Balloon Service. The demand for this service is endless and certainly not limited to only children's birthday parties. Marketing a party balloon service is best achieved by creating a colorful presentation to be distributed to all local event planners, children stores, daycare centers, catering companies, wedding planners, and banquet halls. Likewise, attending local networking clubs or chamber of commerce meetings is also a fantastic way to get the message out about your new service. A small amount of research into your local market will assist you in product pricing as well as determining demand and competition. Should you encounter a great deal of competition in your local community, you may want to add additional services to your enterprise to create a competitive advantage. Great add-on services can include a party cleanup service and an event planning service. This is a business that can be successfully operated from home, however, you will require adequate transportation as the balloons should be filled with helium the day of the event and not prior to.

WEB RESOURCE: www.balloonbasics.com Wholesale distributor of balloons and related supplies and equipment.

VIDEO ARCADE
★★ $$$$

Gone are the days of 25-cent video and pinball games. Today's high-tech games can often cost as much as $2 or $3, and the children (and adults) are still lined up to play. A video arcade is a high investment business to properly establish; nevertheless, the potential profit returns are also extremely high. Like any business that requires a large volume of people to be successful, you will want your video arcade to be located in a high-traffic, highly visible location. Malls and tourist attractions make fantastic operating locations for video arcades. The largest and most successful video arcades also include food concession stands, retail product sales such as theme T-shirts, and family pass options, all of which you will want to consider implementing. Prior to starting a video arcade, complete a full and in-depth market survey into its viability. The investment into this business warrants the expense of such a market study.

WEB RESOURCE: www.arcade-equipment.com Directory service listing manufacturers and distributors of video arcade equipment.

ONLINE NANNY SERVICE
★★ $$$

Operating your own homebased nanny placement service can be a magnificent way to build a prosperous business. Nanny services are in high demand, and busy parents often have no choice but to pay the costs associated with having a nanny care

for their children. There are three major roles to be filled by a nanny service. The first, locating parents who are seeking the services of a professional nanny. The second role is that of an employment screener. You will want to carefully look at all the nannies' résumés, and carry out reference and background checks to make sure they are suitable candidates. The third role is simple; place qualified nannies with parents who seek their services. There are various ways to charge for nanny services. The one that I would suggest is a one-time fee paid by the parents. This is the simplest and most straightforward remuneration option. There are other options such as a percentage of the nanny's wages, but this can be complicated and even lead to potential liability situations. Additionally, by far the best way to bring these parties together is to operate this business as an online venture. Nannies and parents seeking nannies would meet via chat rooms on the site and discuss their qualifications and needs. This cybernanny service will require careful planning and research in order to develop a user-friendly site that can return profits. However, with that said, the Internet is creating new business ventures faster than any other industry.

DOLLHOUSE MANUFACTURING AND SALES
★ $ 🏠 🕐

Manufacturing custom designed dollhouses is a great part-time homebased business venture to set in motion. The dollhouses you build can be sold through retail accounts, flea markets, craft shows, mail order, the Internet, and mall kiosks. The only requirement for this business to succeed is your ability to manufacture a good, high-quality dollhouse. Design plans are available at any hobby shop for dollhouse construction, or you can create you own custom designs. Business start-up cost is less than $500, and the monthly operating overheads are extremely low. The potential profits this business enterprise can produce are varied. However, a well-established dollhouse manufacturing business should have no difficulty generating annual sales in excess of $50,000 per year.

WEB RESOURCE: www.thedollnet.com Directory service listing manufacturers and suppliers of products and equipment for the doll industry.

PUPPET SHOWS

 ★ $$

Jim Hanson's puppet creations made him millions, so why can't yours? Starting a childrens puppet show service is a fantastic way to own and operate your own business. Children cannot help but be fascinated by puppets. Spending a few dollars to purchase or make your own puppets and a portable stage can be the beginning of a rewarding and moneymaking business venture for you. To get business, simply design some fliers and distribute them to local children's stores and daycare centers. Try to stay with current and popular children themes for your puppets and puppet shows, such as space creatures and dinosaurs.

ONLINE BABY NAMES

★ $$$

Some business opportunities have a lot of competition and this business start-up is one of them. However, as an entrepreneur your greatest skill may lie in your ability to take a new and fresh approach to an old business or concept. The old saying in business you can live by is "don't invent a new mouse trap, just build a better mouse trap." That is the case with this business venture. Baby name books in print have always been popular, and maybe you can create and write a new book with a fresh outlook on an old idea and post it online. One idea may be to feature historical names and what they mean or perhaps celebrity names and how they came to be changed or altered to suit the personality. Visitors could browse through the name listings for free, and by renting advertising space or selling products you could earn income. Additionally, seek out interesting ways to make the site more inviting. Perhaps hold a contest or feature a poll to find out the most popular names.

WEB RESOURCE: www.entrepreneur.com Create a business Web site with MySite professional Web site builder.

NATURAL CHILDBIRTH CLASSES

★ $+

Natural childbirth is and will always be a hot topic. This business has limitless possibilities and avenues including natural childbirth classes, seminars, products, and services. This business opportunity will have to be of particular interest to you and will require training and a great amount of research. However, well-accepted professionals who specialize in a field generally are well paid and always in demand. This business may be of particular interest to nurses, childcare givers, and early childhood education teachers. Be sure to do your homework so that your new business will comply with all rules and regulations of your particular community.

SHOPPING MALL PLAY CENTERS

★★ $$$$

Millions of parents go to shopping malls every day across America and usually with their children in tow. While shopping can be a terrific family outing, sometimes a break from the children while shopping can also be a pleasant experience. Starting a shopping mall play center business can fill a couple of demands. The first, of course, gives parents a fantastic place to drop off their children while shopping, The second is that the business can be built into a successful and profitable venture, which is exactly what you want to hear if starting this type of business is a consideration for you. Establishing a children's play center in a mall will take careful planning, especially for legal and liability issues. However, there is a real potential to generate a six-figure yearly income from a shopping mall play center for the owner-operator of this business enterprise.

TALENT AGENT FOR CHILDREN

★ $$

Are you searching for a low investment home-based business opportunity that has the potential to be a lot of fun and potentially very profitable? If so, perhaps you should consider starting a talent agency for child actors. This type of business enterprise is very easy to activate and there will certainly be no shortage of potential clients as many children dream about hamming it up for the camera. Currently, agents for child actors are charging a commission rate of between 10 and 20 percent of their client's earnings. Many agents also represent children in the modeling profession as well as those involved in voice-over work for radio and TV. To gain exposure to producers and directors for the business, start an e-mail, letter, and personal visit campaign promoting your talent agency, clients, and services. Note: Recently talent agencies for children have come under fire because many operate solely to collect money from unsuspecting parents for providing acting lessons and photo portfolios while the children never get a legitimate chance at an audition. Be sure to operate your agency in an ethical manner, and only refer parents to other businesses if they inquire about acting lessons or photograph portfolios.

MINITRAIN RIDES
★ $$$$

Be prepared to invest more than $250,000 to start a minitrain ride business. But also be prepared to generate daily business sales that can easily exceed $1,500. Starting a minitrain ride business for children takes a lot of careful planning, research, and business expertise, and there are numerous considerations including the most important, which is where the business will be located. Good locations include parks, amusement centers, indoor malls, and zoos. Additionally, depending on the business location, sales of products such as hats, T-shirts, and food items can also be added to boost sales and profits. This business has the potential to become a real going concern, and joint venture opportunities with existing businesses that can provide a good operating location for the business should not be overlooked.

ONLINE CHILDREN'S WEB SITE
★★ $$+ 🏠 🕐 🖱

There are literally hundreds of options available in terms of developing and operating a Web site that

focuses on children's topics and/or services. Here are a few suggestions:

- Create an online directory that posts information about Web sites that are operated by children. The site would also include hyperlinks to the sites featured, and charging a listing fee or selling advertising space would earn revenues.
- Develop a Web site that features games and puzzles that children can play online.
- Create an online storybook Web site wherein children can place their names into various story themes and print their own storybooks.
- Start a children's pen pal Web site that enables kids from around the world to select a pen pal and write back and forth online.

Once again, the options are unlimited in terms of developing a Web site with a children's theme.

EDUCATIONAL DAY CAMPS
★★ $$+ 🕐 ⚖ 🌐

Mathematics, grammar, computer training, and arts and crafts can all be included into the curriculum of an educational day camp for kids. The camps can be held in a daylong format on weekends during school months and throughout the week in summers. The main focus on this type of specialized kids day camp business is to provide parents with an alternate choice for additional education as opposed to educational tutoring. The day camps can be run as an independent business or in conjunction with a community program or community center. Start-up costs for this kind of business will vary as to the operating format and size of the business and will range from a low of $5,000 to a high of $25,000. Be sure to seek legal advice in terms of regulations and certifications that may be required to operate a business specializing in educational day camps for kids in your community prior to establishing the business.

PONY RIDES
★ $$$$ 🕐

This is definitely not your typical children's related business opportunity. However, there is a time-tested formula here: "place kids and animals together and your business cannot fail." Mobile might be the key ingredient to this business. Being a mobile business will enable you to travel to where the demand is greatest for the service. Logical locations include high-traffic community gathering places such as malls, fairs, festivals, flea markets, and community parades. You will also want to establish a working relationship with other similarly related businesses that can help support your business. These types of businesses will include carnival companies, kids party services, property managers, clubs, and associations. Additionally, be sure to associate yourself with all the charity events in your area as your service is unique, which can help generate interest for the charity event and profits for you. Furthermore, to gain additional revenue, add a photograph or video service. What parent can resist purchasing a picture of their child on a pony?

REQUIREMENTS: There is a long list of requirements for starting and operating a children's pony ride business including, but not limited to, the following: transportation, boarding space, liability insurance, and of course the ponies. Additionally, you will want to be familiar with ponies and their needs and requirements. The business will take careful planning to put together, but the rewards can be both financially and personally rewarding.

START-UP COSTS: The costs associated with starting a pony ride business will vary depending on the number of ponies and if you will be boarding them or housing them in your own stables. You will also have to take into account the cost and method of transportation. I talked to a person who has been in the business for more than 15 years. He informed me that to start and operate this business properly would take about $25,000 in start-up capital and a fixed monthly operating budget of $2,000 to $3,000.

PROFIT POTENTIAL: The same person I talked to about the business start-up and operating costs also told me that in the 15 years he has been operating his pony ride business he has generally cleared $5,000 per month after expenses. Of course, the profit potential will vary to each operation, but overall this business appears to be fun and interesting.

WEB RESOURCE: www.ponyclub.org Directory listing Pony Clubs in the United States.

HOUSE SAFETY SERVICE
★★ $$ 🏠 🕐

Statistically, the greatest numbers of injury causing accidents involving children happen at home. This creates a fantastic opportunity to remedy this very real situation as well as start your own business as a professional house safety consultant. Your service can focus on all the household items that can potentially harm children and you can provide the service of showing parents how to secure these household items so accidents don't happen. Establishing the service will require a fair amount of research to educate yourself about harmful household chemicals, cabinet safety latches, and overall proper procedures to making a home safe and a child-friendly environment. Begin to market your consulting services by designing and distributing brochures, building alliances with related businesses for referrals, and most important, offer your service for free. Wait, what do you mean free? Exactly that; provide no-charge in-home consultations to potential clients. Once in the client's home, it will be your opportunity to blow them away with your knowledge (the old fear sale) on how to make their homes a child-friendly environment. By the time your "free" consulting visit is over, the chances are good that clients will have committed to hundreds of dollars worth of installed safety products and information manuals.

NOTES

41
CLOTHING
Businesses You Can Start

SENIOR CITIZEN CLOTHING
★★★ $$ 🏠 🕐

Are you searching for a unique clothing retail business that can be operated on a mobile basis and managed from a homebased office? If so, consider starting a business that retails clothing to residents living in retirement and senior citizen homes. Simply build alliances with clothing manufacturers and make arrangements with operators of retirement homes to put on a monthly fashion show for the residents. Additionally, models for the fashion shows can be the residents of the homes, and at the end of the show you can take orders for clothing purchases with delivery to follow within a few days. This could prove to be not only a profitable business to operate, but also a very fun business that provides clients with the convenience of easy shopping as well as a little bit of entertainment at the same time.

DRIVE-THROUGH LAUNDROMAT
★★ $$$$ 🌐

There are drive-through banks, restaurants, and photo finishing stores, so why not drive-through laundromats? A drive-through laundromat is not a new business concept; they have been around for a few years. However, recently they have become more popular, and a few companies have even begun to franchise their drive-through laundromat businesses. Starting a drive-through laundromat does not require a great deal of business experience or knowledge. It does, however, require a good location and a fairly substantial capital investment to establish the business. In terms of a business location, ideally the drive-through laundromat should be established on a busy road, but not so congested with traffic that entering and exiting for customers is a problem or potentially dangerous. Additional location considerations will also include proximity to potential clients most likely to utilize the service such as universities, police stations, hospitals, and industrial business areas. As well as street visibility, accessibility for walk-in customers, parking, and overall building condition and appearance are important. In addition to providing customers with a drive-through service, also provide a walk-in and laundry drop-off service as well as a free pickup and delivery service. The profit potential for this type of business venture is excellent and can easily exceed $75,000 per year, providing the correct steps have been taken to select the right location as well as promoting the service to its full potential.

WEB RESOURCE: www.speedqueen.com Manufacturers and distributors of commercial laundromat equipment.

T-SHIRTS IN A CAN
★★ $$ 🏠 🕐

Designing novelty T-shirts and the can the shirt will be sold in is a very interesting business opportunity to get rolling. The T-shirts can feature jokes, images, or messages based on a variety of themes from political humor to children's cartoon caricatures. Once the silk-screening is completed, the T-shirts can be packaged in tin cans that have a slot in the top to serve a second function of a piggy bank. T-shirts in a Can make a terrific novelty gift and can be sold to retailers on a wholesale basis or directly to consumers via a sales kiosk or the Internet. Furthermore, to keep initial start-up costs to a minimum, the silk-screening aspect of the business can be contracted to a local silk-screener as opposed to purchasing the equipment. In addition to selling T-shirts in a Can, larger sweatshirts can also be printed with humorous messages and packaged in larger one-gallon paint cans.

WEB RESOURCE: www.interchangecorp.com Distributors of new and used silk-screening equipment.

ONLINE BIG AND TALL SHOP
★★ $$$ 🏠 🖱

It is a fact that each generation is physically larger than the previous generation, and this fact creates a terrific opportunity for the innovative entrepreneur

to capitalize by starting an online retail store that stocks and sells clothing and fashion accessories aimed at the big and tall market. The clothing featured on the Web site can be for women, children, and men, and manufacturers of the clothing that you sell can directly ship your orders to customers as a method of reducing the amount of inventory warehousing space that will be required. The profit potential for this type of online retail clothing business is outstanding as the clothing is specialized, so maintaining product markups of 100 percent or more should not be difficult.

WEB RESOURCE: www.smallbizbooks.com Business specific start-up guides and books.

COLLECTIBLE CLOTHING
★★ $$$$

The value and popularity of collectible clothing has been on a steady increase for the past decade, and the demand for collectible clothing from the 1940s to the 1970s shows no signs of diminishing. Starting a business that sells collectible clothing from a retail storefront location is a fantastic business venture to set in motion.

START-UP COSTS: The following example can be used, as a guideline to establish the investment needed for starting a business that retails collectible clothing.

	Low	High
Business setup, banking, legal, etc.	$500	$1,500
Initial inventory	$15,000	$30,000
Business location, leasehold improvements, etc.	$3,000	$10,000
Office equipment and supplies	$2,000	$5,000
Initial advertising and marketing budget	$1,000	$3,000
Working capital	$3,000	$10,000
Total start-up costs	$24,500	$59,500

PROFIT POTENTIAL: The profit potential for a retailer of collectible clothing will vary based on factors such as operating overheads, volume of sales, etc. However, a markup of at least 100 percent should be maintained, and a higher markup on rarer collectible clothing items is certainly not out of line. Maintaining annual sales of $200,000 will create a pretax and expenses profit of $100,000.

ONLINE COLLECTIBLE CLOTHING
★★ $$+ 🏠 🕐 ♂

Create a portal to bring buyers and sellers of collectible clothing items together by developing your own online Web site. As mentioned above, millions of people collect popular clothing items from previous decades, and this online opportunity has the potential to make you rich. There are various options available in terms of how this sort of Web site could operate including an online auction service that exclusively features collectible clothing or an online classifieds service that enables buyers and sellers to list collectible clothing items for sale and wanted. There are also many options for generating revenues and profits including charging a fee to list items for sale, renting banner advertising space, or buying collectible clothing and reselling it via the site for a profit.

WORK UNIFORMS
★★ $$$$ 🌐

There are a few options available when considering starting a business that retails work uniforms and work clothing. The first option is to establish a retail storefront location to stock and sell work uniforms, and the second option is to establish a mobile business that sells work uniforms from a cube van or delivery truck. Both options have drawbacks and benefits in terms of the business. However, the second option of being a mobile retailer of work uniforms will be less costly to establish, as well as operate on a monthly basis. The types of uniforms and work clothing that can be sold include work overalls, health-care uniforms, fire and police service uniforms, and school sportswear. Also stocking and selling specialized work footwear, such as steel toe work boots, can earn additional revenues. Regardless if the business is operated from a fixed location or on a mobile basis, one of the main marketing tools required will be to design and produce a full-color catalog that features the work wear available for sale.

WEB RESOURCE: www.naumd.com National Association of Uniform Manufacturers and Dealers.

ONLINE BLUE JEANS
★★ $$ 🏠 🕐 ♂

Calling all homebased seamstresses. If you are searching for a unique way to profit from your sewing talents then look no further than starting an online business that sells custom made-to-order blue jeans. Blue jeans are an American cultural icon worn by millions of people every day, and for many people the search is never ending for a pair of jeans that fits properly and comfortably. Get started by creating a Web site that features the capability of letting visitors design their own blue jeans. This simply means that your customers select a men's or women's option and enter in the measurements they want: inseam length, waist size, and cuff diameter. Once your customers have completed the online order form and chosen payment option, they would simply click submit and wait for their perfectly fitting jeans to arrive by courier a few weeks later. Should the site prove popular and you have more jeans to make than is possible, you can always hire subcontract seamstresses to work on a piece or performance basis, and order forms for jeans could be forwarded to them electronically.

USED WEDDING GOWNS
★★ $$+ 🏠 ♂

Sell secondhand wedding gowns from home as well as on the Internet for a profit. In a nutshell, the main objective is to purchase secondhand wedding gowns and accessories at bargain basement prices and resell these same gowns for a profit. The gowns can be sold from a homebased location as well as on the Internet by developing your own Web site. In addition to purchasing gowns, you can also accept consignment gowns and retain 25 to 40 percent of the sales value for providing the service. Additionally, to boost profits you can enlist the services of a local seamstress to also provide clients with custom made-to-order new wedding gowns. Advertise your business in your local newspaper and build alliances with wedding planners to promote the business.

SILK-SCREENING SERVICE
★★ $$ 🏠 🕑

The most common use for silk-screen printing is with clothing, especially T-shirts. However, silk-screen printing equipment can be used for printing logos and images on a variety of products such as mouse pads, bumper stickers, heat transfers, shower curtains, binder covers, furniture, and sports items, just to mention a few. Still it is often better to stick with what traditionally will generate revenues and profits for a business, and in this case that means silk-screening T-shirts, hats, jackets, and sweatshirts for corporate promotional wear, gifts, sports uniforms, and special events. The profit potential is great for a silk-screening business as T-shirts can be purchased wholesale for less than $5 each and the ink used to print the image adds up to only a few cents per printed item. Simply securing orders for 500 printed T-shirts a week and charging only $10 each for the shirt and the printing can generate a gross profit in excess of $100,000 per year—a compelling reason to start your own homebased silk-screening business today.

HOMEBASED TAILOR
★★ $$ 🏠 🕑

Retailers of men's formal and business wear generally do not have an in-house tailor, and typically alteration work is subcontracted to outside contract tailors. This fact creates a more than ample opportunity for the individuals with sewing experience to capitalize by starting a tailoring service that operates right from a homebased location. Once again, the fastest way to establish the service is to offer men's wear retailers your services on a subcontract basis, and you can arrange a certain time of the day to pick up garments to be altered and return the garments the following day. Additionally, to generate more revenue for the business, consider purchasing tuxedos that can be rented to clients via the men's wear stores that currently do not provide their customers with this service. Potential income range is $25 to $35 per hour.

WEB RESOURCE: www.paccprofessionals.org The Professional Association of Custom Clothiers, Association representing custom clothiers working from home.

TIE-DYE CLOTHING
★★ $$ 🏠 🕑

If history has taught us anything it is that it will repeat itself, and that is certainly the situation in terms of tie-dye clothing, as these popular cultural icons of the 1960s are once again returning to favor as a fashionable clothing option. Creating tie-dye clothing is extremely easy and training books and videos on the subject are available through most craft supply stores. The business can easily be operated from home, and clothing to be tie-dyed can be purchased from clothing manufacturers on a wholesale basis. Once the clothing has been tie-dyed it can be sold to clothing retailers on a wholesale basis, directly to consumers via the Internet, and through sales kiosks located in malls and public markets.

SPORTSMEN VESTS
★★ $$ 🏠

Manufacturing custom-made sportsmen's vests for hunting, fishing, and boating activities is an outstanding homebased business venture to get rolling, especially for the entrepreneur with sewing skills and experience. The key to success in this type of specialty clothing manufacturing business is to ensure that the sportsmen's vests serve many functions related to the activity they have been created for—as well as ensuring that materials and workmanship used in creating the product are of the highest quality. Once completed, the sportsmen's vest can be sold to national sporting goods retailers on a wholesale basis, or the sportsmen's vest can be sold directly to consumers via mail-order catalogs, recreation trade shows, and even the Internet. Furthermore, the business can be started on a part-time basis and expanded to full-time from the profits that are earned. Be sure to seek exporting opportunities for the vests, as American and Canadian sporting goods and sportswear is extremely popular overseas, especially in Japan and Germany.

SECONDHAND CLOTHING STORE

★★ $$$$ ♂

There are a few options available to the entrepreneur considering a retail business that sells secondhand clothing.

The first and most capital-intensive option is to open a used clothing store from a fixed retail location or storefront. The second option is to sell the secondhand clothing items via a flea-market booth. The third option is to develop a Web site and sell used clothing via the Internet.

Of course, all three options could be combined into one operating format, and combining all three methods of marketing and distribution would greatly increase potential business revenues and profits. I have even recently heard of a few companies that are now selling secondhand designer clothing by way of home parties and independent sales consultants, which could also be a potential avenue well worth investigating.

WEB RESOURCE: www.smallbizbooks.com Business specific start-up guides and books.

PROMOTIONAL WEAR

★★★ $$ 🏠 🕐

Promotional wear such as hats, jackets, and golf shirts emblazoned with corporate and business logos have become very popular for corporations to purchase and resell or give to valued employees and clients as an appreciation gift. Starting a business that sells promotional clothing is very easy to initiate. Not only can the garments be purchased on a wholesale basis, but you can also enlist the services of local silk-screeners and embroiders to carry out customizing the clothing for your clients, thus greatly reducing the start-up investment needed to get the business rolling. Gaining clients can be as easy as arranging appointments with business owners to present samples of the promotional wear along with reasons why these types of promotional items will benefit their business. They can even potentially increase business revenues and profits (great advertising and brand name recognition). Once established, a business that retails promotional wear can

be very profitable, especially when you consider product markups of 50 percent or more are not uncommon in the industry.

ONLINE SPORTSWEAR

★★ $$$ 🏠 🕐 ♂

There are a few approaches that can be taken in terms of starting a sportswear business. The first is to simply retail sportswear purchased on a wholesale basis, via home shopping parties, the Internet, and sales kiosks. The second approach is to establish a business that designs and manufactures sportswear to be sold to clothing and sporting good retailers on a wholesale basis or directly to consumers via the Internet and sales kiosks located in busy malls. Both approaches to establishing the business have their pros and cons. However, the first approach is less capital intensive to start and can be operated on a part-time basis until the business can be expanded to full-time from the profits earned.

EMBROIDERY SERVICE

★★ $$$ 🏠 🕐

Recent technology changes in the embroidery industry have made it very easy even for a novice to start an embroidery service. Embroidery machines are now available in single or multihead units enabling the operator to embroider six items at a time or more. Additionally, modern embroidery equipment is computer assisted, meaning that the designs can be created using specialty software and a computer and then automatically transferred to the embroidery machine to complete the stitching of the design. The business can easily be operated from a homebased location. However, there should still be a small showroom established, even if it is in the home, to display items that can be embroidered as well as samples of embroidery options. Marketing the service can be as easy as creating a catalog and marketing brochure and distributing the package to potential clients such as sports associations, charities, corporations, and clubs. Furthermore, consider hiring a commissioned salesperson to solicit or cold-call for business as this can be a very effective and profitable marketing option.

WEB RESOURCE: www.embmag.com *Embroidery Monogram Business* magazine online.

TEAM UNIFORM SALES
★★ $$

Schools, sports associations, and sports clubs can all be potential customers for a business that specializes in retailing team uniforms. Millions of people across North America participate in amateur sporting events such as football, baseball, hockey, and soccer on a weekly basis. Almost all of these sports teams have one thing in common: the members of the teams dress in a uniform that represents the team. Selling team sportswear with logos, names, and numbers printed on the clothing items is a very easy business to get rolling. You can purchase equipment required to silk-screen and embroider the athletic wear, or you can subcontract this element of the business out to established silk-screen and embroidery companies and concentrate on marketing. Gaining customers can be as easy as creating a catalog of the team uniforms that you stock and setting appointments with decision makers representing the sports teams to solicit business.

ONLINE PET CLOTHING
★★ $$$ 🏠 🕐 🖱

Any pet owner will certainly understand the outstanding opportunity that awaits the enterprising entrepreneurs that start a business marketing specialty clothing for pets, as the spending habits of pet owners often know no bounds. There are a couple of approaches that can be taken in terms of establishing this type of business. The first is to design, manufacture, and market the pet clothing. The second approach is to simply purchase the clothing from a manufacturer on a wholesale basis for resale purposes or to have a local seamstress design and manufacture the clothing for pets. The first approach to establishing the business will be more capital intensive to get off the ground, but

with that said, there are also more options in terms of marketing the products, as well as the potential to generate higher sales and profits. Regardless of the approach taken to build the business, be sure to harness the power of the Internet as a way to advertise and market the pet clothing, as it is without question the easiest and fastest way to reach a global audience and, more importantly, paying customers.

WEB RESOURCE: www.appma.org American Pet Products Manufacturers Association.

BELT BUCKLES
★★ $$ 🏠 🕐

Are you searching for a truly unique homebased business opportunity with a focus on manufacturing? If so, perhaps you should consider starting a business manufacturing specialty belt buckles. The business can be put into action on less than a $3,000 initial investment, and the long-term profit potential is sensational. The key to success in this type of specialty manufacturing business is to ensure the buckle designs are original and to place a concentrated effort on utilizing many marketing methods to ensure maximum exposure for the business and products. Additionally, consider utilizing recyclable materials such as metals and glass for the raw material to construct the belt buckles as not only is this a way to reduce materials' costs, but more importantly, it can be used as a very powerful marketing tool.

HANDBAG DESIGN AND MANUFACTURING
★★★ $$ 🏠 🕐

Creating and manufacturing designer handbags is a terrific new business enterprise to start right from the comforts of home, as not only can the business be run on a part-time basis, but there are also almost no operating overheads to bite into monthly profits. Unique designs and utilizing uncommon materials for the making of the handbags can be your competitive advantage, and completed products can be wholesaled to fashion retailers or placed on consignment in local retail shops. Additionally, the handbags can also be sold directly to consumers by displaying the products at fashion shows or by renting a sales kiosk in a busy mall on weekends. Furthermore, seek big market opportunities by building joint ventures with established handbag manufacturers that can produce and wholesale your handbag designs under a split revenue agreement.

CHILDREN'S DESIGNER CLOTHES
★ $$$

Calling all seamstresses and hobby fashion designers. It is time to start to profit from your good fashion sense and sewing skills by starting a homebased business that designs and manufactures children's designer clothing. Marketing the finished product can be as easy as hosting monthly fashion shows right in your own home. Children from your local neighborhood can be enlisted to work as clothing models and invitations can be sent to parents within the community to attend the fashion show. At the end of the show, simply collect orders for the clothing the parents wish to purchase and set about making the clothes and planning for the next fashion show. To expand the business you can employ independent sales consultants right across the country to also host monthly fashion shows and split the revenues that are earned on clothing sales.

BATHING SUITS
★★ $$

Custom made-to-order bathing suits retail for as much as $150 each while only costing about $20 in material to make. Thus if you have a flair for design and a skill for sewing, starting your own homebased business that specializes in made-to-order bathing suits for clients seeking the perfect fashion look for the beach may be just the business opportunity that can put you on the road to financial riches. Once again, the business can be operated from home simply by converting a room into a workspace and

showroom to display samples of your work for clients. Gaining clients can be as easy as printing discount coupons that can be distributed to travel agents who present the coupons as a gift to their clients traveling to sunny destinations—not to mention the fact that this is the kind of business that will receive a lot of free advertising by way of word-of-mouth referrals.

MOBILE FORMALWEAR RENTALS
★★ $$$$

Take a traditional formalwear rental business, add wheels, and you have the focus of this business opportunity. Who says the customer has to come to you? Why can't you go to the customer? You can, and that is what makes this a very unique business opportunity to pursue. You can offer clients the exact same service and products that a traditional formalwear rental business does simply by converting a delivery van into your operating location. Anyone seeking to rent tuxedos would simply phone in advance and book an appointment for you to go to their home or office. Any alterations could even be completed on site providing time permits. If not, the tuxedo could be delivered to the client the following day. Establishing alliances with wedding and event planners will go a long way to secure business as these professionals can refer your service to their clients.

SUSPENDERS
★★ $$

Suspenders featuring colorful and bold designs are hot selling fashion accessories, and starting a business that manufactures suspenders is a very easy business to set in motion. The business can easily be operated from a homebased work space on a full- or part-time basis. Researching how suspenders are manufactured can be as simple as spending a couple of hundred dollars on competitors' products for closer examination. The complete product can be packaged in a unique style to increase consumer interest and sold on a wholesale basis to fashion retailers or directly to consumers by way of the Internet. Another marketing idea is to display the product at consumer-attended fashion trade shows. Manufacturing and selling related fashion accessories such as hats, belts, gloves, and neckties can also earn additional revenues. Once established, the business could prove to be very profitable, not to mention a whole lot of fun to operate.

LINEN SUPPLY SERVICE
★★ $$ 🏠 🕐

What are the basic ingredients necessary to start and operate a linen supply service? The answer is very easy. A delivery vehicle, a linen inventory, facilities to clean the linens, and good marketing skills. A linen service is simply supplying restaurants, catering services, event planners, hotels, and convention centers with tableclothes, towels, linen napkins, and in some cases entrance carpets. Generally, clients rent the items on a regular or irregular basis, and rental rates include delivery, pickup, and cleaning of the items. If space permits, the business can be operated from a homebased location. However, if space is at a premium at home, consider starting the business as a joint venture with an established laundromat or dry cleaners.

SAFETY CLOTHING SALES
★ $$ 🏠 🕐

Selling safety clothing and footwear on a mobile basis to customers working in factories, at construction sites, and in warehouses is a great business to get rolling. The business can be operated on a full- or part-time basis and managed right from a homebased location. In North America millions of dollars are spent every year by workers, companies, and organizations to purchase safety clothing such as vests, coveralls, and work boots. Securing a small portion of this very lucrative market can be as easy as securing wholesale accounts with manufacturers of these items, purchasing a delivery vehicle, and creating a catalog featuring the items for sale and distributing the catalog to potential clients. Aim to

achieve yearly sales of $150,000 while maintaining a 50 percent markup, and the result will be a business that is generating a gross profit of $50,000 per year.

MATERNITY CLOTHING
★★ $$ 🏠 🕐

More than four million babies are born each year in the United States. Assuming the average expectant mother purchases five new maternity garments while pregnant adds up to a whopping 20 million maternity garments sold each year in the Unites States alone. There are a few ways to cash in on this very large and lucrative market. The first is to design, manufacture, and sell the maternity clothing, and the second is to purchase maternity clothing on a wholesale basis and resell the clothing for a profit. While both options are viable in terms of generating profits for the business, the first option has the potential to generate more sales and profits as well as providing more options for the operator in terms of marketing methods. Profit potential will vary, however, markups of 100 percent are not uncommon in this industry.

COSTUME RENTALS
★★ $$$ 🏠 🕐

A costume rental business can be operated right from a homebased location, and the additional yearly income that a costume rental business can generate is outstanding. I have always been partial to rental businesses. Once the item has paid for itself with five or six rentals, the revenue generated by the rental item from that point on is almost all profit, especially if the business is operated from home with minimal monthly operating overhead costs. The best way to market a costume rental business is to create a marketing brochure describing the costumes in stock and distribute the marketing brochure and rental rate sheet to organizations within the community, such as sports organizations, community theater groups, charity associations, and colleges and universities. Once established, this type

of rental business will easily be supported by word-of-mouth advertising and repeat customers.

WEB RESOURCE: www.promocostumes.com Manufacturers and distributors of costumes.

CUSTOM NECKTIE SALES
★★ $$

Here is an interesting approach to starting a business that sells neckties. Negotiate an exclusive distribution contract with a manufacturer of quality neckties, create a basic marketing brochure describing the neckties along with the retail prices, and distribute samples of the neckties you stock along with the marketing brochures to offices throughout your community. The purpose of this type of direct marketing sales is to leave the samples at offices for a few days along with an order form. Customers wishing to purchase a necktie for themselves or as a gift for others would simply complete the order form and leave it with the receptionist for you to fulfill when you return to pickup the samples. It's unique and could prove to be very profitable.

DRY-CLEANING SERVICE
★★★ $$$$

At one time it was said that the dry-cleaning industry had created more millionaires per capita than any other industry. While I am not sure that this statement still holds true today, one thing is for sure: starting a dry-cleaning service is an excellent business venture to set in motion. Ideally, a dry-cleaning service should be strategically located to be able to take advantage of the target market, and the best locations are generally built-up urban areas in office districts or storefronts with excellent parking facilities in suburban strip plazas. Additionally, as a method to increase business revenues also consider providing clients with a free pickup and delivery service as well as establishing satellite locations or depots where customers can drop off and pick up their dry cleaning the next day.

WEB RESOURCE: www.cleanersonline.com Directory service listing information and links to the dry-cleaning industry.

LINGERIE SHOP
★★ $$$$ ⊕

Heading into the new millennium, specialization is the buzzword for retail "bricks and mortar" businesses, and opening a lingerie shop fits the bill perfectly. Get started by selecting a highly visible store location for your business. Malls are a good choice and you will only require less than 1,000 square feet, so the rent should be reasonable. Next you will want to establish accounts with lingerie manufacturers and distributors. Harness the power of the Internet to locate these companies. The rest is pretty straightforward; you stock your store and sell your products. In addition to selling lingerie from the storefront location, also consider hiring sales consultants to host in-home lingerie parties as a way to bolster sales and profits. A direct mail campaign and mail-order catalog can also be used to increase revenues.

ONLINE LINGERIE SHOP
★★★ $$$$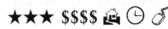

The best aspect about advertising and selling products via the Internet is the fact that it is the great equalizer. Regardless of the size of your business, you can compete with any competition on a level playing field. Lingerie is often a garment that most women and men like to purchase discreetly, and what better way than from a Web site on the Internet. Consider the following steps for establishing an online lingerie shop.

- Secure wholesale purchasing accounts with lingerie designers and manufacturers.
- Develop an easy-to-navigate and interesting Web site featuring lingerie for sale.
- Utilizing a digital camera and a scanner, take pictures of your inventory and post it on the site.
- Establish a secure credit card ordering system for the Web site.
- Develop a packing and shipping program to fulfill orders.
- Have fun operating your new online business venture.

FABRIC SHOP
★★★ $$$$

A fabric shop retailing numerous styles and types of fabrics can be opened in a fixed storefront location, or even from home providing you have the space required and the proper zoning in place. Fabric shops have traditionally been very profitable specialty retail operations as the markups applied to fabrics for retail sales can exceed 100 percent or more. The business needs little in the way of specialized equipment, thus keeping the operating overheads to a minimum. To get going in this business you will need to secure supply arrangements with fabric manufacturers, many of which are located outside of North America, so the business will require quite a bit of research and planning. In addition to fabrics, sewing patterns, buttons, zippers, curtain rods, and even sewing machines can also be sold as a method to increase the selection of goods available to consumers as well as increasing revenues.

WEB RESOURCE: www.textileweb.com Directory service with links to associations, manufacturers, and distributors within the fabric and textile industry.

ONLINE FABRIC SHOP
★★ $$$$ 🏠 🖱

OPTION ONE: Develop a portal that brings fabric manufacturers and distributors together with fabric retailers via an online fabric directory Web site. Worldwide there are thousands of fabric manufacturers and fabric retailers, thus an exciting opportunity exists by bringing these two parties together to buy and sell fabric. Revenues could be earned by charging both fabric manufacturers and retailers a fee for using the directory service. You could even create a password application that would enable both to have their own online warehouse, shipping center, inventory control, and tracking system. This type of Web site would be beneficial to both parties as it would enable them to do business online without the added expense of middlemen, sales consultants, and costly marketing campaigns. Thus, attracting customers to participate in the program should not prove difficult.

OPTION TWO: Focus on the direct to consumer market by creating a Web site that features fabric for sale. Potential customers could include hobby seamstresses, fashion designers, interior decorators, and tailors. The site would be easy to create and could feature pictures and descriptions of the various fabrics you sell as well as a price list. Customers would select the fabric they wanted, add it to their shopping cart, make a payment, and submit the order, all with a few easy clicks of a mouse button. Promote the site by initiating a direct mail and e-mail campaign aimed at fashion designers, sewing clubs, tailors, interior decorators, and smaller more remote communities that do not have a local fabric shop.

LEATHER FASHIONS
★★ $$$$ 🏠 🕐

Selling leather fashions is another great fashion retailing business to initiate. Worldwide there are thousands of manufacturers of leather fashions and accessories, so securing a wholesale source for products should not prove to be difficult. In the spirit of being unique, consider retailing the leather fashions in nontraditional methods including by way of the Internet, home shopping parties, and catalog sales. Like many clothing ventures, the profit potential is excellent for a business that retails leather fashions, as many items can retail for as much as $1,000 each, and the same item can often be purchased wholesale for less than $500.

WEB RESOURCE: www.leatherassociation.com Leather Apparel Association.

WESTERN APPAREL
★★ $$$$

Like country and western music, country and western apparel is currently enjoying a rebound in terms of consumer demand and popularity. Starting a business that retails country and western apparel is a sensational new business venture to put into action. In the spirit of being unique, consider opening a retail business selling country and western apparel in a nontraditional retail environment. Try locating the business within an established country and western theme restaurant or club or establishing the business within a music retailer that specializes in country and western music sales. Forming this type of joint venture with an established retail business often facilitates a lower capital investment and reduced monthly operating overheads, not to mention the fact that the business can capitalize on the existing customer base to drive sales.

EVENING GOWN RENTALS
★★★ $$$

Many designer evening gowns now cost $1,000 or more, placing them far outside the financial reach of many consumers. This fact creates more than ample opportunity for the determined entrepreneur to start an evening gown rental business, which can be easily conducted from a homebased location. Marketing the business can be as simple as creating a full-color catalog featuring pictures and descriptions of the evening gowns for rent and distributing the catalogs throughout the community where they will generate the most interest in the service including business associations and wedding and event planners. Once established, an evening gown rental business should receive a vast amount of referrals from satisfied customers, not to mention a lot of repeat business.

SILK SCARVES
★ $$

Genuine silk scarves can retail for as much as $100 each, yet can be purchased in bulk and on a wholesale basis for as little as $10 each from foreign manufacturers. Herein lies the business opportunity. Simply secure an exclusive import and distribution contract with a foreign manufacturer of silk scarves and set about marketing the product. The scarves can be resold in smaller quantities to clothing retailers on a wholesale basis or directly to consumers via fashion shows, sales kiosks, and the Internet. Thousands of importing opportunities are available for the enterprising entrepreneur to capitalize on. All it takes is some initiative and a desire to become a successful business owner.

MONOGRAMMED BATHROBES
★★ $$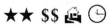

Are you searching for a unique and interesting business opportunity that has minimal competition and can be operated from a homebased location? If so, perhaps you should consider starting a business that sells monogrammed bathrobes and towels. Clients can include luxury hotels and bed and breakfast operations as well as consumers seeking gifts for loved ones or even themselves. You can contract the embroidery aspect of the business to a local company that specializes in monogramming garments. The towels and bathrobes can be purchased in bulk on a wholesale basis from any one of the thousands of manufacturers of these products worldwide. You should have no difficulties in maintaining markup percentages in the range of 100 percent or more, potentially making this a very profitable homebased business that definitely warrants further research and consideration.

SLEEPWEAR
★★ $+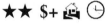

It's a fact that more than six billion people inhabit this planet and the vast majority of people wear some sort of clothing to bed that was purposely designed for being slept in. That is one gigantic potential marketplace, thus creating an exciting business opportunity. Like many business start-ups featured in this directory, there are various options available for starting a particular business, and in the spirit of uniqueness consider these various options for starting a business that focuses on sleepwear.

- Purchase various styles of sleepwear on a wholesale basis and host in-home sleepwear parties that generate orders for your products.
- Design and manufacture your own line of sleepwear and wholesale your products to retailers.
- Create a sleepwear Web site that enables visitors to create their own sleepwear by selecting style, size, and fabric.

- Design and sell patterns used for creating sleep-wear and let consumers sew their own from the patterns they have purchased.
- Secure the licensing rights to popular children's program characters or themes and incorporate them into sleepwear for kids.

NOTES

COMPUTER AND HOME OFFICE
Businesses You Can Start

BOARDROOM FACILITIES

★★★★ $$$$

The increasing trend toward conducting business enterprises from a home office continues to grow at a record pace in North America. Due to this fact an entirely new business requirement has surfaced. What do you do if your business is homebased; yet you require short-term meeting facilities? There is one simple solution to the question if you're an enterprising entrepreneur; you start a boardroom office facility that can be rented and utilized by homebased business entrepreneurs, employees, and traveling business people. The best way to reach your target market, which of course, is homebased business owners, is to join local business associations in your community and start promoting your boardroom rental service. Almost every city and community across North America now has a Homebased Business Owners Association or Chamber of Commerce. Most of these associations host networking meetings and these networking meetings are fantastic forums to meet other business owners and introduce them to your new boardroom service. Likewise, you will want to get the message out to corporate and business travelers that may also require this type of service while conducting business in your area.

REQUIREMENTS: The boardroom facility will have to be well equipped with office fixtures, furniture, and other equipment such as private meeting rooms, computers, Internet connections, copiers, overhead projectors, a catering service, secretarial services, stationery supplies, multi-line and function telephone system, and other related client support services and products. When choosing a location for this business, the following should be considered: a central location, alternately an airport location, good parking, and at least 1,500 square feet of floor space. Prior to establishing the business, a market study should indicate if the business would be supported mainly by homebased business owners or business travelers.

START-UP COSTS: The start-up costs will greatly vary as to the size of the boardroom office rental facility that you intend to open. However, a $25,000 to $40,000 initial investment for equipment, leasehold improvements, and marketing will be sufficient funds to start a medium-size boardroom facility.

PROFIT POTENTIAL: Well-equipped small (6 to 20 people) meeting facilities generally rent for the following rates: $40 to $50 per hour, $100 to $150 per day, $500 to $800 per week. Additionally, you can charge for any special services you provide, such as telephone answering, secretarial services, catering, transportation, and stationery supplies. Furthermore, to maximize profits you will want to have multiple boardrooms and meeting rooms available for rent. Once established, the profit potential for a boardroom rental facility can easily exceed $60,000 per year.

HOME OFFICE PLANNER
★★★ $$ 🏠 🕐

Functional room design is more important for a home office than you may think. Where is my…? I can't work with all this noise. My desk doesn't fit through the door. Many first time attempts to work or operate a business from home meets with frustration and a feeling of "where do I begin?" These very common problems are the basis of starting a home office planning service with a focus on assisting employees or business owners to establish, or make the transition to, a homebased office. You would also work one on one with the client to develop successful work and organization plans and programs that are tailor suited to specific needs. The home office planning service can include assisting employees and business owners with homebased office solutions such as office layout design, storage solution, recycling programs, work routine schedules, computer and telephone integration, and suitable equipment requirements. Remember not to forget to market this service to corporations as many companies are now having key employees work from a homebased office. Corporations can be great markets to tap into as all of these people have to make the adjustment to a new working environment. Furthermore, a home office planning service can be marketed directly to potential clients by all traditional advertising mediums, as well as by joining business associations and promoting the service at networking meetings and events.

ONLINE COMMUNITY WEB SITE
★★★ $$$ 🏠 🌐 🖱

Not all small business owners can afford to develop and maintain an independent Web site. Thus a fantastic opportunity exists for the cybersavvy Web master to capitalize by establishing, promoting, and maintaining a community Web site in your area. The site would feature and promote local merchants and service providers within a specific geographic area. Instead of 50 business owners paying thousands of dollars to develop 50 independent Web sites, they can be pooled together into one community Web site and pay only a small monthly maintenance fee for the service. The site would have to be indexed or categorized to represent the businesses featured on the site. Each business owner would receive a listing that could be linked to an individual pop-up page to promote his or her business, products, and services. Additionally you could also provide customers with a coupon page option. Promoting the Web site within the community it serves can be accomplished by advertising the domain in local newspapers as well as creating signs that promote the site and are displayed at participating merchants' stores. Fifty merchants paying only $100 each per month to participate in the community Web site will create annually revenues of $60,000.

HOME OFFICE RESOURCE GUIDE
★★ $$$ 🏠 🕐 🌐

Are you looking to start a business that can be set in motion with a minimal capital investment, operated from a homebased office, and has the potential to be expanded across North America over a very short period of time with unlimited income potential? If so, perhaps starting a community resource guide for homebased business owners and homebased employees is the right business venture for you. The business is very straightforward; simply design a resource guide that features information on local services, products, and associations that will be of benefit to homebased employees and business owners. The resource guide can be published on a semiannual or annual basis and can be supported by two different revenue streams. The first source of revenue for the community homebased business owner resource guide is generated by way of advertising sales. Local companies can purchase advertising space in the resource guide in the format of an eighth of a page, a quarter of a page, or a full-page advertisement. The second source of revenue for the resource guide is by way of sales of the resource guide; currently similar small business resource books are selling in the range of $25 to $50 each. The guide can be sold through local business associations, as well as on a wholesale basis to local retailers. Additional revenue for this type of business can be gained by also starting or implementing a chapter of a homebased business association that is currently not represented in your community. Overall, this business will take careful planning and research to establish, however, the rewards both personally and financially can be worth the effort.

WEB RESOURCE: www.aahbb.org American Association of Homebased Businesses.

ONLINE CYBERSECRETARIAL SERVICE
★★★ $$ 🏠 🕐 🖱

More people are working from home or operating a business from home than ever before in the history of the United States. This fact creates an outstanding opportunity to capitalize on the ever-increasing demand for secretarial services by starting a secretarial service that specializes in assisting clients by harnessing the power of the Internet. A cybersecretarial service provides the same services that a regular secretarial service provides with one main difference: the services are provided online. Clients seeking typing, editing, or electronic filing services would simply e-mail the work or the outline of the work required. Once the work has been completed, it would be e-mailed back to the client. The business will take some time to establish in terms of securing regular clients and building

templates and an operating format. However, for anyone with secretarial experience, starting this business is a great way to work from home, benefit from your skills, and earn an income of $25 per hour or more.

MOBILE OFFICE SERVICE
★★ $$$ 🕐

Though the target market for a mobile office service is generally limited to individuals and companies taking part in trade shows, seminars, and business conventions, this limited market is still gigantic, creating an outstanding business opportunity for all enterprising entrepreneurs by starting a mobile office service. A mobile office service can be designed to conveniently fit into a display booth that can be set up at trade shows and business conventions, and the services offered to clients can include high speed photocopying, sign making, typing services, Internet browsing, e-mail receiving and posting, and facsimile transmissions. Furthermore, to generate additional revenues for the business, office products and stationery supplies can be sold to trade show exhibitors that have run low or out of needed supplies to complete the show.

ONLINE DOMAIN NAME BROKER
★★ $$$$ 🏠 🕐 ⚖ 🖱

It is estimated that 93 percent of words in the English language have been incorporated in some fashion into a dot.com domain name. As corporations and small business owners race to register or purchase cool, short and effective dot.com names, the resale price goes up. In some cases it skyrockets into the seven-figure range. While a great deal of effective dot.com names have already been registered, many of these same names are now for sale or soon will be, and this fact creates a fantastic opportunity to capitalize on the worldwide race for the perfect Internet address. The key to success in domain name brokering is not to try and register good names, but to simply locate people and companies seeking to sell domain names and convince them you are the right broker for the task.

HOTEL COMPUTER RENTALS
★★★ $$$$ 🏠 🕐

Business travel has outpaced pleasure travel in recent years, and hotels have become a second home and office to many business owners and corporate executives. This fact creates a fantastic opportunity to start a business that specializes in renting computer equipment to people traveling for business purposes. The starting point will be to form a joint venture with one or more hotels. You supply the computer equipment for the rentals, and they market the service to their guest. Rental revenues earned can be split with the hotel on a 60/40 percent basis in your favor. This is a truly a win-win situation as you get to build a terrific business, and hotels get to provide their guests with a great service that requires no initial investment and can generate large profits.

VIRTUAL TOURS
★★★ $$$$ 🏠 🕐 🖱

Producing virtual tours for clients who are seeking the ultimate marketing tool for their Web sites is not only an incredible business opportunity, but the business also has the potential to generate profits far in excess of $100,000 per year. Virtual tours are becoming a very popular feature of many commercial Web sites. These virtual tours can range from a hotel that gives potential guests a tour of their facility, accommodations, and amenities via their Web site to real estate brokers that broadcast house tours of properties they have listed for sale and posted on their Web site. To get started you will need specialized software, a computer, and a digital camcorder, not to mention production and editing skills to produce the finished product. Marketing the service can be as easy as creating a few sample virtual tours and posting the tours on your own Web site for potential clients to view, as well as hiring a direct sales force to solicit business.

NEW COMPUTER SALES
★★ $$$$ 🏠 🕐

Selling computer systems and equipment is one of the most competitive sectors of the retailing industry.

However, with clever marketing in place, it is possible to earn a six-figure income selling new computer equipment from a homebased location. Operating the business from home will give you an enormous competitive advantage and minimal overhead expenses. The key to success in this industry is specialization, concentrate on sales of one particular type of computer or a computer that has been designed for a specific task. Marketing the product line can be by way of the Internet, print advertising, and networking with business owners and professionals at business meetings and functions. Additionally, seek opportunities retailing portable computers or handheld computers as rising consumer demand for these products will soon leave the traditional desktop computer extinct.

COMPUTER REPAIR TECHNICIAN
★★★ $$$ 🏠 🕐 🌐

Computer malfunction or a complete computer network systems crash can cost some companies thousands of dollars in lost revenues for every hour that their computer system is down. This fact alone is more than a compelling reason to start a mobile computer repair business. Operating the business on a mobile basis means that you will never be more than a cellular telephone and a few miles away when a client calls to inform you that disaster has struck and they are in desperate need of your service. In addition to reliable transportation, a cellular telephone, and tools to operate the business, you will need computer repair experience and skills, and plenty of it. Of course, if you lack the skills needed to repair the computer systems, you could always concentrate on the marketing and management aspects of the service, and hire subcontract repair technicians to work on an on-call and revenue split basis.

WEB RESOURCE: www.comptia.org The Computing Technology Industry Association.

MEDICAL BILLING SERVICE
★★ $$ 🏠 🕐 🌐

The medical billing industry is extremely competitive. However, for the determined entrepreneur there is still a good opportunity to earn $40,000 per year or more operating a homebased medical billing service. All medical billing is processed electronically and sent directly to Medicare clearinghouses, so computer equipment will be required as well as medical billing software to operate the service. Additionally, you will have to familiarize yourself with the diagnostic and procedure coding systems used by doctors and health-care professionals on medical claim forms to indicate the type of service being billed. Currently, medical billing services are charging clients in the range of $2 to $3 per claim processed, and the overall profit potential for the service is good, providing you can process medical claims on a volume basis. There is a steep learning curve for operating a medical billing service and careful planning and research techniques will have to be practiced.

WEB RESOURCE: www.smallbizbooks.com Business specific start-up guides and books.

MEDIATOR
★ $$ 🏠 🕐 ⚖

In most areas of the United States a mediator is not required to be licensed or have certificate training, making this an excellent choice for a new business venture. The duties of a mediator are to bring two opposing sides together and find common ground. A mediation service should not be confused with an arbitration service as a mediator does not rule in favor of either party, but remains neutral. The purpose of mediation is to reconcile differences between parties before litigation or arbitration is required to settle the dispute. Securing clients for a mediation service is best accomplished by building alliances with lawyers so the lawyers can refer your service to their clients. Mediators generally bill by the day for mediation services, and the rates average out to approximately $80 to $100 per hour.

WEB RESOURCE: www.mediatorindex.com American Arbitration Association.

BUSINESS CARD CD-ROMS
★★★ $$$$ 🏠 🕐

Do you want to get into a business that is on the cutting edge of technology and has unlimited upside potential market growth? If so, look no further than starting a business that designs and produces business card CD-ROMs. Business card CD-ROMs are simply a smaller version of a standard CD-ROM and are approximately the size of a business card. Additionally, this mini CD-ROMs can be die cut into virtually any shape, and played on any standard disk drive. Best of all, you can add graphics and sound, and they hold the equivalent of about 100 pages of typed information. Now that is a high-tech highly effective business card. There is a learning curve to overcome in terms of creating the end product. However, the business could always be approached as a joint venture with other businesses or individuals in the industry. In my opinion there is only one way to market business card CD-ROMs. Simply create a killer sample card and set appointments with business owners and professionals to present your talents via a laptop computer. One look at the sampling and they will sign up for an initial order of 500 or more.

ONLINE LOTTERIES
★★ $$$ 🏠 ⚖ 🖱

There are an estimated one billion regular lottery players worldwide. Thus, developing a Web site that features and provides site visitors with news and information pertaining to lotteries from around the globe could prove not only to be an interesting enterprise to activate, but also a profitable one. Information and services featured could include lottery games available in various countries, contact information about how to purchase tickets, an "electronic winning numbers forecaster," and stories about hitting it big provided by visitors. Income and profits can be earned by renting advertising space and banner ads as well as selling lottery-related products. Where allowable by law, the site could even become ticket resellers. Be sure to research all legal aspects prior to posting this type of Web site to the Internet as your research could potentially unearth a legal headache that could develop down the line.

WEB RESOURCE: www.entrepreneur.com Create a business Web site with MySite professional Web site builder.

PERSONAL ASSISTANT
★★ $$

Independent personal assistant services are becoming extremely popular and widely utilized by business owners and corporate executives that occasionally have a need for a personal assistant, but not on a full-time basis. Duties performed by a personal assistant include everything from booking appointments to returning telephone calls and, in some cases, even picking up dry cleaning. Additionally, most personal assistants are required to have computer skills as well as their own computer equipment and often travel is required to accompany the client to trade shows, business functions, and out-of-town business appointments.

COMPUTER UPGRADING SERVICE
★★ $$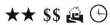

Starting a business that specializes in upgrading existing computer systems with new internal and external equipment is a terrific homebased business to initiate that has great potential to earn an outstanding income for the operator of the business. A computer upgrading service is a very easy business to get rolling, providing you have the skills and equipment necessary to complete upgrading tasks, such as installing more memory into the hard drive, replacing a hard drive, or adding a new disk drive to the computer system. Ideally, to secure the most profitable segment of the potential market, the service should specialize in upgrading business computers as there are many reasons why a business would upgrade a computer system as opposed to replacing the computer system. Additionally, managing the business from a homebased location while providing clients with a mobile service is the best way to keep operating overheads minimized and potentially increases the size of the target market by expanding the service area, due to the fact the business operates on a mobile format.

1-900 TELEPHONE LINES
★ $$

In spite of the fact that 1-900 telephone services have lost some of their appeal in the past few years,

many still continue to thrive and generate excellent profits for the operators of the 1-900 service. For anyone who is not familiar with a 1-900 telephone service, it is simply a business that charges customers a fee to call the service and listen to prerecorded or live messages and conversations via the telephone. Themes for 1-900 telephone services include lucky lottery numbers by phone, astrological readings, psychic readings, and singles dating. Generally, the caller is charged by the minute that he or she is on the phone, and the fees can range from $1 to $4 per minute. Once again, 1-900 telephone services have lost much of their appeal for callers in recent years, thanks mainly to the popularity of the Internet. However, for the determined entrepreneur with a popular theme, good profits can still be earned.

COMPUTER CLEANING SERVICE
★★ $ 🏠 🕐 🌐

Most commercial office cleaning services will not clean computers while cleaning an office. In fact most commercial cleaners will not even dust a desk that a computer is sitting on or near. Why? Simply because they do not want to accept the liability should anything happen to the computer equipment or information and programs stored within. Herein lies the business opportunity. The fastest and most efficient way to establish a computer cleaning service that specializes in cleaning computers used for business is to build alliances with commercial office cleaners so they can recommend your service to their clients. The only requirements for operating a computer cleaning service are to have the proper equipment to clean the computers along with the needed skills and a liability insurance policy.

MAILING SERVICE
★★ $$ 🏠 🕐

The increase in homebased business start-ups and the shift to employees working from home as opposed to a corporate office has created a terrific opportunity to start a mailing service. Good organizational skills, a postage meter, and a desktop computer and printer are about all that is needed to put this business into action. A mailing service provides clients services such as newsletter mailings, mail merge services, parcel shipping, accepting mail and parcels, and mass mailings of direct mail advertisements and marketing brochures. Fees are based on the services provided as well as the amount of mail shipped and received, plus postage charges. The profit potential is good and should average out to the $25 per hour range. Additionally, the long-term growth outlook for a mailing service is excellent simply due to the fact that homebased businesses requiring this type of specialized business service are opening at a record pace.

INVENTORY SERVICE

In spite of the fact that many businesses have a computerized inventory tracking system in place, most businesses still must conduct semiannual or annual inventory counts for tax and inventory shrinkage reasons. This fact creates a fantastic opportunity to capitalize by starting an inventory recording service. The business concept is very basic, and there are specialized handheld electronic recorders that enable the user to rapidly record and document inventory with a business or warehouse. One of the main marketing tools that will be available to you in terms of persuading potential clients to utilize the inventory service is simply the fact that in most cases the inventory counting can be conducted at night. Not disturbing the business or having to pay employees overtime wage rates to conduct the counts, not to mention the fact of accuracy in counting and recording methods, make this attractive to businesses.

ONLINE BEAUTY PAGEANTS

★ $$$$ 🌐 🐭

The world is ready for cyberbeauty pageants and you can bring it to them by creating a Web site that features community beauty pageants from around the globe. This online business concept is straightforward. Host statewide cyberbeauty pag-

eants with the winners of each contest being entered into the yearly Miss Cyber Pageant. Income can be earned by securing sponsors for each local or state pageant. Likewise these same corporate sponsors can also have pageant entry forms on their Web sites and in their stores. This type of cyberventure is going to require a substantial investment into marketing and promotion in order to become a brand name or well-recognized Web site. However, this type of site properly promoted also has the potential to attract millions of online visitors daily. With those kinds of hits, the sky is the limit in terms of ways and options to generate revenues and profits.

USED COMPUTER SALES

★★ $$$ 🕐

Purchasing secondhand computers and computer equipment by way of auction or surplus sales and reselling the equipment for a profit is a terrific new homebased business venture to put into action. Many corporations, government agencies, and educational institutions upgrade and replace their computer equipment on a regular basis. Often the computer equipment is only a few years old and can be purchased for as little as 5 percent of its original cost. Securing surplus computer equipment can be accomplished by attending auction sales, surplus sales, and successfully bidding in tenders for secondhand surplus computer equipment as they become available. Marketing the computer equipment can be by way of classified advertisements, a retail location such as a sales kiosk, a flea market booth, or by way of e-mail and fax blasts targeted at small businesses.

ONLINE RESEARCHER

Do you spend hours every day surfing the Web? If so, why not start an Internet research service and get paid for surfing. This business opportunity was once commonly referred to as information brokering. However, with the introduction of the Internet, the name has changed, but the business remains the same, as the information that used to be researched and compiled from newspapers, trade magazines, and business and industry directories now can all be found on the Internet. In a nutshell, an Internet research service operates in two fashions. The first is the service collects data and facts relevant to just about any topic or subject known to exist. The second is where business owners and corporations enlist the services of an Internet researcher to source data and facts relevant to their particular business, industry, or market. In both cases, clients pay for information they are seeking. Billing rates for the services vary depending on how much research time is required to compile the data being sought; however, many Internet research services base billing rates on $20 to $30 per hour.

WEB RESOURCE: www.smallbizbooks.com Business specific start-up guides and books.

HOLIDAY E-MAIL SERVICE

★★ $$ 🏠 🕐 🌍 ✍

Starting a holiday and special occasion greeting card e-mail service is a fantastic new business enterprise to set in motion, especially when you consider the business can be operated from home and put into action with less than a $3,000 initial investment. Business owners, corporate executives, and professionals lead very busy lives, often not leaving time for the small but important things in life, like sending a card to a family member on a special occasion or thanking a client at Christmastime for their continued support and business. Designing "fill-in-the-blank" templates for a number of occasions such as birthdays, anniversaries, and thanks for your business is the first step toward establishing the business. The templates can be quickly altered and e-mailed to recipients at your client's request. Setting fees for the service will greatly depend on a client's volume of e-mail greeting cards sent on a yearly basis. However, securing 200 clients and e-mailing 100 customized greeting cards for each on a yearly basis can generate gross revenues of $40,000, providing you only charge $2 for each e-mail greeting card sent, or about half the cost to send a traditional prints greeting card via the mail.

PROPOSAL WRITER

★★ $$ 🏠 🕐

Each year government agencies on the federal, state, and local levels put thousands of RFPs (requests for proposals) out for bid. The proposals can range from building government buildings to supplying computer equipment for government offices, and just about anything in between. Though many of these proposals can be very lucrative for the company or individual that successfully bids for the contract, many small- to medium-sized contractors simply do not complete the proposal and bid forms. Due to the fact that the bidding process is extremely involved and usually requires technical drawings, action plans, and contingency plans, business owners and management have neither the time nor abilities to complete them. A proposal writer compiles and completes the proposal documents on behalf of the contractor. It's as simple as that. Proposal writers charge fees based on the amount of time it will take to complete the proposal, typically in the range of $30 to $40 per hour. Some proposal writers even charge a commission on the value of the contract should their client be awarded. Furthermore, most proposal writers specialize in an area of expertise such as nonperishable goods, construction, services, or maintenance. Equipment required for the service is basic and only includes standard office and computer equipment. Additionally, a proposal writer must have access to a wide range of research resources and in most cases a technical writing ability.

TRADE SHOW VISITOR

★ $ 🕐

Did you know that many corporations enlist the services of an independent trade show visitor, or researcher, as a method of keeping track of their competition exhibiting at trade shows? Starting a trade show visitor service is just about as straightforward as any new business venture can be. The duties of a trade show visitor are to collect information for clients about their competition exhibiting at the show. The information collected includes items such as marketing brochures, display booth designs, pictures, traffic counts, special promotions, new product introductions, and just about anything else a client may request. To ensure the business is financially viable, most trade show visitors attend trade shows representing as many as 10 to 15 clients. To establish and operate the service, excellent communication and marketing skills will be needed, and a digital camera and notebook computer will prove invaluable.

ONLINE TRADE SHOW DIRECTORY
★★ $$$ 🏠 🕐 🖱

Worldwide, more than 100,000 trade shows take place annually. Thus a very exciting and potentially profitable business opportunity exists—an online trade show directory. You can easily develop a Web site that lists trade show information such as what type of trade show, when it is taking place, where the show is being conducted, and how to contact the shows organizers. This type of online directory could become very popular as thousands of small businesses and corporations rely solely on trade shows as their main marketing tool for introducing new products and services as well as collecting qualified sales leads from interested parties. You also have options in terms of how your business will generate income and profits including charging a listing fee to have trade show information featured on the site, selling advertising space on the site, or selling an annual trade show directory in print format.

TELEMARKETING SERVICE
★★ $$ 🏠 🕐

Excellent telephone and communications skills coupled with a take-no-prisoners attitude can earn you a small fortune operating a telemarketing service. Best of all, the business can be operated from the comforts of a homebased office. Professional telemarketers are in high demand, simply because they get results, and companies have no hesitation paying top dollar to secure a telemarketing service to promote or sell their products and services via the telephone. Rates vary, however, most telemarketing services charge a fee for each call made, and additional fees if products or services are sold or

appointments booked. Securing clients for the service is very straightforward, and as an initial promotion, consider offering your telemarketing services for free and only charging for results. A client will have nothing to lose by using your service, as you will only get paid if you're earning them money or booking appointments for their sales professionals. Potential income range is $20 to $50 per hour.

WEB RESOURCE: www.atacontact.org American Telemarketing Association.

_____ OF THE MONTH CLUB
★ $$$$ 🏠

Books, toys, tools, CD music, or just about any product can be the basis of a _____ of the Month Club. The secret to success in this type of homebased retail business is to offer good quality products at discounted or less than retail cost. This is to build a large club membership base and constantly expand both the membership base and the selection of products being offered for sale. To keep start-up costs to a minimum, there are thousands of manufacturers and distributors of consumer goods that will drop ship products directly to your customers. To build a club membership base quickly, advertise free memberships as well as a free mystery gift as an incentive for people to become members.

COMPUTER DELIVERY AND ASSEMBLY SERVICE
★★ $ 🏠 🕐

A computer delivery and assembly service is a very easy new business venture to set in action. The best way to market the service is to establish joint ventures with retailers of new and secondhand computer systems and equipment. They sell—you deliver and install it. Furthermore, as a method to earn additional income for the business, consider marketing additional products and services along with the delivery and assembly service. These additional products and services can include retailing computer security items, offering clients a computer cleaning service, as well as offering clients a software installation and explanation service, just to mention a few. The amount of income the business can generate will vary as to the services provided. However, even operating a computer delivery and assembly service alone can easily generate a part-time income of $20 per hour or more.

1-800 TELEPHONE CALL CENTER
★★★ $$$ 🏠

A 1-800 telephone call center is simply an answering service that caters to companies that sell products via mail order, classified advertising, and infomercials. They rely on a 1-800 or toll-free line for incoming inquiries and product orders. Furthermore, a 1-800 telephone service can be operated right from a homebased office. Clients can call-forward their toll-free lines to your office for after hours inquiry, or you can establish toll-free lines and issue clients an extension number for their business and advertising activities. Establishing billing rates can be by way of charging clients a monthly fee for handling their toll-free lines, or by each call that is received. The telephone equipment needed to start this type of specialized communications business is costly, and as a method to reduce start-up costs, consider purchasing secondhand telephone equipment capable of handling large incoming call volumes.

DIGITAL VIDEO E-MAIL TERMINALS
★★★★ $$$$ ⚖ 🖱

Are you searching for a truly unique business opportunity that will place you at the forefront of the computer and technology industry? If so, perhaps you should consider developing Internet video e-mail terminals equipped with a Web cam that enable the user to send video e-mails. The video e-mail terminals can be located in high-traffic community gathering places such as airports, train stations, bus depots, and cruise ships. The unique feature of the video e-mail terminals are that instead of placing telephone calls to friends and family, users of the terminals can send video and audio e-mails to friends and family members. The e-mails would be received by the recipient and opened as an attachment file when checking e-mail. The terminals can take credit card and debit card payments from consumers using the service,

and revenue split or location fee could be paid to the owner or operator of the building where the terminals are installed. Web cams are common and Internet terminals are common. To date I am not aware of any company that has combined these technologies and created a video e-mail terminal. The concept is fresh and will obviously require a lot of planning and research, not to mention investment capital. However, perhaps this type of communications system will someday replace the public pay telephone?

ONLINE WEDDING SERVICE
★★★ $$$$ 🏠 🌐 🖱

Starting a commercial Web site venture solely dedicated to weddings could potentially make you the next online gazillionaire. The site can be indexed by state or even city and be broken down into subsections featuring every imaginable wedding-related product or service including:

- A directory of wedding photographers and videographers.
- A directory of wedding singers, disc jockeys, and musical bands.
- A directory of wedding planners and caterers.
- A directory of formal wear and rentals for both men and women.
- A directory of limousine services and much more.

Site visitors would simply select the geographical area they live in, chose the topic of interest, and start to view the listings and information. Anyone getting married would be able to log onto the site to find a photographer, plan a honeymoon, and book a reception hall all with the click of a mouse.

TONER CARTRIDGE RECYCLING
★★ $$ 🏠 🕐 🌐

Ink or toner cartridges used in many photocopiers, fax machines, and printers are able to be recycled by simply replenishing the ink supply, and this fact creates a terrific opportunity to start a toner cartridge recycling business. The business can easily be run from home, and the only requirements for operating the business is to have transportation, a few basic tools, and the ability to refill the cartridges with new ink. Your competitive advantage over retail operations that sell new toner cartridges for office and printing equipment is the fact that you can offer clients free and fast delivery of recycled cartridges. In addition, clients can save as much as 50 percent by purchasing recycled toner cartridges, as opposed to the cost of new cartridges

WEB RESOURCE: http://fome.fuse.net/gcrane/reman.html Directory service listing manufacturers and distributors of toner cartridge supplies and equipment as well as industry-related information.

COMPUTER KIOSK DESIGNER
★★★ $$$ 🏠 🕐

Computer kiosks are popping up everywhere in North America: movie theaters, malls, retail stores, and grocery stores. Starting a business that designs and constructs specialty kiosks to house computer equipment is a fantastic new business venture to set in motion. The main requirements for operating this type of specialized manufacturing business is to have a good working knowledge of construction, as well as the ability to work in various material mediums. The business can be based from a well-equipped home workshop with a truck, van, or trailer for local delivery of the kiosks. Securing contracts for designing and manufacturing the kiosks can be accomplished by building a few samples, creating a marketing brochure, and distributing the marketing material to potential clients in need of this kind of product. Once established, this type of specialty manufacturing business can prove to be very profitable.

WEB SITE DIRECTORIES IN PRINT
★★ $$$$ 🏠 🌎

Thousands of companies, associations, individuals, agencies, and organizations go online and post new Web sites on the Internet daily, adding to the millions of Web sites that are already vying for cyberspace supremacy. Even with the assistance of Internet search engines, key word searches, and hyperlinks,

the Internet can still be a very confusing, and even a frustrating tool for researching or locating information. Herein lies the business opportunity. Create a monthly Web site directory publication that features useful and practical information such as Web addresses and the type of information contained within the Web site. The publication can be divided into various categories such as sports, business, health, and entertainment for quick reference purposes. Furthermore, the monthly publication can be distributed locally or nationally with the assistance of a newspaper distribution service. Selling the publication to consumers as well as charging a fee to be listed in the publication would earn revenues.

ONLINE JOB POSTINGS
★★ $$$$ 🏠 🕐 🖱

There is stiff competition in the online job postings and career industry. However, there is always room for more creative, useful, and varied services provided via the Internet. In the spirit of uniqueness, perhaps your online job posting service could specialize in a site solely dedicated to employment in the computer programming industry. Or, maybe specialize in the mining and forestry industry; there are unlimited online opportunities for the innovative entrepreneur to capitalize on. Additionally this type of Web venture would also lend itself to selling employment guides and offering online employee training programs.

TEMPORARY HELP AGENCY
★★★ $$$ 🏠 🌐

Starting a homebased temporary help agency is a fantastic new business venture to set in motion. Ideally, the agency should specialize in supplying qualified workers on a temporary basis in one particular industry or area of expertise, such as the construction industry. Recruiting workers prepared to work on a temporary basis should not prove difficult, given that many people have various reasons why they do not wish to seek full-time employment including students, early retirees, and even homebased business owners seeking to gain additional income periodically. Marketing the service can be as easy as creating an information package describing the service and workforce, and distributing the packages to businesses and companies that occasionally rely on temporary workers to run their business. Establishing a billing rate for the workers supplied is based on market value for the job being performed, and the agency representing the worker generally retains 10 to 15 percent or the workers earnings.

WEB RESOURCE: www.smallbizbooks.com Business specific start-up guides and books.

FILING SYSTEMS
★★ $$

Environmentalists once envisioned the computer and its electronic information storage capacities as the absolute final solution for a world that would no longer need to consume paper products. However, as long as an original signature stands as the most binding and unchallenged legal identification for a person, there will always be a need for paper, files, and filing systems. Operating a business that sells and installs filing systems is a great homebased enterprise to set in motion. Not only can you make a profit on the initial sale of the system, but as your client's business grows and expands you will receive repeat sales of filing supplies. Customers can include businesses and professionals whose business or service is document reliant such as lawyers, doctors, advertising firms, financial institutions, schools, and government agencies. Aim for yearly sales of $200,000 while maintaining a product markup of 50 percent. The results will be a terrific homebased business generating revenues of $70,000 per year.

WEB RESOURCE: www.resources.com/storagma.htm Directory service listing manufacturers and distributors of filing systems and storage management equipment.

MOBILE COMPUTER TRAINING
★★★ $$

As a rule of thumb, most computer training schools require the student to come to their business location for training classes. However, for companies that have recently upgraded their computers system or have introduced new software into the business, it is often not practical to have ten or more people going off-site for computer upgrade training or to learn how to maximize the benefits of a new software program. Herein lies the business opportunity. Combining your computer, software, and marketing skills and experience, you can start a mobile computer training service. The classes can be conducted at the client's location as well as using the client's computer equipment. Income potential range is $40 to $50 per hour.

WEB RESOURCE: www.icca.org Independent Computer Consultants Association.

TECHNOLOGY EMPLOYMENT AGENT
★★★ $$ 🏠

Baseball players have agents, writers have agents, and an agent represents even animals that appear on film. So why not start a business that specializes in representing people with computer and technology skills as their agent? High-tech, computer, and Internet companies are scrambling to find skilled employees with technology skills, and the wages paid are entering the stratosphere, not to mention the many benefits and perks that are also offered. A software designer being paid $150,000 per year may be worth twice that amount to a competing software development company, and the designer may not even realize it. The duty of the agent is to seek out and secure the best contract for their client, or in this case, the position that pays twice as much. Billing rates for the service can be by way of a predetermined fee, by a commission based on the value of the contract secured and paid by the client, or by the company that wishes to retain the services of the client. The profit potential is outstanding.

TELEPHONE ANSWERING SERVICE
★★ $$ 🏠

The only talents needed to start a homebased telephone answering service are a pleasant telephone manner and excellent communication skills. Business owners, professionals, and sales consultants are all starting to realize that customers want the personalized service of talking to a live person when they call a business, not a prerecorded message. Many business owners are turning to call forwarding their telephone numbers to a telephone answering service after normal business hours, on weekends, during lunch breaks, and when no one is available to take incoming calls. Services provided by a telephone answering service include: answering incoming calls, answering basic customer questions, forwarding messages, and often additional office services such as sending and receiving facsimiles and e-mail transmissions. Rates are based on the number of services provided for clients, and standard nonbusiness-hour telephone answering rates start at about $200 per month. Securing 10 to 15 clients for the service could easily generate business revenues in the range of $3,000 to $5,000 per month.

ONLINE SOFTWARE DISTRIBUTION
★★ $$+

Worldwide, there are thousands of software designers and manufacturing firms that produce literally thousands of different software applications. This fact creates a very exciting business opportunity by developing a Web site that sells software applications online. However, selling software is extremely competitive. In order to compete, seek to specialize in one type of software application. The first step will be to secure an agreement with a software developer to represent and market their product. Once again, harnessing the power of the Internet is the best way to research and accomplish this task. Once you have selected the software you will be selling and the Web site has been posted to the Internet, you can begin to promote both the software and the Web site. In terms of promoting the software, initiate a direct mail and e-mail marketing campaign aimed at the industry or individual that will benefit from this software application. The site can be promoted by registering with search engines, installing hyperlinks to topic-related sites, joining e-malls, and by participating in rotating banner advertisement programs.

E-BARGAINS
★★★ $

In today's highly competitive retail environment I love the e-bargain business concept. Simply put, you compile an e-mail address list of people that would like to receive your weekly e-bargains newsletter that features discounts on a wide variety of consumer products and services. There are no membership fees or costs associated with receiving the newsletter. It's absolutely free of charge. Income and profits are earned by selling a very limited number of advertising spaces to online merchants and service providers that want access to your newsletter subscribers. In addition to paying the advertising fee, merchants and service providers must also agree that the products and service that are advertised in the e-bargain newsletter will be at least 10 percent less than the normal retail price. You can also spice up the newsletter by including trivia questions, games, jokes, or any other interesting content. Be sure to comply with anti-Spam regulations and remove anyone from your e-mail list that requests so. Securing just five advertisers per week each paying $50 will create a yearly income in excess of $10,000, and best of all this can be accomplished with a part-time effort of less than ten hours of work each week.

WEB SITE QUALITY CONSULTANT
★★ $$

In exchange for a $99 consulting fee, give small business owners the real lowdown on the quality of their Web site. In the rush to get online many small business owners forget that information and services should provide quality in terms of their Web site. In a nutshell, as the quality consultant you would view a client's Web site and submit a full report. The report could include a comparison to competitor sites, a rating on how user-friendly their site is, and suggestions on how the site could be improved. These improvements could range from including a software application, to providing enhanced visitor services, to changing the style of how content is presented. The cost of this very beneficial consulting service is low, but the impact that it could potentially have on a client's site could mean the difference between cyberfailure and cybersuccess. Put in those terms, securing clients should not prove difficult.

WEB SITE DESIGN
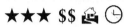

More than 1,000 Web sites a day are being posted to the Internet, and here is your chance to cash in by starting a Web site design service. Fear not if you do not know how to design a highly effective Web site. You can take a crash course in Web site design at your local community college or, failing that, you can hire a high-tech wizard to design the sites while you concentrate your efforts on sales and marketing. Online competition in Web site design and service is steep; thus you may want to take a more hands-on approach to marketing the service right in your own city or community. Start by designing a few sample sites—one in an e-commerce format and one as an information portal. The next step is to initiate a letter writing and telephone campaign to introduce yourself and your service to small business owners in your community that currently do not have a business Web site. The goal is to get a presentation appointment at their place of business. Finally, armed with a notebook computer you can meet with business owners, present your sample sites, and explain the benefits of your Web site design service.

WEB RESOURCE: www.whosontheWeb.com The International Association of Web Masters and Designers.

NOTES

KEY	
RATINGS	★
START-UP COST	$
HOMEBASED BUSINESS	🏡
PART-TIME	🕐
LEGAL ISSUES	⚖
FRANCHISE OR LICENSE POTENTIAL	🌐
ONLINE	🖱

30
CRAFT
Businesses You Can Start

DECORATIVE PARTITION SCREEN MANUFACTURING

★★ $$ 🏡 🕐

If you have an entrepreneurial spirit and a creative talent, starting a business that manufactures and sells decorative partition screens may be just the money-making opportunity that you have been looking for. Partition screens are commonly used in homes, offices, even outdoors as an added decorative flair or to divide and partition any existing space. However, you will need basic knowledge of carpentry, have artistic talent, and the desire to succeed in this business. Once completed there are numerous ways to market the screens, including:

- Selling the screens to specialty retailers on a wholesale basis.
- Placing the decorative screens in retail stores on a consignment basis.
- Selling the screens to residential and commercial interior decorators.

This is truly a unique and inexpensive homebased business opportunity to start that can be operated on a full- or part-time basis. In terms of product pricing, the first step is to check out the competition. A general pricing formula is to take your material and labor costs, which add up to the product cost. Then figure out your markup (anywhere from 50 to 100 percent) and multiply it by your product costs to equal the wholesale or retail selling price.

CANDLE MAKING

★★ $ 🏡 🕐

The popularity of specialty candles has really taken off in the past decade as more and more people are starting to enjoy the relaxing effect that burning scented candles can have. This popularity and consumer demand for specialty candles creates a tremendous business opportunity for the innovative entrepreneur to start a business that manufactures and sells candles. A good starting point for learning how to make candles would be to visit the local library, as well as logging onto the Web site for the National Candle Association located at www.candles.org. A homebased candle making business is best suited for the entrepreneur who is seeking additional income on a part-time basis, with a long-term goal of establishing a full-time and profitable business concern. Selling the completed candles can be as easy as renting a table at a local craft show, placing the candles in retail locations on consignment basis, or even establishing wholesale accounts with national specialty retailers. Furthermore, adding fragrance, coloring, and creating artistic details on the candles will definitely increase consumer demand for the product and result in more profit for you.

WEB RESOURCE: www.candles.org National Candle Association.

CRAFT SUPPLY STORE
★★★ $$$$

Starting a craft supply retail store is a fantastic new business enterprise to set in motion. There are thousands of people across North America working in the craft industry, whether as a hobby or as an artist making a living, and all of these potential customers need a place to purchase their craft supplies. This is the kind of retail business that will require a substantial initial start-up investment, but the profit potential can easily justify the investment. Ideally, this type of business enterprise will be located in a highly visible and easily accessible location within the community. Furthermore, be sure to carry a wide variety of craft supplies. The key to successful retailing is to build repeat clientele, and the best way to ensure this happens is to have the store well-stocked with products and supplies that represent all areas of the craft industry. Marketing this type of enterprise would be by way of traditional advertising mediums like newspapers, fliers, and radio. An innovative approach to generate more income would be to hold instructional seminars after business hours on different crafting techniques such as painting or silk-flower arrangements. Locating wholesalers and distributors for products will not be difficult, and the profit potential is tremendous as product markups can be 100 percent or more.

WEB RESOURCE: www.craftassoc.com National Craft Association, links to manufactures and distributors of crafts supplies.

ONLINE CRAFT SUPPLY SALES
★ $$$$ 🏠 🖱

There are a few options available in terms of selling craft supplies online. The first option is to develop a Web site that features craft supplies of every sort for sale, and stock these items for customer orders. This option would be costly to establish as not only would you have to develop and market the site, but you would also have to invest a large amount of capital into inventory. However, if this route was selected, the Web site could be promoted by running display advertisements in craft magazines as well as by initiating a direct mail campaign aimed specifically at people in the crafts industry. Names for the direct mail campaign could be accessed through crafters associations and clubs. The second and less costly option for selling craft supplies online would be to develop a Web site that featured literally hundreds of various craft supplies for sale with direct hyperlinks or "pop-up" pages to the manufacturers or distributors of these products. This option would enable you to carry a wide selection of craft supplies without having to invest thousands of dollars into inventory as the manufacturers or distributors could ship directly to your customers. Revenue would be generated by either charging the manufacturers and distributors a fee for being listed and featured on the site, or by retaining a percentage on total sales generated.

WEB RESOURCE: www.entrepreneur.com Create a business Web site with MySite professional Web site builder.

POTTERY
★★ $$ 🏠 🕐

Starting a business that designs, produces, and sells pottery items is definitely best suited for the entrepreneur with a creative flair who is seeking a unique homebased business opportunity.

Some of the aspects of this business to be considered are:

- *Ability.* Anyone considering this business venture will definitely need the ability to not only create pottery items, but to create interesting and unique pottery items.

- *Equipment and supplies.* All equipment and supplies required for starting and operating a pottery making business are readily available in almost every community through craft supply stores that stock the items or orders the items on an as-needed basis.

- *Marketing.* Pottery items can be sold by renting a table at craft shows, by selling the pottery to retailers on a wholesale basis, and by placing the pottery items in retail stores on a consignment basis.

- *Business location.* A pottery business is ideally suited to being operated from a homebased studio location. Additionally, if zoning permits, the studio can also act as a retail outlet or factory direct sales outlet for the pottery products. In addition to creating and selling pottery items, you can also generate additional business revenues and profits by holding instructional classes on pottery making and pottery glazing techniques.

CACTUS ARRANGEMENTS

Creating and selling cactus arrangements—what a great and inexpensive homebased business venture to start. As houseplants go, cactuses are one of the most popular. The reason is simple. People love having plants to decorate their homes, but most people do not have the time or the green thumbs required to care for plants. Cactus plants are very easy to grow and require very little in the way of regular maintenance. Purchasing cactus plants and related materials from a wholesale company would be your first step. Be sure to negotiate the best price possible with the wholesaler, and also research the care and

requirements for each type of cactus. Now the fun part starts—creating interesting cactus arrangements that will command top dollar. The selling price of the cactus arrangements will greatly depend on the arrangement itself; however, adding product costs and labor time together, plus a 100 percent markup, is not out of line in terms of establishing a retail selling value. Ideally, aim to establish wholesale accounts with retailers to stock and sell the cactus arrangements, as well as selling the arrangements directly to consumers via rented sales kiosks in a busy mall or market.

WEB RESOURCE: www.growit.com Online directory of nursery wholesalers.

HAND-PAINTED PLANTING POTS

Gardening is one of the fastest growing pastimes in North America. For the entrepreneur seeking to capitalize on the huge demand for garden-related products, look no further than starting a business that creates and sells one of a kind hand-painted clay gardening pots. More and more people are searching for unique and interesting ways in which to display their flowers and shrubs, so why not create extraordinary planting pots for these consumers and start making money. Simply purchase clay planting pots from a local wholesale company, and paint and decorate the pots with unique, interesting, and colorful themes and designs. Once completed, the flowerpots can be sold in various ways, including directly to specialty retailers and garden centers on a wholesale basis and to residential and commercial interior decorators and garden planners. You can also sell them by renting a sales table at a local craft show or flea market and of course directly to consumers by advertising the hand-painted flower pots for sale over the Internet.

MOSAIC TILE CREATIONS

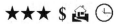

Creating home decoration items featuring mosaic tile designs is an exceptional business venture to set in motion. Not only can this enterprise be started and run from a homebased location, but this business is also very inexpensive to initiate. Best of all, interesting home and office decoration products are always in high demand. Create unique mosaic tile designs; everything from tabletops to mosaic tile picture frames. Your only limitations will be your imagination. Mosaic tiles can be purchased ready to install or you can create your own simply by buying discontinued styles and colors as well as collecting broken tiles from local building and renovation companies. Of course, the latter options would be excellent choices, as most could be purchased at a very low or no cost, not to mention the fact that you will be recycling any unwanted waste product. Marketing the mosaic tile creations can be by way of traditional advertising mediums, as well as by renting a weekend sales kiosk in a market or mall. Additionally, be sure to contact interior decorators in your community to introduce them to your unique decorating product line.

WEB RESOURCE: www.mosaicmerc.com Manufacturer and distributor of mosaic tile equipment and supplies.

HAND-PAINTED STORAGE BOXES

With so many people looking for unique and interesting ways to organize their personal belongings, home office documents, and family keepsakes, hand-painted storage boxes are sure to fit the bill. The options are endless—using materials such as wood, metal, and cardboard you can create designer storage boxes to suit every decor. You will need to have some artistic talent, but with that said, art and craft classes are available in almost every community in North America. Additionally, consider building the storage boxes out of recycled materials, as well as using organic paints to decorate the storage boxes. Not only will you be helping the environment by doing this, but you will also be able to capitalize on an earth-friendly marketing approach.

LAWN ORNAMENT SALES

Not only are lawn decorations easy to make, they are also easy products to sell. Combining these two facts creates a wonderful business opportunity for the innovative entrepreneur to start a business that manufactures and sells lawn ornaments. The first step will be to purchase or make the molds required for manufacturing the lawn ornaments; the rest is very straightforward. Simply practice making and painting lawn ornaments until you are satisfied with the finished product. Next you will be ready to start making money. Lawn ornaments are currently retailing in the range of $25 to $100 each, depending on the size and style of the item, and the profit potential is excellent as it only costs about $5 in material to produce the average sized precast lawn ornament. The lawn decorations can be sold on a wholesale basis to retailers, or you can even sell them directly to consumers right from your own front yard.

WEB RESOURCE: www.concrete-success.com Suppliers of lawn ornament molds and equipment.

WOODCARVING

Do you wood carve for a hobby, and are the carvings good? If so, consider starting a woodcarving business that not only lets you work at what you like best, but also makes you some money at the same time. Original, interesting, and unique woodcarvings sell like crazy in the right retail environment, such as arts and crafts shows, and specialty retail shops. Finding retailers to stock and sell the woodcarvings is simple. Why? Because the owners of these businesses know how well woodcarvings sell and how much money can be made selling woodcarvings. Of course, if you want to keep the bulk of the profits yourself, you can always sell your woodcarving creations directly to consumers by renting a sales kiosk in a mall or even by advertising the woodcarvings for sale, complete with a description and picture, on one of the many online auction services.

WEB RESOURCE: www.chiphats.org National Wood Carvers Association.

KNITTING

★ $ 🏠 🕐

Do you currently knit sweaters, jackets, and more? If so, perhaps you should consider turning your hobby craft into a profitable part-time business enterprise. The business is to simply create beautiful and unique hand-knitted products from sweaters to a clothing line for stuffed animals. The opportunities are endless; all you need is a creative spirit, knitting needles, some yarn, and you're in business. For the truly enterprising entrepreneur aim toward developing a Web site that features premade knit clothing products for sale, as well as a custom made-to-order service where site visitors could simply fill out an order form for the size and style of knit products they want. The income and profit potential will vary in this type of unique crafts business. However, there should be no problem in attaining a part-time income level of $10,000 per year or more after expenses.

WEB RESOURCE: www.tkga.com The Knitting Guild of America.

STUFFED ANIMALS

★★ $$ 🏠 🕐

There are a few different approaches that can be taken when considering starting a business that focuses on selling stuffed animals. The first approach is to design and manufacture the stuffed animals yourself. The second approach is to purchase stuffed animals on a wholesale basis, and resell them for a profit. The third approach is to purchase antique stuffed animals and resell them for a profit. All three approaches have a great opportunity at business success, as stuffed animals new or old are in and will always be in high demand by collectors and consumers alike. The profit potential is outstanding, especially if you can locate a good source for antique stuffed animals, as it is not uncommon for antique teddy bears to sell for as much as $1,000 each.

WEB RESOURCE: www.toydirectory.com Directory service listing toy manufacturers.

CRAFT SHOWS

★ $$ 🕐

Do you want to know how you can make an extra $25,000 per year by hosting only four annual craft shows? It is actually quite easy to host craft shows, and in the spirit of being unique, let me suggest a way that you cannot only make an additional $25,000 per year part-time, but you can also have a lot of fun doing it. The business concept is very direct. Simply, secure 100 craft vendors per craft show that you host, and charge each vendor $100 for table rental. Holding a winter, spring, summer, and fall show will generate total business revenues of $40,000 (4 shows x 100 vendors each show x $100 per table booth = $40,000). The next trick is to keep as much of the gross revenues as possible, and seek out ways of promoting the show so craft vendors will receive maximum exposure. Here is how it can be accomplished:

- *Free location for the craft shows.* Finding a location to hold the craft show without having to pay rent is very easy. Simply negotiate with the landlord of the location that shows' admittance fees and concession snack revenue will be retained by the location or landlord. One thousand people paying $1 each to attend and spending only $1 each on snacks will result in a two-day "same as rent" fee of $2,000. As you can see, finding a location for the craft show should not be hard.

- *Free advertising for the craft shows.* Advertising and promoting the craft show for free is also very easy. Start by negotiating with the craft vendors that 5 percent of their total sales will go to a community charity. The next step is to contact a local newspaper or TV station and negotiate a joint venture in terms of sponsoring the craft show and the local charity. Once again, it will not be hard to find a newspaper or TV station that is willing to give away some free advertising in exchange for the goodwill benefits of being a co-sponsor of a community event for charity.

WEB RESOURCE: www.artsandcraftshows.net Directory service listing arts and craft shows.

ONLINE CRAFT SHOWS
★★ $$$$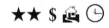

Take craft shows high-tech by starting your own virtual 365-days-a-year online craft show Web site. The concept is straightforward. Many people producing crafts on a full- or part-time basis need a marketing and distribution outlet for their products beyond a few "bricks and mortar" craft shows each year. Additionally, many of these same crafters cannot afford to spend a few thousand dollars to develop their own Web site, and even if they could, there is still the cost of marketing and maintenance to consider. Here is the solution. Develop a Web site that is a virtual craft show or e-crafts mall. The site can be indexed into various craft categories and visitors would simply choose the section they wished to visit. Crafters would receive a listing with an automatic link to a pop-up page that would give details about their particular products as well as show photographs of their products. Consumers wishing to purchase a product would simply click on their selection and be linked to the central e-crafts store to enter payment and shipping information. Revenues would be earned by charging a listing fee to be featured on the site, as well as retaining a percentage of each sale for providing the e-craft store and service. Crafters would be notified electronically of each sale including shipping details so they could send consumers their purchases directly. Marketing the site can be accomplished by registering with search engines including keyword searches and by advertising the site through traditional print mediums like magazines, craft newsletters, and other craft publications. Developing and publishing this type of Web site will require some custom ASP programming and a substantial development and marketing budget. However, the potential for profit is fantastic, and

once the site has been perfected it would be relatively easy to maintain.

QUILT SALES
★★ $$ 🏠 🕐

Quilting has been around for generations and continues to thrive. Like many things today "everything old is once again new and popular," and starting a business that sells custom-made one-of-a-kind quilts could be your opportunity to reap big financial benefits. If you are already familiar with quilting, great— if not, simply research the different aspects of quilting, or a visit to your library should give you enough information to get started. For those of you not familiar with copyright laws, be sure not to infringe on someone else's creation. Selling the quilts could be as easy as renting a table at local craft shows or selling the custom quilts via the Web to a global audience. Additionally, look for opportunities in purchasing antique quilts and reselling the quilts for a profit, as the collector market for antique quilts is hot.

WEB RESOURCE: www.nqaquilts.org National Quilting Association.

BASKET WEAVING
★★ $ 🏠 🕐

Starting a business that manufactures and sells custom-made baskets is an incredible enterprise to get rolling, simply because people from every walk of life are always searching for the perfect piece of functional home decoration. Utilizing a wide variety of raw materials, ranging from rattan to wire, will provide you with not only the material required to make the baskets but also results in a varied and interesting product line. If you do not know how to basket weave, don't worry; you can always take a few instructional classes or locate other basket weavers and sell their finished products. Marketing the baskets can be accomplished by establishing accounts with retailers to stock and sell the baskets, as well as by hiring a direct sales force to host home parties that feature the complete basket product line for sale.

WEB RESOURCE: www.weavespindye.org Handweavers Guild of America Inc.

DRIED FLOWERS

Growing, processing, and selling dried flowers could put you on the path to self-employment independence, and financial freedom. One of the best aspects about setting this business enterprise in motion is the fact that it can easily be started right from your home, using your own garden as the initial source for the flowers to be dried and sold. Once the business is ready to be expanded there are a couple options in terms of the required flowers. The first is to lease vacant land to increase flower production and the second option is to purchase flowers. While the second option is easier, it will also reduce the amount of available profit. Once dried and packaged, the flowers can be sold to retailers on a wholesale basis. Profit potential range is $5,000+ per year part-time.

ARTIFICIAL PLANTS

Designing, making, and selling artificial plants is a terrific homebased business venture to put into action, as the demand for artificial plants is strong and will continue to be strong in the future. Artificial plants are easy to make, and the raw materials required are available in almost every community through craft supply stores. Additionally, many of these same craft stores also stock books and instruction videos on how to make artificial plants for profit. Marketing the artificial plants can be accomplished in a number of ways including: selling the plants to retailers on a wholesale basis, placing the plants at retail locations on a consignment basis, and selling the plants to interior designers and event planners at discounted prices.

SEASHELL JEWELRY

Do you live near the ocean and take daily walks on the beach? If so, you could be walking past thousands of dollars in potential profits and not even realize it. Starting a small homebased business that designs and sells seashell jewelry is not only an easy and inexpensive business to set in motion, it also could prove to be very fun and interesting. The business opportunity is to collect various sizes, shapes, and colors of seashells right from the beach and create beautiful seashell jewelry. Once completed the jewelry can be sold to local retailers on a wholesale basis or placed in retail stores on a consignment basis. A seashell jewelry manufacturing business is not only easy to start and run, but it could also generate an extra income of $10,000 per year or more.

CHRISTMAS DECORATIONS

Each year, billions of dollars are spent on Christmas decorations worldwide, and securing a portion of this very lucrative market is easy. This new business enterprise is very straightforward and can be initiated by anyone, as it does not require any special business experience or skills. Simply design, produce, and sell custom one-of-a-kind Christmas decorations. Go for the high end of the market where consumers are willing to pay $25 or more for one Christmas decoration that will become a family heirloom. The decorations can be made from almost any type of raw material, in almost any popular Christmas theme. The key to success is that the Christmas decorations must be unique and appealing. The decorations can be sold to specialty retailers on a wholesale basis or directly to consumers via renting a sales table at art and craft shows.

PLASTER CASTS

Now a few of you reading this may be wondering how you can start a profitable business that creates and sells plaster casts? Probably many more of you are wondering why someone would purchase a plaster cast? Amazingly enough there are businesses that

not only survive producing plaster casts, but also earn very substantial profits for doing so. Annually millions of plaster casts depicting people, animals, and objects are sold as home decorations. The materials needed to make plaster casts are inexpensive and readily available at most crafts supply stores. Many of these same stores also carry information, books, and videos about how to make plaster casts and, in some cases, even conduct classes on the subject. The potential to earn an income or generate a profit from this very unique business enterprise will obviously vary based on a number of factors. However, providing you can tap into the right marketing and distribution mix, there will be no reason why you cannot only create an income but also a profit, as others have already proven that this can be accomplished.

FLOWER ARRANGEMENTS

Millions of flowers are purchased each year for every kind of occasion imaginable, and all of these occasions have one thing in common, the flowers have to be arranged once they arrive at the event. The opportunity for making money by creating and selling flowers arrangements are endless—everything from creating small bouquets to large center pieces, to establishing joint ventures with interior decorators and event planners. Or you can even simply supply real estate agents with thank-you flower bouquets delivered to their clients who have recently purchased a home. Gaining new clients for the business can be as easy as preparing samples of your work and hand delivering them to potential clients with a full marketing presentation outlining the value and benefits of your service. This is a great part-time homebased business opportunity to set in motion, and the spin off opportunities to earn a substantial yearly income are almost unlimited.

WEB RESOURCE: email~aifd@assnhqtrs.com American Institute of Floral Designers.

CUSTOM BUTTONS
★★★ $$

Are you searching for a unique and inexpensive homebased business opportunity that has little competition and a real chance of succeeding? If so, consider starting a business that specializes in manufacturing and selling custom one-of-a-kind buttons for clothing. The buttons can be manufactured from just about every type of raw material including wood, metal, seashells, and glass. The key to success in button manufacturing is two-fold. First is that the buttons must be unique in design and appearance, and the second key to success lies within marketing the buttons. Consider the following:

- Establish accounts with specialty retailers to purchase the buttons on a wholesale basis.
- Sell the buttons to manufacturers and designers of custom clothing.
- Sell the custom clothing buttons directly to consumers via the Internet.

POTPOURRI SALES
★★ $

Starting a business that makes and wholesales potpourri products is an excellent homebased business venture to set in motion. The potpourri can be made from dried flowers, pine cones, and bark mulch with fragrant essential oils added. Once packaged, the potpourri can be sold on a wholesale basis to specialty retailers or directly to consumers via a sales kiosk or craft show. One important aspect of the business not to overlook is packaging. The packaging for the potpourri should be unique to your business, as a method to separate your product from the competition. Additionally, be sure to use recycled materials for the packaging of the products, as this will not only help the environment, but it can also be used as a fantastic marketing tool.

IRON SCULPTURES

Calling all talented artists with welding skills and a home workshop. It's time to start profiting from your talents by starting a business that produces iron art sculptures. The raw materials required for the sculptures can be purchased from metal recycling facilities for low or no cost. Once completed, the sculptures can be marketed directly to art-loving consumers and art collectors by setting up a sales kiosk on weekends at malls and other community gathering places. Additionally, the iron sculptures can be featured and sold via the Internet and through local art galleries. Furthermore, be sure to craft iron sculptures that have functional value such as weather vanes, coat racks, and partitions.

LAMP SHADES

Are you searching to start a part-time business that has virtually no competition? If the answer is yes, then consider starting a business that manufactures and markets custom-made lampshades. The key to success in this very unusual manufacturing business is to ensure you create really unique lampshades, not only in appearance and design but also in your choice of raw material used in the construction. Get marketing the lampshades by contacting local interior decorators and setting appointments with them to introduce them to your unique product. Additionally, aim to sell the lampshades to retailers on a wholesale basis or place the lampshades into retail stores on a consignment basis.

DESIGNER PILLOWS

Turn your sewing machine and skills into a part-time profit center by creating custom designed pillows. The pillows can be completed on a made-to-order basis, or you can develop standard designs and themes and sell the pillows on a wholesale basis. Be sure to establish alliances with interior decorators, as these decorators could become your best customers for custom designed pillows. Additional income can also be earned by designing and manufacturing custom pillow and cushion slip covers with elaborate themes. Stick with standard sizes or custom made-to-order designs for this side of the business.

STAINED GLASS

Lampshades, sun-catchers, window inserts, and light panel stained glass products are extremely popular home decoration products. In almost every community across North America there are classes available that offer training about how to make stained glass items. Additionally, the materials and equipment needed to start this part-time business are very inexpensive. Completed stained glass creations can be sold by way of craft shows, home and garden shows, or by renting a sales kiosk in malls on weekends. The profit potential is outstanding as stained glass lampshades alone can retail for as much as $1,000.

WEB RESOURCE: www.anythinginstainedglass.com Wholesale source for supplies and equipment.

CORSAGES

Corsages are used as a fashion accessory for hundreds of special occasions, and one of the best aspects about starting a business that makes corsages is the fact that the business can be started for peanuts. A small amount of research and practice will be required for this endeavor to train yourself in the art of making corsages. This information can be obtained at local libraries, craft shops, or even by harnessing the power of the Internet for research purposes. Once completed corsages can be sold to local flower and gift shops on a wholesale basis. Additionally, be sure to build alliances with wedding and event planners in your community, as these special occasion planners can utilize your service themselves or refer their clients to your service.

NOTES

39

DESKTOP PUBLISHING
Businesses You Can Start

KEY

RATINGS	★
START-UP COST	$
HOMEBASED BUSINESS	
PART-TIME	
LEGAL ISSUES	
FRANCHISE OR LICENSE POTENTIAL	
ONLINE	

PHOTOGRAPH RESTORATION SERVICE

★ $$$ 🏠 🕐

Purchasing a good quality scanner, computer, and photograph restoration software will enable you to start a business providing photograph restoration services for clients right from a home-based location. Regardless of whether the photographs are black and white or color, you will be able to restore old and damaged photographs and produce new copies in print format, on a CD, or a floppy disk. The potential market for a photograph restoration service is gigantic in every community across North America, and once established, repeat customers and referrals will be all the marketing required to sustain the business and generate a very substantial income. However, it should be noted that you will need to spend time practicing the art of electronic photograph restoration, as the software is not designed for beginners.

Refer to your local community college to check on the availability of digital imaging training courses.

WEB RESOURCE: www.adobe.com Designers and distributors of specialty imaging software.

SPECIALITY GREETING CARDS

★★★ $$ 🏠 🕐

Millions of greeting cards are sold annually in the United States, and starting a business the designs and produces one-of-a-kind custom greeting cards for clients is a terrific desktop publishing business to set into action. In addition to a high quality color printer, you will also need a computer and design software. Ideally, marketing efforts should be focused on potential customers that would send a lot of greeting cards each year, as well as clients who would benefit the most from sending customized greeting cards. Potential customers would include corporations, associations, organizations, professionals, and individual consumers who would be prepared to purchase the specialty greeting cards in minimum orders of 50 at one time. Potential income range is $20 to $25 per hour.

WEB RESOURCE: www.greetingcard.org Greeting Card Association.

COMPANY NEWSLETTERS

Designing and printing newsletters for companies, salespeople, and stockbrokers is a fantastic low-investment business start-up that can generate a great income. Monthly newsletters are a terrific way for salespeople and business owners to stay in contact with clients, promote monthly specials, and help secure new business. Most business people realize that creating a monthly newsletter and distributing it to valued clients is a very inexpensive and powerful marketing tool for their business. However, very few companies and salespeople utilize newsletters, and those who do often struggle to get the newsletter out on time, if at all. Many business owners simply do not have the skills, equipment, or time to create an effective newsletter. These facts are the reason why starting a business designing, producing, and distributing newsletters for business clients is such a fabulous business enterprise to start. To succeed in this type of venture you will need the following:

- A creative ability, as well as the ability to operate a computer and specialized software.
- Strong marketing and presentation skills.
- A well-equipped home office.
- Clients.

The first three requirements are easy to acquire or learn. However, it is the fourth requirement that is the most important—without clients there is no business. To secure business, simply predesign newsletters featuring local companies, then set presentation meetings at these companies to explain the values and benefits of your newsletter service. This type of marketing and presentation system is extremely effective, as once business owners have seen the finished product it will be difficult for them

not to at least commit to a few months for a trial program.

WEB RESOURCE: www.newslettersonly.com Industry information, resources, and links.

ONLINE E-NEWSLETTERS

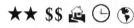

Like printed newsletters, many companies that produce a monthly e-newsletter have good initial intentions, but reality soon sets in and time factors take a toll in terms of getting the e-newsletter to customers on time. Once again, this fact creates a fantastic opportunity to capitalize on by starting your own homebased business specializing in creating e-newsletters. The hard part will be signing on new clients and developing a standard format for their first e-newsletter, but after that it is all straightforward. Maintaining a client's newsletter should require no more than about six to ten hours of work per month. Aim to secure 15 regular customers paying a mere $200 each per month for the service and you can generate an income in excess of $35,000 per year. Also be sure not to limit your potential market and include print newsletter services as well as electronic. The two combined have the ability to earn you six-figures annually.

COUPON BOOKS

Community coupon books are hot, and starting a business that designs and produces coupon books is a sensational new business endeavor to set in motion. The concept is very straightforward. Simply secure 50 to 100 businesses throughout the community that would like to be featured in the coupon book free of charge. Of course, the catch is they must be prepared to provide consumers with a discount on their products or service, either in the form of a percentage discount or a fixed amount of discount on a particular product or service. Revenues for the business are gained by selling the coupon books to consumers within the community, the larger the advertised savings the better. Suppose the discounts offered in the coupon book add up to a total of $5,000. You would want to advertise that fact by promoting a coupon book that costs $10, but will save the purchaser $5,000 on products and services they purchase on a regular basis within their own community.

WEB RESOURCE: www.couponpros.org Association of Coupon Professionals.

ONLINE COMMUNITY COUPONS
★★★ $$$ 🏠 🕒 🌐 ✋

Watch out, Web sites featuring discount coupons are becoming the hottest trend for bricks and mortar retailers to combat Internet cyberretailing. Develop a community coupon Web site; simply charge local merchants in the community to post discount coupons and specials on the site. Residents in the local area would simply log onto the site and print coupons that are of interest to them. In terms of making money, I would suggest that you charge participating merchants a monthly fee. This fee could include designing and posting a coupon page within the site as well as a fixed number of coupon changes each month. Of course, for those of you with ASP programming skills or deep pockets, participating merchants could be issued a password enabling them to update their own coupon page. This method would be more costly to create initially but less costly and work intensive to maintain over time. If this option is chosen and a few page tools were included for users, the site could be easily duplicated and operated in every major city across North America on a franchise basis.

HOLIDAY DRINK GUIDES
★★★ $$$ 🏠 🕒 🌐

Holiday drink books are simply small guides that are published twice per year in the winter and summer and feature recipes for alcoholic and nonalcoholic drinks. The holiday drink books are distributed throughout the community free of charge and are supported by selling display-advertising space in the guides to local companies wishing to advertise their products and services. Starting this type of desktop publishing

business is very easy, as the business can be operated from home and requires little in the way of start-up investment or special skills. Furthermore, to gain additional year round income, consider expanding the business to include publishing and distributing community coupon books as well as a free classified advertising community paper. Both of these opportunities are also featured in this chapter of the directory.

PACKAGE DESIGN SERVICE
★★ $$ 🏠 🕒

Most manufacturers realize that products packaging can be just as important as the product itself in terms of sales and the overall success. This is why many manufacturers enlist the services of a professional when it comes time to design or redesign of packaging for their products. This is a terrific opportunity for enterprising entrepreneurs to capitalize by starting a packaging design service. Once again, potential clients can include just about any manufacturer that is introducing a new product to the market place or any manufacturer that is seeking to redesign existing packaging of a product. As a method to get started, consider redesigning packaging for a product that is produced locally in your area and that you feel could use a makeover in terms of the packaging appeal. Once completed, present your concepts and ideas to the manufacturer of the product along with a presentation of the possible benefits that can be gained by altering or changing the packaging entirely. You may be pleasantly surprised by the outcome of the meeting. Don't forget to ask for the business.

WEB RESOURCE: www.flexpack.org Flexible Packaging Association.

LOGO DESIGN SERVICE
★★ $$ 🏠 🕒

Company or product recognition is a very important aspect of the overall marketing of a company or product. Logos build consumer recognition and brand name image in terms of identifying a particular logo with a business, product, or service. To reinforce this statement look no further than the Nike swoosh, or the golden arches of McDonald's. This fact formulates an outstanding opportunity for the enterprising entrepreneur to capitalize by launching a logo design service. A logo design service can be operated on a full- or part-time basis right from home, and the only requirements needed to succeed will be a creative artistic ability and a computer. Marketing this type of service can be as easy as designing sample logos of fictional companies and distributing the logo designs along with a presentation describing your service to advertising agencies, marketing companies, and at business networking meetings. The service will require time in terms of establishing a client base. However, once established, a logo design service can easily generate an income in excess of $50,000 per year for the owner.

ONLINE E-LOGO DESIGN

Designing corporate and product logos for free has the potential to earn you $25,000 or more each year with only a part-time effort. How? you may be wondering. Simply start surfing the Web for corporate or product logos that could be improved upon or for companies and products that do not have an eye-catching logo. Next, using your design skills and basic computer hardware and software, design new logos for this same corporation. When the logo is complete, simply send it to the company via e-mail with a letter or presentation package describing your service and the fact that if they should choose to use the logo or would like to purchase it, the cost would be ___. Yes in some cases you will be working for free. However, providing the logo you have designed is eye catching and represents the business or product well, in most cases you will get paid for your work. A gamble? Yes, but considering the business can be started for very little and will cost next to nothing to operate, you only have a little bit of time on the line.

INVITATIONS

Are you searching for a desktop publishing business opportunity that can be operated from home

and started with a minimal investment? If so, consider starting a business that designs and produces custom made-to-order invitations. Not only can this business be started for literally peanuts, but there is also gigantic consumer demand for custom-designed invitations. Marketing the business can be as easy as contacting event and wedding planners in your community and presenting them with samples of your work. Additionally, providing your handwriting is excellent, you can also combine calligraphy with custom computer-aided graphics and images to produce truly one-of-a-kind invitations.

BUSINESS PRESENTATIONS
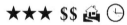

A business presentation or proposal is not only judged on the information contained within, but also on the format, appearance, and the overall flow of the presentation. Due to this fact, many business owners realize the importance of having a business presentation or proposal professionally created as opposed to creating it themselves. Starting a desktop publishing service that specializes in creating and producing business presentations and proposals is a fantastic new venture to get rolling. Marketing this type of business can be as simple as designing sample presentations and distributing the presentations at business functions and networking meetings. The business can easily be operated from a homebased location on a full- or part-time basis, and the only skills needed to make the business successful are computer skills and a determination to excel.

HOME SAFETY GUIDES FOR THE ELDERLY
★★★ $$ 🏠 🕐 🌍

Here is an outstanding desktop publishing venture to start in your community. Every year in the United States thousands of the elderly fall victim to crime or suffer injuries right in their own homes. Starting a desktop publishing business that focuses on creating and distributing monthly home safety guides for the elderly is not only a great way to operate your own business, but it is also a fantastic way of providing a valuable and much needed community information service. The home safety guides can feature tips on how to make a home less of a target for crime, as well as how to prevent needless accidents around the home and what to do in case of an emergency. The safety guides can be distributed free of charge throughout the community and supported by display advertisement sales. Additionally, be sure to build an alliance with local police and fire protection agencies, as this can be a way to gain credibility for the business, as well as useful information and tips for the safety guides.

CATALOGS
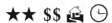 ★★ $$

Millions of catalogs are designed and produced each year in the United States, and securing just a small portion of this very lucrative market can make you rich. The key to success in this industry is not to have all the skills required to produce the catalogs yourself, but to have excellent marketing skills and a good contact base of professionals who can assist in the creation and production of the catalogs from start to finish. In terms of marketing the service, you first must produce sample catalogs to act as a marketing tools. The next step would be to simply show potential customers the sample catalogs whenever and wherever possible. Additionally, aim to join local business associations in your community, as the members of these associations can be a great source of business for your service or as a referral source to lead you to potential business.

MARKETING BROCHURES
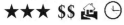 ★★★ $$

Like business presentations, marketing brochures are more than a few words on a page accompanied by a glossy picture, and the importance of effective marketing brochures cannot be over stated in terms of attracting new business for many companies. This fact creates a terrific opportunity for an entrepreneur with a sales and marketing background to capitalize by starting a desktop publishing business that creates and produces highly effective marketing brochures for clients. Once again, this business can be operated

from home on a part-time basis and expanded to full-time as the business grows. Potential clients can include just about any business that relies on marketing brochures to generate all or some interest in their business, products, and services. Potential income range is $25+ per hour.

WEB RESOURCE: www.click-here-now.com/software/mailinglists/brochuresdesign.htm Distributor of brochure design software.

EVENT PROGRAMS
 ★ $$

Seminars, auctions, plays, trade shows, and business conventions generally have one thing in common. They require event programs to be distributed to the people in attendance to let them know what's going on, what's for sale, and what's coming up next. Starting a desktop publishing business that designs and produces event programs is a very easy new business enterprise to launch. A computer and a good printer is about all of the equipment that you will need to get started creating event programs initially, until the business is established, at which point you may want to consider the addition of a scanner, binding machine, and high speed photocopier. Furthermore, specializing in short production runs will give you an advantage on competition, as the larger and more established printing firms typically require larger runs to justify setup time and operating overheads.

BARTER-AND-SWAP PUBLICATION
★★ $$

Barter-and-swap publications have become very popular in the past decade, as people seek more creative ways to get rid of items they do not want or need, and trade it for useful items they would like to have. Herein lies an outstanding opportunity to start a community barter-and-swap publication. The publication can be published on a bimonthly or monthly basis, and in addition to featuring thousands of barter and trade classified ads, the paper could also feature puzzles, games, and facts on local history or trivia. Revenue can be generated in three ways or a combination of any of these methods that include:

- Distribute the paper for free and charge for the barter or swap advertisement.
- Give the barter and swap advertisements away for free and charge for the paper.
- Do not charge for the paper or the ads, and sell display advertising space to local merchants.

ONLINE THANK-YOU CARDS AND E-MAILS

★ $$

The customer is king. Without customers, no business can stay in business. This obvious statement can be used as your greatest marketing tool if your intentions are to start a business that focuses on creating and sending customer appreciation thank-you cards and e-mails for your clients. The easiest way to earn a customer's business for life is to provide top-notch service and to let them know you appreciate the business. Unfortunately, time restrictions do not allow most business owners and professionals to properly thank their clients, even if the appreciation is in the form of a simple thank-you card sent by mail or a thank-you letter sent electronically. Providing this type of unique and personalized service for busy business owners and professionals will not only enable you to build your own business, but it will also assist your clients in retaining customers, building goodwill, and ultimately increase referrals and sales.

INSTRUCTION MANUALS

★★ $$

Worldwide millions of products are manufactured that require an instruction manual be included in the packaging of a product to describe assembly methods or how to use the product. This fact creates an outstanding opportunity to start a desktop publishing business that designs and produces instruction manuals. On the surface this business opportunity may seem somewhat limited in terms of potential clients and profitability. However, consider the following: securing just ten manufacturing clients that produce a total of 100,000 products annually can potentially generate a gross profit of $250,000 per year for your business, simply by maintaining a mere 25-cent

markup on each instruction manual that is sold to the manufacturers and included with their products. I bet that you now see the potential of this business in an entirely different light.

RESTAURANT MENUS

★★ $$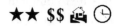

Starting a desktop publishing business that specializes in designing and producing restaurant menus is a fantastic new enterprise to set in motion. Restaurants can be ideal clients to work with, due to the fact that menus regularly change and generally only a short production run of the menus are needed, thus excluding many larger commercial printers. Furthermore, this type of desktop publishing business is also ideally operated on a part-time basis, and it would only require a handful of regular clients to produce a substantial part-time income. In addition to a computer, you will also need a color printer that can produce larger menu pages up to 11-inches by 17-inches. Additional revenues can also be earned by creating and producing restaurant paper placemats and menu inserts describing daily specials.

BUSINESS DIRECTORIES

★★ $$$$

Manufacturers, charity organizations, business organizations, wholesalers, printers, publishers, home-based businesses, tour operators, and engineering professionals are only a few examples of the numerous business directories that can be created by a desktop publishing business that specializes in developing business directories. Generally, revenues are earned in two ways in this type of business. The first is to charge companies, organizations, and individuals a fee to be listed and featured in the directory, and the second way to earn revenues is to sell the directories to companies, organizations, and individuals who are seeking these types of business directories for information, marketing, and resource purposes. The profit potential is good, and a business directories publishing business can be operated from home.

WEB RESOURCE: www.idpa.org National Directory Publishing Association.

ONLINE BUSINESS DIRECTORIES
★ $$$ 🏠 🕐 ✍

Like the printed counterparts, online business directories come in many forms and are very popular. This is a very competitive segment of the online advertising industry. However, with more than 1,000 businesses going online every day, the demand for this type of advertising service continues to grow. In a nutshell, an online business directory is simply a listing service for merchants and service providers in similar industries, such as tour operators and retailers to name a few. In exchange for being listed in the directory, clients pay a monthly or annual fee. The fee will vary as to how much traffic is generated on the site. In some cases the fee is based on how many hits or views the client's listing or hyperlink receives.

WEB RESOURCE: www.entrepreneur.com Create a business Web site with MySite professional Web site builder.

ONLINE CONTRACT FORMS
★ $$$$ 🏠 🕐 ⚖ ✍

Here is a very simple desktop publishing business to put into action. Template or fill-in-the-blank contract forms in print format and on floppy disk are very popular and can serve a wide variety of uses from a residential lease contract to acceptance of purchase contract for a home owner selling a home privately. The template contract forms can be sold to specialty office product retailers on a wholesale basis or directly to the public by creating a Web site that enables visitors to download contract templates for a fee. It will take time and careful research to develop the contract forms, but with that said the saleable life span for the product can be as long as five years or more.

BUILDING HISTORY GUIDES
★★ $$ 🏠 🕐 🌍

Are you seeking to start a very interesting and potentially profitable desktop publishing business that can be operated from home on a part-time basis? If so, perhaps you should consider starting a business that specializes in writing guides about local historical buildings in your community, as well as features display advertisements promoting community businesses. The building history guides can be published each month and distributed free of charge throughout the community. Revenues to support the business would be earned by selling advertising space in the guides to local merchants wishing to promote their products and services. Furthermore, local residents can supply most of the historical information and pictures featured in the guide, thus greatly reducing the amount of time it will take to create the monthly publication.

WEB RESOURCE: www.oah.org Organization of American Historians.

BUSINESS FORM TEMPLATES
★★ $$ 🏠 🕐

Business form templates are simply blank business documents and forms in print format or on CD-ROM or floppy disk that have been specifically designed to be used in a particular business industry, such as automotive sales, manufacturing, or home renovation. The purpose of the business forms and documents are to make it easier for business owners to establish operating and recordkeeping systems for their businesses. The business forms and documents can include items, such as monthly expense reports, estimate forms, work orders, purchase orders, sales receipts, bookkeeping forms, packing slips, and sales reports, just to mention a few. Business form templates can be packaged and sold to specialty retailers on a wholesale basis, or directly to consumers via the Web.

RÉSUMÉ SERVICE
★★ $$ 🏠 🕐

In spite of the fact that more than 50 percent of American and Canadian households have a computer system, starting a résumé service is still a fantastic new business to set in motion, as many people still require a professional touch in terms of the structure and format of their résumé. Once established, repeat business and word-of-mouth referrals will keep the service hopping. However, to initially market the service there are a few methods that can be employed, such as posting information fliers describing the résumé service on community and company bulletin boards, taking out a small print classified ad in a community paper, and networking with people at career expos.

FREE CLASSIFIED AD PUBLICATION
★★ $$$ 🏠 🕐 🌐

Are you seeking to start a homebased desktop publishing business that has the potential to earn you a six-figure income? If so, perhaps you should consider starting a free classified advertisement publication in your community. Not only can the business be started and operated from a homebased office, but the business also has the potential to generate excellent profits and could be potentially expanded across North America on a franchise or licensed-to-operate basis once established and proven successful. The business concept is very basic. People from within the community that are selling cars, furniture, houses, or just about anything could advertise their items for sale free in the paper. Furthermore, the paper would be distributed free of charge throughout the community and published on a monthly or bimonthly basis. Selling larger display advertising space in the paper to local merchants and service providers wishing to advertise their products and services would generate revenues for the business.

FOR SALE BY OWNER KITS
★★★ $$ 🏠 🕐

Millions of cars, boats, homes, and businesses are sold each year in the United States privately by the owners of these items, and this fact creates an outstanding opportunity for the innovative entrepreneur to capitalize by starting a desktop publishing business that specializes in creating for sale by owner marketing kits. For sale-by-owner marketing kits should be created specifically for the pur-

poses of marketing one particular item, such as a car. Furthermore, the kits should also include a guide on how to maximize profits from the sale, sales and marketing tips for that particular product, and offer to purchase and contract forms for purchase in template form. The kits can be in print format or electronic on CD-ROMs or floppy disks, and can be sold to retailers on a wholesale basis or directly to consumers via mail order and the Internet. Once established, the profit potential for this type of unique desktop publishing business is outstanding, as the market for the product is unlimited.

CORRESPONDENCE AND TRAINING MANUALS
★★ $$ 🏠 🕐

Every year in North America, millions of people take part in correspondence and training courses at home, and starting a desktop publishing business that designs and produces correspondence and training manuals is an outstanding new business venture to set in motion. Clients for the business can include all levels of schools, companies with employees that work from home, government agencies, and just about any other business or organization that requires manuals to be produced on a yearly basis. This is the type of desktop publishing business that will take time and patience to establish. However, once the business is established, many clients will potentially become yearly repeat clients, and a special focus to detail and service should be placed on ensuring that clients do indeed become repeat clients.

PUZZLE AND GAME BOOKS
★★ $$ 🏠 🕐

Here is a great homebased desktop publishing business to activate in any community. Trivia, crossword puzzles, and word search games are hot, and starting a business that creates puzzles and game books combined with coupons featuring discounts on products and services provided by local merchants has the potential to make you rich. The booklets could be sold locally through participating retailers that have advertisements and discount coupons featured in the book. Additionally, as a method to drive sales and interest in the game book-lets, consider establishing an alliance with a local charity, wherein a portion of the revenues generated by book sales goes back to support community char-ity programs.

WEB RESOURCE: http://thinks.com/software/cross-words.htm Distributor of software used to create crossword puzzles and games.

EMPLOYMENT AND CAREER PUBLICATIONS
★★ $$$

Starting a desktop publishing business that spe-cializes in producing a monthly employment and career guide newspaper is a fantastic new business venture to set in motion. The business can be oper-ated from a homebased location and even has the potential to be expanded nationally on a franchise or license-to-operate basis once established. The paper can be distributed throughout the communi-ty free of charge and supported by charging com-panies advertising fees to list their employment and career opportunities in the paper. Additionally, the paper should also include useful information and tips for readers on subjects and topics pertaining to securing gainful employment. The tips could include information, such as how to prepare for a job interview, ten secrets to a winning résumé, and more.

SMALL BUSINESS GUIDES
★★ $$$

Small businesses drive the economies in both the United States and Canada. In fact, small business is responsible for 80 percent of all new and existing employment in both countries. Starting a desktop publishing business in your community that special-izes in creating a monthly small business guide is a terrific new business venture to set in motion. The small business guides can be distributed free of charge to small and homebased business owners

throughout the community and supported by selling advertising space to local companies wishing to advertise their products and services in the guide. Furthermore, the information and articles featured in the monthly guide can include tips for improving the performance of a business, legal issues pertaining to business, and other information small business own-ers would find useful.

COMMERCIAL REAL ESTATE GUIDE
★ $$$$

Creating a monthly publication that features com-mercial real estate for sale or lease is a terrific home-based desktop publishing business to put into action. In addition to commercial real estate listings, the paper can also include business and franchise oppor-tunity advertisements. Advertising clients can include commercial real estate agents and brokers, property development companies, and franchise and business opportunity companies. Securing revenue for the monthly paper can be accomplished two ways. The first is to charge consumers to purchase the paper through retail distribution channels, by print, or electronic subscription. Selling the commercial real estate advertising space to agents and brokers will create the second method of revenue.

ONLINE IMPORT/EXPORT DIRECTORY
★★ $$$

Publishing a biannual import/export opportuni-ties directory in printed and electronic format has the potential to make you rich, as millions of bud-ding entrepreneurs worldwide are constantly on the lookout for income and business opportunities. Simply create an import/export directory that fea-tures information about worldwide manufacturers, wholesalers, and agents that are seeking to expand their product lines into foreign countries and new markets, or individuals or companies that are seek-ing to import particular products into their regions. Charging a fee to be listed in the directory, as well as selling the directories to people who are seeking this type of valuable and potentially profitable information and contact sources would earn revenue for the business.

BUSINESS PLAN SERVICE
★★★ $$ 🏠 🕐

Did you know that a recent survey of new business owners revealed that less than 25 percent of the 250 owners surveyed had created a business plan for their new venture? When asked why they had not created a business plan for their new venture, the number one reason given by the business owners was simply that they did not know how to create a business plan. Approximately 700,000 new businesses are started each year in the United States, and this fact creates an outstanding opportunity for the ingenious and determined entrepreneur to capitalize by starting a business that creates business plans for owners of new ventures. Marketing this type of specialized service will take some clever planning, in terms of promoting the service and getting the word out. However, consider the following marketing methods:

- Join local business associations and attend networking meetings to promote your service.
- Attempt to obtain a list of all new applicants for business licenses through your local business service center.
- Build alliances with business training schools to market your services to the students.

CAMPUS NEWSPAPER
★★ $$$ 🏠

The fact that most universities and colleges already have campus newspapers does not mean that they are good papers, or that there isn't room for another campus newspaper. Starting an unofficial campus newspaper is the focus of this business opportunity. Creating and producing a campus newspaper is very straightforward. The paper can be published on a weekly or bimonthly basis and distributed free of charge throughout the campus and community. Selling classified and display advertising space to local businesses wishing to gain exposure to the

paper readership base would support the paper. Information and articles featured in the newspaper can focus on campus issues and events, and most of the information can be obtained for free from students, readers, and freelance hobby writers.

ONLINE CAMPUS WEB SITE
★★ $$$$ 🏠 ✍

Once again, most universities and colleges have official Web sites, but that certainly does not mean there isn't room for another. To be better than a competitor in cyberspace means a few things, such as providing visitors with more useful information and services, promoting the site in unique ways to generate interest and traffic, and maintaining the site regularly to ensure repeat visits. The starting point is research. Go online and see what the local university or college site is lacking or what could be improved on. Are there services such as student housing listings, classified advertising space, free e-mail, up-to-date news and articles about life on campus? Conduct surveys to see exactly what features and information students want on a Web site. Basically, go to the source and ask. Of course, the better the site and the more visitors you get the more you will be able to charge local merchants and service providers for advertising.

DIGITAL PRINTING SERVICE
★★★ $$+ 🏠 🕐

The printing industry has been revolutionized with the advent of digital technology. No longer are business owners and consumers at the mercy of print shops to create their short run marketing brochures, event programs, and invitations as these types of printed items can now all be printed in full-color digital format in quantities of one or more without the expensive print plate making charge. A digital printing service can easily be operated from home and the main requirements to get this business rolling will be a good desktop computer, design software, a high quality digital printer capable of 11-inch by 17-inch printing, and of course the ability to use this equipment efficiently. Once again, you will want to concentrate your marketing efforts on customers that are seeking short run printing services. Potential customers will include business owners, consumers, schools, government institutions, clubs, and associations. The equipment will let you print professional full-color items such as newsletters, invitations, business cards, marketing brochures, event programs, restaurant menus, booklets, and guides. Advertise and promote your digital printing service by joining local business associations to network for clients. Short run digital printing is becoming extremely popular with business owners that routinely change prices, promotions, and products. Once the word is out about your service, the business will easily be supported by referrals and repeat business.

WEB RESOURCE: www.printussa.com Directory listing new and used digital printing equipment, dealers, and supplies.

TV LISTINGS MAGAZINE

Profit from the fast-paced entertainment industry by starting your own weekly TV listings magazine. The magazine can be distributed free of charge throughout the community and supported by selling display advertising space to local merchants and service providers. In addition to weekly TV program listings, the magazine can also feature crossword puzzles, celebrity profiles, and a list of upcoming community events and activities. To keep distribution costs to a minimum, establish outlets for the magazine, such as convenience stores, restaurants, and grocery stores where residents can pick up the publication while shopping or dinning. You can obtain TV programming schedules and reprint rights from media providers such as Tribune Media Services. This business opportunity is perfect for the entrepreneur with a publishing or sales background, and the business can easily be operated from a home-based location. Contracting out the printing and distribution of the magazine will enable you to start this business on an initial investment of less than $10,000, and once established, the business could

even be franchised and expanded into new geographic regions of the country.

WEB RESOURCE: www.tms.tribune.com Tribune Media Services, providers of print and electronic content media, including TV program listings, crosswords, and editorials.

NOTES

KEY

RATINGS	★
START-UP COST	$
HOMEBASED BUSINESS	
PART-TIME	
LEGAL ISSUES	
FRANCHISE OR LICENSE POTENTIAL	
ONLINE	

43 ENTERTAINMENT
Businesses You Can Start

DUNK TANK RENTALS

★★★ $$$$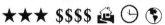

This certainly is not the type of business that jumps to mind when you start the process of thinking about the various types of business opportunities you can start and operate. However, for anyone who is seeking something a little bit out of the ordinary in terms of a new business venture, a dunk tank rental business does have a lot of benefits to be considered including limited competition, low start-up investment, ability to be managed from a homebased office, flexible business hours, good growth and franchise potential, no inventory, minimal overheads, and great profit potential. There are two main objectives to be accomplished in order for a dunk tank rental business to be successful. The first objective is to rent the dunk tank, and the second objective is to make sure no one is ever injured as a result of renting the dunk tank. Providing these two objectives can be achieved, the business will be considered a suc-

cess. The first business objective is that dunk tanks do have a limited target market in terms of rental; so the business owner must apply innovation and creativity to secure the existing limited market, create a larger market, or both. Securing the existing market can only be achieved in one way, you must not be afraid to approach people and promote your business. Potential customers will include sports associations, charities, business associations, schools, fundraising consultants, special event planners, caterers, kid's party planners, and community organizations. Generally the purpose for a group, club, organization, school, or charity to rent the dunk tank is to raise money for an event or program by charging people in attendance a fee to attempt to dunk the unfortunate soul who has been chosen to take the wet seat. With that being the case, what better way than a dunk tank to raise the money. Once again the second and equally important business objective is to ensure that the dunk tank is safe for all participants, and this can be accomplished with careful planning, research, design, construction practices, and material choice. Designing a dunk tank should be left to a professional engineer, as a typical dunk tank contains over 3,000 pounds of water once filled. Furthermore the dunk tank should also be professionally built. There are a few manufacturers of dunk tanks, and research into your local area will probably uncover a company with suitable credentials to undertake the project.

The final considerations for starting a dunk tank rental business are as follows:

- Suitable indoor or protected outdoor storage area for the dunk tank when not in use.
- Transportation capable of towing the trailer-mounted dunk tank to rental locations.
- Liability insurance for the business.

PROFIT POTENTIAL: As mentioned above, the competition for a dunk tank rental business is virtually non-existent, and because of this, it took quite a few calls before I could track down rental information. The following is the result of that call.

Delivery and pickup charge	$75 within 1-hour radius, $125 outside delivery area
One day dunk tank rental charge	$350
Each additional day	$125

WEB RESOURCE: www.twisterdisplay.com Manufacturers of dunk tanks and equipment.

EXTRAS-ONLY AGENT
★★ $$$$ 🏠

The film and TV production industry is booming, and starting an extras-only casting agency can potentially secure you a portion of this multibillion-dollar industry. Extras casting is simply supplying people to act as background performers in a film production. Typically extras or background performers represent every walk of life in terms of race, age, gender, size, and appearance. The key to successfully competing in this very competitive industry is without question to build and maintain a good

contact base and working relationship with film producers, directors, and other casting agencies. These are the people and companies that will call upon your service to supply extras for film work. In terms of revenue generation for the business, an extras agent retains 10 percent of a background performer's wage in the form of a commission, so it is important to work in volume, as extras are generally only paid $10 per hour.

ONLINE ACTORS DIRECTORY
★★★ $$$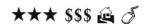

In North America thousands of actors and models are hoping to be "found" and posting your own actors directory Web site might just make you a financial star. You can charge actors and models a small yearly fee to post their headshot and portfolio pictures on the site. Directors, casting agents, and producers who log onto the site would only be a click away from finding the perfect person for the role they are trying to cast. The site will have to be indexed for search purposes by age, gender, race, experience, etc. The key to success for this type of online venture will be to attract people that do the hiring in the film and modeling industry to use the site. This can be accomplished by initiating a direct mail and e-mail campaign explaining the site and the benefits of using it. Once established, you could even branch out and include film crew listings, film prop rentals, and production site information.

USED CD MUSIC SHOP
★ $$$

Do you want to open a business in the fast-paced music industry that really has the potential to earn big profits? If so, perhaps you should consider starting a retail sales business that buys and sells secondhand musical compact discs. The business can be established in a storefront location or alternately in a sales kiosk located within a busy mall or public market. To initially establish an inventory of compact music discs for the business, place classified advertisements in the local community newspaper offering to purchase whole or partial compact disc collections. Currently, secondhand music CDs are retailing for $5 to $12 each, and as rule of thumb, owners of secondhand compact disc shops mark up all products by 100 percent for retailing purposes.

JINGLE WRITER

★ $

Do you have a musical talent for creating catchy little tunes and rhymes? If so, the time has never been better than now to start a jingle writing service, as advertising in all mediums are booming thanks entirely to the dot.com sensation. Potential clients for a jingle writing service can include radio producers, advertising agencies, and business owners. The key to success in this unique business is to go out and ask for business. Select local companies in your community that now have a radio presence, but not a catchy jingle for their advertisements. Next, simply create a jingle and set an appointment with the owner of the business to present the jingle, along with the reasons why a catchy jingle will benefit their advertising, and ultimately their business.

ENTERTAINMENT HOTLINE SERVICE

★ $$

Just about any determined entrepreneur who is willing to work hard and practice good business skills can tackle starting and operating an entertainment hotline service in your community. Simply start an entertainment hotline service that features various events taking place in the community on the specific day and week. Callers to the free entertainment hotline would be able to choose from an index of categories that could include movie listings, community events, restaurants, concerts, and plays. Additionally, if any of the businesses featured on the hotline service wanted to offer discounts or special pricing for events on the service, they would be encouraged to do so. Revenues for the business would be earned by charging the companies featured on the entertainment hotline service a monthly fee for membership to the service. Providing 100 to 150 companies could be secured and featured on the

entertainment hotline, the business could prove to be very profitable.

STREET ENTERTAINER

★★★ $$$$

Do you possess a special entertainment talent such as miming, juggling, or walking on stilts? If so, perhaps you should consider applying that talent to becoming a professional street entertainer or busker, as many buskers routinely earn more than $1,000 per week and, best of all, the earnings come in the form of cash. Becoming a street performer is very easy. However, there are two potential drawbacks to operating this unique entertainment service as a business. The first drawback is that many buskers routinely travel to where the tourists are depending on the season. While this may not be a drawback for all people considering this career, it will be for anyone with a family. The second potential problem is that many communities in the United States and Canada are starting to regulate street performers by issuing licenses or permits to conduct the performances, and generally the permits are awarded on a lottery basis, so research is vital.

MYSTERY DINNER PARTIES

★★★ $$

Organizing and hosting mystery dinner parties is not only a sensational business venture to initiate, but it could also prove to be a lot of fun. "Who done it" or murder mystery dinner parties have become an extremely popular entertainment service in the past few years, and there are many benefits to starting this unique and fun service including:

- The business can be managed from a home-based office and operated on a full- or part-time basis. Additionally, the initial start-up investment is less than $3,000.
- The demand for the service is excellent, and clients can include individuals wanting to host an interesting dinner party, corporations seeking a fun social function for their employees and customers, and event planners searching

for something out of the ordinary in terms of a unique entertainment experience for their clients.

The theme of the party can be created or you can use a popular mystery theme or story that people are familiar with. Currently, mystery dinner party services are charging rates in the range of $15 per person plus the cost of a catered dinner.

WEB RESOURCE: www.killerscripts.com License rights to murder mystery dinner scripts available.

ONLINE BAGPIPES
★★ $$$ 🏠 🕐 🖱

Writing this, I wondered how many people would be curious about what kind of business exactly is an online bagpipe service? For those of you wondering, an online bagpipe service is simply a listing or posting service for bagpipe musicians to utilize for the purpose of marketing their bagpipe playing services. In the past decade live bagpipe music has become extremely popular for entertaining guests at weddings, funerals, trade shows, and just about any other special event or occasion. Starting an online venture dedicated to helping people and event planners find an accomplished bagpiper in their area to play at special events is not only a unique business enterprise to start, but it could also prove to be profitable and fun. Revenues for the business can be earned by charging bagpipers a listing fee to have their service posted on the Web site, or you can act as a booking agent for the bagpipers and retain a commission on the performance fee. Additionally, be sure to always broadcast bagpipe music over the site. You would be amazed by how many people will leave on their computers just to hear it.

BAND REHEARSAL SPACE RENTALS
★ $$$ 🕐

Musical bands and performers have always had a difficult time securing space for rehearsing their acts and numbers, and starting a business that rents rehearsal space to musicians by the hour, day, week, or month is a fantastic new enterprise to get rolling. Ideally, the business will be established on leased premises in an industrial building so that noise will not be a concern or become a problem. Additionally, the spaced that is leased for the rehearsal space should also be subdivided into a few smaller rehearsal rooms to accommodate more than one customer at a time. Current rental rates for rehearsal rooms start at $10 per hour and can go much higher depending if any equipment and PA systems are supplied and included in the rent.

ONLINE STAR SEARCH
★★ $$$$ 🏠 🖱

Here is a novel online business opportunity for the cybersavvy entrepreneur to tackle. Develop a Web site that enables wanna-be movie stars, singers, and performers of all sorts a chance at fame. People with a particular talent could submit digital video footage of their performance and the footage could be placed into the Web site under the appropriate heading. Visitors to the site could select a category and view the performances. Now here is the twist—site visitors vote for which they think is the best performance in each category on a weekly or monthly basis. Each winner would receive a prize that is awarded by a business sponsor of the contest. This is a unique online venture and could prove to be very popular for performers and visitors alike. Thus an outstanding opportunity would be created for renting advertising space on the site to generate revenues.

RECORDING STUDIO
★★ $$$$

The investment required to start a sound recording studio is gigantic. However, the profits that the business can potentially generate are even larger. Starting a sound recording studio is much easier than it was at one time, simply because of the advancement in technology. Many recording studios that specialize in voiceovers for radio advertising, compact disc recordings, and videocassette recording are even homebased operations. Any one who does not have experience in the recording industry is well advised to stay clear of this particular business opportunity—unless the business is approached or established as a joint venture enterprise with a person or company that has experience in the industry, but lacks the financial backing or business experience to ensure the enterprise succeeds. A recording studio can potentially exceed $100,000 per year in profit after wages, expenses, and taxes.

WEB RESOURCE: www.1212.com Directory of products and services for the sound recording industry.

WEDDING SINGER

Unlike the movie, many wedding singers actually do possess a great musical and singing talent, and starting a wedding singer service may be just the new business opportunity that you have been searching for. There are a few options available in terms of starting a wedding singer service. The first option is of course, if you have the talent, then you can be the wedding singer and market your services. The second option available is to start a wedding singer directory service or agency. The second option will be more costly to initiate. However, it also has the possibility to generate higher sales and potential profits for the business, as you would be representing multiple wedding singers and retaining a portion of their performance fee as your commission. Profit potential range is $20,000+ per year.

ONLINE WEDDING SINGER DIRECTORY

You can take a wedding singer directory one step further and put it online. This cyberbusiness concept is very straightforward. Start by developing a Web site that is indexed by state and city for visitor search purposes. Next solicit wedding singers to post information about their service on the site. In exchange for a monthly listing fee singers featured on the site would receive a listing linked to a pop-up page that describes their service, rates, and contact information. Additionally, with specialized programming you could even include audio sound options for the singers as well as a complete menu of the songs they perform. Activating a direct mail and e-mail campaign aimed at

wedding and event planners as well as utilizing the usual Internet marketing could promote the site and advertising methods such as search engine registration and hyperlinks. Also incorporate additional wedding singer information and trivia into the site like top first songs, most requested wedding songs, etc. Incorporating this type of content into a Web site makes the site much more interesting to visitors.

RED CARPET SERVICE
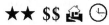

A red carpet service includes individual services such as valet parking, ushers, event planning, and professional emcees all wrapped up into one service for clients. The market for a red carpet service is huge in every city across North America, and clients can include event and wedding planners, business owners hosting special events, seminar and trade show companies, and even political and sports organizations for award ceremonies. Once established, this is the type of business that will be kept very busy by way of repeat clients and word-of-mouth referrals. As there are numerous variables, the profit potential for the business will fluctuate. However, even on a part-time basis the business is capable of $20,000+ per year.

CHARITY CASINO ORGANIZER

There are two options available for generating revenues and profits by starting and operating a charity casino business. The first option is to simply rent casino equipment to charities for their events. The second option is to completely organize the event, supply the equipment, and supply dealers and staff to operate the event, and finally supply the location for the charity casino event. The first option will be less costly in terms of establishing the business, but with that said, the amount of revenue the business is capable of generating will also be less than the second option. Additional aspects of the business to consider prior to establishing the business will be local government regulations in regards to operating the business and demand for the service from local charities.

WEB RESOURCE: www.gamblersgeneralstore.com Casino equipment and supplies distributor.

MUSIC FEST PROMOTER
★ $$$ 🏚 🕐 ⚖️

Music festivals are extremely popular entertainment events across North America, and becoming a music festival promoter is an outstanding opportunity for the entrepreneur that is seeking to start a part-time business. The business concept is basic and you can get started by first deciding what type of music festival or festivals you want to promote; country and western, jazz, rock, or folk. The choices are unlimited, as different music styles appeal to everybody. Consider the following six-step process to establishing the business.

1. Secure a suitable location for the music festival, such as a park, beach, outdoor arena, or farmland.
2. Apply for and secure all required permits from local government agencies.
3. Secure performers and vendors for the festival.
4. Build alliances with co-sponsors for the event, such as TV and radio stations.
5. Assemble a volunteer workforce to assist in operating the event. This can usually be accomplished by joining forces with a local charity that receives a portion of the admission sales.
6. Print and sell tickets.

There is a great amount of research and planning required to organize and host a music festival; however, once established the festival can be held annually and even expanded to additional communities.

SINGLES-ONLY DANCES
★★ $$ 🏚 🕐

How big is the potential market for a business that organizes and hosts singles-only dances? Very big, and to back up this statement, consider the following two facts:

1. People are waiting longer than any other previous generation before they get married.

2. The United States and Canadian divorce rate is at a staggering 40 percent.

Initiating a business that organizes and hosts singles-only dances is not only an easy business to get rolling, it is also a business that can be started from home and operated on a part-time basis. The fastest way to get the first dance organized is to form a joint venture with a nightclub or dance hall on the following basis: You supply the people for the dance event and keep the ticket revenues, while the owner of the dance hall or nightclub profits from the refreshment sales.

ALCOHOL-FREE CLUB
★★ $$$$ ⚖️

There are numerous benefits for starting a dance club or nightclub that does not serve alcoholic beverages, as opposed to a nightclub that does. The benefits include:

- Less investment capital required to start and operate the business.
- Fewer government regulations, and substantially lower liability insurance premiums.
- Less competition within the industry, and a clear definition of the target market.
- Increased choices in terms of operating location.

In addition to the aforementioned benefits, people are also starting to lead a healthier lifestyle that does not include consumption of alcoholic beverages, making this a very timely business get going.

MIDWAY RIDES AND GAMES
★ $$$$ 🕐 ⚖️

Starting a business that owns and operates midway rides or games is a very straightforward business to initiate. The carnival and fair circuits in North America operate on a seasonal basis, starting in May and ending in October. In spite of the numerous entertainment diversions that can keep a family busy, carnivals have fared well, though not as popular or numerous as they once were. A well-promoted carnival or exhibition still receives a good turn out. This type of business does require a lot of traveling and is certainly not a business opportunity meant for the masses. However, if traveling and the bright lights of a carnival appeal to you, a very good income can be earned in the industry, and some ride and game operators are earning as much as $100,000 in a six-month season.

WEB RESOURCE: www.carnivalbiz.com Directory services with links to the amusement and carnival industry.

VOICE OVERS
★ $

Perhaps your voice is your greatest asset, but you do not yet realize it. Do you sound like a silky smooth DJ and can you do multiple impersonations of celebrities and cartoon characters? If so, you may have a well-paying career ahead of you by starting and operating a voice over service. Clients for your vocal abilities can include film producers, advertising agencies, radio commercial producers, radio stations, publishers of audiobook tapes, and corporations for prerecorded telephone messages. Currently people who specialize in supplying their voice or voice over work for various projects are charging rates for the service in the range of $50 to $75 per hour. Joining a performers union is also recommended, as the rates paid to union performers is generally higher than nonunion performers—not to mention the fact that it is also easier to market your service and secure more work.

ONLINE STUDIO MUSICIANS
★★ $$$

Worldwide, there are thousands of full- and part-time studio musicians, and starting an online directory for studio musicians seeking work and for musical bands and music producers seeking studio musicians is a fantastic new business to start that enables you to take advantage of the power of the Internet. Revenues for the business could be gained by charging musicians a fee to post their information on the Web site, and producers seeking a certain type of studio musician for their projects would only be a click away from locating the perfect candidate. Selling

banner advertising on the Web site as well as also creating a directory or classified advertising section that features musical equipment and instruments for sale could also earn additional revenues.

WEB RESOURCE: www.entrepreneur.com Create a business Web site with MySite professional Web site builder.

BUSKERS SCHOOL
★★★ $$$

What could be more interesting and fun than starting and operating a school that trains students to become buskers or street entertainers? There probably is not a correct answer to that question, as it is a matter of personal preference. It could be a wonderful business for any determined entrepreneur that is seeking to start a unique business with great potential to be both fun and profitable. Fun aside, all new business opportunities still require careful planning and research regardless of the opportunity, and starting a buskers training school is not an exception to the rule. Potential students can include both people seeking busker training to become a professional street entertainer and people who are simply looking for a way to learn a fun hobby such as juggling. Furthermore, the teaching staff can include both retired and actively performing street entertainers who would be prepared to work on a revenue split basis. A buskers school is definitely a business opportunity that deserves further investigation and consideration.

OLD-TIME RADIO PROGRAMS
★ $$$$

History always has a way of repeating itself, and old-time radio programs from the 1930s and '40s are no exception to the rule, as these radio programs are once again becoming very popular. Seek to purchase the rights or pay for the rights to re-record old-time radio programs onto cassette tapes and compact discs. Once complete, the tapes and compact discs can be sold to retailers on a whole-sale basis, or directly to consumers via mail order, the Internet, or even infomercials. Providing you can secure the right radio programs to re-record and that demand is high for the programs, the profitability of the business could be outstanding as it only costs a couple of dollars each to mass produce tapes and CDs.

SHORT RUN CD-ROM PRODUCTION
★★★ $$$$ 🏠

Are you searching for a unique business opportunity in the fast-paced technology industry? If so, consider starting a business that produces compact discs for clients that are only seeking 100 copies or less, as the market demand for the service is gigantic and growing by the second. Anyone who has ever tried to locate a company that is willing to produce a short run for compact disks can certainly tell you it is very difficult, due to the fact that most companies specialize in large runs that produce thousands of CD copies a day. This fact creates a terrific opportunity for the creative and technologically experienced entrepreneur to capitalize by providing clients with a short-run compact disc production service. The start-up costs for the business are high, but with that said, most of the required computer equipment can be leased or rented. Once the business is established, the profit potential is outstanding.

SWING BANDS
★★ $$ 🏠 🕐

A recent article in a music entertainment magazine declared "Swing is King." That is probably a very accurate description as millions of people across North America are burning up the dance floor once again to swing music. Herein lies a tremendous opportunity for enterprising entrepreneurs to capitalize by starting a business that promotes swing bands and swing dance contests. Revenues and profits can be earned by retaining a percentage of the performance fees paid to the swing bands that you represent as well as possible royalties from cassette and compact disc sales. Additionally, revenues can also be gained by securing advertisers and sponsors for the swing dance contests. The business will take clever planning and marketing to

establish, but with that said, a successful business is not built on luck.

STUNT SCHOOL
★ $$$$ ⚖️

Like a buskers school, a stunt school is also a very interesting business opportunity to start. However, unlike a buskers school, the market for this type of specialized training is very limited and would only include students that are truly seeking to train for a career as a professional stunt person. Ideally, a stunt school should be formed as a joint venture with professionals within the stunt industry or with a production company within the film production industry. Gaining clients for a stunt school should not prove to be difficult, even though the potential market is limited, as the TV film and movie industry as a whole is presently riding a wave of popularity not seen since the heyday of Hollywood in the 1920s and '30s. Additional considerations in terms of establishing the business will include liability insurance, operating location, training staff, and course curriculum.

WEB RESOURCE: www.stuntscanada.net Stunts Canada Association of Professional Stunt Coordinators and Performers.

ONLINE ENTERTAINMENT COUPONS
★★★ $$$$ 🏠 🖱️

Here is a new business opportunity that combines the entertainment industry with the Internet. Consider starting an online entertainment coupon service. The business concept is very straightforward. Simply design a Web site that is indexed into various entertainment services and products such as musical concerts, plays, movies, etc. The next step is to secure companies and businesses within the entertainment industry to advertise discounts that apply to their specific products and services on the Web site. Visitors to the entertainment coupon Web site would be only a few clicks away from locating and printing a discount coupon for the entertainment event or product they were seeking. The business would gain revenue by charging the entertainment companies a monthly fee to advertise on the site and post their discount coupons.

DVD RENTALS
★★★ $$$$

Opening a store that rents DVDs (digital video discs) is a very exciting business opportunity that has potential for gigantic growth, as DVDs are relatively new to the market and consumer demand for DVD players and movies has manufacturers of these products scrambling to keep up with orders. Furthermore, a DVD rental store is also much less costly to open in terms of the movie rental inventory, as traditional VHS videos can cost as much as $100 for a new release. A new-release DVD only costs between $30 and $70 each. Additionally, as a method to further reduce initial start-up costs for the business, consider establishing the business in an existing retail store such as a large food market. This type of location for the business can have many benefits, including sharing monthly overhead costs, capitalizing on an existing customer base, and forming a joint advertising and promotional program.

ENTERTAINMENT BOOKING AGENT
★ $$

If you are looking for a business opportunity that could prove to be both fun and profitable, look no further than starting a business as a freelance entertainment booking agent. A booking agent is a person that actively seeks out opportunities in the entertainment industry, such as booking music bands for nightclub performances, theater groups for stage performances, and just about any other type of entertainer for live performances. Generally, an entertainment booking agent does not represent or act as management for entertainers, but merely builds alliances with entertainers and retains a portion of the performance fee paid to entertainers for work the agent has secured.

COMEDY CLUB
★ $$$$

Comedy clubs are a very popular entertainment venue, and there are a few approaches that can be taken in terms of starting a comedy club. The first and most costly option is to open a comedy club from a fixed location. The second and cheaper option is to establish a mobile comedy troop and book performances for the troop across the country for nightclub engagements, seminar performances, weddings, universities, colleges, and many other special occasion events. Regardless of which approach is employed to establish the business, comedy clubs and acts are extremely popular as more and more people are seeking to reduce stress in their lives through humor.

DISC JOCKEY SERVICE
★★ $$$ 🏠 🕐

One of the best part-time entertainment businesses that can be started is a disc jockey service, as not only are disc jockey services in high demand, but the business can also be initiated on less than a $10,000 investment and the monthly operating overheads are virtually nonexistent. There are basically four ingredients required to start and operate a successful disc jockey service:

1. An excellent and varied music selection.
2. Suitable DJ equipment and reliable transportation.
3. A talent for public speaking and an outgoing personality.
4. Good marketing skills.

Potential clients for a disc jockey service can include event planners, wedding planners, tour operators, nightclub owners, and the individual consumer seeking to secure disc jockey services for a celebration or event. Potential income range is $200 to $400 per night.

WEB RESOURCE: www.adja.org American Disc Jockey Association.

SINGING TELEGRAM SERVICE
★★ $$ 🏠 🕐

Would you like to start a singing telegram business, but your singing abilities are best left to the shower where no one can hear you? Fear not. For starting a singing telegram service is easy, even for those of us who cannot sing. A singing telegram service is a fantastic choice for a new business venture, especially for entrepreneurs with limited capital available, as this homebased enterprise can be put into action for less than a few thousand dollars. Furthermore, there are numerous accomplished singers in every community across North America that will be more than happy to exercise their singing talents for a fee, so locating the singers should not prove difficult. Once established, repeat business and word-of-mouth referrals will become the main marketing and advertising source. However, until the business is established, fliers, faxes, and e-mail blasts will be a good starting point in terms of marketing. Additionally, for the truly innovative entrepreneur, a cybersinging telegram service can also be initiated, and the addition of this service would only require basic equipment and a Web site.

COMMUNITY ENTERTAINMENT DIRECTORY
★★ $$ 🏠 🕐 🌍

Calling all aspiring publishers. Are you seeking to start a homebased publishing business that has the potential to generate a great profit, as well as be started on an initial investment of less than $10,000? If so, perhaps you should consider launching a monthly entertainment guide that services your community. The entertainment guide can be distributed free of charge and feature articles and information about local entertainment events, movie listings, concert listings and reviews, and horoscopes. Selling display advertising space in the entertainment guide to local merchants can support the business. Once again, this is an ideal publishing business to be operated from a homebased office. Once established and proven successful, the business could be expanded nationally on a franchise or license-to-operate basis.

MUSICAL BAND MANAGEMENT
★★ $$ 🏠 🕐

There are a few approaches that can be taken in terms of starting a musical band management service. The first approach is to start and operate the

business on a part-time basis from home and perhaps only represent one or two musical bands or solo musical performers. The second option is to start a full-time management agency that represents multiple bands or solo performers at one time. Both approaches to establishing and operating the business have their pros and cons, however, careful research will determine the best approach for you. Additionally, be sure to follow current or popular music trends when seeking a band or performer to represent, as the likelihood of success will be much greater.

INDEPENDENT MUSIC LABEL
★★ $$$$

Independent music labels are popping up everywhere across North America, and the rise in numbers of independent music labels rest solely with the creation and subsequent popularity of the Internet. Independent music labels now have the ability to level the playing field with their larger and better-financed competition by marketing new bands, performers, and music via the Internet. Furthermore, never in the history of music has there been such a wide variance of musical styles available to suit everyone's musical tastes. Everything from jazz to hip-hop and back to good old rock 'n roll. The key to successfully starting and operating an independent music label will rest squarely in your ability to secure the right musical acts and performers to sign, market, and promote. The start-up costs is high for this unique entertainment venture, but the profit potential is also very high.

WEB RESOURCE: www.afim.org Association for Independent Music.

ALBUMS AND EIGHT-TRACK SALES
★★ $ 🏠 🕐

Vinyl record albums and eight-track cassettes from the 1940s to the early 1980s have become hot collectible items. Starting a business that buys albums and eight-track cassettes at bargain basement prices, and resells these items for a profit is a fantastic new business venture to set in motion. As the saying goes, "time must be on your side" as it will take a fair amount of time to build an initial inventory for the business. That will mean spending time at flea markets and garage sales to locate and purchase secondhand albums and eight-track cassettes. Retailing collectible albums and eight-tracks can easily be conducted from a homebased office, as the most efficient way to market the products is to harness the power of the Internet and sell them via the Internet. Additionally, be sure to mark up the products by at least 200 percent, and in the case of a truly collectable item, it should go to the highest bidder.

MODELING AGENCY
★ $$$

Some of the world's most profitable and famous modeling agencies started on a shoestring budget. The key to success in this industry is not having deep pockets, but good contacts and knowing how to capitalize on those contacts. When you stand back and analyze a modeling agency, what you find at the core of the business is simply this, a modeling agency represents people of various appearances, shapes, sizes, races, etc., who are used to promote or display a product or service for a paying client. Nothing more. This gets back to my first point, which was industry contacts. Contacts are important in this industry for a few reasons, including the fact that the industry is very competitive or even cutthroat. Reliability is essential, and new modeling agencies find a lot of closed doors unless they have a contact inside. Once established a modeling agency can be very profitable, making this a business opportunity that is definitely worth investing some time into researching the possibilities further.

SATELLITE DISH SALES AND INSTALLATIONS
★ $$$$

Minisatellite dishes are in high demand by consumers, as many of these systems can receive a few hundred televisions and radio stations for the cost of a basic television cable service. There has never been a better time to start a business that sells and installs minisatellite dishes, as the product and service is still relatively new, yet well proven, and saturation of the market place is many years (if ever) away. The first step to establishing this type of business is to secure a sales and installation contract with one of the many manufacturers and subscription providers. The next step is to effectively market the product and installation service, and this can be accomplished by building a direct sales team to represent the products and services, as well as utilizing all traditional advertising mediums to gain consumer interest in the business. Additionally, be sure not to overlook apartment and condominium buildings as potential clients, as it is often easier to market to a captive audience once one or two people are on board and have purchased the product and service.

THEATER PRODUCTIONS
★ $$$ 🏠 🕐

Producing theatrical plays is much easier than you think and many plays have the potential to generate outstanding profits even if they are only small community plays. Producing plays simply means you are the financial backer of the production and you pay for the costs associated with bringing the play to stage. However there is a major benefit for producing these types of small plays in that often the performers, directors, and stagehands will work for little or no financial compensation. Just the fact that they are taking part in the play itself is reward enough. Additionally, many venues for performances can also be secured for free, providing there are benefits for the owner of the venue such as refreshment sales or product sales. The key to success in producing a community play for profit is to retain as much of the ticket revenue as possible while seeking out ways to reduce or eliminate production costs.

ONLINE ENTERTAINMENT LISTINGS AND REVIEWS
★ $$ 🏠 🕐 🌐 🖱

Developing an online entertainment listings and reviews Web site is a very straightforward cyberenterprise to activate. Simply provide visitors within specific communities information about forthcoming entertainment events like concert and movie listings, theatrical play dates, special events, and even restaurant listings. Additionally the site can also include an entertainment review section with feedback and critiques supplied by visitors. The site can earn income by selling advertising space to local merchants. Once established, this type of online business could easily be expanded to other communities and cities on a franchise or license-to-operate basis.

KARAOKE DJ SERVICE
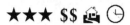 ★★★ $$ 🏠 🕐

Karaoke singing has become wildly popular in the past decade and to back this statement up you do not have to look any further than your own community, as I am sure there is a local karaoke club or karaoke singing night. The requirements for starting a karaoke DJ service are basic: you need karaoke equipment, a good music selection, and reliable transportation. Of course a fairly decent singing voice is not going to hurt business either. You can market your service to event and wedding planners as well as to local nightclubs, restaurants, and pubs that may entertain the idea of a weekly karaoke singing contest.

WEB RESOURCE: www.adja.org American Disc Jockey Association.

MUSICAL INSTRUMENT SALES
★★ $$$$ 🌐

Retailing musical instruments is a fantastic business venture to set in motion for the musically inclined entrepreneur that is seeking for a way to capitalize on their skills and interests. Ideally this type of specialty retailing is best suited to be established and operated from a retail storefront. However, for the financially challenged entrepreneur wishing to start this type of venture, the business could begin on a part-time basis from home or as a joint venture with an existing retailer within the community, such as a CD music shop or home electronics retailer. In addition to retailing musical instruments you can increase revenues and profits by providing instrument repairs, instructional classes,

instrument rentals, and sales of related products such as sheet music. Also be sure to establish relationships with schools, music teachers, associations, and clubs in the community. This can be a fantastic way to promote the business, products, and services you provide quickly as word-of-mouth advertising and referrals really work.

NOTES

KEY

RATINGS ★
START-UP COST $
HOMEBASED
BUSINESS 🏡
PART-TIME 🕐
LEGAL ISSUES ⚖
FRANCHISE OR
LICENSE POTENTIAL 🌐
ONLINE 🖱

46

FINANCIAL AND PROFESSIONAL SERVICE

Businesses You Can Start

STOCK WATCH PUBLICATION

★★ $$$ 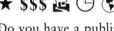 🕐 🌐

Do you have a publishing background and advertising sales experience? If so, you can put it to good use by starting a business that publishes a weekly stock watch report. The stock watch publication can be distributed free of charge throughout the community and feature information and articles on world stock markets, publicly-traded companies, and of course stock tips. The information featured in the publication can be provided by local investment brokers and financial planners. Revenues can be earned by selling advertising space in the publication to stockbrokers, real estate agents, investment advisors, and banks to promote their financial products and services. The time has never been better than now to start this type of publication, as interest in stock investing and trading has never been greater.

PAYDAY LOANS AND CHECK CASHING

★ $$$$ ⚖ 🌐

Payday loans and check cashing have become one of the fastest growing segments of the financial and investment industry, and for good reason; the profit potential is outstanding. To reinforce this statement considers the following: Typically, a check cashing service will charge customers 3 percent of the total as a service fee to cash a check. While 3 percent might not add up to a lot over the course of a week, it sure can over the period of a year. If you started with a mere $1,000 and cashed a check for that amount every day, at the end of the year your $1,000 initial investment would have generated $1,095 in check cashing service fees, or a 1,100 percent return on investment. Now imagine 10, 20, or 30 times that amount on a yearly basis. Furthermore, even a higher rate of return can be earned on short-term payday loans, making this a financial service to seriously consider as a new business venture.

ONLINE LOANS
★★ $$$$ ⚖ ✎

Business start-up loans, home improvement loans, and automotive loans are all types of financing services that can be featured on an online loans Web site. Banks, venture capitalists, and other lending institutions would pay a yearly fee to be listed and featured on the site as well as be given space within the site to promote and give details about their lending prerequisites and other information. People seeking financing for a product or project would log onto the site, select the type of loan and lending institution they are seeking, and complete and submit an application for financing right online. The application would be confidential and secure and be electronically forwarded to the lending institution(s) of their choice. Once again, specialization is the buzzword for business in the new millennium, thus you may want to consider specializing in one particular type of financing, like home improvement loans. If this route were chosen, it could open doors in terms of how you market the Web site. In the case of home improvement loans, home improvement contractors could hyperlink their Web site to yours and their customers seeking financing for a renovation project would be able to complete a financing application right from the contractor's Web site. The contractor would pay you a fee for having the service so readily available.

LEASING AGENT
★★ $$ 🏠 ⚖

In most areas of the United States and Canada a special license is not required to match clients with lending institutions that specialize in providing financing solutions on a lease basis for purchases ranging from automobiles to computer equipment for business use. Operating this service is very easy. Simply secure clients wishing to lease a product and complete and submit the lease documents to two or three leasing companies or financial institutions. The lenders that reply with the best lease rates and terms for your clients are the companies that will earn your clients' and your business. Revenues for the service are earned by charging the financial lenders a fee or a commission based on the value of the total lease amount. Income and profit potential range is $40,000 to $100,000 per year.

BUSINESS FOR SALE BROKER
★★★ $$$$ ⚖

The financial investment and training time required to secure a commercial Realtors license enabling you to start a real estate brokerage specializing in listing and selling businesses and commercial investment properties will be well worth the effort. It is common for business brokers to earn $250,000 or more per year after expenses. Additionally, consider specializing in a particular kind of business sales, such as marketing, manufacturing, or retail businesses. Specialization in the commercial real estate industry is the fastest way to become known as an industry leader, and gain valuable referrals. Marketing listings can be by way of the Internet, trade specific publications, and a wide network of contacts within the industry.

WEB RESOURCE: www.ibba.org International Business Brokers Association.

ONLINE BUSINESS BROKERAGE
★★ $$$$ 🏠 ✎

Thousands of established businesses and business opportunities are bought and sold annually in North America, and now is your chance to cash in on the public's demand for opportunities in self-employment by posting a business for sale Web site. The site will have to be indexed into numerous sections that represent various businesses for sale and opportunities like manufacturing, distributorships, and so on. In exchange for a $100 posting or listing fee, clients would receive a six-month posting on the site that describes their business or business opportunity for sale along with contact information. Once the Web site has been developed and posted to the Net, it can be kicked into high gear by employing subcontract sales consultants to solicit listings. To secure listings the sales consultants could simply scan classified business for sale advertisements in their local area and contact the owner to pursue a listing agreement. Objections should be few, as this is a very low-cost, highly effective method for business owners wishing to sell their business to reach a global audience.

EQUITIES DAY TRADER

★ $$+ 🏠 🕐 🗲

With the advent of the Internet, an entirely new homebased self-employment opportunity has surfaced. This business has the potential to generate six-figure incomes for everyday Americans who become day traders of equities and commodities. However, this opportunity certainly has a risky downside, as the potential is as great to lose money as it is to make it, especially for the novice and inexperienced trader. The key to successfully earning an income as an equities day trader is to gain as much knowledge about the industry as possible. Specialize in a specific type of stock or commodities trading, have considerable investment capital to get rolling, and most importantly nerves of steel and an understanding of what goes up must come down. Remember, most day traders go for short gains, buy in early and sell out the same day. Holding overnight is too much risk, especially for heavily invested traders in unstable market conditions. Of course remember the golden rule of stock and commodities trading: "never risk more than you can afford to lose."

WEB RESOURCE: www.electronic-trader.org Electronic Traders Association.

TAX PREPARATION SERVICE

★ $$ 🏠 🕐 ⚖

An accounting background is preferred; however, there are training and certification courses available that will enable you to start your own income tax preparation service as a qualified professional. As in any business, the more you know and the better your skills are, the more you will potentially earn. Though tax preparation is a seasonal service, additional income can also be gained by providing business clients with year-round bookkeeping services. Once established, word-of-mouth advertising and repeat business will support the service. However, to initially secure clients for the business, consider offering a two-for-one special for your first year of operation, prepare one tax return for the regular fee, while a spouse or partner receives the service for free.

LICENSING SPECIALIST

★★ $$$ 🏠 ⚖

Acting as a licensing specialist, you can seek out opportunities to secure the exclusive rights to use a popular name, product, service, or operating system or formula, and sell sublicenses to qualified business owners wishing to utilize the license in a business venture, product, or service. An example of a licensing situation is as follows: a popular motorcycle is being manufactured and you secure the master license to use the name of the motorcycle in question to promote products and services. You sell a license to a clothing company to use the motorcycle name, image, and logo on their clothing line and charge a one-time fee plus on-going royalties based on the success of the clothing line. You sell a license to a corporation that wants to establish a chain of restaurants using the motorcycle's name, logo, and image. These are only two examples; there are literally hundreds if not thousands of ways to profit as a licensing specialist.

WEB RESOURCE: www.licensing.org Licensing Industry Merchants' Association.

ONLINE AUTO LEASE MATCH-UP SERVICE

★★ $$$$ 🏠 🗲

Thousands of new and used cars are leased each year as opposed to being purchased. A quick glance through the automotive classified section of your local newspaper will tell you that there are a lot of people seeking to get out of their automotive lease agreement. This fact creates a fantastic business opportunity for the enterprising entrepreneur to capitalize on by starting a service that matches automotive leaseholders with people who are prepared to assume their lease. The easiest way to gain clients or listings for the business is to call leaseholders wishing to get out of their lease and offer to find a person to acquire it. Once you have secured a few hundred listings, you can begin to run your own classified advertisements that read, "thousands of used vehicles for lease, most no money down." Revenues for the service are earned by charging the leaseholder a fee once you have located and secured a client to assume the lease. Of course, the best operating format for the service is a specialized Web site posted on the Internet. In addition to classified advertisements promoting the lease match-up service, you can also register the site with search engines, hyperlink the site, and post Internet classified advertisements.

WEB RESOURCE: www.entrepreneur.com Create a business Web site with MySite professional Web site builder.

USED ATM SALES
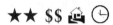

A few years ago, laws governing ownership and operation of ATMs (automated teller machines) were deregulated, paving the way for entrepreneurs from every walk of life to own and operate ATMs as a business concern. Since deregulation of this industry, millions of new ATMs have been sold, and a secondary market is now emerging, which is the sales of secondhand ATMs. While a very lucrative income can be earned by purchasing ATMs and reselling them for a profit, the gigantic profits are made by purchasing secondhand ATMs, locating the machine in a public place where it can generate revenue, and then selling the secondhand ATM as a going business concern. The potential to earn $250,000 per year is attainable for the determined entrepreneur who initiates this very basic business concept.

ONLINE SPOKESPERSON DIRECTORY
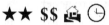

Product endorsements and testimonials are a very important marketing tool for many businesses. Thus activating a Web site featuring spokespersons for hire has the potential to make you rich. Professionals,

industry experts, and celebrities alike from every corner of the globe could post an advertisement on the site that gives detailed information about their qualifications to promote certain products or services and the type of endorsement contracts they are seeking. Corporations and organizations that are looking for a professional spokesperson to endorse or promote their products and service would simply log onto the site and begin to search the listings featured. Sources of revenue for this type of cyberenterprise include charging spokespersons a listing fee as well as selling advertising space on the site.

BOOKKEEPING SERVICE

Bookkeeping is simply the procedure of recording financial transactions, or put differently, a record is made every time money changes hands. Providing you possess accounting or bookkeeping experience and skill, a substantial income can be earned by running a bookkeeping service. Clients will largely consist of business owners that either do not have the time or ability to set up and manage a bookkeeping system for their business. Recent technological advancement has made operating a bookkeeping service very straightforward, as there are many types of small business accounting software available that will not only make your job easier, but also enable you to service many clients at one time. Typically, bookkeeping services charge clients a monthly fee to record and update their financial records on a regular basis. Averaged, this fee translates into $25 to $35 per hour.

WEB RESOURCE: www.aibp.org American Institute of Professional Bookkeepers.

COLLECTION AGENCY
★★ $$ 🏠 🕐 ⚖️

If you have had past experience in the field of debt collection, than a logical new business venture for you to start is a collection agency operating from a home-based location. Generally, the duties of a collection agency focus on collecting financial debts typically owed to a company or business in a nonharassing manner and utilizing the telephone and official sounding letters as your main debt collection tools. Securing clients for the service is extremely easy, due to the simple fact that you will not be paid for your service unless you are successful in collecting the debt owed. Rates for the services are based on a percentage of the amount of money that is collected, and the longer the debt has been outstanding, the higher the fee charge to collect the debt. Typically, a 25 percent fee would be charged on successfully collecting debts that have been in arrears for up to 180 days. Beyond 180 days the fee could increase to as much as 50 percent of the total debt collected.

WEB RESOURCE: www.collector.com American Collectors Association.

IMAGE CONSULTANT

★ $$

Many business owners and corporate executives realize that a book is often judged by its cover and thus have no hesitation enlisting the services of a personal image consultant to ensure they are keeping up with current fashion and social trends to maximize a favorable public image. Beyond assisting clients with wardrobe and etiquette tips, image consultants also assist clients in selecting the best social events to attend. They also help them keep up with current social and political issues. Most importantly, they coach clients on how to avoid situations or conversations that can potentially damage their careers or business. Potential income range is $30 to $50 per hour.

VENTURE CAPITAL BROKER

★★ $$

A venture capital broker is simply a person that brings two parties together that share a common goal. The goal generally and ultimately is to create a profit. One party is the entrepreneur that is seeking capital to start or expand a business. The second party is a venture capitalist who lends entrepreneurs money for business financing in exchange for a high rate of return on the investment or a combination of company shares and a return on investment. The

venture capital broker that successfully brings the two parties together is remunerated by way of commission based on the total amount of financing that was secured. Depending on the amount of money secured, the commission rate will range from a low of 5 percent to a high of 15 percent. Securing clients for the service is as easy as scanning local newspapers for business financing-wanted classified advertisements, and taking over the task of locating suitable capital for the venture. However, finding a source of financing can be difficult, so be sure to only represent clients that have a viable business concept accompanied by a completed business plan that reinforces the business concept.

WEB RESOURCE: www.nvca.org National Venture Capital Association.

ONLINE VENTURE CAPITAL

★★ $$$$

With more than 700,000 new business ventures being started every year in the United States, developing an online venture capital or "angle" forum has the potential to make you rich. A very healthy percentage of these 700,000 new business ventures require money to make them work, and securing financing to start or expand a business is one of the largest challenges facing any entrepreneur. That is what makes this online venture so exciting. This type of site could feature information and services including:

- A classified advertisement section featuring advertisements posted by entrepreneurs seeking business financing and lenders or venture capitalists seeking projects.
- A "pitch a plan" section that entrepreneurs could use to pitch a business plan or opportunity in digital video format.
- Tips and information about business financing topics submitted by successful business owners and venture capitalist financial gurus alike.
- A business for sale and business opportunity section.

The options are unlimited and ways to generate revenues and profits from this type of online venture are also unlimited. Like any Internet enterprise, the key to success lies within attracting visitors to the site to take advantage of and use the information and services provided within.

TENDER RESEARCHER
★★ $$ 🏠 🕒

A tender research service is an outstanding new business opportunity to put into action for the entrepreneur that is seeking to own and operate a home-based business that has the potential to generate an income of $50,000 per year or more. Simply put, a tender research service does exactly that, researches tender information from across North America, and in some cases even the world. The best method for operating a tender research service is to simply charge all clients the same fee, say $50 per month. In exchange for the fee, clients would receive by way of e-mail or fax all tender information related to their business or industry. The main requirement for operating a tender research service is to have excellent research skills, and locating tender information can be accomplished by surfing the Web, as well as subscribing to daily newspapers and trade publications from around the globe. One hundred clients each paying a mere $50 per month for the service will result in business revenues of $60,000 per year.

ONLINE TENDER DIRECTORY
★★ $$$$ 🖰

Corporations, government agencies, and organizations of all sorts place thousands of tender display advertisements in newspapers annually. The cost of one ad can be as much as $1,000. Now imagine if that same corporation could post as many tenders as they wanted to online for an annual cost of only $99. Could this type of Web site become popular for companies and agencies to post tenders as well as for contractors seeking to secure tenders? Of course it could, thus creating a fantastic business opportunity by developing a Web site that exclusively featured tender information and contracts available. The site would have to be indexed by tender subject such as construction, maintenance service, computer hardware, etc. Contractors wishing to bid for a tender

could simply view listing and tender information and even download tender documents right online. This type of online venture will require a substantial investment to develop and market the site. However, once established the profit potential is outstanding.

FRANCHISE SPECIALIST
★★ $$$$ 🏠 ⚖️

Forming a joint venture with a lawyer who specializes in franchise business law could be your first step toward building a successful business as a franchise specialist. A franchise specialist service seeks opportunities in two ways. In the first way the specialist looks for small, independently owned and operated businesses that are ideal candidates to be expanded nationally, on a franchise basis. The second way is when a franchise specialist looks for companies that have already gone through the lengthy and costly franchising legal requirements process, and are now ready to begin marketing the franchises to qualified owners or operators. In both cases, the goal of the franchise specialist is to market the franchises, retaining a large portion of the franchise fee in exchange for providing the service, and in some cases, even securing a portion of the company's shares.

WEB RESOURCE: www.aafd.org American Association of Franchisees and Dealers.

ONLINE FRANCHISE AND LICENSING OPPORTUNITIES
Franchise Opportunities
★★ $$$$ 🏠 🖰

Create an online portal that brings corporations with franchise opportunities for sale together with people that want to purchase and operate a franchise business. The site can be created in a directory format with a main index page that lists the various franchise opportunity categories on the site, such as restaurants and food services, retail, and maintenance services. Income is earned by charging corporations a listing fee to be featured on the site. Additionally an alliance could be established with a lawyer that specializes in franchise agreements to write and post articles pertaining to the legalities of franchising on the site. Promote the site by utilizing Internet marketing techniques such as search engine registrations, hyperlinking, and joining a rotating banner advertisement program. For the truly innovative entrepreneur, you could also host monthly franchise opportunity trade shows that operated in conjunction with the Web site. The trade shows could take place in every major city across North America on a rotating basis.

Licensing Opportunities
★★ $$$$ 🏠 ✍

Licensing is somewhat different than franchising and by definition means "an individual, corporation, or enterprise that has been granted a license by another individual, corporation, or enterprise." Generally the license allows for the licensee to conduct business utilizing the license holder's formulas and procedures, and in some cases logos and names. However, this type of online venture would operate similarly to an online franchise directory. The main objective would be to bring together corporations and individuals seeking to grant licenses with corporations and individuals seeking to acquire licenses. Once again, the site would be supported financially by charging fees to have information pertaining to licensing opportunities featured on the site.

PUBLIC RELATIONS
★★ $$ 🏠 🕐

Many public relation firms are chosen by companies not based on what they know, but whom they know. A good PR person representing an individual, business, product, or service can be the equivalent of having a person in your corner that can pick lottery numbers before they are even drawn. The main duty of a public relations agency is to promote in a positive manner, regardless of who or what is being promoted. Promotion techniques include creating press kits and press releases for clients, organizing media and special events for clients, and around-the-clock networking on the client's behalf. Getting started in the business can be difficult, given that the public

relations industry is fiercely competitive. However, as an entry point consider starting small and representing one or two clients on a local basis until you have mastered the fine art of public relations. Income potential range is $30 to $50 per hour plus expenses.

WEB RESOURCE: www.prsa.org Public Relations Society of America.

EMPLOYEE TRAINING
★★ $$ 🏠 🕐 🌍

The demand from employers for specialized employee training is enormous, and starting a home-based employee-training service is a terrific new business venture to set in motion. The key to success in this business is specialization, and your service should focus on one particular training style or method that you have mastered or can quickly master. Popular employee training course topics include customer service, working without direction, money handling, making the workplace a safe and secure environment, and coping with stress. The training courses can be conducted on the client's site. Marketing the service can be accomplished by attending business networking meetings to promote your service or designing a marketing brochure explaining the service and course curriculum and distributing the brochures to potential clients.

HEADHUNTER SERVICE
★ $$ 🏠 🕐

Unlike an employment agency, a headhunting service does not wait for potential employees or career seekers to send in a résumé for a job listing; a headhunter goes out and actively searches for the ideal candidate. This usually means the first stop is at the client's competitors. Securing clients for a headhunting service is very straightforward, simply due to the fact that the clients only pay for the service if and when the ideal person is located and hired. Fees for the service are paid by the client that is seeking to fill an employment position, and are typically 4 to 8 percent of the employment position's annual salary. In addition to competitor companies, potential employees can also be located at business networking meetings, and even some small business owners can be lured back into the corporate world if the offer is lucrative enough.

FUNDRAISING CONSULTANT
★★ $$ 🏠 🕐 ⚖️

Acting on behalf of charities as a fundraising consultant can earn you as much as $100,000 per year, of course providing you have the skills and abilities to raise funds for the charities that your service represents. The first step required for establishing a fundraising service is to build alliances with local or national charities to represent the charities as a fundraising specialist. The next step is to establish a fundraising program for the charity, similar to a business plan. The plan or program should outline how the funds will be raised, as well as the fee you will charge for your service. Typically, fundraising consultants charge a commission for services based on a percentage of the total amount of money raised, and the commission rate will range from 10 percent on amounts in excess of $100,000 to percentages as high as 50 percent for amounts under $1,000. As lucrative as the business sounds, remember the cost to establish, advertise, and manage the fundraising program comes directly from the fees charged for providing the service.

WEB RESOURCE: www.afrds.com The Association of Fund Raisers and Direct Sellers.

SALES TRAINING SERVICE
★★ $$ 🏠 🕐 🌐

Are you a sales professional who is recognized as a top producer in your industry? If so, in addition to your six-figure yearly commission earnings, you can add another $100,000 simply by training other sales professionals to also become perennial top sales producers. The sales training can be taught at the client's site or in a homebased classroom atmosphere. The course curriculum can be developed by amassing your sales experience, techniques, trade secrets, and methodology into a study guide utilized and practiced by students. Gaining clients for the classes can be as easy as creating a

marketing package. This promotional package should describe the sales training program, highlight your own personal sales achievements, and explain the benefits and value that this type of focused and specialized coaching can have in terms of turning sales order takers into sales order makers. The marketing presentation can be presented to business owners and corporations that rely on a direct sales team to drive business revenues and profits.

COPYWRITER
★★ $$ 🏠 🕐

Copywriters prepare copy or text for advertisements, marketing brochures, press releases, TV and radio commercials, catalogs, and packaging labels, just to mention a few. This business depends on you having a talent for writing in a clear and concise manner that can get the message across, building excitement and interest, and motivating people to take action. The demand for copywriter services is excellent, as most business owners do not possess the skills, time, or inclinations to prepare highly effective copy. Establishing alliances with advertising agencies, graphic artists, and public relations firms is an outstanding method to market a copywriting service, as these types of companies can refer your service to their clients, or utilize the service themselves. Copywriting fees greatly vary depending on the type and size of the copy being created. However, achieving average earnings of $50 per hour should not prove difficult.

WEB RESOURCE: www.copydesk.org The American Copy Editors Society.

PROFESSIONAL EMCEE
★ $$ 🏠 🕐

Do you possess good communications skills and a knack for public speaking? If so, your skills are in high demand from corporations and organizations from around the globe as a professional emcee. Professional emcees are often hired to host an event, open a seminar series, or act as the master of ceremonies for events ranging from charity auctions to general annual meetings for large corporations. A freelance professional emcee service is a terrific business to operate on a part-time basis to supplement business or employment income. Professional emcees can earn as much as $500 for each event they emcee.

WEB RESOURCE: email~nsamain@aol.com National Speakers Association.

INDEPENDENT SALES CONSULTANT
★★★ $$ 🏠

Some of the highest earning professionals in any industry are independent sales consultants working on a freelance basis for clients. Freelance sales consultants represent companies that sell products and services ranging from manufactured goods to home improvement services, and just about everything in between. Securing clients to represent is easy, simply because freelance sales consultants generally supply all the tools of the trade such as transportation, communications requirements, and computer equipment that may be needed to acquire customers and conduct business—not to mention the fact that many freelance sales consultants also generate their own sales leads. Or, put differently, clients have little, if anything, to lose by having freelance sales consultants representing their business. Remuneration for products or services sold is always by way of commission, which will range between 10 and 25 percent of the total sales value.

SEMINAR SPEAKER
★ $$ 🏠 🕐

Corporations, associations, and event planners are on the constant lookout for interesting speakers to lecture at corporate events and seminars. If you possess special life experiences in business, travel, finance, or overcoming the odds, then an outstanding opportunity awaits you by becoming a freelance seminar speaker. Initially to secure speaking engagements, create a resume outlining your experience and related skills, and distribute this information to event planners, seminar organizations, and corporations. This is the type of service that is built on word-of-

mouth referrals, and if your speeches and lectures are good, you will soon be in demand for speaking engagements across North America, and perhaps the world.

WEB RESOURCE: email~nsamain@aol.com National Speakers Association.

PROSPECTING AGENT
★★ $$ 🏠 🕐

In a nutshell, a prospecting agent generates and qualifies sales leads for their clients. However, the service should not be confused with a telemarketing service, as a prospecting service never attempts to close a sale or go beyond qualifying a sales lead for their clients. Prospecting agents are paid for each lead they generate, and the higher the value of the client's products and service, the larger the fee for supplying qualified leads. Additionally, some prospecting agents also generate sales leads first, and then sell the leads to the highest bidder. A example of this would be a prospecting agent that sets up a display booth at a home and garden trade show and collects names, addresses, and contact information from people that are considering a home improvement renovation. The type of renovation they are considering will dictate what kind of home improvement company the prospecting agent will approach to purchase the leads.

RETIRED PRESIDENTS SERVICE
★★ $$ 🏠 🌍

How many novice entrepreneurs would benefit from consulting meetings with business veterans that have 20 years experience or more in the business world? Almost all. The business concept is very straightforward. Simply, retain the services of retired company presidents, corporate executives, and small business owners to work on a consulting basis as needed coaching new business owners in their field of specialty, such as sales and marketing, management, or financial and tax manners. Clients could pay for the business coaching services on an hourly basis, or you could develop a complete program consisting of a guidebook and multiple hours of coaching, and the revenue earned could be split with the retired business consultants.

DEMOGRAPHIC DATA BROKER

★★ $$$

Once a business determines who their target market is for a product or service they will be selling, they have to know where the target market is, how many potential customers are in the target range, and what are the trends in terms of their target market. Starting a demographic data brokerage service will enable you to fill the demand for corporations, organizations, and small business owners for demographics data. Simply, create an electronic filing system that can be used for compiling demographics information. The data can be researched and acquired for free in most cases, via government agencies, the Internet, and with reprint permission right from publishers of almanacs, encyclopedias, and populations directories. The quickest way to secure paying customers that require this type of demographics data to create business, marketing, and advertising plans is to contact companies that create business, marketing, and advertising plans.

GRAND OPENING SERVICE

★★★ $$$$

According to the U.S. Small Business Administration, more than 700,000 new businesses open each year in the United States, and this fact creates a fantastic opportunity for the enterprising entrepreneur to start a business that specializes in providing clients with various grand opening services. Grand opening services can include celebrity visits for grand opening events, a red carpet service, a ribbon cutting service, and a press release service, just to mention a few. As a unique way of marketing the grand opening service, consider initiating a direct-mail advertising campaign explaining the various services your business provides. The campaign can be targeted at owners of businesses that have recently opened or will be opening in the very near future. To obtain this type of contact information for the direct-mail advertising campaign, simply contact your local

business service center and ask for a list of people that have recently applied and been issued a business license.

CONTRACT NEGOTIATIONS SERVICE

★★ $$

The ability to successfully negotiate a business contract can mean the difference of prospering in business or failing in business. Many business owners are quick to realize that contract negotiation skills are an art form and often best left to professional contract negotiators. If you possess a high degree of business ethics, have exceptional communications, negotiations, and closing skills, then an unmatched opportunity waits in starting a contract negotiation service. Securing clients for the service is best approached by creating a marketing package that explains the service, but more importantly your accomplishments in terms of successfully negotiating contracts. Don't be shy. If you have a track record of negotiating multimillion dollar contracts in your past corporate life, let potential clients know. Once the marketing package has been completed, set appointments with companies and business owners that you feel would benefit by utilizing your service and negotiations experience.

OFFICE PROTOCOL CONSULTANT

★★★ $$

The time has never been better than now to start a business as an office protocol consultant. As disputes between employees or between employees and management based on allegations of sexual harassment, racism, and abusive behavior within the office environment cannot only morally bankrupt a business, but also financially bankrupt a business as a result of successful litigation. The business concept is very straightforward. Acting as an office protocol consultant you can advise clients on issues pertaining to these subjects, as well as create a training program for employees and management on how to avoid and react to any potentially unfavorable situation that may arise within the office working environment. The demand for this type of consulting service is gigantic, as thousands of corporations rush to retain the services of a protocol consultant as a proactive measure to ensure they are not caught in politically and socially inappropriate situations reflecting negatively on corporate image.

MARKETING CONSULTANT
★★★ $$ 🏠

Without marketing a business cannot survive, simply because marketing is a combination of sales, advertising, promotion, and publicity, or put differently marketing is an activity initiated by business to generate revenues for the business. Top-notch marketing consultants are in high demand from every size corporation and business across North America. Many marketing consultants will specialize in one particular marketing element, while the more experienced consultants tackle the full range of marketing activities for clients. Securing clients for the service can be accomplished in numerous ways including promoting the service at business networking meetings, initiating a direct-mail advertising campaign, or simply setting meetings with potential clients to present your services. Additionally, if you possess skills and experience marketing products or services via the Internet, be sure to capitalize on this ability, as marketing consultants that specialize in Internet marketing are earning as much as $100 per hour.

WEB RESOURCE: www.the-dma.org The Direct Marketing Association.

ORGANIZATION SERVICE
★★ $$ 🏠 🕐

Helping people to become and stay organized can earn you as much as $40 per hour, and best of all the business can be put into action for less than a few thousand dollars in start-up capital. The main focus of an organization service is to assist clients to develop a system to organize their home, office, business, or whatever else in their lives needs to be organized and put in place. Gaining clients for the service can be as easy as designing a marketing brochure explaining the service and distributing it to potential customers via fax and e-mail blasts, direct mail, or personally

handing out the marketing material at business networking meetings. Once established this is the type of personal service business that will receive a lot of word-of-mouth referrals and repeat business.

ASSOCIATION MANAGEMENT SERVICE
★★ $$$

An association management service is a service that provides office, staff, and management solutions for associations, organizations, and trade unions that are too large to rely on volunteers within the association or organization to carry out the administrative and management duties required to maintain the association. Or, the organization may be too small and lack the financial backing to hire full-time staff and management. The duties of an association management service can include answering telephones, managing accounts receivables and payables, filing documents, corresponding with association membership, and just about any other task required in the day-to-day management of an association. Establishing billing rates for the service will depend on the various services provided for each client, and typically a quote is submitted reflecting the costs for providing the management services in a one-year period. The business can be operated from home, providing the intentions are to only manage a few associations. Larger services will require office space with boardroom facilities for association meetings.

WEB RESOURCE: www.marketingsource.com/association Directory service listing more than 5,000 associations.

SURVEY SERVICE
★★ $$ 🏠 🕐 🌐

Starting a homebased telephone survey service is a terrific new business venture to set in motion. A few of the best aspects about starting this type of business include:

- Homebased business opportunity with very flexible operating hours.
- Growth industry, proven and stable, and no previous experience or special skills requirements.

- Low initial start-up investment and minimal monthly operating overheads.

Once established, referrals and repeat business should drive the marketing. However, gaining clients to establish the business can be as easy as developing a direct-mail marketing program and distributing a marketing package to potential clients. The marketing package should include the various benefits that clients receive with your service, as well as a complete description of the service.

CAREER EXPOS
★ $$$ 🌐

Career expos are simply trade shows that bring potential employers and employees together under one roof, and in one venue. Career expos serve two functions. The first is they give corporations a chance to blow their own horn and explain to potential employees why they are the industry leaders, and more importantly, why working for their company has advantages over selecting the competition company. The second function career expos serve is that they give people seeking to start, change, or upgrade a career an opportunity to blow their horns, and explain to the corporations exhibiting at the expo how they can benefit the corporation and what they can bring to the table. As you can see, there is a whole lot of horn blowing going on at career expos, but without question they are an excellent opportunity for both potential employers and potential employees to come together and seek mutually beneficial working relationships and opportunities.

ONLINE SCHOLARSHIPS
★ $$$$ 🏠 🕐 🖱

Every year thousands of students vie for educational scholarships in North America, and one of the most difficult challenges facing students is trying to keep track and up-to-date with the thousands of different scholarships that are awarded each year. Developing a Web site that features information about scholarships can serve two purposes. The first is that creating this type of Web site and posting it on the Internet is a terrific way to develop your own homebased business. The second purpose is obvious; parents and students would have access to a fantastic resource base to learn more about particular scholarships and the required criteria in terms of the awarding process. This type of online business could earn revenues in a few ways, such as charging students and parents a yearly membership fee for access to the site or charging educational facilities and scholarship advisory boards a fee to post their scholarship information on the Web site. Of course advertising revenues could also be earned by renting banner ads once the Web site was established and proven popular.

ONLINE OFFICE TOWER
★★ $$+ 🏠 🕐 🌐 🖱

Restrictive financial budgets do not enable many professionals providing business services the ability to create and maintain their own Web site. This creates a fantastic opportunity for the cybersavvy entrepreneur to capitalize financially by developing an online office tower that services the local community. An online office tower is simply a collection of professional service providers that serve a particular city or community located in one Web site. In exchange for being featured in the site the client pays a low cost annual fee that includes one time setup, site hosting, and ongoing site maintenance. Ideally each professional would receive a bold headline in the main index that is linked to a page within the site. The professional's page could give details about the service they provide as well as information about how to contact them. Designing this type of Web site will let you be very creative and you will be able to add some really spectacular graphics and images, perhaps even a elevator attendant that whisks visitors to each individual page within the site. Once you have an operational Web site model established, the business could easily be expanded on a franchise or license basis to service every major city across the United States and Canada.

EXPENSE REDUCTION CONSULTANT

★★ $$ 🏠 🕐

Calling all business managers, controllers, and operations managers. You can profit from your business and budget management skills and experiences by starting your own expense reduction consulting service. Expense reduction consultants provide clients with services such as developing long-term budgets, analyzing fixed and variable overheads, controlling product and service costs, and developing expense reduction strategies to suit individual client needs. The objective of the expense reduction exercise is to uncover costs associated with doing business that can be reduced or eliminated while still maintaining the efficiency of the business in terms of operations, customer service, and profitability. Potential clients will largely be small- to medium-sized businesses, but you can also target your marketing efforts toward professionals, nonprofit associations, and privately-run institutions. Additionally, many of these consulting services will specialize in a particular type of business or industry such as fixed location retailing or manufacturing. Get started by developing an expense reduction manual. The manual should be representative of the type of business or industry you will target and include an index of categories you will analyze, such as business location, employees, communications, etc. The purpose of the manual is to act as a road map to guide you through each client's business. You can then tailor the manual to a specific client's business and enter subcategories for each business component that you analyze. Expense reduction consultants present each client with an extensive written report at the end of their investigation. This report typically outlines the consultants suggestions in terms of reducing costs, including relevant supporting data and statistics. Fees for the service vary. Some consultants prefer to charge an hourly rate, while other prefer to charge a percentage based on the amount of money they can save a client. The percentage can range from 10 to 50 percent of first year's saving. Marketing the service can be as easy as joining business associations to network with small business owners.

ELDERLY EMPLOYMENT AGENCY

★★ $$ 🏠 🕐 🌐

Ask any older person seeking employment what the most difficult challenge they face is and nine times out of ten the response will be their age. Opening an employment agency geared toward helping aging members of our society find gainful employment may just be your opportunity to build a successful and profitable business. No special training or education can replace good, old-fashioned experience, and this can be your most powerful marketing tool for recruiting small business and corporations to become clients and post job openings within their firms suitable for elderly people with your agency. There are two methods for generating revenues for this type of business. The first is to charge would-be employers a fee to post a job listing and for you to find a suitable candidate to fill the job. The second option is to charge the person seeking employment a fee when employment is gained through the efforts of your agency. Additionally, you will also want to consider specialization in terms of the types of industries your agency will work in. Choices include a temporary work placement agency, a high-level executive recruitment, tourism and hospitality, and just about any other industry wherein the needs of the employer can be suitably matched to the needs of the aging employee. Given the fact that people are living longer and healthier now than any other time in history, the timing to initiate an employment agency for the elderly could not be better.

EXPERT WITNESS SERVICE

★★ $$ 🏠 🕐

Starting an "expert witness for hire service" is a very unique and interesting business opportunity for the innovative entrepreneur to tackle. The idea is you represent expert witnesses that can be retained by lawyers to give professional testimony in court or legal proceedings. These expert witnesses could include medical doctors, gun and ammunition experts, transportation and automobile experts, private investigators, or just about any other type of professional that can be deemed an expert in their career or industry. The service would work very much like an employment agency, but with extremely high security measures in place to protect both clients and the expert witnesses. You can set presentation appointments with lawyers to introduce them to your service and discuss their needs in terms of experts needed to testify at trials. In exchange for providing the service, you would charge clients a commission based on the amount of money received for providing expert testimony. This is the type of business that will take very careful planning in order to establish. Partnering with a lawyer may be a consideration. However, the effort and expense to properly research and establish this business could be well rewarded financially, as expert witnesses can receive as much as five-figures in some situations to provide professional testimony.

NOTES

KEY

RATINGS ★
START-UP COST $
HOMEBASED BUSINESS 🏠
PART-TIME 🕐
LEGAL ISSUES ⚖
FRANCHISE OR LICENSE POTENTIAL 🌐
ONLINE 🖱

61

FOOD-RELATED
Businesses You Can Start

VENDING MACHINES
★★ $$$ 🏠 🕐

Every day factories, warehouses, office buildings, and recreation centers are being constructed. What do these buildings have to do with a food business you may ask? A lot, especially if you are considering starting a vending business, as all of these locations are perfect spots to install snack and soda vending machines. The snack vending business is a multibillion dollar industry in North America, and continues to grow each year. Entering into the vending industry is very easy. Simply purchase a few vending machines, stock and locate them, and you're in business right? Wrong. This industry also has one of the highest failure rates due to the simple fact that people who start vending routes have often done so at the mercy of vending route business opportunity companies. These companies, in exchange for $10,000 or more, promise huge profits to the operators of these vending

routes. Subsequently the vending equipment is inferior and usually ends up in the operator's garage after four or five months of not producing any income while on location. There is no great science to making a vending route or machine pay for itself. The key to success in vending is the same as opening a retail store: location, location, location. Research and source the right location and a vending machine will not only make money, it will be profitable for many years.

WEB RESOURCE: www.smallbizbooks.com Business-specific start-up guides and books.

ONLINE VENDING EQUIPMENT AND OPPORTUNITIES
★★★ $$$ 🏠 🖱

Once again, food vending in North America is a multibillion dollar industry and, in the spirit of uniqueness, consider the following online business opportunity as a method to enter the vending industry. Develop a Web site that specializes in providing a one-stop source for vending information and details. The site can include a classified advertisement section featuring vending opportunities and vending equipment for sale as well as other information related to the food vending industry like articles on success stories, regulations, and scams in the marketplace. All services and information featured would be free for visitors to the site, and revenues can be earned by charging advertisers a fee for listing or posting their vending opportunities or equipment for sale in the classifieds. Marketing the site to the general public would be as easy as placing small classified advertisements in major daily newspapers under the business opportunity section. These ads give a brief explanation about the Web site and how to find it on the Internet.

USED RESTAURANT EQUIPMENT SALES
★★★ $$$ 🏠 🕐

Did you know that starting a restaurant is one of the most common new business ventures? And, did you also know that more than 90 percent of new restaurants go out of business within the first five years of operation? The combination of these two facts is the basis for starting a business that buys and sells secondhand restaurant equipment like grills, fryers, and coffee machines. Simply put, when one restaurant goes out of business you purchase their equipment, and when another restaurant opens you resell that same equipment for a profit. This type of business venture can be started and operated from home initially and moved to a larger location as the business expands. Furthermore, you can specialize in one particular type of restaurant equipment such as deli equipment or in restaurant equipment in general. The potential to earn large profits from selling secondhand restaurant equipment is outstanding, and this business opportunity definitely warrants further investigation.

PREPACKAGED ENERGY FOODS
★★ $$ 🏠 🕐 ⚖️

The increase in outdoor recreational activities such as hiking, rock climbing, and backpacking is fueling the demand for prepackaged energy foods and nutrition bars, creating a terrific opportunity for the enterprising entrepreneur to start a new business venture that packages and sells these types of high-energy food products. You can get started on a part-time basis packaging and selling basic energy food like mixed nuts, dried fruits, and raisins. As the business grows, so can your product line to include energy drinks and full meals. The food items that you package can be sold through retail accounts such as fitness and health food stores. Furthermore, you can sell the products over the Internet, via your own Web site, or by listing your products for sale on other Web sites.

WEB RESOURCE: www.sfa.org Snack Food Association of America.

POPCORN CART
★★★ $$ 🕐 ⚖️ 🌐

Here is a great part- or full-time business enterprise that can be started on a small initial investment and return excellent profits. Starting a popcorn cart vending business requires little more than a vendor's license, popcorn cart, and a high-traffic location to set up at. Excellent locations include weekend flea markets, sports events, fairs, farmers markets, and all other busy community gathering places. New popcorn vending carts can cost as much as $15,000. However, as a way of keeping start-up costs to a minimum, you may want to consider purchasing a secondhand popcorn vending cart, as used carts are currently selling for approximately $2,500 to $5,000 depending on size and condition. The ability to make a very good living operating a popcorn cart is excellent, and the markup on a bag of popcorn is 500 percent or greater.

WEB RESOURCE: www.classic-carts.com Manufacturers of specialty food vending carts.

SANDWICH DELIVERY ROUTE
★★ $$

If you are searching for a very inexpensive business to start in the food industry that has the potential to generate $1,000 per week or more in combined income and profits, then look no further than starting a sandwich delivery route. Ideally, a sandwich route will be established in an office district or industrial district of a city or community, enabling the business to capitalize on sheer volume of people working in these areas. In terms of operating the business, it is as easy as establishing a working relationship with a catering service or restaurant to supply the sandwiches and salads on a wholesale basis, while building a customer base to purchase the lunch meals. Design a menu featuring all the sandwich and salad items available and distribute the menu to office buildings and factories. Customers would simply place their lunch orders in the morning or the day before. Additionally, lunch orders could be placed by way of fax, telephone, or e-mail and of course delivery would always be free.

WINE RACK MANUFACTURING
★ $

Are you searching for an inexpensive business start-up that can be operated part-time from home? If so you may want to consider activating a business that focuses on manufacturing and wholesaling custom-made wine racks. The business is easy to establish and only requires basic woodworking skills and woodworking equipment. In addition to constructing the wine racks from wood, you could also build the racks from a metal, or even better, all recycled material, such as scrap metal and used building material that can usually be acquired for free with a little bit of detective work. Once you have designed and constructed a few wine racks, they can be wholesaled or consigned to wine stores, furniture stores, liquor stores, u-brew-it wine shops, and even restaurants. The key to success in wine rack manufacturing is to have a unique product that consumers are compelled to purchase for themselves or as a gift for others.

FARMERS' MARKET
★★ $$$

Every community needs a farmers' market, so why not start one in your community? The business is very straightforward to start and operate. Simply secure leased premises large enough to be subdivided into 30 or 40 ten-foot by ten-foot vendor booths. Once completed, the vendor booths can be rented to local farmers, specialty food manufacturers, and crafts people. Current rental rates for booths at farmers' markets are $75 to $125 per day. Assuming you had 30 booths rented once per week, four times per month the business would generate $12,000 per month in rental revenue, prior to operating expenses. The key to success in this type of business venture is to ensure the vendors that are participating in the market have high quality products.

WEB RESOURCE: www.pma.com Produce Marketing Association.

ONLINE FARMERS' MARKET
★★★ $$$$

Take the farmers' market high-tech by going online. Not many farmers producing quality foods have the time or equipment required for developing their own Web site, not to mention the time and costs associated with maintaining a Web site. Thus opportunity calls. Create your own online farmers' market by developing a Web site that features farm fresh products for sale. The site can be indexed by food type and feature farmer listings. In exchange for a monthly fee farmers listed on the site would receive a pop-up page describing their products as well as a listing in the main index. Consumers wishing to purchase products would simply choose their selections, place them in the shopping cart, and head for the checkout. An automatic e-mail response system would notify farmers about product sales and forward the required shipping information. Some day in the not-so-distant future it is possible that all people will shop for groceries online or in an electronic format.

COFFEE SERVICE
★★ $$$

Billions of cups of coffee are sold annually in the United States, and securing just a small portion of this very lucrative market can make you rich. We are a nation of coffee drinkers, and to reinforce this statement you do not have to look further than any commercial district to realize there is a coffee shop on every corner. However, a coffee service is not to be confused with a coffee shop, as a coffee service is a mobile business that supplies medium- to large-size companies with free coffee-making equipment in exchange for the company purchasing coffee and coffee filters from the coffee service. The profit potential for a coffee service is outstanding, providing the service operates on a large volume basis.

WEB RESOURCE: www.ncausa.org National Coffee Association.

JUICE BAR
★★★ $$$ ⚖ 🌐

A juice bar that serves customers fresh squeezed fruit juice drinks is an absolutely fantastic new business enterprise to put into action, as more and more people are striving to lead healthier lifestyles. Ideal locations to establish a juice bar include busy tourist attractions and beach areas, food courts in malls, fitness clubs, and public markets. To boost sales and profits, additional items such as sandwiches and salads can also be added to the menu. Furthermore, for the truly enterprising entrepreneurs, consider adding a home delivery service that specializes in sales and free home delivery of fresh squeezed juices in larger quantities. The profit potential for a juice bar will vary based on factors such as operating overhead and total sales. However, an established and well-run juice bar can easily generate profits in excess of $50,000 per year for the owner/operator of the business, and the profits can go much higher by adding additional menu items and delivery services.

ORGANIC FARMING
★ $$$$ 🏠 ⚖

Is it time to sell the house in the city and move to the country, but you're just not too sure what you could do to earn a living? Well if that's your dilemma then perhaps organic farming is for you. In the past decade organically grown and produced food products have really taken off in popularity and have been scientifically proven to be better for our health. Of course, operating a farm that grows organic foods requires a great deal of consideration and research

prior to committing, not to mention an extremely large financial investment. However, the current demand for organically grown foods shows no sign of slowing down and will only continue to expand as the human population continues to become more concerned about maintaining a healthy and balanced diet.

WEB RESOURCE: www.organichub.com Links to organic farming associations, wholesalers, and retailers.

PIZZA BY THE SLICE
★★ $$$ ⚖ 🌐

There are a lot of advantages and benefits to opening a small pizza by the slice takeout restaurant, as opposed to a full-service sit-down pizza restaurant that provides customers with a varied menu and delivery options. These benefits include a smaller initial investment, lower monthly operating overheads, and shorter operating hours. Ideal locations for opening a pizza by the slice takeout restaurant include food courts in malls, storefronts in office districts, and kiosks in large family entertainment centers. Supplying the pizza slices on a wholesale basis to factory and school cafeterias, as well as providing a free lunchtime delivery service of pizza slices in office districts can also be used as a method for boosting sales.

COMMUNITY RESTAURANT GUIDE
★★ $$ 🏠 🕐 🌐

Starting a business that creates and publishes a monthly community restaurant guide is a very straightforward business venture to set in motion. The guide can feature information and articles about community restaurants, restaurant specials and coupons, as well as forthcoming community event information. Furthermore, the restaurant guide can be distributed throughout the community free of charge, and revenues to support the business can be gained by charging the restaurants featured in the guide an advertising fee. Additional income can also be earned by providing restaurant owners with menu printing options, as well as paper placemat advertising and printing options. Both of these additional business opportunities are also featured in this directory.

ONLINE COMMUNITY RESTAURANT DIRECTORY

★★ $$ 🏠 🕐 ✍

Like its print counterpart, an online community restaurant directory features similar information and content as the guide, but in an electronic format. The biggest advantage for restaurant owners to get on board with the program is the fact that this type of directory will give them an online presence without the cost associated with establishing their own Web site. Once again, the Web site can be developed to serve a specific community or city. Or, the site can be indexed by state and serve many communities and cities, the determining factor will be the amount of investment capital you have available to start the business. In exchange for a monthly fee, restaurant owners would receive a listing linked to a pop-up page on the site and you could even provide menu display and online food order options. This type of Web site could be established in a very basic form for a modest investment. However, the more services you can provide both clients and visitors the better, thus a substantial investment will likely be required to get the site operational and profitable.

CHOCOLATE MAKING

★★ $$ ⚖

Starting a business that creates chocolate candies and treats is a great new enterprise to initiate, and the business can easily be formed as a joint venture with an established catering service or restaurant. The purpose of forming the joint venture with an established business is to greatly reduce the amount of start-up capital required to get the business rolling. A joint venture can enable you to utilize the partner's commercial kitchen, and in some cases the existing employee and customer base. The chocolate candies and treats can be sold to specialty retailers on a wholesale basis, or directly to chocolate loving consumers via a sales kiosk or factory direct outlet. Additionally, be sure to investigate the potential for forming alliances with charity groups, schools, and organizations as the students, volunteers, or members can be enlisted to sell packaged chocolate candies with partial proceeds going back to support community charities and programs.

WEB RESOURCE: www.candyusa.org Chocolate Manufacturers Association.

PACKAGED HERBS AND SPICES

★★ $$ 🏠 🕐

Here is a great little business opportunity that can be started on a part-time basis right from a home-based location. Purchasing herbs and spices in bulk, repackaging the product into smaller quantities, and selling the herbs and spices through local retailers via point-of-purchase (POP) displays, is easily accomplished. The main objective is to ensure the packaging you create for the products are unique, as well as ensuring that the POP displays are located in highly visible areas of the retail stores that you secure distribution rights with. In all likelihood the POP displays and product will have to be consigned with retailers initially until the product is a proven seller, at which point the accounts can easily be converted to typical wholesale supply accounts. Additionally, consider stocking the POP displays with cookbooks and recipe guides as well as the packaged herbs and spices as a method to increase consumer awareness and increase business revenues and profits.

WEB RESOURCE: www.garden.org National Gardening Association.

WEDDING CAKE SALES

★★★ $ 🏠 🕐

Designing and creating one-of-a-kind wedding cakes is truly an art form. However, for the creative entrepreneurs that possess this talent, an incredible part-time business opportunity awaits by starting a business that makes and sells wedding cakes. Many wedding cakes can retail for as much as $500 each or more, and generally only cost about 20 percent of the retail value to make. Building alliances with wedding planners and caterers is the fastest way to establish the business, even though it will probably mean splitting the revenue or selling the wedding cakes on a wholesale basis. Additionally, be sure to check local requirements in terms of operating this business from home, as health board permits may be required. If the business cannot be operated from home, inquire at local restaurants to see if a commercial kitchen can be rented on an hourly basis during nonbusiness hours to make the wedding cakes. Operating this type of specialty food business can generate an income of $300 or more each week on a part-time basis, making this a business opportunity well worth further investigation.

ROADSIDE VEGETABLE STAND
★ $$

A roadside vegetable stand is a fantastic seasonal part-time business to get rolling, as the start-up costs are minimal, the profit potential is great, and the demand for fresh in-season vegetables is high. The key to success in this type of food retailing is to secure a good location to operate the vegetable stand from. Excellent locations include gas station parking lots, industrial parks, and main highways in and out of busy tourist areas. Furthermore, in addition to a highly visible roadside location, be sure and have large and colorful signs made to advertise the stand. Generally, the season for fresh vegetables starts in early June and ends in early September. You can extend your season a month or more by selling cider, apples, chrysanthemums, and pumpkins in the fall.

ONLINE ORGANIC FOOD SALES
★★ $$$

The time has never been better than now to start a business that specializes in organic food sales and home delivery, as organically grown foods have become so popular that growers are having a hard time meeting consumer demand. The first step to establishing the business is to build alliances with organic food growers to supply the inventory needed for the business. The second step is to create and distribute a catalog featuring all the organically grown food products that the business sells and delivers. Additionally, be sure to develop a Web site that will enable clients to place food orders online, as well as accepting food orders via e-mail and fax. The profit

potential for a business that sells and delivers organically grown fruits and vegetables is outstanding, as the products can be marked up by 30 percent to 40 percent. This still enables you to undercut grocery stores and retailers of organically grown foods by 10 percent or more.

WEB RESOURCE: www.organichub.com Links to organic food growers and wholesalers.

SUBMARINE SANDWICH SHOP
★★ $$$$

Submarine sandwich shops are popping up everywhere across the country, and starting your own sub shop may be just the new business opportunity that you have been searching for. The great thing about starting a sub shop is that operating this business does not require a lot of past business experience or skills, making this a business opportunity that just about any determined entrepreneur can tackle. Like any restaurant business, the key to success lies within selecting the right location for the business, providing top notch customer service, and serving good food at reasonable prices. Additional revenues can also be earned by expanding the menu to include salad and soup options, as well as a free home delivery service for food orders over a certain dollar amount.

GOURMET FRENCH FRY STAND
★★★ $$$

French fries are probably the most popular fast food product sold in North America, and starting a gourmet french fry stand may be just the new business opportunity that you have been searching for. Ideally, a french fry stand should be located in busy areas of the community such as mall food courts, beach areas, or close to schools. What separates a gourmet french fry stand from a common french fry stand are the toppings and sauces that are available. Toppings can include cheese, chili, salsa, gravy, or just about any other type of sauce that is currently available or that you want to create. Also, french fries should be fresh cut from potatoes on site to be considered the best. Furthermore, as a method to keep start-up costs to a minimum, consider purchasing secondhand restaurant and commercial kitchen equipment like french fryers and potato chippers, as often secondhand equipment in good condition can be purchased for half of the cost of new equipment.

HOT DOG CART
 ★★ $$ 🕐 ⚖️

The biggest challenge to overcome in terms of starting a hot dog vending business is to secure a vendor's permit in your local community. However, even if a vendor's permit cannot be obtained, you can still operate a hot dog cart on privately-owned property and cater to functions such as flea markets, auction sales, sporting events, and fairs. Currently new hot dog vending carts are retailing in the range of $4,000 to $8,000 each, depending on the features. However, as a method to reduce business start-up costs, consider purchasing a secondhand hot dog vending cart, as they are typically half the cost of a new one. This is a terrific business to operate on a full- or part-time basis, and providing you can secure a good location or local events to cater to, hot dog vendors regularly earn $4,000 per month and more.

WEB RESOURCE: www.classic-carts.com Manufacturers of specialty food vending carts.

CATERING SERVICE
★★★ $$$ 🏢 🕐 ⚖️

A catering service is one of the best food businesses to start. Not only is the demand for catering services at an all time high, but the catering industry as a whole has been proven to be very stable and definitely a growth industry. Additionally, one of the best aspects about starting a catering service is the fact the business can initially be operated on a part-time basis, and expanded to full-time as demand for the service increases. Securing clients for a catering service can be as easy as building alliances with wedding and event planners to refer the catering service to their clients. Also, develop a marketing package that can be presented to corporations

for consideration to cater their next business meeting, seminar, or social function. Many catering companies will specialize in one particular segment of the industry such as weddings, and this may be a good practice to embrace, at least until the business is established.

WEB RESOURCE: www.ncacater.org National Caterers Association.

COTTON CANDY
★★★ $$$ 🕐

Equipment needed to make cotton candy can be purchased secondhand for as little as $2,000, and starting a part-time business that makes and sells cotton candy is a great little business for enterprising entrepreneurs to tackle. In addition to the cotton candy making equipment, a small trailer converted into a booth for sales will also be required to get the business up and rolling. Once the trailer has been outfitted with the equipment, supplies, and advertising signs, there are numerous locations to set up at in every community. Excellent locations include flea markets, sporting events, public markets, fairs, beach locations, parks, community events, and parades. A cotton candy sales cart, trailer, or kiosk can be operated on weekends only, and still generate sales of $1,000 per day.

FRESH PASTA MAKING
★★ $$$

Does your favorite Italian restaurant make pasta fresh daily or purchase premade pastas? If the answer is the latter, then consider proposing a joint venture business opportunity to the owner of the restaurant. You make the pasta at their location, and they use the pasta for meal preparations for the business, as well as sell fresh pasta to their clients. Alternately, a pasta making and sales business could be established in a food market or farmers' market by renting a small booth, storefront, or kiosk, and additional revenues could also be generated by selling freshly made sauces and seasonings. Operating this type of food business does require pasta making experience, or at least a willingness to learn by trial and error. However, for the determined entrepreneur, business and financial success can be achieved by using sound judgment and common sense.

WEB RESOURCE: www.pastamachines.com Manufacturers of pasta making equipment.

MAPLE SYRUP SALES
★ $$ 🏭 🕐

The time has never been better than now to start a business importing and selling Canadian maple syrup. Not only is Canadian maple syrup considered to be the best in the world, but also the Canadian dollar is at an all time low against the U.S. greenback. This means 50 percent more wholesale buying power in favor of the Yankees. Once imported, the maple syrup can be sold directly to consumers via sales kiosks in malls, the Internet, farmers' markets, and even by way of mail-order sales. Aim for annual sales of $200,000, while maintaining a 100 percent markup and this unique specialty importing business will generate gross profits of $100,000.

WEB RESOURCE: www.ontariomaple.com Ontario Maple Syrup Producers Association.

CANDY STORE
★★ $$$$ 🌐

Candy sales kiosks are popping up in every mall across North America, and why not? A basic and easy to run candy sales kiosk can earn the operator a combined income and business profits of $60,000 per year or more. Starting a business that retails candy is very straightforward and the biggest challenge to overcome is selecting the right operating location for the business. Ideally, a candy shop should be in a very busy area of a community so that it can take advantage of foot traffic, as well as impulse buying by consumers. Also consider offering customers a free delivery service to expand the potential market to include customers who want to send candies to relatives in the hospital, loved ones at holiday time, and business owners seeking to reward clients or employees with their favorite box of chocolates or candies.

WEB RESOURCE: www.candynet.com National Candy Brokers Association.

BUFFET-ONLY RESTAURANT
★★ $$$$ ⚖️

One price, all-you-can-eat buffet-style restaurants have become extremely popular amongst the budget-minded dinning crowd, and starting a buffet-only restaurant is a very wise choice for a new restaurant venture. Unlike a typical restaurant, a buffet restaurant has one major benefit for the operator—shorter work hours. Typically, buffet restaurants cater to lunch and supper diners and do not open until 11:00 AM and are closed by 9:00 PM. Based on volume, a buffet restaurant can be very profitable, as often the operating overheads are much lower than similarly-sized restaurants, simply due to the fact that less employees are required to run the business. Additionally, wholesale food items can also be purchased for lower cost based on volume buying, which all add up to beefed up profits.

WEB RESOURCE: www.restaurant.org National Restaurant Association.

EXHAUST HOOD CLEANING
★ $$ 🏭 🕐

In many regions of the country, restaurants are required by health board regulations to have their kitchen exhaust hoods cleaned on a regular basis to prevent bacteria growth and potential grease fires. This fact creates more than ample opportunity for the enterprising entrepreneurs to capitalize by starting an exhaust hood cleaning service. There is specialized equipment available for cleaning restaurant exhaust hoods and filters. However, this equipment can be costly, and as a method to reduce start-up costs you can always resort to the good old "strong arm" method until the business is established and the equipment can be purchased from profits. Cleaning rates vary depending on the size, style, and access to the exhaust hood, but averaged out on an hourly basis there should be no problem maintaining $30 to $50 per hour for providing the cleaning service.

BOTTLED WATER
★★ $$$$ ⚖

Did you know that many water bottling facilities bottle water under private label agreements? While this may seem like useless trivia to most, it certainly is useful information for anyone who is seeking to start a business wholesaling or retailing bottled water, especially on a limited start-up capital basis. Fifty years from now the overnight millionaires and billionaires will not be conquering heroes of dot.com start-ups in the technology industry, but rather entrepreneurs that had the foresight to start a business in the water supply or recycling industry. The world's population now stands at more than six billion people, half of which do not currently have access to clean drinking water. As the world's population expands this disastrous situation is not going to improve. It is possible to get into the bottled water sales business now with a limited start-up investment, and grow the business from the profits that are earned until the business can be expanded to the point that water bottling, and purchasing water rights for bottling can be accomplished.

WEB RESOURCE: www.bottledwater.com Links to the bottled water industry.

HONOR SYSTEM VENDING BOXES
★★★ $$ 🏠 🕐

Look no further than starting an honor system vending box business if your goal is to be self-employed operating your own business that has the potential to generate a six-figure yearly income—not to mention the fact that the business can be set in motion with an initial investment of less than $10,000. Honesty vending boxes are simply pre-designed and colorful cardboard boxes that contain snack food items like candy bars, chips, and gum for sale on the honor system. This means there is a coin box built into the vending box that does not lock and customers are expected to pay for their purchases on the honor system. Ideal locations to place these boxes are in small- to medium-sized companies with 50 employees or less. The vending boxes can be put in lunchrooms or reception areas, and are replenished with new stock on a weekly basis. An honor system box vending business is a very wise choice for entrepreneurs seeking to get into the vending industry on a limited investment basis. It is inexpensive to construct or purchase the boxes used in the business as opposed to purchasing vending machines. There are also more locations that the vending boxes can be located and that traditional vending machines cannot. Snack products are routinely marked up by 100 percent or more for retail sales so the profit potential is outstanding.

SPECIALTY SAUCES
★ $$$ 🏠 🕐 ⚖

Have you been selected as the guardian of age-old family recipes such as barbeque sauces, salsa, and salad dressings? If so, perhaps you should consider sharing the family treasures with others and start a business that specializes in making and marketing specialty sauces. Once prepared, the sauces can be sold in bulk to restaurants, or packaged into smaller quantities and sold to grocery stores and specialty food retailers on a wholesale basis. The main objective in this type of food processing business is very straightforward. The sauces must taste good, and the packaging must be unique to gain consumer's interest in trying the product. Additionally, be sure to enlist the services of a product demonstration service to give away free samples of the sauces in the stores that will be retailing the products as a method of promotion.

SOUP AND SALAD RESTAURANT
★★ $$$$ ⚖

Light and healthy lunches are in, and starting a soup and salad restaurant can potentially put you on the road to financial freedom. Ideally, a small restaurant that serves soups and salads will be located in an office district or office building within a community to take advantage of the lunch crowd. Alternately the restaurant can be located within a mall to take advantage of shoppers seeking a quick meal before going home. If the restaurant is located within an office district, the business will also be able to provide a lunchtime soup and salad delivery service, and orders can come in by way of fax or e-mail to the restaurant. There are no secrets to success in terms of operating a soup and salad restaurant, select a good location, serve good food at reasonable prices, and provide customers with top-notch service, and the business will flourish.

WEB RESOURCE: www.smallbizbooks.com Business-specific start-up guides and books.

FACTORY CAFETERIA
★ $$$ ⚖

Most cafeterias located within factories, institutions, and schools are operated under a lease by an outside contractor, and if you are seeking to start a low-investment restaurant venture, then this type of business opportunity may be just what you have been looking for. Securing a lease for a factory or school cafeteria is generally obtained by successfully tendering the service. Typically, tenders for cafeteria services are put up for bidding every couple of years, and the existing operators do not always successfully tender for the services. Be sure to start the research into the business, and more specifically into the particular cafeteria you wish to operate, early.

DOUGHNUT SHOP AND BULK SALES
★★ $$$$ ⚖ 🌐

Did you know that more than one billion doughnuts are sold each year in the United States? That is more than ample reason to consider a doughnut shop as a new business venture. The first approach is to open a traditional sit-down style doughnut shop that serves customers doughnuts, coffee, and muffins. The second approach is to establish a commercial doughnut bakery that is not open to the public, but specializes in making doughnuts for wholesale to grocery stores, restaurants, school cafeterias, and catering companies. Of course, the enterprising entrepreneur can also combine both operating formats and run a doughnut shop as well as a doughnut wholesale bakery business. The industry is very competitive, so

be sure to practice good research and planning skills prior to establishing the business. Profit potential range is $40,000+ per year.

ICE CREAM STAND
★★ $$ 🕐 ⚖

Like a gourmet french fry stand, an ice cream stand is also an excellent choice for a new business enterprise. You can get started for less than a $10,000 investment and run the business on a part-time or seasonal basis. Good operating locations for an ice cream stand include mall food courts, beach areas, or a small storefront on a main street. Additionally, an ice cream stand can also be operated on a mobile basis by converting an enclosed trailer or delivery van into an ice cream stand. A mobile ice cream stand has many benefits as opposed to a fixed location due to the fact that you can transport your business to areas where demand is greatest for the product. The profit potential is outstanding, and it is not uncommon for an established ice cream stand to generate profits in excess of $50,000 in a three or four month season.

WEB RESOURCE: www.nicyra.org National Ice Cream and Yogurt Retailers Association.

PREPACKAGED VEGETARIAN FOODS
★★★ $$$ ⚖

Calling all vegetarians. Do you find it difficult to find prepackaged meals at your local grocery store that can be prepared quickly and conveniently, and of course that do not have meat or meat by-products in the ingredients? If so, perhaps you should consider starting a business that makes and packages vegetarian meals that can be sold on a wholesale basis to grocery stores and specialty food retailers. If this sounds appealing as a business opportunity, that's because it is. There are an estimated 20 million vegetarians in the United States, and this number continues to grow on a yearly basis as more and more people are starting to understand the benefits of a vegetarian diet. The business will require careful planning and research to establish, but with that said, prepackaged vegetarian foods are a growth segment of the food industry providing tremendous upside potential for long-term business success and profits.

WEB RESOURCE: www.nfpa-food.org National Food Processors Association.

VEGETARIAN RESTAURANT
★★★ $$$$ ⚖ 🌐

There are an estimated 20 million American adults who are vegetarians, and this fact creates an excellent opportunity for the budding restaurateur to capitalize by starting a vegetarian restaurant. Like any restaurant business, conducting a market survey in the area where the restaurant is to be established will indicate consumer demand, and this step is especially important prior to opening a vegetarian restaurant due to the specialized nature of the business. In addition to serving vegetarian meals, many vegetarian restaurants also sell food products as well as vegetarian cookbooks, and this can be a terrific way to increase business revenues and profits. Furthermore, also seek opportunities for a lunch delivery service to offices and homes, as this can also be a way to bolster sales. As a rule of thumb most restaurants operate on a 40–40–20 percent basis, meaning 40 percent of the revenue covers food and consumable costs, 40 percent of revenues covers operating and overhead costs, and 20 percent of revenue is left as the pretax gross profit.

CATERING TRUCK
★★ $$$$ 🕐 ⚖

Secondhand catering trucks in good condition can be purchased for as little as $10,000, and this can be the first step taken to establishing a catering truck route. A catering truck route is a great business to set in motion. Not only are the hours of operation generally limited to 6:00 AM to 3:00 PM, but also the business can also be started for less than $15,000 and can easily generate a combined income and profit earnings of $50,000 per year or more. Additionally, food products can be purchased from restaurants, catering services, and wholesalers and marked up by as much as 150 percent for retail sales. Ideal stopping points for a catering truck route

include construction sites, factories, parks, beaches, and sporting events.

CHUCK WAGON
★★ $$$+ 🕐 ⚖

Purchasing an enclosed trailer or delivery step van that can be converted into a chuck wagon is the first step toward starting your own mobile restaurant business. Chuck wagons or mobile food concessions are everywhere, and initiating this type of business venture is easy. As mentioned, you can purchase an enclosed trailer or step van and convert it into a food concession on wheels by equipping it with commercial restaurant equipment such as fryers and grills. Or, you can purchase a mobile concession truck that has been professionally designed and constructed. Typical chuck wagon menus include french fries, hamburgers, and hot dogs. One of the best aspects about starting this business is it offers flexibility in terms of operating hours and location. Good locations include outdoor auction sales, parades, beaches, fairs, parks, sporting events, or any other busy community event. You will need to acquire a vendor's permit and a health board certificate to operate. However, providing the mobile concession stand meets health board codes, these permits are very easy to get. The profit potential is outstanding as it is not uncommon for mobile food concessions to generate sales of $1,000 per day or more in the right location.

TAKE-OUT CHICKEN AND WINGS
★★ $$$$ ⚖ 🌐

Starting a take-out chicken and wings restaurant is a very easy business venture to set in motion. This type of restaurant requires little experience to operate, and the kitchen equipment needed can be purchased secondhand in just about every community across the country. Like many restaurants, a take-out chicken and wings restaurant can be established in a fixed location such as a storefront or kiosk in a mall food court. The business can also be operated on a mobile basis from an enclosed trailer or van that has been converted into a mobile restaurant. Assuming the restaurant is operating from a fixed location, be sure to provide customers with a free delivery service, as this can potentially increase the size of your market to include customers that may otherwise not frequent the restaurant. Additionally, operating the restaurant in a take-out format will also help to reduce the amount of space required as well as reduce the amount of start-up capital required to get the restaurant rolling.

DESSERT SHOP
★★ $$$$ ⚖ 🌐

Dessert-only restaurants have become very popular in the past decade, both as a new business venture and for consumers seeking to satisfy their sweet tooth. The business concept is very straightforward. Simply open a small sit-down restaurant that offers customers varied menu options including cakes, cookies, tarts, pies, ice cream, and just about any other dessert or treat that you can think of, or create. Ideally, the location selected to establish a dessert shop should be in an area that has a large volume of people walking by, including theater districts, malls, and office and financial districts, as many customers will be attracted by impulse buying urges. Additionally, very popular items on the menu can also be made and packaged under the name of the business and sold on a wholesale basis to grocery stores and specialty food retailers throughout the local community.

FROZEN YOGURT SHOP
★★ $$$ ⚖

Frozen yogurt has been a favorite treat of consumers for years, and establishing a frozen yogurt shop as a new business venture is not only proven, but also very stable. Furthermore, for the entrepreneur seeking to work hard for half of the year, while traveling the other half of the year, opening a frozen yogurt shop is a very wise choice. The business can be established in a beach or busy tourist area and a full-time income can easily be earned operating the business on a seasonal basis only. In addition to frozen yogurt, additional treats such as homemade fudge and ice cream can also be included in the menu to appeal to a wider range of potential customers, and of course to also increase sales and profits.

WEB RESOURCE: www.nicyra.org National Ice Cream and Yogurt Retailers Association.

COOKIE SALES
★★ $$$

Do your family and friends tell you that you bake the best cookies in town? If so, putting your cookie baking talents to work for you has the potential to make you rich. Mass producing specialty or gourmet cookies is a very easy business to put into action. Simply rent or secure commercial kitchen space, perfect the cookie baking process, design interesting packaging for the cookies, and you're in business and ready to start profiting. Specialty cookies can be sold to food retailers on a wholesale basis, or directly to the public via a cookie sales kiosk located in a mall or public market. Also, for the truly enterprising entrepreneur, vending machines can be purchased and installed in high-traffic areas throughout the community to sell the cookies. Once established, the profit potential could prove to be outstanding for the creative and clever cookie maker.

BAKERY
★★ $$$$ ⚖

A bakery can be established as a retail business from a storefront location selling baked goods to consumers, or a bakery can be established as a wholesale business selling baked goods to food retailers and institutions. Additionally, many bakeries will operate both as a retail and wholesale business to increase the size of their potential market as well as revenues and profits. Establishing a bakery is a very straightforward process with one exception, the best bakers possess bakers trade papers, so be prepared to hire a qualified baker, or take the time necessary to become a qualified baker. The profit potential is good for a bakery, especially if the business focuses on both retail and wholesales baked goods sales.

WEB RESOURCE: www.americanbakers.org American Bakers Association.

PEANUT AND NUT SALES

★ $$

You can start making money by purchasing peanuts and other assorted nuts in bulk and repackage the nuts into smaller sizes and sell the packaged nuts to retailers on a wholesale basis. Or alternately, the nuts can be placed into retail stores and sold on a consignment and revenue share basis. Additionally, do not overlook the possibility of selling peanuts from vending machines that can be installed at locations like malls, pubs, and sports complexes. The vending machines will initially cost a few thousand dollars to purchase. However, the return on investment is quick providing the machines are installed in busy areas.

ONLINE COOKING RECIPES

★ $$

Cooking recipes, classes, products, and ingredients can all be provided and sold via your own cooking Web site. This type of cyberventure is sure to be popular, as cooking certainly has mass appeal. To get started first determine the focus and format of the site. There are many choices. The site can provide cooking recipes that can be downloaded for free and supported by selling advertising space and banners. Or you can opt to sell recipes and cooking-related products via the site. The options are limitless.

WEB RESOURCE: www.entrepreneur.com Create a business Web site with MySite professional Web site builder.

HERB GARDENING

★ $

A small plot of land in your backyard can easily be converted into a cash-producing herb garden. Dill, parsley, and chives are just a few of the many herbs that can be grown at home for profit. Get started by spending time at your local library and on the Internet to learn as much as you can about herbs and herb gardening. The rest is very simple. Plant your garden, grow your herbs, design some herb packages, and set out to establish accounts with local merchants to sell your goods. Like any new business venture there will be a learning curve to climb. However, the rewards of a few extra thousand dollars each year can justify the effort.

WEB RESOURCE: www.smallbizbooks.com Business specific start-up guides and books.

RESTAURANT WASHROOM CLEANING SERVICE

★★★ $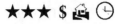

Next to bad food the number one reason people will not return to a restaurant is dirty washrooms. This fact alone can be used as your greatest sales and marketing tool for convincing restaurant owners and managers that they need your washroom sanitation services. Offer the service for fee for the first time as it only takes about 20 minutes to sanitize the average washroom. Managers and owners (not to mention patrons) will be so impressed with the excellent service and positive effects that they will contract with you to return weekly to continue the washroom sanitation program. Income potential once established is $15 to $25 per hour.

GROCERY DELIVERY SERVICE

★★ $

You have a few options available in terms of starting a grocery delivery service. The first is to simply contract with local grocery stores to deliver customer orders for a fee. The grocery store would bill the customer, market the service, and manage the deliveries. You simply deliver the groceries. The second and more lucrative option is to establish a buying account with a grocery wholesaler and resell groceries to your customers at a profit. This method means you will have to create a catalog of the grocery items you stock as well as market the service. However, once again the potential to generate more profit is greatly increased.

Grocery delivery services are often very profitable business ventures, as the convenience of home delivery makes getting customers very easy.

ONLINE GROCERY STORE

★ $$$$

Here is a high-tech option for starting a grocery delivery service. Develop a Web site that features grocery items for sale. To start, offer only the most popular grocery items like milk and bread and as the business expands so can your product line. Contract the delivery aspect of the service to people in your local community seeking to earn a part-time income. The operating format for the site would be very basic and easy to establish. Customers would simply log onto the site, select the items they wished to purchase, enter payment and shipping information, and wait for their groceries. It's that easy. Once established, this type of cyberventure could be franchised and operated in every community and city across North America.

SEAFOOD SALES

★★ $$$ 🏠 🕐 ⚖️

Starting a business that specializes in seafood sales and home delivery is a fantastic new business venture to set in motion. Both frozen and fresh seafood products such as fish, lobster, and oysters can be purchased on a wholesale basis, and resold at a profit to consumers simply by purchasing a delivery vehicle with a refrigeration or freezer unit. Securing customers for the business can be as easy as designing and distributing a menu or marketing brochure that features a description of the various seafood products that are available. Generally, these types of specialty food sale businesses can really flourish. Fresh high-quality seafood is not always readily available in every community, and the convenience of home delivery can be used as a very powerful marketing tool. Potential profit range is $30,000+ per year.

WEB RESOURCE: www.nfi.org National Fisheries Institute Inc. Links to seafood producers.

ONLINE SEAFOOD SALES

★★ $$$$ 🏠 🐭

Take local seafood sales and delivery online and open your business to consumers from around the world. This cyberenterprise is very straightforward. Develop a Web site that features seafood of all sorts for sale. Customers would simply select the seafood they wanted to purchase, enter in payment and shipping information, and wait for delivery. Commercial fishermen in virtually every country can supply the seafood featured on the site. They catch it, you sell it, and they ship it to your customers. The concept is basic but will require a great amount of planning and legwork to be completed prior to activating the business.

WEB RESOURCE: www.nfi.org National Fisheries Institute Inc. Links to seafood producers.

PERSONAL CHEF SERVICE

★★★ $ 🏠 🕐 🌐

Take your pots and pans, cooking skills, and love of food mobile and hit the road as a personal chef for hire. Prepare gourmet meals for people hosting house parties, small special occasions such as birthdays or anniversaries, and for corporate luncheons; basically anywhere there is a kitchen on site that you can utilize for your chef service. Personal chefs are becoming a very popular alternative for people that do not have the budget for a full-scale catered event or for people that are hosting small events that do not require complete catering services. The advantages for starting this type of unique service are apparent: low overhead, low start-up costs, and part-time operating hours. Promote the service by joining business networking clubs and community social clubs to spread the news about your personal chef service. This is the type of business that can easily be supported by word-of-mouth referrals and repeat business once established, leading to a full-time profitable business venture. Typically chef rates are quoted on each job and vary on factors such as the supply of food and the type of menu requested. However, on average personal chefs are generally earnings in the range of $35 to $50 per hour.

INTERNET CAFÉ
★★ $$$$ ⚖ 🌐

In 1994 there were a mere 30 Internet or cyber-cafés in the United States and by the year 2000 the number of Internet café's had swelled to more than 3,000 and still continues to grow. Why? Simply because there is strong consumer demand, and Internet café's can be an extremely profitable business venture. In addition to the usual fare of coffee, snacks, and Web surfing, other services to lure customers from the competition can be employed. These services can include a scanner service, digital printing, and even how to surf the Net instructional classes after normal business hours. The cost to open an Internet café is substantial. However, with a basic cup of coffee and bagel now retailing for $5 or more, the return on investment can be swift and this type of unique retail food business is an ideal candidate to be expanded on a franchise basis.

WEB RESOURCE: www.internetcafeguide.com Information about how to start and operate an Internet café.

PRODUCE SHOP
★★ $$$$

Specialty retailing is the buzzword for the new millennium and nowhere is this more apparent than in food retailing. The bland produce shops of days gone by with their less-than-appealing display methods, boring interiors, and limited product selections are quickly being replaced by what is now called "Produce Boutiques." A sheep in wolf's clothing perhaps, but today's new age produce shops are specifically catering to consumers that have in large become more health wise and want a relaxing shopping experience. Many produce shops now offer customer services such as a juice bar, the ability to sample products before they buy, and an area to sit down and relax with your favorite fruit or vegetable and read the paper. This is the type of retailing business that must be located in a densely populated urban center to thrive. Less cars and more walk-by foot traffic are key location considerations. Furthermore, as a method to increase revenues and profits, be sure to establish supply accounts with restaurants and catering companies that are seeking the best produce available to prepare for their valued customers.

WEB RESOURCE: www.pma.com Produce Marketing Association.

DELI
★★ $$$$ ⚖

Starting and operating a deli has many advantages over a traditional restaurant including lower start-up costs, shorter operating hours, and lower operating overheads. The best delis not only sell varied meats, cheeses, and other exotic gourmet foods but also provide customers with a lunch delivery service, a few seats and tables for the sit-down lunch crowd, and take-out catering options including cold meat and cheese trays. Noteworthy is the fact that many deli proprietors choose a theme for their business such as a New York-style deli, a British deli, or a German deli. Ideal operating locations for delis are generally found in office districts, industrial malls, and mall food courts. The key to success in this type of competitive food business is to provide customers with excellent quality products, exceptional service, and varied products and menu that will appeal to a large segment of the population.

WEB RESOURCE: www.restaurantequipment.net Directory service with thousands of listings for new and used restaurant equipment and supplies for sale.

TEXAS BARBEQUE
★★ $$ 🏠 🕐

Regardless of where you live, a Texas-style barbeque is a surefire hungry crowd pleaser and a great business start-up for the entrepreneur that is looking for a potentially profitable part-time enterprise. Hamburgers, steak on a bun, ribs, and hot dogs are just a few of the menu items that can be included. You can operate this type of business from a large tent, and excellent events to cater to include sports events, corporate functions, parades, auction sales, fairs, and social events such as family reunions. This type of food service business will need licensing in most areas by the health board, but providing you meet and maintain health board requirements, securing this type of license is easy. In addition to a large tent, you will also need a commercial barbeque that operates on propane, or even seasoned wood for the true barbeque enthusiast, as well as other basic equipment such as coolers. You can purchase an enclosed trailer or van to transport the equipment to the event you are catering. This is a great part-time business enterprise for anyone with cooking experience to undertake and operate just a few hours each weekend. This can generate profits of $500 or more at a busy event as these types of food products are typically marked-up by 400 percent or more for retail sale. Market the business by building alliances with business associations, wedding and event planners, and networking clubs. It will not take long to establish a contact and referral base providing the food and service you provide is excellent.

WEB RESOURCE: www.bbqsearch.com Directory service listing information about barbeque food service, recipes, and links to equipment manufacturers and product providers.

GOURMET COFFEE KIOSK
★★ $$$$ 🌍

Millions of cups of coffee are consumed daily in the United States and thousands of entrepreneurs are capitalizing financially because of it, and so can you by opening a gourmet coffee kiosk. Rent a kiosk in a mall or market location and provide customers with the best coffee and tea selections available from around the world. You can purchase or lease coffee grinding and packaging equipment and offer free samples to coffee and tea enthusiasts as a method to get them acquainted with your products. Unlike a coffee shop that serves brewed coffees and teas along with pastries and snack items, your gourmet coffee kiosk can specialize in selling fresh packaged coffee and tea products to consumers. Purchase the specialty coffees in bulk in bean form, grind it on site, and sell it repackaged in smaller quantities. Additionally, be sure to develop your own brand of private label coffee and teas. This

can be a method of increasing revenues by establishing wholesale accounts with grocery stores and specialty food retailers to stock and sell your brand name products.

WEB RESOURCE: www.kaldi.com Wholesale distributors of specialty coffee equipment and supplies.

ROMANTIC CATERING
★★★ $$ 🏠 🕐 🌍

Who needs cupid when they can hire your romantic catering service and surprise that someone special in their lives with a unique and unforgettable romantic dinner for two. Romantic catering is just that. You plan and play host to a memorable dining experience for clients. The evening could start with a romantic ride in a horse-drawn carriage through a park, complete with wine, roses, and mood-setting music. The ride could end on a secluded beach under the stars where the client would dine on lobster and caviar picnic-style. Of course, your service would provide the gourmet meal, make all the arrangements, supply the transportation, and even serve the meal on the finest china while dressed in exquisite formalwear. Best of all, you do not need to be a chef, have the horse-drawn carriage, or even have the ability to serve the meal. All of these can be contracted to qualified people who posses these abilities and equipment. What is required, however, is the ability to market the service and have a creative imagination to plan the best possible romantic dinner adventures available. This type of specialty business will also enable you to be creative in how you go about promoting the service. Perhaps a deal can be struck with the local newspaper or entertainment magazine. You provide a romantic dinner full of surprises for a reporter, editor, or publisher and their guest in exchange for a write-up about your romantic catering service to be featured in their publication. This is the type of business that can enjoy a great amount of repeat business and word-of-mouth referrals.

KEY

RATINGS	★
START-UP COST	$
HOMEBASED BUSINESS	
PART-TIME	
LEGAL ISSUES	
FRANCHISE OR LICENSE POTENTIAL	
ONLINE	

24

FURNITURE
Businesses You Can Start

REFURBISHING ANTIQUE APPLIANCES
★★★ $$$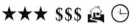

The profits that can be made by turning discarded and abandoned antique appliances into refurbished and functional appliances for today's custom designed residential kitchens are enormous. One of the best aspects of this business opportunity is that you do not even have to know how to repair or refurbish the appliances yourself, as you can hire skilled employees for this part of the business. The market for refurbished antique appliances is absolutely gigantic. Some appliances sell for as much as $5,000 each to interior decorators and homeowners seeking the ultimate designer touch. When you consider many of these same antique appliances can be found in less than perfect condition at garage sales, junkyards, and auction sales for less than $100, that's a very good return on investment; even if it costs a thousand dollars or more to restore the appliance. Once refurbished,

antique appliances can be sold directly to consumers and design professionals via a display booth at home and garden shows, advertisements in home improvement and antique trade publications, and of course through Internet malls and Web auction services.

FURNITURE DELIVERY AND ASSEMBLY
★★ $$

Starting a furniture delivery and assembly service is the perfect new venture for the handyperson with a truck and basic tools to get rolling. The business can be managed from a homebased office and the fixed operating overheads are minimal. Get started by contacting local furniture and office supply stores in your community to see if they are currently providing their customers with a delivery and assembly option. If not, strike a deal to provide their customers with the service and you're in business. Moving companies are also a good source of work, as we all know there is a lot of furniture assembly to be done after a move. Outside of a suitable delivery vehicle and moving carts, the only other requirement is liability insurance.

THEME TOY BOXES

 ★★ $ 🏠 🕐

Manufacturing theme toy boxes is a wonderful homebased business venture, and best of all the business can be kicked into high gear for less than a $1,000 initial investment. The key to successfully manufacturing and selling the toy boxes is to ensure that the designs are original, the material used in the construction of the toy boxes is unique, and the finished product is colorful and depicts an elaborate children's theme such as horses, cowboys, or dinosaurs. The toy boxes can be sold to retailers on a wholesale basis or directly to consumers via the Internet, trade shows, a mall sales kiosk, or mail order. As an additional source of revenue and as a marketing tool also consider making wooden toys and including one wooden toy with each toy box as a surprise bonus gift.

WEB RESOURCE: www.scrollsaw.com Distributor of construction plans for toy boxes.

FURNITURE STEAM CLEANING

★★ $$ 🏠 🕐 🌍

Are you searching for a business opportunity that can be started for peanuts, operated on a full- or part-time basis, and has the potential to earn $30 per hour or more? If so, perhaps you should consider starting a furniture steam cleaning service. A furniture steam cleaning service is very easy to get started, as the equipment needed for furniture steam cleaning is available in almost every community, and the business requires little experience or special skills. One of the best aspects of starting and operating this type of business is the fact that it can be operated on a part-time basis and expanded to a full-time business from the profits earned. Additionally, operating the business from home will enable you to keep monthly overheads to a minimum. This can be an advantage for under-cutting steam-cleaning rates of the larger established

services. As a quick start marketing promotion, print and distribute two-for-one furniture steam cleaning coupons.

WEB RESOURCE: www.theblubook.com Directory service listing manufacturers and distributors of steam cleaning equipment and supplies.

ANTIQUE FURNITURE SALES

Starting a business that buys antique furniture and resells it for a profit is a terrific new venture to set in motion. The following information describes three various methods for starting and operating an antique furniture sales business.

Homebased

 ★★ $$ 🏠 🕐

The first option for starting an antique furniture sales business is to establish and operate the business from a homebased location. This is an excellent way for entrepreneurs with limited investment capital to get into antique sales, then later expand the business from the profits earned. If this approach is taken, be sure to utilize any low-cost advertising mediums available in the local community for marketing the antique furniture, such as free penny-saver classified ads.

Additionally, spend time scouring flea markets and garage sales to locate antique furniture to resell. Providing you have the skills and equipment necessary, you can even offer customers antique furniture restoration service.

Online

 ★★ $$$ 🏠 🕐 🖱

Once again, there are two options for retailing antique furniture via the Internet. The first option is to purchase the items listed for sale on the Web site yourself. And the second option is to operate the Web site as a posting service for individuals and antique dealers to list their antique items for sale. If you choose to promote and operate the Web site as an antique furniture directory, you have two methods for earning income. The first is to charge customers a listing or posting fee to feature their antique furniture for sale on the site. The second option is to retain a percentage of the revenues that are generated through furniture sales.

Retail Storefront
★★ $$$$

The third and most capital-intensive option for starting an antique furniture sales business is to open a retail storefront. This type of specialty retailing has the potential to generate very large profits for the owner-operator of the business. However, careful planning and research are required prior to opening the store. Key to the success of the business will be the location selected for the store. Customer parking, street visibility, size, and consumer demographics all must be carefully considered when selecting the location. In the spirit of being unique, consider a joint venture—perhaps with a store that retails new furniture or appliances. Joint ventures in retailing have many benefits including shared operating overhead costs, joint cost-saving advertising and promotion campaigns, and the ability to draw from each other's customer base.

WEB RESOURCE: www.acda.org Antique and Collectibles Dealers Association.

SLATE TABLES
★★ $$$ 🏠 🕐

Slate and natural stone tables are becoming extremely popular, both as functional designer furnishings for residential homes and as bold furnishing statements for professional offices. This forms a tremendous opportunity for the enterprising entrepreneur with creative design abilities to capitalize by starting a business that designs, manufactures, and markets slate and natural stone coffee tables, end tables, desks, and boardroom tables. The main requirements for starting and operating this highly specialized furniture manufacturing business includes an ability to work in stone mediums, heavy duty equipment for manufacturing and transporting the finished products, clever marketing skills, and an industrial location for manufacturing.

WEB RESOURCE: www.afma.org American Furniture Manufacturers Association.

ANTIQUE SIDEBOARD VANITIES
★★★★ $$+ 🏠 🕐

Antique sideboard cabinets make fantastic washroom sink vanities, especially when used in heritage and Victorian homes. Converting antique sideboard cabinets into washroom vanities is an excellent and potentially very profitable new enterprise to set in motion. The main requirements for successfully establishing and operating this type of unique business opportunity include:

- A well-equipped workshop.
- Carpentry and construction skills and experience.
- Excellent marketing and promotion skills.

Patience will be required, as obtaining the antique sideboards to be used for bathroom vanities could mean spending a fair amount of time scouring garage sales, flea markets, and auction sales. Potential customers or buyers can include custom homebuilders, interior designers and decorators, and contracting and renovation companies. Of course the vanities can also be marketed directly to homeowners by way of home and garden trade shows, print advertising, and the Internet. To minimize start-up costs to get the business rolling as well as the skills required to operate the business, consider subcontracting out the installation and transportation aspects of the business to local qualified plumbers and transportation firms.

START-UP COSTS: The following example can be used as a guideline to establish the investment needed for starting a business that builds and sells sideboard vanities.

	Low	High
Business setup, legal, banking, etc.	$500	$1,500
Woodworking equipment and tools	$2,000	$5,000
Initial antique sideboard and parts inventory	$2,000	$5,000
Initial advertising and marketing budget	$1,000	$2,000
Office equipment and supplies	$1,000	$2,500
Working capital	$1,000	$2,000
Total start-up costs	$7,500	$18,000

PROFIT POTENTIAL: The profit potential associated with operating this business is outstanding, as refinished antique sideboard vanities are currently selling for as much as $3,000 each installed. The cost can be as little as $1,000 to assemble and install. Assuming yearly sales of $150,000 can be achieved, then this very straightforward and unique homebased business opportunity can return the owner-operator as much as $100,000 in pretax income. Once established, the business could even begin to manufacture replicas of the original antique sideboards and establish accounts with national home improvement centers to purchase the sideboard vanity replicas on a wholesale basis.

CUSTOM FURNITURE COVERS
★★ $$ 🏠 🕐

Calling all seamstresses and homemakers with access to a sewing machine, the time is now to put your sewing skills to work and start to earn a living from creating custom fabric furniture covers. There are many patterns available at fabric shops for creating standard-size furniture slips or covers, or the furniture covers can be custom made on a made-to-order basis. Successfully marketing the business can be accomplished in many ways including the following:

- Building alliances and joint ventures with interior decorators for referrals to your business.
- Selling the furniture covers and taking orders for custom-made furniture covers at craft, and home and garden trade shows.
- Advertising for business in traditional print media and on the Internet.
- Working on a subcontract basis for an established furniture upholstery service or retailer of fine home furnishings.

ANTIQUE FURNITURE REFINISHING
★★ $$ 🏠 🕐

Calling all handypeople with a homebased workshop; the time has never been better than now to start an antique furniture refinishing and repair business, as consumer demand has skyrocketed for antiques in a good state of repair. Once again, an antique furniture refinishing business can easily be operated right from a homebased workshop. Finding customers for the service can be as easy as attending antique auctions and sales and handing out business cards to people who have just purchased an antique piece of furniture that requires repairs or refinishing. Additionally, the service can be marketed by establishing alliances with antique retailers who can either use your service or act as a referral for your service to their customers. Purchasing antiques in poor condition yourself, refinishing, and selling them for a profit can also generate additional income.

WEB RESOURCE: Association of Restorers, information and links into the furniture restoration industry.

SPECIALTY RUG SALES
★★ $$$ 🏠 🕐

Here are two options for starting a business that retails Oriental, Indian, and Persian rugs and carpets. The first option is to locate and secure a foreign supplier for the carpets and negotiate an exclusive sales and distribution contract to represent their products in the United States. The second option is to purchase secondhand high-quality carpets and resell them for a profit. The second option is substantially less capital intensive to start and operate. However, the profit potential for the business is also somewhat limited to the availability of a plentiful product source. Regardless of the way the business is approached and established, the fact remains, handmade Eastern rugs and carpets are in very high demand by consumers and professional decorators, and often one single carpet can retail for as much as $10,000. This opportunity definitely warrants further investigation as the potential for huge profits awaits the enterprising entrepreneur who successfully establishes this business.

WEB RESOURCE: www.orrainc.com Oriental Rug Retailers of America.

CEDAR BLANKET BOXES
★ $$ 🏠 🕐

Manufacturing and selling custom-built cedar blanket boxes is not only a straightforward business venture to initiate, it also has the potential to generate a comfortable income for the owner-operator of the business. There are many design plans available for constructing beautiful cedar blanket boxes, making them a very easy piece of furniture to build. Of course, the more experienced woodworker's original designs can also be manufactured and sold. Once completed, the cedar blanket boxes can be sold to specialty retailers on a wholesale basis, or directly to consumers via craft shows, trade shows, and sales kiosks. Consider incorporating recycled wood into the construction of the blanket boxes, as this can be used as a powerful marketing tool.

ART HEADBOARDS

Headboards for beds featuring elaborate art or photographs are beginning to pop up in specialty retail stores across the United States, as well as being featured increasingly in interior decorating magazines and publications. This fact creates a terrific opportunity for the enterprising entrepreneur to capitalize on this new furniture fashion trend by starting a business that designs, manufactures, and sells art headboards for beds. The headboards can feature original art paintings or enlarged photographs that are adhered to the headboard. The art headboards can be sold on a wholesale basis to furniture and decorating retailers or directly to consumers and decorating professionals. Currently, art headboards are retailing for $250 for simple designs and paintings and can retail for as much as $1,000 for more elaborate pieces.

AQUARIUM COFFEE TABLES

Are you searching for a truly unique furniture-related business opportunity? If so, they do not come more unique than starting a business that designs, manufactures, and sells aquarium coffee tables. Aquarium coffee tables are simply a fish aquarium base with a clear glass table placed on top of the aquarium. This type of coffee table makes a welcome

addition and conversation piece for any home or office, and has become very popular in the past few years. The tables can be manufactured in standard sizes, or on a custom, made-to-order basis. Marketing the aquarium coffee tables is also very straightforward. The tables can be sold to retailers on a wholesale basis, directly to professionals in the interior decorating industry, or directly to consumers via a sales kiosk, home and garden trade show, or on the Internet.

MAGAZINE RACK MANUFACTURING

Starting a part-time homebased business that designs, manufactures, and markets magazine racks is not only an easy business to get rolling, it can also be set in motion for less than a $1,000 initial investment. The key requirements in order to make this business successful are to have a workshop and tools available, as well as basic woodworking and construction experience. Once the magazine racks are completed, they can be sold to retailers on a wholesale basis or directly to consumers via craft and trade shows. Be sure that the designs and construction materials utilized in the magazine racks are unique. Consider using recycled materials, as not only will this save money on material costs, but it can also be used as a terrific environmentally-friendly marketing tool.

PLANT STANDS
★ $ 🏠 ⏲

Manufacturing and selling plant stands is not only an economical business undertaking to initiate, it is also a business enterprise that can be easily operated from a homebased workshop, with the potential to generate a sensational part-time income. The key to succeeding in a part-time business that manufactures and markets plant stands for indoor and outdoor use, is to ensure that the stands are of an unconventional design and that the construction material used to build the stands is also interesting. Once completed, the plant stands can be sold to specialty retailers and garden centers on a wholesale basis or directly to consumers via craft and trade shows sales kiosk, and even the on Internet.

HOME DECORATING GUIDE
★★★ $$$ 🏠 🕐 🌐

In spite of its popularity, we have not turned our world completely over to the Internet. Good old print publishing is here to stay, at least for the foreseeable future. A publishing business that creates and distributes semiannual home decorating guides can still earn excellent profits. The business concept is very straightforward. Simply design a guide featuring information, articles, and tips on home decorating and furnishing ideas. The guide can be printed and distributed free of charge throughout the local community it serves twice a year, for example. Revenues for the business would be gained by selling advertising space in the guide to local community businesses, such as furniture retailers, home improvement companies, and interior decorators. As a method of promoting the guide and business on a year-round basis, consider forming a joint venture with a local or community newspaper. In exchange for a weekly home decorating tips column, the paper could promote and print the semiannual home decorating guides. Joint ventures are a fantastic way to potentially increase the size of your market, while decreasing start-up and monthly operating costs for the business. Seek and ask; the worst and most definite answer you will ever get is "no." And with careful planning and good presentation skills, a "no" can become a "yes" very easily.

JUNKYARD FURNITURE CREATIONS
★ $$ 🏠 🕐

If you are looking for a really unique homebased business that has minimal competition and potential to generate a six-figure income, then look no further. Starting a business that manufactures and sells junkyard furniture is a very interesting venture. The key to its success is to create funky, yet functional furniture from discarded items typically found at a wrecking yard or junkyard. The most popular junkyard furniture items are generally couches and chairs that

have been partially assembled from antique auto parts, such as a couch fashioned out of a '57 Chevy front end. Starting this type of business does have its prerequisites—creative and artistic ability, a well-equipped workshop, and design and construction skills. However, for the innovative entrepreneur who possesses these abilities, a fun, interesting, and potentially profitable business venture is waiting.

SHOWROOM PROPS
★★ $$ 🏠 🕐

Many retailers use props for store displays as opposed to the real product. Using props enables the retailer to keep costs down when establishing or updating a showroom, as well as reduce financial loss in the event of damage or theft of the showroom displays. There are two options in terms of initiating a business that sells showroom props to retailers. The first option is to design and manufacture the props, and the second option is to purchase the props in bulk on a wholesale basis from established manufacturers and add a profit percentage for resale. While both options are viable, the second option is far less costly to start and operate. However, the profit potential is also greatly reduced for the second option of operating. Careful research and planning will indicate the preferred method for starting the business for you.

PATIO FURNITURE RETAILER
★★ $$$$ 🌐

Installations of custom-built decks and patios have become the hottest new home improvement. All new decks and patios require one thing to complete them: patio furniture. A retail business that sells patio furniture is a very easy business to initiate, as there are no special skill requirements. Patio furniture will pretty much sell itself, providing of course that the prices are fair and the quality is outstanding. Worldwide, there are thousands of manufacturers of patio furniture products, so securing a product line should not be difficult. Additionally, consider stocking an inventory of locally made cedar or log patio furniture, as traditionally wood patio chairs and tables have always been excellent sellers. Marketing the business can be accomplished by utilizing all local print media, as well as by holding a grand opening sale to let potential customers know where you are and what products you stock.

WEB RESOURCE: www.furninfo.com *Furniture World* magazine online, directory of furniture manufacturers and distributors serving the retail trade industry.

USED FURNITURE STORE
★★ $$$$

Purchasing secondhand furniture at auction sales, garage sales, from classified advertisements, and estate sales is the starting point for opening a used furniture store, or reselling secondhand furniture right from your home. There are a great number of benefits to starting a business that sells secondhand furniture:

- No special skills or equipment requirements.
- Relatively low initial start-up and monthly operating costs.
- Great profit potential, as used furniture can be marked up by 100 percent or more.
- Very little in the way of government regulations beyond a business license.
- Proven stable and profitable retail industry.

ANTIQUE RADIOS
★ $$ 🏠 🕐

Purchasing, refinishing, and selling antique radios is a homebased business that can be started by just about anyone on a full- or part-time basis. Antique radios are highly sought-after pieces of furniture, especially if they are in working order and the cabinets have been restored to their former glory. Many collectors of antique radios are prepared to pay as much as $2,000 for the perfect specimen. The main requirement needed to make this business successful beyond the ability to refinish and repair the radios, will be time. It will take a substantial amount of time to scour flea markets, garage sales, and auctions to

locate the antique radios to be refinished and sold. Marketing the finished products can be by way of the Internet, antique and craft shows, and antique auctions, not to mention word-of-mouth.

FURNITURE UPHOLSTERY SERVICE
★ $$ 🏠 🕐

In spite of the fact that we live in a disposable society, furniture upholstery and recovering is not a dying art. Actually the opposite is true, especially for the upholstery service that specializes in recovering antique furniture. The largest drawback for starting an upholstery service is experience. Furniture upholstery is not an easy trade to learn and this business opportunity is best left tackled by an experienced upholsterer or seamstress. An upholstery service can be operated from a homebased workshop or as a joint venture with an established business such as an antique repair and refinishing service. Providing automotive, RV, and boat upholstery services can generate additional income for a furniture upholstery business. Income potential is $40 per hour or more.

WEB RESOURCE: www.upholster.com *Upholster* magazine online, directory servicing the upholstery industry.

MATTRESS SHOP
★ $$$$ 🌐

Specialization in the retail industry increases the likelihood of success and profitability. Opening a retail mattress store is an excellent example of specialization in the retail furniture sales industry. Mattresses and bedding products have a definite life span of about four to eight years. This is one of the numerous reasons that starting a retail business selling mattresses and bedding products is such a wise choice for a new business enterprise. Furthermore, consider adding institutional sales to the business, meaning hotels, hospitals, and nursing homes. The addition of institutional sales as a sideline for this type of retail business can add a significant amount of revenue to the overall yearly sales of the business, and more importantly, beef up the bottom-line profits.

WEB RESOURCE: www.furninfo.com *Furniture World* magazine online, directory of furniture manufacturers and distributors for the retail trade industry.

UNFINISHED FURNITURE STORE
★ $$$$

Selling "naked" furniture may not be sexy, but it does have the potential to generate huge profits for you. Unfinished furniture appeals mainly to two types of consumers: people on a fixed furnishing budget looking to save a few dollars by staining or painting the furniture themselves and the artisan seeking to create a custom-finished look that will match their interior decor. Target your marketing efforts on one or both of these types of consumers and you can't lose selling unfinished furniture. Unfinished furniture can be purchased on a wholesale basis from manufacturers, or even from local woodworkers and craftspeople. The selection can include tables, chairs, entertainment units, bed frames, and more. In addition to a showroom or a factory-direct approach to displaying and retailing the furniture, also consider providing workspace to your customers for finishing the furniture. Not only will you overcome the "I do not have a place to finish the furniture" objection, but you can also generate additional income by charging a small hourly fee to use the furniture finishing workspace and by selling stains, paints, and accessories such as handles.

WEB RESOURCE: www.buyunfinishedfurniture.com Directory listing retailers, industry information, and links.

NOTES

KEY

RATINGS ★
START-UP COST $
HOMEBASED
BUSINESS
PART-TIME
LEGAL ISSUES
FRANCHISE OR
LICENSE POTENTIAL
ONLINE

37
HEALTH
Businesses You Can Start

VITAMIN SALES
★★ $$$$

Owning and operating your own vitamin store could be the answer to your financial and self-employment dreams. The time has never been better than now to start a health-related business, as more and more people across North America become concerned about their health in general. And selling vitamins is not only a great way to capitalize on consumer demand, but it is also a fantastic way to help others strive for a healthier lifestyle. You will need a great deal of knowledge on vitamin and mineral supplements, but with that said, you can research all of the information you need on the subject and even hire experienced staff or a health consultant to help build and market the vitamin product line. Locating vitamin manufacturers and wholesalers for this venture will not be difficult as there are thousands worldwide who will be more than happy to establish wholesale accounts with new businesses. Start-up costs are high, but the profit potential is excellent. A retail location would best suit this venture, but to keep start-up costs to a minimum, a small kiosk located in a busy mall would be a good alternative.

ONLINE VITAMIN SALES
★ $$+

Do you want to sell vitamins but do not have the investment capital needed to open a retail store selling vitamins? If so, consider developing a Web site featuring vitamins for sale. In addition to selling vitamins you can also include articles and information about the health benefits of vitamin supplements, as well as an online chat room so visitors can exchange information. To keep start-up investment to a minimum you can arrange a direct drop ship agreement with one or more of the hundreds of companies that produce vitamins. Basically you sell the vitamins via your Web site, forward the orders electronically to the vitamin producer, and they fulfill the order and ship the product directly to your customers.

WEB RESOURCE: www.entrepreneur.com Create a business Web site with MySite professional Web site builder.

WEIGHT LOSS CLINIC
★★ $$$$

Starting your own weight loss clinic may be just the type of new business venture that you have been looking for. A recent U.S. government survey indicated that 50 percent of American adults felt their weight was too high and that 80 percent of the respondents intended to start a diet or fitness program within the next six months to correct their weight problem. This survey fact alone is reason enough to start a weight loss clinic. There are two options available to you in terms of business location for a weight loss clinic. The first option for establishing the business would be a retail location where customers come to you, and the second option would be private, in-home consultation where you go to the customer. The first option would require more start-up capital. However, the probability of generating larger revenues and profits is greater in the long run for a weight loss clinic operating from a fixed location, especially once the business is established. The second and less capital-intensive option is a great way to provide your customers with a personalized service and could easily generate an income in the range of $40 to $50 per hour. The largest requirement for starting a weight loss clinic is to be a certified dietitian, or at least have one on staff.

NATURAL HOME REMEDIES
★★ $$ 🏠 🕐

Every year thousands of people turn to a more natural approach to health, and this fact creates a terrific opportunity to start a natural home remedies business, and capitalize on consumer demand and the growing popularity of natural home health remedies. Natural home remedies have been around for hundreds of years, and only recently has the popularity of home remedies really taken off in a big way. Research and planning are definite prerequisites for this type of health business enterprise. To find information on natural home health remedies, start at your local library, harness the power of the Internet, and visit local bookstores. Finding natural home remedy manufacturers and wholesalers for the business will not prove difficult, as there are thousands in North America alone. Innovative entrepreneurs can always create their own line of natural home remedies. Just be sure you follow local and federal regulations in terms of product ingredients and product health or benefit claims. To keep start-up costs to a minimum, consider selling the natural home remedies via mail order.

ONLINE HOME REMEDIES
★ $$+ 🏠 🕐 🖱

Take century-old home remedy medications and health practices into the high-tech world of the Internet by posting a Web site that is dedicated to providing visitors with information and services focused on home remedies. The information and services featured on the site can include an online chat forum for visitors to exchange home remedy information, a directory featuring producers of home remedy products, providers of services, and articles about home remedy topics submitted by visitors. Income can be earned by charging a fee to businesses that want to be included in the directory and by selling home remedy products and books about the subject.

PEDICURE SERVICE
★★ $$ 🏠 🕐

Calling all pedicurists that are tired of working for someone else; the time is now to take control of your financial future and start creating profits for yourself by launching your own pedicure service business. A pedicure service is a great business to start and manage from a homebased location, while operating the service on a mobile basis. In terms of gaining clients for the service, seek out unusual opportunities—go to people who can't come to you. Clients can include busy professionals, residents of nursing and retirement homes, long-term hospital patients, and just about anyone else looking for a terrific in-home or office pedicure service. Providing your clients with exceptional service will guarantee you a very comfortable income and repeat clientele for many years to come. Potential income range is $25 to $40 per hour, plus the potential to sell foot care products.

DIETITIAN
★ $$

Are you a certified dietitian? That is the first qualification for starting this business. Options for operating this sort of health business or health consulting service are almost unlimited. As a certified dietician you could simply subcontract your services out to numerous businesses such as hospitals, nursing homes, weight loss clinics, and fitness centers. The innovative entrepreneur could start up an online dietician service on the Internet via a custom-designed Web site. Profit potential for diet consulting services is outstanding, and achieving an annual income of $50,000 or more is certainly not out of line. To increase business revenues and profits, aim to develop your own exclusive diet programs, books, videos, and software, as all of these products can be sold through the company Web site, as well as to national retailers on a wholesale basis.

WEB RESOURCE: www.cdrnet.org Information about becoming a registered dietitian.

ONLINE DIET AND FITNESS
★★★ $$+

As mentioned earlier in this chapter, a government survey indicated that 50 percent of American adults wanted to lose weight and start a regular diet and fitness program. And given the fact that there are more than 200 million adults in the United States, this means there are potentially 100 million customers for any business venture that specializes in diet and fitness products and services. Thus developing a Web site that is dedicated to providing visitors with diet and fitness information and services can potentially make you rich. The options are unlimited. The site

can provide users with diet and fitness information, products for sale, online fitness training and diet coaching, and offer online fitness evaluations, or a combination of any or all of these products and services. This is one of those rare situations in business wherein the potential marketplace is so large that the products and services provided almost become secondary to the methods used to attract and retain site visitors. Consider the following promotion methods:

- Advertise the site in print publications focused on diet and fitness.
- Build alliances with fitness centers, weight loss clinics, and dieticians.
- Register the site domain with numerous online search engines.
- Create hyperlinks to your site from Web sites relating to diet and fitness topics.
- Join a rotating banner advertisement program.
- Initiate a direct mail and e-mail marketing program aimed at people with an interest in diet and fitness.

SKIN CARE PRODUCTS
★★ $$

Creating and marketing your own skin care product line is a fantastic business venture to set in motion. With so much emphasis on "natural" these days, a skin care line devoted to "all natural ingredients" would definitely be a wise decision in terms of product marketing and consumer acceptance. The starting point for the business will be research, and this can be accomplished with assistance from the Internet, local library, and even the local cosmetics counter. Most cosmeticians will be more than happy to explain the benefits of their products, including what certain ingredients will do for your skin. To keep business start-up costs to a minimum, initially start with basic skin care products (e.g., cleanser, toner, and moisturizer), and expand the skin care product line from there. Good advertising mediums to promote and market skin care products would be the Internet, promotional fliers, newspaper ads, and home shopping parties, but your best advertising will be by way of word-of-mouth referrals. If your clients are happy with the products and service, they will tell others and it will not be long before you are well on your way to financial freedom and self-employment business success. This type of business enterprise is well suited for a homebased business location. To jump start the business, offer free skin care analysis to customers along with free samples of the natural skin care products that you sell.

MEDICAL BOOK SALES

 ★★ $$ 🏠 🕐

There are a few approaches to starting a business that sells medical books, guides, and journals. The first approach is to source publishers of medical books and become an authorized distributor by establishing mail order sales, online sales, and direct sales to consumers via a kiosk established for selling medical books. The second option is to compile information on medical and health issues, write the books, and start a publishing company that specializes in health and medical issues publications. The market for any type of medical or health publication is gigantic. Unfortunately there is also a tremendous amount of competition for the market, so be sure the business is carefully researched prior to starting.

DAY SPA

★★ $$$$ 🌐

With everybody leading such busy and stress-filled lifestyles these days, starting a day spa business is an excellent choice for a new business venture. The initial investment to get a day spa up and rolling is substantial. However, the income potential is outstanding. Location is probably the most important aspect of this new enterprise, so be sure to carefully research the area where you intend to open for business. Providing day spa clients with a wide variety of services such as manicures, seaweed wraps, aroma therapy, and massage options is guaranteed to make the business a popular destination for new and repeat clients. You should have no problem charging top dollar for your services, providing you offer exceptional personalized service to your clients. Marketing a day spa service would be through traditional advertising mediums. Be sure to print and distribute two-for-one discount coupons for the initial grand opening. You may have to sacrifice some revenues, but discount coupons are a terrific way to gain interest from potential customers quickly. The income and profit potential will greatly depend on a number of factors, such as services offered, customer volumes, and business location. However, attaining combined income and business profits in the range of $100,000 per year is achievable.

WEB RESOURCE: www.clubspausa.com Day Spa Association.

ONLINE SPA DIRECTORY

★ $$+ 🏠 🕐 🖱️

Worldwide there are thousands of health and beauty spas that cater to just about any health or beauty treatment or need imaginable. Thus an outstanding opportunity exists to develop an online directory featuring world spas. The directory Web site would have to be indexed both geographically and by spa type for visitor search purposes. However, this is a relatively easy programming task to accomplish. For an annual listing fee, spa operators would receive a headline in the directory index that is linked to a pop-up page that gives visitors details and information, such as services provided, location, and contact information. Sales consultants from around the globe can be employed to solicit spa owners to join the directory. These sales consultants can be remunerated by way of commission. Promote the site in print publications related to health and beauty topics, as well as by utilizing Internet marketing and promotion techniques, such as search engine registrations, hyperlinks, and banner advertisements.

ORGANIC HAIR CARE PRODUCTS

★★ $$ 🏠 🕐

Have you always dreamed about starting your own successful business that can be operated from home? If so, consider starting a venture that specializes in developing and producing natural hair care products. Create, manufacture, and sell natural hair care products such as shampoos and conditioners made from 100 percent natural organic ingredients.

Of course, there will be a steep learning curve in terms of developing the hair care products. However, utilizing research tools such as libraries and the Internet should prove quite useful in this endeavor. The hair care products can be sold to specialty retailers on a wholesale basis, or they can be sold directly to consumers via mail-order advertising, the Internet, and renting a sales kiosk at malls.

HOME-CARE SERVICE
★★★ $$ ⚖

Starting a home-care service is a great business enterprise to initiate, as people are living longer and, more importantly, living longer on their own. This type of new business venture would best suit a person with a background and training in the health-care industry, but with that said, home-care training is available in almost every community across North America. Generally, there are two types of home-care providers, and the training required for each is very different. The first type of home-care service is one that focuses on assisting people with everyday tasks such as cooking, cleaning, errands, and personal hygiene. The second type of home-care service can include the aforementioned with the addition of medication administration, and in some cases, therapy. Income potential will range from $20 per hour to as much as $50 per hour depending on services provided and skill levels required.

WEB RESOURCE: www.nahc.org National Association of Home Care.

MEDICAL BRACES
★★ $$ 🏚 🕐

"Brace yourself" could be your business name or company motto if you're planning to start a business that specializes in retailing medical braces. There are literally hundreds of various types of medical braces used for hundreds of different types of medical conditions; everything from braces for a bad back to knee braces for sports injuries. There are thousands of manufacturers of medical braces worldwide, so securing a wholesale source for the products should

not be difficult. The braces can be sold to consumers in a few different ways including establishing a sales kiosk in a mall or close to a hospital or medical center, selling the braces online, and advertising the braces in specialty publications for mail-order sales. Medical braces are specialized products, so maintaining markups of 100 percent is justified.

WEB RESOURCE: www.hospital-technology.com Directory service listing medical equipment and supplies manufacturers and distributors.

HAIR SALON
★★ $$$ ⚖

There are numerous approaches that can be taken when considering starting a hair salon as a new business enterprise. The first approach is to establish a hair salon that operates from a fixed storefront location. The second approach is to start a mobile hair salon, which is covered in the special services chapter of this business start-up directory. Prior to starting a hair salon, consider the following aspects of the business.

- *Location.* Is there a suitable location available for the business in your community? Good locations for a hair salon can include a home-based hair salon (providing the proper zoning is in place or can easily be secured), a busy mall or strip plaza, and the lobby retail area of a large office building or complex.
- *Competition and price point.* How much competition is there in the local market, and is there room for another hair salon? What is the competition charging for services? Can a profit or reasonable return on investment be accomplished?
- *Services provided.* Will the salon be a full-service hair salon that also provides additional services, such as a manicures and facial treatments? Or will the main-stay of the business be focused on haircuts and hair styling?

There are also additional considerations, such as staff, certifications, etc. However, the three considerations listed above are the main aspects of the business to really consider, research, and plan for. Due to the many variables surrounding a hair salon business, it is very difficult to establish an expected rate of return or potential profit range for the business. Owners of well-established hair salons can easily earn six-figure incomes or very close to a six-figure income. The key to a successful hair salon is the same as any other new business venture: Practice good business skills and judgment and you will be on your way to building a successful business venture. To generate additional revenues and profits, sell hair care products at the salon. The products can include shampoos, conditioners, and all other related hair care products. For the really innovative entrepreneur: seek to develop your own hair care products line, as there are many manufacturers of hair care products who do private label manufacturing. This means that the manufacturer will place its product in your packaging, under your product name. Private label packaging is a fantastic way to not only give your business the look of professionalism and success—it is also a way to wholesale your products nationally.

WEB RESOURCE: www.smallbizbooks.com Business specific start-up guides and books.

COSMETICS RETAILING
★★ $$ 🏠 🕐

The sales of cosmetics generate billions of dollars every year worldwide, and starting a business selling cosmetics is just about as straightforward as a new business venture can get. There are numerous ways to sell cosmetics and make a profit. However, in the spirit of being unique, we will analyze one segment of the cosmetic sales industry that can generate huge profits in a few different ways. The business can be set in motion for less than a $5,000 initial start-up investment. Locate a manufacturer of cosmetic products who does not have representation in your community, state, or even your country. Negotiate an exclusive contract to represent and distribute their cosmetic products in the desired area. Once the distribution contract has been secured, the cosmetics can be sold to retailers on a wholesale basis. Or, you can hire a direct sales team whose main

focus is in-home sales of the cosmetics. Both approaches have the potential to generate enormous sales and profits.

WEB RESOURCE: www.icmad.org Independent Cosmetic Manufacturers and Distributors, Inc. Directory service listing cosmetic manufacturers and distributors.

HAIR REMOVAL SERVICE
★ $$

Hair removal or waxing is a popular procedure that both women and men have done to rid themselves of unwanted body and facial hair. Starting a hair removal service is a good business to set in motion, providing of course that you or a staff member has training and certification as required for the hair removal procedure. The easiest and least expensive way to get the service rolling is to form a joint venture with an established business, such as a hair salon or day spa. A joint venture can reduce the investment needed to start the business, and you can also capitalize on your partner's existing client base to jump-start the business.

MEDICAL EQUIPMENT SALES
★★ $$$$

Millions of dollars worth of medical equipment is sold each year in the United States, and securing a portion of this very lucrative industry is not difficult, especially for the entrepreneur who carefully researches and plans an entry into the medical equipment sales industry. There are a few different approaches that can be taken in terms of medical equipment sales. The first approach is to establish a retail store that sells medical equipment to customers, as well as to online shoppers via the store's Web site. The second approach is to become an independent sales consultant who represents various manufacturers of medical equipment. The main focus of this type of medical equipment sales would be to sell medical equipment to hospitals and health centers by soliciting or using the tender process in which hospitals and medical centers routinely ask for bids to replace equipment. Tenders are usually featured in newspapers or you can call the hospital to inquire about current tenders out for bid. Profit potential range is $50,000 to $150,000 per year.

MOBILE HEARING TESTING
★ $$$$ ⚖️

In many areas of the country workers' compensation boards and workers' insurance and benefits programs require workers to undergo yearly hearing tests as part of an ongoing workers' safety program to ensure that industrial noise is not damaging workers' hearing ability. This fact creates a terrific opportunity for the innovative entrepreneur to capitalize on by starting a business that conducts hearing tests for workers on a mobile basis. Be forewarned that the equipment needed for this type of unique health service is expensive, and the hearing technician to operate the equipment must be certified. However, this is a business opportunity that has amazing growth potential as workers health issues are at the forefront of all levels of governments and industry. The profit potential is outstanding, and this is definitely a business venture that deserves and warrants further investigation.

MASSAGE SALON
★★ $$$$ ⚖️

Starting a massage salon or a career as an independent masseuse requires professional certification, or staff members with professional certification. However, the training to become a certified masseuse generally takes less than one year and costs less than $10,000, making a massage salon venture attainable to just about everyone seeking to start this business. There are a couple of ways to operate a massage therapy business. The first is to work from a fixed location or massage salon, and the second way is to operate the business on a mobile basis where you go to the client. Both approaches to operating the business have their pros and cons. A mobile massage therapy business is by far less costly to establish and operate, but also generates less revenues and profits than a salon.

WEB RESOURCE: www.amtamassage.org American Massage Therapy Association.

MEDICAL SEAT CUSHIONS
★★ $$ 🏭 🕐

Millions of people commute back and forth to work each day in agony, suffering everything from back problems to hip and joint problems. Starting a business that sells specialty automotive medical seat cushions may prove to be very profitable and make you a superstar with commuters. The business is very easy to establish and operate. The first step is to locate a manufacturer of medical seat cushions. This can be accomplished by harnessing the power of the Internet for research purposes, or by acquiring a manufacturers directory. Once you have found a few manufacturers, aim to secure an exclusive distribution contract for their products in the area your business will operate. The seat cushions can be sold directly to consumers by way of mail order and the Internet, as well as by setting up a sales kiosk or booth at car shows and automotive trade shows. The profit potential for this type of enterprise is excellent, as the seat cushions can easily be marked up by 100 percent or more for retail sales.

TANNING SALON
★★ $$$$ 🌐

The quest for the perfect suntan has come under fire in the past decade, as health concerns about skin damage and diseases caused by the harmful ultraviolet rays of the sun have been splashed across the headlines of every newspaper and TV news report. Herein lies the business opportunity. People seek the perfect suntan, but health concerns prevent many of us from sunbathing. So the solution is simple. Start a tanning salon business and capitalize not only on consumer demand for the perfect suntan, but also on public concerns. A tanning salon is a very easy business to get rolling, as there are no regulations or special business skills required. There is also a limited downside, as the demand for the service has been established and proven. There are, however, specific aspects of the business that must be addressed and considered.

THE BUSINESS LOCATION. Like any business that operates from a fixed location and depends on customers to come to the business to generate sales and revenues, the business location for a tanning salon is very important. Consider the following in terms of the right business location:

- Good street visibility, easy access, and customer parking.
- Located in an area with the right customer profile or demographics—an average to higher family income as the people are more likely to travel.
- The location should also be the right size, and not give the appearance of being too cramped or small, or being empty. The building and unit should be in good repair to give clients the feeling of comfort.

ADVERTISING AND MARKETING. How do you effectively advertise, promote, and market a new tanning salon, especially if the advertising budget is limited? Here are a few suggestions.

- Build alliances with all the local travel agents and brokers in your community. The travel agents can provide their clients who are traveling to sunny destinations with 10 percent off coupons for your tanning salon to get a jumpstart on their vacation tans. And, you can provide all of your clients with travel points, meaning that every time they use the suntanning salon you give them one travel point. Each point can represent $1 towards the cost of a vacation booked through a travel agent or cross promotion partner.
- Print and distribute two-for-one suntanning coupons for the initial grand opening promotion.
- Provide customers with a multitanning pass option, meaning that clients could have the option of prebuying ten tanning sessions for the price of eight.

ADDITIONAL PRODUCTS AND SERVICES. Beyond providing customers with a suntanning service, how can a

tanning salon generate additional business revenues and profits? Here are a few suggestions:

- Stock and sell suntan oil and sunscreen lotions.
- Establish a joint venture with a massage therapist. Not only will this reduce overhead by sharing expenses, but also each business can attract new clients from the other business's customers.
- Stock and sell beachwear and sportswear from the tanning salon.

WEB RESOURCE: www.sundash.com Distributors of salon tanning equipment.

ONLINE STORE FOR THE DISABLED
★★ $$$$

People living with physical disabilities often find even life's easy tasks to be frustrating. Starting a business that specializes in selling products aimed at making life easier for people living with physical disabilities is not only a wise choice for a new business venture, it is also a business that can assist thousands of people in leading a better life. Products could include wheelchairs, medical braces, canes, and walkers. The business can focus on both "bricks and mortar" style retailing, as well as developing a Web site for online shoppers. This type of health-related business venture is very costly to set in motion. However, the profit potential is good, and the business can be personally rewarding.

PERFUME
★ $$ 🏠 🕐

Creating, packaging, and distributing your own perfume line can make you rich. Developing your own perfume or perfume line will take some careful planning and research. However, the hard work could really pay off, especially if you can secure national accounts with well-recognized specialty retailers. In terms of the type of perfume your business develops, consider an all-natural approach to the ingredients, as increasing consumer awareness and acceptance of "all natural products" is without question the wave of the future. The perfume can be sold to retailers on a wholesale basis, directly to consumers via the Internet, or by establishing a perfume sales kiosk set up in high-traffic community gathering places. For mail-order sales, advertise the perfume in specialty publications.

MASSAGE OILS
★★ $$$ 🏠 🕐

Like developing your own perfume line, developing your own massage oil line also has great potential. In fact, the two products could be developed together and wholesaled to the same retailers. Given the current popularity of "all natural products" it would be a wise decision to develop the massage oils from all natural and organic ingredients. Seek out joint venture business opportunities with established companies that can assist in the development, marketing, and distribution of your products. Often joint ventures mean that you will lose some control and a portion of the profits of the business. However, having a percentage of something big is better than having all of something small.

HEALTH SEMINARS
★★ $$$ 🏠 🕐

Starting a business that promotes and hosts free informational health seminars can make you rich. You may be wondering how can you get rich by starting a business that gives away free health information to people who attend these seminars? The answer is easy. You promote and host the health seminars, while you have health professionals speak on health issues in their area of expertise. To maximize the profit potential and ensure that the seminar is well attended, the speakers at the seminars should be well known in their field and authors of books on health and wellness programs. The reason is that revenues to support the business and generate a profit will be made by selling the speaker's books and programs at the end of the seminar. Hot topics for these types of health seminars include weight loss and healthy diet, natural childbirth, alternative medicines

and medical treatments, and age-related health issues. It is not unusual for as much as $10,000 worth of products to be sold at health topic seminars, so you can see how this business could become quite lucrative.

NUTRITION GUIDES
★★ $$$ 🏠 🕐

Most health experts agree a healthy diet is the key to a healthy and long life. Starting a business that creates and distributes nutrition guides is a fantastic new venture to set in motion. There are two approaches that can be taken with this business in terms of generating revenues and profits. The first approach is to sell the nutrition guides through bookstores and specialty retailers. The second approach is to distribute the nutrition guides free of charge throughout your community and support the business by selling advertising space in the guides to local businesses that would benefit from this type of advertising exposure. Good choices for potential advertisers in a nutrition guide would include vitamin stores, doctors, health professionals, organic food growers, and health food restaurants. If you choose to adopt the second option in terms of operating the business, the nutrition guides could be published twice per year, making this a potentially very profitable business opportunity.

STAIR LIFTS
★★★ $$$$

Are you searching for a unique and interesting business opportunity that has little competition and the potential to make $100,000 per year or more in profits? If so, perhaps you should consider starting a business that sells and installs specialty stair lift chairs. There are many worldwide manufacturers of stair lifts, so finding a wholesale source should not be difficult. Market the stair lifts using all traditional advertising mediums, as well as by establishing alliances with custom homebuilders and renovation contractors to act as sales agents for the product. Be sure to design a stair lift display that highlights the beneficial features of the product. The display can be set up and used as a sales and marketing tool to collect sales leads from potential customers at home and garden trade shows.

WEB RESOURCE: www.coast-resources.com Directory service listing medical equipment manufacturers.

PERSONAL CARE PRODUCT VENDING
★★ $$$ 🏠 🕐

Starting a vending business that specializes in personal care products is a great choice for a new business venture. The vending machines can be located throughout the community in locations such as public washrooms, restaurants, factories, and all other high-traffic community gathering places. Products sold can include condoms, aspirin, feminine hygiene products, and even disposable baby diapers. The key to success in the vending industry is to secure good locations for the vending machines, and to make sure you carefully watch wholesale product costs. The profit potential is excellent in this kind of vending business, and each machine could easily produce yearly sales in excess of $5,000.

WEB RESOURCE: www.smallbizbooks.com Business specific start-up guides and books.

WIGS
★★ $$$ 🏠 🕐

Many surgical procedures and medical treatments result in patients losing or having their hair removed. While the hair loss is generally short-term, many people still turn to wigs as a way to provide a solution to the problem. The first step in establishing the business is to secure a wholesale or product supply source for the wig, and this should not be difficult as there are thousands of wig manufacturers worldwide. Marketing the wigs can be as easy as establishing alliances with hospitals and medical centers to act as a referral source for the business. The wigs can also be sold directly to consumers via the Internet. Once established, this unique business can generate a very substantial yearly income.

WEB RESOURCE: www.marketwiz.net/wigs_whol/ Directory service listing wig manufacturers.

MOBILE FOOT MASSAGE SERVICE
★ $$ 🕐

It is a proven medical fact that foot problems that are not corrected early can result in additional medical problems later down the road. And this fact creates a terrific opportunity for the budding entrepreneur to capitalize by starting a mobile foot massage service. The target market for a mobile foot massage service is obvious: people who spend a lot of time on their feet. In the spirit of being unique, consider the following method of marketing to gain new clients and generate business revenue. Prepare a full marketing presentation that highlights all the benefits of foot massages, such as happier workers equals increased productivity. Once the marketing presentation is complete, set up proposal meetings with medium to large-sized companies in your community that have employees who are on their feet for most of the day. The pitch to the business owner of why he or she should consider starting a foot massage program for workers will of course be the fact of increased productivity and the possibility of fewer missed work days as a result of foot-related health problems. Once again, a mobile foot massage service is unique and will take some time and careful planning to get rolling. However, once established, an income level of $30 per hour or more should not prove difficult to achieve.

HEALTH TAXI
★★ $$$ ⚖

Starting a health taxi service in your community may be the unique new business enterprise that you have been searching for. The business concept is simply this: Purchase, lease, or rent a suitable mode of transportation such as a passenger van. Set up accounts with local doctors, dentists, and health professionals in your community to provide their patients with a way of getting to and from the doctor's office or clinic via your health taxi service. The doctors would pay a flat fee for every patient that your service taxied to the doctor's location. Not only will the patients benefit from a free taxi service, but the doctors will also benefit by ensuring that patients can get to them to receive proper medical care. Be sure to check out all the legal aspects of the business in terms of liability insurance and special driving permits prior to establishing a health taxi service in your community.

ALTERNATIVE HEALTH-CARE CENTER
★★ $$$$

Do you want to start a business related to alternative health-care, but you lack skills or experience in the industry? You can still be part of the multibillion dollar booming alternative health-care industry, simply by starting an alternative heath-care center. Start by leasing a large professional office space and subdivide the space into smaller offices for alternative health-care practitioners to lease, and in effect, form an alternative heath care center. Attracting heath care practitioners to sublease the smaller individual offices should be no problem, providing you offer services such as a centralized receptionist, parcel shipping, central record keeping, and additional services that the practitioners would typically require for the operation of their alternative health-care services. The alternative health-care services housed within the center could include massage therapy, aromatherapy, herbal medicines, and any other alternative health-care service that is available.

HEALTH FAIR
★★ $$$

Across North America there are thousands of health-care professionals and companies that produce products aimed at the health-care industry. And all of these health-care professionals and industry-related companies could potentially become your clients if your intentions are to start a business that promotes and hosts two-day health fairs across the

country. A health fair is the same as a trade show or craft show. The major difference is that all of the vendors or exhibitors are in the health-care industry. This type of unique health-care related business has a chance to become a profitable business concern, given the recent increased demand by consumers for health-care information, products, and services. Charging people an admittance fee into the health fairs, as well as charging the exhibitors a booth fee to display at the health fair would earn revenue for the business.

HEALTH-CARE NEWSPAPER
★ $$$

Are you seeking to start a unique business in the health-care industry? If so, perhaps you should consider starting a health-care newspaper that is published monthly. The paper can feature stories and articles about health-care in general, as well as new health-care procedures and products that are being introduced. Local health-care professionals covering all segments of the health-care industry can supply the information featured in the paper. The paper could be distributed free of charge throughout the community, and supported by selling advertising space to interested local health-care professionals and companies. Profit potential once established is $25,000+ per year.

ONLINE MEDICAL CENTER
★★★ $$$+

Here is an online business venture that has the potential to be expanded from coast to coast. An online medical center is a collection of health-care providers from one community grouped together into one Web site. Instead of each business or professional having to pay thousands of dollars to develop and maintain individual Web sites, they can join your online medical center for a year for what it typically costs to host and maintain a Web site for one month. The site would have to be indexed by type of medical service or product that is being featured, such as plastic surgery, medical equipment, dental, family practitioners, and home-care providers. Visitors using the site would simply choose an area of interest in the index and be linked to a pop-up page within the site that described the business's medical products and services, including contact information. This type of Web site could be easily expanded by selling the franchise or license rights to qualified operators to host, maintain, and market a clone site in every city or community across the country.

NOTES

KEY

RATINGS	★
START-UP COST	$
HOMEBASED BUSINESS	
PART-TIME	
LEGAL ISSUES	
FRANCHISE OR LICENSE POTENTIAL	
ONLINE	

58

HOME IMPROVEMENT

Businesses You Can Start

ATTIC VENTILATION AND INSULATION

★★★ $$

Most homes built prior to the mid-'70s energy crisis were not properly insulated. The homes that were built after this period until the late '80s suffer from being sealed so tight as not to allow enough air circulation, especially in the attic areas. The bottom line, the market for attic ventilation and insulation installation services is absolutely gigantic. Attic ventilation can be achieved in a variety of installation methods including installations of soffit vents, mechanical and nonmechanical roof vents, ridge vents, and gable vents. Recent studies have indicated that the preferred method of attic insulation is a fiberglass batt format vs. blown-in cellulose insulation, which can shift and/or compact. Checking with local experts, building codes, and building centers will give you the best understanding for which procedure may be required in your region. The business can be marketed through home improvement shows, traditional advertising mediums, contractor visits, and flier distribution. The business is quick to set up and expand based on a word-of-mouth advertising and referral basis.

REQUIREMENTS: Providing that you have experience in home repair or renovation, this trade is very quick to master. You will want to learn all of the local building codes in terms of proper ventilation and insulation specification, and stick to, or exceed these requirements to ensure that the work has been properly completed. This business requires a few basic tools, such as a van or covered truck, step and extension ladders, protective safety gear, and a few hand power tools.

START-UP COSTS: An attic ventilation and insulation installation service can be started for $7,000 to $10,000. This amount of investment would be sufficient capital to acquire a basic truck or van, tools, a small inventory, and provide for an initial marketing budget.

PROFIT POTENTIAL: You can add gigantic markups onto the wholesale costs of the ventilation products, as well as the insulation. In terms of installation rates, there are two methods of billing for this service. The first is to charge an hourly rate that would typically be $40 to $50 per hour for one person, and $70 to $80 dollars per hour for two people. The second method is to calculate a per-square-footage charge, this can be done by way of estimating your time, adding in the product cost plus a markup, then dividing the total number by the number of square feet you will be covering.

FENCING INSTALLATIONS

The desire to keep kids and pets inside a property, and unwanted trespassers outside a property, has created a big demand for companies that provide property fencing installation services. The starting point is to first determine the fencing material(s) and style of fencing your fence installation service will be installing. There are various types of material used in fencing including cedar wood, pressure treated wood, stone, brick, steel or cast iron, recycled plastics, cedar rail, chain link, and aluminum. Likewise, there are also various methods that can be employed to promote and market a fence installation service, such as subcontracting for construction and renovation companies, direct retail sales via advertising, and "installations only" for home building and renovation centers. Perhaps your fence installation service could be different from competitor's by offering the service of installing the fence posts only and supplying the prebuilt fencing panels for the homeowner to complete the installation. This method would save the homeowner money, while having the difficult portion of the job, which is the installation of the fence posts, completed professionally.

ONLINE BUILDING PLANS

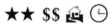

Houses, sundecks, woodworking projects, and just about every other sort of building design plans can be sold online. You can develop a Web site that specializes in one particular type of building plan, like garden sheds. Or you could create an online directory format and list companies that sell building plans. Income would be derived by selling the plans or by charging a fee to be listed on the site. There are millions of do-it-yourself homeowners worldwide and building and design plans are extremely popular. Remember the key to a successful Web site, beyond generating profits, is to attract visitors and keep them coming back. Be sure to use varied and interesting content to ensure as many page views per hit as possible. This is the type of online business venture that, once established, can easily be operated from home on a part-time basis.

WEB RESOURCE: www.entrepreneur.com Create a business Web site with MySite professional Web site builder.

WINDOW INSTALLATIONS

Replacement windows rank sixth as the most frequently completed home improvement renovation, and demand continues to grow. Modern manufacturing methods and materials can be accredited for this booming industry. Today's windows are constructed from maintenance free vinyl and aluminum extrusions that have excellent insulation value, and come in a full range of designs and operating features. People with a construction and renovation background will find this business start-up to be of particular interest, as the investment is low and the profit returns can be excellent.

WEB RESOURCE: www.windoorweb.com Directory service listing window and door manufacturers and distributors.

CERAMIC TILE SALES AND INSTALLATIONS

★★ $$ 🏠 🕐

Here is another great little business venture that you can start for a very small investment and manage from a homebased office. Ceramic tiles will always be a popular choice for a flooring finish, due to their low maintenance and high durability features. Ceramic tile flooring is also very attractive and adds value to any home. To be successful in this venture you will need experience and knowledge in the installation of ceramic tile flooring, or have access to qualified tradesmen to do the actual flooring installations. Operating as a subcontractor service for construction and renovation companies is the logical starting point for this business and as a method of keeping the initial business start-up costs to a minimum.

WEB RESOURCE: www.floorbiz.com Directory service listing ceramic tile distributors and industry information.

SIDING INSTALLATIONS

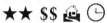 ★★ $$ 🏠 🕐

Siding sales and installations are about as straightforward as a home improvement business start-up can get. Sell the siding, and install the siding. Pricing for siding products and installations are generally based on a per-square basis (one square equals 100 square feet). There are, like any home improvement or renovation service, upgrades to the standard package that can be made available to the consumer. I recently spoke to an owner of a siding installation company, and this business-minded person was very clever in terms of separating his service from his competitor's service. His niche was to use a laptop computer for in-home presentations. He scanned in a "before" picture of the client's house, and by utilizing special construction software, he was able to produce an "after" picture(s) showing the homeowner a multitude of finished looks that could be achieved by installing new siding. Needless to say, he operates the largest siding installation service in the area.

DISPOSAL BIN SERVICE

★★ $$$$

The home renovation and construction industry creates an enormous amount of waste each year that has to be disposed of into landfill sites or taken to recycling facilities for a renewed lease on life. There are a few different approaches that you can take in terms of starting and operating a disposal bin service.

The first and more traditional approach is to own and operate your own roll-off or winch truck that is used in the transportation, delivery, and pickup of the disposal bins. The second option is to own only the disposal bins and subcontract the delivery and pickup service to a trucking firm. The second option is less expensive in terms of start-up capital requirements. However, it will also generate less revenue and profit for the business. The third, and maybe most interesting approach is to use tandem-axle trailers, which can be purchased secondhand relatively inexpensively, and can be towed behind any one-ton pickup truck. This third option enables you to enter into a waste disposal service with less money, while controlling all aspects of the business and revenues. Disposal rates are generally charged on a flat fee basis that is based on distance traveled, plus the cost of disposing of the construction waste.

CARPET INSTALLATIONS

 ★ $$ 🏠 🕐

Not unlike siding sales and installations, carpet sales and installations have been going strong for more than 50 years. The main requirement for this type of home improvement business start-up is to have the ability to properly install carpeting or have access to qualified installers. To be competitive in this industry and keep your overheads low, your best bet may be to stay away from a traditional carpet and flooring showroom and stick to a mobile showroom via your installation van. The business is very inexpensive to set in motion, and you can expect to make a comfortable living, once you have established a client base and referral network.

CAULKING AND FLASHING SERVICE

★★ $$ 🏠 🕐

What makes a caulking and flashing service such a fantastic business start-up is the fact that this business venture can be launched for as little as $500 of investment capital, requires little experience, is a unique service, and has a minimal amount of competition. Caulking and flashings have a definite life span and have to be replaced in order for their intended purposes to be effective. Furthermore, the uses for caulking and flashings are varied and required on just about every standing structure. The simplest method to get rolling and promote your business is to distribute information fliers door-to-door in your community. The promotional fliers should describe all the benefits that replacing caulking and flashings will have for the owner's home. Likewise, residential and commercial property management and maintenance companies can also be a great source to gain new and repeat business.

WEB RESOURCE: www.thebluebook.com Directory service listing caulking manufacturers and distributors.

DRYWALL INSTALLATIONS
★★ $$

Drywall installation and finishing is messy work that not many people enjoy doing; which is great for you, if this is the type of new business you wish to start. The drywall trade does require some practice to master. However, if you are patient, you can master the drywall trade quickly. The fastest way to establish and expand a drywall business is to market the service directly to homebuilders and renovators. Additionally, market the drywall service to home painters and fire and flood restoration companies, as these businesses can also provide you with plenty of work. Drywall repair is an essential part of their service. These companies typically subcontract this work to an outside drywall contractor. At the time this directory was written, drywall rates were $50 per hour plus material for repairs and $1 to $1.25 per square foot for new finished drywall installation. However, you will have to conduct your own market survey in your local area to establish drywall installation and finishing rates.

DECK BUILDING
★★★ $$$

One of the fastest growing segments of the home improvement industry is designing, building, and installing custom sundecks. Many of the sundecks that are now being installed retail for as much as $15,000 and include features such as built-in

planters, areas for sunk-in hot tubs, glass or cast iron handrails, and custom manufactured wood furniture to match the sundeck's design. The most profitable way to operate the business is to sell the sundecks directly to the end consumers. However, this method of operating is also the most expensive to launch and establish. Additional ways to get rolling in your own sundeck installation business also include subcontracting for established building and renovation companies, establishing alliances with designers and architects, and marketing the sundeck sales and installation service directly to consumers via a showroom or trade show displays.

REQUIREMENTS: In most areas of the country, the installation of a sundeck requires a building permit, which must be issued prior to installation. There are building codes in place for the construction specifications of sundecks that have to be closely adhered to. Starting this sort of venture requires a great deal of construction experience and knowledge. In terms of equipment, power tools such as table saws, handsaws, and posthole diggers will be required. To keep initial investment costs down, all the required tools and equipment for building sundecks can be rented on an as needed basis. Be sure to find out if a builder's license is required in your local area for this type of construction business.

START-UP COSTS: The total start-up costs to get going will vary greatly depending on the types of sundecks built and installed. However, an investment in the range of $15,000 to $20,000 will be sufficient to purchase the required equipment and leave enough working capital to fund the business for a few months.

PROFIT POTENTIAL: Once again, the profit potential for a sundeck sales and installation service can greatly vary as to the type of deck manufacturing and installation services that are provided to customers. Potential profits range: $30,000 to $100,000+ per year.

WEB RESOURCE: www.deckindustry.org Deck Industry Association.

CLOSET ORGANIZERS
★ $$

Selling and installing closet organizers is a very inexpensive business you can start and make a pretty darn good living at. Closet organizers are very popular and relatively easy to install. All that is required are a few basic hand tools and reliable transportation. You can market your service to homebuilders and home renovators, as well as directly to the end consumer via trade shows and weekend mall kiosk displays. There is competition in this industry, so you may want to specialize in one particular brand of closet organizer or become a manufacturer's exclusive sales and installation representative. The potential profit range for this type of home improvement business will vary. However, an income of $40,000 per year is easily attainable.

WEB RESOURCE: www.thebluebook.com Directory listing closet organizer manufacturers and distributors.

REFITTING HOUSES FOR THE DISABLED
★★★★ $$$$

Millions of people live with disabilities, and often these physical disabilities can turn life's simplest tasks into stressful and daunting chores. The housing needs and requirements for people living with disabilities are much different from those for people without disabilities. Doors must be wide enough to accommodate wheelchairs, light switches have to be lower, and electrical outlets have to be higher. Kitchens and bathrooms often have to be completely customized, and ramps and other safety items have to be installed in the home. Starting a business that specializes in refitting homes to accommodate people with disabilities can be both a profitable and personally rewarding venture to initiate. The most effective way to market this type of renovation service is to construct a showroom that reflects the alterations and improvements that can be made to a new or existing home to make the house more functional and user-friendly for the disabled person. Alternatively, if your budget does not allow you to implement this type of showroom display, you can still market your services with the use of brochures and other sales aids. However, this type of marketing does not have the same kind of tangible quality that a hands-on showroom can provide for clients.

REQUIREMENTS: This type of specialized renovation service has many requirements that have to be

carefully considered, such as liability insurance, business license, skilled tradespeople or subcontractors, and operating location. The business definitely requires a full business plan, action plan, and market evaluation to be completed prior to establishing the business.

START-UP COSTS: Launching this sort of business venture can be very costly. If your plan is to be completely operational including a showroom, you can expect to invest in the neighborhood of $50,000 to $75,000 for this type of specialty home improvement venture.

PROFIT POTENTIAL: For any home improvement business to be financially viable, you should always strive for a 50 percent markup on all material and labor. If you follow this pricing structure then you will have a 33 percent gross profit margin on all work completed. Depending on sales volumes, 50 percent of your gross profit will be used to cover the cost of operating overheads, leaving approximately 15 percent of your total sales as pretax profits. Providing you can maintain sales of $500,000 per year, that would leave you a gross profit of $75,000 per year.

PET DOORS
★★ $$

There are estimated to be more than 30,000,000 house pets in North America. And if you have a dog or cat, then you are well aware of the fact that they may have to get outside for a host of reasons. Unfortunately, once in a while our schedules conflict with our pets' call to nature conflicts. Enter the solution: the installation of a pet door enabling dogs and cats the freedom to enter the safety of a fenced yard regardless of the time of day. The best way to get this business moving is to market the installation service through all the pet stores in your community. This marketing method can be a great way for you to kick start your new business venture into action. The pet stores should have no reasons not to assist you, as they will be selling the doors and retaining their retail markup. Alternatively, you could also supply the pet doors; or even better, you could manufacture, retail, and install the pet doors for maximum profit returns. To assist in researching the business, I contacted three pet stores; all are well known and established in my community. Two of the stores offered the pet doors for sale. However, not one of these stores offered or provided the service of installing the pet door. Conclusion: Check in your local area, and if your research draws the same conclusion as mine, then this business may be a good opportunity for you to start and operate your own fun, profitable, and independent business.

REQUIREMENTS: In terms of special skill requirements there are few to mention, other than a very basic knowledge of operating power tools. The business also has no requirements that have to be met in terms of building codes, permits, and special government regulations.

START-UP COSTS: A pet door sales and installation service can easily be launched for less than $1,000 including the required tools, product samples, and a small initial advertising and marketing budget.

PROFIT POTENTIAL: For this type of service the pricing structure can be kept very basic. Charge a flat fee for the installation of the door with the only variable being the type of door you will be installing. Should you encounter situations that require the pet door to be installed into wall areas instead of a door, I would suggest that this service be priced on a time plus material basis. Generally for this kind of specialized installation service the installation rates would be in the $25 to $40 per hour range, plus a product markup on any and all pet door sales.

WEB RESOURCE: www.petdoors.com Distributors of pet doors and parts.

STORAGE SHEDS
★★ $$$ 🕐

Building and installing backyard storage sheds is a little known business that generates gigantic profits for the owners of these businesses. Sheds are an affordable method for a homeowner to add additional storage space, workshop space, an art studio, or guest accommodations to a home without having to get plans and permits from local government. Working from a small industrial space you can build shed kits for homeowners to buy and install, or you can build the sheds in a controlled environment and

transport them to the site to install for the purchasers. The business only requires basic construction knowledge and equipment to implement, and the profits that can be generated are outstanding. An elaborate sample shed can be built and displayed in a high-traffic area in your community with proper signs identifying your business. This type of advertising and promotion would be an excellent way to gain attention and attract new customers.

WEB RESOURCE: www.amerished.com Distributor of storage and garden shed construction plans.

SKYLIGHT INSTALLATIONS
★★★★ $$ 🏠 🕐 🌏

The old plastic bubble style skylights are out, and demand is booming for the new high-tech skylights that are now available. Some skylights not only open and close with the push of a button, they also have sensors that will automatically close the skylight if it begins to rain. Some have additional features like smart heat reflective glass, custom shades, and availability in a multitude of shapes and sizes. I talked to one skylight installation company, aptly called "Skylights Only." The owner told me that demand was so great for skylight installations, his company was booked for the next six months straight, and demand showed no signs of slowing down. This business opportunity gets four out of four stars, as not only is there high demand, but the entire venture can be set in motion for less than $5,000. Once again, the income and profit potential will vary. However, skylights have a good gross profit margin, and installation rates average in the range of $35 to $50 per hour. Combined income and profits for a business that sells and installs skylights could easily reach $100,000 per year or more.

WEB RESOURCE: www.thebluebook.com Directory service listing manufacturers and distributors of skylights.

INTERIOR AND EXTERIOR HOUSE PAINTING
★ $$ 🏠 🕐

The business of painting houses has been around for years, and will continue to produce excellent profits for the owners of house painting services for many years to come. Why? Simple. Heights, ladders, and slow tedious work are enough reasons to scare off even the most hardcore of do-it-yourself home-owners. House painting is a very simple business to set in motion and only requires a small investment to get going and even a smaller learning curve to master. Like most labor-intensive business ventures, you can pretty much be guaranteed of work regardless of economic conditions. Providing a free value-added service such as cleaning the gutters or windows while on the job site, is a great way to separate your company from the competition. Often small free value-added services will increase the numbers of referrals your business will receive.

WEB RESOURCE: www.pdca.org Painting and Decorators Contractors Association.

GARAGE ORGANIZERS

Millions of people, myself included, can no longer fit the car into the garage because of the treasures (junk) that the garage seems to magically collect. This strange, but true force of nature can make you rich. To start your own garage organizer service requires no special skills or equipment other than some basic hand tools. Ideally, you can start close to home by providing the service to family and friends, while building a sound referral base. Home improvement trade shows will also be a valuable source of leads, and a "before and after" display can generate an enormous amount of interest in your products and services. The display can be designed and built for less than $1,000. The lack of competition in this industry should allow you to mark up your products such as shelving and storage cabinets by at least 40 to 50 percent, while maintaining an hourly rate for installations in the range of $25 to $30.

MIRROR INSTALLATIONS

Mirrors are required for just about every residential and commercial washroom application, and a mirror sales and installation business can easily be operated from a home garage. All that is required is a truck with a basic glass rack, a few tools, and the ability to cut glass (or hire an assistant who can cut the glass). The current rate to install bathroom mirrors is in the range of $5 to $7 per square foot, while the wholesale cost of the mirror is only $2 per square foot. Your math skills do not have to be good to know that leaves around $4 per square foot just for installing the mirror. For example, if the average installation job is four mirrors with an average size of nine-square feet per mirror, then this would leave you and a helper $150 for installing the mirrors, which would take about an hour to do. Once you have established the business, you can begin to market the services to commercial and residential construction companies, and it should not take long to build up a solid customer base.

WEB RESOURCE: www.glasslinks.com Directory listing information and links to the flat glass industry.

PATIO COVERS
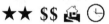

Patio covers are a great low cost, high value home improvement project, as not only can a patio cover be an attractive add-on to any home, more importantly it can provide protection and relief from the heat of the sun. The first step to marketing this type of home improvement business is to establish the target market for the product. Potential customers will include residential homeowners with southern exposed yards and patios, and commercial businesses such as cafés. A display booth set up at a local mall or home and garden trade show that shows the benefits and value associated with the patio covers will be the best approach to attaining qualified sales leads.

REQUIREMENTS: Most manufacturers of aluminum patio covers ship the finished product as a kit including an instruction guide on how to install the product. Due to this kit format, there is not a lot of technical or construction experience required to assemble and install the patio covers. Additional requirements will be power tools, ladders, and a van or trailer to transport the patio covers to the installation site. Almost all areas of the country do not require a building permit to be issued for the purpose of installing a patio cover. Of course, you will always need to check regulations in your local community.

START-UP COSTS: An initial investment of less than $10,000 will kick this new business venture into high gear.

PROFIT POTENTIAL: The following is a suggested retail pricing formula.

1. Installation time should be based on a minimum of $30 per man-hour.
2. Add wholesale product costs to labor costs. Remember to include consumables, such as screws, nails, caulking, and all flashings.
3. Add the labor and materials total and add on 50 percent of that number, which will give you the retail or contract selling price. Maintaining this pricing formula will generate a 33 percent gross profit margin prior to operating overheads being factored.

WEB RESOURCE: www.thebluebook.com Directory service listing patio cover manufacturers and distributors.

WOOD SCREEN DOOR MANUFACTURING

Old-fashioned decorative Victorian wood screen doors are all the rage for an inexpensive home improvement. You can capitalize on the demand for Victorian wood screen doors by starting a business that manufactures, sells, and installs screen doors. The business can be established and operated right from a garage or basement workshop. All you will need is woodworking equipment and some screen door patterns to get rolling. Once again, marketing the doors at home improvement shows and mall kiosks will probably be your best bet, in terms of attracting customers to purchase the finished products. Additionally, check with local homebuilding centers to see if they stock the old-fashion style screen doors. If they do not carry this item, then what a great opportunity for you to set up retail distribution accounts with them.

GAZEBOS
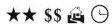

Sales and installations of garden gazebos is a wonderfully inexpensive way to start your own business enterprise. The demand for custom-built gazebos has never been higher, and the demand continues to grow, especially for gazebos used to house hot tubs. The business can be started for a very modest investment, and has the potential to return big profits. You can design your own line of gazebos to sell and install, or you can purchase plans for gazebo construction and use these designs to get started. You may want to build an alliance with an existing gazebo manufacturer that specializes only in sales. This would allow you to carry out the manufacturer's installations and capitalize on their customer base. Profit potential range: part-time $10,000+ per year; full-time $25,000+ per year.

WEB RESOURCE: www.niagaradesigns.com Design plans for gazebos and garden structures.

HOT TUB INSTALLATIONS

★ $$ 🏠 🕐

Hot tubs make a great addition to any home. However, the focus of this new business opportunity is not aimed at hot tub sales, but at the installation of hot tubs. In order for a hot tub to properly work and be safe for the occupants, it must be installed correctly, including the electrical hook-up and a solid foundation base. Starting your own business that specializes in the delivery and installation of hot tubs is a great little business venture to launch. You can charge a flat fee or hourly rate for the installation service. Potential customers for the service can include hot tub retailers who require additional installation contractors and homeowners who are moving and require their hot tubs to be relocated. Income potential range: $25 to $40 per hour plus delivery charges.

SAFE INSTALLATIONS

★★★ $$ 🏠 🕐 ⚖️

Crime is on the rise, and people are now more proactive in terms of protecting themselves and their families from becoming victims of crime and against the loss of their valuables or personal property through crime. The time has never been better to start and operate a business that specializes in the sales and installations of safes used in the prevention of property loss by burglary. Safes typically come in two forms. The first is the traditional floor model safe that can be cemented into place as an additional safety measure. The second is wall-mounted safes, which are generally concealed behind furniture or installed in unlikely places, such as attics and closets. In the research of this business, I interviewed a former locksmith who now exclusively installs safes into residential homes. In an average week he installs four to six safes with a profit margin after expenses of $150 to $200 per safe. That is an excellent income level to achieve for a one-person business that operates from home with virtually no overhead. The only system he uses to market his business is directly through homebuilders and renovation companies. These contractors sell his product and service to their clients as an upgrade feature. In return, the contractors keep 20 percent of the total sales value.

REQUIREMENTS: Installing safes does not require any special certificates, with the exception that the person who is carrying out the installation should be bonded for insurance purposes. However, you must first find out all of the regulations in your area in terms of safe sales and installations. The additional requirements for this business start-up include dolly equipment capable of moving heavy items and a few basic power tools to be used for the safe installations.

START-UP COSTS: The total capital required to activate this venture is in the range of $2,000 to $5,000, excluding transportation requirements.

PROFIT POTENTIAL: The safe installer mentioned previously, charges a flat fee of $200 to install a floor or wall-mounted safe. Additionally, he adds 30 percent markup to the wholesale cost of the safe. Even if you allow for commissions to be paid to a third party for initiating the sale, this is still a very profitable business to start and operate.

DOOR INSTALLATIONS
★★ $$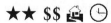

Like windows, doors also rank number six as the most frequently completed home improvement

renovation. Once again, modern manufacturing methods and materials have helped to fuel the desire for this type of home improvement. Newly installed doors not only have better safety and insulation features, these doors are also highly attractive and can improve the appearance of the home for a relatively small investment. Due to the fact that this is a competitive industry, you may want to consider specializing in one particular type of door or become an exclusive agent or representative for one door manufacturer. Specialization in any industry will generally result in lower wholesale product costs and higher returns, in terms of both product and service demand. Do not overlook the apartment or condominium market for this product. Many of these buildings were constructed during the early '80s, while the construction industry was booming, and the quality of the doors at that time was very inferior to today's doors.

WEB RESOURCE: www.windoorweb.com Directory listing window and door manufacturers and distributors.

INTERIOR DECORATING SERVICE
★★ $$

Starting an interior decorating service is the perfect business enterprise for the person that has artistic abilities and a creative flair. Generally certification from a recognized institution in the field of interior decoration and design is required. However, the service can be launched without the certificate, but it will be much better received by potential clients as a professional service with proper accreditation. Not required is a lot of start-up investment, as equipment purchases are minimal and the business can be operated from a homebased or shared office location. Most interior decorators prefer to specialize in providing either a commercial or residential decorating service. Residential decorators establish alliances with new homebuilders and renovation contractors as a method to gain access to their clients. Commercial decorators generally build alliances with commercial property managers and commercial contractors and architects. Home and garden trade shows are also a fantastic forum to promote the service and collect sales leads. Starting this business will require a great deal of patience and time, but with good business and design skills utilized, the determined entrepreneur can establish a very rewarding and profitable business providing interior decorating services.

WEB RESOURCE: www.iida.org International Interior Design Association.

BATHROOM AND KITCHEN VENTS

Prior to building codes establishing mandatory installations of kitchen and bathroom ventilation systems for all new construction projects, many houses were built without ventilation systems. This fact creates a fantastic opportunity for an inexpensive homebased business venture that has the potential to generate a very lucrative income. Installation of ventilation systems generally only requires a few hours of time and basic tools and materials that can be purchased at any local building center. Designing simple door-hanger fliers and distributing them throughout your community can help promote the service. It won't take long for the phone to start ringing, as anyone who does not have kitchen and bath vents realizes the damage it causes in terms of mold, mildew, and odors. Total start-up costs will be less than $1,000, and an income level of $600 per week is easily attainable.

ROOF INSTALLATIONS

The best aspect about starting a roofing service is that unlike a new kitchen, a new roof is usually a need, not a want. Residential and commercial roofing manufacturers use many different materials, such as asphalt, steel, cedar, and composite materials. The first step to get the business set in motion is to decide what type of roofing, and on what type of building you will be concentrating your marketing effort on. Regardless of whether you concentrate on residential or commercial, a roofing service will always be in high demand. Simply put, to get business there are many options available to you, including subcontracting for a new homebuilder, advertising directly

to the end consumers, and becoming a manufacturer's authorized installation representative.

REQUIREMENTS: Depending on the type of roof replacement service you will be operating, the requirements will vary in terms of skilled staff, equipment, regulations, and operating location. In some areas of the country, a builder's license is required to carry out roofing installations. Liability insurance is also an absolute must, regardless of the type of roofing installations you specialize in.

WEB RESOURCE: www.nrca.net The National Roofing Contractors Association.

GLASS TINTING SERVICE

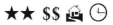

Glass tinting is a very affordable business enterprise to launch, and with a little bit of practice it can be mastered by just about anyone. The best aspect of the business is the fact that it can be operated on a year-round basis, regardless of weather conditions, right from a mobile installation vehicle. The market for glass tinting is endless in terms of residential, commercial, and automotive applications, including cars, boats, house windows and skylights, retail store windows, and recreational vehicles. A fast start method to get rolling in this business is to build alliances with used car dealers, boat brokers, and commercial property managers, as these businesses can offer glass tinting options to their customers.

CUSTOM FIREPLACE MANTELS

★★ $$ 🏠 🕐

One of the hottest home improvements right now is upgrading or installing new gas fireplaces. Most newly installed fireplaces have one thing in common: they require a mantel to suit the fireplace. Building and installing custom fireplace mantels is a great business to start for a person who has expertise in construction, or more specifically, cabinetmaking. This sort of business can easily be started for less than $1,000 and be operated right from a truck or van. In terms of marketing the mantels, there is an endless supply of potential customers who can provide you with work, including homebuilders, interior designers, renovation companies, gas fireplace retailers, architects, and utility companies.

SOLAR TUBE INSTALLATIONS
★★★ $$ 🏠 🕐

Solar tubes are a low-cost alternative to installing skylights. These miniskylights are available in a few different sizes and are packaged complete with roof flashing, expandable tunnel, interior finishing ring, and all required installation hardware. What makes this a terrific business start-up is the fact that solar tubes are easy to install, require no permits or special tools, and cost the homeowner less than $600 for the complete installation, including the product. The benefit of the solar tube is that they can add a tremendous amount of natural light to areas that are normally dark, such as closets, stairways, bathrooms, and hallways. The market for solar tubes is unlimited for both residential and commercial applications. Solar tubes are a relatively new product to enter the home improvement market. The potential growth is excellent and current competition is limited. The best way to promote the product and your installation service is to build a mobile showroom on a trailer, keeping it completely free from light inside the trailer with the exception of a solar tube. Both you and your customers will be amazed at the amount of light that is generated by the solar tube, which of course is a great sales tool.

REQUIREMENTS: Only basic construction knowledge and power tools are required to install solar tube skylights. Currently there are no regulations for the installation of solar tubes, but check with local building officials in your area. Note: A few of the solar tube manufacturers have a night light option. If you are considering providing this option to your customers, ensure that you are, or you have access to, a licensed electrician to complete the electrical hookups.

START-UP COSTS: A solar tube sales and installation service can be established for less than $5,000 including the cost of tools, inventory, and a mobile showroom display. Once you have established contact with manufacturers, attempt to acquire exclusive installation rights for your community, as this

will often reduce wholesale costs you pay for the product.

PROFIT POTENTIAL: Installed solar tubes are currently retailing in the $500 to $600 range and cost less than $200 for the complete kit. This is a great one-person business that can easily generate an income in excess of $60,000 a year for the entrepreneur who is willing to go for it.

WEB RESOURCE: www.thebluebook.com Directory service listing solar tube manufacturers and distributors.

HOME IMPROVEMENT DIRECTORY
★★★ $$$$ 🏠 🕐 🌐

The basis of this business opportunity is straightforward. Home improvement contractors pay you a fee to advertise and promote their services and products in your annual home improvement directory. You create the directory in print or CD-ROM format and distribute the directory free of charge in the community that the home improvement directory is intended to serve. The directory can be distributed via home and garden shows and a local promotion tied in with a newspaper or TV/radio station. This new business venture could not only prove to be very profitable, but it also lends itself perfectly to expand nationally on a franchise basis, once a working model has been proved successful. Start-up costs will vary depending on factors such as print or electronic directory format, etc. However, this venture will not require more than $25,000 in initial capital to get it rolling.

ONLINE CONTRACTORS DIRECTORY
★★ $$$ 🏠 🕐 🌐 🖱

Not all contractors and renovation companies have the time, budget, or skills required to create and maintain their own Web site. Thus there is a fantastic opportunity awaiting the cybersavvy entrepreneur by launching a "contractors online directory." The Web site can be indexed by the various construction or renovation services featured, such as a painting section, flooring section, and sunroom section. Ideally, the site would service one particular community or city, thus allowing for future growth by franchising or licensing the operating format to qualified webmasters across the country. People would simply log onto the site and view the service and product listings that were of interest to them. Each contractor could receive a listing in the index hyperlink to a pop-up page to describe their business, or even link to their Web site if they have one. Charging clients a monthly fee of $100 including site maintenance and coupon page options is not out of line. Providing you can secure 100 clients, you will generate sales in excess of $100,000 annually.

PAVING CONSULTANT

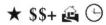 ★ $$+

Starting a full-scale paving contracting business is extremely investment capital-intensive. However, starting a business as an independent paving consultant is a very inexpensive business to get rolling, and can generate an income in excess of $100,000 per year. Simply put, market and sell paving services, and subcontract the paving to a qualified and well-equipped paving contractor while retaining 10 to 20 percent of the contract value. Door knocking, word-of-mouth, and distributing door-hanger fliers throughout the community will best accomplish marketing a paving service. Additional income can be earned by providing a driveway sealing service, and driveway sealing work can be subcontracted to a qualified contractor. Maintaining yearly gross sales of $400,000 will produce a pretax income of $40,000 to $80,000 per year.

WINDOW BOXES AND SHUTTERS

 ★★ $

Sales and installations of exterior window flower boxes and decorative window shutters is a fantastic little business to get going that can be started for peanuts and operated right from home on a full- or part-time basis. You can design and build your own products or purchase prebuilt window boxes and shutters. All that is required to install these items are a few basic tools and a ladder. These window boxes and shutters can be sold to homebuilders, architects, and homeowners. One interesting marketing method

may be to pick a highly visible and attractive home in your community and offer these products to the homeowner for free in exchange for allowing you to use their home as a show home, or reference home. This method will allow other potential customers to drive by to have a look at the dramatic difference that installing window flower boxes and shutters can have on the appearance of their homes. Giving away a few hundred dollars worth of installed products may return you a few thousand dollars in profits.

CUSTOM FRENCH DOORS

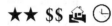 ★★ $$

Starting your own business that manufactures, retails, and installs custom-made interior French doors is an excellent way to be self-employed and generate very lucrative profit returns. There is very little competition in this business; yet the demand for high quality and unique French doors is very good, especially in the higher-end markets, such as expensive homes and professional offices. A great way to market the French doors and installation service is to work with homebuilders who are prepared to offer your French doors to their clients as an upgrade finishing option.

DESIGN TIP: To make your custom French doors unique and different from your competitors, you may want to consider a few of the following: Gold-plated or solid brass hardware, stained glass or sandblasted glass lites, stainless steel or mosaic tile covers, and curved or shaped tops. One thing is for sure: this business will allow you to be creative in your designs, which can assist you in building a solid reputation and client base.

LAMINATE FLOOR INSTALLATIONS

★★★ $$

Laminate flooring that is manufactured to resemble hardwood flooring is an incredibly popular alternative to the high cost of installing real hardwood flooring. Laminate flooring is available in a wide range of finishes and is virtually impossible to damage or destroy. Best of all, laminate flooring is extremely easy to install even if your knowledge of flooring installation is limited. To set this business in motion, first check to see if the home improvement centers in your area provide an installation service of this product. If they don't, then it's a marriage made in heaven. They sell it, and you install it. You can talk to interior decorators and designers to promote your service and establish a client base. The fastest way to market this business if you intend to concentrate on commercial applications will simply be to knock on doors and sell your product and service on the many benefits this type of flooring finish can provide to their business establishments.

REQUIREMENTS: A few basic tools including a jig saw, cordless drill, portable table saw, tape measure, chalk line, transportation, and most importantly, a good set of knee pads. Though it is not required, you will probably want to familiarize yourself with local building codes and safety regulations.

START-UP COSTS: Total business start-up costs, including tools, sales samples, and brochures will be well less than $2,000 providing that you already have suitable transportation, such as a truck, van, or station wagon.

PROFIT POTENTIAL: The profit potential is excellent. Laminate flooring is currently retailing for $4 to $6 per square foot, while the wholesale cost of materials is in the $1.50 to $2 range. Typically, for this type of installation service you can expect to earn $35 to $40 per hour after expenses. Selling and installing new baseboard moldings while you are on the job site can earn additional business revenues and profits.

GLASS BLOCK INSTALLATIONS

Glass block is back in vogue for two reasons. The first: having glass block windows installed is a cost-effective way to beautify your home and add real designer flair. The second reason is that installing glass block into basement window areas is a great way to let the light shine in, and at the same time burglar proof windows. Starting your own glass block installation service does not require a lot in terms of investment or expertise. Almost all home improvement centers will now make up glass block

windows on a custom order basis to fit any size opening. However, the installation techniques still do require some experience, but this can be self-taught starting with your home, or a friend or relative's home. One thing is for sure; it does not appear as though glass block windows will be falling from popularity any time soon.

MOLDING INSTALLATIONS

The fastest and least inexpensive way to improve a home's interior appearance is to install decorative baseboard, crown, and door moldings. The market for interior moldings and installation services is absolutely huge, both for home renovations and new construction. You can market your products and services to homebuilders, interior decorators, or directly to consumers seeking to upgrade their homes.

MARKETING TIP: Building contacts with window and door installation companies is the quickest way in which to launch your own molding installation business. These companies often will subcontract the molding installations, which have to be completed after the windows and doors have been installed. Alliances established with two or three of these companies can easily supply you with more work than a single owner-operator in this business can handle. The total investment to start your own molding installation business will be less than $2,000 including all required tools and equipment. This business can be managed from a homebased office and operated from an installation vehicle.

WALLPAPERING SERVICE

The demand for residential wallpapering has been on a steady decline for the past decade, with the exception of wallpaper decorative ceiling and wall borders. However, the demand for commercial wallpaper applications is on the rise, due to the fact that a wallpaper finish as opposed to a paint finish, lasts longer, is easier to maintain and, calculated over a usable life span, is half the cost of painting.

Specializing in commercial wallpaper applications is a very inexpensive business venture that you can initiate. It can return a comfortable living for many years. Commercial builders, renovators, and property managers can be your best source of leads to secure work.

CABINET DOOR REPLACEMENTS
★★ $$ 🏠 🕒

The average new kitchen costs in the range of $20,000 to install, not including appliances. Not everyone can afford this expensive home improvement; however, it only costs a few thousand dollars to update a kitchen's look with new cabinet doors and hardware. Starting this business does not require a great deal of expertise or capital, and you can generally be completely ready to roll for under a $5,000 investment. I talked to one very crafty gentleman in this business. His solution to building a client base fast was to hold a contest, which he advertised, in his local paper. The contest was for a free kitchen update. You sent in pictures of your existing ugly kitchen and why you thought it needed an updated look. In the first two weeks, he had more than 100 entries for the contest, complete with name, address, and telephone numbers. Not only did he choose a winner and install the kitchen update for free, more importantly he had a base of more than 100 potential customers that he could now market to, as he knew that they were in the market for his type of service.

INTERCOM INSTALLATIONS
★★ $$ 🏠 🕒

Recent technology changes in intercom systems have made them extremely easy to install, as intercoms are now available in wireless form. Due to these recent changes in the product, starting a business that sells and installs wireless intercoms is a fantastic business opportunity for just about anyone, regardless of construction or business experience. Intercom systems have a wide range of uses including:

- Installations in baby nurseries, residential and commercial.
- Business applications for warehouse to office communications.
- Security applications for residential and commercial door entry use.

Overall this is a very good choice for a new low-investment business start-up that has the potential to generate a very lucrative income for the owner-operator of the business.

HOME IMPROVEMENT TRADE SHOWS
★★★ $$$ 🕒

Why not organize and host your own semiannual home improvement trade shows. Now is the time to capitalize on the popularity of home improvement trade shows. Construction and renovation companies do not hesitate in paying as much as $200 per day for a 10-foot x 10-foot display booth, and the attending public will gladly pay $10 to get inside to see all the latest home improvement products and services.

MARKETING TIP: Find a major sponsor to co-host and promote the event, such as a radio station, TV station, local building center, newspaper, or construction association. Securing this type of sponsorship can help reduce your up-front capital outlay as well. You can utilize the resources that these sponsors already have in place. Profit potential range is $10,000+ per home improvement trade show that the business organizes.

HOME THEATER ROOMS
★★ $$$ 🏠 🕒

Home theaters have become a very popular home renovation. Big-screen TVs, surround sound, and full contact audio products are all helping to fuel the demand for the perfect family entertainment room. Thus, starting a business that specializes in designing and renovating existing rooms into home theater rooms is a fantastic business enterprise to set in motion for the new millennium. To keep business start-up costs to a minimum, consider establishing an alliance or joint venture with an existing audio/visual electronics retailer. Your company would provide the room designs and construction, while the retail business would provide the home theater electronics products. This type of joint venture would be very beneficial to both businesses and increase the profit and market share potential overall.

GREENHOUSES
★★ $$$ 🏠 🕒

In the past decade greenhouses have become a very hot home improvement product and project. As the baby boomer generation slips into retirement they are looking for ways to keep busy, physically fit, and enjoy life. Greenhouse hobby gardening provides them with exactly what they are seeking. There are various approaches that can be taken for starting a greenhouse installation business. These approaches include:

- Designing, building, selling, and installing greenhouses.
- Designing and selling U-Install-It greenhouse kits.
- Selling and installing greenhouses for existing manufacturers.

Profit potential range is $20,000 per year part-time and $50,000+ per year full-time.

WEB RESOURCE: www.ngma.com National Greenhouse Manufacturers Association.

DEMOLITION SERVICE
★★★ $$ 🏠 🕒

A demolition service is a fantastic business venture to set in motion—not the traditional large-scale demolition service—but a small demolition service that specializes in residential and commercial renovation projects. What makes this a great business opportunity is simple. Contractors and renovation companies typically will carry out the demolition needed to get started on the rebuilding process involved with a renovation. The problem, however, is the fact that these companies are often forced to pay over-qualified carpenters' huge salaries for doing

the demolition work that could be completed by laborers receiving a much lower hourly rate. The results often mean less revenues and profits for the contractor. Herein lies the business opportunity: Forming a crew of construction laborers and subcontracting for renovation companies and contractors for demolition work has the potential to pay off big. Paying the crew $8 to $10 per hour each, while charging the contractors $15 per man-hour can leave you with a profit of $30 per hour based on a five-man demolition crew. Operate two or three crews and the profit potential increases dramatically. *Note*: Be sure to acquire workers' compensation insurance for employees and general liability insurance to safeguard against the costs of potential accidents.

WEB RESOURCE: www.demolitionassociation.com National Association of Demolition Contractors.

CONSTRUCTION PROJECT MANAGEMENT
★★ $$ 🏠 🕒

"Have construction knowledge and management skills, will travel," can be the motto of your new business if you start a construction management business. The market for construction project management services is huge and includes residential and commercial construction projects. However, due to the nature of the construction industry, you would be well advised to specialize or focus on either residential or commercial construction project management. Currently, subcontract project managers are charging fees based on the construction project itself. Typically, fees are in the range of $300 to $600 per day, and can go as high as $1,000 per day for specialized construction projects.

FIREPLACE INSTALLATIONS
★★ $$$$ 🏠 🕒 ⚖

Wood-burning, gas, and alternative fuels—you can sell and install all of these types of home fireplaces if you are considering starting a fireplace sales and installation business. The best way to operate and market this kind of new business venture is with the assistance of a fully operational fireplace showroom. There are hundreds of fireplace options, mantel options, and fireplace accessories options for home-owners to choose from, and a retail showroom is the best way to display these products and build customer interest. Considerations for this type of retail and installation business include business location, qualified installation staff, and liability insurance, just to mention a few. Be sure to utilize home and garden trade shows for exhibiting purposes, as they are wonderful forums for collecting qualified sales leads. The profit potential will greatly vary for a fireplace sales and installation business. However, there should be no problems maintaining profit margins of 25 to 35 percent on all retail sales. Fireplace installation rates are currently in the range of $35 to $60 per hour, all of which adds up to a potentially profitable business opportunity for the resourceful entrepreneur who is prepared to work hard.

CONSTRUCTION ESTIMATING SERVICE
★★ $$ 🏠 🕐

Calling all handymen, carpenters, and home improvement gurus. The time has never been better than now to start a construction estimating service, and the possibility to earn more than $100,000 per year is very real. Unlike a home inspection service that provides a detailed report on what is wrong with a home, property, or building, a construction estimating service provides a detailed report on how to fix the problems and what the renovation or construction work will cost. The main market for this type of service is home buyers, who not only want to know what is wrong with a home, but also want to know how it can be corrected and what the costs involved will be. A secondary market is existing home and property owners who would like to have an initial cost analysis completed in regards to a home improvement or construction project to assess the value of the project. The main requirement for establishing and running this type of unique consulting service is to have a good understanding of all areas of the construction industry and trades. Rates for a construction estimating service will greatly depend on the size and value of the potential project. However, charging a fee in the range of $50 per hour is certainly not out of line.

PAINT AND WALLPAPER STORE
★★ $$$$

Starting a retail paint and wallpaper store is a relatively stable retail business venture to start, as there is no real threat from Internet sales of these products. However, the big threat comes in the form of big box retailers, so business location is of critical importance to the success and survival of this kind of retailing venture. To increase sales and profits beyond just selling paint and wallpaper, also provide customers with unique services, such as after-hours instruction classes in various home decorating mediums and other products and services, such as equipment rentals for do-it-yourself painters. Factoring in considerations such as competition, start-up investment, operating costs, and profit potential, a paint and wallpaper store is a good choice for a new business enterprise, but best left to those of you with retailing experience.

ABOVE-GROUND POOLS
★ $$$$

Above-ground pools have enjoyed a resurgence in popularity in the past few years. This is a business opportunity for the careful and innovative entrepreneur who is prepared to invest both time and money into selling and installing above-ground pools. The first step that needs to be taken for this business start-up is to locate a manufacturer of above-ground pools and negotiate an exclusive distribution and installation agreement for a selected geographical area. Once that has been successfully achieved, the business can be advertised, promoted, and marketed utilizing all the traditional methods. Additional revenue can be gained by providing clients and above-ground pool owners with a pool maintenance service, as well as a pool dismantling and reinstallation service for customers relocating.

CUSTOM COUNTERTOPS
★★ $$ 🏠 🕐

Laminates, stone, ceramic tile, concrete, or metal kitchen and bathroom countertops can and are being manufactured from a wide variety of raw materials to suit every interior décor and budget. Designing, manufacturing, and installing custom countertops is a relatively uncomplicated process that requires only basic tools and a homebased workshop. Once again, kitchen and bath renovations rank as the two most common home improvement projects carried out by homeowners, and countertops are an important component of these renovations. Most manufacturers and installers of custom-made countertops work on a subcontract basis, mainly for interior designers, architects, homebuilders, and renovation contractors. However, custom countertops can be sold directly to homeowners by displaying samples at home improvement trade shows and by initiating an advertising campaign locally in the area you service. The key to success in this type of unique home improvement business is to provide clients with exciting designs, material selections, and top-notch installation services. Retail prices of custom countertops vary greatly depending on size, shape, complexity, and materials used to construct. However, installation rates are standard in the industry and generally range from $30 to $50 per hour.

CABINETMAKING SERVICE
★★ $$ 🏠 🕐

Time devoted to learning the craft of fine cabinetmaking could be time very well spent considering professional cabinetmakers routinely charge $40 to $70 per hour for their service. Market your cabinetmaking services to contractors of luxury homes, architects, interior designers, and directly to homeowners by placing newspaper advertisements and by displaying your products and skills at home improvement trade shows. Remember not to limit your marketing efforts only to residential prospects, as there is also great demand for custom cabinets and shelves in commercial applications for store fixtures and professional offices. Get started learning cabinetmaking by enrolling in courses, purchasing books and how-to videos, and by practicing constructing cabinets for your own home and for family and friends. Many cabinetmakers work from a well-equipped homebased workshop as a method to keep

start-up costs and operating overheads to a minimum.

WEB RESOURCE: www.cabinetmarkers.org Cabinet Makers Association.

SEAMLESS GUTTERS
★★ $$$ 🏠

Seamless rain gutters are quickly becoming the eavestroughing of choice for most contractors, architects, and homeowners simply because it's inexpensive, quick to install, and available in a wide range of designer colors. The best aspect about starting a seamless gutter service is the fact that it requires little experience. There are portable roll form machines available that will form the gutters in the desired profile right on the customer's job site. In a nutshell, a coil of aluminum metal in the chosen color is loaded into one end of the machine and the finished rain gutter comes out the other end. Currently, gutter installation contractors are charging in the range of $2.50 to $3.50 per linear foot of gutter installed, $1.50 per linear foot of downpipe installed, plus a premium for jobs that require extensive ladder work or have numerous inside and outside corners. As a way to increase the average selling price, many gutter contractors also quote to install aluminum fascia and soffit while on the job site. Promote the products and services by way of traditional print advertising and by establishing alliances with new home contractors, renovation companies, and siding and roofing contractors. Many gutter installation contractors work exclusively on a subcontract basis for the above-mentioned companies.

WEB RESOURCE: www.knudsonmfg.com Manufacturers of gutter making machines.

CONCRETE STAMPING
★★★ $$+ 🏠 🕐

Concrete stamping and coating are one of the hottest home improvements being carried out by homeowners and contractors alike. This just may be the right new business for you to start and succeed with. Generally concrete stamping is done with installations of new concrete driveways, walkways, and patios. Once the forms are in place, dyes have been added, and the concrete is poured using various tools to create the desired pattern and appearance on the surface as it cures. These patterns can range from a cobble stone look to the look of blue Vermont slate. The advantage of concrete stamping is that it costs much less to create a concrete driveway stamped to look like slate than it does to install a real slate driveway—not to mention the fact that the concrete-stamped slate driveway can be completed in a fraction of the time it would take to install the real deal. Concrete stamping is not limited to new installations, as there are surface coatings that can be applied onto existing concrete surfaces to create various patterns and textures. Learning the art of concrete stamping and coatings will require an investment of time on your behalf in order to master it. However, if you are seeking to start a home improvement business that is in demand and has the potential to generate lucrative profits, concrete stamping is one of the best bets.

WEB RESOURCE: www.stampcrete.com Manufacturers and distributors of concrete stamping equipment and supplies; also have concrete stamping training courses available.

GARAGE DOOR SALES AND INSTALLATIONS
★★ $$$ 🏠 🕐

Many single-family dwellings have at least one garage door, some even have as many as three. When you start to multiply the number of single-family dwellings by the average number of garage doors per dwelling you begin to understand why starting a business that sells, installs, and repairs garage doors could prove to be a very profitable new enterprise. Garage doors and accessories are not difficult to install. In fact most manufacturers of these products include detailed step-by-step instruction that outlines the installation procedure. This makes a good business opportunity for just about anyone with basic construction abilities and tools. Like many home improvement and repair businesses, the key to success lies within securing a distribution or installation agreement with one or more manufacturers of the product you intend to sell and install. Thankfully, in

the case of garage doors, securing this type of exclusive agreement should not prove difficult, as there are hundreds of companies that manufacture garage doors in just about every style, material selection, and price range available. As great as that sounds, however, the real challenge will be marketing the product and service. This can be accomplished by building alliances within the construction and real estate industries. These alliances should include new home builders, renovation and general contractors, home and property inspectors, real estate agents and brokers, and property managers, all of whom can refer your service or in some cases supply you business with subcontract installation work. In addition to basic construction skills, you will also need power tools, such as drills, a mitre saw, and transportation like a truck or large trailer capable of moving the product to the installation site. The repair aspect of the business can be equally as lucrative as the sales and installation side.

WEB RESOURCE: www.thomasregister.com Directory service listing garage door manufacturers and distributors.

SUNROOM INSTALLATION
★★ $$$$ 🏠 ⚖️

The addition of a sunroom is a terrific way for many homeowners to increase living space, add an all-season retreat, and increase the value of their home for a relatively low investment. Sunrooms have become one of the most popular home improvement projects in the past decade, and this fact is what makes starting a sunroom sales and installation business such a wise choice for a new business enterprise. There are basically two options available in terms of starting this business. The first is to locate a manufacturer that designs and prebuilds kit sunrooms that can be sold and installed at customers' homes, and negotiate an exclusive dealer's agreement with the manufacturer. The second option is to design and build custom sunrooms to meet customers' needs and requirements. In both cases, a building permit is generally required in all regions of North America for the installation of a sunroom, so be sure to check local building codes and regulations before you get started. Sunrooms are very easy to build and install and only require basic construction knowledge. For anyone wishing to start this business and does not have any construction experience, you can always hire qualified subcontractors to carry out the installations while you concentrate on sales, marketing, and management aspects of the business. Home and garden trade shows are fantastic venues to display your products, and more importantly, collect qualified sales leads. Like most renovation and construction ventures, you should strive to maintain a 50 percent markup on all products and services you sell. Using this pricing formula will result in a 33 percent gross profit margin on sales prior to operating costs and taxes.

WEB RESOURCE: www.sunrooms.com/nsa/htm National Sunroom Association, industry information and links to manufacturers and distributors of sunroom kits, parts, and plans.

DRAPERY STUDIO

Starting a drapery studio is a fantastic new business venture to put into action, and there are three excellent options for operating this home decoration business. The first option is to run the business on a mobile basis wherein you travel to clients' locations equipped with samples of fabrics, rods, and accessories and conduct the presentation on site. The second option is to open a small boutique where customers come to you; or a combination of in-home presentations and boutique presentations. The boutique can even be operated from home providing you have the space and zoning will permit. The third option is to partner the business with an existing interior designer or decorator within the community and utilize their office or showroom for display purposes. Of course all three options can be combined to make it as easy and convenient as possible for customers to do business with you. Once again, like many businesses where a product is manufactured on a custom basis, you can hire subcontract seamstresses and installers if you lack the ability to create and install the drapery products. Utilizing qualified subcontractors will enable you to concentrate on the sales and marketing aspects of the business. Also, be sure to harness the power of the Internet to seek out a wholesale source for curtain rods and drapery accessories. The profit potential is excellent in this business simply due to the custom aspect, and you should have no problem maintaining a 100 percent markup on all products sold and installed.

NOTES

KEY

RATINGS	★
START-UP COST	$
HOMEBASED BUSINESS	
PART-TIME	
LEGAL ISSUES	
FRANCHISE OR LICENSE POTENTIAL	
ONLINE	

43

HOME REPAIR

Businesses You Can Start

GRAFFITI REMOVAL SERVICE

★★★ $$$ 🏠 🕐 🌐

The time has never been better than now to start a graffiti removal service. Why? Simply because graffiti is everywhere; on the walls of buildings, sidewalks, and fences. Starting this new business venture does not require a great deal of working experience, and the market for this service is unlimited, untapped, and graffiti vandalism shows no sign of slowing down or stopping. The equipment required for this business enterprise will be a portable pressure washer and a portable sandblaster, both of which can be conveniently mounted on a trailer for easy transportation to job sites. Successfully marketing a graffiti removal service is best accomplished by visiting businesses that are often the victims of graffiti vandalism and offering the business owners a low-cost graffiti removal solution. Provide the business owners with a monthly graffiti removal option; meaning,

for a fixed monthly fee, you will check in on the business once per week to see if there is any new graffiti to be removed. If new graffiti is present, you would simply remove the graffiti. If no graffiti is present then you would move on to your next client's location. A graffiti removal service could easily generate sales in excess of $6,000 per month, which could be achieved by securing only 100 customers paying an ongoing monthly fee of $60 to ensure that their business never has to worry about unsightly graffiti on their buildings. Additionally, a graffiti removal service could be marketed to schools, libraries, and all other agencies and associations that have problems with graffiti vandalism.

MOBILE SCREEN REPAIR

★★★ $$$ 🏠 🕐 🌐

Every year millions of window and door screens have to be repaired or replaced entirely. Starting a mobile screen repair business could put you on the road to riches. Activating a mobile screen repair service only requires a few basic tools and materials, such as a miter saw, screen rollers, various screen materials, and screen replacement parts. The business can be operated from an enclosed trailer or truck to provide shelter from inclement weather. The key requirement, in terms of marketing a mobile screen repair service, is to establish alliances with companies and individuals that require window screen repairs and replacements on a regular basis. These companies can include residential and commercial property management firms, strata corporations, government agencies, and community associations like recreation centers and schools. The profit potential for a mobile screen repair service is excellent, as there is limited competition and consumer demand is high for screen repairs and replacements. Furthermore, screening materials are very inexpensive to purchase; yet the retail selling price of window and door screen repairs and replacements is typically five to eight times as much as the material costs to produce the screens. The income that can be earned in this business venture will vary as to the total number of screen repairs. However, a well-established mobile screen repair service can generate sales in excess of $100,000 per year.

WEB RESOURCE: www.thebluebook.com Directory service listing manufacturers and distributors of screening material and parts.

PROTECT-A-CORNER SERVICE

★ $

Thousands of children, adults, and pets are injured each year as a result of falling or running into a wall corner. Starting a "protect-a-corner service" is a terrific way to be independent and provide a much needed home and business safety service to clients. There are various products available that can be used to protect wall corners and make them safer in the event of a human impact. Alternatively, you could design and develop your own product that could be used not only as wall corner protection, but also to protect furniture and equipment corners. The potential is unlimited in this business, as to the various products that can be used as corner protection and the multitude of corners they can protect.

DRIVEWAY SEALING

★★ $

Here is a great new business start-up for the university student seeking part-time business earnings to help offset the high cost of attending school. Starting a driveway sealing service is just about as easy and straightforward as any new business venture can possibly be. As mentioned earlier in this chapter, there are an estimated 75,000,000 building structures in the United States, and it's probably safe to assume that at least 25 percent of these buildings have a pavement or asphalt driveway. Assuming this is the case, that equals in the neighborhood of 18,000,000 potential customers for a driveway sealing business. To keep initial start-up costs to a minimum, simply use asphalt driveway sealer in a bucket as opposed to purchasing expensive asphalt spraying equipment. You will find that all the necessary supplies and equipment required for this business are available at any local home improvement or building center. Income potential range is $20 to $30 per hour.

ROOF REPAIRS

★★★ $$

Did you know that there are an estimated 75,000,000 building structures with roofs in the United States? And all of these building structures have one thing in common: at some point they all require the roofs to be repaired. This fact creates an extraordinary opportunity for the ambitious entrepreneur to start a residential and commercial roof repair service. The main requirement needed to operate a roof repair service is to have experience in roofing repairs, or to have an employee on staff that has experience in roof repairs. Secondary requirements include liability and workers' compensation insurance, and a few basic tools and roofing safety equipment. There are various approaches to marketing the business and securing customers, including the following:

- The roof repair service can be marketed to residential homeowners via distributing promotional fliers, or by utilizing traditional advertising mediums, such as newspaper and yellow page advertisements.
- Subcontract your roof repair services to home repair associations and clubs who already have an existing membership base that can utilize this service.
- Establish alliances with residential and commercial property management and maintenance companies and provide these companies with 24-hour roof repair services for their clients.
- Establish working relationships with existing residential and commercial roofing companies that only specialize in roofing replacements and not roofing repairs. This approach is an excellent way to establish the business quickly, as most of these roof replacement companies can act as an excellent source of referrals for the service.

START-UP COSTS: The following example can be used as a guideline to establish the investment required for starting a roof repair service.

	Low	High
Service vehicle (used)	$5,000	$10,000
Tools and equipment	$1,000	$2,500
Business setup, banking, legal, etc.	$500	$1,500
Initial advertising and marketing budget	$1,000	$2,000
Working capital	$500	$1,500
Total start-up costs	$8,000	$17,500

PROFIT POTENTIAL: The profit potential for a roof repair business can greatly vary as to a number of factors, such as the types of roof repair being completed and the manner that the business is being marketed. However, the following is a simple pricing formula that can be used in this business to establish a billing rate.

Material cost to complete roof repair	$20
Flat call-out service rate including travel	$50
2 hours labor required to complete roofing repair	$50 (@$25/hour)
Total costs to complete roofing repair	$120
Markup 50% on repair costs	$60
Total retail selling price for completed roof repair	**$180**

HANDYMAN SERVICE
★★ $$

Handyman services have been around for hundreds of years, and will continue to be around for hundreds more, simply because there is a demand for the service and this type of business venture can make money. The business requires very little in terms of explanation. The main requirement for starting a handyman service is, of course, the fact that you have to be handy and a jack-of-all-trades. Currently, handyman billing rates are in the range of $20 to $35 per hour, plus materials and a markup on materials cost. The service can be promoted and marketed to both residential and commercial customers through all traditional advertising mediums, such as the yellow pages, home maintenance clubs, newspaper advertisements, and flier distribution.

ONLINE HANDYMAN DIRECTORY
★ $$$$

Unite the handymen of the world by posting an online handyman directory. The Web site can be indexed by city and state, as well as by handyman specialty like carpentry, painting, etc. In exchange for a monthly listing fee, handyman services featured on the site would receive a listing as well as a link to a pop-up page to promote their service. The site could be promoted by placing display advertisements in print publications, as well as by linking the site to related Web sites and registering with numerous search engines. Add additional information to the site, such as home maintenance tips and a regular home repair column to increase site visitation.

WELDING

★ $$$$

The main and most important requirement to starting a welding service is that you must have a welding trade certificate. Providing you do, owning and operating a welding service can be extremely profitable. A welding service can operate from a fixed location or on a mobile basis. Of course, a full-service welding business will provide both options to its clients. Establishing a billing rate for welding is accomplished in two formats. The first billing method is to charge per job, which means that you will give your client a cost estimate prior to starting the work. The second and more common billing method is to charge an hourly rate for welding services. The current welding rate ranges between $45 and $65 per hour. All raw welding materials should be marked up by at least 50 percent to establish a retail selling value. Overall, a well-established welding service can easily generate yearly profits in excess of $70,000.

WEB RESOURCE: www.amweld.org American Welding Association.

HOME STORAGE SOLUTIONS

★ $

There are hundreds of home storage solution products on the market, and you can profit by starting a business that specializes in selling and installing these products. The business does not require a lot of investment capital to set in motion, and can be very profitable, as you can charge an hourly rate to install these products as well as add a markup onto all the products that are sold. Search the Internet and directories for manufacturers of these products. Next, simply contact them and inquire about becoming a sales agent or representative for their products in your community. This is the type of business that, once established and you have a few clients, word-of-mouth and referrals will fuel the business growth and expansion.

ZINC STRIPS AND MOSS REMOVAL

★★ $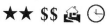

The biggest requirement to starting a zinc strip and moss removal service is that you must live in a wet and rainy area of the country where moss accumulations on rooftops can cause building and structure problems. Providing this requirement is met, the business is very easy to set in motion. Simply put, this business venture involves removing moss from rooftops and installing moss preventative zinc strips and flashing. The fastest and most economical way to market this service is to design a highly effective informational flier explaining the benefits of moss removal and prevention, as well as your service. Distribute the fliers to homes and businesses in your community that have a visible moss problem. Providing you have included the right information in the marketing flier, it will not take long for the phone to start ringing and profits to start coming in. Potential income range is $20 to $30 per hour, plus a markup on installed moss prevention zinc products, such as ridge strips and flashings.

MOBILE PAINT SPRAYING

★★ $$

Prior to researching information for this book, I did not even realize that there was such a business as a mobile paint spraying service. However, there is, and it can be a very profitable business to start and manage. The business, in a nutshell, is just as it sounds: providing paint spraying services to clients on a mobile basis. The enterprise can be operated in two fashions. The first is to use an enclosed trailer or truck to house the equipment, as well as to use as a mobile paint-spraying booth. The second option is to transport the paint spraying equipment in a smaller truck or trailer and paint items outside utilizing portable walls that, when erected, form a mini paint-spraying booth. Both operating methods are extremely effective. However, the latter is less expensive in terms of start-up investment. Mobile paint spraying services can be marketed to both residential homeowners and business owners. The following list is just a few items that can be included in your promotional brochures as items that can be spray painted.

- Fencing
- Wood siding
- Garden equipment
- Appliances

- Handrails
- Flag poles
- Metal roofing
- Store fixtures
- Patio furniture
- Steel boats
- Signs
- Trailers
- Construction equipment
- Concrete floors
- Outdoor toys
- Parking lot lines

The income potential will greatly vary for this type of unique service. However, the companies I contacted that provided mobile paint spraying services all quoted rates over the telephone in the range of $35 to $50 per hour, plus the additional costs of paint.

GUTTER PROTECTION
★★★ $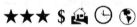

Do you want to make $50,000 or more per year, and be independent within a week from now? If so, then starting a gutter protection business may be exactly the type of new business enterprise that you have been searching for. What is a gutter protection business? Gutter protection is a product that quickly snaps into place over the top of four- and five-inch gutters. Once installed, gutter protection allows water to pass into the gutter, but not debris, such as leaves and small branches. Of course, the greatest benefit to a product like this is the fact that the homeowner no longer has to risk life and limb on a ladder to clean the rain gutters two or three times per year. If this product is so easy to install, then why would the homeowners not simply install it themselves? Because of the fact that many homeowners do not even realize that this product is available, and because it still requires a lot of ladder work to install. To effectively market this product and service, you will want to design and distribute a promotional and informational flier. The flier should highlight all the benefits of having this product installed, as well as indicate your contact information for your

business. A demonstration booth, which can be assembled for use at home and garden shows and malls, is a fantastic way not only to demonstrate the product benefits, but also to generate sales leads from potential customers. The following are reasons why a homeowner should have this product installed; you may want to include these benefits in all advertising and promotional information that you create for the business:

- No more cleaning rain gutters yourself or hiring people to do so, which saves money and time.
- No more risking personal injury by having to clean your rain gutters from an unstable ladder.
- Debris prevented from entering your home's drainage system, which can eliminate any chance of costly repairs to the drainage system.

START-UP COSTS: There are various brands of gutter protection systems available on the market, all of which are stocked at just about every home improvement and building center. This means you will only have to carry a small amount of inventory. Providing that you already have an installation vehicle, the business can be started for less than $1,000. Additionally, you will need a few ladders and basic power tools, such as a cordless drill and jig saw.

PROFIT POTENTIAL: Typically, gutter guard installations are sold on a linear foot basis. Currently, installation rates are anywhere from $2.50 to $10.00 per linear foot depending on the style of gutter guard and the complexity of the installation. To calculate an easy installation rate, simply estimate the time that it would take you to install 100 feet of the product, and use that number to calculate the installation rate. For example, we will assume that it takes two hours to install 100 feet.

50 feet/hour @$25/hour	$0.50 per foot
Product costs	$2.00 per foot
Total cost including labor and materials	$2.50 per foot
30% markup	$0.75 per foot
Retail selling price	$3.25 per foot

WEB RESOURCE: www.permaflow.com Manufacturers of gutter protection products.

REACH TRUCK SERVICE
★★ $$$$ 🏠 🕐

Starting a reach truck service is a fantastic small business for someone who is seeking to operate his or her own business on a part-time basis. The service is very straightforward: you purchase a used small bucket reach truck in good mechanical condition, and rent your services out for small residential and commercial building and structure repair jobs that are not easily or safely reached by a ladder. The possibilities are endless as to the variety of services you can provide with this type of equipment. You can include window washing, painting, gutter cleaning, and sign maintenance. You can rent your services to construction and renovation companies who need to remove and install products on second and third floors of buildings that do not otherwise have good ground or working access. This kind of unique service has little competition, and you should have no problems commanding $50 to $60 per hour for your service.

FIRE AND FLOOD RESTORATION
★★ $$ 🏠 🕐

A small kitchen fire or a burst plumbing pipe can be common occurrences in the lives of homeowners. Starting a fire and flood restoration service means that you may soon be able to assist these homeowners in repairing the damage that can be caused in these unfortunate circumstances. The main duty of a fire and flood restoration service is to initially go to the job site and carry out immediate, or sometimes temporary measures, to limit any further damage to the home. These measures can include boarding up broken windows, covering roofs that have been damaged, and removing water that may have accumulated inside the buildings. The secondary duties can include repairing the damage or hiring subcontractors to repair the damage. The largest requirement in successfully establishing a restoration service is to build contacts with insurance companies and brokers, as insurance companies and brokers will authorize the repair work in 90 percent or more of all fire and flood restoration situations.

WEB RESOURCE: www.ascr.org National Institute of Disaster/Fire and Flood Restoration Contractors Directory.

GLASS SHOP
★ $$$$

Windows, tabletops, and mirrors—the need for glass is everywhere. That's why a glass shop in your community is a good business to start. Operating this kind of specialty business requires experience in glass cutting and glass installation techniques, which is called glazing; or a person with these skills is called a glazier. Providing you or your staff possess this sort of work experience and ability, then opening a glass shop can be a very profitable business to own. There are a great many types of glass installations the business could focus on. Or you may want to specialize in one or two specific areas, such as custom glass table tops or only installing construction equipment glass, such as windshields. This business venture can be costly to establish. However, once you have identified the market that you will be catering to, the business can easily generate profits that can exceed $75,000 per year.

WEB RESOURCE: www.gwiweb.com Directory of wholesale glass and glazier supplies.

ATTIC ROOMS
★ $$$ 🏠 ⚖

There are millions of homes in North America that have some usable attic space that could easily be turned into a home office, children's play room, organized storage room, or just a small reading corner. Starting a business that specializes in the installation of small and basic attic rooms may be the business opportunity that you have been searching for. Providing that you have a good working knowledge of construction practices, as well as knowledge of the most common type of home construction in your community, there is a good chance that you will be able to predesign and construct one or two models of the basic attic rooms. These can then either be sold to customers on a do-it-yourself basis, or the customer could hire you to do the installation. Entry into the attic space can be easily gained with installation of a simple pull-down attic staircase. Prior to starting this type of home improvement venture, you should check with local building officials in terms of compliance with building code regulations.

MASONRY REPAIRS
★★ $$

Calling all masons, it's time to put all of your job experience to work for you and start earning profits in your own masonry business. Starting a business that specializes in small masonry repairs can be extremely profitable. Many of the larger masonry companies cannot service small masonry repair jobs as their overhead requires larger masonry contracts to provide adequate cash flow. This fact creates a terrific opportunity to capitalize by specializing in small masonry repairs such as brick repointing, concrete step and sidewalk repairs, and the installation of stone and brick fireplaces. You can subcontract your masonry services to construction and renovation companies. Or, market your mason repair business directly to residential and commercial customers by utilizing traditional marketing and advertising formats. While operating a small masonry repair business may not make you a millionaire, it can provide a comfortable living with a yearly income that can easily exceed $60,000.

FENCE REPAIRS
★ $

Fences are very easy to repair, and securing work for a fence repair service is even easier. Design a standard fence repair estimate form, leaving a blank area for the description of the repair to be completed. Once you have printed 50 or so of these estimate forms, simply start driving around your community in search of fences that are in need of repairs. The completed fence repair estimate can be left attached to the homeowner's mailbox with a business card and brief cover letter explaining your fence repair service. Aim to close 25 percent of the fence estimates that you complete, and I will guarantee that you can make more than $25,000 per year repairing fences, which is not bad for a business that can be started for less than $1,000.

ONLINE RECYCLED RENOVATION PRODUCTS
★★ $$$ ⌂ 🕐 ♂

Here is a unique business start-up for the cyber-savvy webmaster. Thousands of homes are demolished annually in the United States to make way for new houses and buildings. Many of these same homes have items like hardwood flooring, bathroom fixtures, and doors and windows that are of value and can be recycled. You can profit by developing a Web site where these valuable items can be listed for sale. The site should be indexed by product with a section for hardwood flooring, a section for windows, etc. This would enable visitors to easily navigate the site and find what they are looking for quickly. In terms of making money, there are a few options. The first is to charge contractors and homeowners a fee for listing the recycled building products on the site. The second option is to let customers list the items for free and retain a commission upon successful sale. Another option would be to make the site free to use for both visitors and people wishing to list items for sale and sell or rent banner advertising space to merchants and service providers seeking exposure to your Web site users.

WEB RESOURCE: www.entrepreneur.com Create a business Web site with MySite professional Web site builder.

CEDAR SHAKE RESTORATION
★★ $$ ⌂ 🕐

There are millions of cedar shakes and shingle roofs in North America, and the average lifespan of a cedar roof is about 15 years. However, if cedar roofs are restored prior to reaching their life expectancy, then these same cedar roofs can last for 25 years or more. The process of restoring cedar roofing is not complicated. The roof is first pressure washed to remove all accumulated moss and debris. Once this has been accomplished and the roof dries, a coat of wood preservative is sprayed over the entire roof surface. The average-sized cedar roof costs $10,000 to replace; however, the same cedar roof can be restored to give the roof an additional life of five or more years for approximately $1,500. This fact is what makes this such a good business to start. Not only can you save homeowners a considerable amount of money, you can also use this cost savings analysis as your main marketing tool. The equipment required for the business venture is a few ladders, a pressure washing unit, and a couple of backpack spraying units that are the same type as those used in lawn fertilization. To keep start-up costs to a minimum this equipment can even be rented for the first few jobs, until the business is established. Current rates for cedar roof restoration are in the range of $1.50 to $2.00 per square foot. Additional revenues can be generated by providing clients with gutter and skylight cleaning options while on the job.

WINDOW AND DOOR REPAIR SERVICE

The target market for a window and door repair service is owners of older homes that have wooden sash doors and windows. The reason to target these homes for this type of business is due to the fact that old wooden windows and doors require yearly maintenance, such as new putty, paint, and removal and installation of storm windows. The demand for this type of repair service will always be strong, as many of these homeowners would not consider replacing the windows and doors because the heritage value the wooden doors and windows add to the home's appearance. Potential income range is $20 to $35 per hour.

AWNING CLEANING

An awning cleaning service is a fantastic new business enterprise to put into action, as it requires no special skills or technical experience, and the income potential is outstanding. If the following list appeals to you in terms of excellent reasons why to start a business, then you may have found the right business venture to start in your community.

- Extremely low initial investment, and a fast return on investment.
- Easily managed from a homebased office.

- Flexible full- or part-time work hours.
- No special skills requirements.
- Unlimited market demand, with minimal competition.
- No inventory to warehouse.
- Potential to earn $75,000 per year or more.
- Excellent growth potential, with franchise possibilities.

In the past decade more and more business owners have been switching to commercial awning signs, as opposed to the traditional box sign for advertising their business. All of these awnings have one thing in common. They all have to be cleaned on a regular basis in order to project a good corporate image for the businesses they are promoting. This fact creates an enormous opportunity for the enterprising entrepreneur to cash in and profit, by starting an awning cleaning service. The best way to market, promote, and gain clients for this business is to simply start knocking on doors. Visit all the businesses in your community that have awning signs and talk to the business owners. Explain the benefits of keeping the awnings clean and maintained, as well as the benefits of using your service. This may seem to be an old-fashioned and time consuming marketing method. However, if you set a goal of visiting ten potential clients per day and can close two of these presentations, you will then have 40 new clients in a month's time and be well on your way to establishing a solid and profitable business concern.

START-UP COSTS: The following example can be used as a guideline to establish the investment required for starting an awning cleaning service.

Power washer with all cleaning attachments	$1,000
2 10-foot stepladders, 2 small extension ladders	$ 500
Miscellaneous equipment, such as buckets	$ 250
Business setup, stationery and marketing materials	$1,000
Total setup cost to establish business	**$2,750**

PROFIT POTENTIAL: The key to a successful and profitable awning cleaning service is to secure clients that will be using your service on a regular basis. It is much easier to establish the business and generate a profit from having 400 regular clients who use your service four times per year than it is to find 1,600 new clients each year. Assuming the average awning is $50 to clean, and you have 400 regular clients and you clean their awnings four times per year each, the business could generate gross sales of $80,000 per year.

HARDWOOD FLOOR SANDING
★★ $$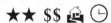

Many do-it-yourself homeowners are more than happy to stain hardwood floors. However, when it comes to sanding new hardwood floors or sanding off old finishes and scratches from old hardwood floors, that's another story entirely. Let's face it, sanding hardwood floors can be a backbreaking task, not to mention the fact that it requires a certain amount of experience, skill, and ability to sand the floors correctly. Perhaps these are good reasons for starting your own hardwood floor sanding service. As previously mentioned, there is a skill requirement that must be taken into account. However, with practice on your own hardwood floors, this skill can definitely be learned in a relatively short period of time. To keep start-up costs to a minimum you can rent the required floor sanding equipment as needed, until the business is profitable and established. Generally, floor sanding is billed on a per square foot basis, so you will want to check current rates in your local area. Successfully marketing a hardwood floor sanding service can be achieved by promoting your service to the end user or by subcontracting your services to local construction and renovation companies. Once the business is established, the owner-operator of this type of specialty construction service should have no problems in creating a yearly income in the range of $40,000 to $50,000.

TIN SHOP
★★ $$$$

The demand for custom-manufactured tin flashings and products is enormous, and starting a tin shop that fabricates these items can put you on the road to financial freedom. The business can be launched right from a basement or garage workshop and only requires a minimal amount of equipment, such as a metal break, tin sheers and a spot welder. Of course, the main requirement for this type of new business venture is that you have to be a tinsmith or have a lot of experience working with tin and various metals. Establishing alliances with roofing and heating companies will supply you with all the work that you need, as these types of construction trades often require custom manufactured tin flashings and products.

SANDBLASTING SERVICE
★★ $$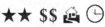

There are two approaches that can be taken when considering starting a sandblasting service. The first approach is to operate a sandblasting service from a fixed location. The second approach is to purchase a van and operate the service on a mobile basis. The second option is less costly to establish. Operating a mobile sandblasting service will also enable access to a larger variety of sandblasting work. The cost to purchase basic sandblasting equipment is minimal, and the required equipment is generally available at industrial supply centers. There are many different types of sandblasting work that can be secured in every community. However, in the spirit of being unique and in an attempt to limit competition and seek a niche, pinpoint one particular sandblasting specialty, such as headstone sandblasting. It is a common practice for headstones to be installed in cemeteries while the person they are intended for is still alive. When the appropriate time arrives, the headstone is completed with the date sandblasted into the headstone at the cemetery. The business is best marketed by visiting all the monument companies in your community and offering this type of mobile sandblasting work. Current rates are in the range of $30 to $60 per headstone and each one requires one to two hours to complete.

WEB RESOURCE: www.thebluebook.com Directory service listing construction equipment manufacturers.

HOUSE NUMBERS ON CURBS
★★ $$ 🏠 🕐

Here is a fantastic moneymaking venture that just about anyone can start for less than $100. The business is simply painting house numbers in reflective paint on the road curb in front of the house. The purpose of having the house number painted on the curb in reflective paint is so that in the event of a 911 call the emergency personnel can locate the house easier day or night. Additionally, address numbers often become hidden by overgrown trees and shrubs. Having the numbers clearly and professionally painted on the curb makes life much easier for home deliveries, such as the Friday night pizza. The only equipment requirements to set this venture in motion are a set of good quality vinyl number stencils and a paintbrush. To market the service, simply design an effective door hanger marketing brochure that details all the benefits of your low-cost service, and start hanging them on every door handle in the community. This is the type of business that can be summed up as a numbers game, meaning the more door hangers you distribute, the more house numbers you will paint. Typically, this method of marketing will result in a two to three percent closing rate. However, given this valuable service is a particular fear sell, and because this service is also unique, there should be no difficulty in securing a five to ten percent closing rate from the door hangers. Providing you secured ten clients per day and charged each one $20 for the service, the business could generate revenues in excess of $50,000 per year.

BATHTUB REGLAZING
★ $$$$ 🏠 🕐 🌐 🔵

The popular colors for bathtubs in the '70s were pink and blue; brown in the '80s; white in the '90s; and now black, as we head into the new millennium. Not all homeowners can afford to replace their bathtubs just to keep up with new and popular remodeling trends. However, many of these same homeowners can certainly afford to have their bathtubs reglazed as a method of inexpensively updating their bathrooms' appearance. Starting a bathtub reglazing service requires very little working experience, and the equipment is readily available through paint and industrial supply stores. The service is best marketed by establishing alliances with industry-related businesses, such as construction companies and property maintenance companies who can utilize the service for their clients. The bathtub reglazing can also be marketed to end consumers via a display and demonstration booth that can be setup at home and garden trade shows to collect sales leads. The potential to profit will vary greatly in this business and be determined by factors such as material cost markup, number of bathtubs reglazed, and operating overhead. However, once established, the business can easily generate an income in the range of $40 to $50 per hour.

WEB RESOURCE: www.otsm.com/links.htm Directory listing bathtub refinishing equipment and opportunities.

APPLIANCE REPAIR SERVICE
★★★ $$$ 🏠 🕐 ⚖️

Stoves, washers, dryers, and dishwashers—repairing home appliances is a service that has been, and will always be, in high demand. There are many instruction courses available that can train you to become an appliance repair technician, and some instruction courses take as little as one year to complete. That's a very strong argument for starting an appliance repair service, especially given the fact that appliance repair rates are now in the range of $50 to $80 per hour. A friend of mine in the appliance repair business generates a yearly income of more than $100,000. This is not bad, considering he only has two regular customers, works from home, and has no employees. How does he earn so much money with only two customers, you may ask? Easy. Prior to starting the business ten years ago his research into the industry revealed that most large property management companies did not have a full-time appliance repair technician on staff, even though these same companies would routinely contract for appliance repair services 100 times per year or more. The next step was easy, he simply designed a professional marketing presentation that explained his service and started to solicit all of the large residential property management companies in the area for work. To secure exclusive service contracts for appliance repairs, he provided these firms with a 10 percent discount on labor and would use refurbished parts whenever possible. Of the five residential property management companies he initially approached, two said yes, and after ten years remain his only customers.

WEB RESOURCE: www.nasa1.org National Appliance Service Association.

CARPORT CONVERSIONS

Did you know that most carports share the same footprint size and dimensions? While this may not seem important to most people, it is very useful information if you plan to start a business that specializes in converting carports into garages. Due to the fact that so many carports share the same dimensions, it creates a terrific opportunity for the innovative entrepreneur to predesign and build standard carport conversion kits that can be sold on a you-install or we-install basis. This type of business is an ideal candidate for starting from home on a part-time basis until the business is established and profitable. To gain customers, simply design a promotional marketing brochure describing your unique product and service, and distribute these brochures to all of the homes in your community that have carports. Prior to initiating this kind of business venture, check local building codes and regulations to ensure that your carport conversion kits will comply with all building code regulations.

CHIMNEY REPAIRS

Providing you have basic masonry skills and experience, starting a chimney repair service can be a very profitable business to own and operate. Brick

and stone chimneys all require maintenance in order to stay structurally sound and perform to their design specifications. The best types of chimney repairs to focus on are repairing or replacing damaged rain pots, rebuilding crowns, installing new base and counter flashing, and repointing and sealing brick and stone chimneys. The tools and equipment necessary for repairing chimneys are also very basic and include ladders, roof jacks, stone chisels, and a few hand tools. Providing you already have a vehicle, the business can easily be started for less than $1,000. Chimney repair services can be marketed to homeowners by designing and distributing door hangers and fliers describing your service. Or you can work as a subcontractor providing roofing companies and home renovation contractors with chimney repair services for their clients. The raw and manufactured materials required for chimney repairs are extremely inexpensive and available at most building centers. Visiting used building material yards can supply you with all the old and various colored bricks that will occasionally be required to replace broken or missing bricks while repairing chimneys. A chimney repair service can be a very profitable business to operate. There should be no problem in maintaining a billing rate of $50 per hour to provide chimney repairs, as well as a markup of at least 50 percent on all the material required for the chimney repair.

WEB RESOURCE: www.chimney.com Directory listing links to equipment and supply manufacturers in the chimney industry.

GARAGE WORKBENCHES
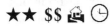

Starting a business that manufactures and sells garage workbenches requires very little investment capital and only basic carpentry skills. The business can be operated from home utilizing a basement or garage workshop for manufacturing and assembling the workbenches. The key to success in this type of manufacturing venture is to include as many custom design features as possible in the workbenches, such as tool racks, clamp-on vices, and locking casters that allow the workbenches to be easily moved. The workbenches can be pre-built and sold through retail accounts, or they can be manufactured on a special order basis. Make sure to approach new homebuilders in your community, as they can offer the workbenches to their customers as an upgrade option.

BASEMENT REMODELING

 ★ $$ 🏠 🕒

The easiest and least expensive method of adding livable square footage to a house is to remodel the basement into usable living space. Launching a new business that specializes in basement remodeling is the focus of this business enterprise. The main requirement for successfully operating this sort of business is to have considerable construction knowledge and practical experience. The business can specialize in one particular type of basement remodeling, such as recreation rooms, or the business can deal in basement remodeling in general. The profit potential for a basement remodeling business can be excellent once the business is established and has a good client referral base.

WATERPROOFING SERVICE

★★ $$ 🏠 🕒

Starting a waterproofing service for residential homes means that you can specialize in one or two particular types of waterproofing, such as concrete foundations or solariums. Or, the service can focus on waterproofing solutions in general for residential homes. Waterproofing services can be promoted and marketed to both residential homeowners and property management companies by employing traditional advertising and marketing mediums and methods. The service can also be offered to renovation and construction companies on a subcontract basis. The key to success in this type of repair business is to have a good working knowledge of construction practices and the ability to properly assess water ingress problems. As this type of repair business is highly specialized, true professionals will have no problem in creating a business income that can easily surpass $100,000 per year. A great additional

revenue source for the service is to also become an exclusive agent representing manufacturers' waterproofing products. Many of these types of specialized waterproofing products can be used in your business, as well as sold to architects, contractors, and the general public.

WEB RESOURCE: www.apk.net/nawc National Association of Waterproofing and Structural Repair Contractors.

STUCCO REPAIR SERVICE

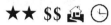 ★★ $$ 🏠 🕒

A stucco repair service is perfectly suited for the person with a minimal amount of construction knowledge and investment capital, but who is seeking to be independent by operating a home repair business. The tools and equipment necessary for this venture are readily available at home improvement centers, as is the material required for completing stucco repairs. Owners of this type of home repair service should have no problems in generating an income in the range of $30 to $40 per hour. Plus, you will be able to add a markup onto the materials that are used in the stucco repairs. The business can be marketed to homeowners by all traditional advertising mediums, as well as to home renovation companies on a subcontract basis.

ILLUMINATED HOUSE NUMBERS

 ★ $ 🏠 🕒

Starting a business that sells and installs solar-powered illuminated house numbers is not only a very inexpensive business venture to set in motion, it also does not require any special repair or construction skills. The solar-powered illuminated house numbers can be purchased from various manufacturers on a wholesale basis and resold to homeowners. The business can be marketed by designing and distributing promotional fliers or by displaying the product at home and garden trade shows. The product can be sold via the Internet or mail order to do-it-yourself homeowners who can install the product themselves. While this business enterprise may not make you a millionaire, it is a great business to start and operate part-time from a home-based office, and can generate substantial extra income.

DRAINAGE REPAIRS
★ $$

Prior to the 1970s, many ground drainage systems were primarily constructed from clay tiles. Over time, these clay tiles can be damaged by tree roots, or collapse under compacted weight or corrosion. These facts create a terrific opportunity to start a new business that specializes in repairing and replacing ground drainage systems for residential houses. The business can be initiated on a small capital investment. Most of the equipment that is required for this home repair service can be rented on an as-needed basis. The materials to carry out drainage repairs, such as big 'O' perforated and non-perforated plastic piping are available at almost any home improvement center. To successfully operate a drainage repair service does not require a great deal of special skills or construction experience. However, research on the subject of drainage and drainage systems should be completed prior to establishing the business.

CONCRETE CUTTING SERVICE
★★ $$ 🏠 🕐

Starting a part-time concrete cutting service is a terrific way to earn additional income and gain valuable business experience. Potential customers for concrete cutting services will include construction and renovation companies, homeowners, property maintenance companies, and driveway installation companies. Simply put, the best way to gain clients and promote the business is to start knocking on doors and soliciting for business. Be sure to establish alliances with plumbing contractors, as they often have to cut concrete basement floors to repair or add additional plumbing pipes, and they will generally subcontract out this work to a concrete cutting service. Current rates for concrete cutting are in the range of $30 to $50 per hour, making this an excellent choice for a new business venture.

HOME REPAIR NEWSPAPER COLUMN
★★ $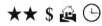

Working as a freelance journalist writing a newspaper column on home repair tips and techniques may not be as difficult to establish as you think. Never in the history of the United States have people taken such an interest in home improvement and repair as they are right now, and the time has never been better to capitalize on this popularity. Getting started in this business will take some time, a few rejections, and a little bit of clever self-promotion. However, once established, there are many methods to make the business pay, and pay big. No names mentioned, but I have a friend who has built a small empire writing about home maintenance and repairs, and starting out, he did not know which end of a screwdriver to hold. However, he did have writing ability and saw an opportunity to capitalize on it. Newspapers, magazines, trade publications, and newsletters are all potential customers to purchase the rights to a home repair advice column. Providing you can accomplish building a regular following, do not overlook product endorsements, because that is where the real money is.

ONLINE HOME REPAIR ADVICE
★★★ $$ 🏠 🕐 🖱

A common term used by Web developers is "site stickiness" basically meaning what level of unique and interesting content or user features can be incorporated into a Web site to increase visitor page views and entice visitors to return to the site regularly. Home repair tips and advice fits that bill perfectly. Utilizing your construction and renovation expertise you can develop a syndicated home repair advice column—syndicated meaning you can plug the column into as many Web sites as possible. The benefit to the site operator is obvious: increasing site stickiness. Aim to have your column featured on 200 Web sites and you could earn an extra $2,000 every month by charging customers only $10 each.

VICTORIAN MOLDINGS
★★★ $$$$ 🏠

Restoring heritage and Victorian homes has become the major focus of homeowners and community leaders across North America. And the time has never been better than now to start a business that manufactures, installs, and sells exterior reproduction Victorian moldings. The business can be operated in the following formats:

- Manufacture, retail, and install reproduction Victorian exterior moldings and decorations.
- Manufacture and retail the Victorian moldings via retail accounts, the Internet, and mail order.
- Manufacture Victorian moldings and decorations on a custom per-piece basis.

The options for this type of specialty business are unlimited for the enterprising entrepreneur.

START-UP COSTS: The major requirement to set this business in motion will be woodworking equipment. The following list represents some of the required woodworking equipment, as well as the current retail selling prices and additional business start-up costs.

Professional table saw	$2,000
Band saw	$1,000
6-inch joiner	$1,000
12-inch planer	$1,000
Drill press	$750
Radial arm saw	$1,500
Air compressor and accessories	$1,500
Compound miter cut-off saw	$500
Various hand power tools	$2,000
Sawdust collection system	$1,000
Miscellaneous equipment	$1,000
Fixed and portable workbenches	$1,000
Installation equipment	$1,000

Installation truck	$10,000
Total equipment costs	**$25,250**
Business start-up expenses	$2,000
Marketing budget	$2,000
Working capital	$5,000
Business setup costs	$2,000
Total start-up investment required	**$36,250**

The business can be started for less than the above-mentioned amount providing that you already have the required equipment, or you purchase good-quality used woodworking equipment.

PROFIT POTENTIAL: While the profit potential will greatly vary in this particular business due to a number of factors, such as local market demand and competition, volume of completed work, etc.; overall, this can be an extremely profitable business to own and operate. Not only can you charge a healthy markup percentage on all completed products you manufacture, you can also charge installation rates which start in the range of $30 per hour and go up from there, based on the complexity of the work being performed.

DRAFT PROOFING SERVICE
★★★ $$$ 🏠 🕐 ⚖ 🌐

1. Save homeowners money.
2. Help the environment by reducing energy consumption.
3. Create a more comfortable living environment for homeowners.
4. Build a successful and profitable business.

You can accomplish all four of the above-mentioned activities by starting your own residential draft proofing service. To get started simply employ current technology and equipment to first assess the home in terms of where the drafts are originating from and what measures can be taken to reduce or eliminate the source. A draft proofing service can function in two fashions. The first option is to carry out the assessment and create a document detailing recommendations and solutions. The second option is to carry out the assessment as well as the recommended draft-proofing repairs. In the case of the first option, you would simply charge the homeowner a fee for creating the assessment report. This report would explain and detail the recommended draft proofing measures that could save money on heating and cooling energy costs. The second option would generate revenues from creating the assessment report as well as carrying out the recommended draft proofing repairs. These repairs could include increased insulation and ventilation, caulking, installation of door and window weather stripping, replacement of electrical wall receptacles to "draft-proof" versions, and even replacement of doors and windows to new high-efficiency models. Providing you have the experience and tools required, you can carry out these repairs. If not, the repairs could be contracted to a local qualified handyman or renovation contractor. Both operating models for this business venture have the potential to be very profitable. Ideally, draft-proofing services are best marketed by establishing working relationships with utility companies, real estate brokers, home inspectors, renovation contractors, and property management firms.

MILLWORK SHOP

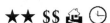

Working on a part-time basis from a homebased workshop you can earn a tidy sum by operating a custom millwork shop. Custom millwork shops service renovation contractors and homeowners that are looking to restore or duplicate a piece of antique molding, handrail, spindle, or any other type of wooden ornament while renovating or restoring a home. Additionally, millwork shops often duplicate larger items for customers such as hardwood floor planks, wooden sash windows, fireplace mantels, and interior doors. The main requirements for operating this type of business is to have woodworking experience and a well-equipped shop. Tools required will include joiners, planers, table saw, miter saw, band saw, drills, clamps, and all other equipment commonly found in a woodworking shop. Market

the service by contacting renovation companies in your local area that specialize in restoring heritage homes. Also contact antique dealers and auction services, as both can also refer your service for restorations and repairs of antique building products and furniture to their clients. Typically billing for this type of specialized work will be done on a per-job basis. However, on average the fee will equal approximately $35 to $50 per hour, plus materials.

FABRIC RESTORATION

Fabric repair and restoration is big business in North America, and securing a portion of this very lucrative market may be easier than you think. Get started by leaning the trade. This can be accomplished in a few ways. You can purchase books and videos on the subject, take training courses, or you can even purchase a franchise or business opportunity in the fabric restoration industry that includes a full training program. Types of fabric repair and restorations include leather repair and dying, fabric repair and dying, and carpet repair and dying. I have a friend in the fabric repair business, and he specializes in only repairing cigarette burns in car upholstery and makes a very comfortable living doing so. For anyone that is new in this business I would suggest offering clients a wide variety of repair and restoration services until the business is established and can be supported by repeat customers and word-of-mouth referrals. Initiate a flier delivery campaign, cold calling and telemarketing program, and advertising program in your local newspaper to kick the business into high gear. Additional sources of revenue can be generated by providing other services, such as blind cleaning, carpet cleaning, and furniture steam cleaning.

WEB RESOURCE: www.fiberenew.com Franchise opportunities in the fabric restoration and repair industry.

NOTES

KEY

RATINGS	★
START-UP COST	$
HOMEBASED BUSINESS	🏠
PART-TIME	🕐
LEGAL ISSUES	⚖️
FRANCHISE OR LICENSE POTENTIAL	🌐
ONLINE	🖱️

29

HOME SERVICE

Businesses You Can Start

POWER WASHING SERVICE

★★★ $$ 🏠 🕐 🌐

Establishing and operating a power washing service is an outstanding business opportunity to set in motion. There are many benefits for the person who is considering a power washing service as a new business enterprise, including low initial investment, proven consumer demand, and no inventory to warehouse. There are literally hundreds of items that can be cleaned using power-washing equipment, and to get you thinking, the following are a few suggestions:

- Driveways
- Recreational vehicles
- Mobile homes
- Signs
- Awnings
- Headstones
- Cars
- Boats
- Decks and patios
- Construction equipment
- Metal roofs
- Bricks and siding
- Outdoor furniture

The key to success will lie in your ability to secure repeat customers. It costs 100 times as much to find 100 clients, as opposed to finding one client who uses your service 100 times. Focusing marketing efforts on companies and individuals that could become regular customers is the best approach, and potential repeat customers could include the following:

- *Construction companies.* Power washing heavy equipment on a regular basis.
- *Cemeteries.* Power washing headstones yearly.
- *Retail stores.* Power washing signs and awnings three or four times per year.
- *Boat dealers.* Power washing their land displayed boats monthly.

- *Trucking firms.* Power washing fleets on a weekly or biweekly basis.
- *Residential and commercial property management companies.* Power washing underground parking lots, decks, driveways, and patios on an annual basis for their clients.

START-UP COSTS: The following example can be used as a guideline to establish the investment needed to start a power washing service.

	Low	High
Van or truck (used)	$3,500	$5,000
Power washer and accessories	$1,000	$2,500
Miscellaneous equipment and tools	$250	$500
Initial marketing and promotion budget	$250	$750
Business setup, banking, legal, etc.	$250	$2,500
Working capital	$750	$1,500
Total start-up costs	$6,000	$12,750

PROFIT POTENTIAL: A power washing service can be extremely profitable, and the only fixed overheads are a telephone, liability insurance, and transportation. The income level that can be achieved will depend on a great number of factors, such as customer volumes, overhead, and pricing structure. However, a well-established power washing service can easily provide the owner-operator of the business with an income in excess of $40,000 per year, after business operating expenses.

WEB RESOURCE: wwwcarvedstone.com Site dedicated to serving professionals within the power washing industry.

DO-IT-YOURSELF WOODWORKING SHOP
★★ $$$$

A do-it-yourself woodworking shop is a fully equipped woodworking shop that customers rent on an hourly basis to complete personal woodworking projects. This type of business is ideally suited to be located in a densely populated urban center where most people do not have access to a home workshop. The business can be marketed to potential clients by initiating a direct-mail campaign and by distributing promotional fliers and discount coupons throughout the community. Approaching organizations and associations like sports clubs, retired persons organizations, and other community groups and offering their members group discounts can also be a fantastic way to market the business. While this type of new business venture is very easy to start, additional business requirements that are of critical importance will include acquiring general business and liability insurance as well as installing on-site safety and first-aid equipment.

START-UP COSTS: The following example can be used as a guideline to establish the investment needed to start a do-it-yourself woodworking shop.

	Low	High
Leased location (F&L)	$1,500	$3,000
Leasehold improvements	$2,500	$5,000
Woodworking equipment (new and used)	$10,000	$20,000
Hand and hand power tools	$2,500	$5,000
Business setup, banking, insurance, legal, etc.	$2,000	$4,000
Office equipment, stationery, etc.	$2,500	$5,000
Initial advertising and marketing budget	$1,500	$3,000
Working capital	$2,500	$5,000
Total start-up costs	$25,000	$50,000

HOUSESITTING SERVICE
★ $$

Students, bachelors, and single seniors are all ideal candidates to start a housesitting service. Millions of North Americans go on business and pleasure holidays each year, often departing with an uneasy feeling that their unoccupied homes are prime targets for potential disasters, like burglaries and fires. To get work, simply build alliances with travel agents who can refer or recommend your housesitting service to their travel clients. Be sure to compile a reference list to hand out to potential clients, as well as having yourself bonded as an extra precaution, to give clients the peace of mind of knowing their homes are well taken care of in their absence. Currently, housesitting rates are in the range of $15 to $25 per day and can go higher if there are also pets to look after. While a housesitting service will not make you rich, it can create a few hundred extra dollars each month.

RUBBISH REMOVAL SERVICE

 ★★ $$

The first step in establishing a rubbish removal service is to ask yourself, who are my potential customers, and how do I effectively target my marketing efforts? While there are many potential customers for this type of home service, one particular segment of this group is certainly new homeowners, or people who are preparing their homes to be sold. Gaining access to this particular group of potential customers can be as easy as building alliances with real estate companies and sales people to refer or recommend your rubbish removal service to their clients. Equipment requirements will include a truck, van, or trailer, garbage cans, and a few shovels and rakes; but that is about all that is needed to start a rubbish removal service.

ROOF TUNE-UP SERVICE

★★★ $$

A roof tune-up service should not to be confused with a roof repair service or roof replacement contractor. Roof tune-ups are a proactive maintenance measure as opposed to reactive measure, such as repairing a leaking roof. The average roof now costs in excess of $5,000 to replace, and roof repairs can cost as much as $1,000 to correct a leakage problem, not including the costs to repair any interior water damage that may have been caused as a result of the water ingress. These facts can be the basis of your advertising and marketing programs should you decide to start a roof tune-up service. A roof

tune-up service is simply carrying out an annual roof inspection and correcting minor problems, such as recaulking a chimney flashing before it becomes a major leakage problem. Clients can include both residential homeowners and commercial building owners. A great method to gain customers year after year for a roof tune-up service is to provide clients with a one-year warranty on their roofs. The warranty would be provided to clients on the basis that should a roof that has been "tuned-up" leak within one year from the date of inspection, then the roof would be repaired free of charge. Warranty exclusions or terms and conditions should include situations that would not be covered under the warranty, such as acts of God, defective manufactured material, and damage caused to the roof by objects or unusual foot traffic. Creating a warranty for this type of service is an incredible marketing tool, as it gives customers and potential clients additional security in terms of the perceived value of the service.

PROFIT POTENTIAL: Charging customers a mere $125 for the annual roof tune-up, and securing only two roof tune-up jobs per day, can generate yearly sales in excess of $65,000. And best of all, almost all of that is profit. The operating overheads for the business are minimal, and only around 5 percent of the service charge will be needed to cover consumable items, such as caulking. Once established, hiring qualified subcontractors to service the accounts on a profit-share or even franchise locations can substantially expand a well-managed roof tune-up service.

POOL AND HOT TUB MAINTENANCE

★★ $$

There are millions of swimming pools and hot tubs in North America, and they all have one thing in common—they must be cleaned and maintained on a regular basis in order to work properly and be safe for the occupants to use. A pool and hot tub maintenance service can be marketed in all traditional advertising mediums. However, as a fast start method to gain customers quickly, consider distributing fliers or coupons throughout your local community. The fliers or coupons should feature free pool and hot tub water safety tests for owners of these items. The safety test would simply be checking the water for toxins and recommending any corrective measures that can be taken to fix the problem. The true purpose of the free water safety test is, of course, to gain clients for the service on a regular monthly basis.

FIRE EQUIPMENT TESTING
★★ $$ 🏠 🕐 ⚖️

Many communities across North America have regulations that require residential and commercial fire-safety equipment, such as alarms and extinguishers, to be tested and inspected on a regular basis. Providing that you have experience in fire safety equipment testing, starting a business that conducts fire-safety equipment inspections can be a terrific, and potentially profitable, business to get rolling. Additional revenues for this type of business can also be gained by selling fire-safety products and equipment to residential and commercial clients, as well as installing the equipment that is sold to customers.

WEB RESOURCE: www.nfpa.org National Fire Protection Association.

CHIMNEY CLEANING SERVICE
★ $$ 🏠 🕐 ⚖️

Anyone who suffers from fear of heights should skip this business opportunity. But for those of you who are not scared of heights, read on. Cleaning wood-burning fireplace chimneys and oil-burning furnace chimneys is very straightforward, and the equipment necessary for this task is available to be purchased in almost every community. Currently, chimney cleaning rates are in the range of $50 to $125 depending on the size of the chimney and on how complicated the cleaning job is. If this is the business opportunity for you, consider building alliances with local firewood delivery and oil delivery companies to initiate a cross-promotional campaign. You would recommend their businesses to your clients, and they could include a discount chimney cleaning coupon in with their monthly invoice mailings that promotes your service.

WEB RESOURCE: www.chimneys.com Directory listings of chimney sweep associations and industry information.

CONSTRUCTION CLEAN-UP SERVICE
★★ $$ 🏠 🕐

Starting a construction clean-up service not only has the potential to generate profits in excess of $60,000 each year, the business can also be set in motion on an investment of less than $1,000. Each year thousands of new homes are built in the United States, and all of these new homes have to be cleaned prior to the new homeowners moving in. A construction clean-up service should be all-inclusive—meaning that the windows are cleaned, the entire house is dusted and vacuumed, and all leftover construction debris is removed from the site. This type of service is very easy and inexpensive to promote. Get marketing by simply setting presentation appointments with all property developers and contractors in your community and giving an in-depth explanation about your construction clean-up service and why it would greatly benefit their company and clients.

WEB RESOURCE: www.smallbizbooks.com Business-specific start-up guides and books.

MOVING SERVICE
★ $$+ ⚖️

The investment needed to start a moving or a moving and storage business can be very large and will vary depending on the size and operating format of the business venture. However, a small moving service that specializes in short-distance residential moving can be launched for less than $10,000 and has the potential to generate an income of $25 to $35 per hour for the owner/operator of the business. Once you have established that there is a need for an additional small residential moving service in your community, the next step is to ask yourself, "How do I gain access to potential clients for the business?" Gaining access to potential clients for a moving service is best accomplished by establishing alliances with companies and individuals that already have access to customers that need a moving service. These companies can include furniture stores, real estate brokers and agents, and property management firms. Establishing strategic alliances with companies, associations, and individuals can often make the difference between business success and business failure, so be sure to build these vital contacts.

ONLINE MOVING DIRECTORY

★ $$$

This cyberconcept is straightforward. Simply develop a Web site that features information relating to moving and relocation, or an online moving directory. The site can be indexed by state and city and feature individual listings for moving companies, packing services, and relocation consultants. The site can also provide visitors with helpful information, such as weather charts, community services, schools, sports clubs, and social associations related to specific communities. Revenues are earned by charging service companies an advertising fee to be listed on the site. The objective is clear: provide visitors with the most up-to-date and useful information available in terms of moving and relocation, and you will succeed.

HOME SERVICE CLUB

★★★★ $$$$ ⊕

A home service club is a business or association that provides its members with a referral service for locating reputable companies that provide home improvement, home repair, and additional home services, such as lawn maintenance. Your next question is probably, why would homeowners and contractors pay a membership fee to belong to this type of club? Because each year, thousands of homeowners find themselves caught in situations or even scams where they have paid in part or in full for home renovations or services only to find the company that is providing the service has not lived up to the contract obligations, or the work completed has not been done properly. Likewise, firms that provide these home services would also be

happy to pay a membership fee because they would have limited competition for the contracts, and the leads would be prequalified by the home service club. The basis for operating a home service club is simple. In exchange for a yearly membership fee, homeowners receive access to reputable contractors who provides an automatic 5 to 10 percent discount on all labor and materials, as well as written warranties on all work completed. Contractors who are members in the home service club receive access to the membership base with limited competition—meaning that there are only two or three firms represented in each category, such as two lawn-maintenance firms. Additionally, the leads that contractors receive have been prequalified by the home service club.

Marketing a home service club is best achieved by using two different methods. The first is to set up a display booth at malls and home and garden trade shows to attract homeowner members. The purpose of the display kiosk is to provide potential members with information about the home service club, as well as to close the sale on site. Closing the sale on site can be accomplished by providing a value-added product or service like reduced first-year membership fees or a free monthly club newsletter. To gain contractors for membership in the club, simply set presentation appointments with the owners of these firms or hold a general invitation meeting and present the benefits of club membership to a large group of contractors at one time. Marketing a home service club can also be done by hiring subcontract sales consultants to promote and sell memberships. While this marketing method reduces the overall profitability of the company, it can provide a faster approach to establishing the needed homeowner and contractor membership base.

Once a home service club has been established, the business has the potential to generate very large yearly profits. as the cost to operate the business is minimal. The business can be started and operated from a homebased office. Providing a home service club can be successful, and once all the operational bugs have been ironed out, this type of business lends itself perfectly to national expansion on a franchise or license-to-operate basis.

NONSLIP SURFACES
★ $$

Thousands of people are injured each year in North America as a result of falling due to a slippery floor surface. This is fact, and starting a business that supplies and installs floor and surface coating can not only prevent a great number of these accidents, it can also make you rich. Trying to manufacture, invent, or produce your own antislip products and coatings is not the best approach to this business start-up as it will cost thousands of dollars in research and development. Instead, locate a manufacturer of these products and coatings and become their exclusive representative in your community, state, or even country. Not only will this arrangement enable you to devote time solely to marketing products, it will also cost you a lot less investment capital to get the business rolling.

To find and source manufacturers of these types of products simply enlist the services of the Internet for research purposes or use one of the various manufacturer directories that are available to find a manufacturing source. Once a distribution agreement is in place with a manufacturer, you can begin to market and install the antislip products and coatings.

Potential customers will include all commercial and residential building owners and, more specifically, those who have the most to lose by a resulting accident at their place of business. Any product that can be effectively used to reduce potential liabilities resulting from a fall at a business place is the perfect product to be sold on a "safety precaution" basis, which is always a good business practice to pursue. Or like they say in the life insurance business, "If you do not already have this product (life insurance) it may already be too late." One of the benefits of becoming an authorized distributor and installer of a product or products on an exclusive basis is that it allows you the potential for larger markups to be placed on the product for retail sales purposes, especially if the product performs well.

DUCT CLEANING SERVICE
★★ $$$

Cleaning furnace and air-conditioning ducts has become a routine home maintenance practice for many homeowners. Duct cleaning is relatively inexpensive, and the health benefits are numerous, as anyone suffering from allergies or other breathing-related health problems will tell you. Perhaps these facts are what makes starting a duct cleaning service such a good choice for a new business venture. A duct cleaning service can be set in motion on a modest investment and does not require a great deal of special skills or knowledge to operate, which makes this a very attractive business opportunity for just about anyone. Establishing alliances with related firms, such as heating contractors, real estate agents, and property management companies can go a long way in establishing a client base for a duct cleaning service.

WEB RESOURCE: www.dmcdist.com Manufacturers and distributors of duct cleaning equipment.

STORM WINDOW INSTALLATIONS AND STORAGE
★ $

Anyone seeking a part-time low-investment and easy business start-up may find this opportunity to be of particular interest. Starting a business that provides residential homeowners with a service of installing storm windows in the fall and removing the storm windows in the spring is a very straightforward business to initiate. While this business will not make you rich, it can provide a great seasonal income of $15 to $25 per hour, with the potential for additional income if the storm window installation service also provides homeowners with optional window cleaning and window repair services. The equipment necessary to get rolling includes a few ladders and basic tools, such as hammers and screwdrivers. Ideal customers for this service are owners of Victorian and heritage homes, as wood storm windows often do not open or provide air circulation in the summer, requiring them to be removed and reinstalled later.

BLIND CLEANING SERVICE
★★ $$

More and more residential and commercial property owners are now using window blinds as opposed to window curtains, and this fact creates a fantastic opportunity for the enterprising entrepreneur to capitalize on by starting a blind cleaning service. There are a couple of different approaches that can be taken for starting a blind cleaning business. The first is to remove and label customers' blinds and take them to a central cleaning location. The second option is to clean the blinds on site using cleaning tanks that can be mounted in a truck or trailer, or cleaning the blinds on site by hand using dusters and cleaning agents. Both operating formats will cost approximately the same to establish. However, a mobile blind cleaning business has a better chance to produce more profits, as the transportation time will be cut in half, allowing for a higher volume of blinds to be cleaned. Potential income range is $20 to $30 per hour.

WEB RESOURCE: www.omegasonics.com Manufacturers and distributors of blind cleaning equipment.

MAID SERVICE

A good-old traditional residential maid service is still a very good business enterprise to set in motion, as there will always be a demand for house cleaning services. Best of all, a maid service can be started for peanuts and requires no special business skills or experience. The equipment needed to operate a maid service is not costly and can be purchased in any local community hardware store. Currently, house cleaning rates are in the range of $12 to $20 per hour, and the enterprising entrepreneur can potentially generate a very good income by hiring experienced house cleaners and paying them on a subcontract basis of 75 percent of the house cleaning contract value. Providing you can keep ten house cleaners working on a full-time basis, this scenario can generate an income in excess of $75,000 per year prior to expenses.

WEB RESOURCE: www.smallbizbooks.com Business specific start-up guides and books.

ROOF SNOW REMOVAL SERVICE

Every year thousands of building structures collapse under the weight of snow and ice, and simply put, there are only two ways to prevent this from happening. The first is to build all buildings with roof pitches so steep that snow and ice cannot accumulate. The second and more viable method (as the first will never happen) is to simply remove the snow and ice from the roof before it can accumulate and cause potential weight problems for the building structure. The best time of year to promote and market a roof snow removal service is in the summer or fall, as this will enable you to build a customer base prior to winter. Ideally, customers should be charged a predetermined flat rate to clear snow from their roofs. A written or verbal contract should also establish at what point the roof will be cleared in terms of snow accumulation. On the surface this may seem to be a business that cannot provide a very lucrative income. However, with careful planning and research, you will soon see that it is very possible to create an income in excess of $20,000 per snowy winter, which is not bad when you consider the business can be started for less than $300.

AIR CONDITIONING SERVICE

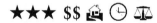

Calling all air conditioning service and repair tradespeople, it is time to stop making money for the boss and start putting your talents to work for you with your own air conditioning service and repair business. And for those of you who are worried about job security and income: don't. Simply premarket your service and build a customer base prior to leaving your job. How you may ask? Easy. Design a presentation package that outlines your abilities and special skills along with air conditioning repair and service rates, and begin to circulate the package to potential clients, such as residential and commercial property management firms as well as directly to residential and commercial building owners. You may be surprised and encouraged by the results, as a small homebased repair business such as this can really compete with larger firms, especially when it comes to service rates, product markup, and service response time.

WEB RESOURCE: www.acca.org Air Conditioning Contractors of America.

DE-ICING SERVICE

★ $

Here is another great part-time seasonal business opportunity that would go hand in hand with a snow removal service, a roof snow removal service, or both. Starting a de-icing service is about as easy as a business start-up can get. The basis for the business is simply sanding or salting sidewalks, driveways, and steps to prevent people from slipping on ice that may accumulate in these areas in the winter. While salting or sanding trucks can cost a hundred thousand dollars or more to purchase new, it certainly is not required if you plan to focus your marketing efforts on owners of residential homes and small commercial properties for a de-icing service. A truck or trailer can be used to transport the sand or salt, and shovels or small mechanical salting machines can be used for spreading it. Aim to secure long-term repeat clients, and a de-icing service can potentially be a profitable seasonal business to start and operate.

PEST CONTROL

★★ $$$

Starting a pest control service does require some careful planning and a license in most areas of the country. However, for an enterprising entrepreneur, this can be a small sacrifice to make, as a pest control service can be extremely profitable to own and operate. There are various types of pest controls that can form the basis of the business, such as insect or rodent control, or the business can specialize in providing all pest control services. There are also various methods now being used to control pests, such as chemical-based sprays and organic-based sprays. This will also have to be a consideration in terms of the types of methods your business will utilize. Overall, a pest control service can be a very profitable business venture and can easily generate profits in excess of $75,000 per year.

WEB RESOURCES: www.pestworld.org National Pest Management Association, Inc.

HOME INSPECTION SERVICE

★★ $$

Providing you have construction experience, and you are also prepared to invest some money and time into an instruction course that will enable you to become a certified home inspector, then you can earn a very good living from owning and operating your own home inspection business. Millions of homes are bought and sold each year in North America. As a condition of sale or subject to sale, most of these homes have to be inspected by a professional home inspector to make sure the home does not have major structural or mechanical problems prior to completion of the purchase. Currently, home inspection rates range from $150 for a small and basic residential home to more than $1,000 for large commercial buildings. The business can be managed from a home office, and the monthly fixed overhead costs are minimal, making a home inspection service a great choice for a new business start-up venture.

WEB RESOURCE: www.smallbizbooks.com Business-specific start-up guides and books.

WINDOW WASHING SERVICE

★★★★ $$

Window washing is the granddaddy of all home service businesses to start. Some of the reasons why are as follows:

- Proven consumer demand with millions of potential repeat clients.
- Low start-up investment and low fixed operating overheads.
- No special skills or business experience required, and the business can be managed from a homebased office with or without staff.
- Flexible full- or part-time hours, no inventory to stock or warehouse.
- Can be operated on a year-round basis offering interior and exterior window cleaning.
- A window washing service can generate sales in excess of $50,000 per year.

- Unlimited growth potential and even franchise expansion possibilities.

Individually each one of these reasons represents a good argument for starting a window washing service. However, when you combine all of these reasons, it creates a very strong argument for launching a window washing enterprise. Marketing a window washing service is simple. However, be sure not to overlook residential and commercial strata properties (a cooperative of owners, such as a condo building), as these corporations usually budget for window cleaning once or twice per year, and securing a few of these contracts can really beef up yearly sales and profits. Access to the strata corporation market can be gained by establishing contact with property management firms. These firms will indicate when and when window washing contracts are becoming available and the tendering or estimating process that will be used to award the contract to a qualified contractor.

START-UP COSTS: The following example can be used as a guideline to establish the investment needed to start a window washing service.

	Low	High
Transportation (used)	$2,500	$5,000
Equipment, ladders, squeegees, buckets, etc.	$250	$500
Initial advertising and marketing budget	$250	$1,000
Business setup, banking, legal, office, etc.	$250	$2,500
Working capital	$250	$1,000
Total start-up costs	$3,500	$10,000

PROFIT POTENTIAL: A large or a small window washing service can both potentially be very profitable. Additional revenues can be generated by providing clients with optional power washing or gutter cleaning services. A well-established and managed window washing service can easily create an income in excess of $50,000 per year after all business expenses, prior to income taxes.

WEB RESOURCE: www.window-cleaning-net.com Directory of window washing equipment suppliers.

GARDEN TILLING SERVICE
★ $$

During the off season when you're not installing Christmas lights or removing snow from roofs, why not start and operate a garden tilling service, as this service is in demand and the business is very inexpensive to get rolling. The terrific thing about many small seasonal business start-ups is the fact that they do not require a great deal of investment or practical business expertise. And a garden tilling service falls into this category. The equipment needed to operate the business can be purchased new or used, or even rented on an as-needed basis to keep start-up costs to a minimum. Furthermore, a garden tilling service is very easy to market and only requires a little bit of marketing ingenuity, such as creating and distributing fliers and door hangers throughout the community promoting the service. You can also establish and build contacts with garden centers and landscape companies that can refer your service to their clients. This business opportunity is not guaranteed to make you rich, but when you consider the low start-up investment, a seasonal income level of $20 to $30 per hour is excellent.

CHRISTMAS LIGHTS INSTALLATIONS
★ $

A roof snow removal service was featured earlier in this chapter, and a good fit with that business is to also provide clients with a service that installs Christmas lights, as well as taking the lights down after Christmas. Even though millions of people decorate their houses each year with Christmas lights, there would probably be millions more, if it was not for the fact that a lot of people simply do not have the time to install Christmas lights, not to mention the old problem of the lights being installed 20 feet off the ground. This is why starting a business that installs and removes Christmas lights is a great small business venture to set in motion. While this business is not guaranteed to make you rich, it can, however, create an extra income of a few thousand dollars each year just when we all seem to need it the most.

BUDGET DECORATING SERVICE

 ★★ $$

Calling all would-be interior decorators. Starting a budget interior decorating service can be profitable as well as a whole lot of fun, especially if you like to spend your free time scouring flea markets and garage sales for the perfect, interesting, and unique home decoration items. The business can easily be set in motion on an initial start-up investment of less than a few thousand dollars and operated from a homebased office. Potential customers for a budget decorating service can include just about anyone seeking to decorate their home or office, especially for people or companies on a tight or fixed decorating budget. In addition to the revenue that is earned by providing decorating tips, guidance, and products, budget decorating instruction classes can be held for homeowners wishing to learn the trade secrets on how to find, and place, that perfect home decoration.

SKYLIGHT MAINTENANCE SERVICE

 ★★ $

There are literally millions of skylights installed in residential homes and commercial buildings across North America. In fact, having skylights installed ranks as one of the most popular home improvements today. However, most homeowners never stop to consider how they will maintain these skylights once installed. That's why starting a business that specializes in skylight cleaning and maintenance is such a fantastic new enterprise to get rolling. A ladder, some cleaning equipment, basic tools, and a little bit of construction knowledge is all you will need to set this money making service into action. There

are a few methods to market the service. The first is to establish alliances with companies and other service contractors that can supply you with work or refer your service to their customers. These companies include property managers, window cleaners, and house painters. The second method to market the service is to simply design promotional brochures describing your service and drop off these brochures to every house in your community that has skylights. Either marketing method will work for one simple reason; skylights are generally 20 feet in the air, thus many people will have absolutely no desire to risk life and limb to clean or repair them.

ODOR CONTROL SERVICE

 ★ $$

Believe it or not, odor control and elimination is big business. Insurance companies and homeowners spend millions of dollars annually in North America to rid their homes and buildings of less-than-favorable odors. Fires, floods, leaky roofs, and pets are a few of the culprits in terms of the origins of these bothersome odors, and eliminating these odors can earn you big profits. The best method for marketing an odor control and elimination service is to establish working relationships with insurance companies and fire and flood restoration companies, as these sources can potentially supply you with more work than you can handle.

CARPET CLEANING SERVICE

 ★★ $$

There are nine major reasons why a carpet cleaning service is a great business start-up.

1. Low investment
2. Proven consumer demand
3. Great profit potential
4. No inventory
5. Homebased
6. Excellent growth potential
7. No special skills
8. Flexible business hours
9. Minimal operating overheads

As a fast-start marketing method to promote a new carpet cleaning service consider printing and distributing coupons featuring a free carpet cleaning offer. The catch: have one carpet cleaned at the regular cost and receive free carpet cleaning for another room of similar size. You can also market the service directly to commercial and residential property management firms for apartment and office carpet cleaning.

WEB RESOURCE: www.carpetcentral.com Directory listing carpet cleaning equipment manufacturers and business and franchise opportunities.

NOTES

30
IMPORT/EXPORT AND MAIL-ORDER
Businesses You Can Start

IMPORT/EXPORT MICROGUIDE

There are a great number of considerations prior to starting an import/export business or a combination of the two. However, the following six steps are the golden rule for successfully establishing an import/export business.

1. Research

Every new business venture has to be carefully researched, in terms of its ability to succeed. However, research is the single most important aspect of starting an import/export business, and the very likelihood of survival will greatly depend on the amount of initial and ongoing research that was used to establish the business, product line, transportation methods, suppliers, agents, legal requirements, and more. Simply put, research is the backbone of an import/export business, and ongoing research will always be an important aspect of the business, even once established.

INTERNET RESEARCH SITES

- International Business Forum: www.ibf.com
- Trade Port: www.tradeport.org
- Export Tutor: www.nemonline.org/tutor
- U.S. Department of Commerce International Trade Administration: www.ita.doc.gov

2. Supply and Demand

Research will establish the demand for a product, however supply is often overlooked in the research process. Consider the following:

SUPPLY

- Stability of foreign suppliers, backup, or contingency suppliers
- Stability of foreign government
- Stability of foreign economies and workforce
- Stability of foreign currency, and possible effects on pricing
- Supplier's ability to fulfill orders, and quality of product

- Supplier's ability to meet time lines

DEMAND
- Projected lifespan of product
- Increasing, decreasing, or stable consumer demand and acceptance of product
- Competition, locally and internationally
- Seasonal or year-round product demand, and demand beyond North American Markets

3. Legal Requirements

It is very important to learn the laws, rules, and regulations in all aspects of the industry, and in terms of the countries you intend to do business with, as not all countries have the same import/export rules and regulations. Furthermore, additional legal requirements can include:

- National and international employee laws
- Protection from legal liability
- Government product approvals
- Customs policies and procedures

4. Contacts and Alliances

Never overlook the importance of good contacts and related business alliances, especially if you are considering starting an import/export business. The following are contacts and alliances that should be established and maintained, nationally and internationally:

- Lawyers
- Accountants
- Transportation firms
- Import/export agents
- Marketing specialists
- Suppliers
- Wholesalers
- Retailers
- Distributors
- Import/export brokers
- Travel Specialist

5. Transportation

How will you be transporting the products, locally, nationally, and internationally? Transportation to an import/export business is like a law degree to a lawyer, you must have a clear and concise transportation plan as well as a backup transportation plan for your business.

Additional transportation considerations include choosing freight forwarder, cargo insurance, product packaging, and product lifespan (if applicable).

6. Profitability

Profit is not a dirty word, and businesses must be able to generate a profit in order to stay in business and continue to provide valuable products and services to fill consumer demand. The gray areas that can arise in the import/export industry can make profitability of the venture strained at the best of times. Transportation delays, union strikes, and government and political unrest can all have an effect on the profitability of your import/export products as well as your business. Once again, the greatest tool you have in your business arsenal to help you ensure the profitability of import/export products and your business is research.

WEB RESOURCE: www.smallbizbooks.com Business-specific start-up guides and books.

IMPORT/EXPORT BUSINESS VENTURES
Import Agent

Do you have excellent and numerous business contacts in North America? If so, why not capitalize on your contact base and become an import agent? An import agent is simply a person who represents products from a foreign country and works as the middleman to get these products distributed to wholesalers and retailers. Once again, the key to success in becoming an import agent is having the ability to build a business contact base. Manufacturers and exporters from foreign countries will want assurances that their product will be receiving the best exposure possible in the North American market. Researching for products, companies, and manufacturers to represent in North America is very straightforward. A good starting point is to join the WTO (World Trade Organization) for research purposes, or start surfing the Internet to search for import opportunities.

Toys

As previously mentioned in this directory, it is possible to earn a six-figure annual income importing low-cost toys and wholesaling or retailing these toys for gigantic profits. It is not uncommon for a $1 toy purchased abroad to sell in North America for 10 to 15 times that much. Be sure to obtain exclusive import or export rights for the products you are dealing with as well as exclusive distribution rights, even if you intend to sell the products to national wholesalers, retailers, or distributors. Furthermore, be sure that the exclusive contract states the distribution contract can be sold, as this is good will that you have developed for your business and this good will should be protected.

Construction Equipment

Thousands of dollars in profits can be made on one single transaction in construction equipment. Look for depressed areas with a weak dollar. The same construction equipment that can be purchased in these slow economies at bargain basement prices can often be resold at a profit in countries with a strong economy or where the construction industry is booming. Entering into the construction equipment import/export industry requires a great deal of construction equipment knowledge, import/export knowledge, and patience, as one single transaction can take up to a year to complete. However, as with all well-devised business plans, the wait can be well worth the effort, as it is possible to make $250,000 or more per year dealing in used construction equipment worldwide.

Building Supplies

Building materials and construction supplies are an excellent choice for products to be imported or exported. Once again, following world economies and world news can be the basis of importing and exporting building materials. I have heard stories of common $100 exterior doors being sold in unstable "feuding" countries for as much as $1,000 each. Building products to consider: lumber, windows and doors, roofing material, construction sealant, flooring, siding, and specialty woods.

Clothing

Importing and exporting clothing is a terrific venture to pursue. The key to success is to source exclusive and unique apparel products that will have mass market appeal. Once again the Internet can be used as a fantastic research tool. Seek small independent clothing manufacturers from around the world as well as in North America and simply contact them concerning their policies in terms of import/export representation. Additionally, be sure to follow market trends in terms of popularity of clothing types.

Automotive Equipment

According to the Automobile Manufacturers Association, there are more than 130 million cars and trucks registered in the United States. Finding the right automotive products to import cannot only be the start to building a successful business, it can make you rich. As with any product that is imported for the purpose of resale for a profit, the product must have mass appeal and be in demand, or a demand for the product be effectively established. Finding the right automotive product to import into North America may indeed take time, substantial financial investment, and careful research. However, once again, North Americans have a love affair with the automobile. There are 130 million potential customers in the United States alone, making this an importing venture certainly worth further investigation.

Computers

In North America we generally think nothing of replacing our computer equipment every few years to keep up with changing technology, or just to have the latest and greatest toys. However, rapid computer upgrading is certainly not practiced worldwide, as people in many different countries simply cannot afford to do so. This situation creates a tremendous business opportunity for an exporting business with a focus on used computer equipment that can be sold around the world. The best aspect about this type of exporting business is the fact that computer equipment in North America that is two years old has no value here and can be purchased extremely inexpensively, or in some cases can even be acquired for free. This same equipment can still command excellent wholesale and retail prices in countries that are now just becoming more technologically advanced. The profit potential for this type of exporting business can easily exceed $250,000 per year, providing the research and homework has been completed.

Food

Food: Every person on the planet needs it to survive, and until a new pill is invented to supply us with the nutrition we need, food will always remain a solid product choice for an import/export business. The following are choices for food import/export: processed food products, food products and ingredients used in food processing, crop products, fruits, vegetables, grains, beverage products and ingredients for beverage processing, food packaging, and containers.

Importing/Exporting Consulting Service

Phrases such as "global marketplace" and "world business community" are just that—phrases. Generally these phrases are loosely used when describing Internet technologies and electronic business opportunities and unfortunately have very little real impact on the average small business that wants to pursue importing and exporting opportunities. Why? Well, it's true that the global marketplace has become much easier to compete in and for. But it cannot be said that entering the global marketplace is easy to do, in spite of the popularity of the Internet. What all of this has created is a very exciting business opportunity focused on providing import and export solutions and programs for companies interested in doing business in the "global marketplace." Corporations need to know how to import or export, where opportunities exist, competitive advantages, and legal and cultural information about countries that they intend to do business in. Starting and operating an import/export consulting service will require previous experience in this industry, or a great deal of research to be conducted in order to be considered an expert in the field.

MAIL-ORDER MICROGUIDE

To those of you thinking that the mail-order industry is dying, think again. Mail-order sales are at all-time record highs and continue to expand at double-digit rates annually, thanks solely to the creation of the Internet. When you order a product from a Web site, you are in fact ordering products by way of mail order, regardless of how the product is delivered to you.

What Is Mail Order?

Simply put, mail order is a product that is purchased by a consumer and delivered to the consumer via the mail service, courier, or by facsimile or e-mail transmission. To initiate a mail-order purchase, a consumer has viewed, heard, or read an advertisement about the product that they are ordering.

Why Start a Mail-Order Business?

Starting a mail-order business will always remain a popular choice for a new business venture, as there are many benefits to starting this type of new business enterprise, including:

- Low initial start-up costs, and potential profits.
- Can be operated and managed from a home-based location.
- No special skills or requirements; proven and stable industry.
- Very little regulation or licensing requirements, and flexible work hours.
- Great growth potential by way of adding additional products.

What Are the Advertising Mediums Used for Marketing Products to Be Sold Via Mail Order?

There are various advertising mediums used to attract interest and produce orders to be shipped. Traditionally, print advertisements were the only way to advertise or promote a mail-order product. However, technological advances have created numerous ways to advertise and sell products via mail order, including:

- Print advertising, newspapers, magazines, and trade-specific publications.

- Home shopping TV clubs and programs and infomercials.
- Radio infomercials.
- Flier and catalog distribution.
- Fax and e-mail blasts.
- Internet, classified ads, newsgroup advertising, and Web sites.

What Are the Best Mail-Order Products?

The best products to be sold via mail order are products that are unique and generally not available from local "bricks and mortar" retailers. Products to be sold via mail order should have as many of the following qualities as possible:

- Unique and interesting.
- Not available from local retailers where the product is being advertised.
- Products with large markups and profit potentials.
- Easy and inexpensive to pack and ship.
- A consumable; meaning the customers may have to reorder.
- A product that serves a purpose with mass appeal.
- A product that unlocks a mystery or formula.

Additionally, keep profit in mind; do not try to sell a $5 item via mail order, as the cost to market the product will likely be more than the potential profits that can be generated by sales of the product, even in large volumes. A good price point for mail-order products is between $25 and $50, with a wholesale, manufacturing, or production cost of 10 percent to 20 percent of the retail selling price.

What Are the Steps Involved in Starting a Mail-Order Business?

INVESTIGATION

- Research the industry.
- Research the legal aspects.
- Research products, advertising mediums, and market.
- Research start-up and operating costs.
- Research profit potentials.

SETUP

- Create business plan.
- Create business identity.
- Establish business management, warehousing, and shipping location.
- Establish product source, contacts, and alliances.
- Develop operations manual and business procedures.
- Establish shipping methods and payment terms.
- Create and develop methods of advertising and advertising copy.

ACTION

- Secure inventory.
- Place ads.
- Filling orders.
- Search for additional products and mail-order opportunities.
- Review entire business process and operating methods.

WEB RESOURCE: www.smallbizbooks.com Business-specific start-ups guides and books.

MAIL-ORDER BUSINESS VENTURES

Kitchen Items

Kitchen products have always been popular items to sell via mail order simply because they meet the criteria: small and easy to ship, mass appeal, and the potential for very large product markups. Many mail-order entrepreneurs have become multimillionaires by selling kitchen gadgets via late night TV infomercials. The key is to source or design the right kitchen products to sell. The Internet can be of great assistance to source these types of products, especially from foreign manufacturers. Additionally, seek joint ventures with companies or individuals who may already have designed and developed a great kitchen gadget, but need an entrepreneur with exceptional marketing skills to assist them in bringing the product to market.

Sewing Patterns

Sewing patterns are a terrific product to be sold via mail order. They cost very little to produce and they can be grouped together and sold for fantastic profits. The best types of sewing patterns to market and sell are as follows:

- Sewing patterns for children and teen clothing.
- Sewing patterns for popular celebrity fashions.
- Sewing patterns for comfortable casual wear.

The sewing patterns can be marketed by placing advertisements in related trade magazines, by placing advertisements throughout the Internet, and on your own Web page.

How-To Books

How-to books, tapes, and software can retail for as much as $50 each and cost as little as $3 each to buy wholesale or produce, and that is what makes how-to books, tapes, and software such great mail-order products. Many publishers, authors, and companies sell master copies of these products with reprint rights, which means that you can place ads and receive orders before you even have to spend money on printing or production costs and inventory. Popular "how-to" titles have always been anything related to business, relationships, child raising, crafts, health and fitness, and self-improvement. Catalogs can easily be produced featuring many titles on these subjects, and with purchased mailing, fax, and e-mail lists you can be in the mail-order business and filling customer orders in a matter of weeks.

Special Fishing Lures

There are more than 20 million fishing enthusiasts in North America alone, and with that many potential customers, it's no wonder that millions of dollars of specialty fishing lures are sold by mail order every year. Fishing lures are best sold by creating a fishing lure kit that "guarantees results." The kits can include lures for all types of fishing and can be advertised and promoted by all the traditional mail-order marketing methods. Locating fishing lures to sell is very straightforward, as there are more than a thousand companies and individuals in North America

alone that specialize in designing, manufacturing, and wholesaling fishing lures. To locate the manufacturers and wholesalers of fishing lures, use the Internet, yellow pages, and manufacturers directories for researching purposes.

Business Opportunity Guides

By far the number-one selling mail-order product is anything related to business opportunities: guides, books, and success formulas sell in the millions every year by mail order. Business opportunity guides can be developed, or business opportunity guides can be purchased on a wholesale basis from the thousands of publishers that handle these types of products. The competition in this sector of the mail-order industry is very heavy, and well-seasoned. However, with careful research, solid business principles, and by developing or providing an excellent product there is absolutely no reason to fear, as this segment of the mail-order industry continues to expand and double in size every decade.

Cooking Recipes

Cooking recipe guides containing 20 or so cooking recipes can easily be produced for less than $2 each and sold via mail order for as much as $15 each. The key to successfully marketing cooking recipes is to be unique and follow a central theme throughout the guide, such as "25 great French recipes," or "20 family meals that can be made from scratch for less than $5 and take less than ten minutes to make." In addition to selling the cooking recipe guides via mail order, often large commercial food processors and packers will purchase these types of guides on a volume basis to include with their products, so be sure to look at all your options and seize all business opportunities.

Astrological Products

Charts, guides, and astrological symbol products sell like crazy through mail order, and while a few of you may be asking why, remember as entrepreneurs: "Ours is not to question why; only to supply, if there is a demand." Millions of people worldwide base some or all of their daily lives, careers, and decisions on astrological readings and interpretations, and starting a mail-order business catering to this extremely large market is very easy to establish and run. There are thousands of manufacturers producing various astrological products; so finding a source to purchase wholesale items should not be difficult. Seek a product that must be updated and repurchased by customers on a regular basis, and once again, with astrological products, this should not be difficult to achieve.

Building Plans

Building plans for homes, additions to homes, decks, and garden sheds are terrific products to sell by mail order, and you have two ways to generate revenues and profits. The first way to make money selling building plans is to create a book containing 50 to 100 building plans on various building topics (homes, decks, etc.). The books will costs around $3 to $6 each to have printed in bulk and can easily be sold for $15 to $25 each. The second way to generate revenues is to sell complete blueprint plans from the book of plans, meaning once a customer has received the plans book they can order the specific blueprint they like from the book. The blueprint plans can include the complete materials list, as well as a scaled building plan. This method of marketing is terrific, as about one-quarter of the customers who initially ordered the plans will submit an order for specific and complete building plans for the project or item of interest.

Casino Game Strategies

Like winning lottery strategies guides, winning casino strategies guides are another great product to be sold by way of mail-order sales. There are more than one billion people worldwide who play casino games and wager money in some form every year, and tapping into this very lucrative market could potentially make you rich. You could develop the winning casino strategy guides, or you can hire a casino games specialist to develop the guides on a consulting and subcontract basis. In addition to selling the guides by mail order, this type of product could also be sold at numerous retail locations and

displayed in a colorful and well-designed point-of-purchase (POP) display.

Fireworks

Selling fireworks via mail order takes extra special research into shipping and legal requirements. However, once established, there are absolutely gigantic profits to be made by purchasing fireworks on a wholesale basis and retailing the fireworks for as much as 20 times the wholesale costs. *Note*: Recently more and more Web sites can be found on the Internet promoting homemade fireworks, as well as plans or recipes on how to make fireworks. Avoid this segment of the fireworks industry at all costs, as the potential liability is enormous. Purchase the fireworks only from a recognized and well-established fireworks manufacturer or wholesaler.

Gourmet Foods

Maine lobster, French mushrooms, Italian olives, and more gourmet foods are sold daily via mail order and the more rare and unique food items are, the higher the profits can be. One of the best aspects about starting a mail-order business that markets gourmet food is the fact that many gourmet food manufacturers and processors will warehouse and drop ship the products directly to your customers. This distribution system is fantastic, as you can reduce start-up costs by not having to purchase and warehouse inventory. Additionally, look to create a catalog featuring many types of gourmet food, dealing with a variety of food producers and manufacturers. Of course, the catalogs will be sent free of charge to all interested potential customers. Selling gourmet food via mail order gets an additional star, as it meets all mail-order criteria, especially because it is a consumable product.

Vegetarian Cookbooks

It is estimated that 5 percent of the United States population are vegetarians, and 5 percent translates into approximately 15 million people, which are a lot of potential customers for any business to focus on. Selling vegetarian cookbooks via mail order is a relatively simple business venture to start and operate. The books can be written and developed by you, or the books can be purchased on a wholesale basis and sold to customers at a profit. Like many mail order products, there are thousands of publishers and book distribution companies that will gladly warehouse and drop ship books directly to your customers. Most of these companies work on the same basis, you market the product and receive customer orders, and the company ships direct to your clients and bills you for the inventory on 30-day terms, once credit has been established.

Health-Care Products

Health-care products such as home remedy guides, health-care books and manuals, as well as products that assist the disabled make terrific items to be sold by mail order. A catalog describing all the products that you sell can be developed and distributed for a minimal cost. Due to the unique and one-of-a-kind nature of many home health-care products, the markups or profit margins can be fantastic, because there is usually little, if any, competition to compare the product to for pricing purposes. However, be warned that trying to develop your own health-care product can be very costly. You may be better off to market existing health-care products.

Diet and Fitness

A recent survey conducted by the U.S. government indicated that a full 50 percent of American adults felt their weight was excessive and that 80 percent of respondents intended to start a diet or fitness program within the next six months in an effort to correct the weight problem. Providing the survey results are accurate, this means there are as many as 100 million American adults that are potential customers for any business that specializes in products and information aimed at assisting people with weight loss and becoming more fit. The options are unlimited in terms of the different types of diet and fitness products that can be marketed and sold by mail order, such as weight loss guides, healthy eating cookbooks, fitness programs that guarantee results, or fitness equipment. This market is huge, and a good starting point is to source or develop an exclusive diet or fitness product and then get rolling.

Military Goods

Military goods, such as uniforms, outdoor survival gear, and training guides are fantastic products to be sold via mail order for the simple reason that there is always a demand for these types of items, and the supply is usually very limited. The best method to acquiring the products to be sold is to tender for a government contract selling the decommissioned goods or to purchase the items at the many auction sales that take place each year featuring these items. Once again, the profit margins can be excellent, as an item that can be purchased for $5 or less can often be resold for as much as $50.

Career Guides

Career guides have always been hot mail-order sellers. We have all seen the advertisements: "Hundreds of cruise ship jobs available. For the complete information package send . . . ." These types of guides are very inexpensive to create and print and can retail for as much as $30 each. The following are career guides that traditionally have been great mail-order sellers.

- Cruise ship and airline jobs.
- Construction flag persons training and jobs.
- Overseas hotel personnel jobs.
- High-tech careers.
- TV and film production positions.

Mailing Lists

Compiling and selling mailing lists, fax blast lists, and e-mail lists can make you rich. Millions of companies worldwide rely on these types of lists as their main marketing and business solicitation tools. To truly succeed in this very competitive segment of the mail-order industry, be sure to go high-tech. Companies who purchase these types of marketing lists now want them to be compatible with their computer systems, meaning the lists have to be on disk, or already pre-entered into a shareware mail merge, fax blast, or e-mail blast program. Additionally, be sure to market different types of mailing lists representing all the various consumer and business demographics groups. Prices for mailing lists vary widely, however, good lists can be sold for as much as $1 per name.

Acne Medications

Teens and adults who have facial acne problems will spend any amount of money for a potential cure, and that is why selling acne medications by mail order is a terrific business enterprise to launch. Acne medications, acne home remedies, and guides to curing facial acne all sell very well. The key to success is, like most mail-order products, the product is secondary and marketing is king. However, with that being said, imagine the strength of a mail-order business that sold acne medications or products that really did work at curing the problem. The business would be well received and have a hard time keeping up with replacement and new orders. Perhaps changing the age-old mail-order rule to "marketing is secondary and product is king" may have very beneficial business and financial results.

Stamps and Coins

Selling coins and stamps by mail order is a very easy business to set up and run. The coins and stamps that sell the best and have the most profit potential are the average, not rare, coins and stamps that are from various countries, creating a mystery or sense of increased value. The coins and stamps should be sold in a limited-offer set or collection to maximize profits.

Left-Handed Products

An estimated 5 percent of the world's population is left-handed, while an estimated 99.5 percent of the world's products have been designed and developed for right-handed people. Starting a mail-order business that specializes in selling products specifically for left-handed people is not only a great business venture to set in motion, but also a business venture that makes a lot of sense, given the discrepancy in the aforementioned numbers. Locating left-handed products to be sold should not prove difficult, as there are still thousands of manufacturers worldwide who specialize in manufacturing products specifically

for left-handed people. This type of mail-order business is perfectly suited to and would likely support a commercial Web site venture, as well as all traditional mail-order marketing mediums.

Magnets

Claims for the healing power of magnets range from curing cancer to helping arthritis sufferers rid themselves of the painful disease, and whether true or false, magnets sell by the thousands every day. Initiating a mail-order business that specializes in selling healing or health magnets is very easy to establish and only requires a business start-up investment of around $3,000. Currently there are numerous types of magnets available including magnets that you wear as bracelets, in your shoes, as a headband, etc. Locating a source for the magnets should also prove effortless, as there are thousands of manufacturers and wholesalers of these products worldwide. The best aspect about selling magnets by mail order is the simple fact that one health magnet can be purchased wholesale for as little as $2 and sold retail for as much as $20, or ten times the cost.

NOTES

KEY

RATINGS ★

START-UP COST $

HOMEBASED
BUSINESS 🏠

PART-TIME 🕐

LEGAL ISSUES ⚖️

FRANCHISE OR
LICENSE POTENTIAL 🌐

ONLINE 🖱

50

INSTRUCTION

Businesses You Can Start

HOME SCHOOLING

★★ $$ 🏠 🕐

Thousands of parents each year in the United States are making a decision to remove their children from the public school system in favor of home schooling their children. This fact creates a fantastic opportunity for an individual with a teaching or education background to start a new consulting business that assists parents in establishing a home-schooling educational program for their children. The home-schooling programs can be designed to specifically meet the educational needs of children at various stages of development and age, as well as feature subject testing, suggested educational field trips, and recreational and social interaction activities. The business can focus on developing and marketing home-schooling programs for children and parents. Or, the business can focus on in-home consulting on a one-on-one basis with parents to specially design a home-schooling program for their individual children. This type of unique consulting service is best marketed directly to parents who are at presently home schooling their children or who are considering it in the near future. The best way to gain access to this market is to join home-schooling associations and utilize the associations' memberships or roster lists as a basis for a direct mail campaign for your home-schooling consulting business. The following are two such home schooling associations:

United States
National Home Schooling Association
P.O. Box 327
Webster, New York 14580
Telephone: 513-772-9580
Web site: www.n-h-a.org

Canada
The Association of Canadian Homebased
  Education

P.O. Box 34148, RPO Fort Richmond
Winnipeg, MB R3T 5T5
Telephone: 815-366-5342
E-mail: homeschool-ca-admin@flore.org

ONLINE HOME SCHOOLING

★ $$+

Take home schooling into the high-tech world of the Internet by developing a "home-schooling" Web site. The Web site can feature information and services that can be utilized by parents wishing to school their children at home. This can include home-schooling programs in print format, an online chat forum for parents to discuss home-schooling issues, and articles submitted by parents on home-schooling topics. In general, the site could become an online support and information service for parents schooling their children at home. Income can be earned by selling textbooks and home-schooling programs and guides that outline suggested curriculums and social activities.

WEB RESOURCE: www.entrepreneur.com Create a business Web site with MySite professional Web site builder.

BALLROOM DANCING

★ $

Big bands and ballroom dancing are back in style, and starting a business that teaches students how to ballroom dance may be just the type of business opportunity that will enable you to make money utilizing your ballroom dancing skills. The business can be established as an independent venture or in association with a community recreation center or club. Students wishing to learn how to ballroom dance would pay a course fee and attend the classes on nights and weekends. Typically, these types of instructional courses cost in the range of $75 to $100 and are held once per week for four or five weeks in duration. This is a terrific business to launch, and could easily generate a part-time income in excess of $1,000 per month.

WOODWORKING CLASSES

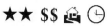 ★★ $$

Calling all craftsmen and woodworkers. It is time to put your woodworking skills to work for yourself and start an instructional business teaching students how to use woodworking equipment and complete woodworking projects. The business can be operated from a homebased workshop or from a small industrial rental location. Woodworking classes can be taught in a group format or a one-on-one basis. Additionally, you can provide various levels of woodworking instructional classes ranging from a beginner level all the way to an advanced course for the serious woodworker seeking to master the required skills to complete more complicated woodworking projects. Additional revenues for a woodworking instruction service can be gained by providing students the option of purchasing wood for their projects, as well as purchasing woodworking tools once they have completed the course.

STOP SMOKING CLINICS

★★ $$$

According to the U.S. Department of Health and Human Services, 29 percent of Americans smoke cigarettes. That means a whopping 80,000,000 potential customers for a stop smoking clinic in the United States alone. Even with the assistance of stop smoking aids, such as nicotine patches, gums, and pills, smokers often need additional guidance and support to be able to kick the habit. And, as a reformed smoker, I can attest to the difficulties and challenges a smoker faces when she or he decides it is finally time to butt out. Starting a stop smoking clinic or counseling service is not difficult. The classes can be conducted in a group format or a one-on-one in-home consulting basis. The business is obviously best suited to be started by an ex-smoker, as they can better understand their clients' situation. The best way to approach this type of instruction business is to develop a course manual: a "guide to quit smoking." The manual can be the basis of the stop smoking program that is offered to clients.

ICE SCULPTURE CLASSES

★★ $

Who would possibly want to learn how to make ice sculptures? The answer is thousands of chefs and caterers. Providing you have the skills and abilities to produce ice sculptures and can teach other people, then you have overcome the first hurdle in establishing a new business venture that teaches students how to make ice sculptures. Ice sculpture classes are best suited to being marketed directly to restaurant and catering company owners by arranging a presentation appointment to display and demonstrate your service. The business does not require an operating location, as you can travel to your client's business location and teach the ice sculpting classes on-site. This is an inexpensive business to establish and there should be no problems charging clients $40 to $50 per hour for the classes.

RIVER RESCUE INSTRUCTION

★★ $$

On the surface, starting a business that specializes in training students river rescue techniques may not seem to be a very viable business opportunity. However, if careful thought is given, you soon realize how important and profitable this business can be. Did you know that more than 4,000 people in the Untied States drown each year, and the leading category of drowning deaths is fishermen who are swept away in moving water—often witnessed by others? Many of these deaths could have been prevented had the witnesses of these drownings been taught river rescue techniques. The business requires the instructor of the program to acquire a river rescue instruction certificate, which can be gained by successfully completing a practical and written examination. Equipment such as throw bags, ropes, and safety harnesses will also be needed to conduct the instructional courses. Most of the equipment is available for purchase at recreational outdoor retailers. Potential clients for a river rescue instruction service include police and fire departments, sports clubs and organizations, fishermen, search and rescue

teams, canoe and kayak associations, and all other outdoor enthusiasts.

WEB RESOURCE: www.nasar.org National Association for Search and Rescue.

GOLF INSTRUCTION

★★★ $$ 🕐

Golf is one of the most popular sports and recreational pastimes in the United States, and millions of people hit the links on a weekly basis. Utilizing your golf expertise and skills, you can start an instruction business that teaches people to golf, or golf better. Most public and private golf courses have on-staff golf professionals who teach golfing lessons to members and visitors. However, this should not be viewed as a negative for starting your own golfing instruction service. There are a multitude of ways to start the business without being stationed or located within an existing golf course, such as a mobile golf pro who teaches proper golf swing and stance on an in-home consulting basis. Or, a golf pro can teach golfing techniques broadcasted live over the Internet via a specially designed Web site that utilizes a Web cam for the broadcasts. There are an infinite number of options for a golfing professional to start and operate a business that teaches students to golf. Furthermore, the business can be started on a small capital investment and can be managed from a homebased office. A well-established golfing instructor should have no difficulties earning an income in the $30 to $50 per hour range. Additional revenues for this business can be gained by manufacturing custom golf clubs, as well as repairing golf clubs for clients.

WEB RESOURCE: www.nagce.org National Association of Golf Coaches and Educators.

ONLINE LANGUAGE INSTRUCTION

★★ $$$$ 🕐 ♂

The world has become a smaller place, thanks to the introduction of the Internet, and starting a cyberventure that teaches students around the globe various languages may be the new business opportunity you have been searching for. Design and construct a Web site featuring foreign language instructional classes that are broadcast over the Internet. Students would simply log onto the site and choose the language they wish to learn. The teaching segments could be filmed using a digital camera and later entered into the correct category on the Web site. All courses could be taught by qualified professionals who provide their teaching service in exchange for a percentage of the revenue that is collected from the students who enroll for their specific language training program. Charging students a monthly membership fee for joining one of the foreign language instruction programs would generate revenues. Additional income could be earned by selling advertising space on the Web site, as well as selling related instructional books and programs. Ideally, the marketing of the business could be directed at large international corporations who have an international sales staff that must be multilingual.

STRESS MANAGEMENT COURSES
★★ $$

During the 1970s, many futurists were predicting that, due to the rapid gains in technology, the average workweek would shrink to only 30 hours by the year 2000. I wonder if these same futurists are now rubbing their heads in disbelief. According to the U.S. Department of Labor, the average American employed full-time is now working 47 hours per week, as opposed to 42 hours per week in the 1970s. This fact, coupled with an increased workload and potential financial and family complications, makes it no wonder that the average person is at the end of their rope and suffering from stress-related health problems. Without question, starting a business that assists people in learning how to cope with stress and how to avoid stressful situations is a business venture with an unlimited number of potential clients. The marketing of the stress management classes could be targeted at individuals seeking to reduce or eliminate stress from their daily lives. However, seeking corporate clients for the stress management courses may be a preferred approach,

as you would have the ability to gain perhaps as many as ten clients with the same amount of marketing effort and costs put toward gaining one individual client. The business can be conducted from a homebased or rental office location, or the stress management classes could be held at the client's business or home location. As with any instructional business, the key to success is to develop an exclusive course manual and program for your clients to use and follow. By developing your own program, you become the owner of the information. And should the program become very popular, it could become an excellent opportunity to put the program into print or electronic format and market the product worldwide.

TRUCK DRIVING SCHOOL
★ $$$$ ⚖

The trucking and delivery transportation industry is enormous. To gain employment in this industry drivers must first acquire a special drivers permit or endorsements on their drivers license to enable them to become professional truck drivers. In most cases, the applicant must successfully pass a written test and a practical road test before they can acquire these special driving permits. Make no mistake, the written examination and practical road test are difficult, and due to this fact, most people who are seeking a career as a truck driver enroll in a truck driving instruction program prior to attempting to obtain the required permits and licenses. Starting a truck driving school necessitates a very large capital investment to establish and operate the business. However, the profit potential is excellent for this type of business endeavor, as truck driving instruction programs cost as much as $3,000 for each student to attend. Further revenue for this business can be generated by providing transportation companies with yearly refresher driving courses for their employees. The benefit to the companies for participating in this type of program is simply the fact that their employees can become improved drivers, which can reduce road accidents, missed work days, and damage to vehicles, which in turn, can increase productivity and yearly profits.

NEW PARENTS SCHOOL

★ $$

According to the U.S. Department of Health and Human Services, almost four million babies were born in the United States last year. While many second- and third-time parents completely understand how to care for a newborn baby, there are hundreds of thousands of first-time parents who could certainly benefit from a little support and guidance on how to be a new parent. Ideally, the person who starts a consulting business teaching first-time parents methods and tips on practical child care will have a nursing or child-care background. The business can work as an independent consulting firm or can be established to work in conjunction with existing hospitals and social service programs. Once established, the owner of this type of consulting service can easily generate an income in excess of $50,000 per year.

THEFT PREVENTION

★★ $$ 🏚 🕐 🌐

Shoplifting, employee theft, delivery trucks that mysteriously lose their cargo along the way, and theft in any form costs companies billions of dollars in lost revenues and profits each year, eventually costing all consumers higher product prices to help offset theft losses. Initiating a consulting service that trains business owners and staff how to prevent thefts and what to do in the event of a theft is a very good venture to set in motion, especially for individuals with a law enforcement or security background. The instructional classes can be taught in a group format that would include the business owner, management, and staff at the client's location during nonbusiness hours. Many theft prevention firms specialize in very in-depth and costly theft prevention programs as a method to separate their service from potential competitors. Perhaps a low-cost, but highly effective theft prevention program could be developed and marketed to business owners who are on a restricted budget, but who would still like to participate in an effective theft prevention program that can

benefit their business. This type of condensed program could be marketed at an affordable price—say $159—and could include two hours of on-site instruction for the owner and employees, as well as a theft prevention manual that has been specially developed for the program. A shortened instructional program such as this is ideally marketed by enlisting the services of a telemarketing firm to promote and sell the service. Alternatively, designing and launching a direct mail promotional campaign, aimed at small business owners and companies with less than 20 employees, could market the program.

SURVIVAL TRAINING

★★ $$ 🏚 🕐 ⚖

What would you do if you were trapped on a mountainside, in subzero weather, with an impending blizzard approaching? This may not seem to be a likely scenario for many of us. However, to the millions of outdoor enthusiasts who take part in recreational activities such as hiking, skiing, and rock climbing, this is a very real and dangerous threat. A survival training service can be marketed directly to potential customers by establishing alliances with recreation-related businesses and associations, such as hiking clubs and rock climbing schools. You could provide their members and customers with survival training instruction courses by way of specially designed informational brochures. In addition to recreational enthusiasts, survival training courses can be offered to police forces, fire departments, and forest service employees. The main requirements for this type of business venture are that the trainers will have to be skilled and experienced survival training instructors, as well as hold a first-aid instructor's certificate. The survival training course could be instructed over a weeklong period with the theory aspect of the course being conducted weekday evenings, and the practical aspect of the course held the following weekend.

This type of instruction business also requires a survival training manual to be developed and utilized in all facets of the complete training program. The factors determining the profit potential for a survival instruction business are too numerous to pinpoint an accurate figure. However, due to the specialized nature of this business opportunity, it can be assumed that a well-promoted and established survival training service has the potential to generate great earnings.

WEB RESOURCE: www.nasar.org National Association for Search and Rescue.

HOW-TO BOOKS
★ $

There are thousands of people who specialize, or have an interest in, a craft, trade, hobby, sport, art medium, or method of doing a particular task or job. And many of these people would love the opportunity to put their experiences, skills, and know-how into print and by writing a book on their subject of expertise. What is stopping these gifted individuals from writing a book? The answer is simple. They don't know where to start or what to do next. Starting a business that teaches people how to write "how-to books" is a terrific venture to put into action. Classes can be held on nights and weekends, enabling the operator of this business venture to manage a daytime business or work a daytime job. The how to write a "how-to book" instruction class should include details and practical tips on information such as popular topics for the books, writing styles and formats, publisher contacts, research techniques, and organizational and time management skills, as well as additional information and guidance to assist students in reaching their "book-writing goals." This type of instruction class is ideally promoted in conjunction with a community institution such as a college, recreation center, or continuing education program.

ACTING LESSONS
★★ $$

Calling all actors, part-time actors, agents, production crew members, or producers. Why not share your experience, skills, and knowledge with the mil-

lions of other people who are seeking to start a career in the acting profession or the TV and film production industry, and start your own instruction business in your field of expertise? The instruction classes could focus on acting, TV, and film industry in general, or could focus on more specific sections of the industry, such as how to audition for a film role or how to become a production grip. Training classes and seminars could be held on an independent basis or be provided to students in conjunction with community programs or related school programs. This type of instruction business is very inexpensive to establish; yet the income potential even on a part-time basis is outstanding.

ONLINE ACTING SCHOOL
★ $$$$

Acting classes via the Internet: why not? Demand for acting classes and courses is certainly large enough for this type of online enterprise to become popular and succeed. Get started by building an alliance with an established acting school. The school's students can digitally video the school's acting classes that can then be broadcast over the Internet via your Web site. You can charge cyberstudents a monthly fee for full access to archived footage of the acting classes featured on the site. You can also incorporate additional information and details about the film production and acting industry into the Web site. This information could include director and producer contact lists, film production schedules, and actors and literary agent listings, all of which can be used as valuable resources by site members.

PHOTOGRAPHY COURSES
★★ $$

A photography instruction service can train students in both traditional print film photography as well as in digital-imaging formats. Courses could be provided for students from a homebased photography studio, or the business could be operated as a joint venture with community training programs or educational facilities. One marketing method may be to approach retailers that sell cameras and digital cameras and offer a free two-hour photography course for all of their customers who purchase a camera. Of course the objective of this type of free promotion is to have a large percentage of the students who take advantage of the free class sign up for extended photography courses and training (on a paid basis).

WEB RESOURCE: www.arct.com/arcatcos/cos37/arc37624.ctm National Photography Instructors Association.

COOKING CLASSES
★★ $$ 📸 🕐

Does everyone tell you what a good cook you are? If so, perhaps you should consider starting your own business that teaches people how to cook. The business can be started on a shoestring budget, yet has the ability to generate a yearly income in excess of $40,000. Providing you can secure the necessary zoning and licensing, the business could be established from a homebased location, or alternatively, the business could be established as a joint venture with an existing retail store that sells cookware and housewares. If the joint venture route is taken, the cooking classes could be conducted at night or during nonbusiness hours. Establishing a business as a joint venture with an existing business that is already successful is a terrific way to minimize start-up investment, capitalize on an existing client base, and share overhead costs. Joint ventures and amalgamations are without question the business trend of the future.

GARDENING CLASSES
★★ $$ 📸 🕐

Teaching "how-to" gardening classes can be a fun and profitable instruction business to start. The classes can be conducted right from home utilizing your own garden as the basis of the instruction class. Successfully marketing this type of instruction business is best achieved by establishing alliances with local garden centers that can refer your "how-to garden" classes to their customers. Additionally, writing and publishing an annual gardener's handbook that features local gardens, gardeners, and gardening tips is also a fantastic way to increase business revenues and profits. The gardening book can be sold through local retail merchants and can be partly supported by selling advertising space in the book to local gardening businesses. Securing a mere 20 clients per week, each paying $50 for a day-long "how-to garden instruction course" will result in yearly business sales of $50,000.

HOME RENOVATION CLASSES
★★★ $$$

Home renovations can no longer be classified as a method to improve a home in terms of function or livability. Home renovations have become a national craze and a hobby practiced and enjoyed by millions of American homeowners annually. There are various approaches that can be taken when considering starting a business that teaches homeowners home renovation skills and techniques. The first is to establish an independent school and charge students a fee to learn a specific home renovation trade such as "how to paint." The second approach is to build an alliance or joint venture with a local building or home improvement center and hold the classes at the building center. The classes can be free, which are then supported by the retailer, or there can be a fee charged to the students for the class. In both cases this is a truly win-win-win situation. The students receive practical and helpful training to improve their homes and save money by not having to enlist the services of a contractor to complete the renovation. The retailers where the training classes are conducted receive fantastic exposure and a lot of long-term future clients. The innovative entrepreneur that establishes the home-renovation training program can capitalize on the building center's existing client base as a quick-start method to attract students, as well as utilize the building center's infrastructure and resources to reduce start-up investment and overheads.

FLYING SCHOOL

★ $$$$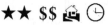

The wide availability and relatively low cost of small prop and ultralight airplanes is fueling a craze for people wanting to learn how to fly a plane. And starting a flying school is the best way to capitalize on this craze. Without question, there are a lot of hurdles, both financial and regulatory, to overcome when considering starting a flying school as a new business venture. However, the long-term rewards can be well worth the effort if starting this type of instruction business has always been a personal dream. In addition to generating revenue for the business from training students, small airplanes and pilots are in high demand for the film industry and are commanding as much as $1,500 per day for supplying themselves and the planes for film work. Additional considerations for starting a flying school will also be location, liability insurance, equipment, and marketing. Good luck and let me know how you are doing.

WEB RESOURCE: www.nafinet.org National Association of Flight Instructors.

CAMPING CLASSES

★★ $$ ◷

Camping is an outdoors recreational pastime enjoyed by millions of people across North America. Thus, starting a "how-to camp" instructional business that teaches novice campers and hikers practical information and tips on how to safely go camping is an extremely low-cost business start-up that can potentially generate fabulous profits. One of the best aspects of starting this business is the fact that the classes can be held outside and, in most cases, without having to pay a fee or rent for the class location. The business can be marketed directly to potential students by distributing fliers and informational brochures through local retailers such as outfitters. The business can also be marketed through a partnership arrangement with community and recreation centers. For a business that can be initiated for an investment of less than $5,000, this one is a very good choice that also promises to be a whole lot of fun.

SKIING INSTRUCTION

★★ $$ ⌂ ◷

Downhill skiing, cross-country skiing, and snowboarding have become some of the most popular winter sports that are enjoyed by millions of participants in North America each year. Starting a business that trains people in one or all of these terrific outdoor sports is a fantastic seasonal business enterprise to set in motion. The business can be established as a joint venture with an existing ski operation, resort, or even an equipment manufacturer; or the business can be an independent venture with a mixture of in-class theory training and outdoor practical training. Once established, a well-managed small- to medium-size "ski school" can easily generate a seasonal income for the owner in excess of $25,000.

WEB RESOURCE: www.psia.org Professional Ski Instructors of America.

DOG TRAINING CLASSES

★★★ $$ ⌂ ◷

Becoming a dog trainer and starting a business teaching people how to train their dogs can be both a personally rewarding lifestyle and a profitable business to operate. There are millions of dogs in North America and, while a great number of them are well trained, there are an equal number of dogs and owners that would certainly benefit from participating in a training or obedience instruction program. As the adopted owner of a 90-pound, extremely strong and stubborn Rottweiler, I can personally attest to the many benefits that both myself and Dana have received by enlisting the services of a professional trainer who ran both of us through the trenches, so to speak. The starting point for launching a dog training business is to first become a professional certified trainer. While this is not an expensive or difficult certificate to acquire, it does require you to have a love for dogs and a desire to assist dogs and dog owners to lead a more rewarding and enjoyable coexistence. The training classes can be conducted from a fixed training location or on a mobile basis wherein you go to the client's home. In both cases the current rates for one-on-one training are in the range of $30 to $40 per hour, while group rates (up to six) work out to approximately $5 to $10 per hour per student. Selling books on training and obedience topics to clients, as well as specialty dog foods and equipment such as leashes and collars, can also generate additional revenue.

WEB RESOURCE: www.nadoi.org National Association of Dog Obedience Instructors.

ONLINE DOG TRAINING

 ★★ $$+

It is time to roll up your sleeves and get to work building a Web site that specializes in providing dog owners with helpful dog training tips and techniques. There are many options in terms of the type of information and services this type of Web site could provide to visitors, including:

- An online directory of dog trainers from coast to coast.
- Digital video broadcasts of live dog training demonstrations and online instruction.
- New articles and information about dog training posted daily by the top dog trainers in the country.

There are also many ways for this type of Web site to generate income including selling advertising space on the site, selling dog training programs, books, and videos, or charging dog trainers a fee to be listed in the online directory.

MUSIC LESSONS

★★★ $$

Do you play a musical instrument, and play it well enough to teach other people how to play? If so, why not start your own business providing music lessons to the thousands of people who take up playing a musical instrument each year. Starting a business that teaches students how to play a musical instrument is a fantastic business to set in motion. Not only can the venture be started on a shoestring budget, it can also be operated from

home or on a mobile basis with virtually no overhead costs. As with any business enterprise, duplication is often the best way to expand the business and create more revenue and profits. In the case of music instruction this can be a difficult task to accomplish given that you are only one person and can only be in one location at a time. Well, lets think about that. What is the easiest way to expand a music instruction business, beyond the obvious answer of having more than one student at a time? Here are a few suggestions: The classes could be taught over the Internet via your own specially designed Web site, you could produce your own music instruction videos and sell them worldwide, or you could hire other musicians for the business and they could work on a profit-share or subcontract basis. The options are limitless when you apply the entrepreneurial spirit that drove you to starting your own business in the first place.

WEB RESOURCE: www.mtna.org Music Teachers National Association.

SAILING SCHOOL

★★ $$$$

Calling all salty sea dogs. Stop working 9 to 5 and making profits for someone you probably do not even like. The time is now to take the bull by the horns and start your own business. Sailing is a sport and recreational pastime that is enjoyed by thousands of people across North America, with thousands more joining the ranks each year. Many of these novice sailors share a common bond: they have enrolled, or will in the near future enroll themselves, spouses, and family into training courses to learn all the vital techniques and skills required to safely operate and sail a sailboat. Providing you have sailing experience and, better yet, a sailing instructor's certificate, then the business is very straightforward to set in motion and does not even require you to have your own sailboat, as you can provide sailing training for students who already have a sailboat. Generally sailboat instruction courses are comprised of two elements: classroom theory, such as basic navigation, and practical on-the-water training.

Additionally, courses are generally conducted over a two- to three-day period on a full-time basis, and a two- to three-week period on a part-time basis. Securing only 20 to 30 clients per year can generate an income, prior to taxes and overhead expenses, in excess of $30,000 per year.

WEB RESOURCE: www.american-sailing.com American Sailing Association.

SCUBA DIVING INSTRUCTION
★★ $$ 🕐 ⚖

Like sailing, scuba diving is a sport and a recreational pastime enjoyed by millions of Americans, and like sailing, thousands more people are taking scuba-diving lessons each year, so they too can enjoy recreational scuba diving. The number one requirement for starting a scuba diving instruction business is, of course, to be a certified scuba diving instructor. There are many training facilities in the United States. However, the best and most recognized scuba diving instructors' program is one that is provided by PADI (Professional Association of Dive Instructors). The course will take a few months to complete and will cost a few thousand dollars. Once certified, scuba diving instruction classes can be marketed directly to potential students via all traditional advertising and marketing mediums. Or, the business can be partnered with an existing scuba diving retailer or charter boat operation. The bottom line is that you can have a lot of fun, make a decent income, and really enjoy your work.

WEB RESOURCE: www.padi.com Professional Association of Dive Instructors.

FIRST-AID TRAINING
★★★ $$ 🏠 🕐 ⚖

Make no mistake, starting an instruction business that focuses on teaching first-aid training has the potential to generate profits in excess of $100,000 per year. Best of all, the business can be managed from a homebased office and started for less than a few thousand dollars. Clients can include construction companies, warehousing and distribution companies, and clubs and organizations. Furthermore,

the first-aid courses are best taught on the customer's site in a group-training format, as this can keep the cost per student to a minimum while keeping business volume and profits to a maximum. Additionally, be sure to offer all clients yearly refresher courses for their employees. The first-aid refresher courses can be slightly discounted as a method of ensuring a 100 percent yearly retention rate. Marketing first aid training services is as simple as designing a high-quality presentation brochure and setting appointments with potential customers to explain all the benefits to their firms by having employees receive occupational first-aid training.

WEB RESOURCE: www.redcross.org American Red Cross.

LOG HOME BUILDING SCHOOL
★★ $$ 🏠 🕐

Year-round home or a seasonal cottage in the mountains or by a lake; thousands of North Americans dream about building and owning their own log homes. And starting a business that teaches people how to build and maintain log homes is a very interesting and unique business venture to launch. The log home building school can be advertised in all the traditional print media, as well as promoted and advertised on the Internet, to attract the attention of potential students from around the world. The requirements for starting this type of business are numerous and the investment is large. However, as a method to reduce start-up costs and share expenses, a possible consideration is to start a joint venture with an existing log home builder.

WEB RESOURCE: www.loghomes.com Directory service listing log home builders and industry information.

FLOWER ARRANGING CLASSES
★★ $$ 🏠 🕐

Thanks in part to craft gurus like Martha Stewart, flower arranging and dried flower products have become extremely popular as home decorations, gifts, and as a hobby. Starting a flower arranging instructional business can be fun, and easily operated from home. The business requires only a minimal investment to get things rolling. Students are currently paying as much a $50 to $75 for one three-hour course, making this a potentially very profitable business venture. Building alliances with flower shops, garden centers, and retail gift stores is a great way to market the business initially, as these types of businesses can act as a referral source or even a joint venture partner, with the flower arranging courses being conducted nights and weekends from their locations. Securing only ten new students per week, and charging a mere $60 for the flower arranging course, will create business revenues of more than $30,000 per year.

DANCE STUDIO
★★ $$$ 🌎

Starting a dance instruction school is a wonderful new business venture to set in motion, as dance schools have been proven financially sound for decades. The business can focus on dance instruction in general, or on specific dance styles such as tap or swing. If you are not a dance instructor yourself, professional dance instructors can be hired on an as-needed part-time, revenue-sharing basis to conduct the instruction classes. The innovative entrepreneur who starts and operates a dance school can also increase revenues and profits by videotaping the instruction classes and selling the videos by way of mail order and the Internet. The potential to create a six-figure yearly income by starting and operating a dance studio is very achievable, providing sound business and marketing judgment are practiced.

EDUCATIONAL TUTOR
★★ $ 🏠 🕐

Education is a major element of a child's development. For parents wanting the peace of mind that their child is receiving the proper education, extracurricular tutoring can be the preferred method of extended educational training beyond public school. There is one main requirement for starting this type of instruction business; you have to be an expert in the field in which you intend to teach or

tutor. Beyond that, the business is very simple to start. The business can be operated on a mobile basis going to the client, or a tutoring business can be operated from a homebased office with the client coming to you. Building a customer and referral base for this type of business can be accomplished by joining community business associations and parent teacher associations. Networking and self-promotion is probably the best marketing strategy. Tutoring is a competitive industry and to gain the upper hand requires explanation and disclosure of credentials firsthand. Current rates for a professional tutoring service vary from a low of $18 per hour to a high of $35 per hour depending on course material and complexity.

ONLINE TUTORS
★★ $$+ 🏠 🕐 🖱

Harness the power of the Internet to take educational tutors from around the globe online via your own specially designed "tutor directory" Web site. You can create a Web site that exclusively specializes in helping people find qualified educational tutors in their community. The site will have to be indexed by tutor type and geographic location for internal search purposes. However, this is a relatively easy programming challenge to overcome. Once again, these sections could include math tutors, science tutors, English, English as a second language tutors, and more. Visitors to the site who are seeking a tutor to help them or their children with their studies would simply select the category of interest and view the listing to find an appropriate candidate. In exchange for an annual listing fee, tutors would receive a headline listing that is linked to a pop-up page. The pop-up page could give full details and information about their tutoring programs, qualifications, and contact information.

STAINED GLASS
★★ $$ 🏠 🕐

Launching a business that focuses on teaching people how to make stained-glass items, such as lampshades and sun catchers, is a terrific low-investment business opportunity to initiate. The business and instruction classes can be operated from a home-based workshop, or the classes can be provided for students and operated in conjunction with a community institution, such as a college, recreation center, or community center. One of the main requirements for starting a business teaching others how to make stained-glass products is, of course, the ability to make and teach others how to make stained-glass items. Beyond that, the business is very simple to start. Selling students the materials required to make the stained-glass items, such as art glass, cutters, and glass grinders, can earn additional income.

WEB RESOURCE: www.stainedglass.org Stained Glass Association of America.

AUTO MAINTENANCE COURSE
★★ $$ 🏠 🕐 ⚖

Calling all certified mechanics. Put your automobile repair skills to work for you and start a business that teaches students how to do general maintenance on their cars and trucks. The auto maintenance courses could be conducted in association with a community or educational facility, such as a community college, or on an independent basis by leasing a small work and training space. Course instruction can include how to change your oil, change a flat tire, and carry out regular brake and steering checks, as well as any other small automotive related maintenance tasks. Providing you can secure ten paying clients per week for a three-hour auto maintenance class and charge the students $50 each, this great part-time business would generate sales in excess of $2,000 per month.

MARTIAL ARTS
★★★ $$$ ⚖ 🌐

Martial arts as a sport is second only to golf in terms of number of new participants over the past decade. Typically, a martial arts school will focus on one particular type of training such as kung fu or kick boxing. A martial arts school can be an expensive new business venture to set in motion. However, the average cost now paid by a student per year for

martial arts training is in excess of $600. Providing the business could train 200 students per year, this would result in revenues exceeding $120,000, based on an average of $600 per year per student. Needless to say, this type of specialized instruction can be very financially lucrative. In addition to group training, one-on-one martial arts training is also becoming popular for the serious student who is prepared to pay $40 per hour or more for an intensive training session.

WEB RESOURCE: www.mararts.org United States Martial Arts Association.

JEWELRY MAKING INSTRUCTION
★★ $$ 🏠 🕐

Starting a jewelry making instruction business could prove to be very profitable and fun. To keep initial start-up costs to a minimum, build alliances with local businesses such as craft stores, clothing retailers, and community centers. By establishing these alliances, you can hold the jewelry instruction classes on the site of your new business partners and split the sales revenues with the owners of these businesses—not to mention the fact that this will also provide you with the opportunity to capitalize on the business's existing customer base to attract new students for the jewelry making classes. A mere four classes per week with ten students paying $20 each will create business revenues in excess of $40,000 per year.

DRIVING SCHOOL
★★ $$$$ 🏠 ⚖ 🌐

Training new drivers how to be good drivers is a multimillion dollar industry in the United States. The main requirement for starting a driver training school is to be, or have on staff, professional driving instructors. Many driving instruction schools now subcontract out the driving instruction to trained professionals who supply their own automobiles, insurance, and gas in exchange for a percentage of the revenue paid by their students. Using this type of operating format can be a terrific way to reduce the overall start-up and operating costs for the business. Currently, revenue split rates range from a low of 60 percent for the instructor and 40 percent for the driving school to 75 percent for the instructor and 25 percent for the school. This is a very competitive industry and the only way to succeed is to secure contracts with high schools providing driver education courses for students. The contracts for this service are usually awarded on a tender-for-service basis every one to three years.

WEB RESOURCE: www.driving.org The Drivers Instructors Association.

SEWING CLASSES
★★ $$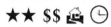

Calling all seamstress and hobby sewers, starting a sewing instruction business is a fantastic opportunity to earn a great part-time income while operating your own homebased business. A sewing instruction business can be set in motion for less than $5,000 and has the potential to easily create an income in the range of $25 to $35 per hour or more. Sewing classes can be marketed directly to students via all traditional means of advertising. You can also initiate a joint venture with a local fabric store to hold the classes evenings and weekends or even as a joint venture with a community or recreation center. Joint ventures are a fantastic way to reduce the overall start-up capital to open a business, as well as capitalize on the partner's existing customer base. Overall, it's a great little business that can generate additional revenue by selling sewing patterns to students, as well as by mail order.

WINDSURFING SCHOOL
★ $$

Windsurfing is a sport and recreational pastime that roared to popularity in the early 1980s, and after a few years of steady growth in the popularity of windsurfing, began to decline. However, that was then, this is now. The popularity of windsurfing is again on the rise. This is mainly due to the fact that once the equipment and training have been paid for, windsurfing is a very inexpensive sport to

participate in, not to mention the thrill of gliding over waves at 30 miles per hour. The first step in starting a windsurfing training school is to be a windsurfer or to hire professional instruction staff on a revenue-split basis. The business is best established in a busy tourist area: one that preferably draws year-round crowds to the beach. In addition to the equipment requirements, it is well advised to seek out liability insurance, due to the nature of the sport and the potential for serious accidents. With the right training location, additional revenues can be generated by renting windsurfing boards to tourists on an hourly and half-day basis. Overall, this can be a great new business venture to establish, providing you have the right location. The profit potential for a seasonal wind surfing training school is in the range of $20,000 per season, while a year-round training school could easily generate profits two to three times that number. The revenue generated by the rental aspect of the business could add an additional $10,000 to $15,000 per year, bringing the total potential profits for a year-round operation to $50,000 or more.

WEB RESOURCE: www.awia.org American Windsurfing Industries Association.

BUSINESS START-UP INSTRUCTION
★★ $$$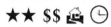

A recent survey conducted by the U.S. government indicated that a full 40 percent of American adults wanted to start and own a business. With 100 million potential clients waiting, there has never been a better time than now to start a business that trains people how to start and run a business. The business start-up instruction courses could be conducted over a week-long period and the classes could be held at night. Of critical importance for this type of instruction business is to design and develop a course manual that will be used for training purposes, as well as form the backbone of the business. To expand the business beyond any particular geographical area, consider broadcasting the training classes over the Internet via your own Web site. This would enable potential clients and students to partake in the business start-up training courses from around the country, as well as increase the profit for the business.

FASHION DESIGN SCHOOL
★ $$$$

Starting a fashion school is very straightforward. However, there certainly is one main requirement. You or your instructors must be fashion designers. There are many approaches that can be taken when considering a fashion school as a new business venture. The first approach is to start a full-service fashion school that is recognized by fashion designers and clothing manufacturers. A less costly and less complicated approach to starting a fashion design school is to target students who have an interest in starting their own fashion label or clothing manufacturing business. The training provided could be over a shorter period of time and could be less costly than traditional fashion school courses. Additional revenues can be created by selling the fashions designed by the students through your own fashion shows, as well as over the Internet via your own Web site. This type of business is costly to establish. However, the potential to generate a six-figure yearly income is certainly within reach for the hard-working entrepreneur.

PUBLIC SPEAKING INSTRUCTION
★★ $$ ⏲

Public speaking is an art, and unfortunately many business owners do not realize the importance of being able to project a positive image of their business and themselves, whether it is speaking in front of one person or a group of 500 people. Starting an instruction business that specializes in training business owners, managers, and employees to become effective public speakers is a great new business venture to set in motion. The best way to market this type of instruction service is to design a complete marketing presentation and distribute the presentation to the most likely potential clients. A good segment of the market to focus on is businesses and companies with medium to large sales forces.

Furthermore, the training courses can be conducted right at the client's location, eliminating the need for costly office rental. Aim to secure three clients per week for a specialized half-day public speaking course, and you can be well on your way to earning $100,000 per year.

FIREARMS TRAINING
★★ $$ ⏲ ⚖

Like the saying goes "guns do not kill people, people kill people," and this saying clearly indicates why a person who owns a gun should learn how to safely use, store, and maintain the gun. You must be a certified instructor in order to provide clients with firearms training, thus this will be the first step you need to take to start the business if you are not already a certified instructor. Marketing your firearms training courses is best accomplished by building an alliance with a gun club or shooting range. You can also hold free seminars in your community with a "gun safety" theme and discussion. These types of seminars are a terrific way to collect leads from potential customers interested in participating in a complete in-depth firearms training and safety program.

CUSTOMER SERVICE TRAINING
★★★ $$ 🏢 ⏲ 🌐

We have all been in situations where we have been treated poorly by a food server, service manager, receptionist, or product installer. The end result of such an encounter is typically a vow to never return to or refer that particular business again. Rude and poorly trained employees cost companies millions of dollars each year in potential future business and referrals. The companies that benefit from this are the ones that take proactive measures to ensure their staff has received proper customer service and appreciation training. You can earn an incredible income by starting a consulting service that provides companies, organizations, and associations with various customer service training programs that have been specifically designed to meet their individual needs and that target how to become a good, helpful, and customer-appreciative employee. To get started, decide if your instruction program will focus on one specific industry for training, such as food servers, or be a general instruction program that trains all service employees, regardless of the industry or position they work in. Once you have chosen an operating format, the next step is to design and publish an instruction manual and course description that will become the basis of the program. This step is extremely important, as it is the foundation for the entire business venture. The manual should be designed in such a way that it is a comprehensive "A to Z" program that covers all the bases in customer service and customer appreciation training and can be easily and quickly customized to meet individual client needs. The training programs can take place at client locations during nonbusiness hours in a group or one-on-one format.

A prerequisite for starting this type of business is to be a customer service specialist. While this does not mean that you must possess a specific certificate, it does mean that you must posses a great deal of customer service experience, common sense, and a creative imagination to develop role play sketches for the purpose of training. Market the service by joining local business groups to network for clients, as well as build alliances with other types of employee training services that do not presently provide clients with customer service training options. Fees for the service will be in the range of $40 to $60 per hour, based on the average training program.

SELF-DEFENSE TRAINING
 ★★ $$

Self-defense training is a booming multimillion dollar industry in North America, and this business opportunity will appeal to anyone with a military or police service training background. Once again, providing that you are qualified to teach self-defense, an excellent income can be earned by doing just that. The classes can be conducted in a one-on-one basis at clients' locations, or alternately you can offer the training classes in conjunction with a community

center, school, or fitness center. Also, do not overlook the possibility of marketing the classes directly to medium- and large-sized corporations. If you choose this route, you can develop a complete self-defense and personal safety program for your client's employees and even conduct the classes at the corporate location during nonbusiness or office hours. Expanding the business is as easy as hiring other qualified instructors to conduct the classes, and you can even add additional types of instruction courses, such as first aid, wilderness survival, and river rescue to your roster. Unfortunately, women are often the target of attacks and violent crime, so be sure to pay extra attention to marketing the classes to this segment of the population. Currently fees for this type of specialized training are in the range of $25 to $40 per hour taught on a one-on-one basis, and approximately $100 for a one-to-two hour course taught in group format.

TIME MANAGEMENT CLASSES
 ★★ $$

Unlike the hit song of the '60s, time is not on our side! Hectic work and home schedules can leave even the most organized members of our society in a state of constant chaos. The 70-hour workweek, little league games, social commitments, and even simple grocery shopping all are the villains that make managing time near impossible for some. Here is where you can come to the rescue and build a successful business at the same time. Provide clients with time management training that can teach them how to manage their time better, identify time wasted, organize their daily routines, and build a system that is more productive when working and get more enjoyment when not working. Classes can be taught on a one-on-one basis, or in group format. Group format training can be marketed to small- and medium-sized businesses and corporations. The individual classes can be targeted to high-level executive positions and professionals. A prerequisite for starting and operating this business is to have experience in the field and, more importantly, excellent organizational and management skills. Additionally, be sure to develop a standardized time management manual that can be customized quickly and easily to suit individual client needs. The manual is an important aspect of the business as it is the backbone for all the training classes, follow-up sessions, and ongoing exercises. The manual should be included and given to clients as part of the training program.

SPORT COACH TRAINING

Here is a unique business opportunity that really has big market potential as there are currently hundreds of thousand of amateur sports coaches across North America, and thousands more joining their ranks every year. The title of this opportunity may be somewhat misleading. You do not want to provide the service of training sport coaches how to be better in their particular sport; in most cases they already have a vast knowledge of the sport or they would not be coaching. But you want to teach them how to be better coaches and mentors in terms of interacting with players on the team, parents, spouses, and game and league officials. The idea is to organize, market, and conduct seminars for sport coaches with specialized management, interaction, and social responsibility themes to help train them to be better mentors and coaches. You can enlist the services of professionals, such as motivational speakers, psychologists, and management specialists to speak at the training seminars and hand out printed material on the subject they are teaching. The seminars can be marketed directly to amateur sports associations, clubs, and organizations by initiating a direct mail campaign. Objections from coaches and sports association members to the seminar training should be minimal.

NOTES

KEY

RATINGS	★
START-UP COST	$
HOMEBASED BUSINESS	
PART-TIME	
LEGAL ISSUES	
FRANCHISE OR LICENSE POTENTIAL	
ONLINE	

62

MANUFACTURING

Businesses You Can Start

PATIO FURNITURE MANUFACTURING

★ $$

Custom-designed and manufactured cedar patio furniture is highly sought after by homeowners who enjoy comfortable and fashionable outdoor patio furniture. Launching a business venture that builds custom cedar patio furniture is a relatively inexpensive enterprise to establish. The business can be run from a garage or basement workshop and requires only minimal woodworking equipment such as a table saw, band saw, planer, basic power hand tools, and sanders. There are thousands of design plans available to assist in constructing the patio furniture, or the seasoned carpenter can certainly manufacture his/her own custom designs. The patio furniture can be sold on a wholesale basis by establishing accounts with garden centers and designers. Or, the custom patio furniture can be sold directly to consumers by marketing the products at home and garden trade shows.

WEB RESOURCE: www.scrollsaw.com Design plans for patio furniture.

ONLINE MANUFACTURERS DIRECTORY

★★ $$$

Manufacturers directories in print have served as a valuable resource tool for many corporations and small businesses for decades. Now it is your opportunity to merge old ways with high-tech solutions. Taking manufacturers directories into cyberspace is relatively easy to accomplish. Start by selecting a segment of the industry you want to concentrate on, like machined fasteners or fabric. Next, design the site into various categories or sections representing manufacturers products, businesses seeking manufactured goods, and agents seeking to represent manufacturers. Once the site has been developed you can go about marketing the listing service. Typically, manufacturers that list with this type of service pay a monthly or annual fee and receive a listing on the site linked to a promotional pop-up page or hyperlink to their site if applicable. Remember, manufacturers will only pay for this service if it is of value to them, meaning that exposure on the site ultimately must result in increased or new sales. So be sure to aim marketing efforts at those who will purchase the type of manufactured goods featured on the site.

KITCHEN CUTTING BOARDS
★ $

Kitchen cutting boards are easy to make, and there is a strong market demand for the product from both homeowners and commercial kitchen chefs. Once you have mastered the art of producing high-quality kitchen cutting boards, you can then move on to butcher block tables as the market demand for this specialty product is huge, and a well-made butcher block table can easily sell for $1,000 or more. This new business venture is an ideal candidate for starting from home on a part-time basis. Not only can you enjoy the benefits of earning extra income, you will also be gaining valuable business experience that can be applied when it's time for the business to expand. Potential income range is $5,000 to $10,000 per year part-time.

BOOKENDS
★★ $

Manufacturing bookends? Why not? They fall into the category of a great gift for someone who has everything. And best of all, the business can be set in motion for less than $500 and operated right from home. One of the key elements for this manufacturing venture to take off and fly will be your ability to design and create very unique and different bookends. One idea may be to capitalize on the ever-increasing environmentally friendly theme and manufacture all the bookends out of recycled materials. If this route is chosen, be sure to include the fact that your products are manufactured from recycled materials in all packaging and promotional material, as this can be utilized as a fantastic

marketing tool. The finished product can be sold through retail stores, such as gift shops, bookstores, and the Internet.

WEATHER VANES
★★ $$

Weather vanes adorn millions of homes worldwide. These functional and attractive features add charm to any home and harken back to the days of old. Manufacturing weather vanes can clearly be accomplished by utilizing a garage or basement workshop, and the vanes can be manufactured from a whole host of materials, such as copper, iron, wood, and plastic. Weather vanes best suit the architectural style of Victorian and heritage homes. Gaining access to owners of theses types of homes can be achieved by advertising the weather vanes in heritage home and antique publications, as well as antique shows. Additionally, the weather vanes can be sold through the traditional channels, such as establishing accounts with retailers and displaying the vanes at home and garden trade shows. A good starting point for this venture will be to acquire a few antique weather vanes to be used as the templates for constructing the new replicas.

WATERBEDS
★ $$

Waterbeds helped form the social culture of the 1970s and though they are not as popular as they once were, if history has taught us anything, it is that it will always repeat itself. Starting a business now that manufactures and sells waterbeds may just put you ahead of the competition when waterbeds once again become all the rage. Parts for waterbeds, such as liners and heaters, are available from numerous manufacturers on a wholesale basis. You simply design and construct the waterbed frames and assemble the other parts to fit. Waterbeds are still in demand and can be sold directly to consumers via placing advertisements in all traditional mediums, as well as selling the beds through the Internet and at furniture trade shows.

WEB RESOURCE: www.waterbedreplaceparts.com Wholesale source of waterbed parts.

CUSTOM PICTURE FRAMES

Manufacturing and wholesaling custom-designed picture frames is another great part-time homebased business opportunity. Ideally, the picture frames will be manufactured from a unique material, such as copper, molded clay, plastic, or wood. The more interesting the materials and more unique the design of the picture frames, the better. Consumers are always attracted to different and one-of-a-kind products, especially if the item is going to be given as a gift to a friend or family member. Establishing wholesale accounts with photography stores, photofinishing stores, gift shops, and other specialty retailers is the best avenue to market the custom picture frames. The picture frames can even be placed into these stores on a consignment basis to really get things moving fast. While consigning products is not always the best marketing method available, it does enable a business owner to get the product established in retail stores much quicker.

WOODEN SIGNS

There are a few methods of manufacturing highly attractive and functional wood signs. The first is to use a router to remove wood and leave the message or words raised, or concave. The second method requires a design stencil and sandblasting equipment to remove the wood around the message or words. This manufacturing method can also produce a raised or concave appearance to the sign. Initially, a novice wood sign-maker should have the wooden blanks for the signs produced by an outside firm, unless you have the required woodworking skills and equipment to construct the sign blanks. All types of businesses and professional services can utilize wooden signs. Traditionally, wooden signs are extremely popular with bed and breakfast lodgings, lawyers, accountants, doctors, antique shops, cafés, and gift shops. Currently, high-quality wooden signs are selling at prices starting at $500 each and up depending on size, complexity, and the type of wood used for the sign.

WEB RESOURCE: www.signsupplyusa.com Distributors of wholesale sign-making equipment.

SCRATCH POSTS

Scratch posts—cats love them, and cat owners love them even more. Starting a manufacturing business that focuses on building cat scratch posts is probably the easiest manufacturing business featured in this chapter to start. This enterprise requires virtually no special skills and only basic hand or power tools. Logically, the best venue for selling this type of product will be local pet stores and cat shows. Purchasing a few scratch posts can give you a good idea in terms of how this product is constructed and the various types of materials required. Once again, if possible try to incorporate recycled materials into the construction of the cat scratch posts, as it will serve as a good marketing tool and, of course, help the environment. This business venture is ideal for the person who is seeking a few extra dollars each month, earned by running their own homebased business.

WOODEN SASH WINDOWS

Many owners of Victorian and heritage homes will never make the change to new windows manufactured from aluminum or vinyl, regardless of how bad the condition of the original wood windows is. This fact is why starting a business that manufactures, sells, and installs wood sash windows is such a wise choice for a new enterprise. As mentioned before, most owners of heritage homes would never even consider installing new windows manufactured from aluminum or vinyl. However, almost all would gladly replace the old wood windows in poor condition, with new wood windows that still retain and reflect the home's original appearance and charm. The main qualification for launching this venture is to possess a good deal of carpentry experience and knowledge. The wood windows can be marketed directly to homeowners or to home renovation companies on a subcontract basis. A well-established wood window manufacturing business can easily generate profits in excess of $75,000 per year.

BIRDHOUSES

While building and selling birdhouses may not make you rich, it can provide a good source of additional part-time business income. The only requirements for starting a business that manufactures birdhouses is to have basic woodworking equipment and skills. There are birdhouse design plans available, or you can design and build your own birdhouses. The finished products can be sold at craft shows, flea markets, and to community merchants. The choices are unlimited in terms of how the birdhouses can be marketed. More important is the fact that this is a good homebased business venture that can be started for peanuts and produce a good part-time income.

WEB RESOURCE: www.scrollsaw.com Design plans for birdhouse construction.

ONLINE BIRDHOUSE SALES

Why not sell birdhouses online? Develop a Web site to sell your own birdhouse creations as well as other hobbyist birdhouse builders. Market and promote the site via the usual Internet advertising mediums as well as in print publications relating to crafts and home and garden decoration. Part-time birdhouse builders from all around the country can have their products listed for sale on the site, and you can charge a flat monthly fee or commission for this service. The best aspect about this type of online enterprise is the fact that once the Web site has been created and posted to the Internet it will require little maintenance.

WIND CHIMES

Seashells, glass, metal, or bells—wind chimes can be manufactured from almost any kind of material. Starting a business that manufactures wind chimes can be a great way to turn spare time into extra income. The wind chimes can be sold to retail stores, garden centers, and gift shops on a wholesale basis. Or, the wind chimes can be sold directly to the end consumers via a booth at a busy flea market, mall kiosk, or an Internet mall.

While there may not seem to be a lot of potential for profit in this type of manufacturing business, consider the following: 50 retail accounts that sold only four wind chimes each month would produce total unit sales of 200 wind chimes. A $10 gross profit on each wind chime sold would produce gross profits of $2,000 each month for the business venture. Now imagine if there were 500 retail accounts established across North America that achieved the same sales volumes, this simple manufacturing and wholesaling business would then be generating gross profits of $20,000 per month.

SAUNAS

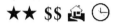

Designing, manufacturing, and wholesaling custom-built you-assemble sauna kits is a fantastic business venture to set in motion. You can design, manufacture, and package the saunas complete with assembly instructions for delivery all around the world. Parts such as the heater boxes are available on a wholesale basis. Additionally, milling your own cedar boards for the sauna construction can be an effective method in keeping manufacturing costs to a minimum. In addition to establishing accounts with national retailers to stock and sell the sauna kits, you can also sell the sauna kits directly to consumers by displaying the saunas at home and garden trade shows, Internet malls, and by setting up a sauna display on weekends in busy community malls.

WEB RESOURCE: www.saunasite.com Sauna design plans and information.

PROTOTYPE DESIGN

Do you want to start a truly unique manufacturing business that has unlimited potential for growth and profits? If so, perhaps starting a business that designs and constructs manufacturing prototypes is the right enterprise for you. Designing and building prototypes is a highly specialized business that requires a great deal of construction knowledge, ability to work with various mediums, and all required equipment necessary for building a host of various products. The following steps can be taken to establish and market this type of new business enterprise:

1. Decide if the business will focus on designing and building manufacturing prototypes in general or cater to a more specified segment of the manufacturing industry, such as mall kiosks.
2. Design a complete marketing and promotional package including highlights of experience, capabilities, and specialized equipment and know-how.
3. Join manufacturing and business associations.
4. Acquire membership lists of the associations and initiate a direct mail and introduction telephone call campaign utilizing the newly designed promotional package.
5. List your company in manufacturing directories and trade-related publications.

Following these five easy steps will place you in front of your potential market for this type of business venture. Generally, clients will want an estimate for their projects prior to awarding the contract, and this can be extremely difficult given the nature of prototype design. However, this is one of the few industries that allows for a certain percentage of gray area, in terms of a cost estimate. The objective is to always enter into the contract with a clear and concise estimate that includes a scope of work, product details, manufacturing time lines, and the potential pitfalls associated with the client's project.

ROOF TRUSSES
★★ $$$$ ⚖

Most new home construction now utilizes pre-engineered and built roof trusses, as opposed to traditional rafter framing to form the roof structure of the house. This type of framing construction is faster and generally costs less money than rafter framing, making it a popular construction choice for contractors. While this is one of the more costly manufacturing businesses featured in this chapter, it also has the potential to be one of the most profitable. The target market for this product is general contractors, home renovation companies, and architects. Setting introduction meetings with the owners of these firms

is the best route to take in promoting and marketing the business. Additional considerations in establishing a business that manufactures roof trusses will be business location, equipment requirements, and most importantly, learning local building codes and regulations in terms of roof truss manufacturing.

WEB RESOURCE: www.woodtruss.com Wood Truss Council of America.

FLOATING DOCKS
★ $$ 🏠 🕐

Building floating docks and swim platforms is a manufacturing business that can be started by just about anyone with construction knowledge and a well-equipped woodworking shop. Most of the components that are required to build a floating dock, such as the floats and anchors, can be purchased on a wholesale basis from the manufacturers of these products. To locate manufacturers of dock floats, etc., simply refer to one of the many directories available for a detailed listing of parts suppliers. The market for floating docks includes marinas, waterfront campgrounds, homeowners, and government agencies, such as the Parks Department. While this business enterprise may take some time to establish and build a solid customer base, the potential financial rewards can be well worth the wait.

CANOE PADDLES
★ $$ 🏠 🕐

Millions of people around the world enjoy canoeing as an outdoor recreational sport, and as a canoeist I can attest to the fact that the search for the perfect paddle is a never-ending quest. A business that manufactures wooden canoe and kayak paddles can be established right from a homebased garage workshop, and requires only a small investment into woodworking equipment to get going. The canoe paddles can be sold on a wholesale basis to recreation retail stores, as well as directly to consumers by displaying the paddles for sale at outdoor and recreation trade shows. Additional revenues for this type of manufacturing business can also be gained by manufacturing and selling related canoe and kayak products such as yokes, canoe replacement seats, and custom wood gunnel trim kits.

CD RACKS

Like many of the products featured in this chapter, manufacturing CD racks is a very easy and inexpensive business venture to set in motion. The CD racks can be manufactured from wood, plastic, or iron in various shapes and sizes and CD storage capacities. Like many manufactured specialty products, the design and type of materials used will often dictate the products' popularity and lifespan, so be sure to give this aspect of the business careful consideration. Ideally, the best method of marketing and distributing the finished CD racks is to establish wholesale accounts with national multilocation retailers to stock and sell them. Providing this can be achieved, the business can become an overnight success.

ART EASELS

Hobby artists rank in the millions, and starting a business that builds and sells art easels is a very easy and inexpensive enterprise to get rolling. The business can be operated from a small homebased workshop, and the art easels can be sold to artist supply stores on a wholesale basis. Furthermore, once the business has been established and all of the manufacturing bugs have been ironed out, approach various manufacturers of all-inclusive painting kits to check out the viability of including an art easel with these painting kits. Providing this can be achieved, the business could become a large and profitable concern in a very short period of time.

PICNIC TABLES

Building and selling picnic tables is about as easy as a manufacturing business start-up can get. The business needs only basic construction knowledge, and can be readily operated from a small homebased

workshop. Of course, the fact that this business is so easy to establish means that in all likelihood there will be a great deal of competition in your community—not only in the form of other picnic table manufacturers, but also from do-it-yourself homeowners. But that's ok; it's a part of our great free market and free enterprise business system that all entrepreneurs expect. In the spirit of being unique and as a method to separate the business from competitors, consider adopting a different method of manufacturing the picnic tables or a different type of raw construction material, such as beach driftwood or recycled building materials. The key to success in business often lies in our ability to create our own market out of a competitive, proven, and existing marketplace.

WEB RESOURCE: www.toolcenter.com/JERs/picnic.html Distributor of picnic table construction plans.

WOOD MOLDINGS

One of the most popular and least expensive ways to upgrade a home's interior appearance is to install new wood trims and moldings. Starting a business that manufactures custom wood moldings with standard profiles, as well as made-to-order wood moldings, is a terrific business start-up for the skilled and well-equipped carpenter to initiate. Customers can include home renovation and construction companies or sell the moldings on a wholesale basis to local home improvement centers. Additionally, to capitalize on the heritage home renovation market, antique replica wood moldings can be manufactured from recycled wood and sold directly to do-it-yourself homeowners via product advertisements placed in newspapers and related trade magazines. To gain additional revenues and profits for the business, a wood molding installation service can also be offered to clients. Potential profits for a moldings manufacturing business will vary based on a number of factors, such as sales volumes, overheads, and product markup. However, a well-established wood molding manufacturing business can easily generate profits in excess of $100,000 per year for the business owner.

OLD ENGLISH TELEPHONE BOOTHS
★ $$

Calling all carpenters and hobby woodworkers. Starting a business that manufactures replica antique English phone booths is a business opportunity that can easily earn you an additional income of $20,000 or more part-time. Best of all, the replica phone booths can be manufactured right from a small homebased workshop. The demand for this style of phone booth is surprisingly large. Real antique phone booths sell for as much as $5,000 at auctions across North America. The main markets for this unique product are restaurants, office buildings, pubs and bars, and homeowners seeking a unique decorating feature. The completed phone booths can be marketed by placing advertisements in antique publications and by promoting and posting the phone booths for sale on the Internet. The phone booths can also be rented to trade show companies, event planners, and as props for the TV and film production industry. The profit potential is very good for this kind of manufactured product. There is minimal competition and the replica English phone booths can easily be sold on a retail basis for as much as $2,000 to $3,000 each. *Note*: Be sure the finished product is painted red.

HIDE-A-BEDS
★★ $$$

In many urban areas of the country small apartments and condominiums are often the only affordable housing options for people living on a tight budget. These small residential living quarters always have one drawback: Where do overnight guests sleep? The solution: a pull-down hide-a-bed. Starting a hide-a-bed manufacturing business will enable you to capitalize on the ever-increasing consumer demand for this functional furniture product. The beds can be sold directly to consumers by placing product advertisements in local newspapers and the yellow pages, as well as constructing a hide-a-bed display, which can be setup at furniture and home and garden trade shows to generate sales leads. A potentially huge market for this product that must

not be overlooked, is new homebuilders, architects, and property development companies. Securing contracts, not only to manufacture the beds for these clients, but also to install the product, can put you on the path to future financial freedom and security.

PACKING CRATES
★★ $$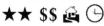

Designing and building custom made-to-order packing crates is a great business to initiate and has an almost endless supply of potential customers. Every year millions of products are manufactured and shipped in packing crates that have been specially designed and built to protect the cargo. The easiest way to get new clients for a packing crate manufacturing business is to simply design and distribute a promotional package to all the manufacturers in your community. The information package should outline and give details about your specialty service as well as include all vital contact information. Additional revenue for the business can be generated by manufacturing and selling wood shipping pallets to business clients. Once again, try to include recycled wood materials into the finished product.

WEB RESOURCE: www.nwpca.com National Wood Pallet and Container Association.

STORE DISPLAY CASES
★★ $$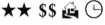

Starting a manufacturing business that specializes in custom-designed and constructed store display cases and fixtures is a fantastic business that can be set up and conducted right from a homebased workshop. There are many predesigned and prebuilt display cases available to retailers. However, often merchants require display cases and store fixtures that have to be specially constructed to highlight or merchandise their inventory. There are a few marketing techniques that can be used to promote the business including joining retail business associations, networking with the association members to gather potential leads, and establishing alliances with companies that specialize in commercial store openings and renovations. Both can become an excellent source for new business and business contacts.

FUTONS
★★ $$$

Consumer demand for futons has been on a steady increase for the past decade and shows no signs of slowing down. Futons are a functional, yet inexpensive piece of furniture that can serve a multitude of uses. A futon manufacturing business can be setup and managed from home. However, renting a small industrial location can serve not only for a manufacturing location, but also a "factory outlet" for retail sales of the futons. Books that feature futon design plans and construction tips are readily available. These books can be used as a valuable guide for assisting in the design and construction process of the futons. Futon cushions and mattresses are also available from a number of wholesale suppliers, which can be found listed in various manufacturing print and online trade directories. Overall, this is a good choice for a manufacturing business start-up, especially if the factory outlet route is chosen.

WEB RESOURCE: www.futonfurnitureplans.com Distributors of futon construction plans.

WOODTURNINGS
★ $$ 🏠 🕐

Fruit bowls, candlesticks, stair spindles or baseball bats—there are literally hundreds of different products which can be manufactured simply by purchasing a wood-turning lathe and mastering the art of wood turning. While the finished products can be sold directly to consumers, a better choice in terms of merchandising the wood-turning products is to arrange accounts with retailers, such as gift shops, to stock and sell the products. On a recent visit to a gift shop, I was amazed to find out that wooden bowls made from exotic hardwoods were selling for as much as $300—and even more surprised when the shop owner told me that he routinely sold one or two a week. Some quick math will tell you that just a dozen or so accounts with retailers like this can

generate a very comfortable living manufacturing and wholesaling wooden bowls.

WEB RESOURCE: www.woodturner.org American Association of Wood Turners.

WINDOW SASH MIRRORS
★★ $$  🕐

Every year millions of old wood windows are replaced in houses, and these old and often discarded wood window frames have the ability to generate incredible profits, providing they are turned into beautifully refinished wooden sash mirrors. The mirrors are very easy to make. Simply remove all the glass and putty from the window frame, and sand and refinish the frame in a stain or natural finish. Once this has been accomplished, place clear or tinted mirrors into the wooden window frame, and presto!— you have a highly saleable product ready to command top dollar. The mirrors can be sold at flea markets, craft shows, and through retailers, such as antique shops and gift stores, on a consignment basis. This is an ideal business venture to be started by someone who is seeking a low-investment home-based business opportunity that can generate a fantastic part-time income and still allow you to maintain a full-time job.

MAGNETIC SIGNS
★ $$$ 🏠 🕐

Magnetic signs are an incredibly handy advertising tool, especially for the business owner or sales person that uses their automobile for both business and pleasure, as the signs can be quickly installed or removed for storage in the trunk. Magnetic signs are also very easy to design and produce, making this an ideal business venture for just about anyone seeking to start a homebased business enterprise that requires little in the way of start-up capital and experience. The signs are actually manufactured from a vinyl material with a magnetic backing, which enables the signs to be lightweight and pliable. The signs are simply cut to size and shape, and vinyl letters are placed on them to finish the sign making process. The only equipment required for manufacturing the signs is a computer, page layout and design software, a vinyl printer, and a plotter that cuts the letters. Required equipment can be purchased used or new in most communities through printing and sign supply companies. Currently, small to medium magnetic signs are retailing for $30 to $60 each and cost about $8 to $12 each to make.

SPECIALTY SOAPS
★★ $$

Making and selling specialty soaps is a business enterprise that can include the entire family. The business can easily be set up and run from home and will not require very much investment capital to get rolling. There are hundreds of soap making recipes available, or you can create your own recipes for making soap. The equipment needed for the manufacturing of soap is inexpensive and can be purchased at many craft supply stores. In addition to manufacturing the soaps, be sure to give careful consideration to how the product will be marketed. One idea may be to design a POP (point of purchase) display and establish accounts with local retailers to stock the POP displays and sell the soaps. Providing the POP displays are in the right retail locations to attract maximum customer interest and the packaging of the product is unique and attractive, you will be well on the way to establishing a profitable and personally rewarding homebased soap manufacturing business.

WEB RESOURCE: www.soapcrafters.com Soap making recipes.

MAILBOXES
★ $

"Wanted: craftspeople to build custom-designed mailboxes. Flexible homebased work hours and a wage of $20 per hour offered." If this is the type of employment advertisement that would attract you, then why not start your own mailbox manufacturing business? The business can be launched on an initial investment of less than $500 and operated on a part- or full-time basis right from home. The completed mailboxes can be sold on a wholesale basis to retail-ers or directly to consumers via a booth at a busy weekend flea market or craft show. Remember the financial goal of operating a business does not always mean that you necessarily desire a $100,000 per year income. Sometimes just the fact that you are making a few extra dollars operating your own business is all the financial reward and personal satisfaction you need.

SILK-SCREENED MOUSE PADS
★★★ $$

Purchasing silk-screening equipment and a few hundred blank mouse pads is all that is necessary for starting your own business that produces mouse pads emblazoned with printed images, logos, and slogans. The business can be operated from home and does not require a great deal of special skills or investment capital to establish. The silk-screened mouse pads can feature generic images and slogans and be sold to retailers on a wholesale basis. Or, the mouse pads can be sold to companies with corporate logos printed on them for use in their own business or to give or sell to their clients. Blank mouse pads can be purchased in bulk for about $1 each, and the cost of ink to silk-screen an image will also be less than $1. Providing you can sell 1,000 mouse pads each week at a wholesale price of $3, the business could potentially generate profits in excess of $1,000 per week, prior to overhead and taxes.

WEB RESOURCE: www.printusa.com Distributor of equipment and supplies for screen-printing mouse pads.

STAIRCASES
★★ $$$$

Starting a business that manufactures and installs residential and commercial staircases not only has the potential to generate enormous yearly profits, the business can also be started and operated from a homebased workshop. Providing you have the necessary skills and equipment, you can build and install staircases made from various construction materials, such as hard and soft woods, steel, concrete, or any combination of these materials. The stairs can be sold directly to homeowners building new homes or renovating existing homes. However, a more suitable marketing approach is to establish alliances with contractors, architects, and renovation companies, and sell the stairs to these firms, as well as install the stairs on a subcontract basis. A staircase design and manufacturing business can be operated as a company that manufactures staircases in general, or the business can specialize and manufacture specific styles of stairs, such as spiral, pull-down attic stairs, or rolling staircases for warehouse applications.

PORCH COLUMNS
★★ $$$

Manufacturing decorative porch columns can be a very profitable business once established, especially if the main focus of the manufacturing business is to design and build Victorian porch column replicas. The porch columns can be manufactured from fiberglass, wood, or compressed injection foam. A good starting point in terms of manufacturing the antique replica porch columns is to purchase a few porch columns to be used as the template for designing and building the new columns. The antique porch columns can be purchased at used building materials yards. There are many different approaches that can be taken for marketing this type of unique specialty building product, including selling the porch columns to local and national building centers on a wholesale basis as well as construction and renovation firms. Or, the porch columns can be sold directly to do-it-yourself homeowners by advertising the columns for sale in newspapers and trade publications and displaying the columns at home and garden trade shows.

THEME BUNK BEDS
★★ $$ 🏚 🕐

Bunk beds are extremely easy to design and build, and right now children's theme bunk beds are hot sellers. The key to success in this type of manufacturing business is to choose the right theme and make

the beds unique and colorful. Theme bunk beds can be manufactured to resemble race cars, space ships, treehouses, or just about any other popular theme that sparks the imagination of children and gets parents to open their wallets. The theme bunk beds can be sold to furniture retailers and children's retail stores on a wholesale basis. Or, the finished product can be sold directly to parents via traditional advertising mediums, Internet malls, and product display and demonstration booths at home and garden trade shows.

FIRST-AID KITS
★★★ $$ 🏚 🕐

Two of the best aspects about starting a business that assembles and markets first-aid kits are the facts that the business can be set in motion for less than a $3,000 investment and first-aid kits are in high demand. First-aid kits can be assembled, packaged, and sold to retailers on a wholesale basis. Or, the first-aid kits can be specially designed and marketed to specific industries, such as construction and transportation. Furthermore, fantastic markets for first-aid kits include manufacturing and warehousing firms, as these types of businesses are required by law to have first-aid kits on site. Providing you can maintain a 100 percent markup on the first-aid kits that you assemble and achieve $100,000 per year in gross sales, this inexpensive and simple business start-up can generate profits of $50,000 per year, prior to overhead costs.

CHRISTMAS ORNAMENTS
★★ $ 🏚 🕐

Starting a business that manufactures Christmas ornaments can provide you with a fabulous part-time seasonal income just when you need it the most—Christmas time. Christmas ornaments such as tree decorations and door wreaths are very simple and inexpensive to make, and can be sold in various ways including to retailers on a wholesale basis or directly to consumers at a sales kiosk in a mall or at craft shows. The business is ideally operated from home and the overheads are virtually nonexistent. While manufacturing and selling Christmas decorations on a part-time, seasonal basis may not make you rich; it can potentially generate an extra income of $5,000 to $10,000 per year.

CUSTOM DOORSTOPS

Now here is a unique and interesting business opportunity. Manufacturing custom designer doorstops is a very easy and straightforward business venture to set in motion. The key to success in this type of manufacturing venture is that the doorstops must be unique in design, and the marketing methods employed must be innovative and clever. The demand for custom and one-of-a-kind home improvement and home-decorating items is gigantic, and this is the kind of product that has real potential to catch on in a big way. The doorstops could be fashioned after antique doorstops, or they could be manufactured from 100 percent recycled materials. The options for manufacturing doorstops are endless and only limited by imagination. Marketing methods that can be utilized are to establish wholesale accounts with national retailers, and the custom doorstops can also be sold directly to high-end homebuilders, architects, and interior designers.

WEB RESOURCE: www.ahma.org American Hardware Manufacturers Association.

WOOD CLOTHES HANGERS

Designing and manufacturing custom wood clothes hangers for high-end, expensive men's and women's fashions is a terrific little business enterprise to set in motion. Typical clothes hangers can destroy expensive clothes, so the potential market for custom-made clothes hangers to specifically fit one particular item of clothing is huge. The coat hangers should be made from aromatic cedar wood and stainless steel for the curved hanger. Marketing the coat hangers should not be difficult, given there are thousands of retail clothing boutiques that specialize in high-end custom-made fashions.

MOLD MAKING

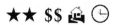

Thousands of different products require a mold in order to be manufactured. Canoes are made from a mold, lawn ornaments are made from a mold, many car body parts are made from a mold, and these are just a few examples. Initiating a business that specializes in making manufacturing molds for clients is not a hard business to establish. However, there is definitely one main requirement: you or an employee must be able to design and build numerous styles of molds. Typically, molds used in manufacturing are constructed from fiberglass, so a well-vented workshop will also be a requirement for this business. Gaining clients can be as easy as purchasing a manufacturers directory and soliciting the manufacturers for mold making contracts, as molds do not last forever and have a predetermined lifespan based on the number of times they are used. The profit potential in mold making is very good, as a single mold can sell for as much as $10,000 for a small product and over $100,000 for a large product, such as a sailboat.

TRADE SHOW DISPLAYS

★★★ $$$ 🏠

Trade shows are a multibillion dollar industry in North America. All companies and organizations that display or promote products and services at trade shows each year have one thing in common. They all need to have an exhibit display designed, constructed, or rented in order to display and promote their products and services. And the best way to capitalize on the demand for trade show displays is to simply start a business that manufactures custom one-of-a-kind trade show displays and off-the-shelf, mass-produced, generic trade show displays. This type of manufacturing business is very easy to establish, as the components needed to build trade show displays are readily available from a wide range of manufacturers. Additionally, a homebased workshop is more than sufficient space to construct the displays, at least initially. Profit margins are excellent for this type of product, especially on the custom one-of-a-kind orders, and finding clients should not be difficult, due to the simple fact that there are an estimated 100,000+ trade shows each year in the United States alone.

WEB RESOURCE: www.epda.com Exhibit Designers and Producers Association.

SNOWBOARDS
★ $$$$

Since the introduction of snowboards about a decade ago, there has been no looking back for the sport, as snowboarding now rivals skiing in terms of popularity and appeals to just about every age group, from 5 to 100. Manufacturing snowboards is not a difficult task. The work lies within the design and composition of the snowboard, making a snowboard manufacturing business best suited to individuals with a manufacturing and designing background. However, with that being said, experienced staff can always be hired or brought in on a consulting basis to help implement the design and manufacturing process. The snowboards can be sold on a wholesale basis to national retailers, as well as directly to consumers via the Internet and at sports and recreation trade shows. One important aspect of the business that should not be overlooked is to secure a spokesperson for the snowboards. The spokesperson should be a recognized person in the world of snowboarding as a sport. Building this type of public exposure will be one of the best marketing tools that can be implemented.

RUBBER STAMPS
★★ $$ 🏠 🕐

In spite of the popularity of easy to make and print computerized labels, there will always be a market for rubber stamps that are used for business purposes, as well as in the hobby craft industry. Starting a business that manufactures predesigned rubber stamps is as easy as 1–2–3.

1. Research the industry, market, and business.
2. Establish a manufacturing process, and secure retail accounts for the stamps.

3. Manufacture the stamps and ship to retailers.

The key to success in manufacturing rubber stamps is to be unique and make the stamps interesting. In addition to the traditional business rubber stamps, also manufacture stamps for use in crafts and for personal use. Right now, animal stamps are very popular and feature just about every kind of animal.

CLOCKS
★ $ 🏠

Calling anyone that is seeking to start a manufacturing business that can be operated from home, costs less than $1,000 to set in motion, does not require special business or manufacturing skills, and has the potential to generate profits of $50,000 per year or more. Does this sound like the business opportunity that you have been looking for? If so, perhaps you should consider starting a business that manufactures clocks. We all need them, and the market demand and product acceptance from consumers has been proven for well over a century. The components needed to build the clocks can be purchased on a wholesale basis from manufacturers of these items, while the housing for the clock itself can be manufactured by your business. The key to success is to make the clocks different and appealing to consumers. Try a different manufacturing process, or use a unique raw material to construct the clocks from. In other words, find your niche.

BROOMS AND BRUSHES
★ $$ 🏠 🕐

Manufacturing brooms and brushes is another business opportunity that just about anyone can tackle. The business has the capability to produce a very substantial income for the owner-operator. The brooms and brushes that can be manufactured can cater to one specific industry that uses a specialty broom or brush, such as the chimney sweep industry. Or, the business can manufacture all types of brooms and brushes. Of course, the largest market is ordinary brooms and brushes used in everyday household cleaning. Once established, this type of manufacturing business is easily capable of producing yearly sales exceeding $100,000.

WEB RESOURCE: www.abma.org/industrial.htm American Brush Manufacturers Association.

WINDOW SHUTTERS AND BLINDS

Manufacturing interior and exterior wood window shutters is a very simple manufacturing business to establish and run. Best of all, only a small home-based workshop is required for manufacturing space. The demand for wooden window shutters and blinds is enormous, especially with recent news that plastic miniblinds can give off toxic fumes into a home. The demand for exterior wooden window shutters used for home decoration and shutter replacements for heritage home renovations is also very large. The completed shutters can be sold to national home improvement center retailers on a wholesale basis, or the window shutters can be sold directly to home-owners on a custom order and installation basis. The profit margins can be terrific on this type of product, as there is not a lot of competition in the industry that focuses on manufacturing wooden window shutters and blinds exclusively.

TREEHOUSE KITS

Time to mix childhood memories, business, and profits. That is exactly what can be achieved by starting a business that manufactures treehouse kits for the do-it-yourself homeowner to purchase, assemble, and install. The treehouse kits can be packaged and sold to retail outlets on a wholesale basis or directly to consumers via advertising the treehouse kits for sale on the Internet, in newspapers and publications, and by establishing a display model that can be exhibited at trade shows. Seek to build a joint venture with companies that are already in the business of manufacturing and whole-saling children's toys and playground equipment, as there will be the possibility to capitalize on their customer base, distribution channels, and business expertise and experience.

STORE DIRECTORY BOARDS

Large retailers, office buildings, malls, and sports complexes all use directory boards to show visitors where they are, where items can be found, and where the various departments are located. Manufacturing store and office directory boards is a very artistic process, simply because the requirements for each location varies. This means that in most cases you do not have to compete against mass-produced directory boards. However, this is still a very competitive segment of the manufacturing and sign industry, so be sure to take a unique and innovative approach to the manufacturing process and appearance of the finished product. Recently, some companies have been selling and installing electronic directory boards for free into high-traffic locations. Of course, the catch is that the boards also feature advertising, which is sold to local businesses that serve the community. This may be a route to consider.

PLASTIC DISPLAYS
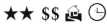

Brochure holders, publication holders, point-of-purchase displays, menu racks, etc., are just a few of the display holders that can be manufactured from plastics. The market demand for custom designed and manufactured product and information display holders is gigantic, and starting a business that specializes in manufacturing plastic displays is very easy. The business can easily be operated from a small homebased workshop. The finished displays can be sold in numerous ways including establishing wholesale accounts with national office products retailers, direct to companies via a direct sales team, or by designing and distributing a product catalog featuring all the various designs and displays your company manufactures. The plastics used to construct the displays can be purchased inexpensively on a wholesale basis, and the equipment used for the manufacturing process is also very inexpensive and available at all glaziers supply stores.

ONLINE FACTORY DIRECT

★★★ $$$

In North America there are thousands of home-based manufacturing businesses. Two of the largest challenges facing these entrepreneurs are marketing and competing against much larger and better-financed competitors. Herein lies the business opportunity. Develop an online "factory direct" Web site that features products for sale manufactured by these homebased entrepreneurs. Not only will you be giving these small manufacturing businesses a fantastic marketing and distribution channel, but you will also be giving them a chance to compete for business without having to blow a bundle on developing and marketing their own Web site.

Products sold via the site can be shipped to purchasers directly from the manufacturer, thus eliminating the need for warehousing inventory. In exchange for providing manufacturers with a marketing channel, you can retain a portion of the sales that the site generates; in the range of 10 to 15 percent would be fair. This type of cyberventure could really prove to be successful, as "factory direct" pricing attracts consumers and securing manufactured goods to be featured on the site would be very easy.

OFFICE DIVIDERS

★★ $$

Starting a business that designs and builds office dividers is a fantastic homebased manufacturing business to get rolling. The latest trend in office layout is no walls; only dividers to create a really communal workplace. This means the time has never been better than now to start this type of manufacturing business. The office divider designs could incorporate handy features, such as adjustable shelving, built-in waste and recycling receptacles, and built-in message and white boards. Once established, this is the kind of small home-based manufacturing business that has the potential to survive and generate a substantial income for the owner.

ANTENNA ORNAMENTS

★ $

Automobile antenna ornaments have become really popular; depicting everything from a cactus with a cowboy hat to cattails. Starting a business that manufactures antenna ornaments is a very easy and low-cost business enterprise to launch. Some of the best aspects about this type of manufacturing business start-up are that the business can be started on a part-time basis and easily operated right from a small homebased workshop. Ideally, the ornaments will be sold on a wholesale basis to national and specialty retailers. The antenna ornaments can also be sold directly to consumers via the Internet, and some clever advertising and marketing. Maintaining a 100 percent markup on all sales and generating revenues of $50,000 per year will create a gross profit of $25,000 per year for the business.

DOGHOUSES

★★ $

A workshop, woodworking equipment, and basic carpentry skills are all that you will need to start building doghouses for profit. You can build doghouses from your own plans or purchase design and construction plans. Consider incorporating recycled materials into the construction process, as you can play upon the benefits of recycling for marketing purposes. The completed doghouses can be sold to retailers on a wholesale basis or you can opt to sell them directly to consumers via pet fairs and craft shows. Be creative in your designs and include features that normally would not be found in a doghouse. Remember, when it comes to pets, many people know no limits in terms of spending money on their pampered pooches.

WEB RESOURCE: www.woodcraftplans.com Distributors of doghouse construction plans.

JEWELRY BOXES

★★ $

Jewelry boxes can retail for as much as 10 to 20 times of what it costs to build them, making this a potentially very profitable homebased manufacturing venture. This is the type of manufacturing business that will let you be very creative in design and in the materials selected for the construction process. Or in other words, "think outside the jewelry box." Consider using materials that normally would not be used for building this product, like recycled items, seashells, glass, or plastic. You can market the boxes by renting table space at crafts sales and flea markets, sell them to retailers on a wholesale basis, and even get the jewelry boxes featured for sale on numerous Web sites. The sky's the limit.

FENCE PANELS
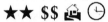

Almost all new wooden fences that are being installed today are constructed from prebuilt fence panels in 4-, 5-, and 6-foot heights. Typically these prebuilt fence panels are constructed from pressure treated wood or from cedar wood, and are available in a wide range of styles. To get started building and selling fence panels you will need a homebased workshop, basic power and hand tools, and some design plans, but that's about it. The fence panels can be sold to fence installation companies, landscape contractors, to do-it-yourself building centers, or directly to homeowners by placing advertisements in your local newspaper. Once established, and the manufacturing bugs have been worked out, there should be no problem averaging $20 to $30 per hour for building the fence panels.

GARDEN ARBORS
★★ $$ 🏠 🕐

Garden arbors have become a very popular landscape feature that thousands of homeowners are opting to include in their gardens. This creates a terrific business opportunity for the innovative entrepreneur to capitalize on by starting a homebased business that manufactures and sells garden arbors. If you have the ability, you can design your own trademark arbors. Or, if you are lacking in design talent, plans are readily available at most building

centers for constructing garden arbors. Only a small workshop space and basic tools will be required for this endeavor. Establishing alliances with architects and landscape designers will enable you to capture the custom made-to-order arbor market. Or you can opt to create standard arbors that can be sold to building centers wholesale. Do not overlook the power of the Internet in terms of marketing the arbors, as this is the type of home improvement product that is not readily available in every community, so some people will seek out the product via the Web.

LATTICE MANUFACTURING

Wood, vinyl, and metal lattice has become an extremely popular landscaping and interior design building product in the past decade. There are many uses for lattice including decorative interior partitions for residential and commercial applications, exterior garden partitions and design features, and interior and exterior handrailing components, just to mention a few. Manufacturing custom lattice can easily be conducted right from a homebased workshop with minimal tools and experience, making this an excellent business start-up for entrepreneurs with minimal available start-up capital. Sell the finished product to building centers on a wholesale basis or directly to contractors, landscapers, and interior designers. The key to success will be in your ability to separate your product from that of competitors. Seek to create interesting lattice designs, sizes, and shapes that are not usually available. Most lattice products generally are sold in standard sizes, material selections, and designs. Venturing from the norm in terms of the design and appearance of your finished product can be your competitive advantage.

DRIFTWOOD AND LOG FURNITURE
★★ $$ 🏠 🕐

One of the best aspects about starting a business that designs and manufactures driftwood and log furniture for the home and patio is the fact that much of the raw manufacturing materials can be acquired for free or for very little cost. There are literally hundreds of different household and patio furniture products that can be manufactured from driftwood, rough cut logs, or even waste wood. These furniture products and home decorations can include coffee tables, benches, serving trays, side tables, chairs, planters, storage boxes, bunk beds, and picture frames; and these are only a few examples. One unique product that is very easy to manufacture is driftwood coffee tables. Basically all that is involved is to locate a suitable piece of driftwood, clean with bleach, level and sand as required, and add a shaped glass top. Presto!—a highly saleable and unique piece of functional furniture. Once created, you can sell your furniture and decoration items by renting booth space at home and garden shows, flea markets, and even a kiosk in a mall on weekends. Be sure to contact interior decorators in the area to introduce them to your unique furniture product line. A basic homebased workshop and tools will be required to get started, as well as some creative design abilities, but that is about all that is needed to get this business off the ground and earning profits for you.

AIR FRESHENER MANUFACTURING

★ $$

Gel packs, mist sprays, scented products, and air fresheners can come in many forms. Manufacturing air fresheners is simple, and there are many books dedicated to the subject. Harness the power of the Internet for research purposes to locate books and how-to manuals about creating air fresheners. It will be best to shy away from using chemical compounds in creating the air fresheners and stick to natural and organic ingredients. The air fresheners can be sold to retailers on a wholesale basis or directly to consumers by displaying your products at home and garden shows, as well as automobile shows. The start-up costs are low for this business. It can be operated from a well-vented home workshop, and through trial and error you can potentially create an air freshener product and scent that will appeal to a mass market.

ALUMINUM DOOR AND WINDOW MANUFACTURING

★★ $$$

Manufacturing aluminum storm windows and doors is a relatively simple process that can even be conducted right from a well-equipped homebased workshop. This business start-up will appeal to entrepreneurs with some construction and mechanical aptitude. Once again, aluminum storm windows and doors are easy to manufacture as the material required is referred to as extrusions. It is a simple process of cutting the window framing rails to length, wrapping the glass in a rubber gasket, and attaching the rails that are screw-fastened in the corners. The same basic procedure is used for constructing both aluminum storm windows and doors. Additionally, glass cutting experience will also be required. However, this is also an easy trade to master and most stained-glass retail shops even offer glass cutting courses on nights and weekends. Equipment requirements include a compound miter saw, flat glass-cutting table, a few basic hand tools, and, of course, a small initial inventory of aluminum extrusions, glass, and mechanical parts to get started. One of the best aspects about this business is that the start-up costs are low and only a minimal inventory must be stocked, as all the window orders will be custom sizes, and doors can also be manufactured on an ordered basis.

You can sell the storm windows and doors directly to homeowners by initiating an advertising campaign in your local newspaper, as well as displaying products at home and garden trade shows to collect sales leads. Additionally, be sure to establish alliances with contracting and renovation firms as these types of companies can become very good customers. You can measure and install the finished product yourself, or hire subcontractors to carry out the installations. As a general rule, storm windows and doors are sold on a united inch basis (U.I.), meaning you add the height of the window to the width of the window and multiply the sum in inches by the U.I. price. Check with other manufacturers and glass shops in your area to find out what the current U.I. price is, and providing your overhead structure allows, you should be able to offer clients a similar product at a cost that is less than that of the competitions.

WEB RESOURCE: www.thebluebook.com Directory service listing manufacturers and distributors of aluminum extrusions, equipment, and supplies used in the manufacturing of aluminum windows and doors.

AWNING MANUFACTURING
★★ $$$$ 🏠

A terrific full- or part-time opportunity exists in an awning manufacturing business for entrepreneurs with good marketing skills and design and mechanical abilities. Providing you have the workshop space and zoning permits, you can even manufacture awnings right from a homebased location. There are basically two types of awnings: residential and commercial. Residential awnings are generally constructed from an aluminum or steel frame and covered with a canvas or vinyl fabric shell. Often residential awnings are mechanical, meaning that they can be manually or electrically extended and retracted to suit weather conditions and the user's needs. Commercial awnings are also constructed using an aluminum or steel frame and covered with a canvas or vinyl fabric shell. Most are stationary, and many also act as signage for the business or office and are often electrically backlit to illuminate the sign at night. Skills required for this business include welding of both aluminum and steel pipe, commercial sewing, basic electrical knowledge, and good design skills. Of course much of the manufacturing work can be completed by employees or subcontractors. Equipment requirements will include a suitable workspace, transportation capable of moving large awnings, a welder and welding supplies, power hand tools, a chop-off saw, and pipe-bending machinery. In addition to sales and installations of awnings, you can also increase revenues and profits by offering clients additional services, such as awning cleaning and repairs.

WEB RESOURCE: www.thebluebook.com Directory service listing manufacturers and distributors of awning manufacturing equipment and supplies.

NOTES

46

OUTDOOR SERVICE

Businesses You Can Start

FLOWER KIOSK

★★ $$

Diamonds may be a girl's best friend, but flowers are a close second, and cost a whole lot less. Starting and operating a flower kiosk can be a very profitable business to set in motion, providing the kiosk is located in a highly visible and high-traffic area of your community. Various types of flowers such as roses, mums, and carnations can all be purchased on a wholesale basis from flower suppliers. The markups that are applied to flowers for retail purposes can exceed 200 percent, which can make this a very profitable business to run. A flower kiosk can be operated on a year-round basis, providing you have the right location, such as an indoor mall, busy farmers' or food market, airport location, or in the lobby of a large office tower complex. Professionally manufactured kiosks are available for this particular business. However, to minimize start-up costs you may want to consider designing and constructing

your own kiosk. The key requirement to building your own kiosk will be making the kiosk attractive, portable, and durable. With the right theme, name, and kiosk appearance, this sort of business is an incredible candidate for expansion into various geographic markets on a franchise basis. The franchises could be sold to qualified operators right across the country, and all franchisees would operate under specific rules and guidelines. Once franchised, additional revenues for the business can be achieved not only by charging operators a monthly franchise fee, but also by setting up a centralized flower distribution center that would service all franchisees.

WEB RESOURCE: www.flowersource.net Directory service listing flower growers and distributors.

LAWN MOWING SERVICE

★★ $

Calling all high school and university students, do not work for someone else this summer for minimum

---

239

wage; instead start your own lawn mowing service. Mowing lawns is not a glamorous business to run. However, it's better than flipping burgers, and I'll guarantee that you can make three or four times as much money. Providing you already have transportation to move yourself and equipment from job to job, the start-up investment needed to get a lawn mowing service rolling will be less than $1,000. For those of you on a really tight budget, you can do it for half of that amount if you are willing to take the time required to locate and purchase good quality, secondhand lawn mowing equipment. Marketing a lawn mowing service is as easy as knocking on doors in the neighborhood or designing and distributing fliers in the community describing your service. Likewise, a good source for potential clients is to contact all residential and commercial property management companies in your area to acquire a list of upcoming tenders for required lawn mowing services. The tender process can take some time, so be sure to start researching this potential market early in the year, prior to the kick-off of the lawn care season.

WEB RESOURCE: www.smallbizbooks.com Business-specific start-up guides and books.

PARKING LOT LINE PAINTING

For the university students who are not going to start a lawn mowing service, perhaps you should consider starting a parking lot line painting service. It costs about the same to start this business and can produce a similar income to lawn mowing. The main necessity for starting a parking lot line painting service will be to design stencils that will be used for painting the lines and symbols. The stencils should be cut out of quarter-inch plywood, which will make them sturdy but still light and easy to move. The stencil selection should include straight lines, straight arrows, turning arrows, handicap parking only, no parking, reserved parking, loading zone, and one way. Customers will include any property owner who requires well-marked parking and driving instruction painted onto their parking lots to reduce the chance of accidents and liability claims.

SNOW REMOVAL SERVICE

There are a few methods for removing snow including a plow mounted on a four-wheel drive truck, a self-propelled or standard snowblower, and a good old snow shovel. Assuming you are not working out for the Olympics, I suggest that you stick with the snowblower or snowplow as your choice of equipment for this business venture. While a snow removal service is not likely to make you rich, it can generate an income of $30 per hour or more when the service is in season. Additional revenues for the business can be gained by providing a roof snow removal service for homeowners, as well as a sidewalk and driveway de-icing service. Snow removal services can be offered to both residential and commercial customers.

FIREWOOD DELIVERY
★ $$ ⏱

In spite of the rising popularity in gas fireplaces, wood-burning fireplaces will still be around for some time to come. All wood-burning fireplaces have one thing in common; they need wood to burn. The only requirement for starting a firewood delivery business is to have, or purchase, a truck capable of delivering the firewood. Due to the weight of firewood, I would suggest that you purchase a one-ton pickup truck or a heavy-duty tandem-axle trailer for this task. While there are a few approaches to starting a firewood delivery service, the least costly and quickest to establish is simply purchasing split firewood in bulk and having it shipped to your yard or location. Once this has been completed, you can go about selling and delivering the firewood to customers in smaller quantities.

ROCK AND GEM SHOP
★★ $$$$

Rock and nonprecious gem collecting is an outdoor hobby enjoyed by millions of people around the world. Starting a rock and gem retail store that stocks equipment used by these hobbyists, such as picks, shovels, gold-panning equipment, and informational books can put you on the path to financial freedom. The main requirement for starting a rock and gem shop is to have an interest in the subject as well as working experience. Beyond retail sales, additional income can be earned by conducting evening and weekend instructional classes on the subjects of rock and gem collecting, as well as how to successfully locate valuable rocks and gems. A rock and gem shop is certainly not the right new venture for everyone. However, specialty retailing, such as a rock and gem shop, has a tendency to produce better profits than traditional types of retail operations.

ONLINE ROCK AND GEM SHOP
★ $$$ 🏠 🕐 🖱

As mentioned previously, rock and nonprecious gem collecting is a hobby enjoyed by millions of people worldwide, and you can cash in financially by posting a Web site that sells products used for rock and gem collecting. These products can include books on the subject, picks, shovels, and equipment used for gold panning. Promote the site by placing advertisements in print publications that focus on hobby rock and gem collecting as well as utilizing online marketing options such as search engine registrations, banner advertisements, and hyperlinks on Web sites of a similar nature.

WEB RESOURCE: www.entrepreneur.com Create a business Web site with MySite professional Web site builder.

GARDEN WORKBENCHES
★★ $$ 🏠 🕐

Designing, manufacturing, and retailing garden workbenches is the focus of this new business start-up. Gardening has never been more popular than it is now. Well organized and serious gardeners love to utilize professionally designed and manufactured multipurpose garden workbenches for various gardening tasks, such as potting plants and storing garden implements and fertilizers. The garden workbenches can be designed to include many handy features, such as an easy-clean surface, drawers and bins with rollers, and casters on the bottom of the workbench to enable the user to move their new garden workbench to various areas of the yard. The workbenches must also be manufactured from durable and lightweight construction materials. The garden workstations can be marketed by establishing wholesale accounts with national garden centers, as well as displaying the product locally at trade shows.

SPECIALTY TREE SALES
★★★ $$ 🏠 🕐

Selling rare specialty trees such as the Black Arkansas Spur, Anna Apple tree, or the Mexican Dwarf Banana tree can make you a lot of money. The market for these types of specialty trees is literally every household in North America, as many specialty trees and shrubs can be grown indoors and outdoors. The key to successfully starting this business is to establish a source of growers for the types of trees that you will be selling, and in some cases, importing and exporting. The business does not require a great amount of investment capital to set in motion and can easily be conducted right from home. A well-designed informational presentation describing your business and the specialty trees and shrubs can be distributed to potential clients such as architects, custom homebuilders, and landscape design companies. With the right trees and shrubs and a well-planned marketing program working for you, it should not take long for the telephone to start ringing and orders to start rolling in.

WEB RESOURCE: www.growit.com Directory service listing tree growers and distributors.

ONLINE SPECIALTY TREE SALES
★★ $$ 🏠 🕐 🖱

It is time to roll up you sleeves and get to work building a Web site that features specialty trees from around the world for sale. One of the best aspects about this type of online retailing is that it does not require you to purchase and warehouse an inventory of trees. Customer orders can be electronically forwarded to the grower and they can ship the product directly to your customer. Market the Web site and your products by placing advertisements in garden grower and landscape magazines as well as by initiating a direct mail and e-mail marketing campaign aimed at landscape designers and contractors. The key to success in this type of online venture is to offer trees and shrubs for sale that are difficult to find locally in most communities.

STUMP REMOVAL SERVICE
★★ $$

The fastest and most efficient way to get rid of a tree stump is to grind or cut it out. Purchasing a stump grinding machine is the first step on the way to starting a stump removal service. The cost of a new stump grinding machine starts at a few thousands dollars and generally requires a trailer or truck to be used for transporting, as the machines are very heavy. Contacting and soliciting firms, such as construction companies, landscape companies, architects, and property maintenance companies for stump removal work will generally secure all the business that a one-person stump removal service can handle. Currently, tree stump removal rates are in the range of $35 to $50 per hour. The more difficult stump removal jobs are usually estimated prior to starting the job.

WEB RESOURCE: www.stump-grinding.com Distributor of stump grinding machinery.

PATIO LIGHTING
★ $$

Why not start a business that specializes in installing custom patio lighting? The business is inexpensive to initiate, and patio installations and upgrades are one of the leading home improvement projects undertaken by millions of homeowners each year. The key to success in this business is to seek a manufacturer of high-quality patio lighting products, and become the manufacturer's exclusive distributor and installer for the lighting products in your area. The lighting products and installation service can be marketed to the end consumer, or you can provide your services to architects, homebuilders, and pool and patio contractors on a subcontract basis. Installing patio lighting can easily produce an income of $25 per hour or more, and the lighting products can be marked up by at least 25 percent to generate additional revenue and profits.

TREE PLANTING SERVICE
★ $$

On the surface, starting a tree planting service may not seem like a very lucrative business to operate. However, each year forestry companies cut down thousands of trees and replant thousands more. Typically, the task of replanting these trees is left to subcontractors who either have successfully tendered for the job or have established a working history and relationship with forestry companies to provide tree-planting services. A good starting point in this industry is to compile a list of all forestry companies and commence contacting them to inquire about forthcoming tenders and the status of their particular tree-planting programs. Providing you are successful in securing tree planting contracts, be prepared to work hard and form a crew of tree planting laborers. The work is physically demanding and usually requires the operators of these businesses to be away from home for extended periods of time. However, it is common for tree-planting contracts to exceed $100,000 in value.

LANDSCAPING SERVICE
★★ $$

Depending on the region of the country that you live in, launching a seasonal or year-round landscaping service is a terrific way to stay physically fit, and potentially financial fit. A basic one- or two-person landscaping service can be set in motion for less than $10,000, while a full service landscaping design and installation service can costs ten times that amount to start. A lot of the skill and experience needed to successfully run a landscaping service could be learned on the job. However, operating a landscaping service still requires some past landscaping skills and experience to initiate and to give clients "peace of mind." Potential customers for a landscaping service include commercial property owners, residential property owners, and subdivision property developers. While an established landscaping service can complete work for all three of these types of customers, a new landscaping service should focus on one particular type of customer until the business has established a successful performance record. Most landscaping contracts are completed based on an estimate for services prior to starting the work, so be sure to practice your estimating skills, as it is very easy to underbid and overbid, both of which can be very costly in terms of bottom line business profits.

WEB RESOURCE: www.alca.org Associated Landscape Contractors of America.

ONLINE LANDSCAPING TIPS

Many homeowners across the country are turning their once barren yards into an outdoor oasis leisure area. As the popularity of this type of do-it-yourself home improvement soars, now is your chance to cash in on the landscaping craze. Develop a Web site that provides visitors with valuable landscape design and maintenance tips.

Provide site visitors with landscaping information and services including:

- Landscape design plans that can be downloaded and printed by the user.
- A directory of landscape designers and contractors from coast to coast.
- Top landscaping tips of the week featuring information such as how-to and maintenance topics.
- An online "ask the expert" section that enables visitors to ask experts questions about landscaping in general.
- An online chat forum that can be utilized by visitors to swap information with other landscape hobbyists.

Income and profits can be earned in a number of ways, including charging a fee for landscape designers

and contractors that want to be listed in the directory and by selling products related to landscaping like books, design plans, fishponds, and landscaping equipment.

PATIO PAVING STONES

★★ $$$ 🏠 🕐

Paving stones have become a very popular choice for use in the construction of walkways, patios, and driveways and starting a business that installs patio paving stones can be a very profitable venture to own and operate. The business can be marketed through all traditional marketing and advertising channels including yellow pages, newspapers, flier distribution, and radio and television advertisements. For entrepreneurs on a tight marketing budget, consider offering your service to construction, renovation, and landscape companies on a subcontract basis to supply and install the patio stone for their projects. While subcontracting for other firms will substantially reduce profits, it is a quick-start method to get the business established and generating cash flow.

LAWN SPRINKLER SYSTEMS

★★ $$$ 🏠

At one time the installation of an underground lawn sprinkler system was reserved only for the wealthiest of homeowners. However, times have changed, and new installation techniques and mass-produced plastic pipes have brought the costs of supplying and installing underground sprinkling systems down to a point where they are now within the financial grasp of almost all homeowners. Starting this business requires that the installers of the sprinkler systems be experienced and knowledgeable. Equipment used in this business can be very expensive. However, equipment and tools can be initially rented as a way of controlling start-up costs, and experienced staff can be hired and paid a slight premium as a way of guaranteeing quality work. The service can be marketed directly to consumers via all traditional ad mediums or the service can work for homebuilders and property developers on a subcontract basis.

WEB RESOURCE: www.thebluebook.com Directory service listing equipment and supply manufacturers and distributors.

WISHING WELL PLANTERS

★★ $

Utilize your carpentry skills and start a business that manufactures and sells wishing well planters. The business can be conducted from home and requires only a minimal amount of capital to get rolling. The wishing wells can be displayed and sold at flea markets, gardening trade shows, or by establishing accounts with merchants to stock and sell the wishing wells. Utilizing recycled construction material for building the wishing wells has two benefits. The first is obvious: you will be helping the environment. The second benefit is the fact that utilizing recycled material in construction of any product creates a fantastic platform for a promotional campaign. And in the case of a wishing well, perhaps the slogan could be, "Wish for a Healthier Planet. All materials used in the manufacturing are recycled."

GARDEN PLANNING SERVICE

★ $

Many people, myself included, would love to have a vegetable garden and enjoy fresh in-season vegetables in our daily meals. However, the only problem with this is the fact that most people, once again myself included, do not know the first thing about how to grow vegetables and maintain a productive vegetable garden. Assuming you know how to grow vegetables, maintain a garden, and have some basic marketing skills, there is a better than average chance that you would succeed in starting and operating your own garden planning service. This type of specialized service certainly does not require very much investment capital to get started and can be managed from a homebased office. You provide your gardening expertise and experience on an in-home consulting basis for people who are seeking to establish a productive vegetable garden. The service could be marketed and promoted by establishing alliances

with garden centers that would refer your service to their clients in exchange for supplying you and your clients with the required seeds, plants, and gardening equipment. Depending on the region of the country the business is located in, a seasonal or year-round income of $20 to $25 per hour could easily be charged for the garden planning service.

GOLD PANNING

★★ $$

"There's gold in them dar hills," or at least that's what you can tell your clients. Providing you live in an area of North America that is known for gold panning and gold mining, you already meet the first requirement for starting your own "How to Gold Pan" instructional business. The business can focus on teaching people who are serious about wanting to learn how to successfully gold pan, as well as tourists seeking a fun and entertaining outdoor experience while on holidays. The business can be broken into two categories and fee schedules. Serious students could be provided with a weeklong gold-panning course, while the fun-seeking tourist would be offered a two-hour instructional gold-panning course. This type of enterprise can certainly be set in motion on a minimal capital investment, and the potential earnings for the owner-operator could be fabulous, once the business has been successfully established.

WEB RESOURCE: www.goldprospectors.org Gold Prospectors Association of America.

STONE SALES FOR LANDSCAPING

★★ $$

Natural stone is used every day for landscaping, both for retaining walls and just for an attractive garden feature. The best aspect of starting a business that supplies landscaping stones to contractors and garden supply centers is the fact that the stones can be acquired for free. A short drive into the countryside will reveal that natural fieldstones are everywhere, and simply striking a deal with a few farmers to provide a free stone removal service will provide you with an ongoing and unlimited inventory of stones to sell. The main piece of equipment required for this business is a good-quality used flatbed truck with a hydraulic cherry picker. A cherry picker is a mechanical arm that is controlled by an operator, enabling heavy items to be picked up and moved easily. Additional revenues can also be gained by offering a delivery service for the stones, as well as a stone removal service for property owners.

BOBCAT® SERVICE
★★★ $$$$

Bobcats are a small version of large bulldozers and earth moving machinery. Bobcats can be used for a number of landscaping and construction tasks, including snow removal, topsoil moving, tree planting, excavating earth, digging postholes, removing tree stumps, and clearing brush and debris. The key benefits to owning a Bobcat is the fact that they can easily be maneuvered in small work areas. They can cost as much as one quarter of the amount to operate larger earth moving machinery. A Bobcat service can be offered directly to the end user, such as a homeowner who wishes to have a hole dug for a small addition to their home. Or, the service can be provided to building contractors and landscape installation companies on a subcontract basis. Bobcats are relatively easy to operate and can certainly be mastered by a novice operator with only a small amount of practice. However, as easy as the machines are to drive, they are not easy to repair, and repairs can be very costly. Be sure to purchase a secondhand Bobcat only if it has had a full and independent mechanical inspection.

One of the main requirements to operate a Bobcat service is to acquire liability insurance to protect your assets in the event of an accident.

START-UP COSTS: The following example can be used as a guideline to establish the investment required to successfully start a Bobcat service. For the purposes of providing an example of investment requirements and as a method of minimizing start-up costs, costs shown reflect current prices of used equipment.

	Low	High
Heavy-duty truck or van	$5,000	$15,000
Tandem-axle trailer	$1,000	$2,500
Bobcat, including various equipment attachments	$7,500	$15,000
Safety equipment and miscellaneous tools	$500	$2,000
Business setup, banking, legal, etc.	$1,000	$2,500
Liability insurance coverage	$500	$1,500
Initial marketing and advertising budget	$1,000	$3,000
Working capital	$1,000	$5,000
Total start-up costs	**$17,500**	**$46,500**

PROFIT POTENTIAL: The profit potential for a Bobcat service is outstanding, and currently rates for the service are in the range of $50 to $80 per hour and $350 to $500 per day. Securing a mere 25 hours of work each week can produce business revenues in excess of $80,000 per year. Additional business income can also be gained by providing topsoil, sand, and gravel sales and delivery, as well as furnishing clients with an optional rubbish removal service.

WEB RESOURCE: www.bobcat.com Ingersoll-Rand Inc. Manufacturers of Bobcat construction equipment.

WHOLESALE SHELL DEALER
★ $

Like natural stones for landscaping, starting a business that wholesales seashells to retailers is also a business that can acquire free inventory, providing you live close to an oceanfront community. Collecting seashells to be sold requires no more than a $5 bag for carrying the shells and an early morning stroll down the beach to pick up the seashells. The seashells can be sold on a wholesale basis to craft supply stores for use in making crafts and costume jewelry. While in all likelihood this type of new business venture will not make you rich, it can supply a few extra dollars each month, be operated from home, and will definitely cost less than $50 to set in motion.

SPORTS COURT INSTALLATIONS
★★ $$$$ 🌐

Installations of multipurpose sports courts are the latest rage to enter into the home improvement industry. All-in-one sports courts include features that enable the court to be quickly reformatted to suit alternate sports, such as tennis, basketball, hockey, badminton, and racketball. The sports courts also feature high fencing, durable impact-resistant playing surfaces, and even changing room facilities in some cases. Generally, sports courts are constructed for outside use. However, recently some companies that install sports courts are also providing clients with an optional court enclosure for year-round use in colder climates. Sports court sales and installations not only requires considerable investment capital to start, it also necessitates very careful planning and market research to ensure success.

Sports courts can be marketed in various ways, including designing and constructing an elaborate demonstration display model that can be set up and exhibited at fitness, recreation, and home improvement trade shows and establishing alliances with builders of custom homes that can provide sports court optional upgrade packages to their clients. Other markets for the sports courts include clubs, associations, and corporations. A simple method to establish a retail selling price for the sports courts is to calculate the total cost of material and labor that will be required to complete the installation, and add a 40 to 50 percent markup onto the base labor and material costs. Utilizing this pricing formula will result in a 28 to 33 percent gross profit margin on total sales volumes, prior to subtracting operating overhead and taxes.

SEED PACKAGING
★ $$ 🏠 🕐

Vegetable and flower seeds can be inexpensively purchased in bulk from numerous seed suppliers and packaged into smaller quantities for retail sale purposes. The best method of marketing the seeds is to design and build a point of purchase market-ing display that can be located inside retail stores, such as garden centers, food markets, and flower shops. Some retailers may request that the POP displays be stocked on a consignment basis. If possible try to provide the retailer with a larger wholesale discount as a method of enticement not to consign the seeds. This is a business that requires a high volume of sales to produce generous profits. However, the business should expand quickly, once a few POP seed displays have been placed and they start to generate revenues and profits.

WEB RESOURCE: www.amseed.com The American Seed Trade Association.

MINIGREENHOUSES
★ $$ 🏠 🕐

Starting a business that manufactures and installs "minigreenhouses," is a terrific business venture to launch. Minigreenhouses are smaller versions of their larger counterparts, and typically are around 25 to 30 square feet in total size. These minigreenhouses can be constructed to be free standing or be built onto the side of a shed, garage, or house. Design plans are available for the construction of minigreenhouses, or of course, you can design and build your own. The business is best marketed by establishing alliances with a local garden supply center that will allow you to construct and assemble a minigreenhouse display model on their site. Once completed, the pint-sized greenhouses can be sold to garden center clients on a "you install kit" basis, or "we install for you" basis.

GARDEN CURBING
★★ $$ 🏠

Cement curbing machines are available that produce fast, easy, and inexpensive curbing for gardens, walkways and driveways. Curbing machines are available in two styles: self-propelled, and not self-propelled, which require the operator of the machine to maneuver it manually. The neat aspect of curbing machines is that they have interchangeable extrusion heads that can form the concrete into various curbing profiles. Currently, installation rates for on-site curbing start at about $3 per linear foot. Extra costs are charged to customers for preparing the ground for the curbing, as well as for creating elaborate curves and curbing designs. A curbing service is ideally suited for the individual who has landscape installation and design experience, as well as general construction knowledge. While the profit potential will greatly vary because of the amount of curbing that is sold and installed, a well-established residential garden curbing service can produce monthly sales exceeding $6,000.

WEB RESOURCE: www.borderlinestamp.com Manufacturers and distributors of curbing equipment.

ORGANIC LAWN AND GARDEN FERTILIZER
★★ $$

As environmental correctness sweeps the country, an increasing number of people are now using organic lawn and garden fertilizers as opposed to chemical fertilizers, and the trend toward switching to environmentally friendly lawn and garden products is on the rise. This fact alone should be enough reason for anyone who is considering starting a new business to take a serious look at initiating a business that wholesales and retails organic lawn and garden fertilizer products. With careful research and development practices being implemented, a recipe can be achieved to produce an effective organic fertilizer. However, locating an existing manufacturer of organic lawn and garden fertilizer products and negotiating an exclusive distribution contract may better serve an entrepreneur who is new to this industry. Once the distribution agreement is in place, the organic lawn and garden products can be wholesaled to retailers to stock and sell in their stores. The potential for profits and growth are excellent for this business venture.

WEB RESOURCE: www.ota.com The Organic Trade Association.

LIVING CHRISTMAS TREES
★ $$

Selling living Christmas trees is a terrific part-time seasonal business to initiate that can produce excellent profits for a few months each year. The first step is to secure a supply of good-quality evergreen trees that are approximately 4 to 6 feet high, that the grower has already potted individually into inexpensive plastic pots. The next and very critical step is to secure a visible indoor or outdoor location, such as a busy parking lot, mall, food market, or recreation center, to setup and sell the living Christmas trees. Without question, environmentally concerned consumers will gladly pay out a few extra dollars for a Christmas tree that can be planted in the back yard when Christmas is over, as opposed to a tree that will end up shredded or in the landfill. Once again, selling living Christmas trees is strictly a seasonal business. However, the innovative entrepreneur who launches this new business venture should have no problems in creating extra income in the range of $10,000 each Christmas season.

WEB RESOURCE: www.christree.org National Christmas Tree Association.

TREE TRIMMING AND REMOVAL SERVICE
★★ $$$

Starting a tree trimming and tree removal service is a great business enterprise to activate, especially if you have past work experience or knowledge in tree trimming and removal practices. The equipment needed to successfully operate the service includes a truck, ladders, safety gear, chainsaws and pruning shears. A number of measures can be used to gain customers, such as designing and distributing promotional fliers, placing advertisements for your service in newspapers and the yellow pages, as well as competing for tree trimming and removal contracts and tenders. One aspect of the business that must not be overlooked will be to make sure the operation is covered by a suitable amount of liability insurance, as well as disability insurance for the owner and employees of the business.

LAWN AERATION SERVICE
★ $

The easiest way to keep a lawn in tiptop condition is to aerate the lawn twice per year. And starting a lawn aeration service in your community is very straightforward. The equipment necessary to start this service is available at most industrial supply centers and is relatively inexpensive to purchase. The most effective way to market a lawn aeration service is to simply design and distribute promotional fliers throughout the community. Once again, this is not the type of business that should be started if your goal is to earn $100,000 per year. However, a realistic earning potential is certainly in the $25 to $30 per hour range.

HAMMOCK SALES

Hammocks are everywhere, and starting a business that sells hammocks can be a very inexpensive way to have your own business. While hammocks are certainly easy enough to manufacture, a better route is to import the hammocks from a manufacturer located outside the country. Manufacturing hammocks is a very labor intensive job, and countries that maintain a lower wage structure for workers can generally (not always) produce a product for a fraction of what it may cost to produce in the United States. To source an international supplier for hammocks, simply consult foreign trade commissions or research the topic on the Internet. Both methods will quickly produce a manufacturer who will be more than happy to enter into an importing agreement with a U.S. company. Once an importing agreement has been secured, the hammocks can be sold on a wholesale basis to specialty retailers such as outdoors and recreation stores and leisure shops. The hammocks can also be sold directly to consumers by setting up a sales kiosk in malls, busy flea markets, and camping and recreation trade shows.

FISHPOND INSTALLATIONS

Many people are now including fish ponds in their home landscape designs. Fish ponds are not only an attractive landscape element, they can also provide hours of relaxing time spent watching the fish. The fishponds can be designed for interior and exterior garden spaces, and can be stocked with a multitude of various fish species. Top-notch fishponds always include recalculating water pumps, rocks, water plants, and pond ornaments. There are many books available on the subject of how to design and create basic and elaborate fishponds. These books will be an invaluable source of information and assistance for anyone considering starting this type of business. In my opinion, there is only one way to market this type of business. Create an award winning fishpond display highlighting as many features as possible, and assemble the display at home and garden shows, as well as at malls on weekends to collect sales leads from people who are interested in purchasing a fishpond.

MANURE SALES
★ $$ 🕐

A quick trip to the garden center will tell you that manure is a popular choice for garden and plant fertilizer. Providing you live close enough to a rural farm area, you can certainly get enough "raw materials" to get you started in the business of packaging and selling manure-based fertilizer products. To keep the family happy, I strongly suggest this business not be established at home. Perhaps a partnership could be negotiated with a farmer to enable the product packaging to be conducted on the farm site. The largest expenses to establish a manure sales business will be in the design and manufacturing of the packaging. Unless you have the ability to design an outstanding package, this task is probably better left to a professional designer, as this is a very important element of the business. The manure can be sold on a wholesale basis to garden centers locally and nationally.

WILDFLOWER GARDENS

Thousands of homeowners are turning away from traditional flower and shrub gardens, in favor of low maintenance and inexpensive wildflower gardens. There are many benefits to a wildflower garden over a traditional garden, including lower regular maintenance and less costly yearly maintenance to keep the garden in top shape. Additionally, wildflower gardens have gained in popularity because of their heritage value and varied appearance. Working as a consultant, you can provide clients with wildflowers, garden design tips, seeds, and even the complete installation of the garden. Establishing a billing rate for the consulting service will greatly depend on the various requests of the clients. However, a base rate for the consulting aspect of the business should be set at $25 to $30 per hour.

WEB RESOURCE: www.onr.com/wildflowers.html National Wildflower Research Council.

WATER WELL DRILLING
★ $$$$ 🏠 ⚖️

The average water well now costs in excess of $5,000 to drill, and while starting a water well drilling business certainly requires a large capital investment and a lot of practical well drilling experience, the profit potential can be enormous. The first step to establishing a well drilling service is obvious: the business must be located in a rural area as opposed to an urban center. Additional considerations for establishing this business will also be local weather conditions, quality of local ground water, and the availability of experienced local well drilling labor. All of these things can have an impact on the business. The business can be marketed in all traditional methods, as well as directly to homebuilders that specialize in developing country properties.

WEB RESOURCE: www.nda-4u.com National Drillers Association.

CHAIN SAW SERVICE
★★ $$ 🏠 🕐

There are literally hundreds of chain saw jobs, such as stump removal, tree and brush clearing, tree removal, and building demolition. Every community could use a reliable person with a chain saw service. The chain saw service can be marketed directly to homeowners by placing small classified advertisements under the work wanted section of local newspapers. Or, you can also provide your chain saw services on a subcontract as-needed basis to property maintenance firms and landscape contractors. A chain saw service

is not likely to make you rich. However, it is still a great low-cost business start-up that can produce a part-time income of $25 per hour or more.

WILDLIFE CONTROL SERVICE
★★ $$ 🏠 ⚖️

Raccoons, squirrels, and other small critters cause millions of dollars worth of damage to homes and properties each year. New wildlife control policies are springing up across the country, which enable operators of wildlife control companies to trap and relocate these unharmed animals into rural areas outside urban centers. The first requirement to starting this business will be to check local regulations in terms of licenses that may be needed to operate the business. Additionally, be prepared to work long and irregular hours, as this type of service typically provides customers with a 24-hour, seven-days-a-week service by way of an emergency hotline. The equipment needed to start this business includes animal traps, baiting and handling gear, and a service vehicle. Once established, this type business has the potential to earn the owner-operator an income that can easily exceed $50,000 to $60,000 per year.

RETAINING WALL INSTALLATION
★ $$ 🏠 🕐

Designing and installing retaining walls for residential and commercial landscaping projects is not only a great business to start, it is also guaranteed to keep you fit. There are various types of materials used in the construction of retaining walls including cement blocks, pressure treated lumber, and reclaimed railroad ties. The simplest construction materials to work with are the new style of concrete retaining wall blocks that systematically lock into each other. This business can be marketed directly to residential and commercial clients, or the business can work with contractors on a subcontract basis. Installing retaining walls is a relatively straightforward building task. However, the entrepreneur considering starting this type of business should possess construction and landscaping knowledge and practical experience.

SOIL TESTING SERVICE
★ $$$ ⚖

There are many potential customers for a soil testing business including commercial farmers, property developers, and homeowners, just to mention a few. The main requirement needed for this type of service is to be or have an employee who is experienced in soil testing. Beyond that, the rest of the requirements are the same as any new business enterprise. Soil testing is the sort of business that does not explode out of the blocks so to speak; it can take many years to build a client and referral base. With that in mind, be sure you have both the time necessary and the patience required for starting this type of business. Due to the types of chemicals used in soil testing, this business is not suitable to be a homebased business and should be located in an industrial rental unit.

FISHING LURES AND TIES
★★ $$ 🏠 🕐

Calling all homemakers, retirees, students, and anyone else looking to earn extra income from a part-time business venture. If this describes you, maybe starting a business venture that makes specialty fishing lures and fishing ties is the business opportunity that you have been searching for. The market for fishing lures is absolutely gigantic, and the potential to earn $30 or more per hour from making and selling fishing lures is not only achievable, it is being done by thousands of people around the world right now. Getting started in this business only requires research into the construction of fishing lures and ties. Currently, there are hundreds, if not thousands, of books available on this subject so there should be no difficulty learning the trade. Once the fishing lures and ties have been designed and produced, there are numerous ways to sell them. The first method of sales and distribution is to sell the fishing lures to retailers, tackle shops, and fishing camps on a wholesale basis. The second method of sales and distribution is to sell the fishing lures and ties directly to fishermen, and this can be accomplished by mail-order sales or going directly to the source and establishing a sales kiosk that can be set up at fishing and outdoor trade shows. Given the fact that this business can be set in motion on an initial investment from as low as $500, the profit potential is excellent and can well exceed $30 per hour.

SAND AND GRAVEL DELIVERY
★★ $$ 🕐

Ideally a sand and gravel delivery service should be established in a densely populated area in order for this type of microdelivery business to be successful. A small storage yard and suitable delivery transportation, such as a one-ton dump truck, will be needed. Sand, gravel, and topsoil can all be purchased in large quantities on a wholesale basis from a large producer. These same products can then be resold to consumers and business clients in smaller portions at a profit. Clients for this type of service and product will include homeowners, landscaping firms, and garden centers. Maintaining a 100 percent markup on all products sold and delivered, as well as achieving annual sales of $200,000, will result in gross profit for the business of $100,000 prior to taxes and operating costs.

WEB RESOURCE: www.quarryworld.com Directory service listing sand and gravel producers.

FISHING BAIT SALES
★★ $$ 🏠 🕐

There are an infinite number of options available to an entrepreneur, in terms of starting and operating a business that involves stocking and selling fishing bait. My wife's family successfully operated a bait and tackle shop and a complete fishing tourist camp for more than 20 years. The following list highlights a few of the options for operating a business that stocks and sells fishing bait:

- *Minnows.* Bait minnows, like shiners, can be caught in rivers and creeks by using minnow traps or a seine net. Bait minnows can also be raised in ponds. The key to keeping the minnows alive and healthy is to have a good oxygen aeration system in place. The minnows can be sold on a wholesale basis to local bait shops or directly to fishermen, providing you have retail space and facilities. A license to catch or trap bait minnows is generally required, so be sure to check local regulations.

- *Dew worms.* These are also commonly called night crawlers and are also excellent fishing bait that can be raised or picked for a bait supply business. Raising dew worms requires worm boxes to be constructed, and the soil used in the boxes must be nutrient rich and changed on a regular basis. Dew worm picking is best accomplished by forming a crew to pick the worms from the ground. Golf courses are ideal locations, as the worms will come out at night, especially after a light rain. Worm picking is an extremely labor intensive job. The worms can be packaged in flats and wholesaled in bulk to fishing bait shops, or packaged in smaller quantities and sold directly to fishermen.

- *Leeches.* These interesting creatures are once again rising in popularity for medical uses. However, for the purposes of our explanation we will stick to raising leeches for a bait supply business. Leeches can be caught or raised for a fishing bait business, and the leeches can be sold on a wholesale basis to bait shops, or they can be packaged in smaller quantities and sold directly to fishermen, providing you have a retail bait and tackle shop.

Like any new business start-up, careful planning and research prior to establishing a business will always increase the chances for success, and starting a fishing bait supply business is no different. The business can be operated from home under the right conditions, or the business can be established in a rental location, which can include enough space to allow for both retailing and wholesaling bait and possibly fishing tackle and fishing equipment. As mentioned previously, there are an infinite number of options available in terms of starting a fishing related business, and with careful planning and research, a fishing bait supply business can be extremely profitable for the innovative and creative entrepreneur.

MOSS SALES
★ $ 🏠 🕐

Many of you reading probably do not realize that collecting ground moss can provide you with a part-time income. Plain old ordinary moss can be collected for free and sold for cash. Moss is dried and used by crafters for creating flower arrangements, wreaths, and all sorts of craft projects. Moss is also the perfect product to use in the packaging of bait worms for fishing, simply because your hands do not get dirty digging around for a worm to bait your hook with. The only thing you will need for collecting moss is a good pair of hiking boots and a plastic garbage bag. The down side to collecting moss is that it has a "green or hydrated" life span of only a few days and must be kept in a cool place out of the sun. So you will want to get orders from craft supply stores and fishing bait retailers prior to going out and collecting the moss.

RV WASH SERVICE
★ $$ 🏠 🕐

Many campgrounds, overnight RV parks, and even some hotels have RV wash centers right on site, but not all, and the ones that do not are the ones that you want to aim your marketing efforts toward. Simply establish alliances with campgrounds and overnight RV parks to provide their visitors with an optional RV wash service. You can joint venture with various locations and set specific days of the week that you will be on site to offer the service. This is a really beneficial service for campgrounds that do not have an RV washing area, thus they will be more than happy to build the alliance and promote the service. In terms of equipment, all that's required to get started is a portable power washer, a few buckets, and a ladder. You should have no difficulties charging in the range of $15 to $25 dollars to wash the exterior of the average-sized RV and this will only take 30 minutes or less to complete. This is a good business opportunity for someone that is looking to start a business with a minimal investment and on a part-time basis.

CHIPPER AND MULCH SERVICE
★★ $$$$

Starting a portable chipper and mulch business is a terrific venture that can keep you busy on a full- or part-time basis earning a great income. Portable chippers are simply a trailer-mounted wood chipper that is gasoline powered and used to chip branches, brush, and waste woods into saleable mulch. Some chipper models can even accept branches up to 12 inches in diameter, but like any piece of heavy equipment, the bigger the capacity the higher the cost to purchase. Money is earned two ways in this business. The first is to charge customers a fee to turn brush and branches into mulch, and the second is to sell the mulch. The mulch can be sold to landscape contractors, garden centers, farmers, and riding stables for animal bedding. In addition to a chipper, you will also need a large truck to pull the chipper trailer and to act as the bin for the mulch that gets blown out of the chipper. The business can be costly to start. However, chipper fees are in the range of $45 to $60 per hour for operator and equipment. Potential clients will include landscape contractors that do not provide this service, government contracts for cleaning brush from the sides of roads, and property developers. Of interest is the fact that some chipper services are also starting to work with re-roofing contractors that specialize in cedar roofing. Instead of sending the old shakes to landfill sites, they are chipped on site and the mulch is sold providing the shakes have never been chemically treated. Great idea, good for the environment, and a good way to earn extra profits.

WEB RESOURCE: www.woodchuckchipper.com Manufacturers of wood chipping equipment and machinery.

NOTES

KEY

RATINGS	★
START-UP COST	$
HOMEBASED BUSINESS	
PART-TIME	🕐
LEGAL ISSUES	⚖
FRANCHISE OR LICENSE POTENTIAL	🌐
ONLINE	👆

45

PET-RELATED

Businesses You Can Start

DOGGIE WASH

 ★★ $$$$ 🌐

When I think of a doggie wash, visions of Dana, my 90-pound Rottweiler, soaking wet, shaking like mad, and on the run in my home jump to mind. Dog owners like myself share a common dilemma, when it's time for the dog to have a bath, where do you bathe the dog? This dog-bathing problem is magnified if you live in an apartment or condo. The solution is a doggie bathhouse, and starting one of these businesses in your community can put you on the road to financial independence. The business is similar to a coin-operated car wash, except instead of washing the car, you wash your dog. The business can be established in a retail store location of approximately 800 square feet, which would allow for the installation of at least four dog washing booths and a small retail area at the front for product sales. A quick-start marketing method is to distribute free dog wash coupons throughout the community, as this method of promotion can be excellent for letting potential clients know where you are located as well as introducing them to your very unique business.

START-UP COSTS: The following example can be used as a guideline to establish the investment required for starting a doggie wash business.

	Low	High
Lease requirements (F&L)	$1,500	$3,000
Leasehold improvements	$5,000	$10,000
Equipment and fixtures	$5,000	$10,000
Inventory	$2,000	$4,000
Business setup, legal, banking, etc.	$1,000	$2,000
Promotional material	$500	$1,000
Initial advertising and marketing budget	$1,000	$2,000

	Low	High
Working capital	$3,000	$6,000
Total start-up costs	**$19,000**	**$38,000**

PROFIT POTENTIAL: The profit potential can be excellent for this type of business venture, as people usually wash their dogs every four to six weeks. Additionally, you can sell related products such as pet foods, books, pet toys, treats, walking collars, and leashes as a way to increase sales and profits. The key to success in this type of business is to have the doggie wash located in a densely populated urban area that is comprised mainly of apartment and condominium residences. Most dog owners will be more than happy to pay $10 to have the ability to wash their dogs in a safe and friendly environment.

WEB RESOURCE: www.appma.org American Pet Products Manufacturers Association.

MOBILE DOG WASH SERVICE

The purchase of a secondhand van or enclosed trailer is the first step toward starting a mobile dog wash service. You will have to outfit the truck or trailer with a water tank and some other basic equipment such as a hose and brushes. You can market a mobile dog wash service by creating promotional fliers and placing the fliers on display at pet retailers, vets, and the local SPCA. This type of unique service should be established in a densely populated urban center where many people live in apartments and condominiums, simply because these people that own dogs are your main target market. Like many pet services, word-of-mouth referrals will become your main marketing tool so be sure that a quality service is what you are providing. Also seek to build an alliance with a local charity, as they can host monthly dog washes as a method to generate revenues for the charity and you can provide the service for a 50 percent split of revenues generated.

DOG WALKING SERVICE

A dog walking service is perfectly suited for the person who has the time, patience, and a love for dogs. Best of all, this business venture can be initiated for less than $100. There are various styles of multilead dog walking collars and leashes available that will allow three or more dogs to be walked at the same time without becoming tangled in the leash. Acquiring this equipment will be important to your new business, as it will reduce frustration and enable you to walk multiple dogs at the same time, thus increasing revenues and profits. To secure clients for the service, simply design a promotional flier that explains your dog walking service and qualifications. Distribute the fliers to businesses that are frequented by dog owners such as grooming locations, kennels, pet food stores, community animal shelters and town halls. Once word is out about your dog walking service, it should not take long to establish a base of 20 or 30 regular clients.

ONLINE TALENTED PET DIRECTORY

Thousands of dogs, cats, and just about every other type of animal are featured in movies, commercials, and television programs each year. If you are seeking to start an online business enterprise that is a little bit out of the ordinary, then an online talent agency for pets may fit the bill. In a nutshell the concept is to create a portal that brings animal owners and trainers together with the film production industry via your Web site. The site should be indexed as to the various types of animals that are featured such as a dog section, a cat section, and so on. Furthermore you will have to create subsections for search purposes within each category like the breed or size of the animal. Each animal listing would include a headline that is linked to a pop-up page that features a picture of the animal, special skills, contact information, and any previous experience in the film industry. Producers, directors, or casting agents that are seeking to fill a particular animal role for a film project would simply log onto the site and view the listings that were of interest to them. Animal owners and trainers would pay a yearly listing fee to have their pets or animals featured on the site.

PET TAXI
★ $$$ 🏠 🕐 🌐

A pet taxi service could be a difficult business to operate for a profit, unless you are located in a very densely populated urban center. However, a pet taxi service that is operated in combination with another business, such as a delivery service, can be a fantastic way to diversify and profit. The main requirements for operating a pet taxi service is to have suitable transportation such as a van or station wagon and a good communications system to enable you to quickly respond to customers' calls for pet pickup and delivery. Using a cellular telephone for incoming and outgoing calls and inquiries can easily fill the communication requirements. A pet taxi service can be marketed and promoted by using all the traditional marketing methods such as print media. Furthermore, a well-designed and informative promotional brochure that explains the service and pricing structure displayed in local pet-related businesses and retailers can go a long way to securing new and repeat customers.

DOG RUN SALES AND INSTALLATIONS
★★ $$ 🏠 🕐

Initiating and operating a business that focuses on manufacturing and retailing predesigned and constructed dog runs can be a very lucrative enterprise to start. The business can be started by anyone regardless of experience. Dog runs are not only easily designed, but equally easy to build. Once the dog runs have been constructed, they can be disassembled and packaged for convient shipping and fast installation on a customer's site. A key requirement in the design process of this type of product is to separate your product from the competitions'. In the case of dog runs, this could simply mean installing a sunshade or building in a food and water dish. Dog runs can be sold through local or national retail accounts, such as pet stores and animal shelters. Furthermore, this type of specialty product is also suited to Internet marketing, mail-order sales, and related exhibition trade shows. The profit potential will greatly vary on a number of factors including product pricing, num-ber of units sold, and market demand. However, dog runs are a necessary piece of equipment for many dog owners, breeders, and kennels, and the market has already been proven and established.

CUSTOM COLLAR AND LEASH MANUFACTURING
★ $$ 🏠 🕐

Government statistics estimate that there are more than 30 million domesticated household pets in North America, and while I could not get a clear number on how many dogs there are, I would assume a safe estimate would have to be at least ten million. Providing, my estimate is relatively accurate, and assuming the average dog lives to be 12 years old and requires at least two collars and leashes over its life span, then some quick math will tell you there must be somewhere in the neighborhood of one to two million dog collars and leashes sold each year in North America. Starting a business that manufactures and sells custom dog collars and leashes could prove to be a very profitable business venture to get rolling. The only requirement to set this enterprise in motion is a sewing machine and the ability to sew. Nylon webbing, leather, and the required collar and leash hardware can all be purchased on a wholesale basis. The next step is to simply design the collars and leashes and begin to manufacture and market your products. While the potential to get rich from this type of business is not great, there should be no problem establishing a very lucrative part-time income that, with some clever promotional ideas applied, could even be turned into a full-time and very profitable homebased business.

PET GROOMING
★★ $$$ 🌐

The main requirement for starting a pet grooming service is obvious. You or an employee must be a pet groomer. Many pet groomers are not officially certified, however, those who take the time to register and complete a pet grooming certification course will be doing themselves, their clients, and their customers (pets) a great favor. A pet grooming service is very inexpensive to start, and has the potential to be extremely profitable, as pet grooming for medium-sized dogs now costs in the range of $30 to $80 per visit. Additional revenue can be gained for the grooming service by selling related pet grooming products such as flea powders, shampoos, and even specialty pet foods.

WEB RESOURCE: www.nauticom.net/www/ndga National Dog Groomers Association of America.

BEST WALKING TRAILS BOOK
★★★ $$$ 🏠 🕐 🌐

Harnessing the power of the Internet and technology can enable you to write books about the best pet walking trails for every community across North America, or even the world for that matter. How? Simply visit as many Web sites as possible that focus specifically on pets or dogs. By utilizing the Web site chat rooms you can ask site visitors questions that pertain to the best pet walking trails and areas in their specific community. The information gathered can become the basis for the "best pet walking trails" book. Make no mistake, this is a fantastic business opportunity, as many communities now limit the places where dogs can be walked and exercised, on or off-leash. The series of books that are written can be self-published and distributed for sale through retail outlets such as book stores and pet stores. Or, you can approach a publisher with the idea and sample of your work to print and distribute the various best pet walking trail books. Additional revenue for this type of unique business venture can be gained by soliciting pet-related businesses in the communities that the book serves for advertising. For a fixed advertising cost you will promote and highlight their business in the book. The advertisement can be by way of a discount coupon or a traditional advertisement, which promotes the business, products, and services. This type of business enterprise is ideally suited for the creative entrepreneur who is seeking to generate a very lucrative income while working mainly from the comforts of home.

HOUSE SAFETY SERVICE FOR PETS
★★ $$ 🏠 🕐 🌐

It is extremely important for households with young children to put safety measures in place so that children cannot open cabinets and gain access to potentially harmful products and chemicals. It is equally important for households with pets to take these same safety measures and precautions. Starting a business that focuses on securing households to prevent pet injuries can be a very personally rewarding and profitable business to initiate. The service is best marketed by designing and distributing information fliers about this unique service to local pet-related businesses and organizations in the community, such as the SPCA, pet food stores, and veterinarians' clinics. You can charge clients a fee for the in-home pet safe consulting visits, as well as sell products that may be required to make the home pet safe.

ENGRAVED PET TAGS
★ $$ 🕐

Engraving pet name and identification tags is a terrific little part-time business that anyone can start and successfully operate for a profit. Engraving tags requires no special skills or experience, and only basic metal engraving equipment that can be purchased at industrial supply stores will be needed. Ideally, an engraving service is best promoted and marketed by designing a portable sales kiosk that can be set up in malls and flea markets on weekends and during holiday times to engrave and sell the pet name tags. Currently custom-engraved pet name tags sell for $5 to $20 each, depending on the type of metal tag used and the amount of engraving that has to be completed. The retail selling price leaves a lot of room for profit, as the blank tags can be purchased in bulk on a wholesale basis for less than $1 each. This type of specialty retailing gives the operator a lot of flexibility in terms of working hours, operating location, and expansion potential, which can all add up to a fun and profitable part-time business opportunity.

PET DAY CARE
★★★ $$$$ 🌐

Day-care centers for dogs are becoming extremely popular as more and more caring dog owners are starting to realize that money spent on doggie day-care while they are at work is money well spent. Dogs, like people, are social creatures and need to have contact with people as well as other dogs to become better behaved and more confident family pets. A doggie day care is the perfect place for pet Rover to learn important and beneficial socialization skills. This type of business venture should not be confused with a kennel service, which is featured later in this chapter. This is a pet day-care center with a focus on dogs that are dropped off in the morning and picked up the same day, no overnight stays. To market the business, simply establish alliances with all local pet-related businesses in your community, such as pet food stores, pet grooming shops, and vets. A pet day-care center is not suitable as a home-based business venture, unless you have the space and the proper zoning. Ideally, the business location would have 2,000 to 3,000 square feet of indoor space and the same amount of outdoor space. To really give your clients the feeling of security so they know they have made the right choice in terms of pet day care, install a digital Web cam and broadcast live images of the day-care center activities over your company's Web site as this can be used as an amazing marketing tool for the business. Imagine, pet owners at work could simply log onto the pet day-care Web site and check on their dogs any time they wanted to. There are no limits on the beneficial use of technology in any business.

START-UP COSTS: The following example can be used as a guideline to establish the investment needed for starting a pet day-care center.

Leased operating space 2,000–3,000 square feet (F&L)	$4,000
Leasehold improvements	$10,000
Kennels and fixtures	$5,000
Office equipment	$5,000
Initial marketing, promotion, and advertising budget	$2,500
Working capital	$10,000
Business setup, legal, accounting, banking, etc.	$2,500
Total start-up costs	$39,000

PROFIT POTENTIAL: Currently rates for dog day care are from $14 to $20 per day, which generally includes two walks, one meal, and a drop-off time of 6:00 AM and a pick-up time of 6:00 PM.

PET MEMORIALS

★★★★ $$$

Starting a pet memorial business is a fantastic opportunity for the enterprising entrepreneur to establish and build into a very successful and solid business venture. The basis of the business is very straightforward. Select four various styles of rocks or monuments that are approximately one foot square. They do not have to be expensive. Once you have selected the stone that will be used for the memorial, select an artist to draw ten designs that will be used as the standard for the memorials. The only part of the memorial that will be customized will be the pet's name and possibly a date. Next, you will want to set up accounts with retailers such as veterinarians, pet food stores, and pet grooming salons who will act as the authorized distributors of the pet memorial. All the distributors should have an order catalog, as well as a sample of the memorial on site. These retailers will simply take orders from their customers and fax a completed order form for the pet memorial to your office. You can subcontract the sandblasting of the memorial to a local firm as well as the delivery. Aim to establish 100 accounts with local pet-related stores and it will not take long to build a very solid and profitable business.

START-UP COSTS: The following example can be used as a guideline to establish the investment needed for starting a pet memorials business.

Business setup, legal, banking, etc.	$1,500
100 sample memorials @ $25 each	$2,500
100 sample and order catalogs @ $10 each	$1,000
Office equipment and supplies	$3,500
Initial marketing and promotional budget	$1,000
Working capital	$2,500
Total start-up costs	$12,000

PROFIT POTENTIAL: The profit potential is excellent for a pet memorial business enterprise due to the fact that most of the work is on a subcontract basis and the monthly overhead costs are minimal. The following outline can be used as an example to establish both projected monthly overheads, as well as sales forecasts.

Overhead

Advertising and marketing	$500
Management wage	$2,000
Telephone, fax, etc.	$250
Office supplies	$250
Total monthly operating costs	**$3,000**

PROFIT PROJECTIONS. To establish a profit projection, assume the following:

Stone cost	$10
Sandblasting and engraving cost	$10
Delivery and setup cost	$15
Retailers commission	$30
Total product cost	**$65**

The following is based on a retail sales value of $125, and reflects monthly targets.

# Retailers	# Memorials Sold	Sales Value	Product Costs	Operating Overhead	Profit
100	100	$12,500	$6,500	$3,000	$3,000
100	150	$18,750	$9,750	$3,000	$6,000
100	200	$25,000	$13,000	$3,000	$9,000

100 retailers selling 200 pet memorials per month could net the owner-operator of this type of business in excess of $120,000 per year, including management fees and profits, prior to taxes.

ONLINE PET MEMORIALS

★★★ $$$$

Take pet memorials into the high-tech world of the Internet and open your business to a global marketplace. Millions of pets die each year and to most owners these furry little creatures are more than pets, they are cherished members of the family. What better way to remember a family member than with the purchase of a memorial that will stand the test of time as a sign of respect and fondness. Here is how this online business enterprise could work. Create a Web site that features pet memorials, perhaps ten styles in varying sizes, shapes, and price ranges. Visitors to the site could select the style of memorial for their pet as well as typing in exactly what they want to say on the memorial. They would make payment via the site and submit the memorial order form. Once you have the completed order form, you can set about inscribing the memorial as outlined and ship it to the purchaser via courier when the memorial is completed. This type of Web site could be promoted by way of the usual online marketing and promotion options as well as placing display advertisements in print media relating to pets. Also be sure to initiate a direct mail and e-mail campaign aimed at veterinarians, pet store retailers, and pet breeders as word of this type of unique service will spread fast in the pet industry.

ONLINE SPECIALTY PET FOODS

★★★ $$$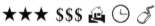

Specialty pet foods such as all-natural organically grown foods and special dietary foods for animals with health problems are the latest rage to stock the shelves of pet food stores everywhere. Starting a business that sells specialty pet foods is a straightforward enterprise to set in motion. You can produce your own recipes for pet foods by researching the subject. Or, you can locate a manufacturer of these types of specialty pet foods and become their exclusive sales representative in your local area, state, or even country. This business is ideal for starting part-time from a homebased location and expanding the business from the profits that are generated. Furthermore, this type of business is also ideally suited for sales via the Internet and your own custom-designed Web site featuring specialty pet foods for sale. Internet retailing for this type of venture would enable the business to become global overnight, and the products could be shipped through the postal service or a courier company. While this particular business will require a fair amount of time to establish, the future profit could be worth the wait.

WEB RESOURCE: www.appma.org American Pet Products Manufacturers Association.

EVERYTHING FOR BIRDS
★★ $$$$ 🏚 🕐

The title of this business opportunity may have a few of you confused. What exactly is an "everything for birds" business venture? The business opportunity is simply this, bird watching, feeding, and bird ownership in the United States is big business that generates millions of dollars each year in related sales. An everything for birds business is a retail operation that sells everything to do with birds, both wild and domesticated, but not the birds. The store can be setup and located in any one of the following retail sales formats: a mall kiosk, an individual store, or kiosk within an existing retail business such as a supermarket. The focus of the business is to purchase bird-related items such as bird feed, birdhouses, and books on bird watching on a wholesale basis, add a generous markup, and retail these items to consumers. The profit potential for this type of specialty retail operation is terrific, as the overheads can be kept to a minimum and the markups that can be applied to these types of product for retail sales are in the range of 100 to 200 percent.

In addition to retail sales from a fixed location, the innovative entrepreneur could also sell bird-related products over the Internet utilizing a specially designed Web site for product sales, or post the products for sale in the many Internet malls. Finding products for the business can be accomplished by purchasing one of the many manufacturing directories that are available. These directories focus on information such as the type of product, the uses for the product, manufacturers contact information, and the person to contact within the company. Manufacturing directories are available for North America or worldwide. Once established, this type of specialty retail business is an ideal candidate for franchising nationally to qualified operators or franchisees. Aim to achieve yearly gross sales of $200,000 in an everything for birds store and the business can easily generate gross profits in excess of $100,000 providing you can maintain a 100 percent markup on products sold.

PET TRICK BOOKS AND VIDEOS
★★ $$$$ 🏚 🕐

Pet owners are always searching for ways to teach their pets new and interesting tricks, and this is the basis of this new business start-up. You can work with established pet trainers to produce your own pet trick videos and sell the videos through retail merchant accounts, mail-order catalogs, and Internet Web sites. You can assemble this same information and put it in the print format of a book, which can be sold utilizing the same retail channels as the video sales. Additional revenues for this type of venture can be sought by soliciting national pet food and pet equipment manufacturers for advertising purposes in the videos as well as in the book. Due to the fact that pets are so popular, this business has an enormous potential to generate very sizable profits, and ideally the video and books could become a yearly series.

PET EMERGENCY KITS
★★ $$ 🏚 🕐

Are you seeking to start a business that only requires a small initial investment to get rolling; yet the profit potential is extremely good? If so, perhaps you should consider starting a business that manufactures, assembles, and wholesales emergency first aid kits for pets. The business does not require any experience, and the only skill requirement is the ability to be an effective marketer. The kits should include simple products and medications that can assist in a pet emergency, such as a cut paw. The kits can be sold to pet-related businesses on a wholesale basis, as well as directly to consumers via mail order and the Web. The key to success in this type of business enterprise is to make the packaging of the kits very effective, as well as establishing as many wholesale accounts as possible.

PORTABLE SUNSHADES FOR PETS
★★ $$ 🏚 🕐

The sun and pets are generally not a suitable match, and that's why a portable sunshade business for pets is a great idea. Portable pet sunshades are perfect items for any pet owner to purchase and take along on vacations or a trip to the beach with Rover. Not only can these handy little items potentially save some dogs lives, they also make the dog's day at a park a whole lot more comfortable. Ideally, the pet sunshades would be manufactured to be smaller than a traditional sun umbrella, but larger than a rain umbrella. The sunshades should feature colorful images of pets, as this can create an emotional type purchase from many pet owners. The pet sunshades can be sold to pet retailers and veterinarians on a wholesale basis, as well as sold directly to consumers via mall kiosks, the Internet, and mail order. This is a terrific small homebased business concept that really has the potential to grow and become a very profitable business concern.

WEB RESOURCE: www.avma.org American Veterinary Medical Association.

SPECIALTY FISH SALES
 ★★★ $$$

Becoming a specialty fish breeder is easier than you might think. The only requirements to start this business in motion are to purchase large breeding tanks or construct breeding ponds. Then purchase additional equipment, such as water and air circulatory machines, a few various species of breeding tropical fish, and you're in business. Some tropical fish breeds sell for as much as $100 each, so once established a specialty fish breeding operation can become very profitable. Marketing the specialty fish is also very straightforward. Simply establish accounts with local pet stores to purchase the tropical fish on a wholesale basis. A mall kiosk selling the fish on weekends and holidays could also prove to be an excellent method for marketing the tropical fish.

DOG SADDLE BAGS
 ★★ $$

Calling all innovative entrepreneurs. Activating a business that manufactures and wholesales saddle bags for dogs may just be the kind of unique business enterprise you have been seeking to start. The dog saddle bags could be manufactured with comical

messages printed on them such as "Dog-in-Training," or "I'm with stupid" with an arrow pointing at the walker. The saddle bags could feature various compartments that can be utilized by the pet owners for carrying items like water, dog biscuits, and balls. This business would not take a lot of investment capital to get rolling and could easily be operated and managed from a homebased location. The options to marketing the saddle bags are limitless and include establishing accounts with pet retailers, mail-order sales, Internet sales via your own custom-designed Web site, or displaying and selling the saddle bags at flea markets and dog shows.

INTERIOR AND EXTERIOR PET FENCING
 ★★★ $$

Manufacturing and wholesaling portable pet fencing is a very inexpensive business venture to launch and operate. The business can be run from a homebased location and also requires very little in the way of special skills or requirements. Basically, the business is preassembling fencing for pets that can be used inside and outside the home, as well as easily packaged and transported for the occasion when pet and owner are on vacation and a detainment system is required. The key to success in the portable pet fencing business is the fencing must be durable and well designed and constructed to allow for easy assembly, shipping, packaging, and portability. The market for this type of product is limitless, and a good starting point once the fencing has been designed and a prototype built is to market the product to a major national pet retailer, with an objective to secure national retail distribution accounts.

PETTING ZOO
★ $$$$

There is something special about a petting zoo that lures both children and their parents. Starting and running a petting zoo is certainly not for everyone, as a petting zoo requires a great deal of knowledge and special handling skills in terms of the animals. Additionally, this type of business can be somewhat costly to start and operate. However, a properly established and managed petting zoo business, whether operated from a fixed or portable location, can be both a personally and financially rewarding business to own and operate. Traditionally, popular animals featured in a petting zoo have always been sheep, deer, ponies, and rabbits.

WEB RESOURCE: www.pettingzoofarm.com Directory service listing nationwide petting zoos and industry information.

PET FOOD STORE
★★ $$$$ 🌐

More than one billion dollars worth of pet food is sold every year in North America; thus opening your own pet food store may just put you on the road to financial freedom. There are various approaches that can be taken to launch a pet food store. The first is to open a store that sells all types of pet foods. The second approach is to open a store that sells organic pet foods only, and the third approach is not to open a retail store but provide customers with pet food catalogs and free home delivery. The third approach is by far the least expensive to start of the three. Profit potential will vary as to the operating approach that is taken with opening a pet food store or supply business. However, maintaining annual sales of $200,000 and 100 percent markup will create annual gross profits of $100,000.

WEB RESOURCE: www.appma.org American Pet Products Manufacturers Association.

PET FOOD BOWLS
★ $ 🏠 🕐

Designing, manufacturing, and wholesaling pet food bowls is a great homebased business venture to get rolling. The key to success in this type of business is for the pet food bowls to be interesting, made from a unique construction material, and perhaps serve a specific need, such as bowls that are higher than normal for dogs with arthritis. The pet food bowls can be sold to pet stores, veterinarians, and pet groomers on a wholesale basis, as well as directly to consumers via the Internet and mail order. Additionally, utilizing a mall kiosk, pet names can be silk screened directly onto the pet food bowls for customers right on site. This type of kiosk is very inexpensive to construct and sales could easily top $1,000 a day.

PET NAME BOOKS
★ $$ 🏠 🕐

Writing a pet name book is almost guaranteed not to make you rich, but it is guaranteed to be a whole lot of fun. There are many different approaches that can be taken with a pet name book. The book could focus on one particular type of pet, such as cats or dogs, or feature historical pet names or celebrity pet names and how they came to be. Other items to consider are whether you will self-publish the book or have a commercial publisher take on the project. Self-publishing will add additional start-up costs to have the book printed and distributed, however the profit potential is also greater. If you choose to go the commercial publishing route the current commission or royalty rate is typically 4 to 8 percent of the total gross volume of sales.

TROPICAL FISH AND AQUARIUM RENTALS
★★ $$ 🏠 🕐

Gigantic profits can be earned by starting a tropical fish and aquarium rental business, and best of all, this very unique enterprise can be set in motion for less than $5,000 and managed right from a home-based office. At this point, I am sure you're wondering exactly who would rent tropical fish and an aquarium? The list is very long, and if you think about waiting rooms, the list of potential clients can include doctors, lawyers, restaurants, and business offices. The concept behind the tropical fish rental is this. People who must wait in a waiting room need something to keep them occupied, and believe it or not it would be less expensive for businesses and professional offices to rent tropical fish every month than to supply customers and patients with costly newspapers and magazines. Once a regular clientele base has been established for a tropical fish and aquarium rental business, the yearly profits that can be earned could well exceed $50,000 or more.

PACKAGED CATNIP
★ $$ 🏠 🕐

Cats go crazy for catnip. Starting a business that produces catnip or purchases it in bulk and wholesales the catnip in smaller quantities is a homebased business venture that just about anyone can tackle. The prepackaged catnip can be sold to pet food stores, pet retailers, veterinarians, and pet grooming companies on a wholesale basis. This is a product that can be marked up by 100 percent or more, even for wholesaling. Providing you can achieve gross yearly sales of $100,000, the business would generate a gross profit before taxes and expenses of $50,000, which is not bad for a low-investment business venture.

WEB RESOURCE: www.appma.org American Pet Products Manufacturers Association.

KENNEL
★★ $$$$ 🏠 ⚖️

Starting a dog kennel has numerous and varied requirements that must be carefully planned for and researched prior to starting the business. The investment needed to establish a dog kennel from the ground up can easily exceed $150,000, making this business venture one that should only be tackled by a seasoned business pro with experience in the industry. However, with that having been said, I have a close personal friend who has successfully operated a professional dog kennel for more than 15 years, and the business never fails to generate a pretax income of less than $80,000 per year after expenses. Additional revenues for a dog kennel can be earned by also providing customers with services, such as training instruction for their dogs, and selling related products, such as dog foods and leashes. Profit potential range is $25,000 to $150,000 per year.

WEB RESOURCE: www.abka.com American Boarding Kennels Association.

PET TOYS
★★ $$ 🏠 🕐

Designing, manufacturing, and wholesaling pet toys could put you on the path to financial freedom, and best of all this is a business opportunity that can be started part-time from home on a minimal initial investment. There are literally thousands of different pet toys on the market and this is definitely a situation where it is not important that you build it first, only better. The toys can be sold on a wholesale basis to pet retailers, or even directly to consumers via the Internet and mail order. I purchased two glow-in-the-dark balls for my dog from a man who was selling them right out of a knapsack in the park. The key to success in this type of business is to have a high-quality toy and the ability to get the pet toy in front of as many potential customers as possible. Remember, pets are like children to most people and generally people will spare no expense when it comes to the happiness of their pets. That is why starting any new business that involves pets, or that is related to pets in any way, has already got a head start on the road to financial success.

PET TRAVEL KITS
★★ $$ 🏠 🕐

Starting a business that prepackages everything an owner will need for a long car trip with their pet is a terrific small homebased business to get rolling. Pet travel kits can include water, a sunshade for the car windows, and plastic bags for treasures, messes, and treats. The travel kits for pets can be sold on a wholesale basis to pet store retailers, truck stops, veterinarians, and pet grooming companies. In the world of business ventures there is not a lot that can be started for less than a few thousand dollars that has the potential to earn profits of greater than $25,000 per year. However, this business opportunity is one of the very rare as it can be started for less than a few thousand dollars and selling a mere 5,000 car kits for pets per year with a gross profit of $5 each will generate an income of $25,000.

PET FURNITURE COVERS
★ $$ 🏠 🕐

Calling all homemakers with a sewing machine and sewing skills. Put your sewing experience to work for you and start making made-to-order furniture covers for pet owners. This type of specialized service can be marketed through pet stores, furniture stores, and veterinarians. Simply design and distribute information and marketing brochures that highlight all the benefits of your custom-made furniture covers. The furniture covers can be sold by mail order, over the Internet, and directly to interior designers. Additional revenues can also be earned by creating made-to-order pet clothes for clients seeking something a little bit different for their pets.

ONLINE ALL FOR DOGS WEB SITE
★★ $$$$ 🏠 🖱

Develop a portal to bring dog lovers together with retailers of products for dogs and service providers that specialize in services for dogs via a specially designed Web site. This type of Web site can be referred to as a "dog mega site" and can feature just about any sort of product or service available relating to dogs and dog ownership. The site will have to be indexed by products, services, and geographic area, and subindexed by types of dogs, types of products, and types of services featured on the site. Income is earned by charging retailers and service providers a fee to be listed on the site and each client should receive their own Web page within the Web site that they can customize to best promote their specific products and services. The site should also include interesting dog content for visitors to view such as articles and information pertaining to dogs—perhaps an online dog show or polls that let visitors vote for the best dog breeds of all time.

PLAY CENTER FOR DOGS
★★★ $$$$ 🌐

Anyone, who owns a dog will tell you the most frustrating aspect of walking a dog is trying to find a suitable and safe area that the dog can run off-leash, play, and socialize with other dogs. More and more communities are banning dogs from parks, beaches, and playing fields making it an almost impossible chore to find an off-leash area for dogs, especially if you live in a densely populated urban center. I will guarantee that a play center for dogs would be a welcome addition in any community by both dog and

nondog owners. The play center could be conducted from an indoor or outdoor location and feature grassy surfaces, ponds, and a lot of running space for dogs and their owners. Customers would pay an hourly fee for using the play center and for the really hardcore customers, a discounted monthly pass could be offered for sale. The business can be marketed by distributing promotional fliers and discount trial offer coupons throughout the community for the dog play center services. However, do not spend too much money on initial advertising because word will spread very quickly. Dog owners are fast to tell other dog owners about unique and beneficial services for their pets. Once established and proven profitable, this business is an outstanding candidate to be expanded on a national basis by selling franchises to qualified operators.

PET GROOMING KITS
★★★ $$$$ 🏠

Are you looking for a pet-related business start-up that has the potential to make you rich? If so, perhaps you should consider starting a business that designs, packages, and wholesales pet grooming kits. Simply package pet grooming supplies into one convenient kit. The kits should be animal-breed specific and include a booklet on grooming tips for the particular breed as well as grooming equipment and supplies, such as brushes, shampoos, and nail clippers. The pet grooming kits can be sold to pet store retailers nationally on a wholesale basis, as well as directly to consumers via the Internet and mail order. Providing careful planning, research, and marketing skills are practiced, this type of business concept has the potential to generate millions of dollars in annual sales.

BREED BOOKS
★ $$ 🏠 🕐

Thousands of new pet owners have numerous questions after purchasing or adopting a new pet in terms of the particular breed's habits, health needs, dietary needs, and training tips. Starting a business that publishes and distributes breed specific pet books is a terrific homebased business venture to initiate.

Fear not if you do not have the skills required to write the books yourself, as you and the business will be better served by having professional dog breeders and trainers write the books on the breeds they specialize in. Once the books are complete and printed, they can be sold on a wholesale basis to pet stores, pet breeders, veterinarians, and even the SPCA. This type of new business venture will require a substantial amount of investment capital, planning, and research in order to be successful, however, the potential financial rewards could be well worth the effort.

WEB RESOURCE: www.hometown.aol.com/bstofshw/wccm.html American Dog Breeders Association.

POOPER SCOOPER SERVICE

Believe it or not, you can make a very comfortable living by starting a doggie pooper-scooper service in your community. The business is extremely easy to set up and has no special requirements in terms of skills, equipment, or business experience. As crazy as this may sound, how difficult would it be to find 200 customers willing to pay a mere $30 each per month to ensure that all little treasures have been cleaned up and removed on a weekly basis from their yard? The answer is not difficult at all. The result would be creating an income of almost $75,000 per year from a business that can be put in motion for less than $1,000. This type of service can be marketed through veterinarians, pet food retailers, and most of all, word-of-mouth.

WEB RESOURCE: www.pooper-scooper.com Directory listing hundreds of pooper scooper services in North America.

PET BREEDER

If your motivation for starting a pet breeding business is purely for profit, then buzz off. The last thing the world needs are more puppy mills. However, if your motivation for starting a pet breeding business is because you have a keen interest in a particular breed of animal and you also have a keen interest in ensuring that the animal is sold to a caring family,

then this is the business for you. Chances are you are going to have a very rewarding business future both personally and financially. Additional considerations for starting a pet breeding business include qualifications, business location, registration, association memberships, and marketing skills and abilities. Once established, a professional animal breeder might not need to advertise, as word-of-mouth and referrals spread fast in this industry.

WEB RESOURCE: www.hometown.aol.com/bstofshw/wccm.html American Dog Breeders Association.

ONLINE PET BREEDERS DIRECTORY

A Web site that features a directory of pet breeders nationwide is a very straightforward online enterprise to initiate. The site can be divided into sections such as type of animal or pet and geographic location. In exchange for a yearly posting fee you could give pet breeders two price and service options. The first would be a simple headline listing in the directory with a hyperlink to the breeder's own Web site. The second option would include a headline listing linked to a pop-up page within the site that could detail information such as type of breeding, qualifications, location, contact information, and pictures. These types of directories are very popular for small business owners especially if option number two is chosen simply because, in effect, they are receiving their own Web site within a Web site at a yearly cost that usually equals what it would cost to host their own site for just one month.

PET MATS

Selling dog and cat specialty mats is a fantastic homebased business to start that really has the potential to earn some serious cash. You can purchase the pet mats in bulk relatively inexpensively and silkscreen on the customer's pet name in bright colors. The mats can be sold directly to consumers via a specially designed sales kiosk that can be setup on weekends at malls and flea markets. This business has the potential to generate sales in excess of $1,000 per day, and best of all, the entire business can easily be set in motion for less than $5,000. Additional revenues can be earned by silk-screening pet names for clients on other types of products, such as pet clothes. These products can also be sold right from the silk-screening kiosk. Once established and proven successful, this business venture is another ideal candidate for expansion by selling franchises to qualified operators right across the country.

PET FAIRS
★★ $$$ ⏲

Calling all pet lovers who are seeking to start a unique and interesting pet-related business venture. Starting a pet fair trade show business is a great new enterprise to set in motion that has the potential to earn you a very comfortable six-figure income every year. The business concept is to simply host pet fair trade shows and charge vendors a fee for table or booth rental, as well as visitors an entrance fee into the pet fair. The show can feature retailers of pets, pet clothing, pet toys, pet foods, and just about any other product or service that is related to pets. The shows should also feature workshops on pet training, as well as pet shows for entertainment, such as trained dog routines. The great aspect about a business that organizes and hosts pet fairs is it can be started small on a local basis with an annual or a semiannual pet fair in your community, and expand into various geographic regions of the country from the profits the business generates.

ONLINE PET FAIRS
★★ $$$+ 🏠 🖱

Like its real world counterpart, online pet fairs can provide site visitors with many of the same products and services. The site can be divided into sections including products for sale, training workshops, and a service providers directory. The concept behind this type of online business is to provide small business owners within the pet industry an affordable alternative to the high cost associated with developing and marketing their own online presence. Promote the site by placing advertisements in publications geared toward pet owners. Also use traditional online marketing techniques such as search engine registrations, hyperlinks, online classified ads, rotating banner advertisement programs, and newsgroup postings. Securing business owners to participate in this online marketing program can be achieved by initiating a direct mail and e-mail campaign aimed at small business owners in the pet industry.

ONLINE ALL FOR CATS WEB SITE
★★ $$$ 🏠 🖱

As mentioned earlier in this chapter, you can create an online portal to bring dogs lovers together with merchandisers of dog-related products as well as service providers that specialize in providing services for dogs. Well, you can also create the same online portal for cat lovers.

Once again this type of "mega site for cats" will have to be indexed by types of products, types of services, and geographic area. Income is earned by charging retailers and service providers an annual fee for being featured on the Web site. In addition to a bold index listing, each client should receive a linked pop-up page within the Web site that they can customize to best promote their specific products and services. Make the site attractive for visitors by adding interesting cat content such as polls that let visitors vote for the best breed of cat and a veterinarian corner that can be established as an "ask the expert" talk-back line.

ONLINE PET ADOPTION
★ $$$ 🏠 ⏲ 🖱

For a host of various reasons, sometimes pet owners are forced to give their cherished pets up for adoption, and you can help by developing a Web site that is focused on finding good families for good pets. In a nutshell, this sort of site would operate in a classifieds advertisement format and include various headings such as dogs for adoption, cats for adoption, pets wanted, and more. I would suggest that this posting service be offered for free and opt to earn business revenues by selling products for pets or by renting advertising space on the site. Promote the site by initiating a direct e-mail marketing campaign aimed at veterinarians, pet breeders, pet trainers, pet groomers, and all other businesses, associations, and agencies relating to pets.

WEB RESOURCE: www.entrepreneur.com Create a business Web site with MySite professional Web site builder.

INVISIBLE PET FENCING
★★ $$$

Indoor and outdoor invisible pet fencing has become an extremely popular purchase for many pet owners in the past decade. A great business opportunity exists for entrepreneurs that start a service that sells and installs the fencing. Invisible pet fencing is a wire loop that is buried in the ground, or in the case of indoor applications is hidden under floor coverings. The wire loop is connected to a low-voltage transmitter and a separate wireless battery transmitter that is in the pet collar. When the pet gets too close to the boundaries as determined by the wire loop, the transmitter sends a conditioning signal to the collar and the pet stops, or retreats back. The best invisible fencing programs are ones that not only include the installation of the fencing, but also instructs pet owners in training and conditioning exercises that help the pets acknowledge the boundaries. Ideally, an alliance can be established with a professional dog trainer who would provide instruction exercises for the dog and owner. Once established, the business will expand quickly by way of repeat business and referrals. However, to kick things into high gear be sure to enlist the services of other business owners in the pet industry, such as groomers, kennels, and trainers to assist in promoting your business.

WEB RESOURCE: www.contain-a-pet.com Manufacturers and distributors of invisible fencing products, also have certified dealer territories available.

NOTES

KEY

RATINGS	★
START-UP COST	$
HOMEBASED BUSINESS	
PART-TIME	🕐
LEGAL ISSUES	⚖
FRANCHISE OR LICENSE POTENTIAL	🌐
ONLINE	🖱

34

PHOTOGRAPHY

Businesses You Can Start

CONSTRUCTION PHOTOGRAPHY

★★ $ 🏠 🕐

Do you have $1,000 to invest in a new business enterprise that can potentially earn you thousands of dollars in profits each year? If so, coupled with basic photography skills, you can start a construction photography service. What exactly is a construction photography service you may ask? The answer and the business opportunity are very straightforward. Each year thousands of new homes are built in North America, and a construction photography service is providing new home owners with a complete photo album of their home's construction, right from the hole in the ground, to the moment the moving truck arrives. The photography service can be provided both in traditional film format, as well as digital format utilizing a digital camera. There is only one way to market this business. Do not waste your time chasing down the individual person who is building a new home. Instead, go after the real market, which is homebuilders and property developers. Why? Simply, because many of these companies build hundreds of new homes each year, and not only will securing photography contracts with these companies generate a handsome profit for you, it is also goodwill and a great marketing tool for the construction company. Imagine once the new house is completed, the owner or manager of the construction company presents the new homeowners with a complete photo album chronicling the home's construction start to finish. The best part of this scenario is the homeowner does not even realize they are going to receive this fabulous gift from the builder until the end of the project. Now that is powerful marketing, not in the aspect of attracting clients, but rather in the aspect of receiving referrals to attract new clients. Once explained, most construction companies will certainly have no hesitation in securing your photography services, as well as paying a few hundred dollars for each new home they build to be professionally photographed so they can provide their clients with a unique, special, value-added product.

WEB RESOURCE: www.nabb.org National Association of Home Builders.

COIN-OPERATED PHOTO BOOTHS
★★ $$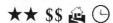

The old three black and white photographs for a dollar coin-operated photography booths are still popular, the only thing that has changed is the price. It has increased to $3 or $4 for the same three black and white instant photos. Secondhand coin-operated photo booths can be purchased for a few thousand dollars and can produce really great profits, providing they are placed in the right locations. Good locations for a coin-operated photo booth include malls, large retailers, food stores, amusement parks, and movie theaters. There are a lot of benefits for people who start and operate this type of vending business, including low investment, potential for good financial returns, all cash business, managed from a home-based office, no special skill requirements, and flexible part-time work hours. Furthermore, the business is fast to establish and expand from the profits that are generated.

WEB RESOURCE: www.aimsintl.org The Amusement Industry Manufacturers and Suppliers International Association. Links to manufacturers of coin-operated photo booths.

PET PHOTOGRAPHY
★★ $$

I am going to share an interesting business concept with you that involves photographing pets. My wife and I were out walking our dog Dana in a local waterfront park. It was approaching dusk and as we were standing there admiring the sunset a man approached us and asked if we minded if he took a few pictures of Dana and us with the sunset as a backdrop. Assuming he was a tourist or a photographer for the local newspaper we said sure. Once he was finished he asked for our address so he could mail a few of the pictures to us. Once again we said

sure and gave him our mailing address. Approximately two weeks later we received a large brown envelope in the mail. Upon opening it we found a beautiful 8 by 10 photograph of Dana and ourselves, along with the photographer's business card and order form for additional prints of the photograph. Having our picture taken with our dog is something that never even entered our minds. However, that day my wife called the photographer and ordered six more prints of that picture in various sizes, as well as booked an appointment with the photographer to take further pictures of Dana. In the end the photographer spent about $8 dollars on a gamble that paid off, in our case to the tune of $200. I am certainly not implying that this type of marketing is suitable for everyone or every business or service. However, once again, the creative and innovative entrepreneur can create market demand, when there is none.

ONLINE STOCK PHOTO SERVICE
★ $$$

Starting a stock photo service is a great business to launch, as it can be operated from home on a full- or part-time basis. The initial investment is small and the operating overheads are minimal. The photographs can be sold to newspapers, advertising agencies, marketing companies, publishers, and directly to individual consumers. The best method of marketing this type of business is to harness the power of technology and go online with a stock photo Web site. This would enable customers to shop for the photograph they need for a project and simply download the file to their location. Be sure to copyright all of your photographs, as you never know when one will be used for a major marketing campaign and become very popular. Once established, a stock photograph business has the potential to generate profits in excess of $25,000 per year, which is excellent for a low-investment homebased business.

PHOTOGRAPH SALES
★★ $

Calling all hobby photographers. Is everyone always telling you what great photographs you take?

If so, why not consider turning your photography hobby into a part-time and profitable business. Selling photographs as art for home and office decorations to consumers is a very easy task to accomplish, providing the photos are good, unique, and interesting. The framed or unframed photographs can be sold at art and craft shows, home and garden shows, to stock photograph services, and to retailers for resale purposes on a wholesale basis. Furthermore, the photographs can be featured in restaurants and other high-traffic community gathering places for sale on a consignment basis. Selling only ten photographs a week, with a gross profit margin of $15 each can generate an additional part-time income of $7,800.

ONLINE PHOTOGRAPH SALES
★★ $$$

Start an online photograph gallery that can be used by hobby and professional photographers to sell their photographs. This type of Web site is very easy to develop and post. The site can be indexed by photographer or by photograph theme or style such as portrait, landscape, or objects. Securing photographs to be sold should not prove difficult as there would be no cost for the photographer to post the picture for sale, only a small commission fee paid upon successful sale. You can boost revenues and profits by also selling camera equipment and supplies.

EXTREME SPORTS PHOTOGRAPHER
★★ $$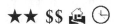

Millions of people worldwide are participants in adventure or extreme sports, and starting a photography business that catches the sheer terror and thrills of these sports is sure to be a profitable and fun business to launch. The photographs can be sold directly to the people involved in the sport, or they can be sold to advertising agencies, newspapers, magazines, and as collectable art. The biggest prerequisites for starting this type of photography business are to be a very good photographer and to enjoy the sports that you will be photographing, as in all likelihood you will have to be a participant yourself to get the truly amazing action shots.

CD-ROM PHOTO ALBUMS
★★★ $$

How many photographs are there in the United States, and how many family memories and stories do each of these photographs represent? The answer for both questions is billions. Starting a business that transfers standard print photographs to CD-ROM photo albums is the focus of this business opportunity. Photographs are scanned into a computer software program, formatted, and transferred onto a CD-ROM disk. Once completed, the customer simply places the CD-ROM into the disk drive of their personal computer and open the CD-ROM containing all of their cherished photographs, professionally indexed and ready for viewing. The market for this type of photography service is unlimited, and best of all you do not have to possess any photography skills or experience to set this business in motion. An interesting approach to marketing this type of business is to design and construct a mobile kiosk display that can be set up in busy community gathering places such as malls, recreation centers, and grocery stores. The portable kiosk is ideal for live demonstrations of transferring the photographs to electronic file. While the kiosk may not generate same day sales and revenues, it will certainly get a lot of attention from shoppers and enable you to collect leads from potential clients.

START-UP COSTS: The following example can be used as a guideline to establish the investment required for starting a CD-ROM photo album transfer service.

	Low	High
Business setup, legal, banking, etc.	$500	$2,500
Personal computer, monitor, keyboard, etc.	$1,500	$2,500
Design software and quality scanner	$1,050	$2,500
CD writer	$200	$400
Office equipment and stationery, etc.	$1,000	$2,000
Initial advertising and marketing budget	$500	$2,000
Working capital	$1,000	$2,000
Total start-up costs	$5,750	$13,900

PROFIT POTENTIAL: In addition to generating sales and profits from transferring photographs to CD-ROM electronic photo albums, the business can also generate additional revenue by providing clients with a photograph restoration service and a photo ID service. Providing the business is marketed and promoted correctly, the owner-operator should have no problem creating a yearly income that can easily exceed $50,000, and much more if additional services are also offered to clients. The business can be operated from home and on a mobile basis, which will also help to keep operating overheads to a minimum and increase the profitability of the business.

REAL ESTATE PHOTO SERVICE
★★ $$

A real estate photography service is a terrific and inexpensive homebased business to start and operate. Thousands of real estate agents and homeowners simply do not have the time, equipment, or skills necessary to take professional photographs of a home or building they are selling or listing to be sold. The best method of marketing a real estate photography service is to simply arrange appointments with real estate agents and present a portfolio of homes, buildings, and properties that you have photographed. Ideally the service should be provided to clients in both film and digital image format. Amazingly, photographing a mere 50 homes per week, and charging only $25 for each home photographed, will produce sales in excess of $50,000 per year.

VIDEO EDITING SERVICE
★★ $$$

Millions of North Americans now own camcorders or digital camcorders and use them on a regular basis for filming important family milestones, vacations, and special events. Starting a video editing service that takes a client's raw film footage and turns it into a fantastic video production including music, titles, and special effects is a fantastic business venture to put into action. A video editing business can easily be operated from a homebased studio, and the business can focus on both video film editing as well as digital film editing.

Utilizing a demonstration kiosk that can set up in a mall or grocery store is a fantastic way to promote a video editing service, as it can give potential clients a firsthand look at how their treasured family videos will look after being professionally edited. Starting a video and digital editing service does require special skills and equipment. However, like any great business opportunity, hard work, research, and planning can pay off in terms of personal and financial rewards.

WEB RESOURCE: www.omegamultimedia.com Distributors of video editing software.

AERIAL PHOTOGRAPHY
★ $$$

There are a few approaches that can be taken when considering an aerial photography business as a new self-employment venture. The first approach is to take photographs of the subject, property, or building from an airplane or helicopter. The second approach is to purchase a remote controlled inflatable that has an automatic camera mounted on it that can be operated from the ground. The second approach has become very popular, as it is a less costly option over the long-term. Potential clients for an aerial photography business can include homeowners wishing to have a picture of their homes from a different perspective, land developers for subdivision and property development purposes, and business owners for a unique outlook on their business that can be used for promotional purposes. Rates vary largely for aerial photography that is conducted from an airplane. However, current billing rates for photography pictures that are taken utilizing a remote controlled inflatable are in the range of $150 to $200 per half day, and more than $300 for a full-day rental of operator and equipment.

WEB RESOURCE: www.floatograph.com Distributor of remote controlled photograph and imaging systems and equipment, as well as industry links.

PHOTO ID SERVICE
★★★ $$

A photo ID service is a terrific homebased business venture to set in motion, and has the potential to generate a six-figure income per year once established. The business concept is very straightforward. Each year millions of dollars worth of personal property such as TVs, stereos, home computers, and other household items are stolen from homes and businesses. The photo ID service is simply taking digital pictures of a client's personal property and storing the images on a CD-ROM. Clients receive one copy of the CD-ROM while a second copy is archived in storage. Should the client's home or business be burglarized and questions arise about the property stolen, the client would simply produce a copy of the CD-ROM for the police and insurance company featuring the items that have been stolen, leaving no doubt as to the type and value of the stolen items. The service could be provided both to residential homeowners as well as business owners. A fantastic way to market this type of unique service is to establish alliances with companies that sell and install home alarm systems. The alarm companies could offer this service as a free added-value for their clients or charge only a small fee for the service. A joint venture such as this would be a win-win-win situation. The home or business owner would receive a terrific service that could potentially save them thousands of dollars or result in the stolen items being returned. The alarm company would have a sales and marketing tool second to none for promotional use, which would definitely separate them from their competition, and you would benefit by establishing a successful business that is being marketed and promoted by a team with great built-in contacts and resources. Once again, a photo ID service is very simple to establish and does not require a great deal of photographic skill. However, some computer and software skills will be needed to successfully transfer the digital images to the CD-ROM.

ACTORS PHOTO PORTFOLIOS
★★ $$ 🏠 🕐

Taking photographs of actors and models is a sector of the photography industry that generates millions of dollars in revenues each year. Providing you have the photography skills and equipment necessary to take professional actors' head shots and create photograph portfolios, then starting a photography business that specializes in actors' and models' portfolios is a terrific business venture to set in motion. The business can be operated from a home photography studio or on a mobile basis going to the actors' and models' locations. Marketing this type of photography service is best accomplished by establishing alliances with acting and modeling agencies and acting and modeling schools. Currently the rate for taking actors' headshots are in the range of $100 to $150 plus $5 to $8 per 8-inch by 11-inch. Modeling portfolios start in the range of $250 and go up in price depending on the complexity of the portfolio.

PHOTO CALENDARS FOR BUSINESSES
★★ $$ 🏠 🕐

Are you looking for a very unique photography business to start? If so, perhaps you should consider starting a photography business that produces specialty calendars for clients to give away to valued customers as a business promotion. At some point we have all been given a generic calendar from a business, club, or organization. The focus of this business, however, is much different, as the calendars that are produced for each client's business is unique and exclusive to the business. Why would a home-builder give away a calendar to a client that featured animal pictures? Obviously the calendar should feature photographs of the homes the builder has completed; this would be a far more powerful marketing tool for the business. The business is very easy to market. Simply design sample calendars and set appointments to present the product to local companies you feel would greatly benefit from this type of specialty marketing tool. Providing you have dynamite product and presentation skills, there should be no problem gaining customers for this type of photography business.

NATURAL DISASTER PHOTOGRAPHY
★ $$$ 🏠 🕐

There are many different approaches that can be taken, in terms of starting a natural disaster photography service. The first approach is to travel the world and take pictures of the numerous natural disasters such as earthquakes, floods, and fires that happen annually, and use the photos to create a yearly natural disaster coffee table book. The second approach is to use digital camera equipment to take the photographs, which could then be posted on a Web site and sold to news agencies and publishers. Both approaches to this photography business require sizeable investment capital, photography skills, and excellent marketing skills. However, this is a very unique and interesting business that has the potential to generate an extremely large income, providing the business can be properly established.

PERSONAL POST CARDS
★★★ $$$

Once again, this is a business opportunity that could not have been started a decade ago simply because the technology to create instant post cards simply was not yet available. Get started by building a custom sales kiosk and equip the kiosk with computer equipment, software, and a digital camera. Then take pictures of tourists at tourist attractions. The pictures can be produced instantly in the format of a post card complete with text captions and graphics. Instead of tourists purchasing generic post cards to send home to family and friends, they purchase post cards featuring themselves in front of a tourist attraction or involved in a tourist activity. Outside of having the ability to run the camera and computer equipment, the main business requirement will be a very good and busy tourist location to set up the kiosk in order to take the pictures. Excellent locations can include tourist attractions, amusement parks, sports tours such as white water rafting centers, busy outdoor parks, and natural wonders.

U-FILM-IT MOVIE STUDIO
★ $$$$

Are you looking for a fun, interesting, and unique business opportunity that has minimal competition? If so, perhaps you should consider starting a movie studio that provides customers with props, clothing, and equipment on a rental basis so they can film and

produce their own movies. Additionally, the movie studio can be rented to film production companies, theater groups, acting students producing their own short films and audition tapes, and just about anyone else seeking to film their own movie, play, or commercial for profit or fun. A U-Film-It movie studio will require substantial investment capital for equipment and to get it rolling. However, there should be no difficulties charging rental rates in the range of $150 to $250 per hour for the use of equipment, location, and props.

CORPORATE VIDEOS
★★★ $$$$

Corporate videos have become a very popular marketing and training tool for companies worldwide, and starting a business that films and produces high-quality corporate training and promotional videos could put you on the path to financial freedom. Without question this is another business venture that requires a great deal of planning, research, investment capital, and experience in order to successfully operate. However, with the ever-increasing demand for corporate videos, the time to start a corporate video production service has never been better. The service can be marketed directly to potential customers, or it can be established as a joint venture with an existing advertising agency or marketing agency. This would be a great business opportunity to start in conjunction with the U-Film-It movie studio, as the corporate videos could also be filmed in the same studio when the studio is not being rented.

CUSTOM PHOTO ALBUMS
★ $$

In spite of the popularity of digital cameras and CD-ROM photo albums; traditional photo albums will always be used to showcase cherished family photographs as they are handy and can easily be passed around a room full of interested onlookers (tough to pass around a full-size computer, or to have a group of ten people crowd around a computer). The photo albums that you design and manufacture should be interesting and constructed from unique building materials. The completed photo albums can be sold to local and national retailers on a wholesale basis, or directly to consumers via a weekend sales kiosk established in a mall or market. While creating and selling custom photo albums won't make you an overnight millionaire, it can provide a good part-time income.

PHOTO MUGS AND PLATES
★ $$ 🕐

Starting a part-time business that photographs people and pets and places their image onto plates, mugs, or plaques is a terrific small business opportunity that does not require a great deal of photographic experience or investment start-up capital to get rolling. Best of all, the business can easily create an income of $25 to $30 per hour. This type of business is best suited to be operated from a small kiosk located in a busy area such as a mall on the weekends, flea markets, trade shows, and outdoor community events. The equipment needed to run the business is available to be purchased new or used and can be located in most business opportunity magazines, or by special order through photographic equipment supply businesses. If you are considering starting this type of business be sure to market the service and products to businesses, clubs, and organizations as photo plaques make great achievement awards and corporate gifts.

WEB RESOURCE: www.printusa.com Distributor of equipment and supplies for imaging transfers and printing.

COMMERCIAL PHOTOGRAPHY
★★ $$ 🏠 🕐

Every year there are millions of catalogs, marketing brochures, and information pamphlets distributed in the United States, and many of these promotional mediums use photographs of a product, person, or place to highlight the product, service, or information that is being promoted or sold. Starting a photography business that takes professional photographs for commercial use in catalogs is a very easy business to initiate and operate. A commercial photography service can be marketed directly to end users via distributing presentation brochures to businesses, or it can be part of a joint venture and work in conjunction with an existing advertising agency. The second approach to marketing the service can be better in the short-term as it will reduce the amount of investment capital needed to start the business, as well as providing a client base instantly.

WEB RESOURCE: www.apanational.com Advertising Photographers Association of America.

PORTRAIT PHOTOGRAPHER
★★ $$ 🏠 🕐

Calling all hobby photographers. Why not start a part-time business as a portrait photographer and start profiting from your hobby? A portrait photography business can be easily operated from a home-based studio, or as a mobile photography service going directly to the client's location. A portrait photography service can be marketed by all traditional means of advertising, as well as by establishing alliances with large retail stores and setting up a portrait photo studio on weekends. The second option of marketing will generate fewer profits as you will have to negotiate a revenue split with the retailer, however, this can be a terrific joint venture as it will enable you to capitalize on the retailer's customer base. Part-time potential income ranges from $10,000 to $25,000 per year.

WEDDING PHOTOGRAPHER
★★ $$ 🏠 🕐

There are a number of different approaches that can be taken when starting a wedding photography business. The first option is to be the wedding photographer, and the second option is to start an agency representing wedding photographers. If you choose the second option, a Web site could be established that would list wedding photographers from across North America along with samples of their photography work. Anyone seeking a wedding photographer would simply log onto the Web site and search the index for photographers in their area. Revenues for the Web site can be generated by charging the photographers a yearly fee to be listed on the site, and the site could generate substantial advertising revenue from related businesses such as wedding planners, caterers, and formalwear rental companies seeking additional exposure.

WEB RESOURCE: www.weva.com Wedding and Event Videographers Association International.

ONLINE PHOTOGRAPHERS DIRECTORY

★ $$

Launching a Web site featuring a photographers directory is a very straightforward cyberbusiness to establish. The site is simply a listing service for professional photographers, and can be indexed by city or state and by photography style, such as commercial, portrait, and pets. A photographer wishing to be listed in the online directory would pay a small $20 to $30 yearly fee. The site can be promoted in the usual ways, including hyperlinks, search engine registration, and banner advertising. You could also initiate a direct mail campaign aimed at those who would benefit by having access to this type of directory such as event and wedding planners, advertising and marketing agencies, and insurance companies. This would be a good choice for a new online enterprise for the entrepreneur seeking to earn a few thousand dollars each year with only a part-time effort.

THEME PHOTOGRAPHY STUDIO

★★ $$$

Providing you can secure the right high-profile retail location in a busy year-round tourist area, then starting a theme photography studio can be an outstanding business opportunity that has the potential to generate profits in excess of $10,000 per month. The key to success with a theme photography studio is to have a wide and interesting range of backdrops and costumes for customers to choose from for their photographs. Harnessing current technology can enable you to produce all the photographs as digital images and augment the pictures for the client. Ideal locations to establish a theme photography studio include beach areas, amusement parks, and on a mobile basis traveling from mall to mall on weekends.

Additionally, this type of business can be marketed to clubs and associations seeking fun photographs for their members.

PHOTO BUSINESS CARDS

★★ $$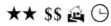

Designing photo business cards is a fantastic homebased business to set in motion. The equipment needed to operate a photo business card enterprise is inexpensive and includes a computer, scanner, design software, and a digital camera. Potential clients can include any person who is in business, or requires a business card for their job. The most efficient way to operate the business is to simply supply the service of taking the photograph to be used in the business card and designing the layout for the card. Printing the cards should be done by a professional printer as it will cost less to produce mass quantities and the overall quality will be far superior. Currently photo business cards are retailing for approximately $150 to $200 per thousand, and cost around $40 to produce that same quantity. Quick math will tell you that leaves around $100 to design the cards and take the picture, or about $50 per hour, making this a potentially very profitable business venture to start and run from a homebased location

HOLIDAY GREETING CARDS

★★ $$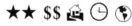

Love them or hate them, holiday greeting cards featuring employees of a business or a family standing in front of a fireplace at Christmas are here to stay. Some people find picture greeting cards to be silly, while others swear by them and have them created every year. Starting this type of photography business does not require a great amount of photographic experience as most of the digital images can be improved or cleaned up with specialized software right on your computer. Gaining clients for this type of business can be accomplished with the use of a sales and promotion kiosk that can be setup in malls and trade shows to demonstrate and promote the service. Overall, a photo greeting card business is a good choice for a homebased business opportunity that has the ability to create a part-time income of $20,000 or more each year.

SCHOOL AND BUSINESS PHOTOGRAPH YEARBOOKS
★★ $$$ 🏠 🕐

Each year millions of school yearbooks are sold across North America, and business photo yearbooks are starting to become popular for medium to large companies to have produced as gifts to their valued employees. The best aspect about starting a yearbook photography business is the fact that you do not have to be a photographer to make the business work, as the photography aspect of the business can be subcontracted to a professional photographer. The real key to success in this type of photography service is to possess excellent marketing abilities, as this is a very competitive segment of the photography industry. Once again, potential clients for a yearbook service can include grade schools, high schools, colleges, universities, companies, clubs, sports leagues, associations, and charity organizations. As a method to separate your yearbook service from the competition, perhaps you could specialize in digital yearbooks on a CD-ROM format.

ONLINE CAMERA SALES
★ $$ 🏠 🕐 ✍

Millions of cameras are sold each year in the United States, and this raises the question: What do people do with all the used cameras they are replacing? It's time to get the old cameras out of the basements and closets and start a business that sells used cameras over the Internet via a custom-designed Web site. The business can be initiated with a minimal amount of investment capital, and promoting and advertising the Web site can be accomplished almost for free by utilizing the various newsgroups with free advertising sections. The Web site could generate revenues from two sources: (1) by people who would pay a small fee to advertise their secondhand camera equipment for sale; and (2) by way of selling advertising space to companies seeking exposure on this type of Web site.

WEB RESOURCE: www.entrepreneur.com Create a business Web site with MySite professional Web site builder.

PHOTO KEY CHAINS
★★ $$ 🕐

Once again, here is a fantastic photography business opportunity that can be started simply by purchasing a digital camera, notebook computer, specialty software, and a couple hundred blank key chains. Photo key chains are very popular with tourists, who can't resist a picture of themselves with a loved one while on vacation. They key to success with this type of business venture is to be located in high-traffic areas with loads of tourists. Utilizing the above-mentioned equipment will enable you to produce a finished photo key chain in less than five minutes, and for less than $1 in costs. Considering the photo key chains sell for $10 it is a very good return on investment. Good locations for this mobile photography business include pubs, restaurants, comedy clubs, beaches, malls, amusement parks, sports events, concerts, and just about every other high traffic community-gathering place.

LITTLE LEAGUE CARDS
★★★ $$ 🏠 🕐 🌐

Baseball, football, soccer, and hockey each have literally hundreds of thousands of little league teams. Who wouldn't want their very own little league trading cards featuring all the team players? Little league photo trading cards present an outstanding opportunity as a business venture. You can operate from a homebased location and service the little league teams in your community. The business could even be expanded nationwide on a franchise or license-to-operate basis. The investment to get going adds up to little more than a camera and photo supplies and marketing the service is as easy as contacting amateur sports clubs and associations in your area to present your product. To keep start-up costs to a minimum the printing of the trading cards can be contracted to a local printer.

BABY PHOTOGRAPHER

★★★ $$

The learning curve to become a baby photographer is relatively short and the potential profits this business can produce are excellent. When combined, these two facts create a pretty strong argument for starting a baby photography service. The business can be managed from home and operated on a full- or part-time basis. Equipment needed is inexpensive, and operating overheads are minimal. If you posses photography experience you are one step ahead of the game. If not, don't worry as there are photography courses available in every community that will put you on the path toward starting this business. There are numerous options in terms of how it will operate. You can go to clients' homes to take the photographs. You can set up a small studio in your own home providing you have the space and zoning permits. Or you can partner with one or more retailers in your community and set up a small photography studio within their store that operates one or two days per week. Of course you can also combine all three options and make it as convenient as possible for your customers to have their baby photographed. In addition to camera and developing equipment you will also need backdrop scenes, props, and a few toy diversions to keep the babies attention on the camera.

Of interest, baby trading cards are really starting to become very popular and this is a service you may want to consider providing to your clients. Baby trading cards are a photograph of the baby complete the baby's name printed on the front and "baby stats," such as date born, height, weight, favorite food, etc., printed on the back. Parents love to give these baby trading cards to friends and family, as well as receive other cards from parents. The baby trading cards also provide a good opportunity for repeat business as the cards and photographs can be renewed annually, newborn, one-year-old, right up to the teenage years.

ONE-HOUR PHOTO LAB

★★ $$$$

In spite of the increasing popularity of digital imaging, print or negative photography will be around for many years to come. A good income can still be earned by starting and operating a one-hour photo lab. Of course the resourceful entrepreneur will also provide customers with digital imaging services in addition to traditional film development services. Like any retail business, location will be a major consideration. Good operating locations for a one-hour photo lab include stand-alone kiosks in malls, small storefronts in strip plazas, and kiosks within existing retail stores such as grocery stores and pharmacies. One-hour photo lab equipment is easy to operate and most distributors of this equipment will include some training when new or used photo lab equipment is purchased. The title of the business suggests that all film developing is completed in one hour or less. However, this is inaccurate as it is best to give customers film development options. The faster they want their film developed the higher the costs. There are also incentives that you can offer to secure new and repeat business such as two prints for the price of one, a free roll of film with each three rolls developed, and a free 8-inch by 10-inch blowup of one picture per roll of film developed. Also to increase revenues, be sure to establish drop-off and pick-up satellite locations. Satellite locations simply mean that customers can drop off their film at various locations throughout the community and pick up their photos at a later date. You simply drive to these location daily and pick up the film to be developed and drop it off the next day when you return to pick up film again.

WEB RESOURCE: www.usedphotolab.com Broker listing secondhand one-hour photo lab and photographic processing equipment for sale.

FREELANCE PHOTOGRAPHER

★ $$

Calling all hobby photographers, it's time to start to earn profits from your photography skills by cashing in on the huge demand for still pictures. Thanks in part to the popularity of the Internet, still pictures are once again in huge demand for media publishing. Why? Simply because there are in excess of two billion Web pages worldwide and many of these pages feature photographs of every imaginable person, object, or place. If that's not enough to convince you that photographs are in high demand, consider that there are millions of print publications distributed every month that also feature photographs. I am sure you get the message, millions of photographs are published in print or electronic media every year. Freelance photographers have various options open to them in terms of selling their photographs. You can sell them directly to brokers who will pay you a one-time fee for the photograph and all copyrights. You can feature your photographs in one or more of the numerous online stock photo services, wherein every time your photograph is downloaded you receive a small fee. You can develop your own online stock photo service. Or, you can select what you believe to be your best photographs on varying subjects and send them to media publishers in the hopes that they will get purchased. The options for selling the photographs are almost as unlimited as the number of things that can be photographed.

WEB RESOURCE: www.aipress.com International Freelance Photographers Organization; site contains information about how to earn money as a freelance photographer as well as industry information and links.

NOTES

KEY

RATINGS ★
START-UP COST $
HOMEBASED BUSINESS
PART-TIME
LEGAL ISSUES
FRANCHISE OR LICENSE POTENTIAL
ONLINE

33
REAL ESTATE
Businesses You Can Start

PROPERTY MANAGER
★★ $$

Here is the perfect new business venture for someone who wants to start a business on a limited investment and manage his or her new enterprise from the comforts of a home office. Becoming a property manager is relatively straightforward. Simply find residential and commercial landlords who are seeking the services of a property management firm, negotiate a service contract, and start the business. The duties of a property manager can include organizing tradespeople to conduct repairs on the building structure, receiving and replying to tenant and owner inquiries, leasing vacant units, and negotiating lease terms and details. A property management service is ideally suited for a person with a real estate background. However, anyone can start this venture on a small part-time basis and gain valuable on-the-job experience and knowledge, which can be later

applied to grow the business into a large and profitable going concern.

WEB RESOURCE: www.npma.org National Property Managers Association.

COMMERCIAL LEASING AGENT
★★★ $$

Educating yourself about the laws of commercial real estate leases and contracts can really pay off, especially if you apply this newfound knowledge and become a commercial leasing agent. A commercial leasing agent service can be set in motion for less than $10,000, and can return as much as $100,000 per year in income. The main focus of this enterprise is to source buildings, stores, and offices to list for lease, and find suitable tenants to occupy these locations. In exchange for your services you charge the landlord of the building one month's rent as your fee, or leasing commission. Should another real estate or leasing agent be involved in the transaction, you would simply split the fee with that person or company. Commercial leasing is very straightforward, but you will still want to extensively research the topic as well as check local regulations in terms of the legalities of becoming a leasing agent in your community.

HOUSE PREPARATION SERVICE
★★★ $$

Every real estate agent will tell you that a home that has been professionally prepared to be listed for sale will sell fast and for top dollar. That is why real estate agents will become your best source of referrals if you are considering starting a house preparation service. There is only one objective to be achieved in this type of service for your clients. Make the home ready, so that it will sell quickly and as close as possible to the full asking price. Best of all, this can be easily accomplished if you place yourself in the shoes of the potential purchaser. How? Look for things that standout and could have a negative impact in the eyes of a potential buyer, such as loose boards on the front porch, a broken pane of glass in a window, dull paint in the living room, or a cracked tile in the kitchen floor. A thousand dollars spent to repair a few minor deficiencies prior to listing a home for sale can easily fetch the vendor ten times that amount in a higher selling price. Why? Deficiencies begin to add up financially in a potential buyer's mind, which usually results in a lower negotiated sale price for the home.

Charging for your service should be done on a pre-estimated basis. That means you will estimate the job prior to commencing with your services. Additionally, your estimate should clearly state exactly the work to be performed, so there won't be any difficulties arising after the work has been completed. There should be a signed agreement by both parties to govern any discussions or miscommunications. This type of specialized service can easily command $40 per hour for labor, plus a 100 percent markup on all materials that may be required to fulfill the agreement. Without question, a home preparation service is a fantastic new business venture to start for any person who is

handy with repairs and possesses marketing skills. The business can easily be operated from a home-based office and even has the potential to be expanded nationally on a franchise basis once the business is established and proven successful.

HOUSE FOR SALE BY OWNER PUBLICATION
★★ $$$

Many homeowners are forgoing the services of a real estate agent when selling their homes as a method of saving money on commission fees. This situation creates a great opportunity for business-minded entrepreneurs to capitalize on by starting a "For Sale by Owner" publication in your local community. The publication can be printed and distributed free of charge on a weekly or monthly basis and supported by selling advertising space to owners of the homes for sale. As well as selling advertising to local companies, such as moving and storage firms, consider adding home renovation businesses seeking to gain exposure to potential new clients. As a quick-start method to get the first publication in print and distributed, you can give away the "home for sale" advertising spaces for free. This kind of grand opening promotion not only gets you rolling, but it also builds good will with the free advertisers, of which many will become paid advertisers for the next issue of the home for sale by owner publication.

ONLINE HOUSE FOR SALE BY OWNER
★★ $$$

Providing your local community with this type of online advertising service is a fantastic way to get into a cyberenterprise. Not only will you be renting low-cost, highly effective advertising space to homeowners selling privately, but you will also be providing them an alternative to high-price print advertising. You will want to index the site into various sections such as residential homes for sale, condominiums for sale, and vacant land for sale. In addition to the advertising revenues created by home seller listings, you can also earn extra advertising income by developing a community service providers section in the site. This section of the site can list local companies in the real estate, home improvement, and moving industry—basically any type of business that is associated with home ownership.

MINISTORAGE CENTER
★★ $$

The ministorage industry is booming. Why? Simply because with homebased businesses opening at a record pace, homebased business owners require storage space for products, displays, and equipment. Likewise, the baby boomer generation is scaling down to smaller residences and require storage space for their personal belongings. Without question, starting a ministorage business involves an enormous investment on behalf of the entrepreneur. However, the income that can be earned from a well-established ministorage business can exceed $150,000 per year or more. A possible solution to combat this high investment dilemma may be to form a group of investors to back the business venture financially, with you as a minority share holder and the operator of the storage business.

WEB RESOURCE: www.selfstorage.org Self Storage Association.

SHARED OFFICE CENTER
★★★ $$$$

Shared office facilities are very popular, and the demand for low-cost shared office rentals continues to increase right across North America. As an alternative to working from home many small companies are utilizing shared office space as a way to keep monthly overheads manageable, and shared office centers usually consist of 20 to 30 small individual offices housed within one location. A shared office center can be started on a reasonable investment of about $25,000 and can return very good profits. Additional revenue can be generated from providing your tenants with a wide range of "extra services," such as reception and secretarial services, high-speed photocopying, parcel shipping and receiving, and boardroom facilities. The individual offices can be rented furnished or unfurnished—providing this

option to tenants is also an excellent way to increase your business income with furniture and equipment rentals.

ONLINE FURNISHED ACCOMMODATION RENTALS
★★★ $$$

Renting furnished accommodations to corporate executives on a short-term or long-term basis can provide you with an income that can match your corporate clients' staggering salaries. Every year thousands of homes and luxury condos sit vacant while the owners are away on extended holidays or short-term job transfers. Many of these same homeowners would gladly rent out their homes while not in use, especially if they knew the house was going to be rented to a responsible corporate executive. The above-mentioned scenario paints a very profitable business opportunity picture for the creative entrepreneur. Once again, this type of business venture is ideally suited for the Internet via a custom-designed Web site featuring furnished homes available for rent to corporate executives. Revenues can be generated for the business by charging homeowners a listing fee to post the rental information on the site. Or, you can list the accommodations for free and accept 50 percent of the first month's rent as the fee.

REAL ESTATE SIGN INSTALLATION SERVICE
★ $

Installing real estate signs is a very inexpensive way to get into business for yourself. This enterprise requires no special skills, and only a few basic tools are needed to complete the sign installations. Most real estate agents and companies do not install their own signs, as generally they do not have the time or the proper vehicle to transport the signs or the necessary equipment to carry out the installation. A great way to separate your service from a competitor's service in this industry is to provide your clients with not only a fast and reliable sign installation service, but also free regular checks to make sure the signs have not been damaged or removed from the building or property site.

VACATION PROPERTY RENTAL AGENT
★★★ $$ 🏠 🕐

Do you live in a busy tourist area where there are literally thousands of seasonal and year-round vacation homes? If so, this business start-up will be of particular interest to you. Many people purchase vacation homes in the hopes they will be able to rent the property to tourists for part of the year as a way to reduce the costs of owning and maintaining their vacation property. Unfortunately, rental income often fails to materialize, as the property owners do not realize how much time and work is involved to rent their properties effectively. As a result the property sits vacant, or is sold due to the lack of rental income. This fact creates a terrific opportunity to start a vacation rental service that also provides property maintenance and management services for the owners of vacation properties. The business can be managed from a home office and started on a part-time basis while the business is establishing a good reputation for service and reliability in the vacation property rental industry.

ONLINE VACATION RENTALS
★★ $$+ 🏠 ✍

By designing and posting a "vacation homes for rent" Web site you will not only be assisting people in finding the perfect vacation destination, but this type of online venture can also be expanded to include every major tourist area within the United States and Canada. The focus of this online business opportunity is to seek out owners of vacation homes that routinely rent these homes as a method to help finance the purchase and ongoing cost of ownership. Persuade them to list their vacation home for rent on your Web site. You can do this or you can employ sales consultants right across the country to solicit listings. Index the Web site by geographic location and type of rental accommodation for search purposes. In exchange for an annual listing fee, vacation homeowners would receive a bold heading that links to a Web page within the site that gives details and contact information including photographs about their vacation home for rent. Promote the site by placing low-cost classified

advertisements in community newspapers under vacation properties for rent. Your ad could read, "Thousands of vacation homes for rent. Check them out at www...." There are advertising programs available that will enable your ad to be featured in as many as 1,500 newspapers per month for less than $1,000. Contact your local community newspaper for details.

PETS-ALLOWED APARTMENT RENTALS
★★★ $$ 🏠 🕐

The most common phrase in house or apartment for rent advertisements is "no pets allowed." If you have a dog or cat, then there is a good chance that you have dealt with the very frustrating task of finding a new rental home for yourself and your pet. This business opportunity comes to the rescue of all pet owners who are seeking rental accommodations that allow pets. To get going, contact landlords and property management companies in your community to inquire about their particular regulations in regards to renting residential units to people with pets. The landlords who indicate that they do allow pets in their units are the ones who will benefit. Why? Simply because you can save the landlords money in advertising costs. How? By providing free advertising via your pets-allowed property rental service. The money earned in this business is derived from the pet owners seeking the rental accommodations, as they pay you a fee to locate an apartment or house for them that allows pets. The most effective marketing method for this rental service is to simply run a classified advertisement under "Houses for Rent" and "Apartments for Rent" in your local newspaper. The ad should run every day and simply read "Hundreds of houses and apartments for rent that allow pets" (plus your telephone number).

STUDENT HOUSING SERVICE
★★ $$ 🏠 🕐

Locating suitable living accommodations can be very difficult for students, especially if they cannot arrange dorm or campus housing. While there are many sources of information in regards to apartments for rent for students, this business start-up focuses on locating room and board accommodations for students. Many people who live in close proximity to colleges and universities have space to accommodate students in a room and board situation. This business venture simply provides the service of bringing these two parties together via a student room-and-board housing service. The business can be marketed and promoted in all traditional print publications. Revenue can be obtained by charging the students and landlords a small fee, say $50 each, for providing this very valuable student housing service.

ONLINE TIME-SHARE BROKER
★★ $$$

Time-share vacation condos are generally sold by the week, meaning that when you purchase a time-share, you are purchasing a particular week or weeks of the year. While time-shares are very popular, the purchaser within a couple of years of the original purchase date typically resells them. This fact creates a terrific business opportunity for the enterprising entrepreneur to start a business that focuses on selling time-share properties. A vacation time-share brokerage is ideally suited for the Internet as an operating format, via your own specialized "time-share for sale" Web site. The Web site can generate revenues by charging the time-share owner wishing to sell a listing or posting fee. Or, you can charge a commission on the total sale price of the time-share that is sold.

REAL ESTATE AUCTIONS
★★ $$$$ ⚖

Real estate auctions are becoming extremely popular, as an auction is a very effective method to sell a property quickly and effortlessly. The main requirement for starting a real estate auction service is that you, a partner, or employee must be a licensed auctioneer. The business can focus on real estate in general, or be more specific and specialize in one particular type of real estate such as vacation properties or commercial buildings. The business creates revenue by way of a commission percentage that is based on the total selling price of the property be auctioned,

and the commission rate charged often varies between 3 and 10 percent. The key objective is obvious: sell the property for as much as possible, as this will earn the business a higher commission fee. This will make your client very happy, which in turn helps to build a good reputation in the industry and guarantees future real estate auction clients.

WEB RESOURCE: www.auctionmarketing.org Real Estate Auctioneer Certification (AARE).

REAL ESTATE PRESENTATIONS
★★★ $$

High-end real estate properties deserve a custom-designed marketing presentation to highlight all the special features contained within these homes and properties. Starting a business that designs and produces specialized real estate marketing presentations is not only a very unique service, it is also a new business venture that requires only a small investment to get going and can be operated right from the comforts of a home office. The requirements for starting a real estate presentation publishing business are very straightforward. You will need computer equipment and presentation design software, as well as the ability and expertise to operate the computer and software. Many homes are now selling in the million-dollar plus price range, and while a great deal of effort and money are spent marketing these properties, the listing agents typically will only provide an interested or potential purchaser with a basic one-page information leaflet on the property for sale. Why? Simply because most agents do not have the equipment or ability required to design and produce a good marketing presentation with exceptional visual-impact qualities that properly showcase the property for sale. That is what makes this new business venture so exciting. Not only is there virtually an unlimited demand for the product and service, there is also almost no competition to contend with for securing paying customers. The presentations should utilize all of today's technologies and include vital information in regards to the property being marketed, as well as colorful images and pictures. Likewise, the presentation should be printed on medium to high-gloss paper and be bound in a creative fashion, such as colored string. Gaining new clients for the business can be very easy. Simply design sample presentations featuring local properties for sale and set appointments with the listing agents of these properties to "present" your sample "marketing presentation." I will guarantee that nine out of ten of these agents will be so blown away with the product that they will become instant and repeat clients.

START-UP COSTS: A real estate presentation publishing business can be started on a modest investment of about $10,000. This should easily cover the costs to purchase the required computer and printing equipment, as well as the software and design programs. One of the greatest benefits of starting this business is that once the equipment has been purchased there is very little additional capital needed to start making money right away.

PROFIT POTENTIAL: An hourly fee of $50 to design the presentation is certainly recommended. Additionally, if each presentation costs $3 to produce, the retail-selling price of the presentations should be two to three times the production costs. Remember that you will be dealing with million-dollar properties, so a few hundred dollars to properly present a high-end property is not out of line. To maximize profits, be sure to copyright the entire presentation that you have designed and produced. Copyrighting these presentations means the real estate agents will not be able to have the presentations reproduced by anyone but you. This will guarantee that each time they require an additional presentation for that particular property you will be making a profit by selling the presentations to the client.

RESIDENTIAL RENTAL SERVICE
★★ $$

A residential rental service can be operated from a small office location, and does not require a lot of investment capital to start. Once the business has been set in motion, the fastest way to get landlords to list their properties for rent with the service is to provide the service for free. This approach saves the landlord money by not having to advertise their properties for rent. It also provides you with a method to acquire a few hundred residential rental

listings for the rental service very quickly. A fee paid by the person seeking the rental will generate revenues for the business. This can best be achieved by charging potential clients a membership fee to gain access to your rental listings. The fee would be small, perhaps $100, and the membership would last for a month or two, which should provide the client with ample time to search and secure a new rental accommodation.

REAL ESTATE TOURS ON CD-ROM
★★ $$

This business start-up is similar to the real estate presentation business enterprise analyzed earlier in this chapter. However, designing real estate tour presentations in a CD-ROM format utilizes current technology to its fullest capabilities. The business concept is very straightforward and focuses on applying technology to create a virtual tour of luxury homes and properties, presented in a CD-ROM viewing format. The greatest benefit to this type of promotional presentation is its ability to showcase the entire property. The compact discs are small enough that they can easily be shipped to a potential purchaser half way around the world within a few days. Creating the CD-ROM presentations does require a great deal of equipment and knowledge. However, some of the more difficult tasks can always be contracted to an outside professional editing company. Filming the moving images and still pictures can easily be accomplished with the aid of a digital camera. Once the footage and text have been created for the presentation, then it is simply an editing job to mix everything together in a coherent and interesting manner including the use of background music and titles.

Marketing presentations such as these are definitely reserved for homes and properties for sale in the million-dollar-plus price range, as each presentation including 50 discs can easily cost the home owner or listing agent $5,000 to produce. But, with that said, there are literally thousands of homes and properties for sale that this type of unique presentation system would be of great assistance in attaining top price for the property. Producing and distributing a sample presentation in CD-ROM format, will be your greatest marketing tool for acquiring new clients. Providing the finished product is professional and without flaw, the potential profits that can be realized from the business could easily surpass $250,000 per year.

MOBILE HOME BROKER
★ $$

Working as a mobile home sales broker does not require a real estate license in most areas of the country, and that is one of the many reasons making this a very good low-cost business venture to initiate. The business can be operated from home on a full- or part-time basis, and promoting the broker service can be by way of designing and distributing promotional information pamphlets to all the mobile home parks in your community. You can charge clients a 5 or 6 percent commission upon successfully selling their mobile homes. Becoming a mobile home broker does not require a lot in terms of equipment, and the main requirement to make the business successful will be outstanding marketing skills.

WEB RESOURCE: www.mobilehomeparkstore.com Directory service listing mobile home associations, parks, and manufacturers.

INDEPENDENT LISTING AGENT
★ $

Here is a very inexpensive business enterprise that anyone with a phone book and telephone can start. Working as an independent listing agent for real estate professionals means that you cold call or telemarket for various real estate agents. Starting at "A" in the telephone book and calling people in anticipation that they are now or will be soon considering listing their homes for sale is all that is required in terms of job description for this business. Once you have established that a person may be interested in listing their home for sale, you simply turn this information over to a real estate agent to complete the negotiations. For every confirmed listing the real estate agent receives as a result of you initiating the procedure, the agent would pay you

$250. For every property sold that was listed via your service, the real estate agent would pay you an additional $500. It would only take 30 listings and sales in order to generate an income of more than $20,000 per year.

ARTIST WORKSPACE RENTALS
★ $$$

Renting a large warehouse space and dividing the space into smaller sections to rent to artists as work studios is a great way to start your own business and be self-employed. The work studios can be rented on a daily, weekly, or monthly basis, providing they are used for work areas only and not residential units. The business does not require a great deal of investment capital to get rolling, and the monthly profits can be terrific. That is, if you assume a 3,000-square-foot warehouse was rented for $2,000 per month, and the same warehouse could be divided into 15 smaller 200-square-foot artists' workspaces and rented for $300 per month each. This simple scenario could create a gross monthly income of $4,500 each month before expenses. The main requirement prior to starting this venture is to check local zoning and fire regulations to make sure the venture is legal in your local area.

DEVELOPER HOME SALES
★★★ $

Providing you have excellent sales and marketing skills, a career as an independent new home sales consultant may be right up your alley. In most areas of the country a real estate license is not required to sell new homes, townhouses, and condos for the developer of these housing and subdivision projects. The main obstacle to overcome in establishing yourself as an effective and results-oriented professional is to convince the developer that you are the right person for the very important task of marketing their capital-intensive developments. However, once established, persistence and results are generously rewarded, as top producers in this industry routinely earn six-figure incomes year after year. Marketing your consulting expertise is like marketing any business. Prior to contacting developers to solicit for sales consulting contracts, make sure that you have done all your homework and have prepared a complete presentation as to the projected sales forecasts and marketing methods you will be implementing in the merchandising of their development project.

WEB RESOURCE: www.nahb.com National Association of Home Builders.

FOR SALE BY OWNER CONSULTANT

★★★ $$+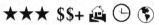

Thousands of people across North America attempt to sell their own homes and properties each year. Some are successful, but many more are not, creating a business opportunity. Starting a business that assists homeowners in selling their own homes not only is a service that is in high demand, but it is also a business venture that can make you rich. A for sale by owner consulting service assists clients with tips and techniques to not only sell their homes, but to do it quickly and for top dollar. The consulting service can include information about how to prepare the home for sale, what the asking price of the home should be, how to advertise and market the home, and all legal matters and documents required to sell a home. Additional revenue for this type of consulting service can be generated by publishing a for sale by owner publication and a for sale by owner Web site, both of which can provide substantial sources of advertising revenues and profits.

START-UP COSTS: The following example can be used as a guideline to establish the investment needed for starting a for sale by owner consulting service.

	Low	High
Business setup, legal, banking, etc.	$250	$500
Web site and/or publication	$1,500	$3,000
Office equipment and stationery	$2,000	$4,000
Initial adverting and marketing budget	$2,000	$4,000
Working capital	$2,000	$4,000
Total start-up investment	**$7,750**	**$15,500**

HOUSE TOURS

★★ $$

Homes featured on the home tour can include historical interest, celebrity homes, homes that were once lived in by a famous personality, homes of heritage interest, technologically advanced homes, and homes that have had a checkered past, such as the location of a murder. Starting this type of tour business is very easy and inexpensive to do. Clients can include local residents, tourists, organizations, and school students. Additionally, for the really innovative entrepreneur, the business could go virtual and offer clients a glimpse of these homes over the Internet via a specially designed Web site. Mainly this is the type of business that would really be of interest to tourists, so be sure to establish contacts and alliances with hotels, motels, and restaurants throughout your community. The profitability will greatly vary as to the popularity of the house tours and the frequencies the home tours are operated. However, a mere 200 clients per week paying an average of $10 for the tour each will create business revenues in excess of $100,000 per year.

FIRST-TIME HOME BUYERS GUIDE

★★ $$$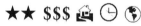

Many of us remember, and many more will soon find out, that purchasing your first home is a major decision and task; the questions that arise about a home purchase are numerous. However, the answers always seem to be few and hard to get. Starting a business that writes and publishes an annual guide for first-time home buyers and features information such as mortgage details, home repair tips, and legal matters is a terrific homebased business venture to initiate. The guide should be widely distributed free of charge throughout the community it serves and can be supported by advertising sales made to community merchants and service providers that wish to be featured in the guide. Potential advertisers can include real estate agents and brokers, home improvement companies, landscape contractors, moving and storage firms, and just about any other business that is related to housing or real estate in general. Typically, these types of guides will cost in the neighborhood of $10,000 to $15,000 to publish, print, and distribute on an annual basis, but can easily generate advertising revenues of five or six times that amount. Once established, this type of business is perfect to be expanded on a national basis serving many communities by franchising the business operating systems to qualified operators.

MORTGAGE BROKER

★★ $$ 🏠 🕐 ⚖️

The main requirement to becoming a mortgage broker is to check in your community to see if there is a registration or certification requirement that must be met to legally arrange mortgages for potential clients. Providing you can arrange mortgages or can acquire the necessary certification, then this can be a very profitable business to launch. You can charge clients a flat fee or percentage of the total mortgage that you arrange for their home purchase.

WEB RESOURCE: www.namb.org National Association of Mortgage Brokers.

ONLINE MORTGAGE BROKER

★★ $$+ 🏠 🖱️

Applying for new mortgages or renewing an existing mortgage online has become a very popular practice for many homebuyers and homeowners. An online mortgage broker is a very competitive segment of the financial lending industry, thus for anyone considering this type on new online business venture you will have to employ some clever marketing strategies or seek niche markets in order to succeed and profit. In the spirit of seeking a niche market consider the following options for establishing a Web site focused on mortgage lending.

- Build a directory of mortgage brokers that specialize in high-risk property financing.
- Create a portal that brings private investors together with mortgage brokers to purchase new and existing mortgages.
- Feature mortgage brokers that lend exclusively for second and third-mortgage financing.

- Develop a directory of mortgage brokers and lending institutions that finance property purchases with zero down payments.

These are only a few suggestions as there are many ways to seek or create a niche market within the mortgage financing industry. Regardless of the type of site you create, the revenue stream will mainly be generated by charging brokers listing fees and selling advertising space.

HOUSE PHOTOGRAPHY

★ $$ 🏠 🕐

Calling all hobby photographers. Are you seeking a way to earn an income or extra money utilizing your photography skills? If so, perhaps you should consider starting a house photography service. The business could be started for less than a few thousand dollars and operated right from a homebased studio. The business concept is very basic. Simply photograph houses in your community at the right time, such as Christmas, during sunsets, or during storms. Pictures taken under these conditions are excellent "one-of-a-kind" photos that almost any homeowner would be proud to have, and more importantly be happy to pay for. Potential income for part-time is $10,000+ per year and full-time is $25,000+ per year.

REAL ESTATE ADVERTISING KIOSK

★ $$ 🏠 🕐 🌐

Designing and constructing an unmanned real estate advertising kiosk is a fantastic way to get started in your own business. The kiosk can be located in high-traffic community gathering places such as malls and recreation centers. These same kiosks can feature advertisements for houses that are for sale locally. The advertisements would include a picture and brief description of the property for sale. Charging real estate agents a fee to utilize the kiosk for advertising the properties they have listed for sale could generate revenue. The kiosk would have to be constructed of low maintenance materials and feature lighting and safety glass fronts to deter vandals or tampering with the advertisements. Ideally, the kiosk would be four-sided and have the ability to hold 48 letter-sized ads. The advertising space can be sold for $50 per month, and the kiosk could generate an income of $2,400 per month prior to expenses.

ONLINE ROOMMATE SERVICE

★ $$+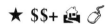

We have all heard the expression "roommate from hell." Perhaps this phrase can be incorporated into your motto or mission statement in a positive way if you intend to start an online business that brings people looking for roommates to share rent expenses together with other people seeking this type of living arrangement. This type of Web site is very easy to develop and would only require basic programming to create a search index by geographic location. A modified classifieds advertisements program would be sufficient. In terms of generating revenues there are many options including charging a fee to post a notice, renting advertising space, or charging visitors a membership fee to search available roommates-wanted listings. Promote the site by registering with search engines, join a rotating banner advertising program, and post notices in online chat forums.

RELOCATION SERVICE

★ $$

Put your organizational skills to work for you by starting a homebased relocation service. Annually, millions of people in North America move locally or sometimes across the country. For anyone that has undertaken a relocation or two in the past, I'm sure that you can easily identify with the need and demand for a professional relocation service. The main objective is clear. Providing relocation services for clients means you are responsible for coordinating the move, ensuring telephone and utilities connections have been completed, and in some cases providing school and other community services information. But also, and most importantly, you

remove the anxiety from what can be a very stressful situation. A relocation service can be promoted by a few methods, including direct solicitation of large corporations that routinely shuffle management and employees around, building alliances with moving companies, and by joining your local chapter of the chamber of commerce, as many people will phone the chamber to find out more information about the community they are relocating to. Currently, rates for providing relocation services start at $500 each and can go much higher depending on the size and complexity of the move as well as unusual or special requests. For the entrepreneurs seeking big market opportunities, specializing in international relocations can be extremely lucrative. Ideally, operating a international relocation service will mean establishing a working relationship with a lawyer that specializes in immigration. You will also want to specialize in a specific country of origin.

REAL ESTATE APPRAISAL SERVICE

★★ $$$

Canada requires all practicing real estate appraisers to undertake training and secure a license to practice. However, in the United States not all states have licensing requirements for real estate appraisers. Anyone considering a self-employment career as a professional real estate appraiser should receive the necessary training and secure the appropriate credentials. Additional considerations will also include the type of appraisal service or area of expertise you will provide, such as residential homes, commercial buildings, farms, or income-producing properties. The licensing requirements are different for each field. Real estate appraisal rates vary widely based on the type of property, the purpose of the appraisal, and the research required. Typically, appraisals start at $150 to $200 and go up from there. A good annual income level can be achieved with many real estate appraisers routinely earning six-figures per year after operating overheads and expenses.

WEB RESOURCE: www.iami.org/narea.cfm National Association of Real Estate Appraisers.

TRAIN-CAR COTTAGES
★ $$$$ ⚖

Old railroad freight cars and cabooses make fantastic cottages, guest homes, and studios. Starting a business that converts railroad cars and cabooses into useable living or work space is certainly not a venture that can be tackled by everyone. It requires substantial investment capital, careful planning, and most importantly, clever marketing. However, providing that this business enterprise is properly researched and capitalized, the profit potential could prove to be outstanding. Get started by checking building and zoning codes in the area that you would like to market this type of unique live/work space buildings. Assuming the first step is viable and the train cars can be converted into habitable dwellings that comply with local building codes and regulations, then you will want to start to contact railroad companies and private collectors to secure the railcars for their transformation. Initially, to keep startup costs to a minimum you can provide the rail-car cottages or studios to people who already have land and that are seeking to build a cottage, add a guest home, or create a studio to operate a business or office from. Renovations and refurbishing the railcars can be contracted to local qualified contractors, and in most cases you will be able to pre-sell the rail-car and let your customer decide about the features and amenities they would like built in. One thing is for sure, once you have a few train-car cottages on location, interest and demand will soon follow.

WEB RESOURCE: www.caboosenut.com Information and links about railroad cabooses and transformations into living space.

NOTES

KEY

RATINGS	★
START-UP COST	$
HOMEBASED BUSINESS	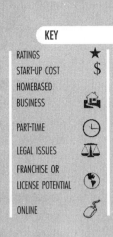
PART-TIME	🕐
LEGAL ISSUES	⚖
FRANCHISE OR LICENSE POTENTIAL	🌐
ONLINE	🖱

33
RECREATION
Businesses You Can Start

PAINT BALL GAMES

★★ $$$ 🕐

If you have ever participated in a paint ball war game, you know how popular and fun these events can be that place you in direct competition with family, friends, and co-workers. The business structure is quite simple. People pay you a fee for transporting them to a site, so they can form teams and use paint ball guns to shoot paint balls at each other in a strategic game of war or cat and mouse. Market the business by going directly to large groups of people who will use a day of paint ball war games as an opportunity to take part in an event that can include a large portion of their entire group. Ideal candidates are corporations, schools, clubs, and sports associations. To really kick things into high gear attempt to enlist local high-profile politicians and business people to take part in a charity game. Place the citizens of the community in direct competition with these high-profile community leaders. Not only will this give you a real shot in the arm in terms of exposure for your new business, it can also raise a great deal of money for a local charity.

REQUIREMENTS: The main requirement for this business venture is land to operate and host the paint ball game events. Additionally, an enclosed trailer can also be located on the event site to serve as a portable office and for equipment storage. Secondary requirements include liability insurance, first-aid equipment, and emergency action plans. The transportation of the participants can be contracted to a local transportation company to reduce start-up costs.

START-UP COSTS: Including the cost of equipment, advertising, land lease, and a portable trailer, the complete business can be started for less than $15,000. To reduce investment requirements, it may be possible to negotiate a profit-split arrangement with the owner of the land where the games will be played.

PROFIT POTENTIAL: Participants pay a flat fee for the game, usually including transportation to the site, a basic lunch, and the game itself. The fee can vary between $30 and $50 per person. Participants also pay for the paint balls used in the game. This business, even operating on weekends only, can easily generate profits in the range of $20,000 to $30,000 per year. This venture also lends itself to selling T-shirts, hats, and jackets to the participants at the end of the game. Generally these keepsakes would have captions such as "I survived the Third World War" with your company logo and a business name printed on the item of clothing.

WEB RESOURCE: www.npbs.com Distributors of paint ball equipment and supplies.

HOUSEBOAT RENTALS
★ $$

There are numerous options available to you in terms of starting a houseboat rental service. The first option is to purchase the houseboats ($20,000 to $30,000 each secondhand). The second, and more viable option is to locate houseboat owners and see if they are prepared to enter their boats into a rental pool that is managed and operated by your service. Houseboat rental rates are in the range of $750 to $1,000 per week and the person who is renting the boat must pay for additional operating costs such as gas and insurance. In exchange for the boat owner allowing their houseboat to be used in the rental pool, they would receive 50 percent of the rental revenue and pay no moorage or maintenance fees for their boats. You would keep 50 percent of the rental fee and maintain the houseboat for the owner. Including operating overheads, boat maintenance, and moorage, a pretax net of 20 percent of the total rental fees per year should be the profit. Providing you have at least ten houseboats in the rental pool that were rented for an average of 25 weeks each per year, this example would leave you a profit of $50,000. The business can be started for less than $10,000 providing you are not intending to purchase the houseboats.

ONLINE HOUSEBOAT RENTALS
★ $$ 🏠 🕐 ✍

Take houseboat rentals online by posting your own "houseboat for rent" Web site on the Internet. There are thousands of houseboat owners right across the country that would be more than willing to rent their houseboats when they are not using them as a method to help offset the high cost of ownership and maintenance. Likewise there are also thousands of people that rent houseboats every year for a unique family getaway. The objective is clear, bring these two parties together via the Internet. A Web site can easily be developed that is formatted as a houseboat for rent directory. In exchange for a small listing fee, houseboat owners seeking to rent their boats could post a for rent advertisement describing their boat, rental rates, and contact information on the site. Visitors to the site seeking to rent a houseboat would simply select a location from an index and start viewing houseboat rental information in that geographic area.

BUNGEE JUMPING
★ $$$$ 🕐 ⚖

Bungee jumping is becoming very popular with those people who seek adventure. The biggest downside to starting this business is the very high investment to get the business going, and the very high cost of liability insurance to keep it operating. You will easily require an initial investment of $50,000 to start this business. However, at $75 to $150 per jump, you can very quickly recoup your investment plus sizeable profits.

MARKETING TIP: For some very strange reason, nude bungee jumping is the latest craze. I would certainly think that you could charge a $25 premium per jump for anyone who wished to take the leap of faith, the natural way.

MOBILE ROCK CLIMBING
★★ $$$$ ⚖

We all know how popular rock climbing has become in the past decade, and here is a business that you can start based on a successful and proven theme. A mobile rock climbing wall that is mounted on a trailer and designed for fast assembly and dismantling can be used both for instruction and business promotion purposes.

INSTRUCTION: This aspect of the business is very straightforward. Market the rock climbing instruction classes to corporations, organizations, clubs, and schools who pay a flat hourly, half-day, or full-day fee, as opposed to a per person instruction fee.

BUSINESS PROMOTION: The second aspect of the business is much more unique. Companies within the local community hire the mobile rock climbing wall and your instruction capabilities to promote their own business for sales events, grand openings, and special occasions. Imagine the advertisement, "Climb to the top of the wall, ring the bell, and receive 25 percent off the retail price." The possibilities are endless for this type of unique promotion service.

REQUIREMENTS: You or an employee will have to be a certified rock-climbing instructor. Furthermore, you will also need the expertise to build your mobile rock-climbing wall. Liability insurance and safety equipment are an absolute must in order to run a mobile rock climbing business.

START-UP COSTS: A mobile rock-climbing business can easily be started for less than $30,000, including the cost of designing and building the rock climbing wall, safety equipment, and the trailer.

PROFIT POTENTIAL: Once the business setup is completed, the monthly overheads are minimal and the business only requires one part-time employee. The following is a good example of the rates that can be charged for this service. All rental rates include instructor and assistant, the setup and dismantle time, as well as the use of the required climbing and safety equipment.

- Hourly instruction and rental rate: $150
- Half-day instruction and rental rate: $350
- Full-day instruction and rental rate: $500

Providing the average sale is based on a half-day rate and you are booked 15 half days per month, the business would generate revenues in excess of $60,000 per year.

WEB RESOURCE: www.amga.com American Mountain Guides Association.

DOG SLED TRAINING AND TOURS
★ $$$+ 🏠 🕐

Learning how to dog sled is becoming increasingly popular, and not just in the winter. You can start your own dog sledding school for less than a $20,000 investment, and operate the business on a year-round basis using sleds with runners in the winter and sleds with wheels in the summer. I made inquires into one such type of operation. This business offered all-inclusive dog sled training for a fee of $2,200 per person for one week. As well, they also offered a two-day mini vacation tour for people that wanted to be involved in the action, but were not interested in learning how to dog sled. Promote the business by advertising in travel and recreation magazines and on a Web site, as well as by establishing alliances with travel agents and other tour operators and training schools. Additionally, be sure to initiate a direct-mail advertising campaign aimed at sports associations and clubs, as you may be able to attract multiple students or guests by providing group discounts. However, keep in mind that starting this type of business will take a great amount of research, planning, and training as you will have to know a lot about dog sledding and even more about northern breed dogs.

WEB RESOURCE: www.sleddog.org The Alaska Dog Mushers Association.

CROSS-COUNTRY SKIING
★★ $$$+ 🕐

Cross-country skiing is a fantastic way to stay fit while enjoying the great outdoors in the wintertime. A low-cost method to start your own cross-country ski facility is to rent agricultural land in the winter and setup a portable trailer to operate your business from. A cross-country ski facility can be marketed to just about anyone who is seeking a wintertime activity including sports associations, clubs, corporations, schools, and individuals. To really give this business a shot in the arm, give away thousands of two-for-one single-day ski pass coupons or free rental equipment with the purchase of a day ski pass. The intention of this type of promotion is to acquaint your business with as many people as quickly as possible. You will be surprised how many people return as full-paying customers once they realize how much fun and enjoyment they can get out of this sport.

REQUIREMENTS: The first requirement for this business is snow, and lots of it. Locate in the northern climates of the United States or Canada, in an area known for large annual snowfall. The longer the winter season the more revenue your business will generate. Additional requirements will be obtaining liability insurance, securing rental land for operations, and checking to make sure that the zoning of the land allows for this type of commercial business venture. Furthermore, you will also need someone on staff with first-aid training and transportation, such as a snowmobile for emergency situations and for use in grooming, maintaining, and marking ski trails. The onsite trailer can serve as the office, concession, pro-shop, equipment storage, and classroom training facility. Providing the business is successful and capital is available, the business can be relocated to owned land with service buildings constructed. If the land is owned, the business could operate on a year-round basis offering mountain biking trails, equipment rental, and camping in the summer.

START-UP COSTS: The total cost to establish this type of business and kick it into high gear will be between $20,000 and $30,000. This includes a portable site trailer, equipment, and initial advertising budget. The start-up cost does not reflect the purchase or lease of land.

PROFIT POTENTIAL: The potential to profit in this business is outstanding. You can operate on very tight overheads and once the rental equipment has paid for itself, it will act as residual income for a great number of years. Revenue can be generated by the sales of day and season passes, equipment rentals, and cross-country ski lessons.

BOAT CHARTERS
★ $$$$ 🕐 ⚖️

Owning and operating a boat charter business can make you the envy of any burned-out corporate employee. The requirements for a boat charter business are very straightforward. You must own a suitable boat and have a certificate that allows you to operate the charter boat. There are various types of boat charter businesses that can be started, and providing you meet the requirements, they include dive charters, sightseeing, business functions, weddings, whale watching, and fishing charters. Typically, a boat charter will include catering, an itinerary, and often some form of entertainment or social activity. Generally, boat charter rates are calculated and charged on a per person basis, and the rate will vary depending on the type of boat charter business you are operating and the services or activities that are included. The start-up costs for a boat charter business are high, in the $50,000+ range. However, the business can be profitable and afford you a rewarding lifestyle that money sometimes cannot buy.

EXTREME ADVENTURE TRIPS
★★ $$ 🏠 🕐

Does taking a hot air balloon trip over Australia interest you? How about a kayak trip down the Amazon River? You can start a business in which you act as an agent or broker on a local basis for adventure travel companies located around the world. Starting this type of unique business requires very little in the way of investment capital to initiate, and the service can be marketed directly to consumers via the Internet or through traditional mediums of print advertising. Once you have secured a paying customer and all the travel accommodations and activity plans have been confirmed, you would charge the adventure tour company a 20 percent commission of the total trip value. Providing you can maintain yearly sales of $500,000 (which shouldn't be difficult given the fact that many of these adventure tour trips are selling for as much as $10,000 per person), the business would generate gross sales of $200,000, which is outstanding for a homebased owner-operator business.

ROWBOAT RENTALS

★ $$

Here is a great little business that can be started for peanuts and operated on weekends and holidays on a part-time basis. Secondhand good quality rowboats can be purchased for as little as $500 each, yet the same rowboats can be rented for as much as $10 per hour to fishermen and sightseers. With that kind of return on investment, it will not take long to get back your initial start-up costs and reap a healthy profit. Obviously the business has one main requirement in order to be operated: water. If the business is established within close proximity to a river or lake, the boats can be rented from a marina location, beach, or even right from a riverbank. A rowboat rental business also requires that you carry liability insurance and the boats are outfitted with safety equipment such as life vests, paddles, and a whistle.

ONLINE ADVENTURE TRIP DIRECTORY

★★ $$+ 🏠 🖱

How about a white-water rafting trip down the Snake River or perhaps a hot air balloon trip over Africa? Or for the truly adventurous maybe an ascent on Everest. Around the globe there are hundreds if not thousands of tour companies that specialize in high adventure tours and trips, and even if you are the nonadventurous type you can still profit by starting your own online adventure trip directory. The site can be indexed by type of adventure trip and geographic area. In exchange for a listing fee, adventure tour operators would receive a full-page listing in the site that describes their tour, their qualifications, and contact information. You can employ sales consultants to solicit tour operators to become members in the site and pay the consultants by way of commission based on sales revenues. Promote the site in travel publications and by registering with search engines. Become a member in a banner-

advertising program and initiate a direct e-mail campaign aimed at frequent travelers.

CAMPGROUND

★★ $$$$

A big investment capital outlay but with the potential for even bigger profit returns. This is the best way to describe starting a campground. Campgrounds remain the single largest family vacation destinations in the travel industry. North Americans spend billions of dollars at campgrounds and on camping-related products each year. There are various types of campground operations that can be started, including a seasonal campground, a year-round operated campground, tent-only camping, trailer and motor home-only, and campgrounds that cater to one specific industry such as fishing. All of these campgrounds have one thing in common, the greater number of services and products that are offered to the campers, the higher business revenues will be. This means you will want to have a pool or swimming facilities, an on-site store, firewood, washroom facilities, activity centers, laundry, holding tank clean-out facilities, and more. The better and more expansive your service, the better the chance for return visitors and referrals. Furthermore, seek to join campground business owners' associations such as "Good Sam," as being listed in these types of travel associations are a guaranteed way to have campers stay at your campground.

WEB RESOURCE: www.allcampgrounds.com Directory service listing American Campground Owners Associations.

ONLINE CYBERCAMPING

★ $$$ 🏠 🕐 🖱

Camping ranks as the number one outdoor recreational pastime in North America, thus a very exciting business opportunity can be realized by the savvy Web master who posts a camping Web site on the Internet. The site can feature information such as a directory of commercial and government-operated campgrounds, camping product reviews, camping tips, articles, and stories about camping topics submitted by visitors. Income can be generated by selling camping products, renting advertising banners, or by charging a yearly subscription fee to become a site member.

SNORKEL TOURS
★★★ $$

Tourists, sun, and water are the crucial elements that will make this business start-up a triumphant success. Starting a snorkel tour business is a fantastic way to earn a potentially lucrative income, and enjoy a personally rewarding lifestyle. How do you get customers for this business venture? Easy. Design a very informative and colorful brochure depicting your fun and relaxing snorkel tours, and distribute them to all the hotels, motels, campgrounds, and restaurants in the local area where the business operates. Likewise, you will want to establish pickup times with all of these locations, in terms of starting the tour. You will have to pay the hotels a booking fee, but the business can easily generate enough revenue and then some to cover the costs of booking commissions. Also consider enlisting the services of a tour-booking agent, as these booking agents work beaches and other busy tourist areas promoting and enlisting clients into the different tour activities they represent. Good booking agents can easily sign up 100 or more tourists in one day for various activities.

REQUIREMENTS: The requirements for this business enterprise are very specific. You will need general knowledge and experience in snorkeling as well as first-aid training and equipment. However, due to the nature of this business you will be required to carry liability insurance and possibly a certificate or registration number identifying you as a tour operator. Any business plan should always include research in terms of legal restrictions and registrations. Not required is a waterfront business location, as the idea of the tours is to pick people up at predetermined locations and shuttle them to one or more locations for the snorkeling, or to a boat. Premiere snorkeling areas in North America include Hawaii, the Florida Keys, Texas, and California.

Cold water snorkeling is also becoming popular in areas such as British Columbia, Washington state, and the Great Lakes. However, keep in mind that you will have to invest in two or three milimeter wet suits for customers to wear if you are planning to establish cold-water snorkeling trips. In addition to reef snorkeling, shallow water, surface shipwrecks, and designated marine parks are also popular spots for snorkeling.

START-UP COSTS: Contracting out the transportation aspect of this business to local transportation and boat charter companies will keep the start-up costs for this business to less than $10,000 including the cost of promotional brochure design, equipment, and advertising.

PROFIT POTENTIAL: The profit potential is excellent. A basic format to follow for operating a snorkeling tour business is as follows: Charge a flat fee of at least $40 per person for a half-day snorkeling tour. Include required transportation both by land and sea, the snorkeling equipment, about 30 minutes of basic instruction, and a small bag of fish food. Your total cost to provide this all-inclusive snorkeling tour should average out to approximately $20 per person. Providing the usual snorkeling tour includes ten people and you have two tours per day three days a week, your yearly profit would be in excess of $60,000. However, this business is capable of generating profits of more than $100,000 per year, especially if you sell underwater disposable cameras and underwater video footage.

ADVENTURE CLUBS
★★ $$$

Establishing an adventure club in your local area is an exciting way to capitalize on the growing popularity of adventure trips, activities, and adventure sports in general. The business concept is to start an adventure club offering members discounts on sporting events, adventure holidays, sports equipment, and sporting activities. The hook is that there is no fee for a membership, as business revenues are earned from companies who wish to advertise in your discount directory and on the club's Web site. You will have little resistance from business owners you approach for advertising sales, providing you have a captive market that they want exposure too. This business can be fully operational for an investment of less than $15,000 and has the potential to return excellent profits for the creative entrepreneur. Furthermore, the fastest way to get members in the club, even though the memberships are free, is to set up a display booth at an outdoor recreation trade show for a week. This is the target market you want and there should be no problems acquiring a few thousand new members from a busy recreation trade show.

TRAMPOLINE SALES
★ $$

Trampolines are fun and a good way to get exercise, plus kids love them. Now for the downside. They can also be very hard to find for sale in almost every area of the country. The solution is to start a business that specializes in the sales and repairs of trampolines. This is a fantastic low-investment business that you can start and operate on a part-time basis right from the comforts of your home. Marketing this type of product can be achieved through print advertising, product demonstration displays, and the Internet. Due to the fact that trampolines are a unique product with limited competition, you should have no difficulties securing a healthy markup.

WEB RESOURCE: www.trampmaster.com Manufacturers of trampolines and accessories.

HOBBY SHOP
★ $$$$

Model trains, puzzles, and games of all sorts are big business, and launching a hobby shop retail business can put you on the path to financial freedom. Hobby shops can be operated from a retail storefront, from a mall kiosk, or as an online store via your own Web site. The possibilities are endless. However, one thing is for sure—the markups added onto these types of products are enormous. The investment required to start a hobby shop will greatly depend on the way in

which the business is set up. Likewise, these same variables will also determine your monthly overhead operating costs.

RIVER RAFTING
★★★ $$$$ ⚖

White-water river rafting is a low-cost, mini adventure trip that almost anyone can participate in. White-water rafting excursions can be advertised to the general public as well as schools, corporations, and clubs to gain customers. There is no marketing magic here. This is a good business and a fun adventure that does not require a lot of arm twisting to get people excited about paying you to go rafting. With that being said, you will still want to separate yourself from any competition and seek your niche in the marketplace.

REQUIREMENTS: You and your employees that will be operating either the paddle-style rafts or motorized-style rafts will be required to get a license, which is commonly referred to as a river guide certificate. Likewise, all employees will need certification in first aid and river rescue techniques. You will also be required to carry a substantial amount of liability insurance. All of these certification courses are widely offered by outdoor instruction and certification companies. Additional information about these companies can usually be obtained from local police and fire departments. In terms of equipment, there are generally two types of river rafts used in this business venture. The first is a motorized inflatable raft, and the second is, an inflatable paddle raft. All boats and passengers have to be equipped with safety gear such as life vests and helmets.

START-UP COSTS: The start-up costs for a white-water rafting business can vary greatly. However, a good used paddle raft and trailer will set you back approximately $7,000 to $10,000. In terms of total capital requirements you should have in the neighborhood of $30,000 available to properly set this business in motion.

PROFIT POTENTIAL: The three river rafting companies that I checked with were all charging about the same rate for a one-day trip, which was $85 including a light lunch, but not including transportation to the rafting center. Once again, the potential profit for this type of business will greatly depend on how large your operation is, and your total customer volume.

HORSEBACK RIDING

★ $$$ ◷

Starting a horse riding stable, training, and boarding facility requires an enormous capital investment, and this type of business start-up is strictly for the experienced horse fanatic, not to mention that you must be a seasoned business veteran. However, if your dream is to operate your own horse stable then maybe you could start small with a few horses that can be boarded at a local farm. The same farm may allow you to conduct riding classes on their property for a split of the business profit. The initial start-up costs will still be high, but only a fraction of what it would cost to establish a complete horseback riding facility.

HIKING GUIDE BOOK

★★ $$ 🏠 ◷

Writing your own hiking guidebook relating to your local area is a fantastic opportunity to earn extra money year after year. Hiking as a pastime, hobby, and sport is extremely popular and millions of people receive a vast amount of enjoyment from participating in this fun outdoor activity. Your "Guide to Hiking" book can include explanations on all the local trails and hiking areas, as well as information on how to get to the trails, what to look for, and what to watch out for. Once the book has been printed, it can be sold through local retailers via a point-of-purchase display. Including a few coupon pages in the book can generate additional income, and the coupon pages can be sold to local merchants wishing to advertise their hiking or outdoor-related businesses. The book can be published on a yearly basis with an updated and revised edition on hiking.

ONLINE HIKING TRAIL DIRECTORY

★ $$ 🏠 ◷ ✎

Trail hiking is so popular simply because it keeps you fit, it's fun, and it is one of the few sports and recreational pastimes that does not cost any money to participate in. If this is not a strong argument for starting an online businesses venture that caters to the millions of recreational hikers in this country, then I do not know what is. Like it says in a well-known movie, "build it and they will come," and in this case the build it is referring to is a Web site that is dedicated to providing recreational hikers trail information and tips on topics related to hiking in general. This type of online information service could include a countrywide directory listing popular hiking trails and areas, how to find them, and what you need to know when you get there. Site visitors and avid hikers, via a chat forum, could provide most of this information. Once popular you would be able to rent advertising space as well as potentially selling products related to hiking on the site.

PONTOON BOAT RENTALS

★ $$$ ◷

Once again, this is a great little business venture to initiate. You can purchase used pontoon boats for next to nothing, and rent them out for weddings, corporate functions, or just to people who want to float around and relax on a warm summer day. Pontoon boats do not require much in the way of maintenance and are very economical to operate. You can charge rental rates of $100 per day or more for pontoon boats and moor them at local marinas.

BUSINESS TIP: You can purchase the pontoon boats and let the marina maintain, store, and rent the boats for you. This partnership can work well as it can give you an ongoing income and the marina can generate additional rental revenue without having to spend precious capital purchasing the pontoon boats.

WATER SKI TOURS
★ $$$ 🕐 ⚖️

Sun, surf, and sand. Who doesn't like this combination? For those of you seeking to start a business that will enable you to enjoy the great outdoors, perhaps you should consider starting a business providing water ski tours or rides to vacationers. Purchase a boat and water ski equipment, and charge beach goers and vacationers a fee for 15 or 20 minutes of water skiing up and down the beach. The main requirements for starting the business will be a beach or marina operating location, business license, a boat, and liability insurance. Providing you can satisfy all the requirements, get ready for a lot of fun in the sun that may even earn you a good seasonal income.

ONLINE BACKPACKERS-ONLY STORE
★★ $$$$ 🥾

You can start your own backpackers-only store from a fixed retail storefront location, or as an online store via your own specially designed Web site. This type of retailing is unique and specialized, and products can include backpacks, flashlights, knives, camping equipment, safety equipment, books, and just about anything else that is related to backpacking and hiking. The start-up capital requirements for the fixed retail location option would be in the range of $40,000 to $60,000, while the online version could be launched for considerably less, in the $20,000 to $30,000 range. The business also lends itself to first aid and wilderness training courses, especially if you have a fixed location. The instruction classes could be held nights after the store has closed. Adding related specialty instruction or training classes is a great way to optimize profits while getting the most mileage out of your existing resources.

WEB RESOURCE: www.entrepreneur.com Create a business Web site with My Site professional Web site builder.

BASEBALL BATTING CAGE
★★ $$$$ 🌐

Baseball batting cages have always been, and will always be a popular recreation attraction. Starting a baseball batting cage business could prove to be financially lucrative and fun. The most important aspect of this business venture is location; the baseball batting cage must be located in a very busy area with great exposure in order to become successful. Good operating locations for this kind of recreation or amusement business are hard to come by and often very expensive to lease or purchase. As a way to keep start-up capital requirements to a minimum, and as a method of securing the right business location, consider a joint venture with a company that is already established in terms of location, customers, and in the recreation or family amusement industry. Look for good joint venture partners who are currently involved with golf, sports complexes, amusement parks, and large family entertainment centers.

WEB RESOURCE: www.sterlingnets.com Manufacturers of baseball batting cages.

SKATEBOARD PARK
★ $$$$ 🌐

Skateboarding and in-line skating are two of the most popular sports and recreational pastimes in North America, enjoyed by millions of participants every day. There has never been a better time than now to capitalize on the demand for anything skateboard or in-line skating related. Perhaps one of the best ways to capitalize on this demand is to start a skateboard and in-line skating park. The park can be indoor or outdoor, depending on geographical location. Furthermore, the park can feature areas with obstacles for beginners to advanced skill levels. Additional income can be earned by providing equipment rentals as well as instruction courses for skateboarding and in-line skating. Without question this is an expensive and difficult business to establish in terms of planning, research, and financing. However, the potential profits that can be earned justify the effort.

BILLIARDS HALL
★★ $$$$

Cash flow best describes this business venture. Starting a billiards parlor that provides customers with pool table rentals, a concession stand, and pool lessons is a great business to operate. Not only can a pool hall generate substantial profits, but the payment terms are also great, CASH. The key to owning and operating a successful billiards parlor is location; the business must be located in an area that is likely to attract pool players. Good locations to establish the business include industrial parks, strip plazas, and upscale locations in office districts. Additional income can be gained by selling monthly memberships, and by starting a pool league. Currently pool table rental rates are $8 to $12 per hour for snooker, and $6 to $10 per hour for eight-ball tables. A mere ten pool tables can produce as much as $200,000 per year in business revenues.

WEB RESOURCE: www.arcade-equipment.com Directory service listing billiards and arcade equipment manufacturers.

FISHING AND HUNTING GUIDE
★★ $$ 🏠 🕐

Calling all hunting and fishing enthusiasts. Starting a fishing and hunting guide service is a very low-investment enterprise to set in motion that has real potential to earn a comfortable living. There are a few ways to market a fishing and hunting guide service, including building alliances with motels and hotels in the area where the guide service is located so these types of businesses can refer their clients to your service. As well as promoting the fishing and hunting guide service by placing advertisements in fishing and hunting publications, you can advertise on the Internet, or start a direct-mail campaign aimed at hunting and fishing associations and clubs. Currently rates for this type of service vary depending on factors such as equipment rentals and transportation requirements. However, base rates without equipment and transportation start at $125 per half-day and as high as $400 per day.

WEB RESOURCE: www.streamside.com Directory service listing associations and industry information.

PARASAILING
★★ $$$$

Parasailing is a blast and the only thing I can think of that would be more fun than parasailing is owning a parasailing business. Be forewarned, this is not a cheap business venture to set in motion, as professional parasailing equipment is very expensive and used parasailing boats can cost as much as $50,000 alone. However, with that being said, securing the right high-traffic beach to work from, the investment to start the business will seem small compared to the profits that can be earned by a parasailing business. Parasailing rates vary from location to location and also on the amount of time the person is in the air, but typically parasailing rates are in the range of $30 for ten minutes. In one day a parasailing business can generate sales of $1,000 or more (tandem riders), which is excellent for a business that only requires two people to operate it.

WEB RESOURCE: www.parasail.org Parasail Safety Council.

BOOKING AGENCY
★★ $$

Starting a booking agency for recreation businesses in your area and that are located around the globe is a fantastic business enterprise to initiate, and best of all it can be tackled by just about anyone regardless of business experience. A booking agency works like this: You promote and sell recreational and travel services for existing companies in the industry and charge a commission on the total sales. The tours and packages you promote and sell can be services, such as hotel rooms, dive tours, snorkeling tours, beach parties, car and Jet Ski rentals, etc. For the truly innovative entrepreneur your business could even act as a booking agency for recreation and travel-related businesses from around the world by developing and operating a Web site that promoted these types of activities to would-be vacationers and travelers. Currently recreation and travel booking agencies are charging a 20 to 25 percent commission on all packages and tour services they sell.

SCUBA DIVE CHARTER BOAT
★★ $$$$ 🕐 ⚖️

Calling all dive masters, dive instructors, and boat owners. A financially and personally rewarding lifestyle awaits anyone who starts a scuba dive charter boat business. The two main requirements to get this business rolling are an experienced dive master or instructor on board and a boat. Perhaps you possess one of these requirements, but not the other. This can be the groundwork for a potential business partnership or joint business venture with a company or individual that has what you lack. The business can be marketed by utilizing all the traditional marketing and advertising methods, as well by building alliances with companies and individuals who are already in the travel and recreation industry who can refer your business to their clients for free. Or they can even act as a booking agent for you business and receive a commission for doing so. Ideally, a scuba dive charter boat will be operated in a busy tourist area, or in an area where weather permits year-round scuba diving.

WEB RESOURCE: www.padi.com Professional Association of Dive Instructors.

ONLINE SHIPWRECKS
★ $$$$ 🏠 🖱️

Take underwater shipwrecks into the high-tech world of the Internet by starting your own shipwreck Web site. This type of Web site could feature all sorts of unique information and visitor services like underwater film footage of shipwrecks taken and submitted by visitors or perhaps world maps of bodies of water with icons indicating shipwreck locations. When visitors clicked on the icon, a pop-up page describing the shipwreck including pictures, the dive terrain, and skill level requirements to reach it could appear. The site could be supported financially by selling advertising space to scuba dive instruction

and tour companies as well as by selling scuba dive products and equipment.

LASER TAG
★ $$$$ 🌐

Indoor laser tag is quickly becoming as popular as paint ball games, and starting a laser tag recreation center may just put you on the path to financial independence. Though this is a very costly business to start and operate (well into the six-figure range), the profit potential is outstanding. Revenues are earned by drop-in customers that want to play, as well as by selling monthly memberships to the center. You can also market laser tag games to corporate clients, schools, and clubs, and create special packages that include laser tag games, food, and beverages for corporate and social functions like birthday parties. Additionally, many operators of laser tag centers also create team leagues and monthly tournaments and give away prizes to the winners. Of course you will also want to have a concession counter on site and sell related products, such as promotional clothing and equipment to bolster sales. The initial objective when you first open is to get as many people as possible to come out and try the game, as a great number of these people will return as regular customers. To accomplish this, give away two-for-one play coupons, and create joint promotions with other businesses in the community.

WEB RESOURCE: www.lasertrag.org International Laser Tag Association. Industry information and links, as well as information about how to start a commercial laser tag recreation business.

NOTES

22 RECYCLING
Businesses You Can Start

DRIFTWOOD

★★ $ 🏠 🕐

Driftwood is a recyclable product that has many uses beyond making a nice backdrop for a family picture. It can be used in landscaping as a design feature, chipped for garden mulch, crafted into wood sculptures, and used to build unique custom patio furniture. The best thing about starting a business that utilizes driftwood as the raw material to create a saleable product is the fact that you can collect as much beach driftwood as you like for absolutely free. The starting point is to first decide exactly what the driftwood will be used for. The next step is easy—start to collect driftwood and get the business rolling.

BUNDLED KINDLING SALES

★★★ $ 🏠 🕐

Packaging and selling kindling for fireplace and campfire use is a very inexpensive business to get

rolling and requires no special skills or experience. This is a great business opportunity for any person with limited business expertise and investment capital to pursue. To locate wood that can be recycled into kindling, look no further than building demolition sites, fallen forest brush, manufacturers of wood products (waste wood), beach driftwood, and construction and property development sites. To market the kindling, simply shrink-wrap the kindling into five- and ten-pound bundles. Once packaged, the kindling can be sold to gas stations, food stores, campgrounds, and building centers on a wholesale basis.

RECYCLING CONSULTANT

★★ $$$ 🕐

Taking the time to educate yourself in the subject of recycling industrial and household materials can really pay off, especially if you apply that knowledge and become a recycling consultant. Millions of homeowners and companies now recycle everyday waste material.

However, millions more could be, and people that are now recycling could also be recycling various other waste materials except they do not know how or what. This is the point where your recycling knowledge can start to work for you by teaching homeowners, business owners, and employees how to recycle, what to recycle, and where it can be recycled. The business is very straightforward; you charge corporations and homeowners a fee to design a specially created recycling plan for their business or home. In addition to creating the recycling program, you can also give a brief instruction course on the recycling program that you have created for them, as well as on the topic of recycling in general. The timing to become a recycling consultant has never been better than now, as the need for every person on the planet to practice recycling measures has never been more apparent. Potential income ranges from $50 to $70 per hour.

TELEPHONE AND HYDRO POLES
★★ $$ 🏚 🕒

Due to safety and structural integrity concerns, most wooden telephone and hydro poles are replaced after 30 years of service. In many cases these old wooden poles can be acquired for free from telephone and utility companies, or purchased at extremely low prices. On the surface this may not seem like an exceptional business opportunity, unless you take the time to consider that once the telephone poles have been milled into lumber there is enough wood from one single telephone pole to build more than 100 wooden shipping pallets. Currently new shipping pallets are selling for $12 to $15 each, which means each telephone pole that was acquired for free or purchased for a few dollars contains enough lumber to potentially produce $1,500 worth of saleable merchandise. In addition to shipping pallets, the lumber can also be used to build patio furniture or used for deck planks and fence boards.

ONLINE RECYCLING INFORMATION

Increased environmental concerns and awareness has made recycling a hot information topic. People want to know what can be recycled, how to recycle, and where to recycle. Here is your chance to capitalize financially by posting your own Web site focused on providing recycling information, know-how, and tips on the Internet. Content featured on the site can be created with a little bit of research or visitors to the site can post recycling information and articles. Revenues can be earned by renting advertising space or selling products related to recycling and recycling topics. Advertise the domain address by registering with search engines, posting newsgroup listings, and creating hyperlinks with other Web sites related to recycling subjects.

WEB RESOURCE: www.enyrepreneur.com Create a business Web site with MySite professional Web site builder.

USED MATTRESS SALES
★ $$ 🏚 🕒

Are you searching for a recycling business that can be started for peanuts and has the potential to generate a good part-time income? If so, consider starting a business that purchases good-quality used mattresses and resells them for a profit. There are a couple great sources for purchasing used mattresses at very low prices. The first is hotels and motels, as most replace their mattresses every five to eight years. The second source is retailers of new mattresses as many of these businesses provide their clients with free disposal of the old mattresses. Once the mattresses have been steam cleaned, they can be advertised for sale to the general public. Many first-time homeowners on a limited furnishing budget and students are the prime customers for purchasing a high-quality used mattress. Providing the business can achieve monthly sales of $3,000 and maintain a 100 percent markup on all used mattresses bought and resold, then this very inexpensive business start-up can generate a gross profit each year in excess of $18,000.

MOBILE PAPER SHREDDING
★★★ $$$

Recycling paper is practiced by more than 50 percent of North American companies. However, not all paper products and documents can simply be dropped into the blue bin for recycling. Many must first be shredded as they may contain confidential business, employee, or customer information. Starting a mobile paper shredding service is very straightforward. The main equipment requirement is a step van or five-ton truck outfitted with an industrial paper shredder and a generator as a power supply. This type of mobile setup will enable you to shred paper right at the customer's site. Clients for high-volume paper shredding include large corporations and organizations, such as hospitals, law firms, manufacturers, and education facilities. Once shredded, the paper is simply dropped off at any recycling depot. This type of recycling business requires careful planning, as the investment to get the business rolling is substantial, and not every community has the industrial and business base needed to support the volume of paper shredding considered necessary to make this a profitable venture.

WEB RESOURCE: www.gebco.com Distributors of paper shredding machinery.

PALLETS
★ $$

Starting a business building shipping pallets from reclaimed wood is a fantastic way to help the environment and join the ranks of the self-employed. Shipping pallets are very easy to build and only require basic tools and woodworking equipment to be used in the manufacturing process. Pallets can be built from various types of wood, such as telephones poles and wood reclaimed from house and building demolitions. Once constructed, the shipping pallets can be sold to transportation, manufacturing, and warehousing firms. Currently shipping pallets are selling in the range of $12 to $15 each. If the raw manufacturing material can be acquired for free or purchased inexpensively, this could prove to be a very profitable homebased recycling business to start.

WEB RESOURCE: www.nwpca.org National Wood Pallet and Container Association.

ENERGY MANAGEMENT CONSULTANT
★★★ $$

Corporations and homeowners combined spend billions of dollars annually on energy to light, heat, and air-condition their homes and buildings. Imagine how much healthier the environment would be, as well how much money each of us could save every year, if we could all reduce our energy consumption by a mere 10 percent? The aforementioned is the focus of this incredible business opportunity. Working as an energy management consultant from a homebased office you can teach homeowners and business owners practical and useful energy management tips about reducing consumption and waste. Successfully activating this business will require a great deal of research, planning, and perhaps training. However, with energy costs continuing to soar, the need to take care of the environment and save money is becoming a major concern for most people. This type of venture should have a very favorable future.

RAILROAD TIES
★ $$

Railroad ties are in great demand for use in landscaping to create retaining walls and planters and are currently selling for as much as $25 each. There are thousands of miles of abandoned railroad tracks that are removed every year, and securing a contract to purchase the old railroad ties can be the start of establishing a business that resells railroad ties for a profit to homeowners and landscape contractors. Additionally, railroad ties can be sold to building centers and garden centers on a wholesale basis. The business can be managed from a homebased office, and as a method to reduce the start-up investment needed to get rolling, the transportation and delivery aspect of the business can be subcontracted to an established trucking firm. Like any business, the key to success will be dependent on a number of factors such as railroad tie source, volume purchase discount, market demand, and operating overheads. Providing all of these factors can be researched and proven viable, this can be a financially rewarding and unique business opportunity to pursue.

FLEA MARKET
★★ $$

Reduce, reuse, and recycle. Two out of three is not bad, and that's how many of the three "R's" can be achieved starting a business as a flea market vendor or as a flea market host. Both are simple ventures to start and operate, and necessitate very little in the way of business or special skill requirements. As a flea market vendor you can purchase previously-owned goods and resell these items at a profit to consumers via a flea market booth on weekends. As a flea market host you can subdivide a large indoor or outdoor area into smaller subsections and rent these spaces to flea market vendors on a weekly, monthly, or yearly basis. The key to success in operating a flea market vendor booth is to have high-quality, well-priced goods that are in demand. The key to success in operating a flea market is to have quality vendors, a great location, and for the flea market to be well publicized. Overall, both are good business opportunities to initiate that have the potential to generate great profits.

WEB RESOURCE: www.fleamarkets.org National Flea Market Association.

BOOKS
★ $$$

Opening a retail store that sells secondhand books and publications is a great way to help the environment by recycling a very common and in-demand product. Not to mention the fact that many secondhand bookstore owners earn a very good annual income. The following formula can be used as a guideline to establish the wholesale purchasing price of books, as well as the retail selling value of secondhand books. Of course there are variations to the rule such as condition, rarity, consumer demand, and age. However, this formula is widely accepted and practiced by owners of secondhand bookstores:

If you are purchasing books, estimate between 10 and 25 percent of original retail value new.

When selling books, the price should be about 25 to 50 percent of original retail value new.

SPILL CONTAINMENT SERVICE
★ $$$$ ⚖

There are two main types of spill containment services that can be started. The first is a water-based operation that specializes in containing, cleanup, and recovery of liquid or solid material spills such as oil or chemicals that occur in open waters, lakes, and rivers. The second type of spill containment service is land-based, with a focus on the containment, cleanup, and recovery of liquid or solid material spills that occur on roadways or land in general. You will need either very deep pockets or a very understanding banker to capitalize this type of business venture, in addition to government licenses, certifications, and a whole lot of red tape. However, as a spill containment, cleanup, and recovery service is highly specialized, the potential profits that can be realized are enormous.

WEB RESOURCE: www.onlinenow.com/rayway/ Manufacturers of portable spill containment equipment.

CARDBOARD BOXES
★ $$ 🏠 🕐

Starting a cardboard collection and recycling business is a very easy and straightforward venture to set in motion. Cardboard boxes can be collected from retailers, grocery stores, and manufacturers and sold to local or state cardboard recycling facilities. Prices paid for reclaimed cardboard fluctuates, as cardboard is a commodity and the price is established on a world supply and demand basis. Still, a part-time income of $1,000 per month or more is easily attainable with collecting and selling reclaimed cardboard boxes. Further information on collecting cardboard boxes and the prices paid for the used cardboard can be found at any local recycling depot, or by contacting local government recycling agencies.

WEB RESOURCE: www.recycle.net Directory service listing cardboard recycling facilities.

BARN BOARDS AND BRICKS
★ $$ 🏠 🕐

Thousands of brick buildings and barns are demolished in the United States annually, thus creating a terrific business opportunity by purchasing reclaimed barn boards and bricks at bargain prices and reselling these items for a profit. Reclaimed bricks can be used for landscaping purposes in constructing patios, sidewalks, and driveways, while reclaimed barn board can be used for making antique replica furniture and as a decorative wall treatment. The main requirement for starting this type of recycling business is to have a storage space large enough to hold an inventory, as well as locating a good and constant supply for the reclaimed material. Providing bricks and barn board can be purchased in large enough quantities at volume discount prices, this business can be extremely profitable. These reclaimed items can be substantially marked-up and sold to homeowners, designers, renovation companies, and landscape contractors in smaller quantities.

CEDAR RAIL FENCING
★★★ $

Antique-style split cedar rails are a hot and valuable commodity sought by urban home owners for use in building decorative property fences that add a certain country charm to their city oasis. If you have spent any time driving country roads, then you are well aware of the fact that not only are cedar rails plentiful, in most cases they are no longer serving a fencing purpose for the property on which they are located. The best method to acquire the cedar rails is to approach property owners and negotiate to purchase the fencing. Once a supply has been accumulated, the cedar rails can be sold on a wholesale basis to garden centers, landscape contractors, or directly to homeowners on a retail basis. This is a terrific little business venture that can easily generate profits of $25,000 per year or more for a creative entrepreneur.

OIL RECOVERY
★★ $$$$

Oil recovery and recycling is a multimillion-dollar industry, and starting a business that specializes in reclaiming various types of oil to be sold to oil recycling firms is a relatively easy business to set in motion and operate. The various types of oil that can be reclaimed and recycled are motor oil, transmission fluids, automobile lubricants, and restaurant cooking oil, just to mention a few. The key to success in the oil reclaiming industry is to establish ongoing exclusive contracts with companies that routinely use some type of oil in the day-to-day operation of their business. This is a business that can generate sizable annual profits, providing the business is operated on a high-volume basis, as profit margins are very tight in this industry. Be sure to check licensing and regulations in your local community in terms of compliance that may be needed to operate an oil recovery service.

WEB RESOURCE: www.dep.state.pa.us/dep/DEPU-TATE/AIRWASTE/WM/oil.htm Information about oil recycling and recovery.

SCRAP METALS
★★ $$+

There are a great number of options open to the creative entrepreneur who is considering starting a recycling business focusing on scrap metals. You can specialize and operate a scrap metal depot that sells various reclaimed metals to metal recycling companies. Or, specialize in one particular type of scrap metal collection and recycling. Owning a scrap metal recycling business is like having your company traded publicly the day it opens for business. Metals are commodities and the price fluctuates on a supply and demand basis, often based on forecasts for the supply and demand for certain types of metals a year or more in advance. Overall, this is a good choice for a recycling business start-up, and the investment can vary from a few thousand dollars to hundreds of thousands of dollars.

PINE CONES
★★ $

Calling all hikers. Here is a terrific recycling business start-up that is guaranteed to keep you outdoors and fit. Collecting pine cones is not only easy, but it can also be very profitable. Pine cones can be packaged in one to two pound bags and sold to craft stores on a wholesale basis. Currently pine cones are wholesaling in the range of $2 to $5 per pound depending on the size, style, and rarity. Collecting other types of forest products such as willow branches (furniture making) and mushrooms (gourmet foods) can also add additional income to the venture. Overall this is a terrific business to get started on a full- or part-time basis, and keeping busy collecting pine cones can provide you with an annual income that can potentially surpass $25,000.

SAWDUST
★ $$ 🏠 🕐

Sawdust is readily available and usually free, and this is important information especially if you are considering starting a recycling business with a focus on sawdust. Sawdust has many uses: it can be compacted into pellets and used for fuel for pellet-wood stoves, it can be used for bedding purposes for livestock and pets, and it can also be compressed into molds to create interior trim moldings and home decoration items. Sources for acquiring sawdust can include sawmills, home renovation centers, and furniture manufactures. Additional revenues for this type of recycling venture can also be sought by acquiring wood chips, packaging the wood chips, and selling them to landscapers and garden centers on a wholesale basis.

WEB RESOURCE: www.sorbilite.com Manufacturers of compression molding systems and equipment.

TIRES
★ $$$

It is estimated that more than one billion tires end up in landfill sites and tire storage facilities each year worldwide. Recycling and ridding the planet of used tires remains to be one of the largest environmental concerns facing all countries. Recently, innovative companies have been cropping up that have developed technologies for recycling used tires into products such as fence boards and industrial flooring. The time to develop a tire recycling process has never been better, as many levels of government have special grants and loans available for starting this type of recycling business. Starting this type of business takes time, money, and creative development. In spite of this, the individual or company that develops a useful product manufactured in whole or part from used tires stands a better than average chance of business success and financial rewards.

WEB RESOURCE: www.vitalsite.com/recycle/tires Distributors of tire recycling equipment.

RECYCLED KITCHEN CABINETS
★ $ 🏠 🕐

Secondhand kitchen cabinets can be put to good use as storage cabinets in the garage, workshop, or basement. They can be outfitted in a summer cabin or cottage or even resurfaced and sold as "new recycled cabinets." Finding a good supply of secondhand cabinets to resell for a profit is very easy as kitchen replacements continually rank as the number one home improvement carried out by homeowners. Start by contacting kitchen and bath renovation companies in your area; strike a deal to purchase cabinets they have removed. In most cases you can get these cabinets for free simply by agreeing to pick them up and removing them from the site. Next carry out any minor repairs that the cabinets may require and begin to market the recycled cabinets. Advertise the cabinets for sale by placing free ads in your local penny-saver or barter publication. This recycling business may not make you rich, however, for the determined entrepreneur earning an extra few thousand dollars each year is certainly within reach.

NOTES

KEY

RATINGS	★
START-UP COST	$
HOMEBASED BUSINESS	
PART-TIME	🕐
LEGAL ISSUES	⚖
FRANCHISE OR LICENSE POTENTIAL	🌐
ONLINE	🖱

45

RENTAL
Businesses You Can Start

POWER TOOL RENTALS
★★★ $$$$ 🏠

Simply start by purchasing good-quality commercial-grade power tools, design an information brochure listing tool descriptions, and indicate day and weekly rental rates. The rental price list can be distributed to local construction and renovation companies. Your advantage over the competition is that you can advertise that you guarantee free delivery of the rental tool (if in stock) to the job site in one hour. The entire business can be conducted right from a delivery truck with the assistance of a cellular phone for incoming rental inquiries.

START-UP COSTS: The initial investment to set a tool rental business in motion will be in the range of $20,000 to $25,000, plus the cost of a delivery truck or van.

PROFIT POTENTIAL: Providing you can maintain weekly rental sales of $2,000, there will be no difficulties in generating profits of $1,000 per week after overheads, equipment repairs, depreciation, and replacements.

WEB RESOURCE: www.whsletool.com Wholesaler of power tools representing leading power tool manufacturers.

PERSONAL WATER CRAFTS
★★ $$$$ 🕐

Renting personal watercrafts like Jet Skis® can be a fun and profitable way to earn a living. A watercraft rental business can be established in a fixed location, such as a marina, or the business can be operated on a mobile basis, setting up daily in busy tourist areas like public beaches. You will need to get permission for the mobile operation, as well as securing liability insurance regardless if the business is operated from a fixed location or on a mobile basis. This unique rental business could even be operated on the basis that each watercraft has its own small trailer, and people could rent the watercraft on a daily or weekly basis for extended holidays.

START-UP COSTS: There are numerous variables, in terms of the total investment required to start a personal watercraft rental business including the number of rental watercraft, fixed or mobile operating location, and transportation equipment. However, this type of rental business will require approximately $25,000 to $35,000 to establish.

PROFIT POTENTIAL: Jet Skis generally rent for the following rates: $50 to $70 per hour, $200 to $250 per day, and $600 per week. A well-equipped and established watercraft rental business can easily provide the owner-operator with profits exceeding $50,000 per year. Additionally, the ability to mechanically maintain the equipment will help keep overhead costs to a minimum.

MOBILE HOT TUB RENTALS

Portable hot tubs, such as Soft Tubs® and Lite-Tubs® are a smaller version of traditional hot tubs. Portable hot tubs do not require any special electrical hookups, and only weigh about 60 pounds each, making them ideal for a mobile hot tub rental business. These hot tubs can easily be transported by truck or trailer and it only takes one person about an hour to completely set up the hot tub. Once established, a hot tub rental business can effortlessly sustain itself through word-of-mouth referrals, and repeat customers.

START-UP COSTS: New portable hot tubs retail for $2,000 to $3,000. However, you may be able to go directly to the manufacturer and receive a volume discount if you intend to purchase five or more at one time.

PROFIT POTENTIAL: While researching this business opportunity I found out that portable hot tubs rent for $150 per day and can also be rented on a weekly and monthly basis. Assuming that you had four hot tubs that were rented an average of 100 days per year each, the business would create gross sales of $60,000 per year with only a part-time effort.

WEB RESOURCE: www.softub.com Manufacturers of portable hot tubs.

SPORTING EQUIPMENT RENTALS
★ $$$

There are literally hundreds of different types of sporting equipment that can be rented for profit, such as in-line skates, cross-country skiis, and bicycles. To be very successful in a sporting equipment rental business you need to locate the business in a busy area, with lots of tourists and local residences. Furthermore, having your rental business located in close proximity to parks, beaches, and playing fields is also crucial to the success of this kind of rental venture.

START-UP COSTS: Good-quality sporting equipment can be very expensive. However, these items require little in the way of maintenance and repairs. The type of sporting equipment you will be renting and where your business will be located will be the determining factors, in terms of start-up investment needed to get the business rolling.

PROFIT POTENTIAL: Similar to the start-up costs, profit potential will also greatly vary. However, a well-established and well-equipped sporting equipment rental business can be very profitable.

FURNITURE

Renting furniture on a short- or long-term basis can be a very profitable business to start and operate. There are many reasons why people and business owners rent furniture including short-term job relocations, financial restrictions, and as a way to keep business start-up costs to a minimum by renting reception area furniture as opposed to purchasing it. The key to succeeding in a furniture rental business is to first determine local market conditions and test market all aspects of the business prior to establishing the business.

START-UP COSTS: Start-up costs will vary depending on the size of furniture rental business that you intend to establish. However, as a cost control measure, consider purchasing good quality secondhand furniture as opposed to new furniture, and carry out any repairs or cleaning that may be required prior to renting these items. Additionally, delivery can be contracted to a local moving company to avoid the high cost of acquiring your own delivery vehicle. Investment range is $10,000+.

PROFIT POTENTIAL: As a rule of thumb, in the rental industry always try to maintain rental fees of 10 percent per week of the rental item's value, or maintain a percentage as close as possible to 10 percent. Utilizing this type of pricing formula will make your business profitable, and the rental inventory will pay for itself with a mere ten rentals.

KARAOKE MACHINES
★★ $$

Everybody deserves their 15 minutes of fame, and becoming a singing sensation with the assistance of a karaoke machine allows anyone to achieve momentary stardom. Karaoke machines can be rented to nightclubs, the general public, aspiring singers, disc jockey services, and event and wedding planners.

START-UP COSTS: Good quality karaoke machines retail for about $2,000. Additionally, you will have to build a music library consisting of a wide selection of rock, blues, country and western, and contemporary music. In total an investment of $3,000 will be required.

PROFIT POTENTIAL: Karaoke machines rent for $100 to $150 per day. Additional revenue can be generated if you have the ability to act as an event host or emcee. This extra source of income can be as high as $150 per event that you host. Part-time potential profit range is $10,000 to $12,000 per year and can be attained with a little bit of clever marketing and shameless promotion.

WEB RESOURCE: www.totalkaraoke.com Suppliers of karaoke machines and music discs.

BIG-SCREEN TVS
★ $$

Starting a big-screen TV rental business can be a great way to get into business on a minimal capital investment. Big-screen TVs can be rented to corporate clients for presentation purposes, seminars as visual aids, TV production companies for props, trade shows for video demonstrations, and just

about any sports fan seeking to watch the playoffs in style. Furthermore, the business can be operated from a homebased location, and the monthly overhead costs to run the business are virtually nonexistent.

START-UP COSTS: Big-screen TVs cost between $1,500 and $5,000 depending on how large you want to go. You will also need a van for deliveries, and good heavy-duty dolly equipment to move the TVs around once at the rental site. Investment range is $5,000 to $10,000 for equipment costs and an additional $5,000 to purchase secondhand delivery transportation.

PROFIT POTENTIAL: Once again, the amount of revenue this rental business can generate, will depend on a few factors, such as how many TVs you are going to be renting and the rental rates that your local market will bare. Current rental rates for big-screen TVs are $75 to $100 per day and up to $250 per week. Providing you can secure a total of 40 rentals per month, the business would generate sales in excess of $40,000 per year.

PORTABLE STORAGE SERVICE
★★★ $$$

The home improvement and renovation industry is booming. Due to this fact, starting a portable storage rental business can put you on the path to financial freedom. Almost all homes that are undergoing renovations have one thing in common: Where do homeowners store furniture and personal belongings while their home is in the midst of the renovation? The solution: "Portable storage." I met a very enterprising entrepreneur a few years ago. He realized that there was a need for a portable storage service in his community. Unfortunately his financial situation did not allow him to start this business by way of traditional means of purchasing prebuilt portable storage units, as they cost more than $3,000 each at that time. Here is where the creativity and innovative actions of an entrepreneur can really pay off. His solution was to purchase used one-ton and five-ton truck bodies for about $500 each from a local wrecking yard. Once he had the truck bodies at his home he painted and signed them with his company logo and name, as well as welded two rollers onto the front of each box. Welding the rollers onto the front of the boxes allowed the newly-built portable storage units to be picked up and delivered by a traditional roll-off or winch truck. He contracted out the delivery and pickup of the storage units to a local trucking company. In total he had less than $800 into each portable storage container and was able to charge a premium over the competition because his storage units had almost 50 percent more storage room than traditional portable lockers. At the time of our conversation he had already constructed 12 of these low-cost storage containers and was renting them for $200 each per week. He negotiated a flat fee of $50 to the trucking company for the pickup and delivery of each storage container. Thus he had built a business that had sales in excess of $2,000 per week, from an initial investment of only $10,000. This type of portable storage service is best promoted directly through construction and renovation companies, as they already have contact with the people who will require this service. You may even want to consider a profit-sharing deal with these companies that support and help market your business.

CONSTRUCTION EQUIPMENT
★★ $$$$

Beyond power tools, there is a vast amount of construction equipment that is required to successfully complete a building or renovation project. A great deal of this equipment is rented for this purpose, as opposed to purchasing the construction equipment. Construction equipment rentals can include lift and crane trucks, generators, lighting equipment, ladders, safety equipment, grading equipment, and on-site security equipment. Starting a construction equipment rental business requires a very good working knowledge of the construction industry and of the exact needs and requirements of contractors, in terms of equipment. Additionally, mechanical and equipment repair abilities are an absolute must.

START-UP COSTS: To properly setup and establish a construction equipment rental business you will need a very large investment, in the neighborhood of $100,000 to $150,000. Once again, providing that you have the ability to repair the equipment, you can save a considerable amount of start-up capital by purchasing used construction equipment that is in good mechanical and operating order. However, the name of the game in construction equipment is reliability and speed, and if your equipment is not reliable contractors will rent elsewhere.

PROFIT POTENTIAL: Construction equipment rentals can be extremely lucrative, annual profits can easily exceed $100,000 per year.

ONLINE CONSTRUCTION EQUIPMENT RENTALS
★★ $$$$ 🖼 ✒

What does a contractor or construction company do with their very expensive equipment when it is not being used? If they are smart they will post it for rent on your new Web site that exclusively feature construction equipment rentals. This sort of Web site would be relatively easy to develop and contractors from across the country could benefit by either listing equipment for rent on the site, or by visiting the site to locate a piece of equipment they want to rent. The site could be indexed representing the various equipment for rent and a basic online form could be created that would enable customers to complete and submit an equipment rental listing for posting. Visitors could surf the site free of charge to locate rental equipment they are seeking, while contractors listing equipment for rent would pay a small advertising fee. The site would be best marketed and promoted by placing advertisements in construction-related publications, as well as by registering the site with search engines and hyperlinking the site to related sites and Web topics.

MANNEQUIN RENTALS
★★ $$ 🖼 🕐 🌐

I'll bet that most of you reading this did not realize that new mannequins sell for as much as $2,000 each. Due to the high cost of purchasing mannequins, many retail business owners have to do without the added visual benefits that displaying merchandise on mannequins can have. Starting your own mannequin rental business means that you cannot only come to the rescue of small retailers by renting mannequins, but you can also help small retailers even the playing field with their larger competitors. Simply designing and distributing information brochures to local retail businesses describing your mannequin rental service will be the best way to market the service. Likewise, do not overlook trade shows and weekend mall-kiosk retailers as an additional customer base and revenue source for mannequin rentals.

START-UP COSTS: Start-up costs can be kept to a minimum, if you are prepared to scour flea markets, garage sales, and classified advertisements for secondhand mannequins. Investment range is $5,000 to $10,000.

PROFIT POTENTIAL: Once your initial inventory of mannequins is paid for, the revenue that this business can generate is almost 100 percent profit, as the overheads are minimal and mannequins generally do not require much in the way of maintenance or repairs. Suggested rental rates are as follows: per day $20 to $30, per week $80 to $100.

POOL TABLE RENTALS
★ $$ 📷 🕐

Starting your own pool table rental business could literally be your break into the exciting world of business ownership. Pool playing is a relaxing pastime that unfortunately cannot be enjoyed by all, simply because many people find the cost of pool tables and accessories beyond their financial means. The real question is how to market this as a successful rental business. In terms of marketing consider holding a contest with the winner receiving free use of a pool table for six months including delivery, setup, and accessories. To generate interest in the contest, simply placed the pool table in a high-traffic indoor area, such as a mall. The pool table can have a sign placed on it describing the contest and prize. Also include a ballet box and instructions, as well as contest details. Once you have drawn a contest winner, you will be left with hundreds of potential customers who completed the entry form. You can then start to contact all of the contestants by way of

direct-mail advertising or telephone to sell them on the idea of renting a pool table from your business.

START-UP COSTS: A complete pool table package retails for between $1,500 and $3,000. Of course good-quality secondhand pool tables and equipment can be purchased for about half the costs of the new pool tables and equipment.

WEB RESOURCE: www.brunswick-billiards.com Billiard tables and supplies.

TENT TRAILERS
★ $$+ 📷 🕐

Between roughing it in a tent and resting comfortably in a luxurious RV, tent trailers are the sensible middle ground for camping enthusiasts. Starting a part-time homebased business renting tent trailers is a wonderful way to cut your entrepreneurial teeth. The business can be marketed by word-of-mouth and referral or by traditional advertising print media methods. Furthermore you can promote your business attending homebased business owners association meetings. Renting a tent trailer for a camping holiday is not one of those things that pop directly to mind unless someone plants the seed.

START-UP COSTS: New tent trailers cost in the range of $7,000. However, good used tent trailers can be purchased for $2,000 to $3,000. Investment ranges $3,000 to $15,000.

PROFIT POTENTIAL: Once again, with this type of rental item always strive to rent the item for at least 10 percent of the value. Providing that you have even three tent trailers, which you rent on average of 20 weeks per year, your business could generate sales of $18,000 per year, which is very good for a low-investment business that you can operate from home with a part-time effort.

PARTY TENT RENTALS
★★ $$ 📷 🕐

A party tent rental business can be started as a stand-alone business, or it can make a great add-on to an existing equipment rental business. Additionally, this business enterprise can easily be managed from home on a part-time basis. Potential clients will include wedding planners, caterers, event planers, and charity organizations. Likewise, the party tents can also be rented to community merchants holding outdoor clearance sales.

START-UP COSTS: New large party tents retail for $3,000 to $5,000, while secondhand party tents sell for $1,500 to $2,500. A total investment of $10,000 will secure two or three good quality, large party tents and an enclosed trailer for deliveries and pickups.

PROFIT POTENTIAL: Party tents require about one hour for two people to setup, and about the same amount of time to disassemble. Currently party tent rentals and setup rates are in the range of $250 to $350 per day.

WEB RESOURCE: www.fstents.com Manufacturers of party tents.

PARTY SUPPLY RENTALS
★★ $$$$

The profits that can be earned by operating a party supply rental company are enough to make anybody celebrate. Parties, special events, and social functions all require certain equipment and supplies in order to comfortably accommodate the people in attendance. Tables, chairs, and banners are just a few of these required party items. There are two types of party supply rental services. First, you establish a fixed location for your party rental supply business and open your doors to the general public. The second and less expensive option is to operate the business from home and deal with only industry professionals, such as caterers, wedding planners, corporate event planners, and children's birthday party services.

START-UP COSTS: The terms of capital required to start a party rental supply service are as follows: Option number one will cost approximately $30,000 to start, including the rental inventory and establishing the business from a fixed storefront location. The homebased option catering exclusively to professionals within the event planning industry will cost substantially less to start, in the neighborhood of $10,000.

PROFIT POTENTIAL: Like many rental businesses, once the equipment is paid for, the vast majority of rental revenue will be profit. Profit potential range is

$10,000+ per year part-time and $25,000+ per year full-time.

MUSICAL INSTRUMENTS
★★ $$+ 🏠 🕐

Millions of people across North America play a musical instrument, or are considering taking lessons to learn how to play a musical instrument. You can capitalize on demand by starting a business renting musical instruments to students, and to people who do not have the financial resources to purchase musical instruments, especially pianos. Additionally, musical bands and entertainers often rent musical instruments while they are traveling. On a small scale, a musical instrument rental business can be operated from a homebased office. However, if your plan is to start big, you may want to consider leasing a retail storefront for the business enterprise.

START-UP COSTS: Once again, purchasing secondhand equipment can be a method employed to keep business start-up costs to a minimum. Additionally, you may also want to specialize in only one particular type of instrument rental, such as pianos. Investments range is from $5,000 to $25,000+.

PROFIT POTENTIAL: Rental rates for musical instruments greatly vary depending on the type of instrument that is being rented, and the following is a rental rate guide that you can utilize for establishing rates.

Daily rental rate:	5 percent of the instrument value.
Weekly rental rate:	10 percent of the instrument value.
Monthly rental rate:	10 to 20 percent of the instrument value.

COMPUTER EQUIPMENT RENTALS
★★ $$$ 🏠 🕐

Renting computer equipment on a short- and long-term basis is a booming segment of the rental industry, and customers can include business travelers, companies with limited computer purchasing budgets, businesses with trade show displays, hotels, convention centers, and students, just to mention a few.

START-UP COSTS: People with a good working knowledge of computers will definitely have an advantage starting this type of rental business, as opposed to people who do not have computer equipment knowledge. Providing you have the ability to upgrade computer equipment and carry out any repairs that may be required, secondhand equipment can be purchased for the rental business for a fraction of the cost of new computer equipment. Investment range is $10,000 to $15,000 to get you started in a computer rental service.

PROFIT POTENTIAL: The following are typical rental rates for computer equipment.

	Daily	Weekly
Portable notebook or laptop	$75	$150
Power Point™ presentation projector	$200	$500
Desktop computer system	$40	$100
Portable printers	$25	$60

OFFICE EQUIPMENT
★★ $$$$

Desks, chairs, photocopiers, filing cabinets, and telephone systems are just a few examples of office equipment that is required by most businesses in order to function on a day-to-day basis. The demand for office equipment and furniture has never been greater, and many new business start-ups must rent this equipment, as their budgets do not allow for office equipment and furniture to be purchased out of precious business start-up capital.

START-UP COSTS: A business that rents office equipment and furniture can be initiated on a small scale, and for less than $10,000. Of course, the business can be expanded later from the profits that are generated. On a larger scale this sort of new rental service would require $30,000 to $50,000 to properly establish.

PROFIT POTENTIAL: Rental rates will greatly vary, in terms of local market demand, and the age and condition of the equipment that is being rented. However, assuming the initial investment into the rental equipment for the business was $15,000, then

you should expect rental revenues around $1,500 per month. Office equipment generally rents for 10 percent of its value on a monthly basis, meaning a 20 percent return on investment per year.

CAMPING EQUIPMENT RENTALS
★★★ $$$ 🏠 🕐

Camping is hugely popular in North America as a recreational pastime. However, there is only one drawback to this splendid outdoor family activity. Many families cannot afford to purchase the required equipment to go camping, especially if they are only going to use the camping equipment once or twice a year. This factual scenario creates a great opportunity for innovative entrepreneurs to start a camping equipment rental business, and fill a large market demand that can line your pockets with profits.

START-UP COSTS: For the purpose of projecting business start-up costs, assume that your new camping gear rental business can supply enough camping equipment for ten families with four family members. The investment would be as follows:

Camping Item	Item Quantity	Item Cost	Total Cost
Sleeping tent	2	$200	$400
Sleeping bags	4	$150	$600
Portable stove	1	$100	$100
Food coolers	2	$100	$200
Miscellaneous items			$200
Total package cost			$1,500
Total start-up cost to outfit 10 families			**$15,000**

Additional capital will also be required for marketing and promotional purposes. In total a camping supply rental business can easily be started for less than a $20,000 investment.

PROFIT POTENTIAL: The camping equipment package should rent for 10 percent of the package value per week, or for this example $150. You will be renting single items or multiple items throughout the year. A camping supply rental business can generate profits of $20,000 per year on a part-time basis.

RV RENTALS

★ $$$

To avoid investing hundreds of thousands of dollars yourself into starting a RV rental business, you may want to consider launching this enterprise with the assistance of a pool rental system. An RV pool rental system works on the following basis. Owners of RVs allow you to rent their units to your clients in exchange for a portion of the rental revenue. Additionally, as the owner of the business you may also have to agree to maintain and insure the RVs. However, each rental agreement can be negotiated individually with RV owners. North America remains one of the world's top travel destinations for foreign travelers, and traveling by RV allows them to enjoy and experience a unique and unforgettable holiday.

START-UP COSTS: The total cost to establish an RV rental business using the rental pool format will be approximately $10,000 including a Web site and promotional brochures.

PROFIT POTENTIAL: Class "C" RVs rent for $600+ per week plus gas, insurance, and a mileage charge over a certain number of free miles. Class "A" RVs start at $800 per week and go up from there. In the rental pool system, you keep 50 percent of the rental revenue as the operator of the business.

ONLINE RV RENTALS

★★ $$$

Take RV rentals into cyberspace by starting a Web site that features RV rentals and information. Here is a dandy business opportunity for the innovative entrepreneur with a desire to operate a high-tech homebased business. In the United States there are more than ten million registered recreational vehicles and many RV owners rent their units when they are not using them. An equal number of people rent RVs annually and set out onto the highways and byways on vacation. What an opportunity to bring these two parties together via your specially designed RV rental Web site. The site could be indexed by city or state as well as RV classification. Visitors would simply scroll through the index until they found the type of RV they were interested in

renting. You could charge RV owners a portion of the rental revenue they received. However, to simplify the business and bookkeeping, stick to just charging a small posting or listing fee. Additionally, to increase visitor interest and site stickiness, develop a camping or RV park directory. Good content can go a long way in building a great Web site. Imagine; only 1,000 RV owners paying a mere $15 a month each to have their rental information featured on the Web site will create yearly sales of $180,000.

STORE FIXTURES

★ $$$

Many retail businesses are started on a shoestring budget often not allowing for the purchase of new store fixtures. Renting store fixtures like display cabinets, shelving, and cash registers can be a way that you can get into business in your local community without a lot of previous business experience. Potential clients include businesses who require the use of store fixtures on a temporary basis including inventory liquidators, businesses setting up at local trade shows, and existing businesses establishing secondary satellite locations. A store fixture rental business may not be a good candidate for starting and operating from home due to the storage space that will be required, unless of course you have adequate storage space available at home.

START-UP COSTS: New high quality store fixtures are extremely expensive. However, scanning local newspapers for business closure notices may result in an ability to purchase high-quality store fixtures secondhand for a fraction of their original retail value. Investment range is $10,000 to $25,000.

PROFIT POTENTIAL: The demand is not as high for store fixture rentals as other rental ventures that can be started. You may want to consider adding sales of used store fixtures and equipment as a method of supplementing rental revenue.

CASINO EQUIPMENT

★ $$$$

Renting casino equipment to charity organizations for fundraising events and to businesses for promotional events is big business. The biggest requirement will be to make sure that you will not be bending or breaking any laws, and legal information, in terms of operating a business that rents casino gaming equipment is very easy to obtain on a local basis.

START-UP COSTS: To properly establish a casino equipment rental service will be very costly, in the neighborhood of $50,000 to $100,000 to cover the cost of equipment, transportation, and business setup. There are few short cuts or cost saving measures that can be utilized, as the equipment must be in perfect working condition.

PROFIT POTENTIAL: The casino equipment that you rent can be supplied to charity organizations and companies on a daily, weekly, or monthly basis; whichever will meet your clients' requirements and needs. Additional revenue can be earned by supplying qualified dealers, as well as having your own "learn to become a casino dealer" instruction school. The profit potential will greatly depend on the type of business venture that you will be operating, and also on how diversified the business will be. One thing is for sure, anything to do with gambling and casinos is generally a pretty safe business venture to start and operate.

WEB RESOURCE: www.oneeyedjackgaming.com Distributor of casino equipment and supplies.

FENCING RENTAL
★★ $$$+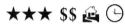

Renting portable fencing solutions to construction companies and outdoor event planers is a fantastic homebased rental business that can be started on a relatively small initial investment. Most rental fencing is in the form of a chain link that is generally six to eight feet high. Additionally, the fencing is typically installed with barbed wire on top to prevent trespassers into the construction site or event.

START-UP COSTS: Ninety-five percent of the start-up costs associated with this business venture will be the purchase of the fencing material and suitable transportation for delivery purposes. The balance of the start-up costs will be used for a simple marketing brochure and establishing the legal aspects for the business, such as business registration and rental

contract forms. Start-up investment range is $15,000 to $30,000.

PROFIT POTENTIAL: Fence rental rates are calculated by the total number of linear feet required for the job. Furthermore, there are additional charges for the complexity of the installation and factors, such as the number of gates and height of fencing required.

CANOE AND KAYAK RENTALS
★★★ $$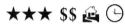

Starting a canoe and kayak rental business will not leave you up the financial river without a paddle, as this is one of the best low-investment rental businesses that can be started. A canoe and kayak rental business can be established in a few different operating formats. With the first, you can supply canoes or kayaks to marinas and waterfront hotels and split the rental revenues that are generated. The second option is you can operate a canoe and kayak rental business from your own rented waterfront location. Or, the third option, you can run the business from home, advertising through print media to attract customers who can simply pickup the rental item from you, or you can deliver the rental equipment to the customer. The second and third options will generate the most income for the business, as well as give you the most control over the business and rental equipment.

START-UP COSTS: A canoe and kayak rental business can be nicely established for less than $10,000. The following is a current retail price list for canoes, kayaks, and accessories.

Fiberglass canoe	$400–$600
Kevlar canoe	$800–$2,000
Ocean fiberglass kayak	$1,500–$2,000
Tandem ocean kayak	$2,000–$3,000
Roto-mold white-water kayaks	$700–$1,000
Life vests	$25–$100
Paddles	$10–$150

Purchasing previously-owned canoes and kayaks generally sell for half of the cost of new ones.

PROFIT POTENTIAL: As is the case in many rental businesses, once the inventory has been paid for there are not a lot of overheads associated with operating the business. Canoes and kayaks have a very long and usable life span and only require the occasional repair. Canoes rent for $40 per day and $125 per week, while kayaks rent for $50 per day and up to $200 per week. A well-established and equipped canoe and kayak rental business can easily generate revenues in excess $100,000 per year.

PORTABLE BUILDINGS
★ $$$$ 🏚 🕐

There are many uses for portable buildings to be set up on a location for temporary business and operating applications. Potential clients for a portable building rental business include construction companies, fairs, outdoor auctions, outdoor liquidation sales, movie and TV production sites, outdoor community special events, sporting events, and roadside vending. The biggest requirement for starting a portable building rental business is the ability to move and set up the portable buildings. However, many of the portable buildings that are rented for the above mentioned applications are modified trailers to suit the client's needs.

START-UP COSTS: The initial start-up investment required to set this business in motion will vary greatly to the number of portable buildings you will be renting as well as the equipment that is supplied or outfitted with the buildings. Investment range is $20,000 to $50,000.

PROFIT POTENTIAL: Portable building rental rates start at $200 per day and $400 per week. Assuming you can meet clients' requirements; a profitable living can be made renting portable buildings. Additional considerations include transportation, storage, and insurance coverage.

BOAT RENTAL
★★ $$$ 🕐

Renting small, motorized, runabout boats to fishermen can be a very lucrative rental business venture to establish in your area. Fishermen travel wide and far in search of the perfect fishing hole. The business can

be water-based and operated from a marina or rented dock facility. Or, the business can be land-based and the boats can be rented with a trailer. To get started, design colorful brochures and distribute them to hotels, motels, and tourist attractions. The brochures should contain information about your boat rentals including rates and the size of boat and motor. The hotels and motels can act as booking agents for the business while providing a great service for their guests. Consider a rental revenue split of perhaps 20 percent for the booking agent and 80 percent for you. This should be more than an adequate financial incentive for any motel proprietor to happily get on board with the program.

START-UP COSTS: Small, secondhand fishing boats with a motor and trailer are selling in the range of $2,500 to $5,000 each. An initial investment of $10,000 to $15,000 will be suitable to get this venture "floating."

PROFIT POTENTIAL: Small fishing boats rent for about $100 per day and include all the safety equipment and gasoline for the day. Three rental boats working for you 100 days per year each can produce a gross business income of $30,000.

ONLINE BOAT RENTALS
★★ $$$ 🏚 🕐 🖱

Starting an online boat rental Web site is a good choice for the land-loving entrepreneur who wants to operate a business from home. To get started, simply create a Web site dedicated to pleasure boat rentals. Boat owners from across North America that are seeking to rent their boats when not in use could post a notice on the site that describes the boat, contact information, and rental rates. People seeking to rent a boat could painlessly view the rental listing until they have found the type of boat that suits their needs. Money will be made by charging boat owners a fee to list their boats for rent, and there is also a good chance that once the site has been established banner advertisements could also be rented to increase revenues. Marketing the site is as easy as placing advertisements in boating-related print publications and Internet advertising options.

MOPED RENTALS
★★ $$$$ ⚖

One ride on a moped is generally all it takes to become a confirmed moped nut. This rental venture is best served by establishing the business in a high-traffic area that caters to and is visited mainly by tourists. The business can be operated from an independent location or in partnership with a hotel or multiple hotels acting as the rental location for the mopeds. A mechanical aptitude will assist with keeping your fleet of mopeds on the road and in good repair.

START-UP COSTS: A fleet of ten new mopeds will set you back about $15,000. Additionally, depending on how you establish the rental operation, an additional $5,000 to $10,000 of working capital will be required.

PROFIT POTENTIAL: Mopeds rent for $50 to $60 per day plus the cost of insurance and gasoline. Once again, providing that your business is located in a busy year-round tourist area and that you have only ten mopeds for rent, you could generate yearly revenues exceeding $100,000. Additional income can be acquired by renting bicycles and in-line skates from the same location. Also, you may act as a booking agent for local tours and tourist attractions, as the commissions earned can really add up and generate excellent additional income for the business.

WEB RESOURCE: www.moped.org Links to Moped dealers and clubs.

PORTABLE SIGN RENTAL
★★ $$$ 🏠 🕐

Just about every retail merchant holds at least one large sale per year and these sales all have to be advertised and promoted to get the attention of consumers. Starting your own portable sign rental business will allow you to cash in on the retailers seeking to promote their sales. Portable rental signs generally feature a flashing arrow or some other type of attention-grabbing feature. These signs have the ability to change messages, either electronically or with the use of individual letters. To kick this business

into high gear, simply check the local newspapers for merchants that are advertising forthcoming sales. You can then call or visit these businesses and present all the benefits that having a portable message sign on site will have in terms of increasing potential revenues for their sales.

START-UP COSTS: Start-up investment range is $10,000 to $15,000.

PROFIT POTENTIAL: Portable message signs rent for $75 per day and $150 per week. Your arithmetic skills do not have to be good to realize that having a few portable signs that are rented on a regular basis can really generate some serious cash flow and profits.

WEB RESOURCE: www.letterperfectinc.net Manufacturers of portable signs and letters.

VIDEO AND CAMERA EQUIPMENT RENTALS
★★★ $$$ 📷 🕐

Digital video and camera equipment is the latest high-tech craze. No film developing costs and you can see the images almost immediately right on your PC monitor. Initiating your own digital video recorder and camera rental business is a great home-based business endeavor to start. The absolutely best way to market the business is through local hotels and motels. Building alliances with these accommodation establishments can make you rich. Simply design a brochure and price list and obtain permission from the hotels, etc., to place this brochure into all of their rental rooms. You can rent the equipment directly to vacationers and business travelers that call you as a result of seeing the brochure in the hotel. Providing your customers with a free one-hour delivery service right to their hotel room is also a valuable method to overcoming any potential resistance to renting the equipment. Of course, you will need to work out a revenue splitting or payment arrangement with the hotels and motels that permit you to post your brochures.

START-UP COSTS: An initial start-up investment of $8,000 to $12,000 can set this business venture into motion.

PROFIT POTENTIAL: Digital camera equipment rents for $30 per day per item and up. This is definitely the kind of rental business that allows you to charge 10 percent of the rental item's value each time the equipment is rented.

ONLINE MOVIE PROP RENTALS
★★★★ $$$ 📷 ✍

Explanation of this particular business start-up really deserves its own complete book. However, here goes with an abbreviated version. Rentals of set or location props are certainly not limited to only the film production industry. Props are also required for trade shows, mall displays, social functions, and the list goes on and on. Starting a prop rental service does not mean that you have to invest hundreds of thousands of dollars into unique and interesting props for inventory. There are millions of people out there with lots of interesting stuff like rare cars, antique jukeboxes, and gadgets of every kind that they would be more than willing to rent for a fee. The problem is how do you get all this stuff into one place and into one rental catalog? Easy. You start a prop-for-rent Web site. Promote the site to those who routinely rent props including producers, event planners, etc. To establish the Web site you will need to index it by category and take pictures of the items up for rent and post the pictures in the proper categories on the site. To generate revenue for your business, simply charge a 50 percent commission on the rental value of all items. One example is a rare car rents for $300 per day for a commercial shoot, and you keep $150 dollars for bringing the two parties together electronically. Of course you will have to work out delivery, pickup, and liability issues. However, done properly, this business could make you a millionaire.

SCAFFOLDING RENTALS
★ $$ 📷 🕐

Almost every building and home service trade needs to rent scaffolding at some point in the course of operating their business. To start this type of business you purchase new or secondhand scaffolding, design a brochure and price list, and distribute the brochure to local home service companies and contractors in your community. Providing a free delivery and pickup service for scaffold rentals will get the telephone ringing and scaffold rental orders coming in.

START-UP COSTS: The investment needed to get the business rolling is very reasonable; $10,000 will suffice initially until the scaffold rental inventory can be expanded from the profits earned. A secondhand truck, van, or utility trailer can be used for deliveries, or the delivery aspect of the business can be contracted to a local transportation firm.

PROFIT POTENTIAL: A small scaffold rental service can achieve profits in excess of $20,000 per year, and additional revenue can be generated by installing and dismantling scaffolding for larger rental contracts.

BOUNCY HOUSE RENTALS
★★ $$$ 📷 🕐 🌐

The focus of this new business opportunity is the rental of portable, inflatable, carnival-style bouncy houses for children's birthday parties and community charity events. In addition to renting bouncy houses, this business start-up can also include operating the bouncy houses in tourist or high-traffic community gathering places, and charging parents a $3 or $4 fee for their kids to spend ten minutes inside bouncing around with their friends.

START-UP COSTS: New bouncy houses retail for about $10,000. However, a good quality secondhand bouncy house can be purchased for approximately half of that amount. Additionally, you will need a truck or trailer to transport the bouncy house to the rental site. In total, this entertaining rental business can be started for less than $15,000.

PROFIT POTENTIAL: Renting without the assistance of an operator, the bouncy house was available for $250 per day plus a delivery and setup charge of $75. The cost to rent the bouncy house with an operator was an additional $25 per hour. Based on the total investment to launch this rental enterprise, one could expect a very quick return on investment given the extremely lucrative rental rates.

WEB RESOURCE: www.800jumping.com Manufacturers of inflatable amusement products.

FARMLAND

★ $$+

The basis of this rental business is maybe not as the name indicates. The idea is to rent or lease farmland that is not being used by its owner. Divide the land into smaller pieces and rent it to people who would like to have their own vegetable garden, but cannot due the lack of space or because they are residing in an apartment. This unique rental business can be potentially very profitable, providing the business is operated close to a densely populated urban center where the majority of potential sublessors clients will come from.

START-UP COSTS: Start-up costs will greatly vary depending on factors, such as the amount of farmland leased and the availability of water on site. The initial investment could be very costly if well water or another water source has to be established.

PROFIT POTENTIAL: Assuming you paid $1,000 per season for the vacant farmland and you were able to divide the land into 100 subparcels that rented for $150 each for the season, you would be left with gross business revenue of $14,000.

ONLINE MOVIE SET LOCATIONS

★★★ $$$$

Like movie and TV prop rentals, renting movie film set locations is ideally suited as an Internet venture via your own specially designed Web site. Location scouts scour the countryside in search of the perfect spot to film movies, music videos, TV productions, and commercials. Starting a movie set location rental business will make you a cyberscout. Once again, the concept is basic. You establish a Web site with various categories for filming locations. These categories could include factories, vacant land, unique houses, and office buildings. The building and landowners of these various locations could supply you with still pictures or video footage of their locations, which can be posted into the various categories on the Web site. Location scouts, directors, and producers would simply log onto the "locate a location" Web site and click their way through the categories that were of interest to them for film production projects.

START-UP COSTS: Establishing a start-up cost for this type of business is difficult, as there is not a lot of competition to use as a yardstick. However, the business does not require a lot of equipment or special software programs to be designed, and the Web site could likely be developed on an initial investment in the range of $30,000 to $40,000.

PROFIT POTENTIAL: There are two billing methods that could be utilized in this business venture. The first would be to charge building and landowners a flat fee for posting their location pictures and information on the Web site. The second option would be to agree upon a split of the location fee from the production company to the landowner.

ONLINE PARKING SPACE BROKER

★★ $$$$

So you live in a densely populated urban center where trying to rent a parking space for an automobile is near impossible? Then becoming a parking space broker may be just the new business opportunity that you have been searching for. Working as a parking space rental broker has the potential to be very profitable business, not to mention the fact that you can operate right from home. Once again, this unique rental venture is ideal for an online enterprise via your own specialized Web site. Owners or lessors of the parking spots who wished to rent their parking spot could simply post a notice on the Web site. People who are looking for a parking spot would simply visit the parking Web site to check availability. This type of operating format for this cyberenterprise would enable you to cover every major city in the world, if you were so inclined. The total start-up cost to launch this kind of online venture would be in the range of $25,000 to $50,000.

PLANT RENTALS

★★ $

Money can grow on trees. Just ask any business owner in the plant rental industry. Renting plants is a pretty uncomplicated rental business. You can operate right from home on a full- or part-time basis, and the delivery and pickup of the plants only requires basic transportation like a small economy car. The target market for plant rentals are trade show planners, wedding planners, seminars, product demonstrations firms, professional offices, TV and movie production sets, entertainment events, political functions, and every other business or event that requires a professional and appealing appearance on a short-term or long-term basis.

START-UP COSTS: A modest investment of a $1,000 or less can get you rolling in your own plant rental business.

PROFIT POTENTIAL: The operating overhead for a plant rental business amounts to the cost of delivery transportation and the occasional plant casualty. The revenue the business generates is basically 100 percent profit. Additional sources of income can be earned by adding a plant care or plant maintenance program service to the plant rental business.

TANNING EQUIPMENT
★★ $$

People love to have a nice tan. Unfortunately, medical studies have proven beyond any doubt that exposure to the sun's harmful rays can cause a whole host of skin-related ailments. That's what makes starting your own business renting in-home tanning equipment such a logical business start-up venture.

MARKETING TIP: This may sound crazy, but working with travel agents to help rent the tanning beds for in-home use is a fantastic way to set this business in motion. The most frequent visitors to tanning salons are people who will be going on holidays to a sunny destination in the near future. The idea is to get a base tan prior to leaving on vacation. Building these alliances with travel agents makes a lot of sense because they know exactly who is going on vacation and when.

START-UP COSTS: Secondhand tanning beds in great condition can be purchased for as little as $1,500 each. An initial investment of $10,000 can get this business underway and working for you.

PROFIT POTENTIAL: Tanning beds can be rented for as much as $200 per week to people seeking the perfect tan. Assuming your rental business had four tanning beds each working just 25 weeks per year would create business revenues of $20,000 per year. To increase sales, add other rental products like portable hot tub and pool tables. Adding these items can enable you to create "packaged fun rentals" by the week or month that could include multiple rental items and be offered to clients as a discount package rental rate.

WEB RESOURCE: www.alwaystan.com Distributors of tanning beds and supplies.

SNOWMOBILE RENTALS
★ $$$

Snowmobile riding is an extremely popular outdoor wintertime activity that is enjoyed by millions of people in North America. A snowmobile rental business is unique and specialized and requires a sound business and action plan put in place prior to activating the business. One absolute must is liability insurance, due to the nature of the activity.

START-UP COSTS: Starting a business that rents snowmobiles on a seasonal basis can be very costly, as new high-powered snowmobiles can cost as much as $10,000. However, if you are mechanically inclined and have the ability to repair and maintain snowmobiles, you can minimize start-up costs by purchasing good-quality secondhand equipment. Generally, late-model secondhand snowmobiles sell for about half of the cost of a similarly equipped new one. Current snowmobile rental rates are in the range of $30 per hour, and $150 to $200 per day.

APARTMENT LAUNDRY EQUIPMENT
★ $$

Many apartment and condominium buildings are constructed without laundry facilities within the residential units. Most of these buildings have a shared or common laundry room that is generally used by all the tenants of the building. You can start your own business that not only installs and services rental laundry equipment, but also retains a portion of the rental revenues. To launch this type of enterprise you will have to build alliances with landlords and property management firms. Laundry room equipment contracts are often tendered to contractors every few years. Starting now to prepare your business will enable you to not only tender for these very lucrative contracts, it will also allow you to establish your business immediately upon being awarded a contract.

START-UP COSTS: Coin-operated laundry equipment retails for about two to three times the amount of residential laundry equipment. A typical laundry room with three washers and dryers will cost in the neighborhood of $8,000 to $10,000 to outfit properly.

PROFIT POTENTIAL: Profit potential will greatly depend on the number of people residing in the building. However, the industry average is $500 per laundry machine per residential unit per year.

PORTABLE SAWMILLS
★ $$$ 🏠 🕓

Operating a portable sawmill rental business can potentially earn you two sources of income. The first source can be derived by simply renting portable sawmill equipment to customers. Renting the sawmill equipment as well as supplying an operator, you or an employee, to operate the equipment for the customer can earn the second source of income. There are a surprisingly large amount of situations that require a portable sawmill to be used for sawing lumber on site, including creating new dimensions from salvaged lumber, log home building, and clearing fallen trees for property owners and insurance companies.

START-UP COSTS: Portable sawmills retail for $10,000 to $20,000, and are generally situated on a flat bed trailer for easy transportation.

PROFIT POTENTIAL: Portable sawmills without an operator rents for $200 to $300 per day. With an operator the sawmills can be rented for as much as $500 per day.

WEB RESOURCE: www.sawmill-exchange.com Directory featuring portable sawmills for sale and related information.

GO-CARTS
★ $$$$ ⚖️

At one time go-cart tracks were all the rage for fun and entertainment for kids and adults alike. Starting your own go-cart track may just put you ahead of future competitors. The business does require a fixed location or track to operate. However, with some clever planning and negotiations, you may be able to secure an operating location that can be partnered with an existing amusement or family entertainment business. Partnerships like this often work well, as each independent business works as a drawing card for the other, not to mention reducing overheads by nonduplication of operating requirements and expenses.

START-UP COSTS: As an independent business venture, a go-cart track could easily require an investment in the range of $250,000 (with leased land) to get rolling. However, as a joint venture with an existing entertainment or amusement type business, the business could be started for less than half of that amount.

PROFIT POTENTIAL: Go-carts are rented in two ways. The first is where the rider pays a fixed amount of money for a certain number of laps around the track. The second method is when the rider pays a fixed amount of money based on the time they are on the go-cart track. In spite of this being an expensive business to start, a popular and well-established go-cart track can produce sizable profits for the business owner that can easily surpass $100,000 per year.

PORTABLE DRESSING ROOMS
★★ $$$$ 🕓

Do you live in or around New York, Los Angeles, Toronto, or Vancouver? If so, then starting a business that rents portable dressing rooms to the film industry could put you on the road to financial freedom. The movie and TV production industry is booming, and operating a portable dressing room rental business can make you a financial star. Eighty percent of all movies, music videos, TV programs, and commercials are shot in or around the above-mentioned cities, and a lot of these film productions require portable dressing rooms for the cast, crew, and directors. Establishing this kind of rental business requires you to have a good contact base in the film industry. Portable dressing room trailers can be very expensive to purchase or build. However, the rental rates are very lucrative, especially once you have established a solid repeat clientele base. Portable dressing rooms can also be rented to businesses and organizations outside the film industry including, outdoor theater productions, and circus and carnival companies. Investment range $50,000 plus. Profit potential of $100,000 per year is attainable in this business.

OUTDOOR BEACH LOCKERS

There has always been one drawback to sunbathing at the beach. Where do you put your car keys when your bathing suit does not have any pockets? Even worse, you have spent the morning shopping and now you want to go for a swim. The only problem is if you leave your new purchases laying around there is no doubt that someone will walk off with them. Outdoor-secured storage lockers can be an amazingly profitable rental business to start. The locations these portable storage lockers can be installed are endless and include beaches, public markets, parks, arenas, fitness centers, trade shows, and sports playing fields, just to mention a few.

START-UP COSTS: This is definitely not a cheap business to start in terms of capital requirements. You can purchase prebuilt storage lockers like the ones at airports. Or, you can design your own lockers to better suit the areas you will be installing the lockers at. One idea may be to have number pads installed on each individual locker that would enable the user to punch in their own entry code upon depositing the coins. This method of locker access would be great, as it does not require the user to carry, and possibly lose, the locker key. Investment range is $20,000+.

PROFIT POTENTIAL: Assume each locker stand has 30 separate lockers that are used twice a day at a cost of $2. Each locker stand could generate $120 per day. Now, if you had only three of these portable storage locker units in place, your business revenue could be

as much as $130,000 annually. Additional considerations may be to arrange a revenue split with the various locations where the storage lockers can be installed. Splitting revenues will cost you money in terms of the bottom line. However, it may be a method that you can use to secure the best possible installation location for the storage lockers.

WEB RESOURCE: www.americanlocker.com Distributors of multipurpose security lockers.

NOTES

86
RETAIL
Businesses You Can Start

BEER COMPANY NOVELTIES
★★ $  🕐

Are you searching for a unique retail business that can be operated from home on a part-time basis? If so, perhaps starting a business that buys and sells beer company novelties will be of particular interest to you. There is an absolutely gigantic market for collectable beer company novelties such as signs, posters, games, coasters, and specialty beer bottles. Scouting garage sales, flea markets, and newspaper classified ads can be the starting point of acquiring beer company novelty items that can be resold to collectors at enormous profits. Finding buyers for the collectibles can be as easy as posting free classified ads on various Internet newsgroups sites, as well as listing the beer company novelties for sale on the numerous online auction Web sites. It is possible to create a part-time income of $25,000 per year buying and selling collectable beer company novelties, providing a 100 percent markup is maintained on all items purchased and resold and yearly sales of $50,000 are achieved.

USED TELEPHONE EQUIPMENT
★★★ $$ 🕐

Buying used telephone equipment and selling it at a profit to new and existing companies is a terrific business venture to initiate, especially if you have experience in the telecommunications industry. Anyone who has ever purchased specialized telephone equipment for a business certainly realizes that this equipment can be extremely costly to purchase and have installed. The basic concept for starting this type of business is very simple. Used telephone equipment is purchased from companies that are closing or upgrading their telephone systems for new equipment. The same telephone equipment that was purchased is marketed and sold to new companies that are opening or existing companies seeking to expand or upgrade their telecommunications systems. Providing clients with a telephone equipment installation service can earn additional revenue. The installation aspect of the business can be subcontracted to a qualified installer working on a profit-share or profit-split basis.

ONLINE E-MALLS

★★ $$$

An online e-mall is a great cyberventure to develop and market. Online e-malls are simply a collection of retailers grouped together into one Web site. What makes this such a terrific business venture to activate is the fact that many small homebased or "bricks and mortar" retailers simply do not have the capital required to develop and maintain their own Web site. You can come to the rescue and earn substantial profits by simply creating an online e-mall site and develop an interesting template for the home page that can feature participating retailers' logos. Visitors to the site would simply click onto a retailer (logo) that interests them and be linked to a pop-up page that describes the merchant's product. Additionally, you can add a shopping cart program and online payment options so that the merchants featured can take product orders right from the site. Income is earned by charging merchants a monthly fee to be included in the online mall or by retaining a small percentage of the sales the site generates. Additionally, consider making your online mall a specialty mall and group together retailers of similar and unique products as a method to differentiate yourself from other online e-malls.

COOKWARE PARTIES

★ $

Hosting home parties that feature cookware and other types of kitchen products for sale is a terrific low-cost homebased business venture to set in motion. There are literally thousands of manufacturers in the United States that market their products on this type of basis, and finding one is as easy

as researching the subject on the Internet. Typically, you can purchase the cookware items for wholesale cost and resell the same items retail at "home cookware parties" at a 100 percent markup or more. In addition to hosting the cookware parties, you can also build a team of cookware party hosts and keep a percentage of the total sales that are generated.

WEB RESOURCE: www.cookware.org The Cookware Manufacturers Association.

RESTAURANT AND HOTEL SUPPLIES

★ $$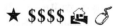

The hotel and restaurant supply industry is enormous and generates billions of dollars in sales of products such as linen, tableware, and paper products each year. Starting a business that sells restaurant and hotel supplies is a very straightforward business venture to set in motion. To get rolling, simply negotiate a distribution contract with manufacturers of these products and begin to establish accounts with hotels and restaurants to supply them. Initially, the business can be operated on a part-time basis from home until enough accounts have been established and proven profitable to expand the business. Remember, this is a very competitive industry and as a small player do not attempt to win business on price only. Establish value-added services to win business such as free delivery, unique products, and exceptional service.

ONLINE CYBERAUCTIONS

★ $$$$

Art, cars, travel packages, or just about anything can be sold by way of an online auction service. Developing your own online auction site has the potential to make you rich. Securing products to be featured in an online auction sale is easy, simply due to the fact that there is no upfront cost to the vendor to list a product or service for auction. Fees are only paid and collected upon the successful sale of the item being auctioned. Online auctions are very competitive and you will have to initiate a very savvy marketing and promotion campaign in terms of attracting visitors to the site to bid on items for sale. Once again, specialization is the key to success. Seek-out a product or service that is not currently being auctioned online, perhaps even dinner dates with eligible bachelors to raise money for charities. The options for an online auction service are limited only by your imagination.

PAWNBROKER
★★ $$$$

Pawnbrokers sometimes get a bad rap, and unfortunately it only takes a few bad apples dealing in stolen merchandise to give the industry a bad name for all operators of pawnshops. However, like any business venture, eventually the bad business operators will disappear and the good operators will flourish. Starting a pawnshop business is a good choice as a business start-up for a few reasons, such as no special business skill requirements, relatively low initial investment, and excellent profit potential. Furthermore, utilizing used product pricing or value guides such as the *Blue Book* take away any guesswork in terms of the wholesale and retail value of products. The key to success for operating and profiting from a pawnbroker business is to keep all transactions legal, establish the business in the right location, deal only in up-to-date merchandise that has real value, and always practice good negotiation skills.

WEB RESOURCE: www.brainerd.net/~ihii/npai.html National Pawnbrokers Association.

USED JEWELRY SALES
★★ $ 🏠 🕒

Purchasing secondhand jewelry and reselling the jewelry for a profit can be a lucrative business. Getting started in this type of retail or resale business is easy. Simply purchase secondhand jewelry from newspaper classified ads that appears to be distress sales. The jewelry can then be resold to individuals that are seeking a particular piece of jewelry such as wedding bands, engagement rings, or for any special occasion as a gift. The one main requirement to make this business work is to have

experience in jewelry in terms of value, quality, condition, and overall industry expertise. Maintaining yearly sales of $150,000 and a 100 percent profit margin will result in pretax and expenses earnings of $75,000 per year.

SUNGLASS VENDING
★★ $$$ 🕒 🌐

Selling sunglasses is a very inexpensive business start-up to get rolling, and the profits that can be earned are excellent. Establishing the business can be as simple as purchasing an initial inventory and selling the sunglasses right from a kiosk set up in a mall, at a beach, or at a busy weekend flea market. There are thousands of manufacturers of sunglasses worldwide, so there should be no problem finding a source for good quality and inexpensive sunglasses. Providing the right sales kiosk can be designed and that the right wholesale-to-retail pricing formula can be established, this simple little retailing venture is a good candidate to expand on a franchise basis and sell franchises to qualified owners-operators nationally in every region of the country. Seek licensing rights to popular people, products, or themes that can help in the marketing of the sunglasses. A pair of sunglasses that feature the name of a popular celebrity printed right on the glasses will sell better and for more money than the same sunglasses without the name or an endorsement.

WEB RESOURCE: www.dezinerwholesale.com Distributor of wholesale sunglasses to the retail trade.

WATCH KIOSK
★★ $$$ 🕒

Retailing wristwatches from a specially-designed sales kiosk is a fabulous low-investment business venture that anyone can own and operate. There are no special skills required to turn this business opportunity into a successful and profitable business enterprise. Watches remain one of the most popular gifts that are given on any number of occasions, such as Christmas, birthdays, graduations, anniversaries, or just for a job well done. Watches can be purchased on a wholesale basis for just a few dollars, and marked up 300 to 600 percent for retail sales. Ideally, the kiosk used for selling the watches should be located in a high-traffic area, such as a mall, busy flea market, tradeshow, or public event. The kiosk can be used on a part-time basis and assembled for special events and holidays. If the kiosk has the right location it can certainly be operated on a full-time basis year round. Once this type of unique retailing business has been established and proven profitable, it can be the perfect business model for franchising purposes or expansion by way of multiple corporate locations.

WEB RESOURCE: www.wwwin.net Directory of wholesalers and distributors of consumer goods.

GIFT BASKETS

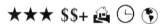 ★★★ $$+ 🖼️ 🕐 🌐

Gift baskets are extremely easy to assemble. Simply select items such as specialty foods, flowers, or personal health products and arrange them in an attractive wicker basket, and the gift basket is complete. The real secret to success in owning and operating a gift basket service is not in the gift baskets, but in the marketing and sales of them. The following are some suggestions on how to market gift baskets.

- Concentrate your marketing efforts on gaining repeat corporate clients, professionals, small business owners, and sales professionals such as Realtors. Hospitals can also become a good client.
- Provide clients with only three pricing options. The first being a nice but economically-priced gift basket in the price range of $30 to $40, the second being a more elaborate gift basket still modestly-priced in the range of $50 to $60. And the third option would be very elaborate and retail in the range of $100+.
- Design and create samples of the three gift basket options. Once completed take pictures of the gift baskets and create a marketing brochure that fully details your business and provides a full description of the gift baskets. The marketing brochure should be in color and printed on high-gloss paper. Furthermore, the

brochure should clearly state "keep in a handy spot, for you never know when you will need to send a gift basket." The desired objective is for the recipient of the brochure not to dispose of the brochure.

- Once the brochure is complete, begin a direct-mail campaign as well as a hand delivery campaign for the marketing brochures. Once again, the marketing should be targeted at businesses, professionals, and salespeople, as these are the most likely candidates to become regular and repeat clients for the business. In addition to the direct-mail campaign, also begin an e-mail broadcast campaign using the same marketing brochure. There are hundreds of companies that specialize in e-mail broadcasting and this type of direct marketing is extremely effective and affordable. The e-mails should be sent on a regular monthly basis until the business is established and generating positive cash flow.
- Provide clients with free local delivery of the gift baskets. Be sure to arrange delivery for gift baskets that are being sent outside the local area. The key is service. Make this a pleasant shopping experience and the clients will become regular customers.

Maintaining a 100 percent markup on the gift baskets sold and achieving $150,000 per year in sales can generate a pretax profit of $75,000 per year for this terrific homebased business opportunity.

WEB RESOURCE: www.smallbizbooks.com Business specific start-up guides and books.

ONLINE GIFT BASKETS

★★ $$$ 🖼️ 🖱️

Here is a simple idea for an online business venture that could prove to be very profitable. Create a Web site that features gift baskets for sale aimed mainly at the corporate market. Keep the site basic and provide perhaps only ten or so preassembled gift basket options. Additionally, try to cover all price ranges, meaning have a basic gift basket at $25 dollars and increase from there in increments of $10. Prices shown for the gift baskets should be all-inclusive including delivery and handling charges. Visitors would simply select the gift basket they wish to purchase, enter payment information, and type in who the basket is for, when they prefer delivery and delivery instruction. The site can be marketed and promoted by initiating a direct mail and e-mail campaign aimed at corporations, event planners, and real estate agents, as often these individuals and companies send gift baskets to clients and business associates. The gift baskets can be warehoused in one central location and courier companies can be contracted for delivery purposes.

AIRBRUSHED HELMETS
★★★ $$$$ 🕐 🌐

I was introduced to this very unique business venture a few years back while on vacation. A very innovative entrepreneur had set up a retail storefront location in a busy beach area that specialized in selling and airbrushing colorful images on helmets used in a variety of sporting and recreational activities. The way the business operated was pure genius. The shop was bright, colorful, and well located. Airbrushing the helmets on site while the customer waited always guaranteed a large crowd of onlookers. The shop sold prepainted helmets as well as painting a customer's helmet while they waited. The helmets they sold included baseball helmets, hockey helmets, bicycle helmets, football helmets, motorcycle helmets, and snowmobile helmets for the vacationing snowbirds. In the two hours that I was there, the shop sold or airbrushed a total of 28 helmets with three artists working. Each helmet took approximately 10 to 15 minutes to complete, and the shop boasted a one-price policy for the artwork of $30 (plus the cost of the helmet). The shop featured binders with pictures and images that clients could choose from for artwork, or customers could provide their own art and supply the artist with a photograph, rough drawing, or even just an idea of what they wanted airbrushed on their helmet. I spoke to the owner who, by the way, was not an artist himself. All the artists were subcontract employees who were paid commissions based on the total number of sales they generated. He told me that in the three years that he had been open, his shop had sold more than 8,000 helmets and painted more than 25,000 images on everything from helmets to beach clothing to motorcycle gas tanks. That is absolutely amazing when you consider this was a seasonal business open only four months a year. Assuming each helmet only sold for $25, the business would have then generated total sales of one million dollars over that three-year period, or more precisely $80,000 for each month that the business was open. The main requirement for starting a business that airbrushes helmets is obvious. You have to have artistic ability or employees in place with the artistic ability to paint the pictures and images. Additionally, the business must be located or operated in a very busy tourist area, or an area with enough local interest to generate sufficient sales.

WEB RESOURCE: www.airheadairbrush.com Distributor of airbrushing equipment and supplies.

CHARITY USED-GOODS STORE
★★ $$$$ ⚖

I'll bet that a lot of you reading this book did not realize that many charity stores that feature secondhand clothing and household goods for sale are really private enterprises operated for a profit. That is right. The same stores that many of us drop off donations of used clothing and furniture to are businesses that are privately-run enterprises. Only a percentage of the total sales that are generated go back to the charity that the business operates under or in association with. This is a good joint venture program, as charities are not businesses and should not have to lose the focus of their intended purpose, while entrepreneurs are better equipped to finance and operate a business with an aim to generate a profit. This scenario also reduces potential financial risk for the charity. To get a charity store up and operating, the first step is to establish an alliance or a joint venture program with a recognized charity, preferably one that serves the community where the business will be located. The second step is to establish a good operating retail location for the business. Thus, when selecting the business location keep in mind who will be purchasing the second-hand goods. Obviously, the business or charity is not best served by locating the store in an area where household incomes average $50,000. Seek to locate the store in an area of the community where a large percentage of the population has good reason for shopping at the secondhand store. The third step is to have an initial charity drive in order to collect as many donations of secondhand goods as possible. The key to a successful drive is to make the donation process as easy as possible for the donors. You will want to establish free household pickup of the items that will be donated. The fourth step is to make sure that the store's inventory changes on a regular basis to keep shoppers interested. This can be accomplished with a couple of methods. The first is to have two stores operating in different areas of a city. This will enable you to move inventory back and forth to where the merchandise sells best. The second option is to build an alliance with an existing charity store and swap inventory on a frequent basis. Lastly, the final step in establishing a successful charity store that sells secondhand goods is to ensure that all merchandise is in good condition and that the inventory has been cleaned prior to placing the items for sale.

ONLINE UNIVERSITY BOOKS

★ $$$ 🏠 👌

New textbooks and course guides are very expensive, especially for students who are struggling to survive on tight education and living budgets. This fact can be the basis of a terrific new online business venture, a Web site that features secondhand textbooks for sale or trade. This type of Web site should be free of charge for anyone to use. Students could post notices or classified ads seeking to buy, sell, or trade university and college textbooks. You can promote the site by posting notices online in university and college newsgroups and chat line forums. To create revenues and profits for the business, seek to feature and sell products via the site that would be of interest to students such as concert tickets and clothing.

Additionally, merchants and service providers that want exposure to these types of consumers would also be happy to pay advertising fees to be featured in some fashion on the Web site.

SILK FLOWERS

★ $$ 🕐

Starting a business that wholesales silk flowers to retail specialty stores is a fantastic homebased business enterprise to set in motion. One of the best aspects about starting this type of business venture is that it enables you to work as the middleperson or agent. Simply source people that make silk flowers and agree to sell their products on a wholesale basis to retailers. Amazingly enough, maintaining yearly sales of $100,000 and a markup of 50 percent will generate a pretax and operating expense income of $33,000 per year. This is excellent for a part-time homebased business that can be established with an initial investment of less than $5,000. The silk flowers can also be sold directly to consumers by establishing a sales kiosk that can be setup at malls and flea markets on weekends.

INVENTORY LIQUIDATION

★★ $$$$

Every year thousands of retail merchants and corporations across North America go out of business, move, reform, and amalgamate, and often this results in billions of dollars worth of stock and inventory becoming available at bargain basement prices. Purchased right and this same inventory can sometimes be bought for as little as five cents on the dollar. Later this can often be resold for as much as five times the purchase price on a wholesale basis, and as much as ten times on a direct-to-consumers retail basis. A good starting point for purchasing bargain inventory (at least until the business builds a reputation and contact base as a liquidator) is to establish alliances with trustees that deal in commercial bankruptcies. Generally the trustee appointed will either arrange to auction off the inventory assets of clients, put out a tender, or offer to purchase the inventory, which usually goes to the highest bidder on a cash basis. Reselling the inventory can be accomplished in a few ways including selling the inventory to retailers on a wholesale basis or selling the inventory in smaller quantities to other inventory liquidators. On a direct-to-consumer retailing basis, the inventory can be sold through a company-owned liquidation store or stores, or monthly inventory liquidation sales can be advertised and held over a few days in short-term rental premises. However, there is a down side to this business, which is purchasing inventory that is difficult to sell regardless of price. This is a very common mistake for first timers in this industry. Traditionally, the best type of products to purchase under inventory liquidation conditions are power and hand tools, nonperishable food items, books, music CDs, toys, building materials, and electronics. Always stay clear of products that have a limited shelf life, or that have special warehousing and transportation requirements. Once again, this is the type of business where the ability to profit will greatly depend on a number of factors such as sales volumes, markups, and product costs. Having personally dabbled in this industry in the past, I can assure you that it is possible to make $10,000 per month or more, providing a carefully planned and well-researched approach to the business is executed.

ONLINE INVENTORY LIQUIDATION SALES
★★ $$$$ 🏠 🖊

This online concept is very straightforward. Simply develop a Web site that can be utilized by inventory liquidation brokers to promote and list their products for sale. The site can be indexed by type of product for sale as well as by geographic location. This type of site would be a popular resource for merchants seeking to purchase discounted inventory for resale, as well as everyday consumers looking for bargains on various products. Across North America there are thousands of inventory liquidation brokers and companies that deal mainly in the resale and distribution of liquidated inventory. Thus securing a few hundred brokers paying a small monthly fee to be featured on the Web site should not prove to be a difficult task.

DOLLAR DISCOUNT STORE
★★ $$$$ 🌐

Dollar or discount stores are popping up everywhere across North America, and that can only mean one of two things. Competition is too heavy and there will soon be a thinning process, or dollar storeowners are making money and expanding into new geographic areas of the country to capitalize on consumer demand. Given the popularity of dollar stores, and the fact that these stores require careful planning and a large start-up investment, my money is on number two. Competition is stiff, but there seems to be unlimited consumer demand for bargains and discount retail stores. The main objective in the discount retailing industry is two-fold, the first is to source and establish alliances with manufacturers of low-cost products, and the second is that the products have to be of reasonable quality and have a useful purpose. The best products to sell via discount stores fit the following profile:

- Inexpensive, retailing for less than $5.
- Kitchen products, toys, and household products.
- Less-expensive versions of popular name brand product.

JANITORIAL SUPPLIES
★★ $$$ 🏠 🕐

Every year companies, government agencies, organizations, educational institutions, and associations spend billions of dollars on janitorial and sanitation supplies such as cleaners, paper products, disposal bags, and janitorial equipment. Starting a janitorial supply business to secure a piece of this very big and financially lucrative pie is not difficult to do. Like many wholesale or middleperson businesses, the key to success is to get out and talk to potential customers. This is a competitive industry and waiting for business to come to you is simply waiting to go out of business. Deal with more than one manufacturer in order to negotiate and secure good pricing. Traditionally, profit margins in the industry are tight and usually products are sold for no more than 10 to 20 percent over costs, so it is critical to build high volume repeat customer accounts.

WEB RESOURCE: www.issa.com International Sanitary Supply Association.

WICKER AND RATTAN SHOP
★ $$$

Wicker and rattan products have always been popular for use as indoor and outdoor furniture, as well as home decoration items due to their low cost, unique appeal, and ability to last a long time. Starting a wicker and rattan retail business is extremely simple. The first step to establishing the business is to decide on the operating format: a retail store, a cyberstore, or a mobile sales kiosk. The next step is to locate a good manufacturing source for the wholesale products. This is best accomplished by utilizing the Internet or directories to find manufacturers of wicker and rattan products. When you open for business, practice good business judgment and marketing skills.

WEB RESOURCE: http://wsmag.com *Wholesale Source* magazine online, directory service listing manufacturers, distributors, and wholesalers of consumer products.

NOSTALGIA STORE
★★★ $$$

Everything old is new again, especially collectibles and novelties from the 1940s, '50s, and '60s.

Opening a nostalgia store is a great retail business enterprise to set in motion. The profit potential is excellent, consumer demand is proven and growing, and the business can be started on a relatively modest investment of less than $20,000. Once again, starting a retail business does not limit you to only a "bricks and mortar" operating format. The nostalgia products can also be retailed or sold on the Web, a sales kiosk or booth, by mail order, or a combination of all of these marketing or retailing methods. As with many business ventures, success lies within the ability to attract customer's attention, not within the method of distribution or sales. Overall, starting a business retailing nostalgia items is a great new business enterprise, and some items depending on their rarity can be sold at tremendous profit markups.

ONLINE HOW-TO BOOKS AND TAPES
★★ $$$

How-to books and tapes have traditionally been excellent products to retail by way of mail order, sales kiosks, and POP displays, and probably will remain excellent products to retail for many years to come, especially when you consider that increased technological gains will result in increased questions from consumers and users of these products. Moving forward into the new millennium requires careful planning and research in the retail sector due to the advent and popularity of the Internet. However, for every traditional product, service, or business that the Internet disables, it creates ten new business opportunities or breathes life into old and proven business opportunities, and retailing how-to books and tapes is an excellent example of this. In terms of the types of how-to books and tapes that are now or will remain popular sellers, these include information or instruction about how to use, understand, and benefit from the Internet, software, and technology in general.

NEWSSTAND
★★ $$$$ 🌐

In spite of the popularity of Internet newsgroups and news Web sites, the good old-fashioned corner newsstand is here to stay. In fact, the arrival of the Internet has only increased the public's desire for information—electronic or print. Starting a newsstand retail business requires getting in touch with one of the many distributors that carry just about every kind of magazine, publication, and newspaper you can imagine, and so building alliances with hundreds of publishers is not required. Additionally, most distributors of publications in every form have a buy-back policy, meaning that once the publication is out of date it is returned and there is no charge levied for it. The key to a successful and profitable newsstand business is diversification; the business should also provide customers with product selections such as lottery tickets, cigars, and snack items.

WHOLESALER
★★ $$$$

A wholesaler is the link between a manufacturer or producer of a product or service and the retailer or reseller of the product or service. There are many different types of products and services that can be sold on a wholesale basis including food items, computers and software, telecommunications services, and even public utilities. Starting a wholesale business is somewhat more difficult than starting a traditional retailing business. Not only do you have to source companies to buy products and services from, you also have to source companies to sell the same products and services to. As competitive as the wholesaling business currently is, the future does look bright, especially when you consider home-based and cyberbased business start-ups are increasing at a record pace. Many of these new business enterprises lack the space required to get their products to market, which means they need the services of a wholesaler with distribution channels, warehousing space, and transportation capabilities.

WEB RESOURCE: www.awmanet.org American Wholesale Marketers Association.

ONLINE WHOLESALERS DIRECTORY
★★ $$$$

Many small merchants rely on wholesalers and distributors to purchase goods for resale simply due to the fact that they do not buy in large enough quantities to enable them to buy in bulk directly from manufacturers. For many small business owners the search for wholesalers and distributors of different products is a never-ending battle. Establishing an online wholesale and distributor directory is the perfect solution to this problem. Simply start by creating a Web site that is indexed for search purposes by product and geographic location. Once this has been completed, employ subcontract sales consultants to solicit wholesalers and distributors to become listing members on the directory Web site. Across North America there are thousands of independent wholesalers and distributors, thus

securing a few hundred to participate in this exciting and beneficial online service will be easy. Marketing and promotion of the site should be aimed at small business owners and merchants. This can be accomplished by acquiring retailers and business association mailing list and initiating a direct e-mail, mail, and telephone campaign.

FLAGS AND FLAG POLES
★ $$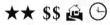

Are you looking for a homebased business opportunity in the retail sector that is interesting, has little in the way of competition, and has the potential to generate excellent revenues and profits? If so, why not consider starting a business the sells and installs flags and flag poles. The time has never been better than now to start this type of unique retail business. The American economy is healthy and with that comes a sense of country pride from every single citizen. What better way to show it than by flying the U.S. flag. Seek a manufacturer of the flags and flag poles, and begin to market. You may just be pleasantly surprised by the results.

WEB RESOURCE: www.flaginfo.com National Independent Flag Dealers Association.

BUMPER STICKERS
★★ $$

In spite of the fact that most new cars and trucks have plastic bumpers, bumper stickers remain very much a cultural icon. Taking the following five steps to establishing a bumper sticker wholesaling business can put you on the path to financial freedom and self-employment independence.

1. Hire an artist and design ten really great bumper stickers, or locate a manufacturer and choose ten bumper stickers from their collection.
2. Design a point-of-purchase (POP) display that is unique and colorful, and that can feature the ten bumper stickers and hold 20 of each (total 200 bumper stickers for each POP display).

3. Establish wholesale accounts with retailers to stock the POP in their stores in a visible area. At first some retailers may want to take the POP displays in on a consignment basis until the product is proven popular and profitable.

4. Service and maintain existing wholesale accounts and expand wholesale base to include additional retailers. Also seek to establish accounts with national multi-unit retailers.

5. Implement a company Web site that features thousands of different bumper stickers that visitors can customize and download for home printing on specialty print paper. (Charge $1 to $2 each for the bumper sticker electronic file transfers.)

PROFIT POTENTIAL: The profit potential for this type of unique business is outstanding once established. Bumper stickers can be printed in mass quantities for less than ten cents each, and retail for as much as $4 each.

ONLINE CELEBRITY AUTOGRAPHS AND PICTURES
★★ $$ 🏠 🕐 ✍

Celebrity autographs and autographed pictures are hot-selling commodities. Starting a part-time home-based business that buys celebrity autographs to resell to collectors and fans for a profit is a fantastic enterprise to set in motion that has real potential to make a lot of money. The key to success in this type of business venture is to buy authentic celebrity autographs at bargain basement prices. This can be achieved by using a little bit of ingenuity like posting advertisements on the Internet seeking celebrity autographs or by acting as a broker for celebrity autographs, where you simply bring the buyer and seller together and collect a commission for doing so. The options are unlimited for this kind of unique enterprise, as celebrity autographs are hot and can fetch top dollar.

LONG-LIFE LIGHT BULBS
★★★★ $$ 🏠 🕐

Do you want to potentially earn a six-figure yearly income from owning and operating your own homebased business? If so, consider starting a business that specializes in selling and installing long-life light bulbs for commercial and residential applications. Long-life light bulbs not only last as much as ten times longer than traditional light bulbs, but they also can consume less than half the energy requirements to run than a standard light bulb. That's good news considering the skyrocketing cost of electricity. These two facts make for a very interesting business opportunity. If you can show home and business owners that they can save utility costs by installing a light bulb that uses less energy and lasts longer than a standard light bulb, then this is the basis of the business and making money. There are many manufacturers of long-life light bulbs, so securing a wholesale source will not be difficult. The only tools required to install the light bulbs will be a couple of ladders and a few basic hand tools to remove light covers. Look to market the light bulbs to potential customers who have the most to gain in terms of cost savings. Good candidates will include retail chain stores, government agencies, school boards, residential strata corporations, property management firms, office buildings, and community and recreational centers.

WEB RESOURCE: www.buylighting.com Distributor of wholesale light bulbs.

SOLAR PRODUCTS
★★★ $$$$

More and more North Americans are starting to realize that we must take care of the environment and look for alternate ways to power our lifestyles. You can sell solar-powered products, such as lights and battery systems, as well as wind-powered generators and solar cell storage systems for big profits. Here are a few suggestions to increase business revenues:

- Hire a direct sales team to call on and solicit business from property developers and contractors for sales and installation of solar-powered products for their new housing developments and construction projects.
- Stock and sell solar-powered products that can be of value to all industries and markets, such

as solar chargers for batteries as used on pleasure boats.

- Design and build an elaborate display featuring solar-powered products, and use the display to promote the business and sell the products at trade shows, home and garden shows, and community events.
- Seek out manufacturers of solar-powered products and establish an exclusive sales and distribution contract for their products to be handled by your company. The products can then be sold to national retailers on a wholesale basis.
- Establish alliances with various government agencies that would be willing to provide consumers with product discounts for switching from electric to solar-powered household products. Of course, your business would be the supplier of the products for the energy conservation program.

WEB RESOURCE: www.seia.org Solar Energy Industries Association.

ONLINE SOLAR PRODUCT SALES
★★ $$$$ 🏠 🕐 🖱️

Solar products are a prime example of a specialty product that sells well via the Internet simply because many specialty consumer products are commonly not found for sale at "bricks and mortar" establishments in small cities and communities. Once again, the main requirement will be to establish a resale or distribution agreement with one or more manufacturers of solar-powered products. The rest is simple. Create and post your Web site on the Internet. Like many cyberventures, the key to success will lie within your ability to effectively market and promote the Web site in such a fashion that the end result is visitor hits and a lot of them. This can be accomplished in the following manner:

- Register the Web site with search engines using key search words.
- Hyperlink the site with sites related to the environment, alternate power sources, and sites focused on recycling topics.

- Rent banner advertising space or participate in a banner advertising exchange program.
- Place articles about the benefits of solar-powered products and promote the site in the numerous online newsgroup forums.
- Place advertisements in traditional print media that focuses on the environment and recycling.
- Acquire mailing lists of people and organizations interested in topics and subjects pertaining to the environment and recycling, and start a direct mail and e-mail campaign.
- List the site with online e-malls and community Web sites.

WEB RESOURCE: www.seia.org Solar Energy Industries Association.

VIDEO GAME STORE
★★ $$$$ 🌐

Video games are hot sellers, and the video game industry rakes in billions of dollars each year in sales. Capturing a portion of the video game sales market is very easy to do. Consider the following options for starting and operating a business that sells video games:

- Buy new video games from manufacturers and sell them at a profit by establishing a retail store or sales kiosk in a mall.
- Purchase used video games and resell directly to consumers by establishing a retail store or sales kiosk.
- Establish a Web site that sells new and used video games that are delivered by mail.
- Incorporate a combination of all of these video game retailing methods.

WEB RESOURCE: www.regalgames.com Distributor of video games to the retail trade.

ONLINE COMIC BOOK SALES
★★ $$ 🏠 🕐 🖱️

Are you looking to start an inexpensive retail business that can be operated from home with flexible hours and really has the potential to generate an excellent part-time income? If so, perhaps you should consider starting a business that buys and sells rare comic books via the Internet. There are a couple of approaches to establishing this type of online business venture. The first is to purchase the rare comic books that will be featured and resold on the Web site. The second approach is to develop the Web site so that anyone can post or list a comic book for sale, and when the comic book is sold you would collect a 10 to 20 percent commission on the selling price of the comic book. Both approaches have their pros and cons. However, there is a very limited downside to this kind of part-time retail business venture, and once established the business could easily generate a full-time income.

AWARD PLAQUES

★★ $$

Manufacturing and selling award plaques is a great homebased business opportunity that really has earning power. Every year across North America, thousands of award plaques are given to thousands of deserving recipients for a job well done, most valuable player, or in recognition of a special event. The business can easily be established from a homebased workshop, and the award plaques can be manufactured from any type of raw material in just about any style and size. Marketing the award plaques can be accomplished by a few different methods including creating a catalog with pictures, costs and descriptions of the plaques available and distributing the catalogs to large companies, sports associations, and school boards. Additionally, a unique approach to marketing the plaques would be to develop a Web site that features all the available designs, so that customers can order and customize the award plaques right online.

FLORIST SHOP

★★ $$$$ ✪

Next to diamonds, flowers are a girl's best friend, and starting a florist shop is a relatively easy business to get up and rolling. There are really three important issues to address in order for a florist shop to

become successful. The first is business location, and the location must be in a high-traffic and highly visible area to increase walk-in business. The second issue is delivery. The business must provide customers with a fast and efficient delivery service. The third important aspect of the business is national exposure. The business must join a florist association that promotes national delivery regardless of geographic location as some florist shops gain as much as 25 percent of their business from people who order flowers from outside the service area of the florist.

WEB RESOURCE: www.flowercource.net Directory service listing flower growers and distributors.

NEON SIGNS

★★★ $$ 🏠 🕐

The investment needed to start a business that manufactures neon signs could easily exceed $100,000. However, starting a business that designs and sells neon signs, while the manufacturing and installation aspect of the signs are contracted to an existing manufacturer, can be set in motion for less than $10,000, and the potential business profits can easily exceed $100,000 per year. Simply go out into your community and take pictures of businesses that are successful, but could definitely use improvement in terms of their business signage. Next, utilizing computer and design software, design a new neon sign for the business that really promotes the business and will become an attraction. Once the design is complete, build a presentation including the proposed new sign look and set a meeting with the owner of the business. You will be amazed at how the business progresses from that point on.

WEB RESOURCE: www.nassd.org The National Association of Sign Supply Distributors.

ICE SUPPLY

★★ $$$ 🏠 🕐

There are many good reasons to start an ice supply business. Consider some of the following:

- No government regulations or certifications required.
- Relatively low initial business start-up investment required with a fast return on your investment.
- Proven consumer demand and flexible business hours.
- Can be operated from a homebased location on a full- or part-time basis.
- No special business skills needed to run the business and excellent growth potential.
- The chance to earn a six-figure yearly income is very attainable.

Starting an ice supply business is a great choice for a new business venture that has limited downside and many benefits. Once the ice has been produced and packaged, there are many options available to market the product, including:

- Selling the ice via ice vending machines located throughout a community.
- Selling the ice to retailers such as gas stations, convenience stores, and food markets on a wholesale basis.
- Selling the ice directly to consumers by establishing the business in a busy beach tourist area.

WEB RESOURCE: www.machineice.com Distributor of ice making machinery and supplies.

COMMERCIAL DOORMATS
★ $$

Starting a business that designs and sells commercial doormats for promotional purposes is a fantastic business venture to set in motion. Simply design doormats for commercial business applications that have a real promotional message, such as welcome to . . . and thanks for shopping at . . . . The doormats can be manufactured from different types of materials and have many different types of messages. The profit potential is excellent for this type of unique business enterprise, and there is limited competition due to the fact that each doormat is custom designed for the client.

KNIFE KIOSK
★ $$$$ 🌐

Retailing products from a kiosk located in a mall, or even within a larger retail store is a terrific way to keep operating overheads to a minimum, thus increasing the profit potential of the business venture. A great product to sell from a kiosk-based location is a specialty knife. The kiosk can stock and sell all type of knives such as ones used in hunting and fishing, custom kitchen knives, wood carvers knives, and knives for collectors. Additionally, to increase revenues and profits you can also provide a knife and scissors sharpening service at the kiosk. Due to the unique nature of the product and business, product markups of 100 percent or more are not out of line and are not uncommon in this type of retailing. Once established and proven successful, a knife kiosk business would be a great candidate to expand nationwide on a franchise basis.

WEB RESOURCE: www.blueridgenives.com Distributor of wholesale knives to the retail trade.

CIGAR SALES
★★ $$+ ⚖

Across the United States millions of dollars' worth of cigars are sold monthly and some of these cigars sell for $250 or more each. Thus securing just a small portion of this very lucrative market has the potential to make you rich. Once you have secured a wholesale source for purchasing cigars, here are a few ways to retail them for a profit:

- Establish a small kiosk in a mall or market location for selling cigars.
- Employ direct sales teams remunerated by way of commission based on their sales.
- Initiate a direct-mail and e-mail campaign aimed at corporations to purchase the cigars to give to valued clients and business associates as gifts.
- Purchase vending machines and stock these machines with cigars for sale. The machine will have to be "minihumidors" and can be located in high-traffic gathering places such as restaurants and pubs.

ONLINE CIGAR SALES

★★ $$$

As mentioned earlier, millions of dollars' worth of cigars are sold every month in the United States and, in the spirit of being unique, perhaps you could develop a Web site that acted as a online portal to bring cigar manufacturers and distributors together with consumers that purchase cigars.

This type of online venture would be very easy to establish and charging cigar manufacturers and distributors a fee to be listed and featured on the site could generate income. Alternately, income could be earned by retaining a portion of the cigar sales that are created, and listed companies could be posted for free. To spice up the site and make it more interesting for visitors, you can also add a chat line forum focused on topics and subjects related to cigars, as well as an online poll that lets cigar smokers vote for the all-time best cigars.

SEASONAL GARDEN CENTER

★★ $$$

A seasonal garden center selling trees, shrubs, flowers, and topsoil can return as much as $30,000 in profits in only a three- or four-month operating season. A seasonal garden center is very easy to establish and set up. The main requirements in terms of equipment will be to purchase or rent portable fencing that can be installed around the perimeter of the garden center. A polyvinyl tent or dome may also have to be purchased or rented to act as shelter for the more delicate plants and as the retail outlet. The inventory can be purchased from various greenhouse suppliers on a wholesale basis, and generally the plants, flowers, and shrubs are marked up by at least 100 to 200 percent. The key to success for operating this type of seasonal retailing business is location. The garden center must be located in a visible location in a high-traffic area of the community. Excellent locations include mall parking lots, gas station lots, and grocery store parking lots.

WEB RESOURCE: www.flowersource.net Directory service listing growers and distributors of flowers and nursery products.

SUNTAN OIL

★★ $$$

Almost every single person in the United States uses suntan or sunscreen protection at some point during the course of a year. This fact creates a tremendous opportunity for the innovative entrepreneur to capitalize by starting a business that wholesales suntan and sunscreen under a private labeling agreement. There are hundreds of manufacturers of suntan oil in the United States and worldwide. Many of these manufacturers are more than happy to bottle their sunscreen in your packaging and under your product name. Private label packaging is very popular and has been commonly practiced by some of America's largest brand-name retailers for many years. The suntan oil and sunscreens can be sold to local and national retailers on a wholesale basis, as well as directly to consumers by establishing a sales kiosk set up at high-traffic areas such as malls and beach retail areas.

ROSES

★ $$

Roses can be purchased in bulk on a wholesale basis for as little as $10 per dozen, and can retail for as much as $5 each or $50 per dozen. Selling the roses is very easy to do. Simply hire individuals to work as street vendors selling roses on a revenue-split basis. Ideal locations for selling the roses include outside restaurants and movie theaters, bus and train stations, and inside pubs and nightclubs, providing permission can be obtained. Consider the following and you'll see why this can be such a profitable business venture to get rolling. You hire 25 street vendors that sell 50 roses each per day at $5 each thus creating gross business revenues of $6,250 per day. Assuming each vendor retains 50 percent of their sales ($125) and the wholesale cost of the roses are $1 each, this example will leave a gross business profit of $1,875 per day. Now that is a lot of profit from a business that is so easy and inexpensive to establish. Additionally, be sure to check into local vending laws in your community as they vary across the country.

WEB RESOURCE: www.flowersource.net Directory service listing growers and distributors of flowers.

SIGN KIOSK
★★ $$$$ 🌐

Signs are as much a part of the North American cultural fabric as cars. In fact there are probably more signs than cars in North America. A sign kiosk is simply this: a sale kiosk located in a mall or other high-traffic area that specializes in selling premade signs and producing custom signs for customers while they wait. Sign making is easy, as there is computer equipment and software applications available that produce excellent-quality vinyl signs in a matter of only minutes. The premade signs that can be featured and sold are house for sale, beware of dog, etc. Of course, the customer's requests and orders will determine custom-made signs. Furthermore, to increase business revenues and profits, the kiosk could also offer key cutting and engraving services to customers.

WEB RESOURCE: www.nassd.org National Association of Sign Supply Distributors.

LUGGAGE SHOP
★ $$$$

Starting a specialty retail business that sells travel luggage and bags, as well as purses, wallets, and briefcases is a fantastic business venture to start. Ideally, the business will be operated from a fixed location such as a storefront or a kiosk in a mall and provide customers with a wide range of travel luggage and bags. There are thousands of manufacturers of travel bags and luggage worldwide, so finding a wholesale product source will not be difficult. Additionally, be sure to establish a Web site that features the travel gear for online shoppers.

WEB RESOURCE: www.luggagedealers.com The American Luggage Dealers Association.

MULTILEVEL MARKETING
★ $+ 🏠 🕐

Most people reading this book have or will at some point get involved with a multilevel marketing

business opportunity, and some will make money and some will lose money. However, the vast majority will lose money. Why? There are many reasons, but without question the number one reason that people will lose money with a multilevel marketing opportunity is lack of planning. Multilevel marketing is no different from any other new business start-up regardless of the promotional hype, and when was the last time you saw a business plan created solely for the purposes of analyzing a multilevel marketing opportunity? I bet the answer is never. If a business plan were created to fully analyze the business and opportunity, it would show that 95 percent of multilevel marketing opportunities simply would not work, thus the creators of the business would not be able to get new people involved based on hype and profit excitement. With that said, I am certainly not suggesting that all multilevel marketing opportunities are bogus. I am simply stating the obvious: a multilevel marketing business opportunity is no different from starting any other business, and sound business judgment and practices must be applied in all aspects of the opportunity, from start to finish.

ONLINE MULTILEVEL MARKETING DIRECTORY
★ $$$$ 🏠 🖱

There are hundreds if not thousands of multilevel marketing (MLM) business opportunities available in this country at any given time. To survive and thrive, these MLM opportunities need new operators constantly. Thus, a potentially profitable business opportunity waits by creating an online portal that features MLM opportunities and MLM operators seeking to build a down line.

The site can be indexed by opportunity and geographic region and revenues would be earned by charging MLM companies a fee to have their opportunity and contact information included and featured on the site. For the truly innovative entrepreneur, the site itself could become a MLM opportunity with the product being Web page creation and monthly hosting. This type of online venture is certainly open to fresh and original ideas as one thing is for sure: MLM is huge and will be around for many years to come.

WEB RESOURCE: www.entrepreneur.com Create a business Web site with MySite professional Web site builder.

VACUUM CLEANER SALES
★★ $$$

A vacuum cleaner sales and repair business is a terrific small business venture to put into action, as the business and consumer demand for the product has been proven for many decades. Like any new retail business venture, store location will top the list of special considerations for this new venture, as well as local competition, potential market growth, and local labor force for the vacuum repair aspect of the business. If you do not possess this ability. It will be of great importance to the success of the business to establish an exclusive sales, service, and distribution agreement with a manufacturer of vacuum cleaners, as this is the only way to compete in a competitive market, keep wholesale product costs low, and build brand-name recognition. Additionally, be sure to also provide built-in vacuum cleaner sales both to residential clients, as well as to commercial customers such as property developers and construction companies. Expanding the product line to include built-in vacuums can greatly increase business revenues and profits.

DISCOUNT TOOLS
★★ $$$$ ⏰

Tools are one of those things that you can never have enough of, regardless of how much they ever get put to use. Starting a retail business that specializes in selling discount tools is an absolutely fabulous business enterprise to initiate. The start-up investment is relatively low, and the profit potential is outstanding. The best operating format for this type of retailing venture is to hold two or three discount tools sales per month that are very well advertised and promoted in the community where the sales will take place. Good locations for the sales include temporarily renting an empty store in a mall

for the week of the sale or having the sale within a large retail store such as a grocery store. There are many excellent locations in every city or community; the key is to secure the best locations in the busiest areas. The tools can be purchased from foreign manufacturers extremely cheaply, especially if the tools are being discontinued or have small flaws. The best types of tools to sell and that have the highest profit margins are tools that retail for less than $50, are small and easy to ship and package, and that are unique.

WIDGET KIOSK
★★ $$$$ 🌐

I am sure many of you are wondering what exactly is a widget kiosk? A widget kiosk is a kiosk that is set up in a high-traffic area such as a mall or busy grocery store on a year-round basis that sells gadgets and gizmos of every kind. The products sold can range from small electronic items like Walkman stereos to handmade wooden toys. The key to success with this type of retail business is two-fold. The first is that the products you sell must be popular and you must be able to purchase them for extremely low wholesale prices allowing for 200 to 400 percent markups to be applied. The second key to success is kiosk location. The kiosk must be located in a high-traffic area frequented by shoppers, and be highly visible for passers-by, and have appeal.

U-BREW STORE
★★ $$$$ ⚖️ 🌐

Beer and wine, U-Brew shops have been popping up everywhere across North America in the past decade, and these shops can make huge profits. Starting this type of specialty retailing business requires a lot of research and planning, not just into the business opportunity, but also into the market conditions in the area where the business will be operating. The profit potential is great once established, and the business even has the possibility to expand across North America on a franchise basis if the right operating and marketing mix are found. Prior to starting this business be sure to check out local rules and regulations within your community to make sure that there will be no problem in terms of opening and running a U-Brew business.

DISCOUNT SPORTS FOOTWEAR
★★ $$$$

Good-quality sports shoes can cost as much as $150 per pair, and that number is multiplied by the number of people in the household. Not every family can afford to spend more than a thousand dollars each year on new sports shoes, and that adds up to an incredible business opportunity to start a retail business that specializes in selling discounted sports footwear. The question is not will people buy good-quality brand-name sports footwear at discounted prices. That is a given. The real question is how do you purchase the sports footwear at low enough discount prices that still will let you make a profit reselling them? The answer is work. It takes time to establish alliances and contacts in this industry. You have to seek out opportunities to purchase manufacturers' seconds, discontinued product lines, and liquidation inventory from out-of-business retailers and retailers seeking to sell older stock. Seek to expand the product line by also providing customers discounted sportswear and sporting equipment to increase business revenues and profits.

WEB RESOURCE: www.nsra.org National Shoe Retailers Association.

PINBALL MACHINES
★★ $$

How do you make money selling pinball machines? You buy them at bargain prices and resell them for a profit. Older style pinball machines from the 1960s and '70s are currently riding a tidal wave of popularity, as collectors from around the globe vie to build the ultimate collection of arcade pinball machines. There are really two aspects to the business, the first being the ability to locate the pinball machines, and the second aspect

is locating the collectors to purchase the pinball machines. Locating the pinball machines will take some legwork and time searching classified sections of newspapers, garage sales, flea markets, and the Internet. In terms of locating purchasers for the pinball machine, look no further than the Internet. You can develop a Web site featuring the pinball machines for sale, or post advertisements in the various newsgroups on the Internet.

MAGAZINE SUBSCRIPTIONS
★ $$

A great part-time income can be earned by selling magazine subscriptions right from the comforts of home. There are literally hundreds of magazine and periodicals publishers across North America that routinely discount the newsstand price of their publications by as much as 60 percent to enable independent subscription sales consultants to sell their publications and pocket the difference. To get started, harness the power of the Internet for researching the subject and gaining contact information for publishers that you can e-mail and inquire about their specific magazine subscription program. Be sure to build a database of customers that you have sold magazine subscriptions to as you can also sell these same people books and guides once you have discovered what their particular reading interests are.

USED HOME ELECTRONICS
★ $$

Purchasing secondhand home electronics equipment at bargain basement prices and reselling them for a profit can earn a terrific part-time income. To get started you will have to devote time to spend at garage and auction sales to locate this equipment for resale. Once you have assembled an inventory of secondhand home electronic equipment, you can begin to place advertisements in free classified papers, such as the community penny savers, to sell your products. Be sure to buy and sell late-model home electronics equipment as older models now have very little resale value.

DISTRESS SALES

★ $ 🏠 🕐

A distress sale is simply an item that a person desperately wants to sell or must sell. You see the ads all the time in the classifieds section of your local newspaper; "pool table for sale must sell now, call...." Amazingly enough money can be earned by purchasing items in a distress sale situation for pennies on the dollar and reselling the same item for a profit. There are basically two methods of buying distress sale items cheaply. The first is you scan your local classified ads early each morning and call what appear to be distress sale ads. Be the first person in line to make a low offer; depending on how desperate the situation is will dictate the outcome of the negotiations. The second method is to collect advertisements of products for sale that interest you and wait at least four weeks. Once four weeks have passed begin to call these vendors to see if they still have this item for sale. If so, often a low-ball offer will buy it simply because the seller is sick and tired of waiting. You must be a strong negotiator and the item you are buying must be bought cheaply and be an easily resaleable item.

COINS AND STAMPS

★ $$$$

Opening a retail store that buys, sells, and trades collectable coins and stamps is a good business venture for the hobbyist coin and stamp collector to get going. The store does not need a great amount of square footage, as the inventory is compact. As a method to reduce start-up and operating costs, consider a joint venture with another retailer. Good matches for this type of shared retail space include pawnshops, comic book retailers, and memorabilia stores. As is the case with any retail venture, the goal is to buy low and sell high; thus you must possess strong negotiation skills and have experience identifying the condition and value of coins and stamps.

ONLINE COINS AND STAMPS

★★ $$$$ 🏠 🖱

Create a portal for coin and stamp collectors from around the globe to get together to buy, sell, and trade coins and stamps by developing an online coin and stamp Web site. The site can feature numerous free information and services for visitors such as a coin and stamp valuation guide, an online chat forum, and a classifieds section featuring coins and stamps for sale or wanted posted by visitors. Now that you have created the site and given away valuable information and services to visitors, you can turn your attentions to making money and here is how. Once the site is established, develop an online coin and stamp auction service. Once again this service would be free for visitors wishing to view auction listings, but collectors wishing to utilize the auction service to sell coins or stamps would pay a fee or agree to a commission upon the successful sale of their items.

ONLINE RARE BOOK BROKER

★ $$ 🏠 🕐 🖱

Rare edition books and celebrity and author autographed books are prized possessions of many rare book collectors. Thus an opportunity exists to develop a Web site that functions as a portal to bring rare book collectors together to buy, sell, and trade books. Once again, this type of specialty site should be designed with the visitor in mind and include information and services that will keep them coming back on a regular basis. These services could include a rare book auction service within the site, a classified advertisement section that visitors could utilize to post notices about books they wished to purchase or sell, and an online chat forum so book collectors can swap information with each other. Revenue sources include fees for classified advertisements and auction services, renting advertising space, and selling books and print format valuation guides.

WEB RESOURCE: www.rarebooks.org International Rare Book Collectors Association.

MILITARY COLLECTIBLES

★ $$ 🏠 🕐

Purchasing military collectible items at bargain basement prices and reselling them to serious collectors for a profit is a fantastic way to earn a part-time business income. Devoting time to scouring flea markets, garage sales, and classified newspaper advertisements is the fist step in terms of finding military collectibles that can be purchased for the right price. Once you have assembled an inventory, there are various methods to resell these items including display advertisements in specialty collectors publications, online auction services, and upscale flea markets. Additionally, there are books and guides available that list the high-low value of every imaginable military collectable item. I suggest that a few of these guides be purchased as they are an invaluable source of information and pricing details.

ONLINE MILITARY COLLECTIBLES

 ★ $$+

Worldwide there are millions of people who collect military items such as helmets, guns, knives, and medals as a hobby and for profit. You can capitalize on this fact and earn money by posting a Web site to the Internet that is devoted to bringing collectors of military items together to buy, sell, and trade. The site can feature a chat room for visitors to exchange information about military collectibles as well as guides that list the value of these items ranked by condition. In terms of creating a revenue stream, you have options, including:

- Developing a military collectibles auction service within the site.
- Charging collectors a fee to post items for sale within the classifieds section of the site.
- Selling banner advertising space to companies that want exposure in this type of site.
- Selling replicas of military collectibles and other items such as print-format valuation guides.

GLAZIERS SUPPLIES

★ $$$

Setting up to wholesale glaziers supplies from home is a terrific niche-retailing enterprise to get going. You supply local glass shops, stained-glass retailers, and framing stores with products and supplies used in the glazing industry, like specialty glass, glasscutters, grinders, and glass drill bits. This type of unique business venture is ideally suited to be established in a smaller community that is currently not being serviced by a large wholesaler. Additionally, like many specialty products you will be amazed at the profit margins there are in these types of glaziers products. To get started, simply book appointments with local glass shops and other businesses that rely on these types of supplies and present your product line and prices. Also be sure to ask these business owners what types of products you could carry that they would purchase on a regular basis.

BINGO SUPPLIES

 ★ $$

Almost every major city across North America has a minimum of 10 to 20 bingo centers operating at any one time. You can start your own business selling bingo supplies to these bingo centers as well as to thousands of regular bingo players. This business venture can easily be operated from home on a part-time basis. Locating manufacturers and distributors of wholesale bingo supplies is as easy as harnessing the power of the Internet for research purposes.

This type of business is not likely to make you rich, however, once established there should be no problem in generating a few extra hundred dollars in profits each month.

GOVERNMENT SURPLUS

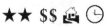 ★★ $$

Purchasing secondhand government products and surplus equipment for pennies on the dollar of the original value and reselling these items to consumers at marked-up prices can make you rich. Every year in the United States various levels of government offices and agencies sell off used equipment, such as fleet vehicles, computer hardware, and office equipment. This surplus equipment is typically sold by way of auction or through a tender process, and providing these surplus items can be purchased at the right price, they can often be resold to consumers for two or three times what you paid the government for them. Using the Internet you can locate these government surplus sales and auctions and begin to purchase surplus equipment. Likewise, the Internet can also be used as a powerful marketing tool for reselling these same surplus items by posting classified ads, listing the items with online auction services, and placing notices in newsgroup forums.

HYDROPONICS EQUIPMENT

★★ $$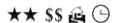

Indoor hydroponic gardening equipment is becoming increasingly popular, especially in densely populated urban centers where privately owned green space for gardening is a luxury that not many can afford. Hydroponic gardening equipment and supplies can be sold right from home. Get started by arranging a dealership or representative agreement with one or more of the hundreds of manufacturers of this type of equipment. Place advertisements promoting your products in your local newspaper, as well as joining community gardening clubs to network for business.

ONLINE SELF-PUBLISHED BOOKS

★★ $$$

Annually in North America there are some ten thousand books and guides that have been self-published by the authors. Without question, the single largest challenge these authors face is finding a suitable marketing and distribution channel for their books. Here is your opportunity to come to the rescue of these authors and launch a Web site dedicated to promoting and selling self-published books and guides. The site can be indexed by fiction and nonfiction, as well as by various sections like self-help, children stories, business, and finance. In addition to marketing books in print format, you can also market books in electronic format that can be downloaded from the site automatically once the purchaser has paid for the product. Furthermore, to eliminate the need for warehouse space, establish an automatic e-mail response system. Every time a book is purchased an e-mail is automatically forwarded to the author to notify them of shipping details. Income is earned by retaining a percentage of sales that the site generates; I would suggest a 60/40 split in favor of the author.

WOODCRAFTS

★★ $

If you love to sell then this is the right low-investment business opportunity for you to start. Most woodcrafts are sold via craft shows and flea markets, and these retailing forums are not suited for wall flowers. You will need to be a showperson in order to make money and not just pass time. Likewise the selling aspect is also what keeps many people that produce beautiful woodcraft items from ever realizing a profit from their work. Now we have a match made in heaven. Find woodcraft artists and use your marketing and sales abilities to promote and sell their products. In exchange for providing this valuable service, charge a 25 percent commission on all products sold. You will be responsible for the costs associated with renting booth space at these shows. However, maintaining sales of $2,000 per show and paying an average booth rent of $100 will still leave you a profit of $400 for a weekend's work.

GUN SHOP

★★ $$$$

In spite of the fact that gun ownership is becoming increasingly restrictive due to government legislation in both the United States and Canada, opening and operating a retail business that buys, sells, and trades guns still has the potential to be profitable. In addition to gun sales you can also sell ammunition and hunting-related products as well as offer a gun repair service. Promote the business by establishing alliances with gun clubs and shooting ranges as well as with firearm instructors, as these clubs and individuals can refer your business to others. Starting this type of retail business will require a substantial investment and you will also have to clear a few legal hurdles before you can open. A well-promoted and operated gun shop could return the owner a six-figure yearly income.

LOTTERY TICKET KIOSK
★★ $$$+ ⚖

Providing you can obtain a lottery ticket vendors permit, then operating a lottery kiosk can be very profitable. Ideally the kiosk will be located in a high-traffic area of the community such as a mall, market, or transportation station. In addition to lottery tickets, you can also sell convenience items like snack foods, newspapers, and cigarettes as well as tickets to local concerts, plays, and sporting events. The investment needed to start this sort of retail business will be in the range of $15,000 to $20,000, not including the cost of the kiosk. If possible, try to find a location with a kiosk for rent, due to the fact that having a kiosk custom designed and built for the business will set you back an additional $15,000.

LIGHTING SHOP
★★ $$$$

Upgrading or replacing interior light fixtures has become a very popular home improvement project for many homeowners simply due to the fact that this type of improvement is relatively inexpensive and can have a beneficial impact on the appearance of their homes. Starting a business that sells interior and exterior lighting products is a wise choice for a new business enterprise. This sort of retail operation does not require a lot of floor space and as a method to reduce start-up costs you may even consider forming a joint venture with an established retailer in your community. Good matches for this type of retailing alliance would include a furniture store or paint and wallpaper store. Also be sure to initiate a direct-mail marketing campaign aimed at architects, homebuilders, and interior designers, as they can also become customers or refer their customers to your store.

WINE STORE
★★ $$$$ ⚖

Retailing wine can be extremely profitable, and this type of business can even be operated from a well-positioned kiosk located in a mall or market. In the right location, walk-in customers will keep you busy selling lots of wine. But as a method to bolster sales and profits, also be sure to establish alliances with event and wedding planners, catering companies, and business clubs and associations as they can become a great source of repeat business. Like any retail business, seek a competitive advantage, meaning offer your customers something the competition does not. Perhaps phone-in orders with free delivery or maybe a weekly wine tasting night. The ability to separate your business from the competitions' often is the difference between business success or business failure.

WEB RESOURCE: www.wswa.org Wine and Spirit Wholesalers of America.

SPECIALTY BUILDING PRODUCTS
★★ $$+ 🏠 🕐

Based on price, quantity, or selection it is nearly impossible to compete against the big retailers of building products. However, on a smaller scale and with specialization you can sell building products and prosper. The key to success is to seek out a building product that is specialized within the industry or marketplace. These types of specialty products can range from a new type of slip-resistant flooring to a fireproof house siding. These sorts of building products are out there, you just have to be prepared to invest a lot of time and a little bit of money to find them. Get started researching by harnessing the power of the Internet and by attending home improvement trade shows and building product trade shows.

LINEN SHOP
★★ $$$$ 🌐

Retailing towels, bedding accessories, and table linens can be extremely profitable, especially when you consider that these products are routinely marked up 100 percent or more for retail sales. However, like any retail operation, success comes to those operators with an eye for detail and a habit for practicing sound business judgment, and a linen shop is no exception to the rule. Considerations prior to opening will include business location, local competition, methods of advertising and promotion, and all management aspects including finances, employees, and inventory. On the positive side start-up costs for this type of business are reasonable, as there are few chattel and equipment requirements. The bulk of available start-up capital can be used for purchasing money-making inventory. For the financially concerned entrepreneur, consider a store-within-a-store approach as a method to reduce start-up costs. Good matches include existing retailers of home furnishings and grocery stores.

KITCHEN AND BATH ACCESSORIES
★★★ $$$$ 🌐

Kitchen and bath accessories shops have become extremely popular in the past decade and are springing up in every city from coast to coast. Like many specialty retailing businesses, a kitchen and bath boutique has the potential to be profitable as it is not uncommon for owners of these businesses to resell their goods for two or three times more than the wholesale costs. In addition to walk-in customers, be sure to promote the store to interior decorators and architects, as they can be both an excellent source for business and will generate referrals via word-of-mouth advertising. Stock items that are commonly found in today's kitchens and bathrooms, such as towel racks and stands, spice holders, specialty soaps, custom cabinet hardware, and more. Ideally, the store will be located in a high-traffic area of the community, such as a mall, strip plaza, or public market. Cross promotions and advertising campaigns with kitchen and bath contractors can also be used as a terrific promotional and marketing method. In the past decade kitchen and bathroom renovations have continually ranked as the first and second most popular home

improvement project carried out by homeowners. The future for this type of specialty retailing can best be described as a growth market with huge upside potential.

FLOORING CENTER
★★ $$$$

In 1999, flooring replacements ranked eighth as the most popular home improvement renovation carried out by homeowners in the United States, generating an estimated ten billion dollars in sales. A tremendous opportunity exists to capitalize on this enormous market by opening a retail flooring center that stocks, sells, and installs a wide range of flooring products, including carpets, area rugs, ceramic tiles, hardwoods, laminates, cork, and vinyl. Flooring installations can be contracted to qualified installers on a subcontract basis, and as a method to bolster sales you can hire flooring sales consultants to work on a commission basis. Do not rely strictly on walk-in store traffic; display your flooring products and services at home improvement trade shows and by setting appointments with new home contractors and architects to present the flooring products and installation services you provide. Be sure to build alliances with property management firms of both residential and commercial buildings. On average, flooring is replaced every 10 to 15 years and property managers and interior decorators can be an excellent work and referral source.

WEB RESOURCE: www.woodfloors.org National Wood Flooring Association.

GREETING CARD KIOSK
★★ $$$ 🌐

In spite of the increasing popularity of electronic or e-mail greeting cards, there are still more than two billion paper and printed greeting cards sold annually in the United States and Canada, generating some six billion dollars in sales revenues. Securing just a small fraction of this very lucrative market can make you rich. There are two options for selling greeting cards from a kiosk: manned and unmanned. The first generally requires a more elaborate kiosk display that also stocks and sells additional products, such as magazines, newspapers, snack items, and tobacco products to justify the labor costs. Manned greeting card kiosks are generally located in public malls and markets. Unmanned greeting card kiosks can range from a small rack-style display to a very large specially-designed kiosk. Typically, these types of kiosks are located within a retail store, such as a grocery store or pharmacy. A jobber on consignment or wholesale basis generally services unmanned greeting card kiosks regularly. Both methods have their pros and cons. However, manned greeting card kiosks are more profitable as single location operation, while unmanned kiosks tend to be a more profitable setup in multiple retail locations. Greeting cards can be purchased in bulk on a wholesale basis very inexpensively. It is not uncommon to retail the cards for two or three times more than wholesale cost. This business opportunity definitely warrants further investigation.

WEB RESOURCE: www.greetingcard.org Greeting Card Association.

BATTERY KIOSK
★★ $$$$ 🌐

The wave of the future for manufactured electronic goods is wireless, and manufacturers have but one option to power these products: batteries. Telephones, computers, radios, and more, consumers want electronic goods that are portable and that they can use just about anywhere. For the innovative entrepreneur an outstanding business opportunity awaits by starting a business that specializes in retailing batteries for consumer electronics products. This type of specialty retailing is ideal for kiosk sales. Get started by having a kiosk professionally designed and constructed and by securing a high-traffic location for the kiosk in a mall or public market. The types of batteries that you can stock and sell are almost unlimited and include batteries for cellular telephones, laptop computers, wristwatches, camcorders, and can even include highly specialized batteries, such as wheelchair and motorcycle batteries. In addition to retailing the batteries from a kiosk location, also be sure to market your products via the Internet, especially for the more highly specialized batteries. Securing multiple wholesale sources for the batteries will not prove difficult, as there are thousands of battery manufacturers and distributors worldwide, and harnessing the power of the Internet for research purposes is a good starting point. The start-up costs for this venture will be high, but the profit potential is fantastic. It is not uncommon for batteries to be marked up by 200 percent or more for retail sales.

WEB RESOURCE: www.batteryweb.com Directory service listing battery manufacturers, industry information, and links.

CONVENIENCE STORE
★★ $$$$ 🌐

In spite of the rising popularity of Internet shopping combined with home delivery of grocery and convenience items, starting and operating a "mini convenience store" is still a good business venture to activate that has the potential to generate respectable profits. The name suggests it all. In order to succeed in this segment of the highly competitive retail industry, the store must be convenient. This means an easily accessible and highly visible business location, well-stocked with the most popular convenience products, and fast and friendly service. Remember, if a customer's shopping experience at the store is not convenient then there will not be any repeat business. In addition to the usual supply of convenience products, such as milk, eggs, bread, snack items, and soda pop, be sure to add other products and services to attract customers to the store and keep them returning as repeat business. These products and services can include lottery ticket sales, tobacco products, newspapers and magazines, a fax service, photocopying, calling cards, postal stamps, and even fresh-cut flowers for sale on a daily basis. Once again, business location is the key to success. The business must be located with easy street access and good parking, or alternately in an area of heavy foot traffic like a mall, transportation terminal, or office district.

WEB RESOURCE: e-mail~nasc1@aol.com National Association of Convenience Stores.

USED APPLIANCE SALES
★★ $$$ 🏠 🕐

A tidy profit can be earned by selling used appliances, such as refrigerators, stoves, washers, and dryers, right from a homebased location. Get started by building a resource library in terms of appliance models, manufacturers, and retail selling prices when new. This type of resource library will prove invaluable when buying secondhand appliances for resale purposes. To secure a initial inventory of used appliances to sell, begin by attending auction sales, garage and estate sales, and scanning your local classified newspaper ads for good used appliances at bargain basement prices. Your target market for resale will include people on a budget, owners of secondary homes, and owners of residential rental and apartment properties. Some basic knowledge of home appliance repair will come in handy, as well as a good, heavy-duty moving dolly and a pickup truck or utility trailer. Aim to maintain a 50 percent markup on all appliances sold and to generate gross annual sales of $50,000 and this simple part-time homebased business will produce gross profits of $15,000 per year.

JEWELRY KIOSK
★★ $$ 🕐 🌐

Billions of dollars worth of nonprecious gem and costume jewelry is sold annually in the United States, and staking your claim in this very lucrative industry may be easier than you think. The jewelry can be sold from a kiosk located in a mall, or by renting booth space at weekend flea markets and community markets. You can also sell the jewelry by employing independent sales contractors to host home shopping parties. Harness the power of the Internet to locate wholesale sources directly from manufacturers and distributors of jewelry items. Additional items that are also very profitable and that can be sold from the same kiosk include watches, sunglasses, and small gift items. It is not uncommon for nonprecious jewelry items to be marked up by 200 percent or more for retail sales, making this a potentially very profitable business to operate even on a part-time basis.

AIR AND WATER FILTRATION SYSTEMS
★★★ $$ 🏠 🕐

Cash in on the clean water and air phenomenon by starting a business that sells and installs air and water filtration systems. The objective for operating this business is crystal clear; buy your air and water filter products and systems on a wholesale basis and resell them for a profit. Installations will not prove difficult as most air filtering devices are simple plug-in models, and water filters are generally installed inline. Inline refers to a quick attachment of the water filter to an existing water line, whether at the intake source into the home or business or under the sink counter. There are many marketing methods that can be employed to sell the air and water filters. These methods include telemarketing followed up by an in-home sales presentation or door-to-door cold calling to both residential and commercial clients. You can also display your products at trade shows and in malls to collect qualified sales leads. Be forewarned this is a very competitive industry and to succeed will require careful planning and clever marketing. However, with that said, air and water pollution is on the rise and the long term prognosis for this industry can only be described as excellent.

WEB RESOURCE: www.ecomall.com Directory service listing manufacturers and distributors of air and water filtering systems and products.

HEAT TRANSFERS KIOSK
★★ $$ 🕐

You can earn as much as $1,000 per day selling designs, logos, and messages that are transferred onto T-shirts, sweatshirts, bags, and shorts via heat press equipment. Of course the key to success in operating a heat transfers kiosk is location. Excellent operating locations include malls, beach areas, public markets, and special events, such as fairs, music festivals, and sporting events. The business is very easy to operate and the heat transfer equipment is widely available through numerous manufacturers. There are also thousands of clothing manufacturers and distributors who will be more than happy to set up an account to supply your garment requirements on a wholesale basis. Generally, the best way to operate this type of business is to design display boards and pin the available designs, logos, and messages to them. Customers simply select the garment they wish to purchase, choose the design, logo, or message they want emblazoned on the garment, and you press it on the garment while they wait. Currently, this product retails for $15 to $25 each and the wholesale cost to purchase the T-shirt and transfer is in the range of $5 to $8, leaving lots of room for profit. All of this adds up to a great business opportunity that can be operated part-time, has the potential to generate enormous profits, and can be started with an initial investment of less than $10,000.

WEB RESOURCE: www.equipmentzone.com Distributors of transfer equipment, heat presses, and heat transfer supplies.

COMMUNICATIONS STORE
★★ $$$$ 🌐

Stake your claim in the multibillion dollar communications industry by opening a communications store. Stock and sell items, such as residential and business telephones, facsimile machines, pagers, Palm Pilots, cellular telephones, and accessories. Ideally, you will want to secure an authorized agents agreement for the wireless side of the business. Securing this type of agreement should not prove difficult given the vast number of communication companies now providing paging, cellular telephone calling, and two-way radio systems. Locate the store in a highly visible area of your community like a store or kiosk in a mall or a storefront on a major street. Additionally, be sure to employ outside salespeople to cold call on businesses in the area to bid on their communication product and service needs. In most cases the salespeople you hire will be more than happy to work on a commission-only basis due to the earnings potential for these types of sales. Thus you will be able to maintain minimal overheads, while having the potential to increase revenues via your outside sales contractors. The communications industry is very competitive. However, with careful planning and clever marketing it is possible to earn a

six-figure yearly income owning and operating a communications store.

COPY CENTER
★★ $$$$ 🌐

The popularity of operating a business or working from home has catapulted a copy center into one of the hottest business start-ups available for the new millennium simply due to the fact that most people working from home lack the resources to purchase this type of office equipment, or can justify the expense for the limited use. Copy centers typically provide customers with a wide range of services, including black and white photocopying, digital color copying, a facsimile transmission service, laminating, booklet and report binding, mail box rentals, courier and shipping options, and small-run print jobs of business cards, fliers, and business presentations. The key requirement for success in this business is unquestionably location. The copy center must be located in a highly visible area with excellent parking facilities and/or lots of walk-by foot traffic. As a method to reduce start-up costs, as this type of equipment is extremely expensive you may want to consider purchasing secondhand equipment or lease new equipment. The industry is competitive and start-up costs are high, but the profit potential is outstanding, and it is not uncommon for owners of copy centers to earn a six-figure income.

NOTES

26

SECURITY

Businesses You Can Start

FIRE SAFETY LADDERS

★★★ $$$$ ⚖

Every year across the United Stated thousands of people are injured or die as a result of fires. Many of these fire-related deaths and injuries could have been prevented had the victims had access to safety ladders enabling them to escape the burning building safely. Starting a business that manufactures, sells, and installs fire safety ladders for residential and commercial applications has the potential to generate profits that could easily exceed $250,000 per year due to an almost unlimited market for the product. The following options are available to the creative entrepreneur that establishes a fire safety ladder business:

- Manufacture and wholesale fire safety ladders; retailers like home improvement centers could act as the distribution channels.
- Manufacture and retail fire safety ladders directly to consumers who carry out their own installation. The fire safety ladders could be sold via the Internet and sales kiosk setup at malls and trade shows.
- Manufacture, sell, and install fire safety ladders directly to consumers via the above-mentioned methods with the addition of a direct-sales team.
- Manufacture and sell the fire safety ladders to construction industry companies only, such as new homebuilders. These companies would install the safety ladders.
- The business could combine any or all of these options into a business operating and marketing format.

REQUIREMENTS: In addition to planning and research, also seek to have the safety ladders certified by Underwriters Laboratories (UL). Not only will this likely be required for selling the ladders to consumers; it also provides consumers with peace of mind to know they are purchasing a proven and safe product. Additional requirements will include manufacturing facilities, transportation, and marketing. Also, seek to have the product endorsed by a professional association such as the Firefighters of America. A product endorsement such as this will greatly assist in marketing, as well as the consumers acceptance.

START-UP COSTS: The investment required to start this business will be substantial and could easily exceed $100,000. However, as a method of reducing the start-up costs for this enterprise, the fire safety ladders could be designed in prototype form and presold to national retailers based on the prototype example. Once this has been accomplished, an existing manufacturer could be awarded the manufacturing contract for the product. This is a terrific way to greatly reduce the capital required.

WEB RESOURCE: www.nfpa.org National Fire Protection Association.

WINDOW SECURITY BARS
★★ $$$ 🏠 🕐

Annually thousands of homes and businesses are burglarized even though many of these same properties have alarms and other types of theft deterrent devices. Many people and business owners are now turning to installing security bars on windows and doors as a method to deter burglars and prevent property entry and theft. The chances of breaking and entering crime stopping or being reduced in the near future is highly unlikely, and this fact is what makes starting a security bar manufacturing and installation business such a good choice for a new venture. The business is very straightforward to get rolling and operate, and security bars can be sold to residential homeowners as well as to commercial property and business owners. In addition to using all traditional advertising mediums to promote the business, you can also establish contacts and alliances with companies such as alarm installers, property management firms, and contractors, all of which can refer your security bar manufacturing and installation service to their clients.

REQUIREMENTS: The main requirements for starting a business that manufactures and installs window and door security bars is to have welding equipment, welding experience, and a workshop large enough to properly carry out the work required to manufacture the security bars.

START-UP COSTS: The investment required to start a window and door security bar manufacturing and installation business will vary. However, an investment of $20,000 to $25,000 will be sufficient funding to establish a small to medium manufacturing facility, as well as provide for the business setup, initial advertising, and marketing budget costs associated with this type of business venture.

PROFIT POTENTIAL: To establish a retail selling price for window and door security bars consider using the following pricing formula as a guideline. This is a common pricing formula used within the construction and renovation building industry.

Material costs + labor costs x 1.5
or 50 percent markup on costs.

Example: material costs are $100 plus labor costs of $50 multiplied by 50 percent markup or $75 equals the total selling price of $225.

Providing this formula is utilized and the business can achieve yearly sales of $300,000, the business would then generate a gross profit prior to overheads and taxes of $100,000 per year.

HOME ALARM SALES
★★ $$$ 🏠 🕐 ⚖

There are various approaches that can be taken when starting a security alarm business. The first is to sell and install alarms that are monitored; the second is to sell alarms for residential and commercial applications that are not monitored. The third approach is to sell security alarm packages to the do-it-yourself homeowner for self-installation. All three approaches have the potential to pay off big in terms of business profits. However, the best approach is to sell and install residential and commercially monitored alarms, which can generate an ongoing residual income by way of monthly alarm monitoring fees, paid by the home or business owner. The first option is the most capital intensive of the three businesses to start, but it also has the potential to return the highest profits. Whichever approach is used to start and establish a security alarm business, one thing is for sure; crime is not going away, making this a great business opportunity to pursue. *Note*: Government licensing required.

WEB RESOURCE: www.alarm.org National Burglar and Fire Alarm Association.

BODYGUARD SECURITY SERVICE
★ $$$ ⚖

Bodyguards are no longer hired just to protect celebrities, they are also hired to protect business leaders, high profile activists, authors, journalists, and just about anyone else who comes under short- or long-term threats. Starting a bodyguard service does require a great deal of careful planning and research in order to ensure business success. However, bodyguard rates can exceed $1,000 per day, and, as an agency that retains 20 percent of the rate, it would not take many bodyguards on staff working only a few days per week to generate business sales in excess of $200,000 per year. Additional revenue for this type of unique business can also be gained by adding an instruction service focused on training students how to become professional bodyguards.

WEB RESOURCE: www.iapps.org The International Association of Professional Protection Services.

RECORDS STORAGE
★ $$$$

Many companies are required by law to retain financial and legal documents and files about their business and clients for long periods of time. In some cases this can be up to ten years or more from the original date of the information or document. This fact creates a huge opportunity for the innovative entrepreneur to start and run a record storage facility, as many companies simply run out of space to store their documents and files. Ideally the business will be established in a location or warehouse that will take the following considerations into account: security, fire sprinklers, building condition, pest control, square footage, ease of accessibility, potential for expansion, central high-traffic location, and

affordability. Rates for record storage vary greatly to the clients specific needs, in terms of volume of record storage and type of documents being stored. However, a well-planned and managed records storage business can post yearly profits that exceed six-figures.

WINDOW ROLLSHUTTERS
★★ $$ 🏠 🕐

Window and door security rollshutters are a terrific alternative to unattractive security bars, and starting a business enterprise that sells and installs window and door security rollshutters is very simple. You can focus on residential or commercial installations, or both. The first step is to source a manufacturer of the rollshutters and secure an exclusive distribution and installation contract. The contract can be for a city, state, or even the entire country. Marketing could consist of a demonstration and sales kiosk setup in malls or at trade shows to generate interest and sales leads for the products. Additionally, establishing alliances with contractors and renovation companies is a terrific marketing approach, as these businesses can offer their existing customers your products in exchange for a commission.

SPECIAL EVENT SECURITY
★ $$ 🏠 🕐 ⚖

Every year in North America there are thousands of special events such as concerts that require security staff present to control crowds and make the event safe for everyone in attendance. Starting a business that provides security for special events is very easy to set in motion, and the security staff used can be off-duty police officers seeking to gain additional part-time income. Contacting event planners and promoters in your community or state to explain the benefits of using your special event security service can help to market this type of security service. Additional revenue for the business can be earned by having the off-duty police officers conduct special instruction classes to students seeking to learn personal security techniques. Overall, a special event security service is a great new business venture for someone with a police or military background and contacts within the industry.

PEEPHOLE INSTALLATIONS
★★ $ 🏠 🕐

Calling all university and college students. Are you seeking to start a business that can generate an excellent part-time income as well as be started for peanuts? If so, consider starting a business that installs security peepholes, as it will sure beat flipping burgers on weekends. Millions of homes, apartments, and condominiums in the United States have older-style solid-wood or metal doors that do not have security peepholes, as the practice of installing peepholes into doors did not take off until the mid-1970s. This means there are millions of potential customers just waiting for you to come by and install a peephole. To market these services, simply go door to door and explain the security benefits of a peephole to the residents of the home. The peepholes are easy to install and generally take less than five minutes to complete.

REQUIREMENTS: The requirements for starting this sort of security enterprise are minimal. There are no regulations to comply with, and the equipment needed for the installations amounts to no more than a cordless drill and a few drill bits. Additionally, consider purchasing liability insurance just in case a door is damaged during the installation process.

START-UP COSTS: The investment needed to get the business rolling is also minimal. Peepholes can be purchased in bulk from wholesalers for less than $3 each. A good quality cordless drill and drill bits will cost less than $200, bringing the total start-up costs to less than $500. The income potential is outstanding, as you can easily charge $20 to $25 for each peephole installed while the cost to purchase the product is less than $5 each.

ONLINE SURVEILLANCE EQUIPMENT SALES
★★★ $$$ 🏠 ⚖️ ✋

Millions of small video cameras, emergency service scanners, night vision glasses, and other types of surveillance equipment are sold to consumers worldwide annually. Starting a business that retails these surveillance devices is very easy to do. Simply locate manufacturers of various types of surveillance equipment and purchase the equipment on a wholesale basis for retail purposes. The best method of marketing surveillance equipment, due to the limited market demand, is to establish a Web site that features and sells the surveillance products. Additionally, advertisements can be placed in newspapers and trade publications for catalog ordering, enabling customers to receive your surveillance equipment by mail order. For the truly innovative entrepreneur, a specialty sales and demonstration kiosk could be designed and constructed. The kiosk could be set up at trade shows and even in busy malls to sell the surveillance equipment to consumers.

WEB RESOURCE: www.entrepreneur.com Create a business Web site with MySite professional Web site builder.

SECURITY STORAGE LOCKERS
★★ $$ 🏠 🕐

There are numerous approaches that can be taken when starting a security locker business. The first is to manufacture and sell the security locker, while the second approach is to purchase the security lockers from an existing manufacturer on a wholesale basis and resell the lockers to clients at a profit. Security lockers have a wide range of uses including companies securing office products, pharmacies securing medications, and short-term security solutions for personal property at airports and other stations. Once again this is a specialty product with a limited market. The profit potential is good and could be in the six-figure range for the entrepreneur who is willing to take the time required to plan and market the business properly.

WEB RESOURCE: www.americanlocker.com Distributors of specialty security lockers.

CRIME PREVENTION TRAINING
★★ $ 🏠 🕐

Crime affects one out of four Americans in some fashion every year, and starting a business that trains people how to prevent themselves from becoming the victims of crime can be a very personally rewarding business venture to set in motion. The basis of the business concept is very straightforward. Simply hold training sessions in a group format for people who are seeking a way of protecting themselves and their families from becoming victims of crime. The classes can be held in conjunction with community services and groups, or on an independent one-on-one basis.

One of the key requirements for starting this type of specialty training business is to design a course manual that will be used as the backbone of the training program. Additionally, a background in police service or the military will help to establish credibility for the business. The profit potential for a crime prevention training service is excellent, as students should be more than happy to pay a mere $100 to learn more about crime prevention tips and techniques they can use to help prevent themselves and their families from becoming victims of crime.

GUARD DOGS
★ $$$ ⚖️

Once again, there are a few different approaches that can be taken for starting a guard dog security service. The first approach is to supply guard dogs with security handlers, the second is to provide guard dogs without security handlers, or both options can be offered to clients. The requirements for starting the business are obvious. You must have trained guard dogs and experience training guard dogs, as well as a suitable operating location. Currently guard dog rental rates without security handlers are in the range of $40 to $60 per eight hours and include delivery and pickup of the dog. Guard dogs with security handlers are supplied to companies and associations for security purposes in the range of $125 to $175 per eight hours.

SECURITY LIGHTING

Calling all electricians. It is time to start earning extra income putting your talents to work for you by starting a part-time business that sells and installs

residential and commercial security lighting solutions. The business can be started for peanuts in terms of investment capital, and has the potential to generate an additional income of $30,000 per year or more on a part-time basis. The best method to market this type of business is to establish a joint venture with home alarm companies. This can be a terrific marketing method as the alarm companies already have the sales force and customer base to assist in building your new business. Simply put, the alarm companies would offer their customers optional security lighting as part of the complete home security system, and you would supply and install the lighting. There should be no difficulties finding an alarm company that would be prepared to go into this type of joint venture, especially when you consider they could earn an additional $2,000 or $3,000 per month in commissions for selling your security lighting solutions.

BOAT ALARM SALES AND INSTALLATIONS

Many alarm companies have skipped installing alarms in boats because there is no effective way to charge a monthly monitoring fee due to the fact that many marinas do not have individual telephone lines to each boat and berth. Starting a business that specializes in only installing boat alarms is a venture that has millions of potential clients, and relatively little competition. Marketing a boat alarm sales and installation service can be accomplished by designing and distributing promotional brochures to marinas and boat dealers, as well as setting up a kiosk or booth at boat shows to collect sales leads. The profit potential is fantastic even as a one-person operation; you could easily surpass $75,000 per year in sales.

LOCKSMITH
★ $$$$ ⚖️

The main requirement for starting a locksmith service is of course to be a certified locksmith. While this may seem like a negative aspect for starting a locksmith service, it is not, because you can become a locksmith relatively easily and the instruction training generally takes less than a year to complete. The best aspect about starting a locksmith service is the fact that this business venture has been proven successful and profitable for decades and is probably one of the most stable business opportunities available to start. Technology is changing the face of traditional locksmithing as many new homes and buildings are being outfitted with electronic locking devices. Like anything to do with technology, it will not take long before electronic locks are widely accepted and common, making this a timely business opportunity. Income potential range is $20,000 to $80,000 per year.

WEB RESOURCE: www.aloa.org The Associated Locksmiths of America.

SECURITY AND SAFETY MIRRORS
★★★★ $$ 🏠 🕐

In spite of the popularity of security video cameras, security mirrors will always be a popular choice for merchants to purchase and install. Unlike security cameras that may indicate a theft or shoplifting problem hours after the incident, security mirrors enable shopkeepers to keep an eye on their valuable inventory in real time. The market for security mirrors is almost unlimited, as there are millions of potential customers right now, and thousands more retail stores open for business on a daily basis in the United States. The easiest way to market this business is to simply design marketing brochures and solicit door-to-door directly. Providing you can explain all the details in regards to the benefits that the security mirrors will have for customers, you should easily be able to achieve a 25 percent closing rate on all presentations.

REQUIREMENTS: Outside of a business license there are no legal restrictions or certifications that must be complied with in regards to starting a business installing security mirrors. The only equipment needed for this business venture is a couple of good quality stepladders and a cordless drill. The best aspect about starting this business is the fact that there are virtually no special skills required; anyone can install security mirrors.

START-UP COSTS: The following example can be used as a guideline to establish the investment needed to start a security mirror installation service.

	Low	High
Installation vehicle (used)	$2,500	$5,000
Installation equipment	$500	$1,000
Initial inventory	$500	$1,000
Business setup, legal, banking, etc.	$250	$500
Initial advertising and marketing budget	$250	$500
Working capital	$1,000	$2,000
Total start-up investment	**$5,000**	**$10,000**

PROFIT POTENTIAL: Even for a small one-person security mirror sales and installation business the profit potential is outstanding. The security mirrors vary in cost as to the size of the mirror and if the mirror is plastic or glass. A small 24-inch security mirror can be purchased wholesale for less than $30, and the current retail price for the same size mirror is $125 for the mirror and installation. Two simple 30-minute jobs per day can create a gross profit of over $4,000 per month.

WEB RESOURCE: www.brossardmirrors.com Manufacturers of safety and security mirror products.

SECURITY ENGRAVING
★★ $ 🏠 🕐

Are you searching for a homebased security business that can be started for less than a $1,000 initial investment? If so, consider starting a security engraving service, as the business is inexpensive to start and operate. This business can easily be managed from a homebased office, requires no special skills or business expertise, and has the ability to produce a very comfortable income for the owner-operator of the business. Well-concealed security engraving identification numbers and names make it very easy for police to return stolen property to the rightful owners, as well as catch the thief that sells the stolen merchandise to pawnshops and secondhand stores. To get working, simply design brochures and fliers explaining your service and distribute them throughout your community. It will not take long for the phone to start ringing.

WEB RESOURCE: www.gravers.com Distributors of engraving equipment and supplies.

PERSONAL SECURITY PRODUCTS
★★ $$

The time to start a business that sells personal security products has never been better than now. Muggings, personal attacks, road rage, and home invasions have people scared to death, and while many people refuse to carry or have a gun in their homes, these same people are more than willing to have or carry personal safety devices that do not have such permanent results. Personal safety products and devices can be purchased on a wholesale basis from the thousands of different manufacturers that manufacture these types of security products, and resold to consumers for a profit. The personal safety products can be sold and distributed in various ways, including over the Internet, mail order, a retail store, sales kiosk, home safety parties, and direct-sales teams. Furthermore, selling these types of products can be extremely profitable as the markups for retailing can be 100 percent or greater.

COUNTERFEIT DETECTION EQUIPMENT
★★ $$

Counterfeit currency remains a problem for retailers, and costs all of us millions of dollars each year as a result of retail prices increasing to help offset these financial losses. Selling counterfeit detection equipment to retailers does not require a lot of experience in the industry, but like any sales-based business it does require good marketing and salesmanship skills. The key to success in this type of security business is not to sell to the retailer with one location, but to target retailers with multiple store locations. Additionally, one of the first steps to be taken prior to establishing the business will be to source a manufacturer of the equipment and negotiate an exclusive sales and distribution contract that services your particular community, city, or state. Providing a 50

percent markup can be maintained on all counterfeit detection equipment sold, and the business can achieve annual sales revenues of $250,000 the business would then generate a gross profit prior to taxes and operating costs of $85,000 per year.

CONSTRUCTION LOCK-UP SERVICE
★★ $$$$

On any medium-sized construction site there are hundreds of thousands of dollars worth of building materials and tools around at any given time, making construction sites a prime target for thieves. Starting a construction lock-up security service is not only a service that is in high demand; the business also has the ability to generate profits that are well into the six-figure range. The focus of the service should be a one-stop approach to construction lock-up and security services, and provide clients optional services like security patrols, security storage locker rentals for tools, portable security fencing rentals, and site trailer rentals. A construction lock-up security service will appeal to a wide variety of potential customers including property developers, commercial contractors, home renovation companies, demolition contractors, and even film and TV production companies. The best way to market the security services is to hire sales professionals on a commissioned basis. The sales professionals can solicit business for the security service, as well as up-sell customers into various security services the business offers. Additional revenues can be earned by providing contractors with employee safety instruction, as well as providing road contractors with flag persons and traffic control service.

REQUIREMENTS: There are few legal requirements for starting a construction lock-up security service except any security staff or guards must be certified and bonded. Also there are the usual requirements such as a business license and liability insurance. Additionally, be sure to purchase business interruption and theft insurance in case your own business becomes the victim of theft.

START-UP COSTS: The investment needed to start a construction lock-up service will greatly vary as to the size of the business, and the number of different services the business provides for clients. However, a small construction lock-up service can be started for less than $20,000 while a larger service will cost in excess of $50,000 to start.

PROFIT POTENTIAL: Profit potential range is $25,000 to $200,000 per year.

COMPUTER SECURITY
★★★ $$ 🏠 🕐

Computer security is big business, and starting a computer security business enterprise can put you on the path to financial freedom. Every year thousands of computers, computer equipment, and software is stolen in the United States, not to mention the valuable and often irreplaceable data that is contained within these computers. One of the best aspects about starting a computer security business is the fact that there are no regulation or certification requirements. Simply research and plan the business and you can literally open for business in a few weeks. Gaining clients for a computer security service can be accomplished in numerous ways including joining business associations and networking with other business owners to promote your services, door-to-door solicitation, direct-mail and e-mail campaigns, and hiring a direct-sales team. Additionally there are various types of computer security services and products that can be provided or offered to clients including tower locks and cages, notebook tracking (GPS), and password identification software. Once established, a computer security business has the potential to generate profits in excess of $100,000 per year.

ELECTRIC SECURITY GATES
★★ $$$ 🏠 🕐

Electric security gates are a popular home improvement upgrade and security feature for many homeowners, strata corporations, companies, and apartment building landlords. Starting a security gate business does not require a great deal of practical construction knowledge, as the manufacturing and installation aspect of the business can be subcontracted to qualified professional tradespeople. However, like almost any business venture, a definite

prerequisite for success is certainly an ability to be or become an effective marketing and sales pro. Building alliances with renovation and construction companies is a good start in terms of marketing and getting the word out about your business. Additionally home and garden trade shows can be an invaluable source for collecting well-qualified sales leads.

BACK-UP GENERATOR SALES
★ $$$ 🏠 🕐

Selling, repairing, and installing emergency back-up generator systems is a fantastic business venture to set in motion. Why would anyone need a back-up generator you may be asking yourself? Floods, earthquakes, ice storms, and power outages are a few of the reasons, not to mention the fact that many businesses rely heavily on a constant energy supply that when interrupted even for a few minutes can cause millions of dollars in damages. Ideally, you will want to sell generator systems to customers who will also sign up for a regular maintenance contract, as this is a method to secure long-term,, ongoing, residual income from the initial sale. It is always easier to succeed in business if you have 100 regular clients utilizing your service ten times per year than it is to have to find 1,000 new clients per year. Profit potential range is $25,000+ per year.

CONSTRUCTION SITE SECURITY
★ $$ 🏠 ⚖️

Millions of dollars worth of tools and building materials are stolen from construction and building renovation sites annually, and this fact is what makes starting a construction site security service such a wise choice for a new business enterprise. This type of security service does not require a great deal of investment capital to set in motion, and the business can easily be managed from a homebased office. Gaining clients for a construction site security service is best achieved simply by soliciting construction and renovation companies for business. Set appointments with these firms and explain all the benefits using your security service will have for their companies.

Additional revenue for this kind of security business can also be earned by providing students with specialized security staff training.

AUTO ALARM SALES AND INSTALLATIONS

In spite of the fact that many new automobiles now come outfitted with auto alarms as standard equipment, starting an auto alarm installation business is still a good choice for a new business venture, especially if the objective is to build a small one-person business that can provide the owner with a comfortable annual income. Establishing alliances with used car dealers is a fabulous way to activate this type of security business, as the car dealers can offer their car purchasing clients optional installations of car alarms, of course provided by your auto alarm sales and installation service. Overall this is a good business start-up for the technically inclined individual, and the income possibility for an automotive alarm sales and installation service is in the range of $25,000 to $50,000 per year.

PHONE-UP SERVICE

Starting a security phone-up service is a very inexpensive business venture to launch that can be operated right from the comforts of a homebased office. A few of you might be wondering exactly what a security phone-up service is, and how this business can make money. A security phone-up service is a security service that telephones clients twice per day seven days per week to make sure that there are no problems in terms of personal security and health. Clients for a phone-up service can include seniors living alone as well as parents who cannot always be home to check up on children. Current rates for a phone-up security service is in the range of $25 to $40 per client per month. Securing only regular customers can produce an income greater than $35,000 per year. Additional revenues for this business can also be from providing clients with a custom telephone memo and paging service.

NOTES

KEY

RATINGS ★

START-UP COST $

HOMEBASED
BUSINESS 🏠

PART-TIME 🕐

LEGAL ISSUES ⚖️

FRANCHISE OR
LICENSE POTENTIAL 🌐

ONLINE 🖱️

76

SPECIAL SERVICE

Businesses You Can Start

BOARD-UP SERVICE

★★ $ 🏠 🕐

Every year tornadoes and hurricanes devastate thousands of people's lives. Being prepared for these nasty forces of nature can save not only property, but also prevent personal injury. The business is quite simple. You measure windows and doors, cut plywood to fit these openings, label each board to its proper location, and install quick-fit installation hardware on each piece of plywood. The next time there is a threat of a hurricane or tornado the homeowner will be prepared; thanks to your very proactive board-up service. Additional revenue for the business can be gained by storing and installing the boards as required. The service can also be marketed to owners of vacation properties and to owners of seasonal businesses who want the peace of mind knowing their buildings will be secure during the off season.

CROWD CONTROL SYSTEMS

★★ $$ 🏠 🕐

Parades, concerts, demonstrations, and fairs all require portable fencing, ticket booths, and barriers to be temporally installed at the site where the event is taking place. You can rent crowd control items by marketing the service to event planners, city management staff, and charity organizations in your community with the assistance of your own specially designed brochure and rental item price list. Likewise, many construction and renovation companies require these same rental items on a periodic basis and these businesses can also be placed on your potential client list. This type of rental business is easily operated from home and you can contract out the delivery of the rental items to a local transportation company in order to keep start-up costs to a minimum.

CHARITY AUCTION SERVICE
★★ $$ 🏠 🕐 ⚖️

One of the best methods for charities to raise funds for their particular need is to host a charity auction. Typically, local merchants will donate products and services to be auctioned.

The focus of this business start-up is to act as the auctioneer as well as solicit local business owners for donations of products and services to be auctioned, and organize the entire auction event. In exchange for your services you would keep 20 percent of the total revenue generated while the charity would retain the balance. If you hold one charity auction per month that generates total sales of $20,000 each, the commissions for your charity auction service would be $48,000 per year. The best charities to build alliances with are local ones that serve the community exclusively. *Note*: An auctioneer's license may be required to operate this service, check with local authorities.

WEB RESOURCE: www.auctionweb.com/aaa National Auctioneers Association.

ONLINE CHARITY AUCTION SERVICE
★★ $$$$ 🏠 ⚖️ 🖱️

Take charity auctions into the high-tech world of the Internet by developing and posting a Web site that exclusively features items for auction with the proceeds benefiting charities. The site would operate like any other online auction with the exception of the endorsement of one or more well-known charities. To get started you will first have to build an alliance with a charity. Ideally, this charity will be nationally recognized. Once you have an agreement with a charity in place and all the legal aspects have been ironed out, you can set about securing products and service to be featured in the online charity. As a method of obtaining products and services for auction, employ subcontract fundraising consultants to solicit corporations and small businesses coast to coast for donations of products and services. The consultants could be paid a commission based on a percentage of the auction value for the items they obtained. Once again, be sure to check the legalities of this system. Keep in mind your cut of the proceeds will have to be large, perhaps even in the range of 75 percent, to cover the costs of marketing and promoting the site as well as the fixed operational overheads of the site. However, the charity would still stand to benefit by as much as 25 percent of revenues generated and should the site create auction revenues in the six-figure range yearly that would add up to $250,000+ for the charity.

BARTENDER FOR HIRE
★★ $ 🏠 🕐

Starting a bartender-for-hire service is a fantastic way to get into business for yourself, without breaking the bank. You can market your services as an independent bartender to catering companies, event planners, hotels, and pubs for relief duties. The business only requires a few hundred dollars of seed capital to initiate, and can return $150 to $200 per day plus gratuities. Ideally, the entrepreneur who starts a bartender-for-hire service will be an experienced one with outstanding social skills. Employing other bartenders on an "as-needed, on-call basis" can generate additional revenue. A bartender-for-hire service has the potential to create annual revenues that can easily exceed $50,000 or more.

WEB RESOURCE: www.bartender.com/link-trade.html Directory service listing industry information and resource links.

DRY CLEANING DELIVERY SERVICE
★★ $$ 🏠

Today's lifestyles are hectic and busy with not enough time for simple tasks like dropping off and picking up dry cleaning. That is exactly what you want to hear if you are considering starting your own dry cleaning delivery service. This business is great. Low investment, high potential earnings, little competition, and very low operating overheads. To get started simply build an alliance with an existing commercial dry cleaner and negotiate the lowest possible per item dry cleaning rates that you can. Once you have accomplished this task, you can then create your own marketing brochure and price list reflecting a 100 percent markup on your wholesale dry cleaning cost. The next phase of establishing the business is to solicit clients. This is best achieved by distributing marketing brochures where they will have the highest impact, such as professional offices, companies with uniforms, and government and non-profit associations. I interviewed one such business owner who in a 12-month period added three sub-contract delivery persons and increased total sales volumes to more than $100,000 per month by following this very basic formula for his dry cleaning delivery service.

OFFICE MOVING
★ $$

Unlike moving residential household furniture, moving office equipment and fixtures requires much more planning in order for the move to be successful and allow the business the fewest possible interruptions to their operation. An office moving service can be marketed through property management companies and directly to business owners via brochures and networking at business association functions. The main requirement is to carry sufficient liability insurance and to check to see if a mover's license is required in your community.

PEDAL BOAT RENTALS
★ $$

A fleet of ten pedal boats can generate as much as $30,000 in rental revenue in a single three-month season. Considering the business can be operated by one person and is relatively inexpensive to launch, that is an excellent return on investment. To establish a pedal boat rental business you will need a water-front location to operate from. The location can be independent or in partnership with an existing business such as a marina. The business can be supported by walk-in traffic as well as two-for-one coupons that can be issued for use on slower mid-week periods. Extra income can be acquired by adding a small catering cart that sells soft drinks and popcorn. This business venture may not make you wealthy, but it

can generate a good income and definitely will be a relaxing work environment.

WEB RESOURCE: www.bwmarineproducts.com Manufacturers of pedal boats and equipment.

BICYCLE COURIER SERVICE
★★★ $

The first step in starting your own bicycle courier service is to check and see if a courier license is required for your vicinity. Providing a license is not required, or you can secure one easily, the second step is to begin marketing your new bicycle courier service. To attract clients simply set appointments with local companies who would require fast, reliable, and local delivery service. Ideal candidates include law firms and design companies. You can charge similar rates for envelopes and small parcels as the motorized couriers charge, with the benefit being your overheads will be a fraction of theirs. One person can easily operate a bicycle courier service with a cellular phone for incoming delivery inquiries. The business can be expanded to include multiple bike couriers with a central dispatch system. Either way, this low-cost business venture is a sure fired way to earn an excellent income and stay very fit.

WEB RESOURCE: www.nybma.com New York Bicycle Messengers Association.

BODY PIERCING
★★ $$

Body piercing started as a fad in the '80s, continued to expand in popularity in the '90s, and looks to be becoming a mainstream industry in the new millennium. Starting a body piercing service does require experience or experienced staff, however, that is about the only requirement. This business venture can be started for peanuts and operated from a fixed location or on a mobile basis in different locations during peak holiday times. An obvious partnership for this kind of unique business is to incorporate your service with an existing business such as a tattoo parlor or hair and nail salon. Business partnerships help to reduce initial start-up costs and ongoing monthly overhead costs. Profit potential will greatly vary. However, once established this kind of business can easily generate weekly sales in excess of $1,000, especially if you also sell the jewelry items.

WEB RESOURCE: www.tattoospa.com Industry information and links to licensing requirements.

REUNION PLANNER

What is the best way to start your own reunion planner service? Acquire ten-year-old school yearbooks and start locating the students of that graduating year. Once you have assembled the list, organize the reunion, and send out the invitations. The attendees will have no idea who organized the reunion, or in most cases will not particularly care. Just as long as they are included and can meet and socialize with past friends and acquaintances. Revenue can be earned by charging an attendance fee to cover the cost of the event (plus a profit). As well, commemorative T-shirts, pictures, and videos can be sold to all in attendance. Organizing and hosting just one reunion per month can easily create a part-time income of $12,000 to $15,000 per year.

WELCOME SERVICE

Here is a business start-up that requires no practical business experience, and very little capital to activate. A welcome wagon service is simply making new residents of your community feel welcome and explaining all the various services and attractions that are available locally. Local companies pay you a small fee in exchange for promoting their products and services to new residents, thus creating a business income. These small fees really start to add up, especially if you are promoting 30 to 40 local businesses at any one time. To source information about new arrivals in your community, build alliances with real estate agents, business associations, and schools.

PRODUCT ASSEMBLY SERVICE

By anyone's estimate, there are far too many products sold that have to be assembled by the purchaser, and these assemblies are never as easy as advertised. A product assembly service can be started for well less than $500 and marketed directly through a retailer who does not currently provide this service to their customers. Of course additional revenue can be created if you also deliver the products that you will be assembling. The business only requires a few basic power tools and perhaps a van if you intend to provide delivery options. Remember that this business can also work in reverse for people who are moving and have to disassemble products and reassemble these same items once relocated. This aspect of the business can be promoted in conjunction with moving and storage companies.

PRIVATE INVESTIGATOR

When you think of a private investigator, images of Sam Spade may come to mind. However, private investigators today do not sleep in their office, carry a flask of whiskey, or wear trench coats and wide brimmed hats. Most assignments now handled by private investigators include spouse surveillance and insurance fraud investigation. The business does require an investigator license, and ideally a police or military training background. A well-established private investigator can enjoy an interesting lifestyle, which can be very well paying in terms of compensation for services.

WEB RESOURCE: www.becomeapi.com Directory service listing industry certification information.

NETWORKING CLUB

Starting a networking club in your community is a perfect way to be self-employed and make a large number of new and valuable business contacts.

Networking clubs are a perfect choice for a new business start-up, especially if the kind of networking club or business association that you are intending to start is currently not represented in your community. The purpose of a networking club is to introduce business owners and their products and services to other business owners. Networking meetings are usually very casual and generally take place in the morning as a breakfast meeting or in the early evening. Members pay a yearly or a monthly fee to belong to the club and to be listed in the club's directory. You can generate additional revenue by providing various services to your members, such as a fax blast service, monthly guest speaker seminars, and minibusiness trade shows that can be open to club members as well as the general public.

ONLINE BUSINESS NETWORKING CLUB
★★ $$$$ 🏠 ✏️

The time has never been better than now to start an online business networking club as homebased and small businesses are starting at a record pace in North America. The main objective is to create a forum where members can exchange business information, sales and marketing ideas, tips, and suggestions between each other; a type of business support group. In exchange for a yearly membership fee, members from around the globe would have full and unlimited access to the online club and its services. Information and services featured within the site could include marketing strategies, demographic research center, question-and-answer chat room, product-and-service marketplace, and online business seminars. To sell memberships employ sales consultants who are currently marketing business association memberships.

TELEPHONE ON-HOLD ADVERTISING
★★ $ 🏠 🕐

Millions of business owners are missing out on a prime opportunity to market their products and services every day. How? By not having prerecorded messages advertising their products and services when their call-in customers are placed on hold. For this business concept you create an on-hold advertising message for your clients and hire a professional voice person to record the message in a studio. The client pays for this service on a one-time fee basis or, on a monthly contract basis that includes a fixed number of changes to their telephone on-hold advertisement. The profit potential is excellent, especially if you can persuade a few hundred business owners to join your unique advertising service on a monthly billing basis.

ASSOCIATION SALES
★★★ $ 🏠 🕐

Business associations and clubs all have one thing in common. They all require members in order to generate revenue. Acting as an independent business association sale consultant is an extremely low-cost businesses start-up that can allow you the opportunity to capitalize on your sales abilities. There are literally hundreds of different associations you can contract your sales services to including boards of trade, chambers of commerce, tourist associations, and networking clubs. Your income will be earned by a commission charged each time you sign a new member into one of the associations that you are representing. A good formula is to charge a 30 percent commission on the first year's membership dues and a 10 percent commission for every year thereafter, providing the member remains active in the association. This billing formula gives you both a real and an annual residual earnings base.

ONLINE ASSOCIATION DIRECTORY
★★ $$$ 🏠 ✏️

Worldwide there are hundreds of thousands of various associations serving an unlimited number of special interest groups, charities, and business industries. Regardless of whether these associations are nonprofit or commercial associations, they all require members paying dues to generate revenues.

This is the basis of a new online business opportunity. Create a Web site exclusively featuring associations of every sort. Index the site by type of association, such as business, charity, sports, and so on. In exchange for being listed on the site, associations would pay a yearly membership fee and their listing could be hyperlinked to the association's own Web site or linked to a pop-up information page within the association directory site. Employ subcontract sales consultants across the country to solicit associations to become members.

PIANO TUNING SERVICE

 ★ $

Pianos are everywhere and they all need to be tuned and maintained on a regular basis in order to work and sound perfect. The main requirement is you have to know how to tune and maintain various types of pianos. Providing you have this skill and a few hundred dollars, you're in business as a professional piano tuner. A piano tuning service can be operated right from your vehicle with the aid of a cellular telephone. Operating a piano tuning service is perfect for the person seeking a good part-time income to supplement an existing one. Contacting local music stores and music schools to promote your service will be the fastest way to earn business via referral and word-of-mouth advertising.

WEB RESOURCE: www.pianoworld.com Directory service listing piano tuners links and industry information.

GIFT-WRAPPING SERVICE

 ★ $

Here is another low-cost business opportunity that is ideally suited to be operated part-time or on a seasonal basis. You can establish your own gift-wrapping service operating from a mall kiosk during holiday times, or in a partnership with a large retailer who will permit you to set up the business within their store. Either way, a gift-wrapping service can generate as much as $1,000 per day in profits during the busy Christmas shopping season. The business can also be operated on a year-round basis by adding additional services, such as a corporate shopping service, gift basket service, and an errand service, all of which are featured in this directory as business opportunities.

PACKING SERVICE

 ★ $

The least favorite task of any moving job is without question all the packing and unpacking of boxes full of personal items. Once again you can start your own packing service for peanuts and be sure of lots of business, because no one likes this necessary chore. Moving companies will be your best source of work, as they can directly supply the jobs or can refer your services to their customers. This is a great business to be partnered with a product assembly service, as operating the two services in one will assure you of ample demand to keep you working on a full-time basis. Generally for this type of service you would charge on a per-hour rate or on a flat rate for the entire job. Either way you should try to maintain at least $20 per hour for your services.

JACKHAMMER SERVICE

★★ $$

A jackhammer service is a very unique business opportunity that has virtually no direct competition, and starting your own jackhammer service is a low-cost way to be self-employed in the construction industry that can easily earn you $30 to $40 per hour. This construction service is required for removal of sidewalks, installation of new plumbing under basement floors, and breaking up small rock formations in the way of construction progress. You can offer your services to construction and renovation companies of every kind on an "as-required basis." The business can be operated from home and a cellular telephone. To really keep start-up costs to a minimum, rent the required jackhammer for your first few jobs until you have established that there is a need and demand for a jackhammer service in your community.

COMMERCIAL DOOR MAINTENANCE SERVICE

★★★ $$

Starting a commercial door maintenance route may be your opportunity to earn in excess of $100,000 per year. Best of all, this business can be started for peanuts. All commercial doors have one thing in common. They all need regular routine maintenance in order to be safe and work properly. Regular maintenance includes adjusting or replacing door closures and pivots, replacing automatic door-mats, and lubricating pivots and concealed hinges. The business does require that you have a working knowledge of commercial door systems. However, the learning curve is short and you can pick up a lot of this knowledge on the job. Additional requirements will be a service vehicle, tools, and an inventory of the most popular types of replacement parts, as these are generally only available through specialty distributors or directly from the door manufacturers. The business is best marketed by providing your services to business locations with commercial door entrances on a monthly service contract basis. Current service rates are in the range of $40 to $60 per hour, plus parts. Commercial property management companies can be your first stop to offer this much-needed service to their existing business customers.

WEB RESOURCE: www.specialtydoors.com Distributor of commercial door systems, parts, and supplies.

MOBILE MAKE-UP ARTIST

★★ $$

Calling all cosmeticians. Why not start your own make-up artist service and start earning profits for you instead of the boss? Providing you have the experience and required credentials, this is a very low-cost business venture to establish. You can market your services to photographers who specialize in actor's headshots, to residents of senior and retirement homes, to anyone in the film production industry, to soon-to-be-brides, and the list goes on and on. The business is best suited on a mobile service basis, so that you can take advantage of wherever your

services may be required. A make-up artist's service can be activated for less than $3,000, and can return profits far in excess of $30,000 per year for the owner-operator.

COAT CHECK SERVICE

★ $

Providing a coat check service for just one social function per week and charging only $125 for the service will earn you an additional $6,500 per year. Best of all it only takes a few hundred dollars and a little bit of legwork to get rolling. You can create your own marketing brochures, complete with pictures of yourself in an expensive tuxedo or evening gown, and distribute the brochures to potential paying customers. Clients can include wedding and event planners, catering companies, and trade show and seminar organizers. This type of event service is always in demand and is a great business start-up for the outgoing businessperson wishing to establish a good part-time income.

BILLING AUDITOR

★ $

How often as business owners or consumers do we miss overcharges on invoices that over time can add up to thousands of dollars? This fact is the only marketing tool you will need to promote a bill auditing service. Getting started will not require a large investment, but operating a bill auditing service does certainly require good bookkeeping and research skills. You can base rates on a percentage of money that may be recouped for clients, or on a flat hourly rate charge. The business can easily be operated from home on a part-time basis, and once established can generate revenues in excess of $20,000 per year.

NAIL STUDIO

★★ $$

There are various approaches that can be taken when considering starting a nail salon. These include:

- An independent nail salon can be established in a fixed retail location like a small storefront or a mall kiosk.
- The salon can be partnered with an existing business such as a hair salon or day spa.
- The business can be established as a mobile nail salon whereas you travel to your client's homes or offices.

Providing you already possess the proper credentials and experience to start this type of business venture, all three approaches to starting and establishing the business are viable. The best of the three is to partner with an existing related business, as you can minimize start-up costs and share monthly operating costs. Likewise, partnering with an established business allows you to take advantage of the client base. Once established, a nail salon can generate profits in the range of $40,000 per year.

WEB RESOURCE: www.nailartstudio.com Nail art designs and industry information and links.

REMOVABLE TATTOOS
★★ $$ 🕐

Here is a great business venture that can keep you busy earning money on weekends and evenings. Starting a removable tattoo business is economical in terms of needed start-up capital, and does not necessitate any special skills or equipment. The business is best suited to be set up on a mobile or portable basis via your own kiosk, tent, or cart. The kiosk can be located in malls on weekends or outdoors during any community event. Furthermore, partnering the business with a tourist attraction can be a fantastic way to create instant sales using the tourist customer base. In terms of profit potential for this kind of unique business venture, that will vary greatly depending on the business location and product markup. However, there should be no difficulties in earning $200 per day on a busy weekend, and even more if you are located in a busy tourist area or mall.

BOAT DELIVERY SERVICE
★ $ 🕐 ⚖

So you're a salty sea dog from way back, are you? Then why not put this experience to work for you and start your own boat delivery service? Depending on your experience you can specialize in sailboat or powerboat delivery. Many boats are sold to novice and inexperienced boaters who are from outside the area in which the boat was purchased. Utilizing your boating and navigational skills means you can deliver these boats to their homeport for the new owners. Additionally, many boat owners in northern climates like to move their boats to sunny southern climates for use in the winter months. Sailing or powering larger boats to a new temporary homeport is much cheaper than transporting the boats by land. Get started by marketing your boat delivery service to local marinas and boat retailers, as well as by joining boating associations to network for business. The business can be initiated for a very small investment, and return a comfortable living in terms of income. Additional revenue can be generated for this business venture by selling and installing electronics and general marine equipment, as well as by offering a rigging service for sailboat owners and a boat cleaning service for all boat owners.

DISTRIBUTION WAREHOUSE
★★★ $$$$

Homebased businesses and the Internet have created a booming market for distribution and warehousing services. Why? Because homebased and cyberventures generally do not have the infrastructure required to store and ship their products that are being sold. Starting a warehousing and distribution service means that you can act as a warehouse, shipping, and receiving agent for as many as 20 or 30 different companies. This business venture does require a great deal of research and investment capital. However, with careful planning and exceptional organizational skills, this type of business venture is capable of creating a six-figure income per year, all within a very short period of time for the enterprising entrepreneur.

MAILBOX CENTER
★★ $$$$ 🌐

Starting a mailbox center is a very easy business enterprise to activate that requires no special business experiences or skills. The main requirement will be a small retail storefront location; approximately 600 square feet will be more than sufficient. Likewise, you will need individually locking mailboxes and a few pieces of office equipment such as a high-speed photocopier, fax, personal computer, and scanner. The purpose for the additional office equipment is so you will have the ability to provide your customers with extra services like a photocopying service. Also, try to acquire the rights to act as a drop-off and pickup depot for courier companies, as this service can also produce sizable extra revenues and profits.

SHOWROOM DESIGNER
★★ $$ 🏠 🕐

Business owners who design their own retail showrooms waste millions of dollars each year. Why? Because in most cases the showroom that they have designed themselves in an effort to save money is very ineffective and as a result, can cost their business lost sales and profits. Showrooms must be visually appealing, customer-friendly in terms of traffic pattern and ease of locating a product, and functional for staff. As a showroom designer you can utilize all your creative talent and design experience to build a very successful and rewarding career. The business does not require a great deal of capital to start. However, experience and design knowledge will be required in order for this new venture to succeed. Teaming with commercial interior decorators is a very good entry point into this segment of the design industry. Additional revenue sources include providing clients with a window display service, renting props for showroom displays, and special sales and promotional events. Be sure not to limit your marketing efforts strictly on new store openings, as for every new store that opens there are 100 times as many existing stores that would benefit from having their showroom redesigned and may be more open to this type of service.

ERRAND SERVICE
★★ $ 🏠 🕐

Busy lifestyles dictate that many business owners and professionals do not have time for even the simplest of errands like taking the dog to the veterinarian. An errand service can be set up for peanuts and operated with the aid of a cellular telephone. Creating a marketing brochure that explains your service can be your best tool to attract new clients. The brochures can be distributed to business owners and professionals. Likewise a few promotional items such as pens and memo pads emblazoned with your company logo, name, and telephone number will go a long way as a gentle reminder of your fast, reliable, and affordable errand service. Attending just a few business association or networking meetings can easily secure a few dozen clients for this service. Remember this is the kind of business that can be supported 100 percent by referrals and word-of-mouth once established. The main objective is customer satisfaction, due to the fact that customer satisfaction is all you are really selling.

ONLINE ERRAND SERVICE
★★ $$$$ 🏠 🌐 🖱

Once again, busy lifestyles means that many people simply do not have enough time to look after life's small tasks, such as running errands. Thus a fantastic online business opportunity is created. Develop an errand service Web site that services your city or community and let people become members for free. All new members would receive a password and a secured errand page. Members wanting errands done would simply log onto the site and their errand page, type in the nature of the errand, and presto! Within 24-hours that task is completed. Errands could include pickup and drop-off of dry cleaning, picking up a bag of groceries, or taking the dog to the veterinarian. You can establish a system wherein all new errands logged in by members would automatically load into one central page of the site. These errands can then be e-mailed or faxed to your subcontract errand drivers and employees for completion. To keep bookkeeping easy a flat rate or fee for each errand can be charged, plus the cost if any for products or services that may have to be paid for in association with the errand.

BOOKING APPOINTMENTS BY PHONE

Are you seeking an easy homebased business to operate that can be started for less than $500? If so, perhaps you may want to consider starting your own appointment booking service for companies who rely on one-to-one sales presentations to drive their business. The concept is basic; you find businesses that require these types of appointments to be arranged, such as a vacuum cleaner sales company. The next step is to open the phone book at "A" and start calling people who would be interested in having a representative from the vacuum cleaner company come and demonstrate the product. Charge your clients a flat fee for every appointment you book for them. You will have no problem finding clients, as they only pay if you book the appointments.

LITTER PICKUP SERVICE

Starting a litter pickup service only requires a small investment and a few basic tools, such as garbage cans, shovels, and rakes. You can create your own low-cost promotional brochure that explains the benefits that a neat and tidy parking lot and entrance can have for a business, in terms of a customer's first impression. Like any service business, your goal should be to establish a monthly service contract with clients for providing the litter pickup service. A good rate to charge for your service would

be about $60 dollars per month for an average size parking lot and entrance area. In exchange the business owner would receive a weekly visit to their site in which you would pick up and remove all litter, as well as remove any simple stains on pavement and sidewalk surfaces. Each visit should only average about a half-hour in time and this quick and simple pricing formula can earn you $30 per hour.

BEACH EQUIPMENT RENTALS
★★ $$ ⏲

Renting beach equipment is not only a fun and relaxing business to operate; it can also be very profitable. The business can be established at any busy tourist beach area, either from a fixed location or a portable one right on the beach with proper permission. Hot rental items always include inflatable intertubes, shade umbrellas, snorkeling equipment, and surfboards. Additional revenue can be earned by providing quick surfing and snorkeling lessons. The profit potential is outstanding from renting beach equipment, as many of the rental items will return their initial purchase cost within as few as six rentals. Generally, this business is operated on a seasonal basis. However, if your lifestyle allows, the business can be established in multiple locations in different climates and operated on a year-round basis.

CONSTRUCTION SITE SAFETY CONSULTANT

Workers' compensation boards and insurance companies usually require that a least one person on a construction site have been trained in first-aid safety treatment. These regulations provide a wonderful opportunity for you to start your own construction site safety consulting service training construction workers in first aid and other related safety applications. The key requirement will be that you will first have to achieve the required certification yourself. This step is easy, and only requires a few months' time and a few certification courses. Your services can be marketed directly to construction companies and factories. Additional revenue can be gained by manufacturing your own first-aid kit, which can be sold to clients that you are providing training instruction courses too.

PORTABLE TOILETS
★★ $$$$

The not-so-sweet smell of success. Implementing a portable toilet business can be very lucrative, especially if you take the time to build a solid contact base. Clients can include event planners, construction companies, charities, sports associations, and just about every other business or organization that holds outdoor events. This is not an inexpensive business to start and operate. However, there is usually a minimal amount of competition, and the service is always in demand. The main requirements will be the purchase of the portable toilets and a delivery or pump truck. The truck will be the largest expense, as a new one can sell for as much as $150,000. To keep initial start-up costs down, a secondhand truck in good mechanical condition will probably be a better choice, at least initially.

WEB RESOURCE: www.nuconcepts.com Manufacturers of portable toilets.

COIN SEARCHING
★ $

This business requires no selling, advertising, managing, or record-keeping. Does this sound too good to be true? Well, it is true. Coin searching can earn you profits in your spare time and few people even know about this money-making secret. Simply start with a $100 float, head down to your local bank, and purchase $100 worth of rolled coins. The rest is easy. Once home break apart the rolls and start searching for valuable coins that have unknowingly been placed in the roll. Keep the valuable coins for resale, roll the left-over coins, and start the process over again with new coin rolls.

CONSTRUCTION FLAG SERVICE
★ $$

There are literally thousands of road construction projects and special events each year, which require the services of traffic control flag personnel. This business start-up lends itself perfectly to the home-based entrepreneur to manage and supply the required personnel to act as traffic control flag people. You can invoice the construction companies a fixed hourly rate for this service, and pay your employees a few dollars an hour less than what you have collected. Providing you can maintain ten people working on a full-time basis, this business can easily produce yearly sales of $60,000. The main requirement for this business venture is that you and your staff have taken an instruction course that will certify you for traffic control duties. This requirement could also produce additional sales revenues by charging all employees a fixed instruction course fee, prior to establishing employment with your firm.

CONSTRUCTION EQUIPMENT CLEANING
★★ $$

You do not often see bulldozers stopping into the local car wash for a quick clean up. It isn't practical, and would cost $20 just for fuel to get there. Investing in portable power washing equipment will give you the ability to start your own mobile construction equipment cleaning service. The main benefit for contractors to keep these pieces of equipment clean is that dirt and mud can affect the hydraulics and cause damage that can cost thousands of dollars to repair, not to mention the costly down-time delays. Market the service by simply stopping into all construction sites and solicit business. You will not have much resistance, as competition is limited for this type of service and all contractors realize the benefits of keeping the very expensive construction equipment clean.

WEB RESOURCE: www.carvedstone.com Directory service listing power-washing equipment manufacturers and distributors as well as industry information.

LIMOUSINE SERVICE
★ $$$$

The two most important requirements prior to starting a limousine service are to check in your local area to see if officials are awarding any further limousine vehicle licenses. If not, how much will it cost to secure one of these licenses through a resale opportunity? The next requirement is to secure a chauffeur driver's certificate. This step is relatively simple and only requires a written exam and practical road test to be successfully completed. Providing you meet these requirements, starting a limousine service is a terrific way to earn a very good living while being your own boss. In recent years many limousine companies have been turning away from the traditional stretch car format in favor of vans and large sport utility vehicles to serve as limousines. There are numerous reasons why this is being done and why you may want to also consider these types of vehicles for your own service. The first is that these vehicles are less costly and more practical. The second and perhaps more important reason is using this kind of transportation offers the occupants more privacy and security, which can be very crucial for corporate and celebrity clients. The financially cautious entrepreneur seeking to get into this business can start by working on a subcontract basis as a driver for companies that have the transportation but need drivers. In addition to providing corporate clients with limousine services, you can also offer wedding limousines, party and prom limousines, and airport shuttles. All can be marketed by establishing alliances with wedding and event planners and with hotels, convention centers, and business associations and networking groups.

WEB RESOURCE: www.limo.org National Limousine Association.

ONLINE DATING SERVICE
★★ $$$

Forty percent of North American marriages end in divorce. While this may be a sad commentary on the state of modern-day relationships, you will find this fact to be very uplifting if you are considering starting your own dating service. A dating service is best suited as an Internet enterprise via your own custom Web site. Choosing this as an operating format opens your dating service to the world, and will not limit your earning potential. One thing to keep in mind may be to specialize your dating service, such as an over-60 dating service. The possibilities are endless, especially for any business that can utilize and harness the power of the Internet as its base of operations and marketing.

BOOKBINDING AND REPAIRS
★ $

Working right from home you can bind books in small quantities and repair antique books. Bookbinding equipment is very inexpensive to purchase and there are even construction plans available that will enable you to build your own bookbinding equipment. Marketing the service can be as easy as establishing alliances with secondhand book retailers and book collector clubs. Likewise the ability to bind and repair books can also pay off in terms of finding valuable collectors books yourself, carrying out any needed repairs, and selling the books for a profit.

WEB RESOURCE: www.a1binding.com Distributors of bookbinding equipment and supplies.

CORPORATE GIFT SERVICE
★★★★ $$$$

Do you have an eye for the perfect gift? If so, starting a corporate gift service can make you a millionaire. A valued employee, existing clients, or wooing a potential client, gift giving is essential for most corporations. You can choose a hundred or a thousand perfect gifts that can easily be engraved, customized, or personalized for your corporate customers to give as one-of-a-kind gifts. Once you have selected the items that you will be retailing, create a catalog and Web site to display and promote the gift items. The catalogs can be distributed to corporations around the world, and the Web site address with a promotional message can be e-mailed to every corporate address you can find. The key to success is the gift items must be unique and ready for fast delivery to your customers. For the very enterprising entrepreneur this concept could be established as a franchise or license opportunity with the rights to all major cities being sold to individual owner-operators.

ONLINE BARTER CLUB

★ $$$

Most barter clubs cater to business owners who use a barter points system to swap products and services for their business requirements. Why not start a barter club for everyday people, so that anybody can barter for services and swap items with each other. This business start-up is definitely best suited as an Internet enterprise via your own custom-designed barter Web site. You can charge the members a yearly flat fee to join, which can give them unlimited access to your site to post items to be bartered as well as search all current barter postings. Likewise, once the site is established, you can sell advertising space to local companies seeking exposure to your membership base. This business is very basic and straightforward and requires little in the way of special skills or equipment, which makes this a great homebased business enterprise.

INVENTOR

★ $+

Are you the type of person who is always thinking of how to do something better? If so, maybe you should give consideration to becoming an inventor. The title is not as ominous as it sounds. Every day thousands of products, formulas, and methods are being invented to make life's tasks easier, or to assist mankind in general. Inventions do not have to be ground-breaking discoveries, they do however, have to have a practical use and be innovative and unique. The potential to profit as an inventor is as varied as the start-up cost of the invention itself. To see first-hand a simple and effective idea of what an invention can be, visit www.lawnbuddy.com. This very enterprising entrepreneur and inventor has a clear and concise understanding of the art of invention.

WEB RESOURCE: www.inventions.org Invention Assistance League.

AUCTION BUYER SERVICE

★ $$

Until the day arrives that all auctions take place via the Internet, there will always be a need for an auction buyer service. In a nutshell, an auction buyer is a person who takes the place of the purchaser at an auction when the purchaser is unable to attend. An auction buyer's service is very inexpensive to start, and clients can be gained through promoting your service in all traditional print media, as well as electronically over the Internet and through e-mails. Remuneration can be by way of a commission on the value of items purchased on behalf of clients, or on a flat-fee basis. Ideally you want to have several clients that you are representing at any one auction. This business start-up will really be of interest to those who have special skills and abilities, such as an art appraiser or antique car appraiser. The more specialized you make your service, the better the chance to eliminate competitors and the greater chance to increase revenues and profits.

PRODUCT DEMONSTRATION SERVICE

★★ $$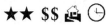

Companies, as a method to promote and introduce new products into the marketplace, often use product demonstration. We have all seen people in grocery stores offering free samples of food or cleaning products to customers. The concept behind this type of marketing is to try and get consumers to like the new product and therefore start to purchase it on a regular basis. The best method of operating a product demonstration service is to hire people to demonstrate the products on a part-time, as-needed basis. Typically, product demonstration services are awarded by companies on a contract basis and include a certain number of demonstration hours and outlets in the contract. Currently product demonstration rates are in the range of $7 to $10 per hour, and the product demonstrators typically receive 80 to 90 percent of the fee. It is vital to the survival of the business that a lot of contracts are secured for product demonstration in order to realize suitable business revenues and profits. The best way to secure product demonstration contracts is not by vying for new or existing contracts with many other demonstration firms, but to go looking for new business by soliciting companies that typically would not use this method of marketing for their products.

The reason for taking this type of marketing approach is that you greatly reduce competition, and number two, you get to utilize all of your entrepreneurial skills in getting potential clients excited about your service and the benefits it will have for their companies. Profit potential range is part-time $10,000+ per year and full-time $25,000+ per year.

SIGN MAINTENANCE SERVICE

★★ $$$

Look around, signs are everywhere and each one can represent money in your pocket. You can start a sign maintenance service on a relatively small capital investment, and manage the business right from a home office location. All signs require maintenance: light bulbs have to be changed, columns and support posts have to be repainted occasionally, and the signs have to be cleaned. Sign maintenance is most profitable when established on a monthly service contract basis. Clients pay a monthly fee in exchange for ongoing and automatic monthly sign maintenance. The monthly charge for maintenance will be as varied as the signs. New signs can range from $500 to $250,000 to purchase, which means there are no set rates; each individual sign must be priced on its own maintenance requirements. The equipment required for this business venture includes ladders, basic power tools, and a bucket-lift truck, all of which can be purchased secondhand for a fraction of the new cost. Market the service by establishing alliances with sign makers to work on a subcontract basis carrying out sign maintenance for their clients. Also simply create promotional brochures describing your service and distribute the information to commercial property management companies and to business owners with signage that must be maintained. Additional revenues can also be earned by purchasing mobile and inflatable signs that can be rented to business owners wanting to promote sales or special events for their business.

GOLD PLATING

★ $$$

Starting a gold plating business can literally give you the "Midas Touch." The equipment required to operate this business venture is readily available and inexpensive. However, the profits that can be earned are extremely lucrative. The following is only a partial list of items that can be gold plated, and a little bit of creative thinking can expand this list to thousands of items: kitchen and bathroom fixtures, cabinet hardware, automobile emblems, musical instruments, baby items, awards, nameplates, and light fixtures. A great way to establish this kind of business venture is to setup a kiosk and gold plate items on site while customers wait. Likewise, building alliances with custom homebuilders and automobile dealers is a great way to network and secure business for your service.

WEB RESOURCE: www.beckerindustries.com Distributors of gold plating equipment and supplies.

FINDER SERVICE

★ $

Starting a finder service is one of the easiest home-based business ventures to get rolling. A finder service simply means that in exchange for a fee you locate products or services that clients are seeking. These items could range from antique cars to military collectibles to a qualified babysitter prepared to work on holidays. Ideally, you will want to market your service to collectors; it does not matter what collectibles they are searching for just as long as they are routinely searching. You can base your fees on an hourly rate or you can charge clients a percentage based on the value of the item you have located for them. Additionally, be sure that you are connected to the Internet, as it will be your research tool for locating items for clients.

ONLINE FINDER SERVICE

★ $$$

Develop a Web site that enables people to post notices about items they are trying to find. These notices could include a particular item, service, or even person. In a nutshell the site would operate like a classifieds Web site, but instead of people selling items, people would place ads looking for stuff. The site could be free of charge for both visitors and people seeking to find something. Furthermore the posting could be kept current for a 90-day period after which time if they were not renewed they would be automatically erased. Providing the site was well promoted, it could become a very busy Web site in terms of the number of daily visitors, so advertising space could be sold to generate income and profits.

MOBILE HAIRDRESSING
★★ $$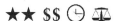

If you have a hairdressing license, starting your own mobile hairstyling business can be a wonderful way to operate your own profitable business. Clients can include all people who either are too busy to make appointments with traditional hair salons or people who for medical reasons cannot travel. You will want to contact seniors and retirement homes in your community to offer your service to their residents. Additional revenues can also be earned by providing clients with manicure and pedicure options. Profit potential can easily exceed $30,000 per year for the owner-operator of the business.

MANUFACTURER'S REPRESENTATIVE
★★★ $$

Industry directories are an invaluable research tool, or in the case of this business opportunity a manufacturers directory can put you on the road to earning in excess of $100,000 per year. Utilizing manufacturers directories can help you identify products that are not being manufactured or possibly even sold in your local community. Once you have identified these products and conducted your own market analysis into their viability in your area, you will be able to contact the manufacturers of these products from the information supplied in the directory. Working as a manufacturer's representative means you promote and market the products on a local, city, state, or in some cases country basis. Always try to negotiate an exclusive service contract with the manufacturer. This means you will be the manufacturer's exclusive

representative within certain geographic boundaries. Remuneration can be by way of a commission charged on total sales, or you can mark up your wholesale costs on the manufactured goods and resell at a higher price. The first method is preferred, as you will not need to warehouse any inventory.

WEB RESOURCE: www.nam.org National Association of Manufacturers.

SAW SHARPENING SERVICE
★ $$$

A mobile saw sharpening service is a great business enterprise to start that does not require a lot in terms of special skills or investment capital. Clients can include construction companies, butchers, ice rinks, landscape contractors, lawn mower repair shops, and just about every other type of company that relies on sharp blades and saws to conduct their business. You can operate the business on a mobile basis right from a van or enclosed trailer converted into a workshop, or you can operate from a home-based location offering free pickup and delivery of the items being sharpened. As a quick-start marketing method consider distributing two-for-one coupons to potential clients.

GLASS ETCHING
★ $$

Glass etching serves a few purposes. First, glass etching can be used as a method to engrave security numbers or names on glass items. Secondly, glass etching is used to create elaborate designs and pictorial themes on glass for interior decorating or artistic expression. Starting a glass etching service does not require a lot of investment capital to get rolling, and a homebased workshop is more than adequate for carrying out the work. Of course, the main requirement for starting this business is to have artistic talent, especially if the business will focus on etching designs for interior decorating. Overall, a glass etching business is a terrific small enterprise that can yield an income of $25 per hour or more.

BABYSITTING SERVICE

 ★ $ 🏠 🕒

There are a couple of options available to the entrepreneur who is considering a babysitting service as a new business enterprise. The first option is to simply become a babysitter, and surprisingly enough this can really pay off, especially during peak holiday times such as New Year's. The second option is to start a staffing service for babysitters, wherein parents can call one number to get a reliable, screened, and professional babysitter. The service would charge a flat rate; say $8 per hour and the babysitter would receive 75 percent of the fee while the service would retain the remaining 25 percent. Providing the service routinely achieved total billable hours in the range of 500 per week, the babysitting service could generate revenues in excess of $50,000 per year.

MORTGAGE PAYMENT CONSULTANT

 ★★ $$ 🏠 🕒

Did you know that paying your mortgage in weekly installments as opposed to monthly installments could save you thousands of dollars in interest charges over the life of the mortgage? While this is pretty basic math, many people never take the time to really calculate out how much money they can save by switching to weekly mortgage installments. Here is your opportunity to do it for them and make a profit for yourself at the same time. Becoming a mortgage payment consultant is easy. Generally there is no special license required and you can operate the service right from home. Begin marketing by hiring a telemarketing firm to set up in-home appointments with clients, or start a direct-mail campaign aimed at first-time homebuyers. Consulting appointments or presentations should only require a few hours in time to identify exactly how much the homeowner can save, so a fair fee for the service would be in the range of $75 to $125 per visit. Providing you can secure a mere ten new clients per week, this low-investment venture can generate a yearly income of $50,000 or more.

WEEKEND COURIER SERVICE

★ $$ 🕒

There are two ways to make money operating a weekend courier service. The first is to simply contract your delivery services to established courier companies on an as-needed basis. The second and more profitable method is to secure weekend delivery contracts with local merchants and professionals. You will need reliable transportation in order to operate this service, as well as a beeper or cellular telephone for incoming inquiries. Many merchants and professionals wait until Friday before shipping local deliveries simply because it is less expensive to ship multiple items than it is to ship one at a time. Waiting until Friday enables them to stock pile deliveries until the end of the week. Joining local business associations and attending networking meetings is a great way to promote your business and secure contracts for the service.

EVENT PLANNER

 ★★ $$ 🏠 🕒

There are basically two types of special events that take place: commercial events that have been specifically created to generate a profit such as a sales seminar, or special events of a social nature such as a wedding anniversary. Many will argue that there are an unlimited number of special events held annually in this country. However, at the core all will fall into one of these two categories. This is the starting point for starting an event planning service. Will the service focus on events of a commercial or social nature, or both? Catering to both is not recommended. To be considered successful, a commercial event must make money for the host or have the potential to pay back in the future. A social event will be considered successful by the number of accolades the guests provide, such as "this was the best picnic I have ever attended." I'm purposely focusing on the two types of events and not on what the duties are simply because the duties of an event planner are obvious, but the purpose is not as obvious. This fact is why you will want to specialize in the types of events you plan. Commercial clients that make money from the event you planned will be quick to refer or use your service again. People who you have planned social events for that went off without a hitch will also be quick to refer your service or use it again. However, as old as this cliché may be, it's true; a happy customer will tell one person about their experience with your business, a dissatisfied customer will tell ten people about their experience with your business. Hence the importance of specialization in business.

WEB RESOURCES: www.event-planner.com Directory service listing event planners, information about how to start and market an event planning service, and industry information and links.

WEDDING PLANNER

"Do you want to take a chance on anything but perfection for the biggest and most important day of your life?" This simple question is the most powerful sales tool you have as a wedding planner to convince potential clients that they need your professional planning service to ensure their wedding day is perfect. The cost of a typical wedding can easily exceed $20,000. Many brides- and grooms-to-be realize spending $1,000 to hire a professional wedding planner is not only money wisely spent, but also a cheap insurance policy on their substantial wedding investment. It is the duty of the wedding planner to plan the wedding, hire caterers and musicians, book a reception hall, and make one heck of a lot of suggestions. In other words, everything that is required to plan and carry out the perfect wedding. Be forewarned, the wedding consulting industry is competitive with more than 8,000 professional wedding planners in the United States. However, more than 2.4 million people tied the knot in 1999, thus a very lucrative opportunity exists for the entrepreneur that practices good research and planning skills when starting a wedding planning service.

WEB RESOURCE: www.nawp.com The National Association of Wedding Professionals.

CEILING CLEANING SERVICE

Starting a ceiling cleaning service is one of those business opportunities that can be a costly venture to set into action, or the business can be started for a modest amount of money. In the spirit of shoestring start-ups, let's choose the low-budget approach. Simply purchase a few buckets, a swivel-head cleaning pad with a telescopic handle, a ladder, initiate a basic marketing program consisting of flier distribution and introduction telephone calls, and you're in the ceiling cleaning business for less than $1,000. Build alliances with commercial property management firms and office cleaners, as both can refer your service to their clients. Do not be afraid to wear out a pair of walking shoes, because a great deal of new business can be secured by simply cold calling on offices and restaurants in your local area and introducing the owner or manager to your service. Ceiling cleaning is a solid choice for a new business enterprise; the industry is stable, there is proven consumer demand for the service, operating overheads are minimal, and the learning curve is quick and easy to master.

WEB RESOURCE: www.icwc.com Manufacturers and distributors of ceiling cleaning equipment and supplies.

AUCTION SERVICE

Did you know that it is estimated that more than 75,000 auctions sales take place each year in the United States? Becoming a certified auctioneer is not difficult, the course is less than two-weeks in duration and costs only a few thousand dollars. Once certified, a world of opportunity awaits the innovative entrepreneurial auctioneers. You can host and arrange your own auction sales or work on a contract basis auctioneering for other services. Many auctioneers like to specialize in one particular type of auctioneering service including real estate, automobiles, fine art, household furnishings, businesses, or heavy equipment. Depending on your experiences and skills you may also want to consider specialization for your service. Typically, auctioneers retain 7 to 12 percent of the value of the goods auctioned and in some cases also charge purchasers a bidders fee that can range from an additional 5 to 10 percent. However lucrative this may sound, be forewarned that hosting and promoting auction sales can be very costly. Directly from the commissions you have to pay for expenses, such as wages for employees, transportation costs, sale advertising and promotion, and administrative costs. Securing clients can also be difficult simply due to the fact that this is a competitive industry and sellers want as much for their products as possible, especially commercial clients. The decision to select one auction service over another is usually based on past performance and experience in the particular goods being auction. But providing research is completed, careful planning is practiced, and you take the time to build a strong and reputable service, a very financially rewarding future can lie ahead.

WEB RESOURCE: www.auctioneers.org National Auctioneers Association, industry information and links as well as certification programs.

FURNITURE ARRANGING SERVICE
★ $

Launching a furniture arranging and rearranging service that caters to residential and commercial clients is a fantastic new part-time business venture to put into action. The business can easily be managed from a homebased office, requires little in the way of experience or start-up capital, and has the potential to generate an income in the range of $15 to $25 per hour. Target your marketing efforts toward people and businesses that are the most likely to use the service, or refer their clients to the service. This can include moving companies, real estate agents, interior decorators, and furniture retailers. You can also market the service directly to homeowners by distributing fliers explaining the benefits of your service, as well as the benefits of having their furniture professionally rearranged (i.e., more visually appealing, better use

of small living spaces, increased functionality, etc.). A prerequisite for operating the business is an eye for design and organization, as well as a strong back. Extra income can also be earned by providing clients with additional services, such as a packing and unpacking service and a budget decorating service, both of which are also featured in this directory.

DISASTER PREPARATION CONSULTANT
★★★ $$$ 🏠 🕐 🌐

Every year in North America earthquakes, flash floods, hurricanes, tornadoes, blizzards, and wildfires reap destruction of enormous magnitude. We cannot control these forces of nature, but with careful planning we can be prepared when these disasters strike. Simply being prepared for a natural disasters when they strike can mean the difference of life or death. Starting your own disaster preparation consulting service not only makes sense, but it can also make you a wealthy entrepreneur. There are two aspect to the business: products and services. Products that can be marketed include first-aid kits, backup generators, emergency lighting, and nonperishable food and water packages. Services can include one-on-one consulting with clients to identify potential threats in disaster situations, how to react in these situations, and drafting emergency action plans to respond to a wide variety of natural disaster situations. The requirements for starting this type of specialized consulting services are numerous including first-aid training, disaster response training, and a varied knowledge of natural disaster situations and how to create proactive action plans. Gaining clients can be as easy as setting up a promotional kiosk in malls and trade shows and collecting leads from interested people. Given the frequency and widely publicized severity of many natural disasters, collecting qualified leads in this type of environment should not be difficult. The profit potential is outstanding as products can be marked up by 100 percent or more for resale, and consulting fees in the range of $50 per hour are certainly not out of line.

MYSTERY SHOPPER SERVICE

★★ $$

No mystery here, the title of this business opportunity explains it all. Go undercover and mystery shop at clients' businesses to assess their employees, operating procedures, and customer service policies. In the past decade more companies, organizations, and retailers have introduced mystery shopper programs into their business than ever before. And for good reason, as mystery shopper programs work very well at uncovering customer service problems and such. Many mystery shopper companies specialize in a particular industry or type of business, such as retail clothing stores and automobile service centers. You may also want to consider specialization for your business. Generally, the mystery shopper will prepare a document detailing their findings, relaying their experiences, and making recommendations to clients upon completion of their visit. Expanding the business is as easy as hiring additional mystery shoppers to work on a "subcontract as-needed basis." The industry is competitive so whatever relevant experiences and training you can bring to the table, the better. These experiences could include managerial training, prior customer service postings, human resources experience, and operations specialists. There are even mystery shopper training courses available that can put you on the path to starting and operating your own business. Once established the income potential is in the range of $15 to $25 per hour, per mystery shopper.

WEB RESOURCES: www.mysteryshopperjobs.com Industry information and links.

INDOOR ENVIRONMENTAL TESTING

★★ $$$

The air you breathe at home and work could prove deadly. As sobering as this statement is, there is truth to these words as more and more cases of indoor environmental toxic poisoning are reported each year. Getting started in the indoor environmental testing industry will mean an investment of time and money on your behalf to become a certified technician, or as known in the industry, a Certified Indoor Environmentalist. The Indoor Air Quality Association offers certification training and the basic course requires approximately one week to complete, costing in the range of $1,000. The association also offers further courses designed to certify technicians with more specific training and testing procedures in various environmental toxins.

Additional start-up costs will include equipment purchases, marketing and advertising budgets, transportation, and licensing. However, as a method to keep start-up costs to a minimum, once the certification process is complete you can subcontract your services to an existing indoor environmental testing company that requires technicians to service their clients using their equipment. Marketing the service can be accomplished by initiating a direct mail campaign, building alliances with commercial and residential property managers, and seeking government contracts to carry out air quality testing in government-operated buildings and institutions. Fees greatly vary depending on the testing that is being conducted, but the starting rate is equivalent to $30 per hour and can go as high as $100 per hour.

WEB RESOURCE: www.iaqa.org Indoor Air Quality Association, industry information and links as well as certification programs.

PLASTIC LAMINATING

★★ $$

Investing a few thousand dollars into laminating equipment is the first step toward starting your own part-time homebased plastic laminating business. This is one of those little known business opportunities that really has the potential to generate excellent profits for entrepreneurs with strong marketing skills. There are numerous items that can be laminated in plastic including restaurant menus, brochures, business presentations, identification cards, and place cards. There are also heat laminating presses available that will enable you to laminate items up to 48 inches in width. Having the availability to laminate items in plastic to that width opens up further opportunities for profits from laminating movie posters, maps, and charts for boaters and divers. Market the service directly to restaurants and to small print and copy shops that do not currently provide laminating options. Great add-on services to boost revenues include bookbinding and repairs, digital color printing, and a scanner service. Once word is out, the business can largely be supported by repeat business and word-of-mouth referrals.

WEB RESOURCE: www.laminators.com Distributors of laminating equipment and supplies.

GARAGE AND ESTATE SALE PROMOTER

Excellent profits await the entrepreneurs that possess good marketing and organizational skills by starting a business that promotes and hosts garage and estate sales. Garage, lawn, and estate sales are a popular weekend event in every community across North America. Operating as a garage and estate sale promoter you can provide clients who do not have the time to hold their own garage sale with the service of organizing and operating the sale for them. Your duties will include promoting, organizing, displaying, and selling the items, and cleaning up after everyone has gone home. In a nutshell, it's your client's sale, at their location, with their stuff for sale, but with you as the ringmaster who has organized and carried out the event. Of course in exchange for providing this valuable service you retain a percentage of the total revenues the sale creates. Typically, the commission will be in the range of 20 percent for larger sales, and up to 50 percent of revenues for smaller sales. Generally you won't find many clients that will complain about surrendering a percentage of the sales, simply because if it wasn't for your service there is a good chance that the sale would not take place.

The key to success in this type of business is promotion. Once you have secured a client, be sure to canvas the neighborhood and solicit for additional business. Why hold a small sale if you can potentially increase revenues and profits by enlisting neighbors to also provide items to be sold? Market the sale by promoting it in local newspapers that do not charge for classified ads or that do not charge for garage sale notices. Also have large signs made that can be tem-

porarily installed on telephone poles in the area that the sale is being conducted. To secure future business simply hand out promotional brochures and tell people in attendance about your service. Imagine, hosting one sale per week that generates revenues of $1,000 can earn you as much as $20,000 per year in gross profits. That is an excellent profit potential when you consider that the business can be operated part-time and started on an investment of only a few hundred dollars.

OFFICE CONTRACTOR

Here is a terrific business opportunity that will appeal to entrepreneurs with a renovation or construction management background. Big profits can be earned operating a contracting business that specializes in office renovations. Having operated a contracting business for many years, I always found that the commercial jobs or office renovation contracts generally produced the highest profit margins, often two times that of residential renovation jobs. The higher profit margins were usually attributed to a few factors including less changes along the way (completion on time), a less competitive marketplace, and a higher grade of products used in finishing (increased average sale).

To truly succeed in this segment of the construction industry will require patience, as often jobs are not put up for tender or bidding and are awarded on the basis of a referral or having completed past contracts for the client. However, once again patience can be rewarded with profits. You can market the service by establishing alliances with commercial property management companies, moving companies that specialize in office relocation, commercial building cleaners, and real estate and insurance agents. In most cases you will find it to be financially beneficial to hire subcontractors to complete the work as opposed to hiring employees. This is simply due to the nature of the construction industry as a whole and trying to maintain employee salaries during the lean times can mean the difference of staying in business or meeting with financial disaster. Additionally, equipment can be rented on an as-needed basis to keep start-up costs in check. Profit potential will vary on a job-to-job basis, but when estimating always try to maintain a 50 percent markup on labor and materials. Using this pricing formula will result in a 33 percent gross profit margin prior to operating overheads and taxes. Aim to generate gross sales of $1 million per year and you can generate gross profits in excess of $300,000.

BRIDAL AND FASHION SHOW PROMOTER
★★ $$

Excellent profits can be earned by organizing and hosting bridal and fashion shows. The shows can take place four times per year and feature bridal and clothing fashions for that season. You can rent a ballroom or banquet hall to host the event and with some clever negotiation skills you may even be able to secure the venue at no charge providing you can convince management that food and beverage sales will be more than sufficient rent payment. Local merchants in the bridal and fashion industry can be easily secured to showcase their products and services, as there is no cost to the merchants to participate in the show. Revenues to support the business and generate a profit are earned by charging an admission fee to the show, as well as by selling advertising space in the event program and in the form of banners and place cards at tables. Additionally, be sure to secure a co-sponsor of the events such as a newspaper or radio station that can assist in promotion. Expanding the business is as easy as promoting and hosting the shows in different communities, and for the truly innovative entrepreneurs you can even establish a Web site that features a year-round online bridal and fashion show, as well as promotes the live versions as they take place.

SMALL CAPACITY BANQUET FACILITIES
★★ $$$$

Small banquet facilities that are suitable for a 100 guests or less are becoming very popular. Starting this type of business just might be the answer to the question of what type of part-time and potentially profitable business can I start? You can get started by leasing a suitable commercial location and carrying out the required renovations and leasehold improvements to turn the space into a small banquet room. The facility will require washrooms, a small well-equipped commercial kitchen that can be utilized by outside caterers, and fixtures such as tables and chairs. These types of small banquet facilities are perfect for corporate functions, social and family functions, weddings, awards ceremonies, stockholder meetings, and seminars. The goal is not to become an event planner or host of the banquet, but to supply a well-equipped and comfortable location for clients that wish to rent an event location. Basically, you rent clients the location and equipment they need to host their event. Market the banquet facility by establishing alliances with catering companies, event and wedding planners, corporations, social and business clubs, and local charity groups. It will not take long until the banquet room is booked well in advance by repeat clients and clients who have heard about the service word-of-mouth. Be sure to check with and conform to local building and health codes when establishing the business. You will need a health board license for the kitchen, on-site fire and safety equipment to meet fire codes, and perhaps a liquor or beer and wine license as well.

SPECIALTY WIRING SERVICE
★★ $$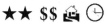

Put your basic construction and wiring experience to work for you by starting a specialty wiring service. Computers, built-in speakers, fire and security alarms, and televisions all have one thing in common—most still require hardwiring in order to work. And until the day that all techno toys, gadgets, and home electronics are wireless there will be a huge demand for the services of a wiring specialist. Starting this business does not mean that you need to be a certified electrician as these types of wiring jobs are nonelectrical or low voltage and do not require a certificate to install. However, basic tools and a good understanding of wiring and networking systems is required. You can provide specialty wiring installation for both new construction and retrofitting of homes and offices. It is obviously easier to install wiring cable and products in a new construction situation, but this segment of the industry is also much more competitive. Additionally, some wiring installation contractors prefer to specialize in one or two types of wiring, such as computer networks or built-in sound and speaker systems. Depending on your experience and local competition in the marketplace you may want to also consider specialization. Market your products and services by developing partnerships with builders of new homes, renovation contractors, and residential and commercial property management companies. Also an excellent income can be earned by subcontracting your services to existing businesses, such as alarm companies (certificate or bonding may be required), electronic and computer retailers, TV cable providers, and satellite TV retailers. Currently specialty wiring installers are charging in the range of $40 per hour for the service, plus materials used.

NOTES

KEY

RATINGS ★
START-UP COST $
HOMEBASED
BUSINESS 🏠
PART-TIME 🕐
LEGAL ISSUES ⚖
FRANCHISE OR
LICENSE POTENTIAL 🌐
ONLINE 🖱

39

SPORT AND FITNESS

Businesses You Can Start

PUTTING GREEN SALES AND INSTALLATIONS
★★★ $$$ 🏠 🕐 🌐

Without question golf has become one of the most popular sports and recreational pastimes in North America. Golf putting greens can be designed for indoor or outdoor installations, as well as sold to both residential and commercial customers. To avoid installation problems and time delays, it is best to predesign six to ten different layouts for the putting greens. When designing the greens, keep in mind the various objects that could potentially be in the way such as tree roots, gardens, and lawn sprinklers. The best way to market golf putting greens and generate the largest profit margins will be to sell the golf greens directly to the residential homeowner or a business owner seeking to install the putting greens at their business for personal and employee use. Sales and marketing options include:

- Direct-sales team with company and self-generated leads.

- Putting green demonstration display set up at home and garden trade shows, outdoor and recreations shows, and at malls on weekends with the purpose of generating interest and sales leads from potential customers.
- Contacting residential homebuilders and soliciting for businesses to include the putting greens as optional upgrades for their clients.
- Business-to-business networking clubs and associations.

The profit potential for a business enterprise that designs, sells, and installs golf putting greens is tremendous as elaborate residential golf putting greens are retailing for as much as $10,000.

INDOOR VOLLEYBALL
★★★ $$$$ 🌐

Are you searching for a fun and interesting sports-related business start-up that has little competition and has the ability to produce a quick return on investment? Search no further, for starting a year-round indoor volleyball center can provide you with that and more. What could be more fun than starting a business that enables customers to have fun and stay fit at the same time? However, with that being said, starting an indoor volleyball center is no different from starting any other business and requires careful planning, research, and good business judgment to be practiced. The business can generate sales and profits in a couple of ways, including selling yearly volleyball memberships and by providing different products and services for members such as a concession stand, clothing sales, and even volleyball training and instructional clinics. Once again, the profit potential for an indoor volleyball center is outstanding, especially when you consider the operating overheads can be kept to a minimum, and a mere 300 members paying only $40 each per month will create yearly sales of $120,000.

WEB RESOURCE: www.usavolleyball.org USA Volleyball is the national governing body for the sport of volleyball in the United States.

SPORTS CAMPS
★★★ $$$

Every year thousands of children and adults attend numerous sports camps across North America, and launching a sports camp has the potential to be a very profitable business venture, not to mention a whole lot of fun. The theme of the sports camp can vary from hockey to baseball to gymnastics, and just about any sport in between. The camp can cater to training kids or adults or both, and can be based on a day camp or weeklong format that includes accommodations for the camps' participants. If possible try to recruit a local sports celebrity to assist in coaching or training at the camp or at least a well-known amateur or professional athlete or coach who will publicly endorse the sports camp. The amount of income that can be earned operating a sports camp will greatly depend on a number of factors, including seasonal or year-round facility, number of participants trained, operating format, and overhead. Market the camp by ways of traditional print advertising and by initiating a direct-mail campaign aimed at sports and social

clubs, associations, and at corporations looking for interesting ways to build a "team player" attitude for employees. There are numerous requirements to starting this type of business, including safety and liability issues, equipment and location, special skills, and experience in the chosen sport. However, for the determined entrepreneur the time spent researching, planning, and setting up this type of business venture has the potential to justify the effort both financially and personally.

WEB RESOURCE: www.sportscampnetwork.com Directory service listing sports camps.

HOME GYM DESIGNER
★★★ $$$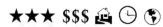

The time has never been better than now to start this business, especially when you consider the fact that a recent U.S. government survey indicated a full 50 percent of American adults were going to start a regular fitness program in the next six months. When you also consider that many of these same people simply do not have the time to go to fitness clubs, working out at home quickly becomes their only option. The focus of the business is not only to sell home fitness equipment such as weights and treadmills, but also to design or transform existing rooms into home gyms.

START-UP COSTS: The following example can be used as a guideline to establish the investment required for starting a home gym sales and installation business.

	Low	High
Business setup, legal, banking, etc.	$500	$2,000
Office equipment, stationery, etc.	$1,500	$3,000
Portable demonstration display	$5,000	$8,000
Initial marketing and advertising budget	$1,500	$3,000
Working capital	$1,000	$2,500
Total start-up costs	$9,500	$18,500

PROFIT POTENTIAL: Establishing a pricing formula for this business is very basic. Simply multiply material costs, labor costs, and equipment costs by 1.5 times, or add 50 percent markup onto the wholesale and labor costs. This pricing formula will result in a 33 percent gross profit margin on total sales volumes prior to taxes and overhead costs being applied. Maintaining yearly sales of $200,000 would result in gross profits of $66,000 using this pricing formula.

WEB RESOURCE: www.whatsthebest-workout.com Buying guide rating home fitness equipment.

PERSONALIZED GOLF BALLS
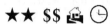 ★★ $$

Personalized golf balls make fantastic gifts, and launching a part-time business that personalizes golf balls can earn you an extra $10,000 per year or more. America is golf-nuts, no other sport or recreational past time is enjoyed by more people than golf, and while this is certainly not enough reason to start a business that sells personalized golf balls, it sure is a good start. The equipment needed to print names, messages, or company logos on golf balls is very inexpensive and available at any silk-screening supply store. Golf balls can be purchased in bulk for as little as $4 per dozen, printed, and resold for as much as $40 per dozen. In addition to gifts for the golf enthusiast, personalized golf balls can also be sold to companies featuring their logo to be given to clients, charity and company golf tournaments, and to tourists with printed messages or images of the place they are visiting. Selling the golf balls can be accomplished by establishing a sales kiosk at malls or even right at busy golf courses and printing the balls while the customer waits. The golf balls can also be preprinted with a humorous golf message and sold to retailers on a wholesale basis.

WEB RESOURCE: www.print-maker.com Distributors of pad printing equipment and supplies.

ONLINE PERSONALIZED GOLF BALL SALES
★★★ $$+

Sell personalized golf balls online to golfers from around the globe via your own Web site. This sort of Web site would be very easy to create and visitors wishing to purchase golf balls emblazoned with a name, logo, or message could simply complete an online order form, submit the order, and wait for their golf balls to be delivered. In addition to the individual consumer purchasing personalized golf balls, be sure to also initiate a direct-mail and e-mail marketing program aimed at corporations and charities for golf tournament balls. You can purchase the printing equipment to personalize the golf balls, or the design and printing aspects of the business can be contracted to an outside source, while you concentrate on the sales, marketing, and promotion aspects of the business.

SPORTS MEMORABILIA
 ★★ $$

Buying sports memorabilia, such as team jerseys, autographed sports celebrity photos, and sports equipment at discounted or bargain prices and then reselling the same memorabilia to collectors and hardcore sports fans at a profit is a terrific little part-time homebased business venture to set in motion. Initiating this business will require some time spent at flea markets, on the Internet, and rummaging through garage sales to find and purchase the sports treasures. However, the payday can be large, especially when you consider rare sports trading cards can fetch $1,000 or more. Once an inventory of good quality sports memorabilia has been assembled it can be resold by establishing a company Web site that sells sports memorabilia at sports trade shows and by even placing classified advertisements in newspapers for the more rare and expensive sports memorabilia items for sale.

ONLINE SPORTS MEMORABILIA SALES
 ★ $$+

Develop an online auction service exclusively for people from around the world wanting to buy and sell sports memorabilia items. Income is earned in a few ways: the first is to charge a flat fee to auction a memorabilia item, while the second option is to retain a percentage or commission based on the selling price of the memorabilia. Of course, you could also provide the auction service for free and rely on selling advertising space as the main source of business revenues. Promote the Web site in sports publications, as well as by utilizing online marketing options such as search engine registrations, hyperlinks, and rotating banner advertisements.

FITNESS EQUIPMENT REPAIRS

 ★★ $

Starting a business that specializes in fitness equipment repairs and maintenance is a great homebased business opportunity to set in motion. Potential customers can include commercial fitness gyms and centers, government-operated fitness centers, companies with on-site employee gyms, and homeowners with home gyms and fitness equipment. Fitness is a huge growth industry, and securing your place in this industry could prove to really pay off in the future as more and more expensive fitness equipment begins to age and require routine maintenance and repairs. The business is very easy to establish and only requires a basic mechanical aptitude to repair the equipment. Ideally, you will want to establish automatic monthly maintenance contracts with fitness facilities; securing only ten contracts at $500 each per month will generate yearly business sales of $60,000.

USED GOLF BALL SALES

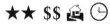 ★★ $$

Securing contracts with public and private golf courses and clubs to retrieve golf balls from water traps could put you on the path to self-employment independence and financial freedom. Every year millions of golf balls are lost in water traps across North America, and reclaiming these balls to be resold as used golf balls is very easy to do. The main requirements for the business are to be a certified scuba diver, as well as have scuba-diving equipment. The golf balls that are retrieved can be sold to the golf course or directly to the public by way of golf equipment retailers and even the Internet. Golf balls that have been used in a celebrity golf tournament are selling for as much as $25 each with the name of the tournament stamped on the ball. Golf balls that have a celebrity golfer's name stamped on the ball can fetch as much as $500 each depending on the popularity of the person whose name is on the ball.

USED FITNESS EQUIPMENT SALES

 ★★★ $$+

Are you a fitness buff, and do you have some extra space around the house and extra time on your hands? If so, why not consider starting a part-time homebased business venture that buys previously owned fitness equipment and resells the same equipment for a profit? The time has never been better than now to start this type of business enterprise, as millions of people across North America are striving to become more fit, and obviously fitness equipment plays a major role in that pursuit. The fitness equipment can be purchased at garage sales, auction sales, and through newspaper classifieds. Reselling the fitness equipment is also very easy as it can be advertised for free in many community newspapers and community information boards, as well as by designing product information and pricing fliers and distributing the fliers throughout the community on a regular basis. This is the type of business that will be promoted by word-of-mouth, and it won't take long until the telephone is ringing off the hook with people calling about fitness equipment they want to purchase or sell.

START-UP COSTS: The following example can be used as a guideline to establish the investment needed for starting a part-time business that sells used fitness equipment.

	Low	High
Business setup, banking legal, etc.	$200	$1,500
Initial used fitness equipment inventory	$2,000	$10,000
Office equipment and supplies	$250	$2,000
Initial advertising and marketing budget	$250	$1,000
Transportation (used utility trailer)	$250	$750
Working capital	$250	$1,000
Total start-up costs	**$3,200**	**$16,250**

PROFIT POTENTIAL: The part-time income potential associated with this type of unique homebased business venture is excellent, and the key to making money will lie within your negotiation skills. The goal is to purchase good-quality secondhand fitness equipment for as little as possible, while selling the same equipment for as much as the market will bear. Aim to get in the habit of establishing a standard pricing structure, or formula. This means you want to create a system for maintaining profitability. This type of system is easy to develop. The first step is to acquire as much information as possible on fitness equipment in general as well as the original cost of the fitness equipment. This information can be used to develop a resource library. A suggested pricing structure would be to rate the fitness equipment first in terms of condition, and purchase the used equipment at 5 to 25 percent of the original cost new. Establishing a retail selling price for the equipment is aimed at maintaining a 100 percent markup. Providing this pricing structure is used and annual sales of $50,000 are achieved, the result would be a homebased business that is generating $25,000 annually prior to overheads and taxes.

FITNESS EQUIPMENT CLEANING
★ $$

Are you looking for a business opportunity that can be managed from home, that costs less than $500 to get rolling, and requires no special business experience or skill? If so, look no further. Starting a business that specializes in cleaning commercial fitness equipment is a fantastic business enterprise to set in motion. As fitness awareness and the number of participants continues to grow, the future for a fitness equipment cleaning service looks terrific. Additionally, combining a fitness equipment cleaning business with a fitness equipment repair service would be a great way to increase customer services offered as well as business revenues and profits. Once established, this unique service with little in the way of competition should easily generate an hourly income of $20 or more.

MOBILE GYM
★★ $$$$ ⚖

Calling all fitness instructors who are looking for a way to start their own fitness instruction business that has the potential to generate a six-figure yearly income. Starting a mobile gym and fitness instruction business is a fantastic new venture to put into action, as the mobile aspect of the business enables you to go and get the clients, instead of waiting for them to come to you. This type of fitness business is highly specialized and the target market though large, is narrow at the same time due to the prohibitive cost associated with one-on-one fitness training and instruction. The ideal target market or customer for this type of fitness training is the professional in business who does not have time to go to the gym, and who is seeking highly focused fitness workouts and instruction. People such as TV and movie actors and crew who cannot leave the set are good candidates, people who operate a homebased business that requires them to be in or very close to their homes every day, as well as people who are seeking to gain fast and effective results from an intensive fitness program. A mobile gym business can be operated right from a five-ton truck or large enclosed trailer and feature the same kind of professional fitness equipment that is found in a commercial fitness center.

REQUIREMENTS: The main requirement for starting a mobile gym business is the instructor must be a certified fitness instructor. There are fitness instructor certification courses available in almost every major city in North America, and the length of these training courses are generally less than a year in duration. Additionally, due to the nature of the venture, general business and liability insurance will also be a necessity.

START-UP COSTS: The following example can be used as a guideline to establish the investment needed to start a mobile gym business. The cost associated with becoming a certified fitness instructor is not included in the example.

	Low	High
Business setup, banking, legal, etc.	$250	$1,500
Transportation, five-ton truck or trailer (used)	$12,500	$20,000
Fitness equipment	$7,500	$15,000
Initial advertising and marketing budget	$1,000	$2,000

	Low	High
Office equipment and supplies	$1,000	$2,000
General business and liability insurance	$1,000	$1,000
Working capital	$1,500	$3,000
Total start-up costs	$24,750	$44,500

PROFIT POTENTIAL: Once established, a mobile gym and fitness training service can generate an incredible income. Currently mobile gym operators limit class sizes to three people at once and charge rates that start at $40 per hour and can go as high as $60 per hour.

WEB RESOURCE: www.body-basics.com National Association for Fitness Certification.

MINIDRIVING RANGE
★★ $$$$ 🌐

A minidriving range is simply a scaled-down version of a traditional golf driving range, and one of the best aspects of a minidriving range is that it can be located just about anywhere. These locations include on top of an industrial building, in the corner of a large parking lot, or even indoors in an industrial warehouse. The concept behind a minidriving range is not driving the golf balls for distance, but more so for accuracy and correctness of swing. The driving range itself does not have to be large and ball nets can be used to ensure the golf balls are kept within the range. Once established, a minidriving range could easily generate yearly profits in excess of $40,000.

WEB RESOURCE: www.sterlingnets.com Manufacturers of golf driving range nets.

ONLINE FITNESS BOOKS AND PROGRAMS
★ $$$ 🏠 🕐 🖱

There are a few approaches that can be taken to start a business that produces and sells fitness books. The first approach is to write the fitness books by compiling information supplied by fitness experts in their field of specialty. The second approach is to purchase fitness books from publishers and book distributors on a wholesale basis and retail the fitness books via mail order, a sales kiosk, or the Internet.

The profit potential will vary as to the selected approach taken in establishing and operating the business, however, fitness is a popular subject and millions of books on fitness and fitness-related topics are sold each year in North America. Securing a portion of this very lucrative market should not be difficult. Should you chose the route of Internet marketing it would be very easy to develop a Web site that featured fitness books and video products for sale. Authors, publishers, and video producers could utilize the site to market their products. In exchange for providing this service you could charge these fitness gurus a listing fee to be featured on the site or alternately a percentage of product sales.

TROPHIES
★ $$ 🏠 🕐

Each year in North America millions of trophies are given to winning sports teams, game MVPs, and to people being recognized for outstanding achievement. The demand for trophies is not only proven, it also continues to increase every year as the population of people and popularity of sports continues to grow. A trophy supply and engraving business can be started for less than $5,000, and purchasing trophies on a wholesale basis should not prove to be difficult as there are thousands of trophy manufacturers worldwide. Furthermore, the equipment needed for engraving name plaques for the trophies is inexpensive and available at most building centers in every community. Profit potential range is $10,000+ per year.

CUSTOM GOLF CLUB SALES
★★★ $$ 🏠 🕐

Big profits await the entrepreneur who starts a business that builds custom golf clubs on a made-to-order basis, as well as repairing golf clubs. A custom golf club manufacturing and sales business is the perfect business to be established on a part-time basis from a homebased location. Later the business can be expanded from the profits that are earned. Manufacturing custom golf clubs may not be as difficult as you think, as there are numerous manufacturers of golf club parts, and the parts can be purchased on a wholesale basis and assembled into a finished product to be sold. As previously mentioned, additional revenues can be earned by providing a golf club repair service to clients.

ONLINE GOLFING WEB SITE

★★★ $$+

The world is golf nuts. Starting an online business venture catering exclusively to the golf fanatic has the potential to make you a cybergazzillionaire. In terms of the golf Web site that you develop, you will want to be creative and seek a niche or untapped market. Here are a few suggestions:

- An online tee time reservation service linked to all the major golf courses across the country.
- A golf coupon site wherein visitors could locate deals and discounts on thousands of golfing products and services.
- An online directory featuring private and public golf course information, such as where they are located, greens fees, and contact information.
- An online golf instruction Web site that enables visitors to log on and learn how to improve their stroke or short game.

The sky is the limit in the online world of cybergolf.

ELDERLY HOME FITNESS TRAINER

★ $$

It is a fact that North Americans are living longer and healthier lives than ever before. This fact creates a fantastic opportunity for the certified fitness instructor to capitalize by starting a mobile fitness training service that specializes in fitness training for seniors. The fitness classes can be conducted right on site at senior citizen and retirement homes, and of course the participants of the fitness classes will be the residents of these institutions. The main requirement for conducting fitness training classes for seniors is to have a fitness instructor training certificate. For those of you who do not meet the requirements for starting this unique fitness service, fear not, a fitness instructor training certificate only requires a few

thousand dollars in course fees and about one year's time to secure. Potential income range is $25 to $40 per hour.

WEB RESOURCE: www.aerobics.com Aerobics and Fitness Association of America.

SPORTS AGENT

★ $$

Finding and representing the next Tiger Woods as a sports agent has the potential to make you a millionaire. Be forewarned that competition is fierce and your contact base in the sports industry in general must be excellent. The main duty of a sports agent is to negotiate for their clients the best possible contracts and product endorsement deals. A simple method to get started working as a sports agent on a part-time basis while building valuable industry experience is to seek out local amateur sports talent on a high school or university level in your own local community. Once you have secured the person you will be representing, you can start to build contacts and alliances within the industry. Becoming a sports agent will take a great amount of time, planning, and research. However, the end results could prove to be a very rewarding career, personally and financially, as an independent sports agent.

ARCHERY RANGE

★★ $$$$

Archery is fast becoming an extremely popular sport in the United States, and starting an archery range is a fantastic way to capitalize on the recent surge in popularity of archery. An archery range can be established as an independent business or as a joint venture with an existing business such as a gun club. In addition to generating revenues from membership dues, the business can also earn revenues and profits by selling archery supplies and providing training instruction. To secure members and customers for a new archery range, offer a grand opening two-for-one special for all new members who sign up in the first month.

WEB RESOURCE: www.usarchery.org National Archery Association.

ONLINE ARCHERY SUPPLIES
★ $$+ 🏠 🕐 ⚖ ✂

Archery supplies are the sort of specialized consumer products that you cannot run out and buy at your corner store in most communities. An exciting online business opportunity exists by posting a Web site to the Internet that is dedicated to selling hard-to-find archery supplies. This sort of e-commerce Web site is simple to create and maintain and could easily be operated part-time from home. You can purchase archery supplies on a wholesale basis and stock an inventory or you can electronically forward customer orders to manufacturers and distributors of these products and have them ship directly to your customers. Promote the site in print publications relating to archery and hunting as well as by establishing alliances with archery clubs and associations.

WEB RESOURCE: www.entrepreneur.com Create a business Web site with MySite professional Web site builder.

FITNESS TRAINING FOR THE DISABLED
★★ $$ 🕐 ⚖

Every industry can be broken down into specialty segments within the industry, and the fitness industry is no different. Starting a business that focuses on providing fitness training and classes for the disabled falls into this industry specialization classification. On the surface fitness training for the disabled may seem to be similar to fitness training for able-bodied students. However, there are numerous differences that must be taken into consideration, such as smaller class size and the location for the classes must be handicap accessible including parking. A minimum of two trainers or supervisors must be present; not to mention the fitness classes will have to be developed to suit various types of disabilities. Starting a business that provides training classes and instruction for the disabled will take careful planning and research, but with a little bit of innovative thinking applied, the entrepreneur starting this business can look forward to a personally gratifying future.

ONLINE SPORTS TRADING CARDS
★★ $$ 🏠 🕐 ✂

Rare sports trading cards can sell for as much as $1,000 each, and this creates a terrific opportunity for the enterprising entrepreneur to start a home-based sports card trading business. Simply put, purchase sports trading cards and resell the sports cards to collectors and sports card enthusiasts for a profit. There are mainly two requirements that are needed to succeed in the sports card trading industry. The first is you have to know or at least have an interest in sports cards and their value. And, the second is you have to have the time available that will be needed to find rare sports cards at bargain prices. This means getting out to as many garage sales and flea markets as possible. Once a sports card inventory has been secured the e-cards can be marketed by placing advertisements on the Internet, as well as listing the more rare cards with online auction services to be sold.

FITNESS CLASSES FOR DOGS AND OWNERS
★★ $$ 🏠 🕐

Are you searching for a truly unique business opportunity that requires a minimal start-up investment, has virtually no competition, and has the potential to generate a great income? If so, perhaps you should consider starting a business that specializes in conducting fitness classes for dogs and their owners. The fitness classes can be held outdoors on a year-round basis and can be designed with a dog and its owner in mind. This type of fitness business is very unique and may take awhile to catch on in your community; however, the profit potential is great. Imagine, a mere 20 students (ten dogs and ten people) paying only $5 per day to take part in a one-hour fitness class will create an hourly income of a whopping $50. Best of all, there are virtually no fixed overhead costs as the classes can be conducted from any outdoor venue for free, and the advertising will certainly be by way of word-of-mouth referral.

FITNESS SEMINARS
★★ $$ 🕐 🌐

There are multiple ways to make money by hosting fitness seminars that are free to attend.

- Sell fitness equipment, diet and fitness programs, and fitness-related products during and at the end of the seminar.
- Charge companies a fee to be a speaker at the seminars and sell their fitness-related products, equipment, and programs.
- Design and develop a seminar program that is purchased by the people who attend the fitness seminar, as well as selling advertising space in the seminar program to companies that are taking part in the fitness seminars.
- Use a combination of all or any of these revenue-generating techniques.

As you can see there are a few options available in terms of generating revenues from a business that hosts fitness seminars that is free for people to attend. The two key words here are "free" and "fitness." People will attend the seminars because the topic is fitness, and even more people will attend the fitness seminars because the seminar is free. The concept behind the business is to create a captive audience, build excitement, and capitalize on the excitement and the fact that you have just created a noncompetitive environment in terms of selling valuable products to consumers or to other businesses.

FITNESS CENTER
★★ $$$$ 🌐

In the past 20 years, fitness centers have not only proven to be popular and very much in demand by fitness conscious consumers, but they have also been proven to be very profitable as a business opportunity. Opening a fitness center requires careful planning and research, and the following are aspects of the business that should be considered:

- *Location.* Where will the fitness center be located, how much square footage will be required, what are the leasehold improvements going to cost, is there good visibility, access, and parking, and is the business located in an area comprised mainly of the target market customers?
- *Operating format.* Will the fitness center cater to all people, or will the focus of the business target one specific group of people? Will the fitness center be full service, meaning optional aerobic classes and one-on-one personal training for clients?
- *Staff.* Is there access to trained fitness instructors and staff in the community where the fitness center is being established, and if so what are the wage and benefit demands, as well as expectancy of staff in terms of career opportunities?
- *Marketing.* How will the fitness center be marketed? Will it be by way of membership drive or a drop-in rate established? What enticements or services will be used as a marketing tool to draw members from competitors' fitness clubs or facilities?
- *Competition.* How much local competition is there in the fitness industry, and is the competition in the form of a chain fitness center, community-operated fitness center, or independently-operated fitness centers? How much does the competition charge? Is there the possibility of a price war? Can the proposed business gain enough clients to be profitable? What is the effect on the business from potential future competitors?

There are many aspects to carefully consider prior to starting a fitness center. However, with careful research and proper planning a fitness center can be a fabulous business to start, operate, and own, not to mention that it also has the potential to be very profitable.

SPORTS SWAP MEETS
★★ $$$ 🕐

Sports equipment swap meets are basically a gathering of sporting equipment retailers and the general public (with used sporting equipment to sell) brought together in one venue to buy and sell the sporting equipment. There are two approaches for generating revenue from this business. The first is to charge vendors rent for booth display space. The second way to generate revenues is to issue vendor numbers and have one central cashier window and retain 10 percent of the total value of the sports equipment sold at the sports swap meet, regardless if the equipment was new or secondhand. Starting a sports swap meet business will take some clever planning and marketing. However, sports in general are part of the North American cultural fabric, and demand for a sports swap meet is guaranteed.

CHILDREN-ONLY FITNESS CLASSES
★★ $$ 🕐 ⚖

Like adults, children need regular exercise to stay healthy and fit, and starting a fitness instruction business that exclusively conducts fitness training classes for children is a fantastic new business enterprise to get rolling. The fitness classes offered should be categorized by the children's age brackets as well as offering classes for beginner through advanced. Once again, this type of unique and specialized fitness training can be conducted as an independent business venture, or as a joint venture with an existing community fitness program. Additional considerations to research prior to starting a childrens-only fitness business include operating location, required certifications, health and safety regulations, and liability insurance.

AEROBICS CENTER
★ $$$$ 🌐

Would you like to start an aerobics training business, but unfortunately you do not have the experience or qualifications required? Fear not, you still can, by starting an aerobics center. An aerobics center is simply a leased location that has been specifically set up to operate as an aerobics training center. The center can have multiple training rooms that are fully equipped and rented on a short- or long-term basis by qualified aerobics instructors to conduct their classes. Alternately, splitting the instruction course fees paid by students with the instructors can

generate revenues. Additional income can be earned by locating a refreshment booth in the aerobics center, as well as selling related products such as sportswear, books, and videos on aerobics training topics.

FITNESS VIDEOS
★ $$$+ 🕐

Countless fitness instructors and fitness gurus have made millions of dollars from producing and selling their own fitness videos, books, and workout programs, and you can do the same. You do not have to be a fitness instructor to produce and sell fitness workout programs, however, you do have to be an enterprising entrepreneur in order to succeed in the highly competitive industry of fitness video production and distribution. There are numerous aspects of this business to consider prior to initiating the venture. The following are basically the steps that have to be taken to establish a business that produces and distributes fitness videos, books, and workout programs:

- Locate a suitable host for the video, preferably a celebrity or an easily recognizable person in the fitness industry.
- Decide upon a particular fitness activity to focus on, such as kickboxing, aerobics, etc.
- Hire a film production and editing crew to produce the videos.
- Decide on a marketing platform to sell the fitness video, such as mail order, infomercials, the Internet, or wholesale accounts with national retailers.

Obviously, there is more involved with producing and distributing fitness videos and workout programs, however, the aforementioned are the basic steps that must be taken.

MINIATURE GOLF CENTER
★★ $$$$ 🌐

There are a few approaches that can be taken for starting and operating a miniature golf business. The first approach is to establish the miniature golf course in a fixed location, indoors or outdoors. The second approach is to conduct the business on a mobile basis, setting up the miniature golf course in high-traffic tourist areas or in a way that people seeking a unique activity for birthday parties and special events can rent the portable miniature golf course. Regardless of the operating format for the business, both enjoy a common feature, which is miniature golf is extremely popular. Consumer demand for miniature golf has been proven successful for many decades, making this opportunity a wise choice as a new business venture for all people seeking self-employment independence.

WEB RESOURCE: www.miniaturegolfer.com Directory service with links and information about the miniature golfing industry.

RUNNERS' STORE
★★ $$$$ 🌐

Long distance running, jogging, and cross training are becoming some of the most popular sports and fitness pastimes enjoyed by millions of participants across North America. Starting a retail business that caters to recreational runners is a fabulous new business enterprise to get rolling. A runners' store can stock and sell products such as sports shoes, sportswear, and running and training books and videos. Beyond retail sales, the business can earn additional revenues and profits by providing running clinics and running instruction programs. To kick things into high gear so to speak, be sure to contact the local sports associations in the community to inform them about the new business and the products sold, as well as the services offered. Also be sure to give members of the various sports associations a preferred customer card, meaning that they will receive a discount on purchases at the store when the card is presented.

WEB RESOURCE: www.arfa.org American Running and Fitness Association.

FITNESS EQUIPMENT MANUFACTURING
★★ $$$

Are you searching for a new business opportunity that will enable you to utilize your design and construction skills? If so, perhaps you should consider starting a business that manufactures fitness equipment. The main requirements for succeeding in this type of manufacturing business is to have a well-equipped workshop, design and construction experience, and good marketing skills. The fitness equipment manufactured can include weight benches, weight stands, and squat stands, just to mention a few. Once the fitness equipment is constructed it can be sold on a wholesale basis to national and specialty retailers, or directly to the public via a factory direct showroom, or over the Internet. Profit potential, once established is $25,000+ per year.

WEB RESOURCE: www.sportlink.com Sporting Goods Manufacturers Association.

MATERNITY FITNESS CLASSES
★★ $$ 🕐 ⚖

There are approximately four million children born each year in the United States. While this statistic may not mean a lot to many of you, it will certainly be useful information for anyone who is considering starting a fitness instruction business that focuses on conducting fitness classes exclusively for expectant mothers. Maternity fitness classes can be held in conjunction with an existing business or community association, or as an independent business. Gaining clients for this type of fitness instruction can be as easy as posting notices at hospitals, community recreation centers, and retailers of children's and baby products. Additionally, be sure to build alliances with any group, association, or organization within the community that is directly related to pregnancy, children, or sports and fitness.

WEB RESOURCE: www.association-of-womens-fitness.org Association of Women's Health and Fitness.

BICYCLE REPAIR SERVICE
★★ $$ 🏠 🕐

How profitable can a bicycle repair service be? Just ask any one of the thousands of bicycle repair shop owners who are now making a handsome profit from their business. A bicycle repair service is a fantastic new venture to start for the following reasons:

- The business can be started and operated from a homebased workshop.
- Low initial start-up investment and minimal monthly operating overheads.

- Proven consumer demand for bicycle repairs that increases each year.
- Ability to earn $40 per hour or more, and additional profits can be made on parts sales.
- Part-time or full-time opportunity that has very flexible operating hours.
- Repair skills needed to operate the business are minimal and can be learned very quickly.

As you can see, there are many benefits to starting a bicycle repair service on a full- or part-time basis. Be sure to establish alliances with bicycling clubs and organizations in the community, as the membership of these clubs can become potential customers of the bicycle repair business.

COMMUNITY SPORTS PAPER
★★ $$$ 📷 🕐 🌐

Starting a business that publishes and distributes a sports paper that features community amateur sports news is a very straightforward business venture to initiate. The information featured in the community sports paper can include team rosters and photographs, game highlights, team stats, and forthcoming sports association news and game schedules. The news and information can be supplied by the various sports associations and clubs in the community, as well as by enlisting the services of a freelance sports writer (chances are, for free). The community sports paper can be published on a weekly, biweekly, or monthly basis, and be distributed throughout the community for free. The paper can generate revenues and profits by selling advertising space to local businesspeople seeking to gain valuable exposure for their companies.

ONLINE COMMUNITY SPORTS DIRECTORY
★★ $$ 📷 🕐 🌐 🖱

Take community amateur athletics into the high-tech world of the Internet by developing a Web site dedicated to bringing sports fans all the local action in amateur sports. Ideally this sort of online venture will service one particular city or community, thus the opportunity for tremendous growth exists by expanding the business to include communities from coast to coast. Local amateur sports information featured and updated daily on the site can include Little League team statistics, game schedules, game commentaries, and more—basically anything to do with local amateur athletics. Sports associations, parents, and team coaches can supply the information posted on the Web site. Income can be earned by selling advertising space on the site to local merchants and service providers, otherwise known as "community sports sponsors."

BOXING CENTER
★★ $$$$ 🌐

Once a sport for the brutes, boxing and kickboxing is quickly becoming one of the most popular fitness activities in North America enjoyed by millions of participants regardless of age or gender. An interest in the sport of boxing or kickboxing is definitely a prerequisite for starting a boxing center. However, a great deal of boxing experience or training is not, simply due to the fact that you can hire certified boxing and kickboxing instructors to conduct classes and oversee the general operation of the business. Build a membership base quickly by distributing two-for-one coupons that entitle the bearer the opportunity to join the boxing center for one month and receive the second month of membership free of charge. You can also add fun and fitness classes to the roster, such as aerobic boxing and kickboxing, self-defense boxing training, and monthly amateur boxing and kickboxing tournaments. In total approximately 4,000 to 6,000 square feet of space will be required to operate the business, and equipment purchases will be expensive, making this a business venture that will require careful planning and research. To bolster sales and revenues beyond classes and training, you can also sell products related to the sport, such as clothing, books, and videos. Imagine, only 500 members paying a mere $30 per month each for membership dues will generate yearly base revenues of $180,000.

WEB RESOURCE: www.aiba.net Amateur Boxing Association industry information and links.

KEY

RATINGS	★
START-UP COST	$
HOMEBASED BUSINESS	
PART-TIME	
LEGAL ISSUES	
FRANCHISE OR LICENSE POTENTIAL	
ONLINE	

TRANSPORTATION
Businesses You Can Start

SAILBOAT RIGGING SERVICE

★ $

Each year thousands of new and used sailboats are purchased by inexperienced sailors. Starting a sailboat rigging service means that you can put your sailing skills to work. Sailboat rigging is not a difficult task for the experienced sailor. However, for the novice sailor, rigging can be a time consuming and frustrating task. A sailboat rigging service is best marketed by establishing joint ventures with marinas, boat brokers, and sailing schools. Sailing clubs can also act as referral sources for the service. Overall, this is a terrific little homebased business venture that can be operated on a full- or part-time basis, and there should be no difficulties in charging and getting $40 to $50 per hour for the rigging service.

HAND CAR WASH

★★★ $$

For an investment of less than $10,000 you can open your own hand car wash service operating in a fixed location. Strike a deal with the owner of a gas station, car dealership, or mechanics garage to set up your car wash in a section of their parking lot that is not being used. Offering a few hundred dollars per month for rent should go a long way in sealing the deal. You will need to purchase a small garden shed for equipment storage and a 10-foot by 20-foot tent to wash the cars under. A water hose can be tied into the building where you establish the business. A small sandwich board sign can be set up at the edge of the lot advertising your car wash. There should be no difficulties in securing a location for the car wash, as it will act as a drawing card for the establishment that you have struck the deal with. Washing only 20 cars per day and charging customers a mere $10 each will generate business revenues of $6,000 per month.

WEB RESOURCE: www.smallbizbooks.com Business-specific start-up guides and books.

MOBILE CAR WASH

★★★ $$+ 🏠 🕐 🌐

The following are five excellent reasons why you should start a mobile car wash service:

1. A mobile car wash business can be started on a modest investment of less than $10,000.
2. A mobile car wash business can produce potential profits in excess of $60,000 per year.
3. Starting and operating a mobile car wash requires no special skills, and there are no legal regulations or restrictions. Everyone with a valid driver's license qualifies.
4. A mobile car wash business can be managed from a homebased office and operated full- or part-time with flexible business hours, no inventory, no staff, and low monthly overheads.
5. The demand is enormous; there are more than 130,000,000 vehicles registered in the United States.

A mobile car wash business is perfectly suited for the entrepreneur who is seeking a simple, profitable and low-investment business opportunity. The business only requires basic equipment and can be operated from a van, truck, or enclosed trailer. To market the business and gain clients, all traditional forms of advertising and promotion can be utilized. However, the real target market for this type of service is to establish monthly car and truck washing and cleaning accounts with companies, organizations, and government agencies who have a fleet of automobiles. Securing only ten monthly car washing accounts can produce a yearly income of $60,000, providing each client has 20 cars or trucks in their fleet.

START UP COSTS: The following example can be used as a guideline to establish the investment necessary to start a mobile car wash business.

	Low	High
Truck or van (used)	$5,000	$15,000
Power washer with accessories	$500	$2,000
Business setup, banking, legal, etc.	$500	$2,500
Equipment, vacuums, etc.	$500	$1,500
Initial marketing and promotion budget	$500	$1,500
Working capital	$500	$2,000
Total start-up costs	$7,500	$24,500

AUTOMOTIVE USED PARTS

★★ $$$$

Starting a business that specializes in used automotive parts is a fantastic business venture to get rolling, especially if the focus of the business is to supply hard-to-find or rare used automotive parts. The business can be operated from a homebased garage location, or a small industrial space can be rented. The used automotive parts can be advertised for sale in traditional media, such as trade-specific publications and newspapers, and by word-of-mouth referral. The profit potential for a used automotive parts business is fantastic, especially if the business specializes in rare or hard-to-find parts, and gross profit margins of 50 percent or more are not uncommon in the industry. A direct-mail marketing campaign targeted at car clubs and owners of rare cars can also be a very effective marketing tool.

WEB RESOURCE: www.autorecyc.org Automotive Recyclers Association

ONLINE AUTOMOTIVE PARTS

★ $ 🏠 🕐 🖱

As mentioned above, selling automotive replacement parts for rare, antique, and sports cars can make you rich. A logical approach to mass market an auto replacement parts business to a global marketplace is the Internet. Like many online business opportunities, you have options. The first is to purchase replacement parts at bargain basement prices and resell them for a profit via your own Web site.

The second option is to create Internet portals that bring people together who are seeking to buy and sell automotive replacement parts. The latter is the less-costly option to choose and will be the focus of this opportunity. Simply create a Web site with information and services pertaining to automotive replacement parts that can be utilized by car collectors and enthusiasts worldwide. The site can include a directory of parts manufacturers and distributors, as well as a classifieds section that enables visitors to post for sale and wanted notices about automotive parts. To spice up the site, include content that visitors would find interesting, such as car maintenance tips, online mechanics instruction training, and a chat forum for visitors to swap information. Income can be earned by selling books and repair manuals, as well as by selling advertising space in the directory in the form of banners.

BOAT BOTTOM PAINTING

★★ $$ 🏠 🕓

Boat hulls must be maintained and painted below the water line on a regular basis in order to maintain performance. Generally, a boat bottom will be painted with antifouling paint every three to four years, and sometimes every year if the water conditions are poor. The process of bottom painting is very straightforward. Remove barnacles and debris by scraping the hull or pressure washing and apply the antifouling paint. A brushed on or roller paint job is generally considered superior to a spray paint job. Negotiating an exclusive distributors contract with an antifouling paint manufacturer is a terrific way to reduce paint wholesale costs and increase the professionalism of the business.

WEB RESOURCE: www.kop-coat.com/handbook.htm Service listing information about boat bottom painting.

AUTO FIRST-AID KITS

★★ $$ 🏠 🕓

Are you searching for a small homebased business opportunity that has unlimited growth potential and that can be set in motion for a modest start-up investment? If so, perhaps you should consider starting a business that specializes in manufacturing and wholesaling automotive first-aid kits. The first-aid kits can include items such as water, bandages, and roadside safety signals, all packaged in a convenient carrying case with a handle. The kits can be sold on a wholesale basis to retailers, direct to car dealers, and to automotive service clubs. The first-aid kits can also be sold directly to consumers via the Internet, and by establishing weekend sales kiosks at flea markets, busy malls, and car and truck shows. Automotive first-aid kits are currently retailing in the range of $25 to $100 depending on the contents of the kit. To generate additional revenues and profits, a roadside first-aid guide could be developed and included with the first-aid kits, or the guide could be sold as an independent product.

PORTABLE SHELTERS AND STORAGE

★ $$ 🏠 🕓

Portable storage systems have become extremely popular in the last few years for anyone that is looking to protect a car, motorcycle, or boat from the weather. Generally, these portable storage shelters are constructed from a lightweight aluminum frame, covered with a water resistant fabric, and are quick to assemble and disassemble. They are available in a wide range of sizes to suit cars, RVs, motorcycles, boats, and just about any other type of transportation that needs protection from the wind, rain, and sun. A potentially profitable part-time business enterprise can be based on purchasing these portable shelters on a wholesale basis and reselling them to car, boat, and motorcycle enthusiasts for a profit. Marketing the shelters will not meet with a lot of resistance, as the cost to purchase one is a mere fraction of what it costs to build a carport or garage. The key to success will lie in your ability to negotiate a dealer's agreement with one of the many manufacturers of these types of portable storage and shelter systems. Your objective should be to secure the distribution rights for a protected territory. You want to be the exclusive sales agent for the manufacturer's product within a defined area. The following are manufacturers that are seeking distributors for their portable storage systems and shelters:

- **PTI Products:** www.thebikebarn.net Manufacturers and distributors of portable motorcycle storage and shelter systems.
- **Tent & Structure International Inc.:** www.classicaltents.com Manufacturers and distributors of portable tents and shelter systems.
- **A.I.S., Inc.:** www.instantshelters.com Manufacturers and distributors of portable storage and shelter systems.
- **Cover It:** www.coveritshelters.com Manufacturers and distributors of portable storage and shelter systems.
- **Shelter World:** www.shelterworld.com Manufacturers and distributors of portable storage and shelter systems.

WINDSHIELD REPAIR

★ $$

What are the benefits of starting a mobile windshield chip repair service?

- Low initial investment and minimal monthly business operating overheads.
- Homebased business opportunity, flexible business hours, and no inventory to stock or store.
- Proven consumer demand with strong future growth potential.
- Full- or part-time business opportunity with the potential to earn $50 per hour or more.
- There are 130 million registered cars and trucks in the United States, which means 130 million potential customers.
- No regulations and quick business learning curve.
- Value priced automotive repair means an easy sell.
- Inexpensive and readily available business equipment that requires virtually no maintenance.
- Excellent potential to expand the business geographically on a franchise or license basis.
- Mainly a cash business with very little accounts receivables or payables headaches.

WEB RESOURCE: www.aegisweb.com Distributor of windshield repair equipment and supplies.

BOAT BROKER

★★★ $$+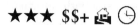

In most areas of North America, certification is not required to start a professional boat brokerage business, and that is extremely good news if this is the type of business venture that gets you thinking. Millions of dollars worth of pre-owned motorboats, sailboats, and personal watercrafts are bought and sold annually in this country. Securing a portion of this lucrative market is very simple to accomplish. The business could be a general boat brokerage business or specialize in a particular type of boats such as commercial fishing boats. It could also be operated from a fixed waterfront or marina location, or on a mobile basis and managed from a home office. The options for starting and operating a boat brokerage business are unlimited, making this is an excellent choice for a new business venture that really deserves further investigation.

START UP COSTS: A homebased or mobile boat brokerage business can be started on an investment of $10,000 or less. A full-service boat brokerage operating from a fixed marina location with birth availability will be substantially more costly to start; in the range of $50,000 to $100,000.

PROFIT POTENTIAL: Generally, a boat brokerage or boat sales consultant will charge the owner of the boat a 10 percent commission fee upon the successful sale of the boat. However, the rate of commission can be as high as 25 percent for boats that are valued at $5,000 or less, and as low as 3 percent for boats the sell in the million-dollar price range. Maintaining a 10 percent commission rate and achieving total yearly sales of $1 million will result in revenues of $100,000 prior to advertising, overheads, and taxes.

ONLINE BOAT BROKER

★★ $$$$

Thousands of pleasure boats are bought and sold privately each month in the United States.

Developing a Web site that acts as a portal to bring boat buyers and sellers together has the potential to make you rich. You can create a Web site that is categorized by boat style, type, and geographic location. Boat sellers wishing to have their boats listed for sale on the site—including a picture, detailed equipment list, and contact information—would pay a monthly fee for this service. People seeking to buy boats would simply log onto the site, select a category of boat they wanted to buy, and start viewing the listings. You could employ subcontract sales consultants to secure boat listings for the site and pay them by way of a commission for each listing they secured. Given the fact that so many boats are bought and sold annually in this country, securing only a few thousand listings should not prove to be a daunting task. To increase revenues and profits, also seek to secure businesses that sell boating equipment and supplies to be featured advertisers on the site.

COURIER SERVICE
 ★ $$

There are numerous approaches that can be taken in terms of starting a courier business. The first is to specialize in small envelopes and small packages only. The second approach is to specialize in local delivery of medium-sized boxes and packages. The third is to specialize in delivery of large equipment and multibox shipments. While all three approaches have their pros and cons, by far the easiest and least expensive courier business to start is one that specializes in small packages and envelopes. Generally, courier drivers work on a commission-split basis, or a flat fee per delivery basis, and are responsible for transportation costs. The responsibility of the courier company is to ensure there is enough work to keep the drivers busy, and to supply central radio dispatched delivery information and instruction. The best way to market a new courier service is to hire direct sales consultants to cold call companies to secure courier services accounts. Profit potential range is $40,000+ per year.

WEB RESOURCE: www.macc.com The Messenger Courier Association of the Americas.

USED BOATING EQUIPMENT
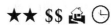 ★★ $$

There are an estimated 15 million pleasure boats and personal watercrafts in the United States alone, and almost all boats have one thing in common. At some point they break down and require repairs and replacement parts. This fact creates an incredible business opportunity for the innovative entrepreneur to capitalize by starting a used boating equipment and parts business. Simply purchase used boating parts and equipment and resell the same parts and equipment for a profit. The business can easily be operated on a full- or part-time basis right from the comforts of a homebased office. Maintaining a 50 percent gross profit margin on all sales and achieving yearly sales of $100,000 will result in a pretax and overhead gross profit of $50,000 per year, which is commendable for such an easy business to start.

WEB RESOURCE: www.nboat.com National Boat Owners Association.

WATER TAXI SERVICE
★ $$$$

Are you looking for a unique, fun, and interesting transportation business venture that will enable you to capitalize on your boating skills and certifications? If so, perhaps you should consider starting a water taxi business. Of course, one of the main requirements is to live by a body of water where this type of service would be in demand. Providing the question of suitable location can be resolved, a water taxi service can be a terrific business venture to set in motion. In addition to the taxi service, you can also provide water sightseeing tours.

FARM EQUIPMENT BROKER
★★ $$$$

International connections can really pay off, especially if you are planning to start a farm equipment brokerage business. Your international connection can not only assist in the marketing of the equipment overseas but also in locating discounted farm equipment for North American purchasers. The market for good-quality used farm equipment such as tractors and hay combines is huge worldwide. Selling just one piece of equipment per week can generate business revenues of $200,000 per year and more. The key to success in this business is to build and maintain vital contacts and alliances with farm equipment dealers and other brokers of farm equipment, as well as to seek international opportunities with booming economies.

START-UP COSTS: The investment needed to start a business as a farm equipment broker will vary based on factors such as initial advertising budget, business location, and overall operating expenses. However, an initial investment of $25,000 to $40,000 is suitable to get the business venture set in motion. As a way to minimize start-up costs, the business can initially be operated from a homebased office and market only local farm equipment to local potential purchasers.

PROFIT POTENTIAL: As a rule of thumb, farm equipment brokers charge a 10 percent commission of the total value of the farm equipment that was successfully sold. There are however, exceptions to the rule. The commission rate will often be higher on lower valued farm equipment, and lower on very expensive farm equipment. Keep in mind that even if a piece of equipment is not sold, the broker is still responsible for the costs associated with attempting to market the equipment, unless a prior agreement has been established with the equipment owner, which is rarely done.

ONLINE FARM EQUIPMENT BROKER
★★ $$$$ 🏭 👆

Unite the farmers of the world by creating a Web site that enables them to buy, sell, and trade farm equipment online. In addition to farmers, farm equipment dealers and brokers could also utilize the listing service. Employ sales consultants in every region of the country to solicit for farm equipment listings for the site. Build a site index that is sectioned into geographic areas and type of farm equipment featured for visitor search purposes. At $30 per month per listing, maintaining only 1,000 listings on

a monthly basis would create a revenue stream of $360,000 per year.

TRUCKING
★ $$$$ ⚖

There are a few approaches that can be taken in terms of starting a trucking business. The first approach is to start a trucking business, secure transportation accounts, and hire subcontract drivers with their own trucks and equipment to service the transportation accounts. The second approach is to purchase or lease a truck and work as an independent trucker, servicing your own accounts or subcontracting for a transportation firm. Both approaches to starting a business within the trucking industry have their pros and cons. However, be forewarned: the trucking industry as a whole is extremely competitive, and the rising cost of fuel, maintenance, and insurance has resulted in drivers having to work extremely long hours to generate any profit beyond a working wage. Profit potential including income, $50,000+ per year.

WEB RESOURCE: www.trucking.org American Trucking Association.

AUTO TOWING
★★ $$$$ 🏭 ⚖

In many areas of North America obtaining a license to start or operate an automotive towing business can be a frustrating task, as auto-towing licenses are heavily regulated. Some operators of towing companies forego the license entirely and do not provide towing services to the general public; instead they only subcontract their services on an exclusive basis to car dealers and property managers. However, this can still be a risky venture given that it may be difficult to secure proper liability insurance for this type of towing operation. The alternative to waiting to be awarded a towing license is to purchase one from an existing towing operator or company. Purchasing a towing license and tow truck in an urban area can cost you as much as $200,000 with no towing accounts in place. Overall, starting an automotive towing business can be a terrific and profitable business venture, providing a license can be obtained or purchased at a reasonable price.

WEB RESOURCE: www.towinfo.com/members/affiliates/traa/traa.html Towing Recovery Association of America.

BOAT MOVING AND STORAGE
★★ $$$$ ⚖

Starting a boat moving and storage business requires very careful planning and research in order to be successful. There are a great number of factors to consider, such as business location, type of boat moving and storage service offered, liability insurance, and transportation and equipment considerations. Probably the easiest and least expensive type of boat moving and storage business to start is one that focuses on small pleasure crafts less than 35 feet in length and 10 feet in width. Boats this size do not have special regulation requirements in terms of transporting the boats on public roads. In terms of boat storage, seek to build alliances with public storage centers on a revenue share basis for storing the boats outside. I have a friend who has been in the boat moving and storage business for more than ten years. He operates his business by subcontracting out all moving and storage aspects of the business to qualified contractors, and focuses solely on selling or marketing the service. Perhaps this approach to a boat moving and storage business can also work for you.

CUSTOM AUTO RACKS
★★ $$$ 🌐

Custom auto racks that are designed to carry golf equipment, skis, mountain bikes, canoes, and kayaks are the latest rage in the automotive accessories industry. Small retail shops that sell and install these types of auto racks are popping up everywhere across North America. Selling and installing custom auto racks is a very lucrative enterprise to get going as there are many manufacturers of these products. Becoming an authorized factory dealer and installer is easily accomplished. The racks are easy and quick

to install and do not require a great amount of mechanical skill or installation equipment and tools. The business is best operated from a small rental location with retailing area and a single garage or drive-in bay for the rack installations. Demand for custom automotive racks is enormous, and securing a 50 percent markup on product costs and charging $30 per hour for installation should not be difficult. Overall this small retail business has the potential to generate a six-figure yearly income for the owner-operator.

BOAT WOODWORK REFINISHING
★★ $$ 🏠 🕐

Many power and sailboats have teakwood decks and trim, and anyone familiar with boating knows that the sun and salt water can really take its toll on boat woodwork. Starting a boat woodwork refinishing service is a fantastic small business venture to set in motion. The business can be operated on a mobile basis and managed from a homebased office. Additionally, the tools and equipment needed for refinishing boat woodwork are inexpensive and readily available at any home improvement center. When marketing a woodworking refinishing service to boat owners, consider the following advertising and marketing options:

- Join boat and yacht clubs and network with boatowners at club social meetings to promote the woodwork refinishing service.
- Hand deliver informational brochures and fliers to boat owners at marinas.
- Subcontract your services to established boat repair yards.
- Cold call and talk to boat owners at marinas.
- Place advertisements in specialty boating publications and newspapers.
- Establish alliances with boat brokers and dealers to provide boat woodworking refinishing services prior to the boats being listed for sale or resold.

To promote the business and create a lot of interest in the woodwork refinishing service, consider purchasing an older wooden boat in poor condition.

Refinish half the boat to perfection, and leave the other half in its original decrepit condition. The end result will be an amazing before and after marketing tool that can be displayed at marinas and boat shows to promote the refinishing service.

CAR STORAGE
★ $$$

Car storage is big business, especially in the northern climate areas of the United States and Canada. And the first step to establishing a car storage business is to secure low-cost indoor storage space, such as a vacant warehouse or manufacturing building. The next step is to simply market the business, and this is best accomplished by joining automotive clubs and associations and attending the clubs' meetings and social functions to network for business. Current automotive storage rates are in the range of $40 to $80 per month. However, of vital importance to the success of the business is to ensure that the storage space is heated and in good repair. Of course, be sure to obtain insurance for the business, as it will be a necessity, and a great marketing tool.

VAN INTERIOR CUSTOMIZING
★★ $$$ 🏠 🕐

Interior customizing of vans and trucks is big business, especially in the commercial sector for delivery and service vehicles. Starting a business that supplies and installs products for van interiors, such as toolboxes and shelving units is an outstanding new business venture to set in motion. The business can be operated right from a homebased workshop on a full- or part-time basis. The total investment required to get the business rolling can be less than $10,000. To truly succeed in this type of business, consider securing an exclusive dealership from a manufacturer of these types of products. Not only will an exclusive product line give you an advantage over the competition, but it also adds credibility to your business and can be used as a terrific marketing tool. To market this business, simply build alliances with new and used car dealers in your area that can refer your business to their clients, or alternatively, car dealerships

can act as sales agents for your products and installation service.

ONLINE CONSIGNMENT CAR LOT
★★ $$$$ 🏠 🖱

Harness the power of the Internet and make your fortune by starting an online consignment car lot. What is an online consignment car lot? An online consignment car lot is a Web site that is utilized by car and truck owners to market their vehicles for sale. Attracting clients to list or post their vehicles for sale on the Web site will be very easy, as there would be no up-front costs associated with marketing their cars. Revenues for the business would be gained by charging only a small commission (2 percent) when the vehicle is successfully sold. The profit potential for this type of cyberventure is amazing. However, the business will take careful planning and research in order to be properly developed and implemented.

BOAT CLEANING SERVICE
★★ $ 🏠 🕐 🌏

Don't want to compete in the highly competitive residential or commercial cleaning industry, but would like to start a cleaning service? If so, why not consider starting a boat cleaning service. The competition is minimal and, providing the cleaning service is established in the right area, the number of potential customers can be almost unlimited. Starting a boat cleaning service could not be easier, as there are no special skills or equipment required to operate the business, and marketing the service requires no more than some printed fliers and a little bit of leg work to distribute the fliers at marinas and boating clubs. Considering a boat cleaning service can be started on an initial investment of less than $1,000, the income potential is excellent at $20 to $30 per hour. Providing customers with a boat bottom cleaning service can also generate additional revenues for a boat cleaning service. This aspect of the service can be subcontracted to a qualified scuba diver to work on revenue split basis.

USED CAR SALES
★★ $$$$ ⚖

The objective is clear in the used car sales game: buy low and sell high. The average new car now costs in excess of $20,000, placing this major purchase out of the reach of many people. Because of this, many people buy secondhand transportation. The main requirement for starting a used car sales business is a car sellers permit. You will need a business location with good street visibility and an initial inventory of cars to sell. Buying used cars for resale can be accomplished in a few ways, including buying from new car dealers who take trades but do not sell used cars beyond a certain age (usually six years old) or by attending automotive auctions for dealers, which generally feature lease returned cars and repossessed cars. Of course, the third option is to scan your local newspaper and purchase privately owned cars for sale. This is a good way of acquiring an initial inventory, providing your negotiation skills are good and you have the time.

WEB RESOURCE: www.niada.com National Independent Automobile Dealers Association.

STEREO INSTALLATIONS
★★ $$ 🕐

A stereo installation service can cater to many potential clients, including car owners, boat owners, car and boat dealers, RV dealerships, and audiovisual retailers. The best way to market a stereo installation service is by providing installations only and not retailing stereos, as this method will enable you to attract retailers of stereo equipment as clients. Two of the best aspects about starting this type of specialized installation service are that it can be operated with virtually no overhead costs, and income in the $35 per hour range can be earned.

CAR FINDER SERVICE
★ $$ 🏠 🕐

Thousands of people spend hundreds of hours each year trying to locate the perfect car or truck to purchase. Many of these people would be more than happy to become clients of a car locating service, especially a service that does not charge clients for vehicle locating services. The business concept is very straightforward. A client is seeking a particular car, truck, or RV, and you locate a few possible choices for the client. Then the client makes their purchase decision. Revenues for the business and your services are generated by negotiating a commission with the vendor of the vehicle being purchased, prior to introducing the vehicle to your client. A car finder service can easily generate an income of $50,000 per year for the operator of the service.

AUTOMOTIVE DETAILING SERVICE

An automotive detailing service is a business that requires little in the way of special skills, experience, or equipment, making this an ideal new business venture for just about anyone who is seeking to become independent. The following are two options available for starting and operating an automotive detailing service.

Mobile Automotive Detailing Service
★★★ $$ 🏠 🕐 🌐

Starting and operating a mobile automotive detailing service has many benefits as opposed to operating the business from a fixed location. These benefits include a smaller initial investment to get the business rolling, flexibility in terms of operating hours, and lower monthly operating overheads. However, there are also two major drawbacks to operating an automotive detailing service on a mobile basis. The business will be at the mercy of weather conditions and the potential to generate business revenues and sales will be limited to what a one-person service can produce, or about $25 to $30 per hour.

WEB RESOURCE: www.smallbizbooks.com Business-specific start-up guides and books.

Fixed Location Automotive Detailing Service
★★ $$$ 🌐

The second option for starting and operating an automotive detailing service is to establish the business in a fixed location, meaning that clients come to you, or you bring the clients' automobiles to your detailing location. There are benefits and drawbacks to operating an automotive detailing service based on this format. The benefits include the business is not affected by weather conditions, it is possible to generate higher sales and profits if the business location has several detailing bays and employees, and the business can also provide additional services to clients that a mobile automotive detailing business cannot. The drawbacks for operating the business from a fixed location include higher initial investment and higher monthly operating overhead costs.

WEB RESOURCE: www.smallbizbooks.com Business-specific start-up guides and books.

BOAT WINDOW REPLACEMENT SERVICE
★★ $$$ 🏠 🕐

Are you a handy person with basic hand tools who is looking to start a small business for less than a few thousand dollars in initial investment? If so, starting a boat window replacement service might not be for you. The business requires a minimal start-up investment, and minimal skills and equipment. Anyone who has ever owned a sailboat will tell you that it does not take long for the boat's plastic windows to discolor and scratch. With millions of sailboats worldwide, a business that replaces plexiglass boat windows should never run out of customers.

VALET PARKING SERVICE
★★ $$ 🏠 🕐 🌐

Starting a valet parking service is very easy. If you have a driver's license and can secure third-party and automobile liability insurance, you are basically in business. A valet parking service can be marketed directly to consumers. However, a more logical marketing approach is to offer the valet parking service to entertainment industry professionals, such as event planners, wedding planners, and tradeshow organizers. The business can be started on a minimal capital outlay. The profit

potential is also excellent, as current rates for valet parking services are in the range of $50 to $70 per hour, not to mention the fact that the cash tips can really add up.

MOBILE OIL CHANGE SERVICE
★★ $$+ 🏠 🕐 ⚖ 🌐

With more than 130 million vehicles registered in the United States, the future looks very bright for the enterprising entrepreneur that starts a mobile oil change service. Assuming the average vehicle is driven 15 thousand miles per year, and that the oil is changed every 5,000 miles, that adds up to a whopping 390 million oil changes each year in the United States. Securing only a fraction of one percent of this market can make you rich. In most areas of the country a mechanics license is not required to perform oil changes, making a mobile oil change service a business opportunity that just about anyone can start. The key to success in this competitive market is not only to provide customers with exceptional service, but also to secure customers who will use the service on a regular basis. Seek to gain clients with large fleets of vehicles, such as taxi companies, courier companies, and utility companies. Once established, a mobile oil change service can provide the owner of the business with a six-figure yearly income.

AUTOMOTIVE MAINTENANCE GUIDE
★★ $$$ 🏠 🕐 🌐

Here is a worthwhile new business venture for the entrepreneur with sales and marketing skills. Excellent profits can be earned by creating and distributing an automotive maintenance guide that is published in the spring and fall of each year. The guide can feature information about how to prepare your car for the upcoming winter or summer months, as well as feature automotive maintenance tips and stories submitted by readers. The automotive maintenance guides can be distributed free of charge throughout the community, and revenues for the business would be generated by selling advertising space in the guide to local business owners who are in the automotive or transportation industry. Once established and proven successful, this would be the ideal business to expand nationally on a franchise or licensed-to-operate basis. Profit potential range is $20,000+ per year.

DENT REMOVAL SERVICE
★★ $$ 🏠 🕐 🌐

Do you want to make as much as $75,000 per year operating your own business? If so, perhaps you should consider starting a dent removal and paint touch-up service. A dent removal and paint touch-up service specializes in removing small dents, such as door dents, hail damage, and touching up small areas of paint that have been damaged. Potential customers can include just about anyone with a small dent that they want removed from their vehicle. However, to truly succeed in this business, alliances should be established with auto dealers of new and used vehicles. Having a small dent removed from a vehicle can increase the retail sales value of a car by $1,000 or more, making this a worthwhile service for auto dealers to use.

MODEL BOATS
★ $$ 🏠 🕐

Large and elaborate models of sailing schooners and war destroyers are highly sought after by individual collectors and by professionals for office decorations. Starting a business that sells completed model boats is a fantastic new money making enterprise to set in motion. Don't worry that you do not have the skills to build the model boats, as there are thousands of people who do, and seeking out only a handful of these hobby model boat builders will keep your inventory levels high. As important as the model boat is to the success of the business, of equal importance is the way in which the model boat is displayed. The display cases should be made of clear glass to properly present the model boats, and in the case of larger models the glass should be tempered safety glass,

especially if the finished model will be displayed in an office or public area. The profit potential is outstanding for this type of unique business, as many model boats sell for as much as $2,500 each or more.

WEB RESOURCE: www.modelboat.com Distributor of model boat kits and tools.

MOPED TOURS
★★★★ $$$$ ⚖️ 🌐

Calling all adventurous entrepreneurs seeking to start a business that could prove to be not only profitable, but also a lot of fun to operate. In almost every community in the United States and Canada, a motorcycle permit is not required to operate a moped under a certain engine size. This fact creates an exceptional opportunity to start a moped tour business. Simply purchase six to ten new or used mopeds, supply helmets for the riders, and plan an interesting sightseeing tour in you local community. The tours can feature stops at historical sites, beaches, shopping malls, or just about any other tourist attraction or point of interest. The profit potential for a moped tour business is outstanding, and providing you can secure a mere 40 customers a week and charge $40 per person for a five-hour moped sightseeing tour, the business would stand to generate yearly gross sales in excess of $80,000.

WEB RESOURCE: www.moped.org Directory service listing moped dealers, tour operators, and clubs.

SAILBOAT RACE PHOTOGRAPHER
★★ $$ 🏠 🕐

Do you have a lust for adventure, good photography skills, and are you seeking to start your own business? If so, then this particular business opportunity will be of interest to you. Every year there are thousands of sailboat races and regattas taking place in the United States. Starting a business that photographs sailboat races, or more specifically a sailboat in action for the boat's owner and captain is a fantastic new venture to get "sailing." Once again, the only requirements to operate the business will be a good camera and photography skills, a strong stomach, and the ability to rent a boat and captain for the day of the race. Utilizing a digital camera will enable you to show the photographs to the boat owners at the end of the race right on a laptop computer. This is a sensational marketing tool, as you would then be able to take orders and payment for the photographs and mail the finished product to the customer at a later date, or place all of the photos taken onto a CD-ROM and edit in special effects and music. The options are unlimited when you apply technology to a strong business concept.

ONLINE USED MOTORCYCLE PARTS
★★ $$$$ 🏠 ♿

In North America millions of people own and ride motorcycles on a daily basis, and like cars, motorcycles breakdown and require repairs and replacement parts. Furthermore, like car owners, not all motorcycle owners can afford to purchase expensive new replacement parts for their motorcycles, especially replacement parts required to repair rare or antique motorcycles. This scenario is the basis of this business opportunity. Start a business that stocks and sells secondhand motorcycle replacement parts. The parts can be acquired relatively inexpensively by purchasing motorcycles from insurance companies that have been written-off due to damage or theft recovery. Likewise, the parts can be marketed for sale inexpensively by developing a Web site that lists all of the available motorcycle parts you have for sale. Motorcycle owners seeking a particular part would only be a click away from locating the part.

MOTORCYCLE SALES
★★ $$$$ ⚖

The time has never been better to start a business that sells secondhand motorcycles, as the popularity of motorcycle riding and ownership is at an all time high. A motorcycle sales business can be operated from home providing the proper zoning requirements have been met. The business can also be operated from a small rental location, or partnered with an existing automobile dealer that does not sell motorcycles. The profit potential for this type of business is great, providing the used motorcycles can be purchased for considerably less than their retail value. This can be accomplished by practicing good research and negotiation skills. Maintaining a 30 percent markup and achieving annual sales of $250,000 will result in a pretax and expense income of $70,000 per year.

IN-THE-WATER BOAT SHOWS
★★ $$$ 🕐 🌐

What is the difference between a "in-the-water boat show" and a boat show that takes place in an arena or complex? Water. Organizing and hosting in-the-water boat shows that feature privately-owned boats for sale is a very easy business to establish and operate. The boat shows can take place at marinas or other docking facilities. Business revenues can be earned by charging boat owners a fee for displaying their boat for sale at the show, or by collecting a commission on the value of the boats sold at the show. Additional revenues can also be earned by renting sales booths to retailers of boating products. The vendor booths can be setup on a floating barge, pontoon boat, or even right on the docks. Marketing the in-the-water boat shows is best executed by advertising the event in boating magazines and publications.

PAINT TOUCH-UP SERVICE
★★★ $$ 🏠 🕐 🌐

Big profits await the enterprising entrepreneur who starts an automotive paint touch-up service. There is an unlimited supply of potential clients and the demand for the service has been on a steady increase for the past decade and shows no sign of slowing down. The equipment required for operating the business is available at most automotive supply centers. The business can be operated right from a truck, van, or even a hatchback car. While it does require some skill to be able to effectively operate the business and perform paint touch-up services, the learning curve is not very steep and, with some practice, can easily be mastered by a novice over the course of a few months. Current rates for automotive paint touch-up services start at about $50 for a basic scratch to be painted and buffed, and can go as high a $200 for more difficult paint touch-up jobs.

SUNROOF INSTALLATIONS
★★ $$

Here is a terrific business opportunity that can be operated on a full- or part-time basis right from a homebased garage. Installing pop-open automotive sunroofs is relatively easy and does not require a lot in terms of expensive installation equipment. Potential customers can include car and truck owners, RV owners, and even boat owners, if the business also provides a mobile installation service. Be sure to establish alliances with car dealers in the local community, as they can act as sales agents for your sunroof products and installation services. Additional income can also be gained by expanding the product line to include the supply and installation of automotive accessories such as sun visors, running boards, and truck canopies.

WEB RESOURCE: www.donmar.com Wholesale distributor of automotive sunroofs and accessories.

IN-THE-WATER BOAT BOTTOM CLEANING
★★ $$ 🏠 ⏱ ⚖

Calling all recreational scuba divers. Do you want to make an extra $40 to $50 per hour in your spare time? If so, then this business opportunity will be of particular interest to you. The easiest way to ensure that a powerboat or sailboat performs to its maximum ability is to keep the bottom of the boat free of barnacles and debris. This fact creates an incredible opportunity for recreation scuba divers with entrepreneurial instincts to start a boat bottom cleaning service while the boat is still in the water. Beyond

scuba equipment and gear, the only equipment needed to operate the business will be a few good quality wire brushes and scrapers. Marketing this type of service is as easy as printing fliers describing the cleaning service and rates, and distributing the fliers to boat owners at marinas and other boat docking facilities.

WEB RESOURCE: www.padi.com Professional Association of Dive Instructors.

AUTO PAINTING SERVICE
★ $$$$ ⚖ 🌐

Automotive painting is not only a proven and stable industry, it can also be a very profitable business venture to set in motion. Starting an automotive painting service has one main requirement to make the business successful; you or an employee must have the skills and experience required to complete bodywork and paint cars. The equipment requirements for operating the business are also numerous, making this a business opportunity best left to professional automotive painters. As a method to reduce the start-up investment needed to get the business rolling, consider a joint venture with an existing automotive repair shop that does not provide clients with automotive painting services. Not only can you reduce the start-up investment, but also greatly reduce the monthly operating overheads by sharing expenses. You can also take advantage of the repair shop clientele base for marketing purposes.

SMALL ENGINE REPAIR
★★★ $$$$ ⚖ 🌐

Many small engine repair shops routinely reward the owners of these businesses with a six-figure yearly income. Repairing lawn mowers and chain saws can be a very lucrative business. Like any business that relies on walk-in traffic to generate sales, the location of a small engine repair shop is critical in terms of the demographics of the area and primary or target markets. Be sure to establish warranty repair services with manufacturers of small engine equipment, as not only does it pay well, but also these manufacturers can send a lot of business to a small engine repair service. Additional income can also be gained for the business by providing customers with optional services, such as saw and blade sharpening, as well as small equipment rentals. Income potential is $100,000.

PILOT CAR SERVICE
★ $$$ 🏠 🕐 ⚖️

A pilot car is a car or truck that travels in front of an oversized vehicle traveling on public roads and highways as a safety precaution. The fact that pilot cars are required by law for oversized vehicles and equipment transport creates a great business opportunity for the innovative entrepreneur seeking a business that's a little bit out of the ordinary. A pilot car service can easily be managed from a homebased office, and the potential to earn a substantial income is great, as the current rates for pilot car services are in the range of $25 to $35 per hour.

REPLACEMENT HOSES AND FITTINGS SERVICE
★★★ $$$$ 🏠 ⚖️ 🌐

Delays in construction due to equipment failures can cost contractors and property developers thousands of dollars for every hour that heavy equipment, such as bulldozers and backhoes, are unable to operate. This fact creates a wonderful opportunity for an entrepreneur with mechanical skills to start a business that sells and installs pressure hoses and fittings for heavy equipment on a mobile basis. The key to success in this service is to provide clients with fast and reliable service. A cell phone for incoming inquiries would be an absolute must. Careful research must be conducted to learn exactly what types of hoses and fittings are the most popular in terms of repair. But beyond that and a good reliable service van, that is all that is required to get this dynamite moneymaker off the ground and earning you big profits.

ONLINE CAR CLUB DIRECTORY
★ $$ 🏠 🕐 🖱️

Across the United States and Canada there are thousands of car clubs and millions of car enthusiasts. Thus an opportunity exists to create an online portal that brings these two parties together to share information about cars and how to join car clubs. The Web site can be indexed both by geographic location as well as type of car club. In addition, the site could also include a chat forum and articles pertaining to collecting cars submitted by visitors. Make the site free to use for visitors as well as for car clubs that want to be listed in the directory. Generate income and profits by selling products related to car collecting, such as books, repair manuals, and die-cast models of cars.

WEB RESOURCE: www.entrepreneur.com Create a business Web site with MySite professional Web site builder.

UTILITY TRAILER SALES
★★★ $$$ 🏠 🕐

Yard work, home renovations, and helping a friend move are all reasons why owing a utility trailer has become extremely popular for many people in North America. This is the perfect time to cash in on the popularity of utility trailers by starting a business that sells new and secondhand utility trailers. The first step for establishing this business is to seek out a manufacturer of utility trailers and negotiate an exclusive sales and distribution contract for your community or state. The next step is to find the right operating location. This can be homebased if zoning permits, an independent location, or as a joint venture with an established business such as a car dealer or RV dealer. The third step is simply to start to advertise and market the utility trailers for sale.

PREPURCHASE AUTO INSPECTION
★★★ $$ 🏠 🕐 ⚖️ 🌐

Are you a certified mechanic who wants to make an extra $25,000 or more each year operating your own part-time business? If so, perhaps you should consider starting an automotive inspection service that operates on a mobile basis. Each year in Canada and the United States millions of previously owned cars and trucks are sold. And with the average cost of a secondhand vehicle now in the range of $8,000, many purchasers are turning to automotive inspection services to inspect the cars for mechanical deficiencies prior to purchasing the vehicle in question. Marketing an automotive inspection service beyond word-of-mouth referrals can be accomplished by utilizing local print mediums for advertising and establishing alliances with car clubs to act as their representatives for the inspection services. Current rates for mobile automotive inspections start at $50 and as much as $250 for RVs and trucks.

AIRPORT SHUTTLE SERVICE
★ $$$$ 🏚 ⚖️

Not unlike a limousine, taxi, or courier service, the largest challenge to overcome in starting an airport shuttle service is to acquire an operator's license. An operator's license can be difficult to get through local government channels in most areas of the country, and very expensive if you plan to purchase one from an existing shuttle service. However, it is certainly not impossible to obtain an operator's license for a shuttle service, and it can be well worth the effort. An airport shuttle service can be a very profitable business to own and operate. Marketing a shuttle service is best accomplished by building alliances and partnerships with companies and local businesses that can supply you with customers, such as hotels, tour operators, travel agents, and large corporations.

MOBILE REFUELING SERVICE
★★★ $$$$ 🏚 ⚖️ 🌍

A mobile refueling service may require a big initial investment, but this business has an even bigger potential to earn enormous profits. That is the best way to describe a mobile refueling service. A mobile refueling service will take a lot of money to establish, as the minitanker truck alone can cost as much as $100,000. However, the truck and other required equipment for the business could be leased as a way to keep initial start-up costs to a minimum. There is one main customer for this type of unique service: contractors with heavy earth-moving machinery. Earth-moving equipment is thirsty for fuel, and you cannot simply head down the road for a quick fill-up in a bulldozer. Most commercial contractors with heavy equipment utilize what is known as a mobile refueling service. The key to success in this business is to be on-call and ready to refuel equipment seven days a week. Revenue is generated by charging a premium for the fuel over gas pump prices, typically in the range of 20 to 30 cents a gallon. There are regulations in this industry, so be sure to carefully research the business and local market prior to establishing the service.

CHILDREN'S COACH SERVICE
★★ $$$$ 🏚 ⚖️ 🌍

A parent's worst nightmare is that their child will become a victim of crime or even worse—abducted. This fact creates a very strong argument for parents to utilize a childrens' coach service within their community. Basically a childrens' coach is a taxi service that exclusively specializes in moving children safely from point A to point B. These specialized services include picking kids up at home and taking them to school in the morning and delivering them home safely after school. Or trips to the mall, a sporting event, to meet friends, and just about any other time parents are too busy to personally pick up and drop off their children for any occasion, can be part of the services you provide. Beyond reliable transportation and a communication system, the main requirement for getting this business going will be a taxi or limousine license and permit. These permits can be difficult to acquire, however. Be sure to plead your case to community officials, as this service is focused on the well-being of kids, and benefits the community as a whole.

CAR RENTALS
★ $$$$ ⚖ 🌐

The car rental industry is extremely competitive, but think about a niche market that the big automotive rental companies are not servicing. Here are a few suggestions:

- Exclusively rent exotic sports cars like Porsches, BMWs, and Corvettes.
- Rent only motorcycles like Harley Davidson or Honda.
- Specialize in convertible cars for rent or perhaps sport utility vehicles.
- For environmentalists seeking car rentals, provide rentals with alternative fuels and electric-powered options.

Promote the business by establishing alliances with hotels, corporations, and business associations, as well as by advertising in local print media. Should you choose the route of exotic sports cars, consider hosting a contest with a local radio station with the prize being a one- or two-day rental of an exotic sports car free of charge. Providing the radio station does its part and publicizes the contest well, then this can be a great way to promote a new business of this nature.

TRUCK ACCESSORIES
★★ $$+ 🏠 🕐 ⚖

Selling and installing after-market accessories for trucks such as box caps, running boards, and roll bars from a homebased workshop is a fantastic money making opportunity that can be conducted on a full- or part-time basis. In addition to these truck accessories, also consider becoming an authorized dealer for one of the many manufacturers of "spray-in liners" for pickup trucks. These types of box liners have become very popular, and there is a 100 percent mark up on the application. As a grand opening promotion you can place advertisements in your local newspaper and offer free installation for all accessories purchased before a specific date. Promotions such as this are costly, but they can attract a lot of business to a new enterprise and the spin off can lead to new business through referrals. *Note*: Be sure to check that the zoning for your home will allow for this sort of business to be operated.

AUTO PARTS REBUILDING
★ $$ 🏠 🕐

Providing you have the equipment and skills required, an excellent part-time income can be earned by rebuilding secondhand automobile replacement parts. You can work from a home-based workshop on an as-needed or part-time basis for existing auto parts rebuilders. Or you can advertise you service locally for rebuilding automotive parts. Also consider specializing in automotive parts rebuilding for parts used in rare, antique, and exotic cars, trucks, and motorcycles.

ONLINE AUTO E-MALL
★★ $$ 🏠 🕐 ⚖ 🖱

Here is a terrific little online business venture you can establish right in your own city. Best of all, it has the potential to be expanded to service every city across the United States and Canada. An online auto e-mall is simply a Web site that contains a grouping of automotive-related businesses from one specific community or city. These companies can include new and used car dealers, mechanics garages, gas stations, auto body paint shops, car rental agencies, car washes, and so on. The purpose of an auto e-mall is to create a convenient one-stop online directory for people looking for automotive products and services within a particular community. This type of community Web site also saves participating businesses thousands of dollars in individual Web site development and maintenance. In exchange for an annual listing fee, your customers would receive a listing or spot in the auto e-mall that when clicked on would link to a separate Web page within the site that outlined details about their products and services. The Web site can be promoted in local print publications and by utilizing Internet marketing techniques, such as search engine registration. Be sure to have signs made that promote the Web site. These signs can be displayed at participating business locations.

BICYCLE TAXI SERVICE (PEDICAB)

★ $$

Peddle your way to profits by starting your own bicycle or pedicab taxi service. Whether a romantic ride through a park or a sightseeing visit around town, tourists love to take in the sights and sounds on their vacation with a relaxing ride in a pedicab. The main obstacle to overcome for starting a pedicab taxi service is licensing. However, if a license to operate a pedicab can be acquired or purchased, you could then be well on your way to establishing a fun and profitable business. There are many styles of pedicabs available ranging from two occupants all the way to six, and the cost to purchase a new pedicab is in the range of $3,500. Ride or rental rates are currently about $8 to $12 per 15 minutes with a minimum $5 charge. This type of business can easily be expanded by hiring contractors to operate the pedicabs on revenue split basis. I would suggest a 50/50 split or a flat rental rate that the operator pays for an entire shift. Ideally, this type of business will be located in an area frequently visited by tourists and with a climate that will allow for a year-round operation to maximize profits. Be sure to build alliances with local hotels, motels, and tourist attractions that will let you display promotional materials in their lobbies as well as park in front of their establishments and cater to their customers seeking to hire a pedicab for an enjoyable ride.

WEB RESOURCE: www.hiwheel.com/pedicab.asp Manufacturers of bicycle pedicabs and accessories.

AUTO PERFORMANCE CENTER

★★ $$$$

With more than 100 million cars and trucks registered in the United States you cannot go wrong with starting an auto performance center that specializes in selling the latest and hottest automobile accessories. Stock and sell items such as mag rims and tires, wheel covers, engine performance parts, audio equipment and alarms, spoilers and body kits, and sport driving lamps. This type of retail business is very costly to establish so planning and research will be of the greatest importance. Also be sure to locate the business in a building that will enable you to carry out installations of these accessories. The installation aspect of the business can be partnered with a mechanic. You sell the products and they install the products at your location. With service and installation space you will also be able to provide customers with additional services, such as detailing, interior cleaning, and window tinting.

BOAT LETTERING

★★ $$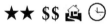

Here is a fantastic little money making opportunity for entrepreneurs with a computer, design software, and a creative imagination. There are thousands of pleasure boats in the United States, and all have call numbers and signs indicating the name of the boat. However, a quick trip to your local marina quickly reveals that the sun and water take its toll. It is common is to see faded and peeling paint and vinyl letters. Here's where your computer and design skills can make you money. Simply design a few sample boat signs featuring great graphics, print them out on paper, and start to show your handy work to boat owners at local marinas. You can sketch out quick ideas for new signage for their boats while on site and return in a day or two with the finished product printed on paper. Once you get the go ahead simply take the digital file with the sign design to a sign shop that specializes in making vinyl peel and stick-on signs and return to the marina to install the new sign for your client. Remember, it costs nothing for the boat owner to find out how good a new sign can look, so you will get little objection to the first step of the process. Providing the sign you design is visually appealing, you will also get little objection from the boat owner when you return to close the sale. Boats are expensive to buy and maintain and very few owners would let $100 stand in their way in terms of improving their boat's appearance.

NOTES

KEY	
RATINGS	★
START-UP COST	$
HOMEBASED BUSINESS	
PART-TIME	
LEGAL ISSUES	
FRANCHISE OR LICENSE POTENTIAL	
ONLINE	

33

TRAVEL
Businesses You Can Start

TOUR GUIDE

★★ $

Do you live in a tourist area, and do you know that area well? If so, why not consider starting a business as a personal tour guide. This type of enterprise can be managed from a home office, started for less than $1,000, and has the potential to produce an income that can easily exceed $50,000 per year. The key to success in becoming a personal tour guide is to promote your service aggressively, build contacts with companies and individuals that can help you succeed, and to provide clients with the best time of their vacation. Currently, tour guides are charging clients around $125 for half-day tours, and as much as $200 for full-day tours, plus the cost to provide transportation and tickets to events or local attractions. Companies and individuals to build alliances with, in terms of generating referrals, are limousine companies, hotels and hotel employees, business event planners, and travel agents.

WEB RESOURCE: www.smallbizbooks.com Business-specific start-up guides and books.

ONLINE TOUR GUIDES

★★ $$

Unite the independent tour guides of the world by creating a Web site that features tour guides from around the globe for hire. Simply develop a Web site that is indexed by country and subindexed by city. Visitors to the site could choose the destination they are traveling to and find a tour guide to show them the attractions once they get there. In exchange for a posting fee, tour guides would receive a listing in the directory as well as a full Web page within the site that would give them the ability to promote their service, state their qualifications, and provide contact information. Promoting the site would be very easy and require you to do no more than initiate a direct-mail and e-mail marketing campaign aimed at travel agents and brokers. Travel agents and brokers would

---

be able to refer their clients to the site to locate a suitable tour guide.

ROAD TRIP DRIVING MAPS
★★★ $$ 🏠 🕐 🌏

Are you seeking to start a fun, unique, and interesting business related to travel? If so, perhaps you should consider starting a business that designs, produces, and distributes road trip driving maps. One of the great icons of American culture is the road trip. It has been the topic of books, songs, and movies, and the more interesting the road trip map, the better. In addition to alternate routes that can be taken from one point to another, the maps can also include information such as the best and worst restaurants, strange and interesting facts about cities and towns along the way, weird roadside attractions, or perhaps fictitious hitchhiker stories. The best way to market the maps is to design a POP display and establish wholesale accounts with retailers as well as truck stops and restaurants that are frequented by travelers.

OFF-ROAD TOURS
★★ $$$$ ⚖

Off-road, or four-wheel-drive, tours have become an extremely popular day excursion for many vacationers, as it is a reasonably priced vacation activity that can be enjoyed by every member of the family. Generally, off-road tours are offered in half-day or all-day packages to clients and are currently priced from $50 to $100 per person. Advertising and promoting off-road or backwoods tours is very easy and is best accomplished by designing and distributing promotional material about the activity to all local restaurants, hotels, and travel agents. This kind of tour business can be very profitable, even if the business associates or partners receive a 10 or 20 percent commission for referring clients to the business.

MOVIE SET TOURS
★ $$$ 🕐

Do you live in an area of the country where many TV productions and movies are filmed? If so, starting a business that takes people on tours of famous movie and TV film locations is a terrific tour service to get rolling. In addition to the movie set tours, also include celebrity drive-by house tours as a method of providing clients with a unique and unforgettable holiday activity. Movie set and location tours can be marketed and promoted in a number of fashions including commissioned booking agencies, listing with travel agents and brokers, and local promotion by distributing fliers to hotels and restaurants.

ONLINE E-TRAVEL BARGAINS
★★ $ 🏠 🕐 🖱

It is time to roll up your sleeves and get to work building an e-mail database of people who like to travel often, and like to travel cheaply even more often. Basically, the goal of this opportunity is to amass a large e-mail database of people to send a weekly travel bargains newsletter to. You are not working as a travel agent; you are simply sending out a free weekly travel e-newsletter that features travel tips, articles, and a limited number of travel bargain advertisements submitted by travel agents. Income is earned by selling advertising space in the newsletter to travel agents, but there is one stipulation: the travel packages or services the agents wish to advertise must be true travel bargains and at least 20 percent off the regular retail selling price. The cost to operate the newsletter adds up to no more than a few hours each week in time. Only five travel agents paying a mere $50 per week each to have access to your e-newsletter subscribers will create an income for you in excess of $10,000 per year.

CUSTOM TRAVEL BAGS
★ $$$ 🏠 🕐

"Have bags, will travel," could be your company motto if you start a business that designs, manufactures, and sells custom travel bags for business and pleasure travelers. The market for unique, functional and good quality travel bags is gigantic, and this business venture is extremely easy to get up and going. The main objective in designing and selling travel bags is for the product to be unique and serve a particular need. Try an all-in-one travel bag that enables business travelers to carry a portable office that can include a notebook computer, printer, paper supplies, cell phone and charger, as well as have a battery power supply built right into the bag. Of course, this is only one suggestion, as there are literally thousands of different ideas that can be incorporated into travel bags to make the product appealing to consumers. To keep initial start-up and development costs in check consider a joint venture partnership with a related business in the industry.

ONLINE HOT AIR BALLOON TRIPS
★★ $$$

Starting a business that promotes and sells hot air balloon tours does not mean you need to rush out and buy a hot air balloon. The business can be successfully operated as a booking agency for balloon tour operators from around the globe. Customers, travel agents, and wedding planners could simply log onto one Web site and be able to book a once-in-a-lifetime hot air balloon tour. It could be that easy. Securing hot air balloon tour operators to be represented by your online booking service would not be difficult, as there would be no charge for tour operators to become a member and be featured on the Web site. However, once a customer has booked a balloon trip or tour, a commission of 25 percent would be charged on the total value, or 75 percent of the trip value would be remitted to the tour operator. In addition to balloon trips the Web site could also provide clients with options to book helicopter and small plane sightseeing excursions.

CORPORATE RETREATS
★ $$

Uniting corporate retreats from around the world into a corporate retreat vacation club may be just the answer to your business start-up dreams. There are thousands of vacation retreats owned by corporations from around the globe, and many of these corporate retreats sit vacant for a great deal of the year. Herein lies the business opportunity. Start a business that manages and rents corporate retreats to business and pleasure travelers when the vacation property is

not in use by the corporation. Revenues could be generated from the weekly and monthly rental rates for the vacation retreats, and the fee for managing and renting the retreats could be 25 percent to 35 percent of the total rental revenue generated. Corporations would save money on property management costs, as well as gain rental revenue, and business and pleasure travelers would have access to a wide range of well-equipped vacation properties around the world.

ECO TOURS
★★★ $$$

The time has never been better than now to start a business that specializes in arranging and conducting eco tours, as we now live in a society that has become more and more concerned and interested in the environment and Mother Nature in general. The first step to establishing this type of tour operation is to decide on the ecology subject or topic, and to determine the way in which the tour will be conducted in terms of transportation, marketing, and accommodations. Additional considerations will also include the possibility of charity endorsement and business location. Overall, ecology and environmental tours are an excellent new business start-up choice for the new millennium and beyond.

WEB RESOURCE: www.ecotourism.org The International Ecotourism Society.

WORKING VACATIONS
★★ $$$

As strange as this may sound, every year thousands of people pay big bucks for an opportunity to work while they're on vacation. Working on a commercial fishing boat, as a farmhand, or as a factory laborer—does not matter. There seems to be interest in all kinds of working vacations, and the stranger the better. Simply seek out companies, businesses, farms, and factories that are interested in forming joint ventures to promote and provide working vacation services. Once the joint ventures have been established, the vacations can be sold via the Internet, through travel agents and brokers, or by establishing a direct commissioned sales team. The biggest business challenge to overcome will be the legal aspect of operating this type of travel business, in terms of workers' compensation laws and liability issues.

CELEBRITY TOURS
★★ $$$ ⚖

Starting a tour business featuring tours that visit or drive by the homes of celebrities, politicians, and the childhood homes of infamous criminals is a terrific travel business venture to activate. And providing you can offer tourists interesting and unforgettable tours, there is a very good likelihood of business and financial success. This type of tour business is best marketed by building alliances with local hotels, motels, and travel agents to act as booking agents for the tours in the area where the business is operated from. To keep initial start-up costs to a minimum also subcontract out the transportation aspect of the business to an established transportation firm. I have participated in many tour activities while on family vacations, and without question the best tours are the ones that combine an interesting topic, good service, and above all, an excellent guide or tour emcee.

TRAVEL COMPANION
★★ $

Do you want to travel the world for free? If so, perhaps you should consider becoming a professional travel companion. Working as a professional travel companion generally does not provide an income; only free travel transportation, meals, and accommodations. There are numerous reasons why people enlist the services of professional travel companions including not wanting to travel alone, to assist in caring for children or elderly members of the family, or wanting a person from their country who is familiar with the area that the person is traveling to. While this type of travel business will not generate much income, if any, it does provide an opportunity to travel the world, make new friends and contacts, and build a lifetime of cherished memories.

ONLINE TRAVEL COMPANIONS
★ $$

Develop a Web site that brings people seeking a travel companion together with people seeking to be travel companions. In addition to travel companions you can also provide space on the site for people who are looking for someone to drive their car to a destination, or share driving duties and costs to go across the country. The site should be a free service for all and income can be earned by selling banner advertising space or even products related to travel, such as books, maps, and accommodation guides. Promote the site by hyperlinking it to sites on the Web that specialize in travel, as well as by registering the site with numerous search engines.

WEB RESOURCE: www.entrepreneur.com Create a business Web site with MySite professional Web site builder.

BICYCLE TOURS
★★★ $$$+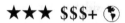

Careening down a steep mountain road at 30 miles per hour on a mountain bike may not be everyone's idea of the perfect vacation. However, there is no denying the fact that bicycle vacation tours are one of the fastest growing segments of the travel industry. The key to success in a bicycle tour business is that the tours have to be unique, fun, and interesting, and should be organized around a central theme. Additional considerations include accommodations, meals, and transportation requirements or services, as well as the length and location of the tours. Advertising in all the traditional media, developing a company Web site promoting the business, and listing the tours with travel agents and brokers can accomplish marketing the business.

START-UP COSTS: The following example can be used as an outline to establish the investment required for starting a bicycle tour business:

	Low	High
Business setup, legal, banking, etc.	$500	$2,000
Company Web site	$500	$2,500

	Low	High
Office equipment and supplies	$2,000	$5,000
Liability insurance	$500	$1,000
Equipment and transportation	$15,000	$50,000
Initial advertising and marketing budget	$1,000	$5,000
Working capital	$1,000	$5,000
Total start-up investment	**$20,500**	**$70,500**

There are cost saving methods that can be employed to substantially reduce the amount of start-up capital required to set a bicycle tour business in motion, these methods include:

- Subcontracting all transportation requirements for the business to a local and established bus or transportation company.
- Negotiating a discount on equipment purchases from a national bicycle manufacturer, as well as the potential to become an authorized dealer of the bicycles.
- Starting the business in conjunction with an established tour operator that does not currently provide bicycle tour options to clients.

PROFIT POTENTIAL: The profit potential for a bicycle tour business varies greatly due to a number of factors, such as length of tour, operating format, customer volumes, and operating overheads. However, the current rates for bicycle tours are in the range of $50 to $70 per person per half day, $75 to $125 per person per full day, and weeklong tours start at $100 per day per person, and go up from there. Additionally, the type of accommodations, meals, and transportation (if supplied) will also have an effect on the overall business revenues and profits. Profit potential range is $20,000+ per year part-time and $40,000+ per year full-time.

WORLD CASTLE VACATIONS
★ $$

England, Scotland, France, Germany, Spain, and Italy all have castles, many of which have been converted to tourist attractions and accommodations.

Starting a travel business that specializes in world castle tours and trips could not only prove to be fun and interesting, it could also make you rich. Promoting and marketing the castle trips and tours can be accomplished in many ways including direct-mail campaign, fax and e-mail broadcasting, on the Internet, and in conjunction with established travel agents and brokers. A suggested commission rate or booking rate for the tours and trips that have been marketed through the Web site would be 10 to 20 percent of the total retail sales value.

TRAVEL CHEAP BOOKS AND GUIDES
★★ $$$

Each year thousands of graduating university and collage students embark on vacations to every corner of the planet as the "last hoorah" prior to starting careers and families. And starting a business that develops, publishes, and distributes "how-to travel cheap" books and guides aimed specifically at this segment of the travel market is a fantastic business enterprise to set in motion. If you're not a well-seasoned traveler yourself, you can still start this business simply by enlisting the services of people who are experts in the field of traveling on a limited budget. The simplest way to get things rolling is to post advertisements on various Internet newsgroups seeking information about ways to "travel cheap" from people who have firsthand experience. Once the information has been gathered, simply compile the information into book form and away you go. Considerations will include publishing, marketing, and distribution methods.

HOTEL PUBLICATIONS
★★ $$$

Are you searching for a unique and interesting business opportunity that will enable you to work from a homebased office and provide you with the possibility of earning a very comfortable living? If so, perhaps you should consider starting a publishing business that focuses on small independent hotel publications. Establish alliances with hotels, and develop and design a two-page publication that can be hand delivered to the hotel guests. To keep printing and production costs down consider using 11-inch by 17-inch paper, as when folded in half, it will give the appearance of a four-page publication. The information and articles featured in the paper can be related to local points of interest, community history, trivia, and a calendar of local activities and events. Selling advertising space to local merchants seeking to capitalize on tourist spending money while on vacation could support the paper.

ONLINE TRAVEL VIDEOS

Calling all innovative entrepreneurs. The time has never been better to start an online business that features travel videos filmed and submitted by amateurs. The online videos would be free of charge for site visitors to view. The travel video footage can be procurred by posting newsgroup advertisements encouraging people to share their travel experiences. Revenue for this type of cybertravel business can be gained by selling advertising space to travel industry companies, as well as by selling related travel products and services. This type of unusual and intriguing Web site has a real possibility of becoming a hit with Web surfers; the key to success will be in promoting and marketing the site to ensure maximum exposure and number of site hits. Revenue can also be gained by selling professionally produced travel videos over the Web site.

SINGLES-ONLY VACATIONS
★★ $$ 🏠 🕐

Business specialization is the buzzword for the new millennium, and the travel industry is no exception. Starting a business that specializes in singles-only vacation destinations could prove to be just the money-making opportunity that you have been searching for. There are inherent differences between a family vacation and one that would be enjoyed by a single person. Catering to this gigantic segment of the travel industry has the potential to make you rich. The key objective in this travel business is to

offer clients original and diverse travel options. Special attention must be paid to marketing and promotion. Seek to initiate joint ventures with established companies that also cater to the single lifestyle. Overall, this type of travel agency has tremendous growth and profit potential.

PETS WELCOME VACATIONS
★★ $$ 🏠 🕐

Starting a travel business that focuses specifically on providing vacation and tour options that include the family pet is the focus of this business opportunity. Most tour and vacation packages that are currently available on the market make no provisions for family pets. In fact, most have a no pets allowed policy, and this situation creates a tremendous opportunity for the entrepreneur with initiative to capitalize on, by starting a travel booking agency that exclusively features "Pets Welcome" vacation packages. The first step to establishing this novel travel business is to organize a list of hotels, resorts, airlines, and tour operators that will allow pets to participate in the family holiday experience. The next step will be simply to start marketing the "pets welcomed" vacation packages and tours. This can be accomplished by advertising and promoting the business and vacation packages via the Internet, and by a direct-mail campaign targeted at pet owners, pet trainers, vets, and all related businesses in the pet industry.

TRAVEL KITS
★ $$ 🏠 🕐

Starting a business that produces and distributes specialty travel kits for business and pleasure travelers could put you on the path to financial freedom and independence. The travel kits could be destination-specific and include items such as maps, language dictionaries, attraction and tour discount coupons, and personal sundries such as a minifirst-aid kit, toothbrushes, etc. Once the travel kits have been designed and produced, they can be sold directly to travel agents and brokers on a wholesale basis, as well as directly to consumers via the Web and mail order.

BACKPACKING VACATIONS
★★ $$$$ 🏠 🕐 🌍

Backpacking and hiking are two of the world's most popular recreational outdoor activities, so it seems logical that a travel business that specializes in operating backpacking and hiking tours would be a wise choice for a travel business start-up. There are various approaches that can be taken in terms of an operating format for the business. One approach may be to offer clients an all-inclusive vacation package, which could include transportation, overnight camping, meals, and numerous activities. An alternate approach is to offer travelers "mini-backpacking excursions" while on vacation. This approach would best be marketed by establishing alliances in the local area of the business operation to act as booking agents for the excursions. Excellent alliances to build would be with restaurants, hotels, travel agents, and local activities booking agents. The one day or mini excursion option would greatly reduce the amount of start-up capital required to set the business in motion. This approach may also enable the business to be operated on a part-time or seasonal basis, which can also be of benefit to the entrepreneur seeking a secondary means of income.

ADVENTURE WEDDING PLANNER
★★★★ $$ 🏠 🕐 🌍

"I do," says the bride, as she is just about to leap off a 200-foot bridge with only a bungee cord separating her and the groom from the ground. Launching a business as an adventure wedding planner could not only prove to be fun and interesting, you are also almost guaranteed of having very little competition. White-water rafting, scuba diving, hot air balloon trips, mountain climbing, and bungee jumping are only a few of the adventure activity choices you can provide to clients who are getting hitched and seeking something out of the ordinary. An adventure wedding planning service can be advertised in wedding publications, as well as on the Internet. It should not take long to establish the business, as this is the type of unique, interesting, and fun service that really gets people talking.

WEB RESOURCE: www.nawp.com National Association of Wedding Professionals.

BED AND BREAKFAST OPERATOR
★★ $$+ 🏠 🕐 ⚖

Providing you can get your home renovated to operate as a bed and breakfast accommodation, and you do not mind having overnight guests, you stand to profit by turning your home into a bed and breakfast tourist destination. Operating a bed and breakfast is a terrific way to meet new people and make new friends. It is also a great way to pay down the mortgage or stash away some extra money for retirement. Rates for B&B stays are typically in the range of $30 to $60 per night and include breakfast the following morning. You can promote your B&B by joining your local tourism association as well as by listing your B&B in online B&B directories and advertising in travel magazines and publications. Beyond a business license, the cost to turn your home into a B&B can vary based on certain factors, such as meeting local fire, safety, and building codes.

WEB RESOURCE: www.smallbizbooks.com Business-specific start-up guides and books.

ONLINE BED AND BREAKFAST DIRECTORY
★★ $$$$ 🏠 🗡

A short decade ago starting an online bed and breakfast directory business could not be accomplished, simply because the technology required to operate the business was not yet available. It never fails to amaze me how new business opportunities can be created virtually overnight, and while being the first to capitalize on the opportunity certainly does have its advantages, it can also have its disadvantages in terms of consumer acceptance and profitability. At first glance it may seem like the Internet is already at capacity for selling consumer products and services; especially in the highly competitive online travel industry. However, the Internet is still in its infancy in terms of consumer acceptance, use, and capacity for new and innovative business concepts. Starting an online or commercial Web site venture requires the same amount of research and planning that a traditional "bricks and mortar" retail business requires. It does however, have numerous advantages, such as generally lower initial start-up costs, ability to level the playing field with competitors, lower operating costs, flexibility in terms of operating location and business hours, and a sharper potential growth pattern. The business concept for starting an online bed and breakfast directory is relatively straightforward. Bed and breakfast accommodation operators would post information such as rates, location, local activities, specials, pictures, and contact information onto the Web site. Visitors to the Web site would simply be a click away from locating the perfect bed and breakfast for their travel plans. Revenue for the business can be generated in a few ways, including:

- Charge B&B operators a yearly posting or listing fee to be featured on the site.
- List B&B operators for free, and charge a commission percentage only on visitor bookings.
- Charge no posting or membership fees and support the business by selling banner advertising on the Web site, and by selling travel products and services.

In addition to a B&B directory, the Web site could also provide information on, or act as a directory for other types of travel services and travel packages including:

- Guest ranch directory
- Cruise ship directory
- Airline flights, train tours, and RV rentals

As with any cyberbusiness, the key to success lies within two areas. The first is to develop, implement, and maintain an interesting and unique Web site. And the second is to get people to visit, utilize, and return to the Web site.

PROFIT POTENTIAL: Based on revenue option number one, the business could potentially generate yearly gross sales of $300,000. This can be done by securing a mere 1,000 B&B operators worldwide to post their business on the Web site, and charging only $25 per month for the service. The potential to not only produce a substantial yearly income, but to also create vast business wealth has never been more attainable than it is now by harnessing the power of the Internet.

TRAVEL AGENT
★★ $$$+ ⚖

The main requirement for starting a travel agency or starting a business as an independent travel consultant will be to check local regulations in terms of certifications that may be required to operate the business. Additional considerations also include:

- Operating a general travel agency, or specializing in a particular type of travel.
- Operating location: storefront or homebased.
- Target markets: the well-heeled traveler or the budget traveler.
- Advertising, promotions, and marketing.

The travel industry as a whole is extremely competitive, especially for businesses that operate as general travel agencies. To limit competition it is important to specialize in this industry and seek a niche market.

WEB RESOURCE: www.astanet.com American Society of Travel Agents.

WHALE WATCHING TOURS
★★ $$$$ ⚖

Whale watching tours are the largest segment of the booming multimillion dollar eco tourism industry. While starting a whale watching tour business is a costly business venture to set in motion, the personal and financial rewards can be tremendous. Beyond having the business located in an area that is excellent for whale watching, the main business requirement is a suitable tour boat and a certified captain at the helm, not to mention substantial liability insurance. Rates for whale watching tours vary as to the length of the tour, meals provided, and additional customer services. They may start at $50 per person and can go as high as $150 per person. The profit potential for a whale watching travel or tour business is exceptional once the business has been established. However, keep in mind that most whale watching tour businesses operate on a part-time or seasonal basis.

ONLINE WHALE WATCHING TOURS
★★ $$$ 🏠 🕐 🐎

Do you want to be part of the multimillion dollar whale watching tour business, but are a little short on investment capital, or you live in a landlocked area of the country? Well don't fret, there is a way to capitalize on the whale watching tour industry without having to invest a large sum of money, or live by an ocean. The solution: start an online whale watching business that features video footage of whale watching tours broadcasted over a specially designed Web site. Whale watching tour operators and tourists from around the world could provide the video footage featured on the site. To generate revenues and profits for the business, simply charge whale watching tour operators a yearly posting or listing fee to be featured on the Web site. Products on whales such as books, music, and apparel could also be sold on the Web site to boost revenues.

DOUBLE-DECKER BUS TOURS
★★ $$$$ ⚖️ 🌐

Antique, English-style double-decker buses have always held a certain mystique and fascination for most people. They are unique, fun, and harken back to an earlier time. Starting a double-decker bus tour business could not only prove to be a whole lot of fun, it could also be a very profitable business venture. The key to success in this type of tour business is to make sure the tour business is operated in a busy tourist area, and that the tour itself is fun, interesting, and unique. Generally with this type of tour business the initial advertising and marketing drive will have to be well researched and planned. However, once established, word-of-mouth advertising from local companies and individuals will

generally be all the advertising required to sustain a suitable customer volume level.

CANOE AND KAYAK TOURS
★★★ $$$+ 🏠 🕐

Are you searching for a travel related recreation business that has tremendous opportunity for growth, profit potential, and a whole lot of fun? If so, why not consider starting a canoe and kayak tour business. A canoe and kayak tour business can be easily operated and managed from a homebased location, or can be operated in conjunction and with existing businesses such as a marina, resort, or waterfront tourist attraction. There are also various options available for the method in which a canoe and kayak tour business can be operated, including day excursion format, overnight, multiday format, or an operating format that combines canoe and kayak instruction as well as a general pleasure tour. A few key considerations in terms of starting and operating this business include:

- Liability and general business insurance
- Transportation and equipment requirements
- First aid and safety requirements and qualifications
- Qualifications for tour leaders

START-UP COSTS: The following example can be used as an outline to establish initial investment required for starting a canoe and kayak tour business.

	Low	High
Business setup, legal, banking, etc.	$500	$2,000
Liability and general business insurance	$750	$1,250
Office equipment and supplies	$1,500	$5,000
Equipment and transportation	$15,000	$25,000
Initial advertising and marketing budget	$500	$1,500
Working capital	$500	$2,000
Total start-up investment	**$18,750**	**$36,750**

Additionally, there are a few options for transportation requirements if the business is operated on a mobile basis, meaning that customers are shuttled to the launch location or starting point of the tour. These options include:

- Purchasing, renting, or leasing the required transportation. Generally a 12-passenger van and a trailer capable of holding an equivalent number of canoes and kayaks is needed.
- Subcontracting the transportation aspect of the business to a local transportation firm.
- Making customers responsible for providing their own transportation, and reflecting this in the rates.

PROFIT POTENTIAL: The following income forecast can be used as a guideline to establish revenue potential.

# of Customers per Week	Tour Rate	Gross Revenue per Month	Gross Revenue per Year
10	$125	$5,000	$60,000
15	$125	$7,500	$90,000
20	$125	$10,000	$120,000
25	$125	$12,500	$150,000

Additional business revenues can be generated by canoe and kayak equipment sales and rentals, as well as by providing clients with extended canoe and kayak instruction courses.

FACTORY TOURS
★ $$$

Do you live in a highly industrialized city or region of the country that has many factories? If so, you could be sitting on a tour business goldmine and not even realize it. Factory tours have become extremely popular in the past decade, as more and more people are seeking different and interesting ways to spend their hard-earned vacation dollars. The first step in establishing a factories tour business is to find companies that will permit tours of their factories. This is not hard to accomplish as the companies can be compensated by way of shared tour revenues. Often factories will sell their manufactured goods to the tourists at wholesale or factory-direct prices. Securing a mere 50 customers per week paying only $20 each will create business revenues of $50,000 per year, which is an excellent start for small homebased tour business.

GUEST RANCH
★★ $$$$

Guest or dude ranches have become an extremely popular vacation destination for thousands of North Americans every year. While starting a guest ranch is a labor and capital intensive business undertaking, there are also numerous benefits, such as a rewarding lifestyle, great income potential, and strong consumer demand. The most popular guest ranches include services and activities such as horseback riding, outdoor barbecues, and sporting activities, such as swimming, mountain bike trail riding, and tennis. Advertising, promoting, and marketing this sort of travel business is best accomplished by utilizing all of the traditional advertising and marketing mediums. Once the business has been established, many guests will become repeat clients as well as generate word-of-mouth referrals for the ranch. The profit potential will greatly vary as to the operating format of the ranch, and the services provided. However, current guest ranch accommodation rates start at $700 per week per person, and can go as high as $2,000 per week per person depending on the vacation package.

WEB RESOURCE: www.guestranches.com Directory listing service of North American Guest Ranches.

NOTES

KEY

RATINGS   ★

START-UP COST $

HOMEBASED BUSINESS

PART-TIME

LEGAL ISSUES

FRANCHISE OR LICENSE POTENTIAL

ONLINE

27
WRITING
Businesses You Can Start

TRUE CRIME WRITER

Murderous tales of love and larceny, or stories about the strangest, stupidest, or most twisted true crimes are spectacles of public fascination. Writing stories about true crimes isn't only a fun and interesting line of work, but it can also potentially earn you a substantial living. Once again, this type of writing is typically done on a freelance basis, unless your intentions are to write a novel about a true crime, or multiple true crimes. Potential purchasers for the articles can include newspapers, magazines, and short story publishers. A good entry point into this type of writing is to document a local crime that has taken place in your community and submit the story to the local newspaper for publishing. This starting method is not likely to generate revenues initially. However, any work that you can get published is a good starting point for building valuable experience and contacts within the publishing industry.

HANDWRITTEN INVITATIONS

The demand for handwritten invitations is gigantic, and starting a business that specializes in handwritten invitations is a fantastic new venture to set in motion that can easily be operated right from the comforts of your own home. Calligraphy is defined as the art of writing beautifully, and if this is a skill that you possess, then why not profit from your perfect penmanship? This type of writing service is very easy to market. Simply design a few sample invitations and set meetings with event and wedding planners to present your talents. The wedding and event planners can act as sales representatives for your service and market the handwritten invitations to their clients. Once established, there should be no difficulties in building this service into a business that generates $40,000 per year in sales or more, and best of all there are virtually no operating overheads to bite into the revenues.

WEB RESOURCE: www.calligraphicarts.org Association for the Calligraphic Arts.

CITY ATTRACTION GUIDES
★★ $$

Every community and city in North America has tourist attractions that deserve to be featured in an attraction guide. Starting a business that creates, produces, and sells city attractions guides is a fantastic new venture to get rolling. The guides can include information such as the best tourist attractions, the best shopping districts, the best restaurants and hotels, and historical information about the city. There are also a couple of options in terms of generating revenues and profits for the business. The first is to sell the guides to local tourist-related business on a wholesale basis, so that the business can retail the guides to their guests and clients. The second and preferred method of generating sales for the business is to distribute the guides for free, and sell advertising space to local merchants wishing to advertise their products and services in the city attraction guide. Once established and proven successful, this type of unique enterprise is the ideal business to expand nationally on a franchise basis to qualified operators.

EDITING SERVICE
★★ $$

An editing service is not limited to publishers and book authors as customers. In fact publishers and authors represent a very small percentage of the potential clients an editing service can be contracted by. The main requirement for starting an editing service is to have computer equipment, editing software, and of course, the ability to edit. Potential clients can include advertising agencies, marketing agencies, publishers, authors, and printers. Actually, just about any company, organization, or individual that needs to ensure that printed or electronic information is spelled correctly, that the grammar is correct, and the information is presented in an easy to read and pleasing format. Potential income range is $25 to $50 per hour.

WEB RESOURCE: www.tiac.net/users/freelance/ Freelance Editors Association.

LETTER WRITING SERVICE
★ $

Not everyone has the ability to write effective letters. And often the effectiveness of a letter can mean the difference between getting and not getting a job, winning or not winning a contract for business, having a book published or not having a book published, and the list goes on. Basically, a letter is the first and sometimes only option for making a good and lasting impression on a business client, or potential employer, etc. Many people, including business owners, politicians, students, and job seekers are more than willing to part with a few dollars to obtain a well-written letter that clearly expresses their intent or purpose. Income potential range is $20 to $30 per hour.

ONLINE ADVICE COLUMNIST
★ $

There are thousands of informational and news Web sites posted on the Internet, and this fact creates a fantastic opportunity for the creative writer and entrepreneur to capitalize by starting an online advice column service. The first step to starting this unique online business is to decide the area of advice the service will specialize in, such as how-to home renovations, social issues, marriage, business, etc. The next step is to create a sample of the advice column and begin to e-mail the sample column to as many online news and information services as possible. The advice columns can be updated on a daily or weekly basis. Securing a mere 100 online companies to feature the advice column on their Web site can create an income of $50,000 per year, providing you charge each subscribing company only $10 per week to post the column.

CHILDREN'S STORY WRITER
★★ $$

Fun aside, writing children's story books can be extremely profitable. To reinforce this fact look no further than the Harry Potter series of books: 30 million copies sold to date and rising. However, as fun and potentially profitable as writing children's story books can be, it is also an extremely competitive industry that demands unique and fresh story lines constantly. There are a few options available in terms of publishing the stories. The first is to find a commercial publisher prepared to take on the story and publish it. The second option is to self-publish the work yourself. The self-publishing option generally has the potential to generate more profits for the author. However, it is also a costly undertaking.

WEB RESOURCE: www.childrensbookguild.org The Children's Book Guild of Washington, D.C.

ONLINE TRIVIA WRITER
★★ $ 🏠 🕐 🖱

Trivia is red hot. Researching and writing about interesting and fun trivia can make you rich. Create a regular trivia column that features trivia information and games on topics that are varied, and begin to market the trivia service or column to as many print and online publishers as possible. Thanks in part to TV shows such as *Who Wants to Be a Millionaire*, it should not be to difficult to secure media outlets to feature the column, providing the trivia information and games are unique, fun, and interesting. Trivia information and games can also be compiled and developed into a book or CD-ROM format to be sold. If you go the route of writing a trivia book, you will however have to decide if the book will be published by an existing publisher, or if you will tackle the job yourself by self-publishing the trivia book and CD-ROM.

LITERARY AGENT
★ $$ 🏠 🕐

A six-figure income can be earned as a literary agent, providing you have a good understanding and knowledge of the publishing industry. You agree to represent authors' works and market the literary works to publishers. Many literary agents will specialize in one or two particular fields of interest, such as business books, children's books, biographies, or

how-to books. There are two ways to generate revenues as a literary agent. Literary agents generally receive a 10 percent commission on all work that is successfully marketed to publishers. Many literary agents charge a reading fee to review manuscripts submitted by authors. This reading fee is not a means of getting rich, but simply a method to get paid for the extensive amount of time spent reading authors' submissions, as they may submit hundreds of manuscripts on a yearly basis.

WEB RESOURCE: www.publishersweekly.com/aar Association of Author's Representatives.

CREATING MAILING LISTS
★★★ $$ 🏠 🕐

Good up-to-date mailing lists sell for as much as $1 per name, and herein lies an exciting business opportunity. The main requirements for getting the business rolling are to have great marketing skills and a computer. The mailing lists you compile should be categorized by industry and target market, as well as being available for companies to purchase in CD-ROM format or on floppy disk. This will make it easier for your customers to utilize the mailing list for mail-merges, fax, and e-mail blasts. Marketing the mailing lists can be as easy as conducting your own fax or e-mail blast campaign describing your service. Include information such as who the people on the list are, what they are looking for, and the types of companies that would benefit most by having access to this information. Profit potential is $25,000 to $100,000 per year.

WEB RESOURCE: http://paml.net Publicly Accessible Mailing Lists, directory with links to industry information.

ONLINE MAILING LIST SALES
★★ $$$$ 🏠 🖱

Let customers go online to select the mailing lists they wish to purchase. Develop a Web site that is indexed into various "mailing list" sections. These sections would be broken down into demographic and consumer buying habit headings such as "people interested in purchasing a business opportunity" or "people who regularly purchase videos by mail." The possibilities are endless in terms of the sections featured on the site. Entrepreneurs that are now in the business of selling mailing lists to other business owners could post their information and lists on the site for a monthly fee or a percentage of the sales generated. This type of cyberventure could prove very profitable, but the key to success is to have good-quality mailing lists. The site must be user-friendly, too. Be sure that downloaded mailing lists also have a program embedded that enables the user to create mailing labels automatically from the list. There are many specialized software applications available that include this function and typically you will only have to pay a one-time licensing fee for the program.

PUBLIC RELATIONS BROCHURES
★★ $$

In this age of political, environmental, and social correctness, starting a business that writes and designs public relations brochures is very timely. The business can be operated from a homebased location. Potential clients can include government agencies, corporations, property developers, and just about any other business, organization, or person seeking professional assistance to create and produce effective public relations brochures. To increase business revenues and sales, a public relations service can also offer one-stop public relations service to potential clients. Like any of the business opportunities featured in this chapter, a prerequisite for starting a business that creates public relations brochures will be a writer's flair, computer equipment, and design software.

ROVING REPORTER
★ $

A roving reporter, or freelance reporter, is an independent writer/reporter who writes human interest stories on a wide variety of subjects. Becoming a roving reporter and getting your stories published by newspapers and magazines is relatively straightforward. Write a few sample articles and submit the articles to as many newspapers and magazines as possible. Providing the stories are interesting and

well written, there is the possibility that one or more of the newspapers or magazines will ask for additional articles, or even a regular feature.

WEB RESOURCE: www.reporter.org Industry information and links.

WHERE ARE THEY NOW BOOKS
★★ $$$

To quote Andy Warhol, "everybody deserves 15 minutes of fame," and if that quote holds any truth, then you will never run out of interesting topics for writing a "where are they now" book. Celebrities, politicians, entertainers, or just everyday folks who are featured in a "where are they now" book can be people from your local community, or people from across the country or around the world. There have been countless books written on this subject, so in order to succeed, be sure that you have created a new twist, in terms of the format, story line, or type of people that are featured in the book. Once again, there are two options for publishing and distributing the book: established commercial publishers or self-publishing. The way in which you choose to publish the book will be based on your own preference and financial situation.

SPEECH WRITER
★★ $$

At some point we have all endured listening to a poorly written and badly delivered speech. Providing that you possess a creative writing flair, good research skills, and are not afraid to ask for business, then there is a better than average chance that you can start and operate a speech writing business that will not only succeed, but will also generate an excellent yearly income. Speech writing is an art form, and many professional speakers and company CEOs realize this. Often they will enlist the services of a professional speechwriter to create a speech that will leave the audience speechless. Obtaining customers is as easy as preparing a few sample speeches on various subjects and distributing the speeches to potential clients. It will take time and patience to establish a speech writing service. However, once established, the business can be personally and financially rewarding; and new clients often remain repeat clients for life.

TRANSCRIPT SERVICE
★★ $$ 🏠 🕐

Starting a transcript service is a unique and interesting business opportunity to pursue. Best of all, it has the potential to generate a substantial income. A transcript service is simply a business that records spoken information, such as a seminar, or TV talk show into a printed document. The document or transcript can then be sold to any person interested in the subject matter. It will take time to establish and build a transcript service, as the industry is competitive and well represented. Once again, starting on a local basis is well advised, as this method enables you and your business to gain valuable experience and industry contacts.

WHO'S WHO DIRECTORY
★★★ $$$ 🏠 🕐

Are you searching for a fun and unique business to start that can enable you to capitalize on your writing skills and imagination? If so, perhaps you should consider writing a "Who's Who Directory" featuring people from your local community. A "Who's Who Directory" is nothing more than a listing of people with information featuring who they are, how much money they make, their claims to fame, their role in the community, etc., formatted into a book or CD-ROM. The profit potential is amazing for this type of writing venture, as almost every person featured in the book will purchase a copy, not to mention their friends, family, and associates. Basically, a well-written and promoted "Who's Who Directory" has the potential to become a best seller within the very community it features.

ONLINE WHO'S WHO DIRECTORY
★★ $$$$ 🏠 🌐 🔧

Take "Who's Who" into cyberspace by starting your own Web site that features the same information

as a printed "Who's Who Directory," but in an electronic format. This is a very exciting business opportunity. Once you have perfected the online 'Who's Who" concept, this same concept can be franchised or licensed to qualified operators right across the country for every community and city. Like its print counterpart, this type of online venture could become very popular. Selling advertising space on the Web site to local business merchants could also create income.

PRESS RELEASE SERVICE
★★★ $$ 🏠 🕐

More than 700,000 new businesses are started each year in the United States. This fact creates an incredible opportunity for the innovative entrepreneur to capitalize by starting a press release service. A press release is simply a document that includes information about a new business enterprise or newsworthy information about an existing business, including expansion plans, new sales contracts, etc. A press release basically serves two purposes. The first is to inform the general public about news of a business, regardless if the business is new or established. The second purpose of a press release is to generate publicity for a business. The key to success in this type of writing service is to establish and maintain an excellent contact base within the media. Beyond your press writing abilities, business owners will pay top dollar to get their business information into the hands of a service that can get a press release printed, seen, talked about, and heard.

ONLINE PRESS RELEASE SERVICE
★★★ $$$$ 🔧

As the saying from a popular movie goes, "build it and they will come." This saying could prove to be very accurate in the case of an online press release service. In a nutshell, an online press release service is simply a Web site that has been specifically design to enable users to log on and create a press release from the many templates available. The press release could then be sent electronically via e-mail to numerous media outlets, all with a click of the mouse. Without question, activating this type of online enterprise will require specialized software programming and countless hours dedicated to researching, formatting, and "plugging in" the media contacts. Additionally, users should have options in terms of the type of media they want their press release to go to, such as newspapers, radio, television, online media, etc. However, this would be relatively easy to format while developing the software application for the site. This type of Web site would be an incredible business tool for all entrepreneurs. Imagine the power of being able to create, edit, and submit a press release to thousands of media outlets all from one user-friendly and convenient Web site. The profit potential could prove outstanding.

SECRETARIAL SERVICE
★★★ $$ 🏠 🕐

The time has never been better than now to start a homebased secretarial service. Homebased businesses are starting in record numbers each year in North America and many business owners and employees working from home lack the infrastructure and resources that traditional offices provide. The secretarial services provided can include typing, electronic filing, scheduling appointments, receptionist duties, etc. Obtaining clients for a secretarial service can be as easy as sending out fax and e-mail blasts describing the secretarial services that are available. Creating résumés for clients, as well as an executive assistant service can also earn additional revenues.

GOSSIP COLUMN
★ $ 🏠 🕐

How do you get started as a gossip columnist? Easy. Write a few sample columns and send them to every print and online newspaper and magazine you can. Chances are, if the gossip column is interesting and well-written, someone will agree to start publishing it on a regular basis. The key to successfully competing in this highly competitive market is to get the dirt, so to speak. So be sure to build and establish as many contacts as possible with people who can

assist in collecting information about the topics or individuals your gossip column focuses on. This type of writing column or service can also be established as an online venture in the format of your own specialized Web site. The options are unlimited for profiting from good old-fashioned gossip.

FAMILY TREE RESEARCH SERVICE
★★ $$ 🏠 🕐

Many people have a keen interest in finding out more about their families and ancestral past, especially if the research reveals past royal connections or connections with characters of dubious distinction or notoriety. Technology, and more importantly the Internet, has made a family tree research service not only an easy business to start, but also a business that can connect you with potential clients worldwide. Clients would pay you a fee for researching and compiling information about their family tree. However, this is a competitive industry and specialization in terms of the business is suggested. This can include focusing on one particular country, race, or time period, such as the 12th century. Income potential range is $20 to $40 per hour.

ONLINE STRANGE NEWS AND TALES
★ $$$ 🏠 🕐 🖱

News of the weird, strange, and fascinating can be the focus of a new and profitable online business enterprise. Society as a whole can never get enough of weird and wonderful tales, news, and twisted facts; thus, an opportunity to profit. There are a few ways to go about getting started. The first is to develop a Web site dedicated to bringing people strange news, stories, and tales online. In addition to the strange stories and tales you post, visitors could also post news of the strange if you include a chat room. Renting advertising space and perhaps plugging in a retail mall or hyperlinking to an online retail mall selling consumer goods would earn income. Another idea is to forego developing a Web site and opt to create a weekly "news of the strange" column that could be sold to numerous webmasters to be featured in their Web sites as content.

WHAT HAPPENED...? WRITER

What happened in your city or community 10, 20, or even 100 years ago? Was bread selling for five cents a loaf, or the first house with indoor plumbing being constructed? Community-minded people love to read about how their community functioned in the past and what the news headline stories of the day were. News and information that happened in the past can generally be uncovered with a little bit of research. Hit the library, museum archives, and start talking to local old-timers as methods for seeking out "what happened" information. This information can be compiled into articles and submitted to your local newspaper for publishing. Or you can develop an entire book from the stories and information you have collected. Do not overlook the possibility of publishing your own "what happened" monthly newspaper. The paper could be distributed free of charge throughout the community and supported by selling advertising space to local merchants.

WRITERS PLOTS

Do you have a creative imagination for developing characters, plots and story themes, but have never had the desire to write a novel, play, or short story? You can still profit from your creative imagination by developing plots and characters for authors and screenwriters who are always on the lookout for fresh and innovative story ideas. Start by developing a few samples of your work: a character study, and a plot outline for a movie, or a theme for a play. On the Internet you will find many Web sites dedicated specifically to posting these types of creative ideas. Writers, producers, and even film directors often visit these Web sites in hopes of discovering their next project. Of course, income is earned when you sell one or more of your story or character ideas. *Note*: Be sure to copyright your stories with the copyright office or register your story with the Writers Guild of America West (www.wga.org) prior to posting them to one of these online writers forums.

WEB RESOURCE: www.freelanceonline.com Directory and online resource center for writers.

SELF-HELP WRITER

We are all an expert at something. Sometimes we just need to take a good look at our lives and accomplishments to discover what we are experts at. Perhaps you have lost 100 pounds and kept it off. Then you would be an expert in the field of weight loss. Or maybe you have sold more cars than any other car salesperson in your area. You then would be considered an expert salesperson. Once you have discovered your area of expertise you can formulate a plan about how you will profit from your expertise. Worldwide, millions of self-help guides, books, and products are sold annually. The creators of these self-help products are generally considered experts in the field of their writings. People purchase these products for the obvious reason; they want to improve some aspect of their lives or want to learn how to do something better and are prepared to follow the guidance and advice of an expert. Take a good look at your accomplishments and see how these accomplishments and successes can be compiled into a book or other type of self-help medium to make you money.

NOTES

RESOURCES

UNITED STATES GOVERNMENT AGENCIES AND BUSINESS ASSOCIATIONS

Small Business Administration (SBA)

409 3rd Street, S.W.
Washington, DC 20416
Telephone: 1-800-827-5722
Web site: www.sba.gov
The U.S. Small Business Administration provides new entrepreneurs and existing business owners with financial, technical, and management resources to start, operate and grow a business. To find the local SBA office in your region log onto www.sba.gov/regions/states.html.

SBA Services and Products for Entrepreneurs

U.S. SBA Small Business Start-Up Kit
To order contact your local SBA to order or log onto www.sba.gov/starting/indexstartup.html.

U.S. SBA Business Training Seminars and Courses
For more information contact your local SBA office or log onto www.sba.gov/starting/index-training.html.

U.S. SBA Business Plan; Road Map to Success
To order contact your local SBA office or log onto www.sba.gov/starting/indexbusplans.html.

U.S. SBA Business Financing and Loan Programs
To order loan forms contact your local SBA office or log onto www.sbba.gov/financing.

United States Patent and Trademark Office

Commissioners of Patents and Trademarks
P.O. Box 9
Washington, DC 20231
Telephone: 1-800-786-9199
Web site: www.uspto.gov

U.S. Copyright Office

Library of Congress
101 Independence Avenue, S.E.
Washington, DC 20559-6000
Public Inquiries Information: 202-707-3000
To order copyright forms and copyright publications call: 202-707-9100
Fax-on-demand service: 202-707-6737
Web site: www.loc.gov/copyright

Service Corps of Retired Executives (SCORE)

409 Third Street, S.W., 6th Floor
Washington, DC 20024
Telephone: 1-800-634-0245
Web site: www.score.org
SCORE is a nonprofit association in partnership with the Small Business Administration to provide aspiring entrepreneurs and business owners with free business counseling and mentoring programs. The association consists of more than 11,000 volunteer business councilors in 389 regional chapters located throughout the United States.

U.S. Chamber of Commerce

1615 H Street, N.W.
Washington, DC 20062-2000
Telephone: 202-659-6000
Web site: www.uschamber.com
The U.S. Chamber of Commerce represents small businesses, corporations, and trade associations from coast to coast. Call 1-202-659-6000 or log onto their Web site to locate a regional branch.

National Business Incubation Association (NBIA)

20 E. Circle Drive, Suite 190
Athens, OH 45701-3571
Telephone: 704-593-4331
Web site: www.nbia.org
In the United States there are more than 900 business incubation programs, and NBIA provides links to these various incubation programs. Additionally, NBIA assists entrepreneurs with information, education, and networking resources to help in the early development stages of business start-up and the advanced stages of business growth.

National Association of Women Business Owners (NAWBO)

1411 K Street, N.W., Suite 1300
Washington, DC 20005
Telephone: 1-800-556-2926
Web site: www.nawbo.org
NAWBO provides women business owner members with support, resources, and business information to help grow and prosper in their own businesses.

American Association of Home Based Businesses (AAHBB)

P.O. Box 10023
Rockville, MD 20849
Web site: www.aahbb.org
Formed in 1991, the AAHBB is a nonprofit organization that provides members with support and networking opportunities. All members operate their business from a homebased location and the organization provides services and products that can be utilized by the home-business owner.

UMass Family Business Center

Division of Continuing Education
358 North Pleasant Street
Amherst, MA 01003-1650
Telephone: 413-545-1537
Web site: www.umass.edu/fambiz/
UMass Family Business Center provides members with training programs, information, and workshops to assist with building entrepreneurial skills that can be best utilized in a family-owned and operated business.

National Association for the Self-Employed (NASE)

P.O. Box 612067 DFW Airport
Dallas, TX 75261-2067
Telephone: 1-800-232-6273
Web site: www.nase.org
Founded in 1981, the NASE is an organization whose members include small business owners and professionals who are self-employed. NASE provides members with support, education, and training to help them succeed and prosper in business.

International Franchise Association (IFA)

1350 New York Avenue, N.W., Suite 900
Washington, DC 20005-4709
Telephone: 202-628-8000
Web site: www.franchise.org
IFA membership organization includes franchisors, franchisees, and service and product suppliers for the franchising industry.

CANADIAN GOVERNMENT AGENCIES AND BUSINESS ASSOCIATIONS

Canadian Business Service Centers (CBSC)

The CBSC offers a wide range of products and services to assist Canadian entrepreneurs to start, manage, and grow a business. The federal government of Canada has partnered with provincial governments and private industry to develop Business Service Centers in all Canadian provinces and territories. CBSC products, services, and publications can be accessed on the CBSC Web site, the info-fax service, or at any Provincial Business Service Center location. Some of the services offered to Canadian entrepreneurs include:

Interactive Business Planner (IBP)

IBP is an online interactive software application that will let you develop and prepare a comprehensive business plan.

Online Small Business Workshops

CBSC online small business workshops have been developed to assist entrepreneurs to start, finance, and market a new business venture, or improve an existing business.

Info-Guides

CBSC info-guides are available free of charge on the Web, the info-fax service, or at the Business Service Center. Info-guides are brief overviews and are industry specific, such as retailing or exporting.

Business Information System (BIS)

BIS is a business resource databank containing more than 1,200 documents pertaining to business programs, services, and regulations. BIS documents are free of charge and can be accessed on the Web site, the info-fax service, or at Business Service Center locations.

CBSC Provincial Office Locations

Alberta Business Link
100-10237-104 Street, N.W.
Edmonton, AB T5J 1B1
Telephone: 1-800-272-9675
Web site: www.cbsc.org/alberta

British Columbia Business Service Center
601 West Cordova Street
Vancouver, BC V6B 1G1
Telephone: 1-800-667-2272
Web site: www.sb.gov.bc.ca

Manitoba Business Service Center
250-240 Graham Avenue
Winnipeg, MB R3C 4B3
Telephone: 1-800-665-2019
Web site: www.cbsc.org/manitoba

New Brunswick Business Service Center
570 Queen Street
Fredericton, NB E3B 6Z6
Telephone: 1-800-668-1010
Web site: www.cbsc.org/nb

Newfoundland and Labrador Business Service Center
90 O'Leary Avenue
St. John's, NF A13 3T1
Telephone: 1-800-668-1010
Web site: www.cbsc.org/nf

North West Territories Business Service Center
Scotia Center, 8th Floor
Yellowknife, NT X1A 2L9
Telephone: 1-800-661-0599
Web site: www.cbsc.org/nwt

Nova Scotia Business Service Center
1575 Brunswick Street
Halifax, NS B3J 2G1
Telephone: 1-800-668-1010
Web site: www.cbsc.org/ns

Nunavut Business Service Center
1088 Noble House

Inqaluit, Nunavut X8A 0H0
Telephone: 1-877-499-5199
Web site: www.cbsc.org/nunavut

Ontario Business Service Center
North York Civic Center, 500 Young Street
Toronto, ON M2N 5V7
Telephone: 416-395-7499
Web site: www.cobsc.org

Prince Edward Island Business Service Center
75 Fitzroy Street
Charlottetown, PEI C1A 7K2
Telephone: 1-800-668-1010
Web site: www.cbsc.org/pe

Quebec Business Service Center
5 Place Ville Marie, Suite 12500
Montreal, Quebec H3B 4Y2
Telephone: 1-800-322-4636
Web site: www.infoentrepreneurs.org

Saskatchewan Business Service Center
122-3rd Avenue, North
Saskatoon, SK S7K 2H6
Telephone: 1-800-667-4373
Web site: www.cbsc.org/sask

Yukon Business Service Center
201-208 Main Street
White Horse, Yukon Y1A 2A9
Telephone: 1-800-661-0543
Web site: www.cbsc.org/yukon

Canadian Intellectual Property Office (CIPO)
Patents, Trademarks & Copyrights
Industry Canada, Place du Portage,
50 Victoria Street, 2nd Floor
Hull, Quebec K19 0C9
Telephone: 819-997-1936
Web site: www.cipo.gc.ca

Canada Customs and Revenue Agency
333 Laurier Avenue West
Ottawa, ON K1A 0L9
Telephone: 1-800-959-2221
Web site: www.ccra-adrc.ga.ca

Information and resources pertaining to small business taxes, corporate tax, tax rebates and programs, payroll deductions, and goods and services tax/harmonized sales tax (GST/HST).

Business Development Bank of Canada (BDC)
150 King Street West, Suite 100
Toronto, ON M5H 1J9
Telephone: 416-395-9014
Web site: www.bdc.ca
BDC provides financial services and programs to Canadians seeking to start or grow a business. Loan application forms can be ordered by calling the BDC or by visiting the Web site.

The Canadian Chamber of Commerce
BCE Place, 181 Bay Street, Heritage Building
Toronto, ON M5J 2T3
Telephone: 416-868-6415
Web site: www.chamber.ca

Small Office Home Office Business Group (SOHO)
2255 B Queen Street East, Suite 3261
Toronto, ON M4E 1G3
Telephone: 1-800-290-7646
Web site: www.soho.ca
SOHO is a nonprofit small business organization, founded in 1995 providing members with networking, education, and incentive programs and opportunities.

Young Entrepreneurs Association (YEA)
720 Spadina Avenue, Suite 300
Toronto, ON M5S 2T9
Telephone: 1-888-639-3222
Web site: www.yea.ca
YEA provides members with peer support, networking opportunities, and business and entrepreneur resources.

Canadian Franchise Association (CFA)
2585 Skymark Avenue, Suite 300
Mississauga, ON L4W 4L5
Telephone: 1-800-665-4232
Web site: www.cfa.ca

BUSINESS BOOKS AND PUBLICATIONS

Suggested Reading

Ben Franklin's 12 Rules of Management: The Founding Father of American Business Solves Your Toughest Business Problems, Blaine McCormick, Irvine, CA: Entrepreneur Press, 2000.

The Best Home Businesses for the 21st Century: The Inside Information You Need to Know to Select a Home-Based Business That's Right for You, Paul and Sarah Edwards, Los Angeles, CA: J.P Tarcher, 1999.

Business Plans Made Easy: Its Not As Hard As You Think!, Mark Henricks, Irvine, CA: Entrepreneur Press, 1999.

The Complete Idiot's Guide to Starting a Home-Based Business, Second Edition, Barbara Weltman and Beverly Williams, Indianapolis, IL: Alpha Books, 2000.

The Customer Revolution, Patricia B. Seybold, New York: Crown Publishing, 2001.

E-Service: 24 Ways to Keep Your Customers—When the Competition is Just a Click Away, Ron Zemke and Thomas K. Connellan, New York: AMACOM, 2000.

Grow Your Business, Mark Henricks, Irvine, CA: Entrepreneur Press, 2001.

How To Dotcom: A Step-by-Step Guide to e-commerce, Robert McGarvey, Irvine, CA: Entrepreneur Press, 2000.

Import/Export: How to Get Started in International Trade, Carl A. Nelson, New York: McGraw-Hill, 2000.

101+ Answers to the Most Frequently Asked Questions From Entrepreneurs, Courtney H. Price, New York: John Wiley & Sons, 1999.

Knock Out Marketing: Powerful Strategies to Punch Up Your Sales, Jack Ferreri, Irvine, CA: Entrepreneur Press, 1999.

Permission Based E-Mail Marketing That Works!, Kim MacPherson and Rosalind Resnick, Chicago: Dearborn Trade, 2001.

Positioning: The Battle for Your Mind, Al Ries and Jack Trout, New York: McGraw-Hill, 2001.

Public Relations Kit for Dummies, Eric Yaverbaum and Bill Bly, Foster City, CA: Hungry Minds Inc., 2001.

Start Your Own Business, Rieva Lesonsky, Irvine, CA: Entrepreneur Press, 2001.

Start Your Own Business: The Only Start-Up Book You'll Ever Need, Rieva Lesonsky, Irvine, CA: Entrepreneur Press, 1998.

Think Big: Nine Ways to Make Millions From Your Ideas, Don Debelak, Irvine, CA: Entrepreneur Press, 2001.

Time Tested Advertising Methods, John Caples and Fred E. Hahn, Upper Saddle River, NJ: Prentice Hall, 1998.

303 Marketing Tips: Guaranteed to Boost Your Business!, Rieva Lesonsky and Leann Anderson, Irvine, CA: Entrepreneur Press, 1999.

Where's the Money? Sure-Fire Financing Solutions for Your Small Business, Art Beroff and Dwayne Moyers, Irvine, CA: Entrepreneur Media Inc., 1999.

Magazines

American Demographics
Intertec Publishing
P.O. Box 10580
Riverton, NJ 08076-0580
Telephone: 1-800-529-7502
Web site: www.demographics.com

e-Business Advisor
Advisor Media Inc.
P.O. Box 429002
San Diego, CA 92142-9002
Telephone: 1-858-278-5600
Web site: www.advisor.com

eCompany Now
One California Street, 29th Floor
San Fransico, CA 94111
Telephone: 1-800-317-9704
Web site: www.ecompany.com

Entrepreneur
Entrepreneur Media Inc.
2445 McCabe Way
Irvine, CA 92614
Telephone: 1-800-274-6229
Web site: www.entrepreneur.com

Fast Company
The Atlantic Monthly Company
77 N. Washington Street
Boston, MA 02114
Telephone: 1-800-688-1545
Web site: www.factcompany.com

Forbes
60 5th Avenue
New York, NY 10011
Telephone: 1-800-888-9896
Web site: www.forbes.com

Home Business
PMB 368, 9582 Hamilton Avenue
Huntington Beach, CA 92646
Telephone: 714-968-0331
Web site: www.homebusinessmag.com

Inc.
100 First Avenue, 4th Floor
Building 36
Charlestown, MA 02129
Telephone: 1-800-234-0999
Web site: www.inc.com

Marketers Forum
Forum Publishing Company
383 E. Main Street
Centerport, NY 11721
Telephone: 1-800-635-7654
Web site: www.forum123.com

Promo
P.O. Box 10587
Riverton, NJ 08076-8575

Telephone: 1-800-775-3777
Web site: www.promormagazine.com

INTERNET AND E-COMMERCE RESOURCES

Entrepreneur Online
www.entrpreneur.com
This is your one-stop source for small business information, products, and services online. View current articles from *Entrepreneur* magazine, get expert advice for all your small business questions, and browse through the thousands of small business and franchise opportunities featured on the site. It's all here in one convenient location and has been specifically developed to help entrepreneurs start, run, and grow their small businesses.

MySite
www.entrepreneur.com
Get a professional Web site for your business today. Entrepreneur has partnered with Vista.com to bring you the most powerful small business Web site development tools and templates available. MySite is fast and easy-to-use, ensuring that you will have your new business Web site up and running in no time. Create an online store, market, and promote your site as well as add high-quality visitor content information and services. Open your new or existing business to a global audience and marketplace with the help of MySite Web site builder.

iSyndicate.com
www.isyndicate.com
Increase revenues, site traffic, and brand loyalty for your Web site by providing visitors with top-notch Web site content. iSyndicate is the place to search for quality content for your Web site, and best of all much of this content can be added to your site for free and it automatically updates. Provide visitors with news, sports, entertainment, health and fitness, and travel information to add some real visitor impact and stickiness to your site.

TrafficBiz.com
www.trafficbiz.com
TrafficBiz provides subscribers with many handy online features and tools for developing and managing

a commercial Web site. These tools include hosting, classified ad systems, reminder systems, and banner exchange programs, just to mention a few.

Netledger.com

www.netledger.com

NetLedger provides accounting options for small business owners without the need for software, as the service is browser-based and can be accessed from any computer. Small business owners will find that this service is handy, affordable, and easy-to-use.

PayPal.com

www.paypal.com

Use the PayPal payment tool on your Web site to receive and send money electronically. PayPal provides many e-commerce payment transfer options and solutions for your online customers and you, including e-checks, credit cards, online auction payment systems, and electronic money transfers. PayPal is easy to install and more importantly easy for your customers to use.

Cafepress.com

www.cafepress.com

Cafepress lets you build a store for your Web site that features promotional products such as T-shirts and hats with your company logo or message emblazoned on them. Unique is the fact that they create your products at their site and ship the products directly to your online customers. No costly inventory to purchase. Cafepress does it all for you and you keep a portion of the profits from every sale.

Submit-it.com

www.submit-it.com

A member of the Microsoft family of products and services, Submit-It enables you to register your Web site with more than 400 search engines and directories quickly and easily. Additionally, there are features such as master forms for simple multi-Web page registrations and 24-hour access via a password to make changes as may be required.

1for1.com

www.1for1.com

1for1.com is a banner exchange program that enables you to advertise your Web site via a banner advertisement on other Web sites. In exchange for the service you provide space on your Web pages to feature banners advertising other Web sites. Banner exchange programs are a very popular method for generating exposure and site traffic for your Web site.

OmniUpdate.com

www.omniupdate.com

Do you want the ability to update or change information, prices, or data on your Web site yourself without having the added cost of a webmaster to maintain your site? OmniUpdate provides browser-based solutions that enable you to update your Web site online from any computer. The service is easy-to-use even for novices and there are many additional handy services and tools that OmniUpdate provides.

MerchantExpress.com

www.merchantexpress.com

Merchant Express provides Internet entrepreneurs, homebased business owners, and retail storefront owners merchant accounts and credit card processing options and solutions. Increase revenues and improve customer services by providing your customers with credit card payment options.

Tradeshownews.com

www.tradeshownews.com

Trade Show News is an online directory that lists the latest trade shows events and news taking place from around the globe. If you want to find industry or product specific trade show to attend or exhibit at, then tradeshownews.com is the place to start your research.

AnimationOnline.com

www.animationonline.com

Create professional animated banners, buttons, and message boards for your Web site quickly and easily using Animation Online banner generator. The service is free and more importantly ,very easy to use.

GolfSyndications.com

www.golfsyndications.com

Golf is one of the most popular sports in North America and if you want to add golf-related "sticky" content to your Web site to boost visitor services then GolfSyndications is the place to find it. Add golfing features to your Web site, such as a course directory, an online pro shop, and more.

Animation Factory

www.animfactory.com

Add real pizzaz to the look of your Web site with clip art, animated gifs, and graphics. Animation Factory features thousands of clip art and graphic images to choose from, and downloading is a snap with their easy-to-understand tutorials.

AuctionBroker.com

www.auctionbroker.com

Want to add an online auction service to your Web site? Auction Broker Software Incorporated has custom software available that will enable you to setup and manage an online auction service right on your own Web site. The software is easy to install, use, and manage.

Gallup.com

www.gallup.com

Studying the response to public opinion and survey polls is a fantastic way to spot potential trends in business and the economy before they materialize. The Gallup Organization (Princeton) is the leader for bringing you the latest and most up-to-date public opinion and survey polls information and data.

Nolo.com

www.nolo.com

Nolo.com is the one-stop source for online law information and forms pertaining to small business, employees, trademarks, and copyrights. If it has to do with the law, you will find it here. This site is large, easy to navigate, and jam-packed full of legal advice, forms, and information.

HelloNetwork.com

www.hellonetwork.com

Talk one-on-one live to your customers online with the helloOperator system. Sales or service questions, you will be able to answer them easily, live, and online.

ichat.com

www.ichat.com

Get your site visitors talking to each other by adding a chat room forum to your site; its easy and fast to do and best of all chat forums can really increase the number of visitors your site gets.

INDEX